Bush
on the Home Front

Bush

on the Home Front

Domestic Policy Triumphs and Setbacks

John D. Graham

Indiana University Press
Bloomington and Indianapolis

This book is a publication of

Indiana University Press
601 North Morton Street
Bloomington, Indiana 47404-3797 USA

www.iupress.indiana.edu

Telephone orders   800-842-6796
Fax orders   812-855-7931
Orders by e-mail   iuporder@indiana.edu

Manufactured in the United States of America

Library of Congress Cataloging-in-Publication Data

Graham, John D.
  Bush on the home front : domestic policy triumphs and failures / John D. Graham.
    p. cm.
  Includes bibliographical references and index.
  ISBN 978-0-253-35436-5 (cloth : alk. paper) — ISBN 978-0-253-22215-2 (pbk. : alk. paper) 1. Bush, George W. (George Walker), 1946- 2. United States—Politics and government—2001-2009. I. Title.
  E902.G743 2010
  973.931092—dc22

2009031619

1 2 3 4 5 15 14 13 12 11 10

Contents

Preface and Acknowledgments   vii

1   Ambiguous Mandate, Polarized Congress   1

2   Lower Taxes, More Spending   27

3   The Social Security Debacle   54

4   Making Sure Kids Learn   63

5   Drug Coverage for Seniors   93

6   Producing More Energy   115

7   Consuming Less Energy   163

8   Cleaner Air, Warmer Climate   194

9   Illegal Immigration: Punishment or Amnesty?   221

10   Tort and Regulatory Reform   251

11   Meltdown and Bailouts   272

12   Taking Stock, with Lessons for Future Presidents   292

Notes   333
Index   403

Preface and Acknowledgments

This book has a dual purpose: to examine what George W. Bush accomplished in domestic policy, and to draw lessons from the Bush experience about how future presidents can be effective in an era of polarized politics. I offer this assessment as both a scholar of public policy and a former participant in the Bush White House.

From 1985 through 2000 I was a professor at the Harvard School of Public Health, where I taught the analytic tools of policy analysis to physicians, nurses, and health policy students. In early 2001 I was asked to join the Bush White House. This invitation came somewhat as a surprise because I had not served on the campaign staff. In fact, I explained gingerly to the Bush-Cheney transition team why I had made an early financial contribution to Elizabeth Dole's short-lived 2000 presidential campaign. I was honored to receive the invitation to serve and eagerly agreed to do so.

From 2001 to early 2006 I served as "regulatory czar" in the U.S. Office of Management and Budget (OMB), a position that placed me at the nerve center of Bush's domestic policy-making apparatus. Technically, the position is called Administrator, Office of Information and Regulatory Affairs, U.S. Office of Management and Budget, one of a handful of Senate-confirmed posts in OMB. In this capacity, I directed a staff of fifty career policy analysts as we oversaw the regulatory, statistical, and information policies of the federal government. I left OMB in early 2006 to become dean of the Pardee RAND Graduate School, the educational arm of the RAND Corporation in Santa Monica, California. Effective August 2008, I became dean of the Indiana University School of Public and Environmental Affairs in Bloomington and Indianapolis.

This book examines Bush's domestic agenda in a wide range of areas: taxes and Social Security, education, health care, energy, clean air, labor and immigration, and policy toward businesses. These particular issues were selected for several reasons: They were each personal priorities of President Bush, they were handled to various degrees by OMB (sometimes by my office), they typically were addressed through a mixture of legislative and executive actions, and they each illustrate, in success and failure, the challenges that a president faces when national politics is evenly divided and polarized on partisan lines. This is not a book about the inner workings of the Bush White House or the personalities of those who served in the Bush administration. Nor is it a book about the internal politics of the Bush administration. Others such as Karl Rove, Andy Card, or President Bush himself are in a better position to offer reflections about how the White House operated and who was most influential on various issues.

This is a book for readers who are interested in the domestic policies of the Bush administration. What did Bush propose to do in domestic policy? What was actually accomplished? Why did some initiatives fail? And how was the challenge of presidential leadership complicated by the partisan polarization in our nation's capital? The case studies presented here will be of special interest to supporters and critics of the Bush administration, reporters who cover the White House and Congress, participants in future presidential campaigns, party leaders, members of Congress and their staffs, governors and mayors, leaders of interest groups who lobby the White House and Congress, and faculty and students who study American politics.

I have drafted the book so that readers can form their own opinions about whether Bush's policies were good or bad for America. In that spirit, I have documented the arguments advanced by both the proponents and opponents of Bush's agenda. My own opinions, with regard to both political strategy and the merits of policy choice, are placed primarily in the introduction or conclusion of each chapter and in the final chapter of the book. In the interests of full disclosure, I note here the issues where I played a significant personal role in policy making: energy (chapters 6 and 7), clean air and climate change (chapter 8), and regulatory reform (chapter 10). Perhaps my strongest influence was on the reform of federal mileage standards for new SUVs and light trucks (chapter 8).

As the book manuscript progressed through numerous iterations, I received helpful comments and suggestions from a large number of thoughtful people: Brent Bradley, Lisa Branch, Christopher DeMuth, Jack Fleer, Jennifer Graham, Susan Graham, Al Hubbard, Charles Jones, Paul Noe, Andy Rich, Michael Rich, Justin Ross, Ronnye Stidvent, Jim Thomson, Elizabeth Vandersarl, James Q. Wilson, and Leo Woerner. The following doctoral fellows at RAND suggested improvements and provided excellent research assistance: Diana Epstein, Jay Griffin, Silvia Montoya, Sabrina Shi, Elizabeth Wilke, and Frank Zhang. Laura Cavagnaro of Indiana University helped perform the analysis of Senate voting in chapter 12. Several peer reviewers commissioned by Indiana University Press also helped me improve the product in numerous ways. The source materials for the book are documented in the endnotes with two notable exceptions: (1) some discussions of White House strategy reflect my impressions based on what I experienced and heard from colleagues in the administration, and (2) the legislative details (including roll-call votes) in each chapter, unless noted otherwise, are drawn from accounts in the *Congressional Quarterly Weekly Report* and *Congressional Quarterly's* annual *Almanac*. All errors and opinions are my responsibility.

I thank President Bush and my immediate supervisors at OMB, Mitch Daniels and Josh Bolten, for the opportunity to serve our country. I also thank the professional staff of OMB and my many colleagues throughout the federal government who educated me about the issues covered in this book. I wrote much of the book before joining RAND and have not relied on findings from any internal RAND studies, but I would also like to thank the RAND Corporation for supporting me during the later stages of writing and editing. My colleagues at Indiana University have also assisted me in the final stages of book production. Maggie Pearson provided invaluable assistance in preparing the manuscript for IU Press.

John D. Graham

Bush

on the Home Front

1

Ambiguous Mandate, Polarized Congress

As George W. Bush's last year in office came to a conclusion, critics declared that our forty-third president was a failure. There are certainly many difficulties to be cited: the prolonged military occupation of Iraq, the messy aftermath of Hurricane Katrina, the burgeoning federal debt, rising fuel prices, a proliferation of home foreclosures, the painful recession that began in 2008, and concerns about health care and income inequality.

Polls indicate that Bush left office as one of the most unpopular presidents in modern history. In 2008 his Gallup Poll approval rating reached a sixty-year low: 28 percent. The previous record low was set by Harry Truman in the midst of the Korean War. Ironically, Bush also holds the record for the highest approval rating in history: 90 percent in the days after the attacks of September 11, 2001.[1] But for most of his presidency Bush struggled to achieve a 50 percent approval rating. Anti-Bush sentiment, coupled with a war-weary public and the scandals in Congress, contributed to the Democratic takeover of the House and

Senate in November 2006. Given the public's mood, the Republican presidential candidates in 2008 all sought to emulate Ronald Reagan more than George W. Bush.[2] Obama's clear win at the polls in 2008 may have resulted in part from Bush's unpopularity and McCain's inability to separate himself from Bush's image.

Bush's national security policies are certainly the subject of intense scrutiny and criticism, both in the United States and around the world. As much as I agree that Bush's activist foreign policy merits meticulous scrutiny, I am struck by how many citizens, opinion leaders, and scholars have little knowledge of Bush's domestic policies or hold misperceptions about them.

The imbalance in the scholarly literature is perhaps most striking. While the "war on terror" literature is huge and growing, there are few assessments of what Bush accomplished, and did not accomplish, on the domestic front. It is curious that some authors seek to explain why Bush had little or no domestic success, without even taking the time to examine his actual domestic record.[3]

Some critics argue that Bush and his domestic aides were so preoccupied with the war in Iraq that there was little sustained attention to domestic policy.[4] Others assert that the Bush White House was unwilling to invest scarce political capital on the domestic front, since his priorities were elsewhere. As evidence for this view, critics point to a comparative study which found that Bush made a smaller number of detailed legislative proposals to Congress on domestic issues than any recent president.[5]

Others allege that Bush was uninterested in domestic policy or that his domestic policy advisers in the White House were weak, ill-informed, or unimaginative.[6] As evidence for this argument, critics point to the high rate of turnover in the White House domestic policy and economics staffs compared to the continuity in Bush's foreign policy team.[7] The implication of these arguments is that Bush didn't really have a meaningful or consistent domestic policy.[8]

Yet another criticism is that Bush had a domestic agenda but was unable to persuade the Congress and the American people to go along with its ideas.[9] For example, the Congress did not enact a constitutional amendment prohibiting gay marriage, even though Bush supported such an amendment. According to this view, Bush's agenda was "hijacked by the right" and was thus unacceptable to most Americans.[10] A related critique is that Bush pushed an "ideologically polarizing agenda" that did more to antagonize Democrats than deliver concrete results for conservatives.[11]

This book offers a different, more positive view. Based on personal experience, I know that Bush was quite interested in domestic policy and devoted a substantial amount of personal time and political energy to domestic issues. In fact, Bush made important contributions to domestic policies concerning taxes, education, health care, energy, clean air, labor, regulatory reform, and financial-sector relief. His successors will change, or even reverse, some of these policies, but much of Bush's domestic work is likely to persist for decades to come. Bush's degree of success as a domestic policy maker is not simply underappreciated. It is remarkable in light of his tenuous standing with the public and the sharp partisan divisions in the Congress.[12]

The book builds upon a small but growing body of scholarship on the Bush presidency.[13] Previous authors have explored the formation of the Bush administration,[14] his performance in 2001–2003,[15] his "second-term blues,"[16] why Bush should be considered a "big-government conservative,"[17] his leadership style,[18] how he differed from Ronald Reagan,[19] public opinion of Bush and the Republican Congress,[20] how Bush intermingled campaigning and governing,[21] and how partisan polarization in Washington defined his presidency.[22] Although this literature touches on selected aspects of Bush's domestic record, it does not provide an in-depth assessment of his successes and failures at home. This book supplies such an assessment.

I define "success" and "failure" by asking three questions: Was Bush effective in enacting his domestic policy agenda? Did the Bush administration make progress in the implementation of his policies? And is there reason to believe that Bush's policies will be effective and worthwhile? I focus more on the first two questions because it is too early to make a definitive policy evaluation of the merits of many of Bush's policies. But I do venture a preliminary evaluation of some policies based on the limited available evidence and the general principles of policy analysis.

In addition to assessing Bush's performance as a domestic policy maker, I draw on modern theories of presidential and congressional power to shed light on how Bush achieved his successes, and why some pieces of his domestic agenda were delayed, weakened, or killed altogether.[23] Much can be learned from the Bush experience, both his successes and his failures. In the final chapter, I derive some useful lessons about how future presidents can be effective domestic policy makers, assuming that American politics continues to be equally and sharply divided along partisan lines.

Contrary to popular belief, Bush's law-making successes were not rooted primarily in Republican "control" of the House and Senate. Single-party control of the White House and Congress is not necessary for lawmaking success, and it certainly does not ensure that success.[24] In fact, Bush achieved more lawmaking success in his first term, when his apparent control of Congress was less secure, than he did at the start of his second term, when the Republican margins in Congress were at their peaks.

My thesis is that Bush was most effective in lawmaking when he recognized his tenuous political standing, analyzed the competing interests in Congress, and chose policy initiatives with broad appeal among Republicans and at least some appeal among key Democrats in the Senate. He was especially effective when he worked the powerful interest groups with ties to the Democratic Party and fostered collaboration with key "crossover" Democrats.[25] Even when his legislative proposals could not be passed, Bush used his executive powers aggressively, knowing that the Congress—an institution that requires supermajorities to act—was too divided to obstruct him effectively.

Future presidents who are elected in landslides may have the luxury to govern differently. It remains to be seen whether President Barack Obama can overcome polarization. For future presidents who aspire to be activists in domestic policy but face partisan polarization, there are constructive lessons here about how to become an effective policy maker. I shall argue that, due to fundamental features of American politics, future presidents may be constrained in ways that Bush was constrained.

It would be a mistake to assume that Bush's domestic policy successes were a side effect of his temporary burst of popularity after the tragic events of 9/11. There was an eighteen-month burst in Bush's job-approval ratings that contributed to his legislative successes on homeland security and military policies, key issues that are beyond the scope of this book. Yet there is little evidence that Bush's temporary popularity helped him on the traditional domestic issues that are the subject of my investigation. For example, the 9/11-induced popularity did not translate into near-term legislative victories on energy policy or the 2002 economic stimulus package favored by Republicans.[26] In fact, the stimulus bill was never passed and the energy bill, which I analyze in chapter 6, was not passed until 2005.

The Governing Strategy

Given that Bush governed with a razor-thin margin in the Electoral College, substantial public disapproval of his presidency, and an ever-present filibuster threat in the Senate, there was good reason to predict that he would fail as a domestic lawmaker. One might have expected that Bush's accomplishments would be confined to foreign and defense policy, where presidential powers (relative to Congress and the judiciary) are large and where the public and Congress are most likely to defer to presidential leadership.[27] Yet this book shows that Bush was frequently an effective domestic policy maker. Bush borrowed from strategies that worked when he was governor of Texas. A two-part governing strategy, which is illuminated by modern theories of presidential and congressional power, was executed in a wide range of domestic policy areas that are illustrated in chapters 2 through 11.

The first part of the governing strategy was frustrating to many people. Bush made a relatively small number of legislative proposals and gave them priority attention. It is much easier to please interest groups by giving each of them its own legislative proposal, and then blaming failure on the Congress. But Bush knew he did not want to blame his fellow Republicans, who controlled the House and Senate for much of his tenure. And Bush did not have the margins in the Congress—especially in the Senate—to pursue a partisan legislative strategy.[28]

Good-government advocates generally prefer the classic bipartisan strategy, where leaders of both parties in the House and Senate are engaged cooperatively by the White House from the outset. On rare occasions (for instance, homeland security policy after 9/11), Bush pursued a classic bipartisan strategy.[29] More often, Bush practiced a "cross-partisan" technique where legislation is passed primarily with votes from the president's party, coupled with the minimum number of votes needed from the other party in order to overcome gridlock.[30] In cross-partisanship, a president does not engage the legislative leaders of the other party, presumably because they are in opposition to the president's agenda or because the negotiating terms they would set for their cooperation are unattractive to the White House. Since Bush often had sufficient Republican votes in the House to pass his agenda without any votes from House Democrats, he frequently coupled a partisan strategy in the House with an outreach to potential crossover Democrats in the Senate.

The Bush White House took creative steps to facilitate cross-partisanship. For example, in many cases the White House chose not to submit detailed legislative packages and instead allowed members of Congress to develop specific bills within broad parameters established by the White House. Bush also selected some domestic issues (such as health, education, and energy conservation) where the national Democratic Party was already eager to enact stronger federal legislation. Interestingly, Bush was not reluctant to reach out to powerful interest groups with ties to the Democratic Party in order to compensate for his tenuous standing in the polls. By driving a wedge between the Senate Democratic leadership and these powerful groups, the Bush White House often found the votes needed to bypass filibuster threats.

Typically, the White House strategy was to pass a bill in the House first, where Bush's Republican base was loyal and in the majority (at least from 2001 to 2006), and where the rules governing floor debate favor the majority party. For example, the House majority leader, in collaboration with the House Rules Committee, can place strict limits on which bills will be debated on the floor, which amendments will be considered, and the maximum permissible time for floor debate. If a bill passed the House, the White House would then pressure the Senate to act, often through presidential speeches scheduled at key locations around the country. The White House would target a limited number of key Senate Democrats and, where feasible, make measured compromises with them to secure the votes necessary to overcome filibuster threats. This delicate balancing act required making enough compromises to secure the necessary Democratic support in the Senate, without making so many compromises that a bill would suffer defections among rank-and-file Republicans in the Senate and House.

On numerous occasions I heard President Bush instruct his advisers: "I will not negotiate with myself." He meant that he would only make modifications to his preferred policy if these were necessary to secure the critical support of key actors and thereby advance his overall policy.

The cross-partisan formula was demonstrated successfully early in 2001 with Bush's top economic policy priority: the largest tax-cut program since the early years of Ronald Reagan's presidency. I shall examine Bush's tax cuts in chapter 2 from a variety of perspectives. But the 2001 tax cut was an enormous accomplishment because it was achieved even faster than Reagan's was in 1981. Unlike Bush, Reagan won his first term in a landslide victory with significant coattails in both the House and Senate.[31] After the 2001 tax-cut victory, the Bush White House repeatedly sought to fashion cross-partisan victories in the Congress. The Democrats countered by seeking greater party discipline against White House priorities.

The second prong of the governing strategy's two parts was the use of executive powers. When legislation was not moving in the Congress (or when it was determined that a legislative proposal would be "dead on arrival"), Bush deployed executive powers to accomplish similar policy objectives. This executive-branch policy making, while less publicized than acts of Congress, can produce the same far-reaching consequences as new legislation or a Supreme Court decision.[32] The most common executive tools are rule making, guidance, enforcement actions, executive orders, and public information campaigns. Bush used executive powers in virtually all policy areas, but they played a critical role in education, energy, clean air, labor, regulatory reform, and tort reform. In his highly aggressive use of executive authority, Bush built on precedents set by Ronald Reagan and Bill Clinton.[33]

Executive actions are often de-emphasized or ignored by scholars because they can be reversed by a future president. In theory that is true, but a future president may be inclined to pursue his or her own agenda rather than spend precious political capital reversing a predecessor's decisions.[34] Congress can also reverse unpopular or unwise executive actions. But the partisan divisions in Congress work to a president's advantage by protecting executive actions from opposition. It is difficult for a divided House and Senate to obstruct a determined president's executive actions.

Casualties in the Bush Agenda

There were plenty of casualties in Bush's domestic policy agenda. When Bush failed to make progress on the domestic front, it was generally because the proposals that were made, whether good or bad on their merits, were not politically feasible given the ambiguous nature of his political mandate and his vulnerability to opposition in the Congress. In some situations, the federal judiciary also played a pivotal role in blocking his executive actions.

Key examples of legislative failure were Bush's "faith-based" legislative agenda, which stalled at the start of the first term, and his Social Security reform effort, which cratered at the start of the second term. The former was only a partial failure, since some of the faith-based agenda was salvaged through the use of executive powers.[35] Social Security reform was a complete failure, despite the fact that Bush elevated it to the status of number one domestic priority in his second term. We shall examine precisely why the cross-partisan technique failed to produce Social Security reform.

When Bush's proposals stalled in Congress, the crucial opposition was often the Senate Democratic leadership. Yet there were also cases where opposition from moderate Republicans was decisive. Bush learned in Texas how to compromise with conservative Democrats, but he learned in Washington, D.C., that compromising with more liberal Senate Democrats was not a sure ticket to success. Conservative Republicans abhorred these compromises and did not hesitate to oppose and ridicule them. There were some crucial situations where numerous defections by House and Senate conservatives blocked Bush's domestic policy ambitions. For example, House conservatives were the key obstacle to passage of Bush's bold proposal to reform federal immigration law.

Some will argue that it is laudable, even courageous, for a president to advocate and fight for a promising proposal and fail.[36] Although this view has merit in unusual cases, I hold a more pragmatic view. It is more important for a president, especially one with tenuous political standing, to target issues where progress can be made. A president's effectiveness needs to be continuously demonstrated because the American people take a largely pragmatic view of presidents. There are plenty of other prominent voices in American society—talk-show hosts, movie stars, ministers, and United States senators—who can take provocative positions simply for the purpose of stimulating public debate. Citizens expect their president to solve problems in domestic policy.

Given the complexities of getting legislation through the Congress, the safer course for the Bush administration was often to enact policy with executive powers. Although Bush used these powers aggressively, my view is that he could have accomplished much more with them. Bush delayed clean-air progress for several years on the faint hope that Congress might pass new legislation, when he could have acted more expeditiously with rule making. At the same time, litigation in federal courts by opposing interest groups sometimes acted as an effective check against executive actions. In several important cases, including the executive actions on clean air and climate change, the federal judiciary slowed or blocked Bush's changes to domestic policy due to procedural or substantive errors committed by policy makers at federal agencies.

Before we turn to an assessment of Bush's domestic record on specific issues, it is crucial to appreciate the political context in which Bush governed. That means the reader should appreciate the basic views of the American people, the makeup of the U.S. Congress, and the growing polarization of Congress along party lines that had begun in the early 1990s and had already complicated the presidency of Bill Clinton.

The Views of the American People

Any assessment of a president's record must begin with an understanding of the people he or she served. The fundamental political views of the American electorate have been largely unchanged for decades. On ideology, about 45 percent of voters consider themselves "moderate" or "middle of the road" or do not know how to describe themselves on the liberal-conservative continuum.[37] The percentage of "conservatives" (about 35 percent) is larger than the percentage of "liberals" (about 20 percent). The only real change in this breakdown since 1970 has been a small but steady growth in the percentage of conservatives.[38] Some analysts argue that the true pool of moderates has diminished, and that they are now a minority of voters.[39]

If instead of using labels we consider opinions on "hot-button" issues (jobs, government spending, welfare, abortion, health care, and affirmative action), surveys again find long-term stability in the views of the American electorate. With the exception of affirmative action, where there has been steady erosion in public support, the distribution of views among today's voters on key issues is similar to voters thirty years ago.[40]

As to party affiliation, there are more Democrats than Republicans. In the 1950s the Democratic registration margin was large, almost 55 percent versus 30 percent. The difference has dwindled over the last thirty years, but the Republicans have still not achieved equality with Democrats in party identification.[41] The percentage of self-described "independents" is about a quarter of the electorate,[42] though the share of independent voters with partisan leanings may have grown since the 1970s.[43]

Most voters have partisan convictions or tendencies, but the "median voter" at the polls is not partisan.[44] The median voter is the person who is in the middle of the spectrum on an issue or group of issues. Sometimes called a centrist, he or she is willing to consider candidates from either political party and does split his or her ticket in different races.

Interestingly, recent U.S. elections have witnessed a growing percentage of straight-ticket voters, a trend that may have begun in the 1970s.[45] The 2000 presidential election produced the highest levels of party-line voting in fifty years. Moreover, the number of congressional districts delivering pluralities to House and presidential candidates of different parties in 2000 was the lowest since 1952.[46]

What is happening? The turnout rates among partisan voters have surged in recent elections, in part due to the concerted efforts of better-funded national political parties.[47] As a result, the percentage of all voters who are party loyalists appears to be rising.[48]

Going into the 2000 election, American voters, based on voting behavior rather than party registration, were about evenly divided along party lines. President Clinton was re-elected with only 49 percent of the popular vote in 1996. (Bob Dole, Ross Perot, and other minor candidates captured the remainder of the votes cast.) The popular vote in the House in 1996 was 49 percent Republican and 48.5 percent Democratic. In 1998 the vote in House races split 49 percent Republican to 48 percent Democratic. Perhaps it should not be surprising that the presidential races in 2000 and 2004 were nail-biters.

What Bush Mandate?

If the extent of an elected president's mandate for policy change is rooted in the margins of his victories in the popular vote or the Electoral College, Bush's mandate could not have been more ambiguous. Among all previous U.S. presidents who served two terms, none did so with the conditions Bush faced: an evenly divided electorate in both November 2000 and November 2004.

Bush versus Gore

The 2000 contest between Vice President Al Gore and Governor George W. Bush resulted in the most inconclusive result in American political history. Out of 104 million popular votes cast, Al Gore received the majority by 540,000. Yet Bush won the Electoral College 271 to 266 (one District of Columbia elector did not vote), barely surpassing the 270 votes required for victory.

Late in the evening on election day 2000, several networks declared that Gore was victorious, based on projections that Florida would fall into Gore's column. Early the next morning, these same networks reversed course and projected that Florida had gone to Bush. Gore first conceded the election, then retracted his concession (as claims of voting irregularities in Florida were voiced), and then pursued a complex recount and litigation strategy to reverse Bush's apparent victory.

The matter was not settled until December 12, 2000, over one month after the election, when a bitterly divided U.S. Supreme Court ruled 5–4 that there would not be another recount and the results would stand as they were. George W. Bush "proceeded to form his presidency with the least political standing in the post–World War II era."[49] Many Democrats felt the 2000 election was stolen rather than won.[50]

Bush versus Kerry

Bush's re-election victory over Senator John Kerry of Massachusetts in 2004, though not as close as his 2000 win, was quite close. In fact, it also stands as one of the closest races in modern American history.

This time Bush won the popular vote 51 percent to 48 percent, but the contest in the all-important Electoral College was neck and neck: 286 for Bush to 251 for Kerry (with one Minnesota elector casting a ballot for John Edwards). If the single state of Ohio, and its 20 electoral votes, had gone for Kerry instead of Bush, Kerry would have won the election. Bush defeated Kerry in Ohio by less than two percentage points. The state-by-state results in the Bush-Kerry race were the same as the Bush-Gore race with three exceptions: Bush won two states (New Mexico and Iowa) that Gore won while Kerry won one state (New Hampshire) that Gore lost.

Bush's success in energizing his base in 2004 was not coupled with an ability to create the kind of political consensus that produced re-election landslides in the Electoral College for Eisenhower (1956), Nixon (1972), Reagan (1984), and Clinton (1996). No re-elected president since Woodrow Wilson in 1916 received such low percentages of the popular and electoral counts as shares of the two-party vote.[51]

Bush's Political Standing

A concept like "political standing" seems highly subjective, but numeric data can be used to score, compare, and rank presidents based on their

Table 1.1. Political Standing of Postwar U.S. Presidents

President	Popular Vote (%)	Electoral Vote (%)	Job Approval (%)	Total	Rank
Eisenhower (1952)	55	83	78	216	4
Eisenhower (1956)	57	86	76	219	2
Kennedy (1960)	50	56	77	183	9
Johnson (1964)	61	90	71	222	1
Nixon (1968)	43	56	59	158	15
Nixon (1972)	61	97	51	209	5
Carter (1976)	50	55	66	171	12
Reagan (1980)	51	91	57	199	6
Reagan (1984)	59	98	62	219	2
Bush 41 (1988)	53	79	57	189	8
Clinton (1992)	43	69	58	170	11
Clinton (1996)	50	70	62	182	10
Bush 43 (2000)	50	50	57	157	14
Bush 43 (2004)	51	53	51	155	13
Obama (2008)	53	67	75	195	7

Notes: Popular vote is share of two-party vote. Job approval is upon entering office.
Adapted from Charles O. Jones, *The Presidency in a Separated System* (Washington, D.C.: Brookings, 2005), p. 52 (Table 3-3).

standing. The approach in table 1.1 uses three inputs: share of the popular vote (%), share of the electoral vote (%), and job approval rating soon after taking office (%). The "political standing" score is simply the sum of the three input values.

As table 1.1 reveals, presidents vary substantially in their scores, and their scores may differ at election and re-election. For our purposes, the rank ordering of post–World War II presidencies conveys the key point: With the exception of Nixon, George W. Bush ranks last in political standing for both election and re-election.[52]

A central point of this book is that low political standing does not necessarily mean that a president will be ineffective. What it means for domestic policy is that the president's agenda must be devised realistically. As we shall see, Bush was often effective in compensating for his low standing with creative cross-partisan strategies and aggressive use of executive powers.

Defining Polarization

Although journalists use the term "polarization" loosely, political scientists use it to refer to conditions where the two political parties are each fairly unified yet hold opposing views on one or more critical issues.[53] America's recent bout of polarization has been accompanied by "conflict extension," the tendency of the two parties to divide on numerous issues, not just a single issue such as slavery, tariffs, a war, or civil rights.[54]

When polarized, activists in one party will tend to hold highly negative views of elected leaders who represent the other party, treating them not just as misinformed but as a source of evil in American life.[55] For example, strong Republicans have become more negative in their opinions of Democratic presidents while strong Democrats have become more negative in their opinions of Republican presidents. The percentage of partisans who "strongly disapprove" of the leaders of the other party has steadily widened, and is higher today than at any other time in recent history, including the months following the resignation of Richard Nixon.[56] Even in the 2008 Obama-McCain contest, pollsters found that more than a third of each candidate's supporters "detest" McCain or Obama so deeply that they would have a hard time accepting as president the one they don't support.[57]

When the two parties are of roughly equal strength, polarization is balanced. When one party is much stronger than the other, polarization is imbalanced. Presidential leadership is always complicated, but balanced polarization, which has emerged as the norm rather than the exception in modern American politics, makes the president vulnerable to opposition from the opposing party and from threats of defection by even a few members of his own party.

Why is American politics becoming more polarized? The drivers are party activists and strong partisans coupled with their allies among opinion leaders and mass media professionals.[58] Activists are more extreme in their policy opinions and less likely to compromise their core beliefs than average Americans.[59] This divergence has been documented by political scientists at every national party convention since 1956.[60] Overall, the differences in views between the average activists in the two parties have been steadily widening for twenty-five years. Devout Republicans have become more conservative; devout Democrats have become more liberal.[61]

Strong partisans and campaign activists are not trivial fractions of the electorate. When voters identify themselves with the Democratic or Republican Party, it often means something. Among Democratic (Republican) Party identifiers in 2004, 25 percent (24 percent) were campaign activists and 46 percent (49 percent) described themselves as strong partisans.[62] What distinguishes strong partisans and party activists from the median voter is that they have some core principles (at least on some issues) that they expect their candidate to uphold. "Compromise" with the opposing party on these core principles is abhorred.[63]

An American politician must win a primary election before he or she can win a general election, unless he or she runs as an independent. These strong partisans and party activists have a crucial voice in determining which candidates make it to the general election. Because they feel strongly about issues, activists monitor the behavior of politicians to make sure they are loyal. The result: Candidates for Congress are responsive to the wishes of activists.[64]

Sorting Liberals and Conservatives into Parties

Through a process of "sorting," ideology and partisanship are becoming more aligned in American politics.[65] Thirty years ago, one could find numerous conservatives and liberals in both parties. But that is changing. Large numbers of conservative whites in the South are now voting Republican rather than Democrat, while large numbers of liberal whites in New England are voting Democrat instead of Republican. Two kinds of voters are becoming endangered: liberal Republicans and conservative Democrats.[66] As a result, the party attachments of voters have become more closely aligned with their ideological self-classifications (for instance, conservative versus liberal) and with their positions on some issues (such as taxes, national defense, religion, and abortion). Coupled with recent trends in voter turnout (disaffection by moderates, enthusiasm by partisans), straight-line party voters make up a larger share of the electorate than they did a generation ago.[67]

Parties matter. In 1975 fewer than 50 percent of voters in the United States saw important differences between the Republican and Democratic parties. That percentage rose to an all-time high of 76 percent in 2004.[68] And the 2006 and 2008 elections witnessed nationalizing forces, whether they are interpreted as anti-war, anti-Bush, or anti-corruption or simply as a determination to give the Democrats an opportunity to change the country's direction. Today, few voters would agree with George Wallace's famous complaint about parties in 1968: There "was not a dime's worth of difference" between them.

Polarization is apparent in congressional voting behavior. Party "unity" scores are rising.[69] A Republican legislator is more likely to vote in agreement with the majority of the Republican members of Congress than he or she was several decades ago.[70] Democratic legislators are also setting record marks for party unity. Accordingly, the percentage of "centrist" members of Congress, defined by voting records on issues, is declining in both parties.[71] According to one definition, a "centrist" is a member whose voting record is closer to the midpoint between the two parties than to the position of the median member of his or her own party. A gradual decline in the number of centrists in Congress is a key feature of polarization.

The Causes of Polarization

There appear to be multiple causes of the polarization in Congress.[72] They are geographical, religious, economic, institutional, and cultural in nature.

Geographically, the South has become reliably Republican in national elections for the first time since the Civil War (excepting Obama's surprising 2008 wins in Virginia and North Carolina). A generation ago, New England was a strong progressive force among congressional Republicans.[73] With the loss of Christopher Shays of Connecticut in 2008, there are no Republican House members from New England. The parties are not simply different names; they are based in different regions of the country with different norms and values.

As southern whites left the New Deal coalition and began to vote Republican in national elections, the Democratic Party lost a conservative influence while the Republican Party acquired another conservative one.[74] Careful studies of southern politics have found economic as well as racial explanations for why the southern states have become realigned in American politics, and are now a loyal base for Republican candidates in presidential elections.[75] Today the strength of the national Republican Party is in the South, where political views on most issues are more conservative than they are in the Northeast and on the West Coast, the centers of liberal Democratic activism.[76]

The growth of evangelical Christian groups and their contribution to grassroots politics is also a polarizing factor.[77] Regular churchgoers in America (especially whites) tend to cast Republican votes while those who never attend church and have a secular view of life tend to cast Democratic votes.[78] Among regular churchgoers, Bush defeated Kerry 64 percent to 35 percent; among those who never attend church, Kerry defeated Bush 62 percent to 36 percent.[79] The Republican Party, which promotes faith-based policies, is increasingly perceived as a friend of religion. The Democratic Party is often perceived as a guardian of the separation of church and state.[80]

Another possible explanation arises from the growing concern about income inequality in the United States.[81] The Republican Party has captured increasing percentages of households with incomes in the top third of the income distribution, without losing its share of lower-income voters. Many of the heads of these wealthier households were born into Democratic families and exerted moderating influences in the "big tent" of the New Deal coalition. Offsetting this trend has been the tendency of highly educated Americans (e.g., those with graduate degrees) to vote for Democratic candidates, even though they have relatively high incomes.[82] Meanwhile, the Republican Party has not responded fully to the growing numbers of low-income immigrants in America because many of them are either living in the country illegally (and hence do not vote) or are disaffected from the political process. A sharper distinction between the two parties along income lines has been accompanied by more polarized views among party elites about what to do about inequality.[83]

Others have speculated that the changing nature of political communication has further isolated party elites and reinforced the extreme views in both parties.[84] The proliferation of cable channels and radio talk shows provides more conservative and liberal outlets for those who like to hear from kindred spirits. Media fragmentation allows elites to listen to people who largely share their views rather than grapple with differences in views.[85] A related theory is that Americans have become more socially segregated in "cultural zones," largely interacting with people like themselves.[86] If true, this phenomenon could also contribute to political polarization among elites and ordinary voters.

Another possible explanation for polarization in Congress is the powerful role of House redistricting procedures.[87] When states "gerrymander" districts, they often favor one party's candidate. States may also work to create more "safe" districts for popular incumbents of both parties. The result is that congressional seats may be virtually guaranteed to be won by one party or the other.[88] If a member running for re-election is not strongly opposed in the general election, he or she has little incentive to moderate positions on issues in order to appeal to centrist voters. To the contrary, many incumbents are more worried about challengers from within their own party than they are about challenges by the other party.[89]

Since national elections now present a meaningful choice to voters, more people are participating. They are urged to do so since the two national parties have new technologies and more resources to find sympathetic voters and get them to the polls. The 2004 presidential election was characterized by a record turnout (about 59 percent), with record numbers of people also involved in some form of political activity beyond voting. In exit polls 85 percent of voters indicated that they cared "a great deal" about who won the election, a passion that is a far cry from the indifference toward national politics that was common a generation ago.[90] Turnout rates rose again in the 2008 presidential election.[91]

For all of these reasons, George W. Bush assumed office in 2001 at a time when polarization in American politics was strong and increasing. The prospects for bipartisan coalitions in Congress were not great.[92] In fact, the number of bipartisan coalitions in Congress on legislative matters had declined steadily for at least three decades.[93] Bush faced a Congress that was just as polarized as the previous polarization peaks in American history: the 1890s and 1930s.[94]

Pressures for "Base Politics"

Independents continue to play a crucial role in elections. In the 2002 and 2006 midterm elections, the turnout rates among Republicans and Democrats were similar. Only 10 percent of party identifiers voted for the House candidate from the opposing party. What appears to have contributed to the big Democratic sweep in 2006 was a shift in the voting of self-described independents, who accounted for about 25 percent of the electorate. Exit polls found that independents broke evenly between the two parties in the 2002 House races, but in 2006, 57 percent of them voted for Democratic House candidates and 39 percent for Republicans.[95]

If the independent voter is the swing voice in close elections, why are politicians spending so much time pandering to their bases? The experience of George W. Bush is instructive.

In 2000 Bush lost the popular vote to Al Gore among independent voters, 55 percent to 45 percent. In 2004 Bush lost independents to John Kerry by an even larger margin: 58 percent to 42 percent. And Kerry did not lose many of the Democratic voters to Bush that Gore captured. The reason Bush defeated Kerry was that, while both campaigns increased turnout among their bases, the Bush campaign was more effective than the Kerry campaign in stimulating turnout.[96]

Moreover, a closer look at ideological "moderates" reveals that they are not what they used to be. Many of these allegedly swing voters are now considered "leaners" because they are consistent in their voting behavior. Some regularly vote Republican; others regularly vote Democratic. The percentage of voters in presidential elections who are not closely aligned with one party or the other appears to have declined from around 15 percent in the 1970s to just over 7 percent in 2004.[97] Some analysts claim that the pool of true "moderates" has been shrinking for thirty years and now constitutes a minority of the electorate in presidential contests (compared to conservatives and liberals).[98]

Although independents and moderates remain crucial in close contests, it is difficult for candidates to appeal to them. Unlike partisan voters, independents tend to be less interested in politics and less ideological in their thinking. On some issues they are liberal; on others they are conservative. As a result, it is challenging for campaigns to reach them with a compelling appeal, particularly an appeal that does not simultaneously offend or alienate a campaign's voter base. In short, independent and moderate voters are as elusive as they are crucial.

We should expect that our national political figures, both presidential candidates and members of Congress, will become more "base" oriented. They will care most about how they are perceived by campaign activists, strong partisans within their parties, and the powerful interest groups aligned with those parties.[99] Politicians still crave support from independent and moderate voters, but a distinctive feature of polarization is an increased focus on the wishes of party activists.

In this polarized era of American politics, activists know how to punish incumbent politicians who engage in offensive bipartisanship (see table 1.2).

Table 1.2. How Party Loyalists Punish Disloyalty

George H. W. Bush

In 1988 Bush pledged to his base voters: "Read my lips: No New Taxes." In office he raised taxes as part of a bipartisan budget deal with congressional Democrats. He lost his bid for re-election in 1992 after many conservatives supported Patrick Buchanan and Ross Perot.

Al Gore

After a career in politics as a consumer advocate and environmentalist, Gore tempered his views on these issues as vice president, reflecting the more moderate stance of President Clinton. Gore offended Ralph Nader, who retaliated by running for president. Nader contributed to Gore's defeat by skimming votes from Gore's 2000 vote.

Arlen Specter

After 24 years as a liberal Republican in the Senate from Pennsylvania, Specter was challenged in his 2004 re-election bid by conservative congressman Pat Toomey. Specter squeaked through the primary 51% to 49% only after promising the Bush White House that he would pay more attention to the wishes of the conservative Republican base.

Joe Lieberman

Veteran senator Joe Lieberman of Connecticut served as Al Gore's running mate in 2000. But he was stunned two years later when he was defeated in the Democratic primary by the wealthy political neophyte Ned Lamont. Lieberman was accused of too much bipartisan collaboration with George W. Bush on the Iraq War, homeland security, and Social Security reform. Lieberman won the general election as an independent largely on Republican votes, and thus his influence in the Democratic Party was damaged.

Lincoln Chafee

As a Republican senator from the highly Democratic state of Rhode Island, Chafee compiled one of the most liberal voting records among Republicans. He was challenged in his re-election bid by the conservative mayor of Warwick, Stephen Laffey, who was backed by the conservative Club for Growth. Chafee emerged from the primary damaged, and then lost the general election 52% to 48%.

These office holders are challenged in a primary by ardent loyalists from their own party.

An incumbent's risk of defeat in a primary is statistically small, as few primary races involving incumbent members of Congress are competitive. Could such unusual events really discourage members of Congress from behaving like centrists? The frequency of primary challenges is small, but that may be because incumbents cast party-line votes that discourage primary opposition.[100]

Three facets of primary challenges are salient to incumbents: (1) when incumbents lose in a primary, it is almost always to a candidate who is from the extreme wing of their party; (2) strong partisans who vote in primaries often vote for kindred spirits on core issues, not for those who might have the best chances of winning the general election; and (3) incumbents who lose primaries rarely re-emerge in national politics. As one pair of scholars put it, "the dreaded CHANCE of being ousted in a primary, however long the odds, now chills the would-be centrists in both parties."[101]

Veteran Republican senator Arlen Specter of Pennsylvania was almost defeated in 2004 by a challenger from his right. He apparently learned his lesson. In 1994 Specter voted with his party 56 percent of the time. In 2005 he did so 84 percent of the time and was diligent in supporting Bush's Supreme Court nominees.[102]

Isn't it true that the 2006 midterm election results will foster more bipartisan political behavior in the Congress? There is a case to be made for this view. Two-thirds of the Republican districts captured by Democratic candidates in 2006 voted for George W. Bush in 2004.[103] In total, Democratic House members now occupy fifty House seats representing districts that Bush carried in 2004. These members may perceive that it is prudent to compile a moderate, centrist voting record.

Of course, there are no guarantees that centrist voting behavior will protect an incumbent.[104] Many of the Republicans defeated in 2006 who had represented districts that voted for Kerry in 2004 had compiled moderate voting records, including a demonstrated proclivity to defy the wishes of the White House on key votes. Notable in this regard are Lincoln Chafee of Rhode Island and Mike DeWine of Ohio in the Senate and Representatives Jim Leach of Iowa and Nancy Johnson of Connecticut. Moreover, the demise of so many moderate Republicans in the 2006 election may have contributed to more polarization in the Congress in 2007–2008, since the minority party in Congress was ideologically more homogeneous and had fewer voices seeking to moderate the stances of the Republican leadership.[105]

On the Democratic side, the ideological composition of the new members of the House and Senate is not nearly as moderate as some commentators have suggested. According to one cursory tally, only five of the more than thirty new Democratic House members in 2006 can plausibly be called social conservatives and, as a whole, the group tends to be anti-war, pro-choice, and very liberal on economic issues. This freshman class of House members may be "more economically liberal than perhaps any since 1958."[106] Moreover, the liberal interest groups allied with the Democratic Party (for instance, proponents of gun control, abortion, free health care, and civil rights) will be determined to produce some results from the new Democratic Congress, thus creating pressure on Democratic members striving to portray a moderate image.[107] The wishes of these liberal groups will be difficult to ignore, since their leaders and rank-and-file members are often campaign activists and strong partisans in the Democratic Party.

Presidents need to fashion policy agendas that sustain enthusiasm among their bases. As presidents reach out to Congress seeking support for their legislative agendas, they will not be able to pass laws on party-line votes. They will need some support from members of the opposite party, although would-be crossovers will see risks in collaborating with a president from the opposing party. Finding crossover votes is a major challenge as the centrists in Congress continue to dwindle in both number and influence.

The House-Senate Chasm

In a representative democracy based on separation of powers, the composition of the Congress must influence a president's agenda. Despite winning the presidency in 2000, the Republicans lost ground in Congress. Bush's "negative coattails" included a net loss of five Republican seats in the Senate and two in the House.[108]

In the House, Bush began with a small partisan edge: 221 Republicans versus 214 Democrats (actually two independents worked with the Democrats). After the 2004 election, this margin increased to its peak during Bush's tenure: 232 Republicans versus 203 Democrats. Much of this gain was attributable to the net effect of redistricting, which favored the Republicans.[109]

Bush was popular among rank-and-file House Republicans and the House leadership (Speaker Dennis Hastert and Majority Leader Tom DeLay). The House rules generally favor the wishes of the majority party more than the Senate rules do. Thus, the Bush administration often looked to the House for leadership on legislative issues, and the House Republicans were generally quite loyal to Bush.[110]

A key challenge Bush faced was finding common ground between the House and Senate. When the bills passed in each house were different, they needed to be reconciled. The typical House Republican was more conservative than the typical Senate Republican and vastly more conservative than the typical United States senator. Speaker Hastert complicated matters by taking the position that no bill should pass the House that was not supported by a majority of House Republicans. If Bush worked too hard to appease moderate Republicans and Democrats in the Senate, he ran the risk of opposition from rank-and-file Republicans in the House.

The dilemma was exacerbated by a long-standing yet peculiar feature of Senate rules, a feature that appears nowhere in the U.S. Constitution.[111] A single United States senator can block progress on legislation by threatening a filibuster. As political analyst Michael Barone has observed: "Journalists speak glibly about who controls the Senate. But no one controls the Senate. It is a body of 100 men and women, most of whom think or thought that he or she should be president. It is a legislative chamber that conducts much of its business under rules that require unanimous consent for many matters and in which a supermajority of 60 votes is required for much of what is routine business."[112]

For many decades the filibuster threat was limited to issues of great national significance, but now it is a core element of the minority party's strategy on a wide range of bills.[113] Greater use of the filibuster was fostered by a change in Senate rules that permits "double tracking": Business is permitted to proceed on one bill while efforts to resolve a "hold" or filibuster threat on another bill proceed. The increasing use of the filibuster threat appears to be both reflecting and exacerbating the partisan polarization in Congress.

Overcoming a Senate Filibuster Threat

When George W. Bush took office in 2001, the Republican margin in the Senate dwindled from 55–45 to a 50–50 stalemate, with Vice President Cheney serving as the tie-breaking vote. On May 24, 2001, veteran senator James Jeffords of Vermont stunned the Washington establishment by changing his party affiliation from Republican to independent. Obviously irritated by both the White House and the Senate Republican leadership (which had recently refused to fully grant his requests for special education funding), Jeffords decided to caucus with the Democrats, who awarded him the coveted chairmanship of the Senate Committee on Environment and Public Works.[114] The leadership of the Senate, and crucial control of the Senate floor agenda, was therefore ceded to the Democrats until the 2002 election. Tom Daschle of South Dakota replaced Trent Lott of Mississippi as Senate majority leader.

The Republicans regained control of the Senate in the 2002 midterm election and expanded the margin of control from 51–49 in 2002 to 55–45 in the 2004 election. Yet a close look at the composition of the Senate reveals why Bush's legislative proposals were highly vulnerable to the filibuster threat, even in the 2005–2006 period.

Sixty votes on the Senate floor are required to invoke cloture, thereby limiting the time for debate and ensuring a vote on the merits of a bill. At peak Republican strength in the 2005–2006 period, there were 55 Republican senators and 45 Democratic senators (counting Jeffords and Sanders as Democrats). Thus, no bill could overcome a filibuster threat without at least a handful of Democratic votes in favor of cloture. The challenge for the Bush White House was to minimize defections among Senate Republicans and maximize the number of crossover Democrats.

Enlisting support from Senate Democrats was no easy task for the Bush White House. As national political parties have been revitalized in fundraising and influence, elections to Congress have taken on a more national character.[115] Party leaders in Congress have more clout.[116] If the Senate Democratic leadership sought to kill a bill through a filibuster threat, a vote for cloture by any Democratic senator was, to put it mildly, looked on with disfavor. Moreover, senators who wished their own filibuster threats to be respected by colleagues were reluctant to oppose those of a valued (or powerful) Senate colleague.

Narrow partisan margins in the Senate actually strengthen the hands of party leaders, who point to the obvious value of party discipline and unity. Although party leaders in the Senate have less power than House leaders, Senate leaders are gaining power over time.[117] Senate majority leaders secure the outcome the party wants about 85 percent of the time. When one or more interest groups "score" a vote, the influence of the majority leader declines.[118]

In 2004 the retirement of key Democratic senators from the South (including John Breaux of Louisiana and Zell Miller of Georgia) exacerbated the polarization because southern Democrats were moderating influences in the Senate Democratic caucus. (As we shall see, Breaux was also highly skilled at forging bipartisan coalitions and brokering constructive compromises among Senate partisans.) As the number of Democratic senators dwindled, the minority became more liberal and antagonistic to the Bush White House. Thus, each additional senator that a party adds near the threshold of sixty has a somewhat diminished expected value to the party.[119]

If the Democratic leadership in the Senate could not be persuaded to collaborate with the White House, the most promising place to look for collaborators was the pool of Democratic senators from states that President Bush carried in 2000 and/or 2004. On occasion, other Senate moderates (such as Tom Carper of Delaware, Jim Jeffords of Vermont, Joe Lieberman of Connecticut, and Herbert Kohl of Wisconsin) were also possibilities. As we shall see in the chapters that follow, support from Democratic senators played a pivotal role in Bush's legislative accomplishments.

Any legislative proposal from the Bush administration was vulnerable to opposition from a determined minority in the Senate. Given that at least a handful of Republican defections could be expected on any controversial matter, Bush typically needed at least ten Democratic senators to join fifty Republicans in a crucial cloture vote. Without those votes, Bush could not be a successful lawmaker. During Bush's last two years in office, the Democratic Party was in the majority in both the House and Senate, forcing Bush to negotiate directly with the congressional Democratic leadership on legislative matters.

The Case Studies

In his first term, Bush set out to make progress on tax cuts, education, health care, and energy.[120] His second-term priorities were reform of Social Security, immigration law, and the tort system. In the chapters that follow, we examine what Bush actually accomplished on these issues.

Chapters 2 through 11 can be considered individual case studies of how Bush governed in domestic policy. In each case study, I consider what Bush sought to accomplish, whether he succeeded or failed, how he accomplished what he did, whether his policies are actually being implemented, and what some of the merits and drawbacks of his policies are.

The case-study approach is attractive because it allows us to capture the richness and political dynamics of an issue as the two terms of the Bush presidency unfold. In each chapter, readers are encouraged to look for whether (and why) the cross-partisan strategy was deployed, whether it succeeded or failed, and whether a modification or alternative to the cross-partisan technique might have been more effective. Readers are also encouraged to compare outcomes on procedural versus substantive votes, since the literature suggests that party pressures are greater on procedural votes.[121] I return to these issues in chapter 12, where I explore why future presidents are likely to find cross-partisan strategies highly attractive.

To the maximum extent possible, I have used public sources to document the legislative and executive developments. On occasion, I disclose White House strategic decisions that are based either on my personal understanding of what happened on the issue or on informal discussions I have had with my colleagues in the Bush administration. In each case study, I also include the key arguments of those who criticized the policies of the Bush administration, including references to relevant studies and articles. When I make preliminary determinations as to whether policies are promising or worthwhile, I provide references to relevant literature.

Since this is a book about Bush's policy-making record, not a book about the internal workings of the administration, I do not discuss the important roles of various members of the White House staff or officials at cabinet departments and agencies. I do capture some of the important interplay between the White House and individual members of Congress, since that interplay is essential to appreciating why the cross-partisan strategy succeeded or failed. I also bring to light the interplay between the White House, interest groups, Congress, and the federal judiciary.

In preparing the case studies, I kept a tally of members of the U.S. Senate who delivered key crossover votes, either Republican senators who voted against the Bush agenda or Democratic senators who voted for the Bush agenda. In the final chapter, I aggregate and analyze the crossover votes on roughly forty roll-call votes covered in the book. I conclude that crossover voting behavior is not random; it is highly correlated with Bush's electoral performance (2000 and 2004) in the states where crossover senators reside. These data provide some useful insights for future presidents who seek to identify wavering members of their own party as well as potential supporters from members of the opposing party.

Although this book covers a wide range of domestic issues, much wider than any previous book on the Bush presidency, it is not an exhaustive account. I have excluded Bush's policy responses to 9/11 and Hurricane Katrina, in part because these responses have already stimulated a substantial literature but also because they address a very different aspect of presidential performance: how well a president responds to unanticipated events. As tragic as these events were for our country, they are so unusual that they are arguably less important for the purpose of making generalizable statements about how future presidents can be effective in advancing their own domestic agendas. Other notable issues that were excluded for practical reasons include agriculture, highways, and information technology. Bush was an activist on these issues as well, but they did not represent his top-tier legislative priorities. I also do not cover Bush's Supreme Court nominations, though the cross-partisan technique was pivotal to his success in two confirmation battles.

2

Lower Taxes, More Spending

The fiscal policies of George W. Bush were decidedly expansionary: multiple rounds of tax cuts combined with substantial increases in the rate of federal spending (both domestic and military). Cross-partisanship was the key legislative strategy, and it was repeatedly successful. There is plenty of good news and bad news in these policies, but there is little doubt that Bush's fiscal policies were meaningful and will change the country for many years to come.

Proponents of the large tax cuts argue that they were each timed in a plausible way to compensate for cyclical weaknesses in the overall U.S. economy. Although they contributed to budgetary imbalance, the annual deficits were modest in size relative to the overall gross domestic product (GDP) and were not out of line with the tenets of textbook stabilization policy.[1] Proponents also argue that the early tax cuts made a significant long-term contribution to U.S. economic performance. The diminished marginal income tax rates, including the lower rate of taxation on income from capital gains and dividends, encouraged work and investment. The strong performance of the U.S. economy from 2003 to 2007 may have been aided by the 2001 and 2003 tax reforms. Whether the supply-side benefits of the tax cuts are fully realized depends critically on which features of the Bush tax cuts, if any, are retained in future tax law.[2]

Critics of the Bush tax cuts argue that they were weighted too heavily at the top of the income scale. This weakened their stimulus effects (since the poor spend more from marginal dollars than the rich do).[3] Critics also argue that the Bush fiscal agenda exacerbated the growth of income inequality in the USA.[4]

The worst aspect of Bush's fiscal policies is that no progress was made toward control of entitlement spending, especially Medicare, Medicaid, and Social Security. Bush deserves limited credit for making some (unpopular) proposals to reform these programs, but he never devised a viable political strategy to move them through a nervous and polarized Congress. Bush also rapidly expanded discretionary spending, especially in his first term. Overall, the combination of unrestrained entitlement spending, more discretionary spending, and lower taxes caused Bush to leave his successors with a more difficult fiscal challenge than he faced at the start of his first term.

At the end of the chapter, I shall argue that Bush did not need to forgo the tax cuts or even the occupation of Iraq in order to achieve fiscal balance. For now, I set the stage with the basic data on the economic conditions in the Bush era and a cautionary note about the uncertain causes of prosperity.

Humility: Economic Performance and Presidential Power

Inferring a president's performance as a policy maker from the state of the economy while he occupies the Oval Office is a dubious line of reasoning. Voters may think otherwise. Incumbents are generally re-elected in times of falling unemployment and ousted when unemployment is rising.[5] But the causal connections between a president's economic policies and near-term changes in U.S. economic performance are murky.

For starters, macroeconomists—especially the "monetarists"—generally assign primary importance to the policies of the U.S. Federal Reserve Board (FRB), which influences the supply of money in the economy and regulates much of the financial sector. The president does appoint the leaders of the Federal Reserve System, including the chairman of the FRB, subject to confirmation by the U.S. Senate. But the FRB chairman does not serve at the pleasure of the president like a cabinet officer does. In fact, there is a long history of the leaders of the FRB asserting their independence from the wishes of the White House and Congress—though determined presidents have, on occasion, had some impact on FRB policy.[6] Thus, if we accept the prevailing view of the monetarists, that monetary policy is the key driver of the economy, then much of U.S. economic performance is outside of any president's formal control.

Likewise, globalization is a reality. While the health of the U.S. economy influences the health of other economies in the world, the U.S. economy is affected by international developments that are outside the control of U.S. policy makers. For example, the U.S. economy can be helped and hurt by events elsewhere in the world (refinery shutdowns in Nigeria, for instance, contributed to a large spike in fuel prices in 2008). Since large segments of the U.S. economy are linked to valuable exports, our economy reaps benefits from growing markets around the globe. Presidents may take, or fail to take, steps that improve economic conditions in the United States, but the state of the U.S. economy cannot be isolated from international developments.

Table 2.1 provides basic economic indicators for the U.S. economy from 1990 to 2009. Those indicators reveal that George W. Bush entered and left the White House as the U.S. economy was faltering. The middle years of his presidency were a period of sustained economic growth coupled with relatively low rates of inflation and unemployment.

From 2001 to 2008, the U.S. economy grew faster than the economies of most advanced countries. Adjusting for inflation, GDP during this period grew 19 percent in the U.S., 14 percent in France, 13 percent in Japan, and 8 percent in both Italy and Germany. In 2005, GDP per capita in the U.S. ($41,813) was 33 percent larger than in the United Kingdom, 37 percent larger than in Germany, and 38 percent larger than in Japan.[7]

But truth be told, it is unlikely that Bush's policies are responsible for all of the good news or the bad news. The 2001 recession actually began in the Clinton years and is typically traced to the "dot-com bubble," the spectacular failure of a group of internet-based companies that were launched in a period of low interest rates, ample venture capital, and exuberant attitudes toward the future of the stock market. It was surely not caused by Bush's policies.

Table 2.1. U.S. Economic Indicators, 1990–2008

Year	% Δ in Real GDP	% Δ in CPI	Jobless Rate %
1990	1.9	5.4	5.6
1991	−0.2	4.2	6.8
1992	3.3	3.0	7.5
1993	2.7	3.0	6.9
1994	4.0	2.6	6.1
1995	2.5	2.8	5.6
1996	3.7	2.9	5.4
1997	4.5	2.3	4.9
1998	4.2	1.5	4.5
1999	4.5	2.2	4.2
2000	3.7	3.4	4.0
2001	0.8	2.8	4.7
2002	1.6	1.6	5.8
2003	2.5	2.3	6.0
2004	3.6	2.7	5.5
2005	3.1	3.4	5.1
2006	2.9	3.2	4.6
2007	2.0	2.8	4.6
2008	1.2	4.1	5.7
2009 (proj)	-2.2	0.1	8.3

Sources: U.S. Council of Economic Advisors, *Economic Report of the President, 2008,* Washington, D.C., Tables B-4, B-64, Table B-42, Table B-73. Also see U.S. Congressional Budget Office, *The Budget and Economic Outlook: Fiscal Years 2008–2018,* Washington, D.C., January 2008, Table 2-1, p. 21. U.S. Congressional Budget Office, *The Budget and Economic Outlook: Fiscal Years 2009 to 2019,* Washington, D.C., January 2009. GDP = Gross Domestic Product; CPI = Consumer Price Index.

There are some efforts to blame Bush's policies for the severe recession that began in 2008,[8] but the dominant view is that the economy slumped due to the collapse of housing prices, the subprime lending crisis, the proliferation of home foreclosures, the global credit crunch, and the rise of oil prices.[9] The oil-price rise was caused by the rapid growth of China and India, coupled with an unwillingness of the major oil-producing countries—especially the OPEC cartel—to respond with rapid increases in oil production. The housing crisis appears to be linked to a variety of monetary policies—easy money, lax oversight—that were initiated by FRB chairman Alan Greenspan in the Clinton years and sustained through the Bush years. Greenspan has questioned some of this criticism but acknowledged in congressional testimony that his regulatory policies were too lax.[10] Another independent agency, the Securities and Exchange Commission (SEC), contributed to the financial meltdown by failing to regulate a variety of complex financial instruments.[11] Without postulating strong White House control of the FRB and SEC, which would be quite a stretch, it is hard to pin the 2008 recession on Bush administration policies.

It was not just the bad times that were largely unrelated to Bush's policies. The good years from 2003 to 2007 were also related—at least in part—to factors outside the control of Bush administration policy.

The fiscal discipline of the Clinton years, an unplanned by-product of a surging economy and a struggle between Clinton and an anti-spending, Republican-controlled Congress, culminated in large budget surpluses in the late 1990s. As a result, financial markets and businesses experienced the reality of low rates of inflation and interest as well as a strong U.S. dollar in world markets. Clinton's relatively permissive trade and immigration policies, enacted with assistance from a Republican Congress, also provided a strong foundation for the U.S. economy as Bush took office. Most importantly, the rapid growth of the global economy, spurred by the booming economies of China and India, helped fuel export-related prosperity in the United States during the Bush years. Thus, although the economy was softening temporarily when Bush took office (in part due to a large stock market correction), Bush inherited an economy with such sound fundamentals that a period of sustained prosperity should not have been a surprise.

Recognizing that the president cannot single-handedly control the economy, I consider Bush's political strategies around tax policy and spending. I focus primarily on the multiple rounds of tax cuts, where Bush applied a daring yet successful cross-partisan strategy in the Senate.[12] I then turn to spending, with a look at why Bush and Congress are justly criticized for overspending.

Groundwork by House Republicans

The Congress delivered five rounds of tax cuts during Bush's tenure. The first, in early 2001, covered personal income; the second, in 2003, was aimed primarily at dividends and capital gains; the third, in 2004, was aimed at both individuals and corporations; the fourth, in 2006, was an extension of some of the prior cuts; and the fifth, in 2008, was a short-term stimulus package designed to boost consumer and business spending. Bush certainly played a central role in each of these legislative victories. But it was the Republican members of the House who, in hard-fought losses to President Clinton's veto power, set the stage for Bush's 2001 success. Thus, the story of the 2001 tax cut properly begins in the Clinton years.

The remarkable prosperity of the 1990s moved the federal budget from deficit to surplus. Prior to 1997, the federal government ran a deficit in twenty-nine consecutive budgets.[13] The surpluses began in 1997 and grew rapidly. (Some experts emphasize that the fiscal restraint after 1995 spurred economic growth, which in turn reduced deficits.)[14] The Congressional Budget Office (CBO) projected in July 2000 that, excluding Social Security, a total of $2.2 trillion of surpluses would accumulate over the next decade.[15] Those projections were based on important yet uncertain assumptions: continued economic growth, no changes in tax law, no changes in entitlement programs, and a rate of spending growth on discretionary programs equal to the projected rate of inflation in the economy.

A partisan battle erupted over how the projected surpluses should be allocated. Republican leaders in Congress proposed that more than one-third of the projected surpluses ($792 billion over ten years) be returned to taxpayers in the form of reductions in personal and corporate taxes. (Governor George W. Bush of Texas, then a presidential candidate, made an early endorsement of the large tax-cut package passed by the Republican-controlled House of Representatives.)[16] Democrats preferred a much smaller tax-cut package, arguing that more of the surpluses should be used for expanded spending programs and payments on the national debt.

A confrontation ensued between President Clinton and the Republican Congress. Clinton could not persuade the Congress to enact his plan, which included only limited tax cuts. Nor did the Republicans have their way. Clinton vetoed a series of ambitious tax-cut plans passed by the Republican Congress in 1999 and 2000. Although there was some Democratic support in Congress for large tax cuts, the Republican-led efforts to override Clinton's vetoes fell short of the required two-thirds margin in both chambers.

During the 2000 election campaign, the presidential candidates from the two major parties—Vice President Al Gore and Governor George W. Bush—

took differing positions on taxes and spending.[17] Both campaigns accepted an updated estimate that $4.56 trillion in surpluses would accumulate over the next ten years. They also agreed that $2.9 trillion should be set aside to shore up Social Security. But they disagreed sharply on the relative size of tax cuts; Vice President Gore proposed $480 billion, while Governor Bush proposed $1.3 trillion.

The Bush-Gore difference on tax cuts was not only a core issue of the presidential campaign. It was at the center of numerous House and Senate election campaigns in 2000, where the candidates of the two parties often echoed the dispute between Bush and Gore.

The 2000 election results were so ambiguous that they led to different partisan interpretations. In January 2001 the newly elected president and the Republican Congress established tax cuts as the number one legislative priority. Democrats saw things differently. The 2000 presidential election was so close and hotly disputed that it was difficult to discern a political mandate for large-scale tax cuts (or any other specific policy agenda). In public opinion polls, one could find little bipartisan groundswell of support for a big tax cut.[18] Since the Democrats actually gained seats in the Congress, they were in a strong position to argue that there was no Republican mandate for a big tax cut.

Overcoming the Filibuster Threat

Inside the White House, the outlook for passage of major tax cuts in 2001 was indeed quite murky. The House was expected to pass a large tax cut again because the Republicans, still the majority party, lost only a handful of seats in the 2000 election. Under House rules, only a majority vote on the House floor is required for major legislation. But the obstacles to passing a big tax cut in the Senate were considerable because Senate rules effectively require sixty votes to bypass filibusters and budgetary points of order. Since some moderate Republicans as well as many Democrats were skeptical of the case for a big tax cut, passing it in the Senate seemed doubtful.

As legislative strategies were considered, the White House rejected the classic bipartisan pathway to legislation. The president's advisers were not inclined to expose the new president's economic agenda to a complex negotiation with Democratic leaders. In this highly polarized setting, the Democratic leadership in Congress had strategic incentives to weaken the new president by blocking his first major economic-policy initiative—just as congressional Republicans weakened President Clinton by opposing in unison his first budget in 1993.[19] Even without this strategic incentive to obstruct, the partisan differences on the substance of fiscal policy were so large at the start of 2001 that there was no basis for a belief that an acceptable bipartisan agreement in Congress could be found.

A partisan strategy was also rejected because the number of Republican votes was insufficient. With the net loss of four seats in the November 2000 election, the Republicans faced a 50–50 Senate in early 2001. Vice President Cheney could—and later would, when necessary—break ties with a vote favoring the White House position. But fifty-one votes are usually inadequate. Under normal legislative procedures, even a unanimous vote for a tax cut by the fifty Senate Republicans would fall ten votes short. Moreover, four moderate Republican senators (Lincoln Chafee of Rhode Island, Jim Jeffords of Vermont, Arlen Specter of Pennsylvania, and George Voinovich of Ohio) cast votes in 2000 to sustain President Clinton's veto of the Republican tax-cut plan. Nobody in the White House was prepared to count on support from these four Republican senators. As expected, when Bush announced his proposal in 2001, Jeffords and Chafee were quick to balk at the size of the cuts.[20] Thus, a purely partisan legislative strategy on tax cuts was not viable in the Senate.

The White House chose instead a cross-partisan strategy with a procedural wrinkle: The tax cuts were included in the budget reconciliation process.[21] The advantage of this maneuver is that only a simple majority in the Senate is required for passage; the disadvantage is that the tax cuts could not be made permanent. By including a "sunset" provision with the tax cuts, set ten years after enactment, Bush's tax package was protected from a budgetary point of order (and a filibuster threat) that would have required sixty votes to waive. Thus, in order to win passage in the evenly divided Senate, the White House needed to win as many Republican votes as possible while finding at least one supportive Democratic senator for each Republican senator who defected.

The White House had good reason to believe that some supportive Democratic senators could be found. In 1999, when the Senate voted 57 to 43 in favor of a $792 billion tax-cut package, there were four Democrats who voted yes (Breaux and Landrieu of Louisiana, Kerrey of Nebraska, and Torricelli of New Jersey). Only two Republican senators voted no (Specter of Pennsylvania and Voinovich of Ohio). However, when a modified package emerged from a House-

Senate conference, a compromise tilted toward the original House version, the conference report ultimately passed the Senate by only one vote (50 to 49). In fact, no Democratic senators cast votes to support the 1999 conference report, and two more moderate Republican senators defected (Collins and Snowe of Maine). This sobering experience suggested that winning some Democratic votes for a tax cut on the Senate floor was possible, but far from assured.

There was some additional evidence that moderate Democrats were "gettable." After the Republicans failed to override Clinton's veto of their comprehensive tax-cut package in 1999, House Republicans responded in 2000 by passing a series of separate bills containing individual elements of the larger package. This strategy forced difficult votes for Democrats in the Congress. A significant number of Senate Democrats voted for one tax-cut provision or another. For example, in 2000 a repeal of the inheritance tax was passed in the Senate 59 to 39, with more than two Democrats supporting the measure for every Republican who opposed it. But these votes are not easy to interpret with confidence because all senators knew that there were insufficient votes to overcome the ensuing veto by President Clinton, which could be overridden only with a two-thirds vote.

In light of the legislative realities, the Bush White House pursued a cross-partisan strategy. Actually, it was a combination of a partisan strategy in the House (there were virtually no negotiations with Democrats) and a cross-partisan strategy in the Senate. The White House negotiated only with a limited number of moderate Republican and Democratic senators who held the key to passage.

The cross-partisan strategy under budget reconciliation irritated many people: the ignored liberal Democrats, conservatives who sought permanent tax cuts, and idealists who see bipartisanship as the model of good government. But the cross-partisan strategy worked in getting the tax cut enacted.

A Trillion-Dollar Tax Cut

A $1.35 trillion, ten-year package was cleared by Congress on May 26, 2001, and signed into law by President Bush on June 7. The rapid speed of congressional action is remarkable, faster than the 1981 tax cuts that occurred after Ronald Reagan's landslide victory over Jimmy Carter in 1980.[22] A confluence of strategic and fortuitous factors contributed to the pace of success.

A key concession from the White House at the outset simplified the political calculations. The focus of the package was personal income taxes.[23] Taxes on businesses were not addressed. Although this omission was a blow to a key element of the Republican base, it also removed the immense complication of balancing the interests of different business sectors.

Unexpected support came in January from Alan Greenspan, chairman of the Federal Reserve Board. Prior to Bush's election, Greenspan took the public position that the projected surpluses should be devoted to reducing the national debt. But as the economy showed signs of weakening in late 2000, Greenspan testified in early 2001 that tax cuts were an appropriate stimulus. The new stimulus rationale opened the door for moderate Republicans and Democrats to reconsider their previous reservations about the fiscal responsibility of large tax cuts.[24]

The House built momentum in 2001 with a series of decisive floor votes favoring key components of the package: rate reductions for individuals (230 to 198), relief from the marriage penalty (282 to 144), repeal of the estate tax (274 to 154), and larger incentives for retirement savings (407 to 24). In a remarkable display of unity, House Republicans were unanimous in the first two votes; the third vote witnessed three Republican defections, and the fourth only one.

Progress was slower in the Senate, where Republican Finance Committee chair Charles Grassley of Iowa worked patiently with moderate Democrat Max Baucus of Montana.[25] Their bill was drafted to appeal to Senate moderates while retaining White House support. Although the tax relief was smaller, and weighted more heavily toward lower-income taxpayers, than Bush had requested, the White House encouraged the effort.[26] Grassley and Baucus won a crucial 14–6 vote in committee, despite skepticism from the Senate Democratic leadership.

Irritated by Baucus's cooperative approach, Daschle and other leading Senate Democrats did not accept the large tax cuts without a contentious Senate floor debate.[27] They argued that the package was fiscally irresponsible because the huge loss of revenue would exacerbate deficits for many years and put the entire Social Security system at financial risk. They also argued that the tax cuts were unfair because they were weighted too heavily toward high-income taxpayers.[28] But a Democratic proposal with more modest tax cuts aimed primarily at lower-income taxpayers did not generate majority support on the Senate floor.

Senate Democrats did bruise Bush by winning a close vote to reduce the size of the tax cut by $448 billion over ten years. This nearly party-line vote included only three Republican defectors (Chafee of Rhode Island, Jeffords of Vermont, and Specter of Pennsylvania) and only one crossover Democrat (Miller of Georgia).

In the vote for overall passage, however, the cross-partisan strategy worked as the White House hoped. The Grassley-Baucus package passed 62 to 38, with twelve Democratic senators joining all fifty Republican senators in a crucial vote. With the exception of Feinstein of California and Torricelli of New Jersey, the crossover Democrats were from the South and Midwest: Baucus of Montana, Breaux of Louisiana, Carnahan of Missouri, Cleland of Georgia, Johnson of South Dakota, Kohl of Wisconsin, Lincoln of Arkansas, Miller of Georgia, and Nelson of Nebraska. Although some moderate Republicans expressed reservations about the package, the unanimous vote by Senate Republicans included some gestures of deference to the top legislative priority of the newly elected Republican president.

The Senate floor action on tax cuts occurred the same day that veteran senator James Jeffords surprised Washington with the news that he was switching his party affiliation from Republican to independent, and caucusing with the Democrats. The result was a dramatic switch of party control in the Senate, with Democrat Tom Daschle of South Dakota replacing Republican Trent Lott as majority leader. Thus, the tax-cut issue went to a House-Senate conference when all participants knew that the Democrats were taking control of the Senate floor.

Four individuals controlled the House-Senate conference: House Ways and Means Committee chair Bill Thomas, and Baucus, Breaux, and Grassley of the Senate Finance Committee. Recognizing that the Democrats were about to assume control of the Senate, the Bush White House and Republican leaders made sure that both Baucus and Breaux, who were perceived as keys to moderate Democratic support in the Senate, supported the conference report. The result was further skewing of the package toward the interests of middle-income and low-income taxpayers.

Table 2.2 summarizes the key provisions of the 2001 tax-cut package. Overall, there were $875 billion in rate cuts, $172 billion in an enlarged child tax credit, $138 billion in cuts in estate taxes, $63 billion in marriage penalty relief, $50 billion in incentives for retirement savings, and $29 billion in tax breaks for educational expenses.

Table 2.2. Key Provisions of the 2001 Tax-Cut Package

Old Law	New Law
Five personal-income brackets: 15%, 28%, 31%, 36%, 39.6%	Created new 10% bracket for low-income filers; New brackets: 10%, 15%, 25%, 28%, 33%, 35% (2006).
Limits on deductions and personal exemptions available to higher-income filers	Phased out limits on itemized deductions and personal exemptions.
Sixty provisions treated single taxpayers differently from married couples filing jointly	Raised standard deduction for married couples filing jointly; expanded upper boundary of 15% for married couples filing jointly; expanded eligibility for earned-income tax credit.
Child tax credit of $500 for each child under age 17	Child tax credit doubled to $1,000 by 2010; refundable credit for families with low income and low tax liability; expanded child adoption credit; expanded dependent care credit.
Alternative minimum tax (AMT)	Raised income limits on exemption from AMT; allowed tax credit for some AMT filers.
Education savings accounts (ESAs)	Raised annual contribution limits; expanded qualified expenses to include some K–12 education as well as college; income limits on use of ESAs raised, especially for married couples.
Estate taxes	Reduced and repealed in 2010.
Unified credit—point at which estate and generation-skipping taxes apply	Raised from $675,000 to $3.5 million in 2009.
Gift taxes (top rate 55%)	Set rate at the highest personal income tax rate (35% in 2010).
Retirement accounts	Raised annual contribution limits.

The final tax-cut package passed the House 240 to 154 as the 211 Republicans were unanimous and 29 Democrats defied the wishes of the Democratic leadership. The Senate vote was 58 to 33. Although Republican senators John McCain and Lincoln Chafee defected, the Bush White House again picked up crucial votes from twelve Democratic senators.

The Quest for Sixty Votes

The fifty-eight votes in the Senate were so close to the sixty-vote goal that tax-cut optimists began to contemplate legislation that would make the tax cuts permanent. In order to do so, they needed to win a majority vote in the

House, persuade Democratic Majority Leader Tom Daschle to schedule a vote on the Senate floor, and achieve the required sixty-vote majority on the Senate floor.

In April 2002 the House voted 229 to 198 in favor of permanence but a Senate vote was never scheduled. Later in the year the House voted 256 to 171 to extend the repeal of the estate tax indefinitely. Daschle agreed to schedule a cloture vote on repeal of the estate tax, but Republicans fell six votes short (54–44) of the required tally. The only Republican defectors were McCain and Chafee, but Daschle limited the number of Democratic defectors to nine (Baucus, Bayh, Cleland, Landrieu, Miller, Nelson of Florida and Nelson of Nebraska, and Wyden of Oregon).

The failure to achieve sixty votes on the estate-tax repeal is an indication that the White House's original tactic of enacting tax cuts as part of budget reconciliation, where only a simple majority of senators was required, was warranted. But, as we shall see, the fight to make the tax cuts permanent did not end in 2002.

Why was the 2001 tax cut such a big political accomplishment? While it was somewhat smaller than Bush's request, it was the largest tax cut since the early years of Ronald Reagan. Recognizing the rising of polarization in Congress, the package represented a major accomplishment for a president who had been elected with the smallest Electoral College margin in modern history. But it should not be forgotten that it was the Republicans in Congress, in the bitter battle with Clinton in 1999–2000, who established the groundwork for Bush's tax-cut victory in early 2001. It was in 2003 that Bush achieved his most unexpected tax-cut accomplishment.

A Win for Supply-Siders

In May 2003 President Bush signed into law a second round of tax cuts totaling $350 billion, the distinctive feature of which was a reduction in individual taxes on stock dividends and capital gains. A new 15 percent tax rate was created, a sharp decline from previous law which taxed capital gains at 20 percent and treated dividends as ordinary income (subject to a tax rate as high as 38.6 percent). To provide near-term economic stimulus, the package also accelerated some of the cuts in personal-income taxes that were passed in 2001. Even more than the 2001 package, this one was a personal victory for Bush because it was more his priority than a priority of congressional Republicans.

The second Bush tax cut is a mystery to some balanced-budget advocates. There was no strong public demand for a tax cut; the budget surpluses from the Clinton years had vanished; and the future budget deficits appeared to be ominous.[29] But the Bush White House was concerned that the recovery from the 2001 recession was still not robust—indeed, many critics were calling it a "jobless recovery." Economic worries about the aftermath of 9/11 were still being felt.

Prior to the 2002 midterm elections, both parties agreed that Congress needed to pass an economic-stimulus package. Yet the two parties moved in different directions on how taxes and spending should be modified to stimulate the economy.

The House, controlled by Republicans, advanced a tax-relief package for businesses as well as individuals. The Senate, led by the Democrats, sought expanded unemployment insurance and more federal government backing of health insurance premiums and Medicaid expenses. Some moderate Senate Democrats (such as Breaux of Louisiana) sought to find a bipartisan compromise for a broad-based stimulus package but no deal was made. While sympathetic with the House Republicans, Bush did not expend much political capital at this stage, in part because no feasible path to legislation was apparent.

The campaigns preceding the November 2002 midterm elections witnessed strong national themes (such as concerns about homeland security and the need for economic stimulus). A highly energetic Bush, buoyed by his post-9/11 surge in popularity, raised large sums of money and actively campaigned for his party's House and Senate candidates in key races throughout the country.[30]

The election result was a stunner in Washington. Most presidents lose support in Congress at the first midterm election, but the Republicans in 2002 regained control of the Senate and widened their margin of majority in the House.[31]

Encouraged by his Council of Economic Advisers (CEA), Bush in early 2003 proposed another massive round of tax cuts.[32] In the fiscal year 2004 budget he sent to Congress, Bush included $1.57 trillion in tax cuts from 2003 to 2013. Almost one-quarter of the package was a bold new proposal: an elimination of federal taxation of stock dividends and capital gains that were already taxed as corporate income.[33] The "supply-side" economists, who had advocated this idea for decades, were now assured that their policy idea would finally be considered.

The supply-side rationale is certainly logical. Taxing corporate income twice—once at the corporate level and again at the individual level—reduces the after-tax reward for saving and investing. It therefore reduces capital formation.[34] It also allocates capital away from the corporate sector, even when gross returns justify corporate investment relative to other types of investment. Thus, the economic case for eliminating the double taxation of corporate income is that it boosts the long-term efficiency of the economy, ultimately producing higher productivity, wages, and employment—not just more corporate investment.[35]

The White House and congressional Republicans made an early decision to pursue a cross-partisan strategy, again using budget reconciliation as a device to avoid the sixty-vote requirement in the Senate. The White House requested that Congress include $726 billion of the $1.57 billion package in the fiscal year 2004 budget resolution, thereby ensuring that at least this portion of Bush's package would be protected against a filibuster (and a budgetary point of order) on the Senate floor.

The Democratic leadership in Congress chose to fight. Their goal was to block or diminish the second round of tax cuts. They argued that the effects of the tax changes on corporate behavior would be limited while the adverse effects of the larger budget deficits (due to revenue losses) on the overall economy would be more serious than any long-term efficiency gain.[36] They also raised fairness concerns, claiming that the majority of the tax savings would go to households with more than $1 million per year in income.[37]

House Republicans quickly rallied in support of the tax-cut request during deliberations on the budget resolution. House Democrats countered that large tax cuts were irresponsible given the growing budget deficit and the unknown future costs of the war in Iraq. Despite the lack of Democratic support, House Budget Committee chairman Jim Nussle of Iowa moved a resolution through his committee on a party-line vote. The resolution provided for $726 billion in tax cuts as both a near-term stimulus for an ailing economy and a long-term, pro-growth measure.

On the House floor, Nussle and the White House found many queasy Republicans raising fiscal concerns. Vice President Cheney was enlisted to help find floor votes for the budget resolution. When the votes were cast, it appeared that Nussle's resolution was going down to defeat. House leaders kept the vote open longer than usual as final pleas were made and arms twisted. When two members from Texas, Republican Larry Campbell and conservative Democrat Ralph M. Hall, switched their votes, the budget resolution passed 215 to 212.

The tussle in the Senate was even closer. At Bush's urging, Senate Budget Committee chairman Don Nickles moved the budget resolution through his committee on a party-line vote. But when the resolution went to the floor, moderate Democrat John Breaux of Louisiana—sometimes a Bush ally—fought to slash the size of the tax cuts, citing concerns about the growing budget deficit. As the floor debate unfolded, it became apparent that Breaux was not simply representing Senate Democrats; he also had the support of some moderate Republicans, including Lincoln Chafee of Rhode Island, Olympia Snowe of Maine, and George Voinovich of Ohio.

Breaux first won a $100 billion reduction in the tax cuts. But then the White House announced the size of their supplemental budget request for the war in Iraq: another $74.7 billion. Breaux then persuaded the Senate to take a much bigger bite, as the tax cuts protected by the resolution were slashed to $350 billion. The Democrats were united while three Republicans defected (Chafee of Rhode Island, Snowe of Maine, and Voinovich of Ohio). In light of Breaux's maneuvers, Bush's proposal to eliminate the tax on stock dividends and capital gains, estimated to cost $395.8 billion, was clearly in jeopardy.

Resolution of the issue occurred in a difficult House-Senate conference negotiation. The House and Senate tax-cut provisions were so different, $729 billion versus $350 billion, that the pathway to agreement was not obvious. House conservatives threatened to walk away from a conference report that did not meet Bush's request. Senate moderates insisted that there were no more than forty-eight votes in the Senate for any conference report with a tax cut exceeding $350 billion.

Conferees appeared to reach an agreement of $550 billion, but Senator Grassley found it impossible to pass that figure through the Senate. In a strange arrangement, Grassley obtained the necessary votes by assuring Senate moderates that the true size of the tax cut would not exceed $350 billion, even though the conferees had agreed on $550 billion. The conference report passed the House and Senate on largely party-line votes (216 to 211 in the House and 51 to 50 in the Senate). Vice President Cheney was forced to cast a tie-breaking vote for the report in the Senate because, while Democrat Zell Miller voted for the report, Republicans Lincoln Chafee and John McCain voted against it.

Passing the budget resolution was only the first step in the process. A specific tax-cut plan also needed to be passed. Bush's allies in Congress warned the White House that they could not deliver Bush's full package.

In the House, Ways and Means Committee chair Bill Thomas of California moved a $550 billion tax-cut package through his committee and the floor on largely party-line votes. But the Thomas package replaced the proposed elimination of the taxes on capital gains and stock dividends with a more modest reduction in the applicable rates.[38]

The obstacles in the Senate were greater. Senator Grassley moved a $350 billion package through the Finance Committee only after he sweetened the package by adding $20 billion in state aid to help attract the support of Republican Susan Collins of Maine and Democrat Ben Nelson of Nebraska. Grassley was able to retain elimination of the dividend/capital gains taxes, as Bush had requested, but only by raising other business-related taxes—a move that sparked controversy among Bush's business allies. Bush helped Grassley by traveling to states with wavering Democrats, making a pitch for crossover Democratic votes in the Senate.[39] Grassley's package squeaked through the Senate 51 to 49, with three crucial Democratic votes compensating for the three Republican senators who defected.

With the House and Senate bills so different, the prospects of a second tax-cut package getting to the Bush's desk were questionable. The House-Senate conference did not begin smoothly due to disagreements between Representative Thomas and Senator Grassley. Vice President Cheney intervened to accelerate progress and broker a deal with Senator George Voinovich of Ohio, a key Republican moderate. The White House reluctantly agreed to a $350 billion ceiling on the net cost of the package, with the $20 billion in state financial relief counted as part of the $350 billion.

Frustrated House Republicans, bowing to White House insistence, passed the conference report 231 to 200. Cheney again cast the tie-breaking vote in the Senate (51 to 50). The previous 51-to-49 Senate vote could not be duplicated because three moderate Republican senators defected (Chafee of Rhode Island, McCain of Arizona, and Snowe of Maine). Two critical crossover Democrats (Miller of Georgia and Nelson of Nebraska) were just enough to enable Cheney's vote to pass the conference report.

The 2003 tax cuts were distinctive because of the focus on stock dividends and capital gains, a Bush priority that many skeptics felt was impossible to enact. Indeed, Democrats argued that this focus skewed the entire package too much in favor of upper-income taxpayers, who do the most investing.[40] But the White House made some progress with the long-run argument that diminished taxes on stock dividends and capital gains encourage investment and enhance economic growth. As a result, Bush and the Congress reduced the rate of federal taxation on dividends and capital gains to its lowest level since World War II.[41] The result, proponents say, was a multiyear period (2003–2007) of rising productivity, falling unemployment, and rising incomes for most Americans.[42]

Failure to Make the Tax Cuts Permanent

In his fiscal year 2005 budget request, Bush again advocated that his 2001 and 2003 tax cuts be made permanent. Recognizing that this request was not likely to be politically feasible, Bush also proposed a $107 billion package of short-term extensions of his 2001 and 2003 tax cuts. Congress responded with modest, noncontroversial steps: extending the child tax credit and the relief for married couples, enlarging the upper income limit for the lowest (10 percent) tax bracket, and providing limited exemptions to the alternative minimum tax (AMT). A tax credit for businesses covering the costs of research and development (R+D) was coupled with the personal tax relief.[43] Election-year squabbles precluded anything more ambitious.

After Bush's re-election in 2004, the Republican lead in the Senate grew from 51–49 to 55–45. Optimists in the White House looked for ways to make the 2001 and 2003 tax cuts permanent. That is in fact what Bush proposed in his fiscal year 2006 budget request to Congress.

In reality, the close 2004 election did not deliver the White House any political mandate for permanent tax cuts.[44] The stark realities were sobering. With a growing federal budget deficit, a large and unpredictable rate of spending in Afghanistan and Iraq, and Bush's austere 2006 request for spending on domestic programs that are generally popular in Congress, many members of the House and Senate questioned the wisdom of additional tax cuts.

In the fiscal year 2006 budget resolution, the best Bush's congressional allies could deliver was a provision for $70 billion in tax cuts over five years, with details to be specified later. After much partisan debate and delays caused by the aftermath of Hurricane Katrina, Congress delivered another small tax-cut package. Tax relief on stock dividends and capital gains was extended for two years (until 2010) while one year of AMT relief was also provided. A two-year extension in the permission for small businesses to deduct up to $100,000 in appreciable assets in one year was also included. The final package, which included $70 billion in net tax cuts over five years, was passed 244–185 in the House and 54–44 in the Senate. Bush lost Republicans Chafee of Rhode Island, Snowe of Maine, and Voinovich of Ohio but picked up Democrats Nelson of Nebraska, Nelson of Florida, and Pryor of Arkansas.

The closest that Congress came to making any of the tax cuts permanent was a roll-call vote in June 2006 to repeal the estate tax. Under the 2001 reform, the estate tax declines and is then repealed entirely for one year (2010). In 2011 it is scheduled to revert to its 2001 level.

The estate-tax repeal was considered a best-case scenario for congressional Republicans because the revenue loss was estimated to be modest ($80 billion over ten years), and an activist group of farmers and other small businessmen with ties to Democratic (as well as Republican) politicians felt strongly about the issue.

After the 2004 elections, the House pressured the Senate by passing a permanent repeal of the estate tax. Even without support from the House Democratic leadership, this initiative passed the House with close to a two-thirds majority: 272 to 162.

In the Senate, Republican Jon Kyl of Arizona teamed with Democrat Max Baucus of Montana on a committee-approved bill to repeal the estate tax. Senate majority leader Bill Frist, the White House favorite who succeeded Trent Lott, delayed a roll-call vote in the Senate several times, hoping for a stronger assurance that the required sixty votes were there. In June 2006 a roll-call vote fell three votes short, thus preventing Frist from bringing the estate-tax bill to the floor or considering any compromise that might expand the tax break rather than repealing it permanently. The Republican defectors were Chafee of Rhode Island and Voinovich of Ohio. Only four Democrats crossed over: Baucus of Montana, Lincoln of Arkansas, Nelson of Nebraska, and Nelson of Florida. It was a big disappointment to Bush and Frist.

When the Democrats captured control of the Congress in November 2006, any faint hope that Bush had of making his tax cuts permanent vanished. The congressional debate quickly shifted to which provisions of the Bush tax cuts should expire, which should be scaled back, and which should be retained. Some Democrats began calling for tax hikes aimed primarily at investors, high-income taxpayers, and corporations.[45] Although some conservatives feared that all of the Bush tax cuts might be repealed,[46] the positions of Democratic presidential candidates Hillary Clinton and Barack Obama became more nuanced. In a televised debate in Indiana, both pledged not to raise taxes on any individual who makes less than $200,000 per year. Meanwhile, Republican candidate John McCain reversed the position he had taken as senator and pledged to make the Bush tax cuts permanent.[47]

Thus, the Bush White House was highly successful in using the reconciliation procedure to achieve the large 2001 and 2003 tax cuts, but there were insufficient votes to make them permanent. Despite Republican gains in the Senate in 2004, the dwindling pool of Senate Democrats became more tightly knit, and they knew they needed to hold together or the Bush White House would divide and conquer them on one issue after another. Indeed, it is doubtful whether the Bush White House could have found even fifty votes in the Senate for making the tax cuts permanent.

Despite the temporary nature of the cuts, they have a substantial political constituency and a cogent supply-side rationale. Given the stances of the presidential candidates in 2008, it appears that the fabric of political debate is turning toward retention of at least substantial parts of the Bush tax cuts. The devil will be in the details of what Congress passes in 2010.

Bush's Final Tax Cut: 2008 Stimulus Package

As the economy weakened in late 2007, the Democratic leadership in Congress and President Bush agreed that additional stimulation of the economy was urgently needed. Ben Bernanke, chairman of the FRB, launched multiple rounds of interest-rate cuts to stimulate the economy while encouraging Congress and the White House to pass a prompt fiscal stimulus package.

Supply-side economists urged the Bush White House to couple any short-term stimulus measures with additional pro-growth incentives to enhance the long-term performance of the economy.[48] Liberal economists objected that more cuts for investors will not spur much consumer spending.[49] They argued that the most effective immediate stimuli would be more federal spending on unemployment insurance or state infrastructure, and tax rebates for low- and middle-income families.[50] Some conservative economists warned that rebates would simply be saved or used to pay off consumer debts.[51] But many liberal economists joined Bernanke in arguing that prompt rebates for working-class families would have a fast-acting stimulus effect on consumer spending.[52]

Bush decided not to insist on further pro-growth policies, such as an extension of his cuts in capital gains taxes or more reductions in marginal tax rates. In a rare instance of bipartisan agreement, Bush and the Congress ultimately settled on $100 billion in tax credits and rebates for 117 million families plus some tax incentives for new business equipment.[53] The package was a rapid response to rising unemployment, a weakening manufacturing sector, a slow holiday retail shopping season, and a weakening stock market. At the end of April 2008, the government began sending stimulus checks to low- and middle-income Americans (at least $600 to individuals, $1,200 to families). The checks seemed to boost retail sales temporarily, but a much larger economic crisis was developing (see chapter 11).[54]

Federal Tax Burdens in Perspective

The Bush administration was persistent about cutting federal income taxes, but the historical relationship between federal tax revenues and gross domestic product was not fundamentally altered. The ratio of federal tax revenues to GDP in the United States has fluctuated around 18 percent for the past forty years. During the Clinton years, it surged to more than 20 percent. Despite Bush's 2001 and 2003 tax cuts, the ratio was 18.8 percent in 2007 and 17.7 percent in 2008, near the forty-year-average.[55] Thus, it is difficult to argue that Bush left the American economy undertaxed, at least by historical standards.

Bush's fiscal policies are vulnerable to the criticism that budget deficits are de facto or implicit tax increases, since they must be financed (for instance, by Treasury bonds or future tax increases). Known as Ricardian equivalence, this point highlights the fact that Bush's success in tax cuts is qualified—at least to some extent—by his practice of running significant annual federal deficits. If informed consumers perceive these deficits as implicit tax hikes, they may constrain consumption in order to pay for them.

Excessive Spending or Misdirected Priorities?

One of the most vociferous objections to the 2001 and 2003 Bush tax cuts is that they exacerbated federal budgetary problems.[56] A commonly held

Table 2.3. Federal Revenues and Outlays, 2001–2009

Fiscal Year	Revenues ($B)	Outlays ($B)	Surplus/Deficit ($B)
2001	+1991	−1863	128
2002	+1853	−2011	−158
2003	+1783	−2160	−378
2004	+1880	−2293	−413
2005	+2154	−2472	−318
2006	+2407	−2655	−248
2007	+2568	−2730	−162
2008	+2524	−2978	−455
2009*	+2357	−3543	−1,186

*Estimates

Sources: U.S. Congressional Budget Office, *The Budget and Economic Outlook: Fiscal Years 2008–2018,* Washington, D.C., January 2008, Table 1-1, p. 2, and Table 1-3, p. 8. Also see U.S. Council of Economic Advisers, *Economic Report to the President, 2008* (statistical tables); U.S. Congressional Budget Office, *The Budget and Economic Outlook: Fiscal Years 2009–2019,* Washington, D.C., January 2009.

view is that the tax cuts exacerbated the annual federal deficits and ensured massive deficits for many years into the future.[57]

In order to assess this argument, it is necessary to examine the spending as well as the revenue side of the ledger. As we shall see, Bush's spending habits contributed substantially to the annual budget deficits. With a somewhat more restrained spending policy, Bush could have retained his tax cuts—which appear to have boosted economic performance in the years prior to the financial meltdown—without creating significant federal deficits.

Table 2.3 presents data on federal revenues and budgetary outlays for fiscal years 2000 through 2009, recognizing that 2002 was the first budget prepared by the Bush administration. The Bush tax cuts did contribute to the growing federal deficits in fiscal years 2003 and 2004, but as the economy recovered, the deficits declined rapidly in absolute terms and as a percentage of gross domestic product. The federal budget deficit declined from a peak of $413 billion in 2004 to $162 billion in 2007 (about 1.2 percent of GDP). Before the U.S. economy slumped in 2008, the federal budget deficit was projected to stay below 1.5 percent of GDP until Bush left office, far below the forty-year average of 2.4 percent of GDP. (The red ink reached a post–World War II high of 6 percent of GDP

Table 2.4. Composition and Growth of Federal Outlays, 2000–2009

Fiscal Year	Mandatory Spending	Discretionary Spending	Non-Defense	Defense
2000	951	615	320	295
2001	1008	649	343	306
2002	1106	734	385	349
2003	1182	825	420	405
2004	1237	895	441	454
2005	1320	968	475	494
2006	1412	1017	497	520
2007	1450	1042	493	549
2008	1507	1133	—	—
2009*	2164	1184	—	—

Sources: U.S. Congressional Budget Office, January 2008, Table 1-3, p. 8. Table F-9, p. 156; U.S. Congressional Budget Office, January 2009, p. 3.

*Estimates. "—" indicates not yet available.

in fiscal year 1983.) Some forecasters were projecting that Bush might actually leave office with the federal budget in surplus, but those forecasts assumed that no recession would occur.[58] The actual 2008 deficit was $455 billion, about 3.2 percent of GDP, due to a sharp decline in revenues from the recession, more spending on unemployment insurance and food stamps, and more revenue loss from the stimulus package.[59]

Overall, the Bush era was a period of heavy spending growth. Compared to the 27 percent inflation of prices from 2000 to 2008, total defense spending rose 106 percent while all other spending rose 55 percent.[60] Discretionary outlays grew sharply from $649 billion in 2001 to an estimated $1,089 billion in 2008 (see table 2.4). Over the same period, mandatory outlays grew from $1,008 billion to $1,550 billion. Bush's policies, in conjunction with congressional decisions, permitted the annual amount of federal spending to increase by more than a trillion dollars.

If spending growth had been somewhat more restrained, the loss of federal revenues from tax cuts would not have led to such large federal deficits. For example, if total federal outlays (discretionary plus mandatory) had risen at just 75 percent of the actual rate from 2002 to 2008, overall spending would have been $254 billion lower in 2008—a savings figure that is larger than the Congressional Budget Office's original estimate of the 2008 federal budget deficit ($198 billion).

The CBO's updated estimate of the 2008 deficit was much larger, around $455 billion, about 3.2 percent of GDP. This estimate accounts for the decline in corporate tax revenues due to the slowing economy[61] and the additional revenue losses from the 2008 stimulus package, which were projected to contribute $151.7 billion in forgone revenue.[62] In a recessionary period, a deficit of around $200 billion in 2008—or 1.4 percent of GDP, below the forty-year average of 2.4 percent—is compatible with textbook stabilization policy. But the actual 2008 deficit was more than twice that amount, and was above the forty-year historical average (when measured against GDP).

Although these calculations are rough and hypothetical, they suggest that the annual Bush deficits would have been tolerable (or even negligible) if the 2001 and 2003 tax cuts had been accompanied by stricter spending restraints. This argument assumes that a slower rate of federal spending growth from 2001 to 2008 would not have harmed the U.S. economy. It might in fact have helped it by buttressing confidence among investors and businesses.

Another way to express the importance of spending restraint is to compare the costs of the wars in Iraq and Afghanistan to the projected size of the federal budget deficit in 2008. Although no rigorous cost estimates were made prior to the invasion of Iraq, Bush's economic adviser was almost fired for suggesting that the war would cost several hundred billion dollars, far more than the rough Pentagon estimates.[63] If Bush's adviser had foreseen the long duration of the occupation, his estimate might have been accurate.

The Congressional Budget Office has placed the overall cost of the wars near $1 trillion through 2007. In fiscal year 2008 alone, Bush sought $196 billion for Iraq and Afghanistan, an original request of $150 billion plus an additional $46 billion in "emergency spending."[64] The military operations alone are equivalent to half the deficit in 2008, and 100 percent of the anticipated 2008 deficit (prior to the unanticipated slowdown and the unbudgeted stimulus package).

From an anti-war perspective, Bush could have proceeded with his tax cuts without creating fiscal problems if he had not insisted on a prolonged occupation of Iraq. Or, from a pro-war perspective, even modest restraints on mandatory and non-defense discretionary outlays would have been sufficient to achieve tolerable deficits in the Bush era while undertaking the invasion and occupation of Iraq.

In short, from 2001 to 2006 Bush and the Republican congressional leadership did not exercise adequate restraint on spending. Bush never vetoed a Republican spending bill, presumably fearing the resulting deterioration in relations with his partisan allies in Congress as well as backlash from adversely impacted constituents. Given his tenuous political standing with the public, his reticence about imposing controversial spending restraints is certainly understandable (if not justifiable).

Spending Politics

Senate voting on budget resolutions reveals that Bush consistently employed the cross-partisan strategy. From fiscal years 2002 to 2007, several budget resolutions were passed in the Senate. The votes were 53–47 (FY02), 51–50 (FY04; Cheney broke a tie), 52–47 (FY05), 51–49 (FY07). With the exception of FY02, the number of Republican defectors exceeded the number of crossover Democrats. The unity of Senate Democrats, combined with the proclivity of a few Republicans to defect (especially Chafee of Rhode Island and DeWine of Ohio), limited Bush's ability to exert his will on budgetary issues. Bush should be criticized for spending, but Congress had an even bigger appetite for it.

Fortunately, the Bush record on spending restraint is not entirely negative. He slowed the rate of discretionary spending growth in his second term, both before and after the Democratic Party captured a majority in Congress. He was certainly not reluctant to threaten and use the veto pen when the Democrats assumed control of the Congress in 2007. Indeed, he vetoed a $25 billion children's health care plan and $22 billion in extra congressional spending on education and health. He also used the threat of the veto to persuade Congress that a variety of discretionary spending ideas should be delayed or shelved.[65]

Critics of President Clinton's security policies argue that a bias against defense spending was pronounced. Bush, delivering on a 2000 campaign pledge, shifted U.S. spending priorities from traditional domestic programs to military programs. When Bush took office, discretionary outlays were 48 percent defense and 52 percent non-defense. The shares steadily changed until, when Bush left office in 2009, the discretionary outlays were 55 percent defense and 45 percent non-defense.[66] Even these categories understate the shift since "homeland security" spending is counted as "non-defense." Whether Bush's decided preference for national security spending over domestic spending is wise is a complicated policy question beyond the scope of this book.[67]

In the long run, Bush's fiscal policy may be faulted more for what he did not do than for the new tax cuts and expenditures that he launched. He proposed to work with Congress to control mandatory spending programs but never devised detailed proposals or an effective political strategy for making those reforms happen.[68] Thus, the long-term fiscal challenges facing President Obama have not been improved by the Bush presidency and will be much worse in the near term due to the severe 2008 recession.

As a fiscal policy maker, there is no question that George W. Bush made a difference. He expanded discretionary federal spending. He shifted the mix of federal spending from domestic needs to the defense sector, mostly due to the prolonged occupation of Iraq. Most importantly, he persuaded the Congress to enact multiple rounds of tax cuts, including some supply-side reforms (such as diminished capital gains taxes) that have substantial long-term promise— if they are retained. Virtually all of Bush's fiscal policies were passed using a combination of partisan voting in the House and a cross-partisan strategy in the Senate.

Over twenty significant federal tax cuts have been passed by the Congress since the end of World War II, five of them at the instigation of George W. Bush. If measured as a percentage of the federal budget, none of the Bush tax cuts are as large as the Kennedy or Reagan tax cuts. But grouping the five Bush tax cuts together, they are about 8.1 percent of the federal budget. That is larger than the Reagan tax cut (5.3 percent of the federal budget) but not as large as the Kennedy tax cut (8.8 percent of the federal budget).[69] Thus, George W. Bush should go down in history as one of the most accomplished tax cutters in modern American politics.

The impact of the Bush tax cuts on the performance of the U.S. economy is difficult to know with certainty.[70] From a classic stabilization perspective, the 2001 and 2008 tax cuts appear to have been well timed to compensate for cyclical weaknesses in the U.S. economy. Given the strong performance of the U.S. economy after Bush's initial eighteen months in office, it is difficult to argue that the tax cuts hurt the economy in the short run.[71] From 2003 to 2007, Bush presided over a sustained period of prosperity and relatively low rates of unemployment and inflation. The economy faltered in late 2007 and collapsed in 2008 but the reasons appear to relate primarily to monetary policy and (to a lesser extent) world oil price movements, not fiscal policy.

From a long-run, pro-growth perspective, Bush's most significant tax-policy changes were the decline in the marginal rates applied to individuals and the reduction in the double taxation of stock dividends and capital gains. By equalizing the taxes on dividends and capital gains, Bush also removed any distorting effects that the discrepancy had on corporate decision making. (Such distortions tend to hurt hiring more than capital investments, since capital is very mobile.) These features of the Bush tax cuts are decidedly pro-growth and are compatible with a future initiative to reform the tax code with a broader base and a uniformly low rate. Even liberal scholars who object to the Bush tax cuts acknowledge that the Bush policies of lowering marginal tax rates on capital income and flattening the rate structure are consistent with the pro-growth objectives of fundamental tax reform.

Bush made the least progress on the corporate income tax, which is much higher (35 percent at the federal level plus an average of 5 percent at the state level) than the rates imposed on firms in other developed countries throughout the world.[72] Some targeted relief aimed at specific sectors was achieved, but Bush never proposed what is arguably needed: a uniform reduction in the tax rates imposed on businesses. The failure of Bush and the Republicans to cut the corporate tax rate provides an opportunity for congressional Democrats.[73]

3

The Social Security Debacle

Social Security is a mandatory entitlement program in the sense that the federal government is required to provide income to all citizens who meet the program specifications. As currently structured, current payees transfer funds to current retirees. In theory, the current payees will one day be transferred funds according to some proportion of what they paid in transfer funds to the previous generation. Some scholars see Social Security as a form of forced savings which nudges lower-income workers to save for their future.

Without reform, the Social Security system will become financially unsustainable as the number of retirees in the United States grows faster than the number of workers. For example, the 2004 Social Security Trustees Report shows the program running cash surpluses until 2018, with trust fund exhaustion projected for 2042.[1] The 2004 forecast was not new; it was quite similar to what forecasters reported to President Clinton in the 1990s.

There are only two ways to solve the problem: cut benefits or raise taxes. Variants on the benefit-cut idea are to increase the retirement age in light of the steadily increasing life expectancies of Americans or to adjust benefits based on income or "need," thus cutting retirement benefits for wealthier citizens. Not surprisingly, none of those ideas have excited elected officials. It is well-known that seniors are politically active and that middle-class workers are sensitive about payroll taxes.[2]

Clinton and the Congress

A relatively new idea in the policy debate is better investment of Social Security revenues. In his 1998 State of the Union message, President Clinton's Social Security plan included a provision calling for the federal government to invest a portion of the program's trust fund in the stock market. Clinton also called for retirement accounts for low-income workers to supplement current benefit plans.

Conservatives advocated a different idea that is more individualistic, allowing each worker some choice over how their funds are invested in the private market and how any residual funds are allocated when they die. For example, conservative House Democrat Charles Stenholm of Texas and Republican Jim Kolbe of Arizona proposed in 1998 a plan to allow workers to invest some of their Social Security in private accounts. The Stenholm-Kolbe plan was adapted from suggestions made by the Cato Institute, a think tank based on libertarian ideals.

Two House committee leaders, Republicans Bill Archer of Texas and E. Clay Shaw Jr. of Florida, crafted an alternative plan in 1999 that permitted individual investment accounts to replace a portion of program benefits. The accounts would be invested 60 percent in stocks and 40 percent in bonds, with the aim of generating new earnings for retirees that might relieve some of the future strain on the Social Security system. Workers were not permitted to draw from these accounts until their retirement.

Despite some interest from the Clinton administration, this plan did not gain any traction in Congress. It attracted little Democratic support and was criticized by conservatives because it did not permit individuals to pass their investment earnings on to their families upon their death.

During the Clinton years, no overhaul of Social Security came close to passage in Congress. The Republican leaders in Congress, Dennis Hastert in the House and Trent Lott in the Senate, were wary of considering any reform plan that did not have bipartisan support. Their wariness was rooted in the knowledge that Democrats have historically used Social Security as an effective wedge issue in campaigns by attracting nervous senior citizens to Democratic candidates. Public opinion polls show that voters trust Democrats more than Republicans on the Social Security issue, and thus many Republicans in Congress feared that highlighting Social Security would only benefit the Democrats.[3]

Democrats, in turn, fear that Social Security "reform" is a code word for either "privatization" or benefit cuts, both of which they see as harmful to lower-income Americans, a core Democratic constituency that depends on Social Security for their day-to-day livelihood. It is estimated that Social Security income is the main means of survival for two-thirds of the elderly, and may prevent almost half of the elderly from being recorded as "poor." Subgroups of Americans who are particularly dependent on Social Security include women, African Americans, and Latinos.[4]

Bush's First Term

When Bush assumed office in 2001, he referred this sensitive matter to a bipartisan commission co-chaired by former Democratic senator Daniel Patrick Moynihan of New York and Richard Parsons of AOL Time Warner.[5] The referral set the stage for some bipartisan input while deferring the issue to a later date.

The bipartisan Moynihan-Parsons commission developed three options for creating private accounts, while emphasizing that some combination of benefit reductions and tax increases would be necessary in the years ahead. The commission also emphasized that private accounts would require $2 trillion in start-up funds over the next seventy-five years, including a new source of revenue to launch the accounts.[6] But the commission was largely favorable to private accounts as a significant component of a long-term modernization of the Social Security system. Some Democrats complained that the White House "cherry-picked" the membership of the commission, making sure that only those sympathetic to private accounts were members.[7]

This report had no near-term impact on policy. Congress struggled with the aftermath of 9/11, other Bush administration priorities, and preparation for the 2002 midterm elections. Given the poor performance of the stock market in this period, few House members and senators were inclined to link their re-election campaigns to the idea that Social Security revenues should be invested in the stock market. Even after the 2002 elections, congressional Republicans resisted White House overtures to make Social Security reform a priority.[8]

In 2004 Senator John Kerry and George W. Bush took markedly different stances on Social Security. Senator Kerry argued that the key to fixing Social Security is a growing economy that will produce more revenues from payroll taxes. What was significant about Kerry's stance is what he pledged not to do: He pledged not to cut benefits, raise the retirement age, or privatize the system.[9]

Bush again called for a fundamental reform that would allow younger workers to divert a portion of their payroll taxes into private investment accounts to build their own nest eggs. (Technically, the Bush proposal did not require workers to invest in private ventures. They could instead choose all low-risk government bonds. But an option was to be offered to each worker.) Although his proposal lacked specifics, it presumably referred to some of the ideas that the Moynihan-Parsons commission analyzed. Bush did not address in detail how the start-up funds for the accounts would be raised. Since the Social Security taxes paid by workers today are used to help pay for benefits received by current retirees, critics of the Bush plan argued that it would lead to more borrowing or benefit reductions to pay for the diversion of funds to private accounts.

As the election campaign intensified in the fall, the Kerry campaign seized on Bush's private-accounts proposal as evidence that Bush planned a "January surprise" to "privatize" Social Security. Referring to the work of the bipartisan commission, the Kerry campaign alleged in October, before the election, that privatization would lead to as much as a 45 percent cut in monthly Social Security checks. The Bush campaign responded that the Kerry campaign was misrepresenting the president's idea in an effort to frighten voters. On the campaign trail Bush said repeatedly that he would not support a reduction in payments to current beneficiaries.[10]

Elevated to Second-Term Priority

Unlike most congressional Republicans, the Bush White House did not fear the Social Security issue. Bush advocated Social Security reform in

2000 against Vice President Gore. He advocated it openly during the campaign prior to the 2002 midterm elections. And he spoke about it passionately in the presidential debates against Senator John Kerry. There is no evidence that Bush was ever hurt by his campaign positions on Social Security, even though some Republican leaders—especially elected officials in Congress—urged the White House to talk about something else.[11]

Soon after the 2004 elections, it became apparent that Social Security reform was not just one of Bush's campaign themes. It was designated as the top legislative priority for the new Congress, and Bush devoted much of his 2005 State of the Union message to the issue.

In theory, Bush needed only five Democratic votes in the Senate for reform of Social Security, assuming he could count on the fifty-five Senate Republicans. When his second term began, Bush did have some hope that limited Democratic support for private accounts could be found. After all, it was President Clinton who opened the door in 1998 to wiser private investment of monies in the Social Security trust fund.

More importantly, a leading Democratic thinker on Social Security, former senator Daniel Patrick Moynihan of New York, co-led the 2001 commission that recommended consideration of private accounts as part of comprehensive reform. Former vice presidential candidate Joe Lieberman, then a Democratic senator from Connecticut, believed that Social Security reform was urgently needed, that bipartisanship would be essential, and that all ideas, including private accounts, needed to be on the table for consideration.[12] A former Democratic congressman from Minnesota, Tim Penny, was an articulate advocate of Social Security reform, including retirement savings accounts for low-income workers.[13]

If Democrats proved to be resistant, the White House believed that Bush could take the case for Social Security reform to the American people, and win the battle of public opinion. If public opinion became largely supportive of reform, it is easy to imagine how the White House could have recruited Democratic collaborators and reassured nervous congressional Republicans.[14]

A confident Bush did take his case to the American people. In a highly publicized tour of the country ("60 Stops in 60 Days"), Bush spoke about Social Security reform in one opportunity after another from January to May of 2005.[15] Bush focused on states that he won in 2004 but that were represented by Democratic senators.[16] Members of the Bush cabinet were also asked to pitch in with the public relations drive. And the campaign was supplemented by a $50 million private campaign, led by the business community, to get the word out.[17] Bush and his allies made their case for "an ownership society," but they were not the only voices speaking.

The most potent constituencies of the Democratic Party, including organized labor and the American Association of Retired Persons (AARP), mobilized quickly against Bush's plan. Commercials sponsored by the AARP railed against Bush's proposal for a "carve out" for younger workers. A broader coalition of 100 groups, dubbed the New Century Alliance for Social Security, worked both the media and key members of the House and Senate.[18]

The critics charged that Bush was, in effect, trying to dismantle Social Security.[19] And these allegations were difficult to refute because the Bush White House never issued detailed legislative language, including a clear mechanism for financing the new private accounts.

From January to May 2005, public support for private accounts did not improve above the 50 percent level and may actually have deteriorated.[20] Perhaps most importantly, those citizens who opposed private accounts held their opinion more intensely than those citizens who favored private accounts.[21]

Unified Democratic Opposition

Immediately after Bush announced that Social Security reform was a second-term priority, congressional Democratic leaders set in motion plans to block Bush's plan in the Senate. They perceived that they had strong philosophical, strategic, and interest-based reasons to stop—rather than negotiate with—Bush.[22] To avoid being defeated by a cross-partisan strategy, the Senate Democratic leadership was determined to impose as much discipline as possible on Senate Democrats.

Without proposing any alternatives, the Senate Democratic leadership closed ranks on the position that no legislation on Social Security should be discussed in Congress until Bush's proposal for private accounts was taken off the table. A letter was drafted demanding that Bush effectively withdraw his proposal, unless the private accounts were designed as a supplement to the current Social Security system (as Clinton had suggested previously).

Some Democrats in the Senate appeared to be willing to discuss reform with the White House but they soon became targets of intraparty attacks. The case of Senator Joe Lieberman of Connecticut is revealing. Lieberman had already developed a reputation for being willing to collaborate with Bush on key issues. On homeland security and the Iraq war, particularly, the Bush White House collaborated with Senator Lieberman. But on other issues ranging from tax cuts to environmental protection, Lieberman joined the Democratic leadership in opposition to Bush administration initiatives. On Social Security, Lieberman began 2005 actively working with Republicans in the Senate and administration officials on a possible way forward on Social Security reform.[23]

Among grassroots liberal activists, Lieberman's behavior on Social Security set off alarm bells, even before the president's State of the Union message in January 2005. Lieberman reportedly told the *Hartford Courant* in January 2005, "If we can figure out a way to help people through private accounts or something else, great." The night of Bush's annual speech to Congress, liberal activists were appalled when President Bush kissed Lieberman on national television. A week later Lieberman praised Republican senator Lindsey Graham of South Carolina for his efforts toward a bipartisan approach to Social Security.

Liberal bloggers began to cite Lieberman as "dean of the faint-hearted faction" because he was considered one of those Democrats likely to break with the party on Social Security. In March 2005 the *New York Times* ran a detailed story describing how Lieberman's efforts on Social Security were "ruffling the feathers" of Democratic leaders.[24] *New York Times* columnist Paul Krugman added a blistering critique of Lieberman's statements on Social Security, including Lieberman's alleged "lie" about the seriousness of the system's fiscal problems.[25] Former Howard Dean supporters in Connecticut were reportedly discussing a "Dump Joe" effort, since Lieberman was up for re-election in 2006. Others began a National Call Joe Lieberman Day, a rallying cry that made its way to *Majority Report,* a liberal radio program.

The prospects for Bush's Social Security proposal died on March 4, 2005, when it was announced that forty-one Democratic senators, including Joe Lieberman, had signed the letter demanding that Bush withdraw his private-accounts proposal.[26] (The only Democratic senators who refused to sign were Kent Conrad of North Dakota, Blanche Lincoln of Arkansas, and Ben Nelson of Nebraska.) With sixty votes required, and only fifty-five Republicans in the Senate, there was no way forward for Bush's top second-term legislative priority.

Ironically, it is likely that many congressional Republicans breathed a sigh of relief, since there was little congressional interest in pursuing Social Security reform in 2005–2006.[27] In fact, Republican leaders in the House and Senate never agreed to bring Bush's proposal forward for floor consideration.[28]

As Democratic opposition to Bush's plan hardened, the Bush White House announced a new willingness to couple private accounts with other reforms perceived as more attractive to rank-and-file Democrats. For example, Bush indicated that he was willing to consider raising the income ceiling on payroll taxes or reducing the growth of benefits to wealthier citizens in order to pay for private accounts.[29] By then, however, the Democrats knew they had drawn blood and they had strong strategic incentives at the start of Bush's second term to make sure that his top priority was a complete failure.

If the Bush administration was truly prepared to propose unpopular tax increases or benefit cuts, the Democrats in the Senate were prepared to wait for details from the White House.[30] No such details were forthcoming. Meanwhile, conservatives in the House were furious that Bush was entertaining some of these ideas.[31] Thus, Bush took the right-wing criticism for suggesting unpopular reforms without the benefit of persuading crossover Democrats to collaborate with him.

Bush's top second-term legislative priority was a debacle. Bush may deserve credit for proposing that Social Security reform be undertaken, but he could not overcome the partisan polarization in Congress, even when the Republican Party had a substantial majority in the House and Senate. Thus, Bush's most serious effort to begin the reform of entitlement programs in the federal government was unsuccessful. The partisan nature of the defeat will certainly not encourage future presidents to venture down the path of entitlement reform.

Why was President Bush more successful cutting personal income taxes than reforming Social Security? The simple answer is that Social Security reform asks voters to experience near-term pain while tax cuts do not. A richer answer can be derived from the 2000 and 2004 presidential campaigns, and the constraints on Bush that were imposed by partisan polarization in Congress.

Given the strategic incentives felt by the Democratic leaders of Congress, the cross-partisan strategy proved to be the only realistic way for Bush to legislate on his top priorities. It worked on tax cuts, as enough moderate Democrats saw political gain (or protection) for themselves. It did not work on Social Security reform because the national Democratic Party successfully discouraged, through party discipline, the crossover support that Bush needed in the Senate. Given Bush's close race against Kerry, his limited political standing, and the lack of any support from powerful interests aligned with the Democratic Party, the Bush White House was overly optimistic to believe that a privatization approach to Social Security had any realistic chance of passage.

If Bush was determined to reform Social Security, he probably needed to pursue a rare bipartisan strategy. With a bold proposal to raise payroll taxes on the wealthy and raise the retirement age for all beneficiaries, he might have created a window of opportunity for his primary interest in private savings accounts. But Bush did not reveal a willingness to make the unpopular proposals until his initiative was virtually dead. By then, any appeal for bipartisan support was too late, and the Democrats were pleased to see his top second-term priority die early.

4

Making Sure Kids Learn

George W. Bush startled many Republicans in January 2001 when he announced his number one priority for social policy: reform of elementary and secondary education. Bush rejected the prevailing view of national conservatives that this issue is not a responsibility of the federal government. Indeed, he had insisted at the 2000 Republican convention that the party platform not include the long-standing plank that the federal Department of Education be abolished.[1] Bush sought instead a major new role for the federal government in public education based on his experience with "standards and testing" in Texas.[2]

There was plenty of reason to question the effectiveness of state-level oversight of public education. Gains in student performance had stalled. National data for nine-year-olds showed no progress in reading and science scores from 1980 to 1999 and only modest gains in math over the same period. The scores from urban schools were below average, and the achievement gaps between white children and black and Hispanic children were large, persistent, and, by some measures, growing.[3] Most disturbing of all was the fact that fewer than half of the states were fully measuring the progress of students against clear academic standards.[4]

The enormity of the challenge is apparent in the achievement gap between white children and black children in the United States. It starts at 1 to 2 standard deviations among three- and four-year-olds and increases by as much as one-third by the end of the K–12 experience. The gap increases less during the school year than during the summer, and is larger for math than for reading. Black children thus start first grade with a disadvantage and then are less likely to be taught by high-quality teachers than are white children.[5]

But how could a fragile, newly elected Republican president persuade a divided Congress to pass legislation aimed at comprehensive reform of public education? In the last year of the Clinton administration, the Congress was unable to pass a reauthorization bill addressing precisely this set of issues.

Bush certainly took some political risks. Opinion polls showed that the public trusted Democrats more than Republicans on the education issue. A repeat of the gridlock of 2000 was more likely to reflect badly on Bush and the Republicans than on the Democrats.[6]

From the standpoint of legislative strategy, there was no realistic hope that Bush could move an education bill through Congress on Republican votes alone. Indeed, opposition from some conservative Republicans was likely, especially in the House. Over in the Senate, where the party split was 50–50 after the 2000 election, any Republican bill was highly vulnerable on the Senate floor to unified Democratic opposition.

To the surprise of virtually everyone, Bush worked quickly and effectively with Congress to create the largest reform of public education since the enactment of Lyndon B. Johnson's Elementary and Secondary Education Act (ESEA) of 1965. The "No Child Left Behind" (NCLB) legislation, with symbolic rhetoric borrowed from the liberal Children's Defense Fund, mandated that 100 percent of U.S. children have basic math and reading skills by the 2013–14 school year.

In this chapter I examine how Bush accomplished this legislative feat and, more importantly, how the White House used executive powers to manage the difficult process of implementation. Based on the initial evaluations of state-by-state implementation, I also consider how well NCLB is working, why it has triggered complaints and intense opposition, what the funding controversy is all about, and why NCLB will need to be refined in the years ahead. Bush's track record on public education includes not just the process of passing and implementing NCLB but his recognition of the need for modification of NCLB as unanticipated problems emerged.

The Standards and Testing Movement

George W. Bush's perspectives on federal education policy were not new. They reflected the standards and testing movement that was catalyzed in 1983 by publication of *A Nation at Risk*. In this report, the National Commission on Excellence in Education sounded the alarm about poor student achievement in the United States.[7] The movement gained further momentum at a 1989 education summit in Charlottesville, Virginia, convened by President George Herbert Walker Bush.[8] Backing his pledge to be the "education president," Bush proposed to a Democratic Congress a voluntary national achievement test, new academic standards, and new federal funds that could be used by low-income parents to send their children to private or public schools. This proposal died in 1990 when Bush could not find an agreement with Senate Democrats, who opposed using federal funds for private schools.[9]

Congress did reauthorize the Elementary and Secondary Education Act in 1994. The bill was strongly influenced by the standards and testing movement. States were required to test children, develop content and performance standards, establish definitions of "adequate yearly progress," and demonstrate "continuous and substantial" progress toward the goal of proficiency for all students in public schools. Thus, many of the building blocks for NCLB were present in the 1994 reauthorization.[10]

When President Clinton was faced with implementation of the 1994 law, he shied away from strict enforcement. He never withheld funds from states that failed to meet prescribed timelines. By 1997, only seventeen states had established clear and specific standards in English, math, social studies, and science.[11]

In April 1999 the Progressive Policy Institute (PPI), the policy arm of the centrist Democratic Leadership Council, released an influential report calling for more teeth in the standards and testing approach. Led by Democratic senator Joe Lieberman of Connecticut, the institute argued that new legislation should call for termination of federal aid to districts that fail to meet performance benchmarks.[12] PPI also called for a major consolidation of the more than fifty categorical federal grant programs into five "performance-based" grants: compensatory education for disadvantaged students, teacher quality, English proficiency improvement, public school choice, and innovation.

Partisan Gridlock in 2000

Despite concerted efforts in 1999 and 2000, Congress failed to reauthorize the Elementary and Secondary Education Act on schedule for the first time in the act's thirty-five-year history. Conservative Republicans argued that the test scores of low-income children exhibited little improvement over three decades, despite the expenditure of $185 billion in federal funds. They pushed for consolidation of the numerous categorical programs into block grants, providing states and schools more flexibility to expend funds where they could do the most good. Liberal Democrats were seeking more federal funds for categorical programs. They feared that block grants would result in many poor children being shortchanged. Meanwhile, President Clinton sought authorization to hire 100,000 new teachers with federal funds, aiming to reduce class sizes in the early grades.[13]

In October 1999 House Republicans advanced a bill based on the principle of block grants, including a ten-state pilot program giving states maximum freedom to spend federal funds as long as academic standards are met. Opposed by the National Education Association, a union of 2.7 million teachers and other educators, the bill also faced a veto threat by President Clinton. It passed the House on a party-line vote of 213 to 208. Only five Democrats supported the bill, while nine Republicans voted against it.[14]

House conservatives fought for authorization of private school vouchers but lost badly in two key votes.[15] Republican Dick Armey of Texas proposed that $100 million be made available to assist parents who sought to enroll their children in private schools. His plan was defeated 257 to 166. Only three Democrats supported the Armey plan; fifty-two Republicans voted against it. (A similar proposal by Armey was defeated in 1997 by a closer vote, 228 to 191.) Republican Tom Petri of Wisconsin also proposed a ten-state pilot plan that permitted parents to use federal funds to enroll their children in a different public or private school. It was defeated by an even larger margin, 271 to 153.

Progress in the Senate was slower, in part because the views of the Republican chair of the Committee on Health, Education, Labor and Pensions, James Jeffords of Vermont, were closer to those of the committee's Democrats than to those of its Republicans. An initial proposal from Jeffords called for new early childhood education programs and expanded federal funding aimed at disadvantaged children. Republican Judd Gregg of New Hampshire pushed an alternative plan with two pilot programs: In one, fifteen states would allow federal funds to be used for any educational purpose as long as better academic results were demonstrated, and in the other, in ten states and twenty school districts parents would be able to take their children out of failing public schools and use federal money to purchase other public or private educational services. The committee passed a Gregg-like plan on a party-line 10 to 8 vote.[16]

When Majority Leader Trent Lott tried to bring Gregg's bill to the floor, he was informed that there would be numerous Democratic amendments, including a controversial one on gun control. Given the strong partisan disagreements and the inability of Republicans to overcome either a filibuster threat or a potential veto by President Clinton, Lott decided against a Senate floor debate. Instead, federal education programs were funded for an additional year through an omnibus appropriations bill. The entire issue was punted until after the 2000 elections.

Delivering on a Campaign Pledge

As the Republican challenger to Vice President Al Gore in the 2000 election, Bush ran explicitly on K–12 education as a priority issue. He raised it repeatedly on the campaign trail, reflecting his confidence in what he had accomplished through "standards and testing" in Texas. Much to Gore's apparent frustration, Bush spoke with passion about elementary education in the presidential debates.[17]

Politically, education played a much larger role in the 2000 presidential campaign than is typical of such campaigns. Bush succeeded in neutralizing the traditional Democratic advantage on education, while also showcasing how his "compassionate conservatism" would benefit Latinos and African Americans. Some analysts argue that education was pivotal in Bush's victory because it helped him make critical progress in the battle for the votes of suburban "soccer moms."[18]

Soon after the Supreme Court resolved the outcome of the 2000 election, Bush invited about twenty members of Congress to the Texas capital of Austin to discuss education policy. At the outset, the White House strategy was to build consensus among key Republicans while reaching out to a limited number of moderate Democrats who saw the need to reform public education. The participating senators included Republicans Judd Gregg and James Jeffords, whose views on public education were quite different. The invitations to Democratic moderates Evan Bayh of Indiana, Joe Lieberman of Connecticut, and Zell Miller of Georgia were clear evidence that the White House was considering a crossover strategy with "New Democrats" in the Senate. The ranking Democrat in the Senate on education issues, Ted Kennedy, was conspicuously absent from the Austin meeting.[19]

Before the Austin session, the key Republican committee chair in the House, John Boehner of Ohio, warned Bush that as many as sixty House conservatives might vote against more federal involvement in public education.[20] Boehner himself had been an opponent of the Department of Education, but he felt it was important that Bush succeed on his number one domestic legislative priority.

At Boehner's insistence, Bush also invited to the Austin meeting one of the most liberal members of the House, George Miller of California, who was assuming the ranking minority position on Boehner's committee. Miller was an advocate of both mandatory national testing and more federal funding for public education. Boehner helped persuade Miller that Bush was serious about improving the quality of public education in America.[21] The presence of George Miller in Austin marked a turning point as the legislative strategy on NCLB began to transition from a cross-partisan to a bipartisan effort, since now a Democratic leader was participating.

The Bush education plan was released in January 2001. Instead of submitting a detailed legislative proposal, Bush released a thirty-page blueprint with principles and aspirations. Following a style he had used effectively in Texas, Bush left plenty of room for bargaining. The key elements of the Bush plan were mandatory testing of kids, strict standards of performance, accountability checks on schools and districts that failed to perform, consolidation of disparate federal funding programs, expanded federal funding for public education, more flexibility for states and localities in deciding how to spend federal money, and more options for parents to access other public and private schools. The estimated cost of the plan was projected to be $47.6 billion over ten years. The ultimate goal of the plan was highly ambitious: 100 percent reading and math proficiency, even among disadvantaged children, within twelve years.

This was a plan well designed to attract the interests of Democratic members of Congress affiliated with the centrist Democratic Leadership Council. One aide to Senator Joe Lieberman of Connecticut said it differently: "GWB basically plagiarized our plan."[22]

The White House encouraged formation of a bipartisan Senate coalition of Judd Gregg of New Hampshire, Joe Lieberman of Connecticut, and Evan Bayh of Indiana. Early in the deliberations, Senators Lieberman and Jeffords registered their strong opposition to any bill that contained vouchers for private schools. The Bush White House responded with a pivotal concession: the president would not insist on vouchers as a precondition.[23]

As centrist Senate Democrats became more interested in NCLB, Senator Ted Kennedy of Massachusetts also became interested. Kennedy met with Bush in the White House in January 2001. In exchange for assurances that the White House was serious about more federal funding, with an emphasis on funds for poor school districts, Kennedy also became a principal in the Senate deliberations. He agreed to more consolidation of programs, more flexibility for states, and more accountability checks on failing schools.[24] With Kennedy at the table working with the White House, the legislative strategy had, in effect, become fully bipartisan.

Kennedy and Miller as Allies

Committee Democrats cooperated with a bill based loosely on Bush's core principles with one key adjustment: The increased federal spending on public education was targeted at the neediest schools. Party-line votes defeated a series of Democratic amendments aimed at securing even larger increases in federal spending, more money to hire teachers, more money to renovate schools, and more money to reduce class sizes. With Kennedy encouraging his Democratic colleagues, the bill cleared the committee on a 20–0 vote.[25] Both sides agreed to reserve two tough issues for Senate floor debate: federal support for private schools (a priority among conservatives) and special-education funding (a priority for Jeffords).

In early May 2001 Boehner negotiated delicate compromises with Miller to secure bipartisan support in the House for Bush's initiative. Boehner agreed to double federal assistance to the poorest schools by fiscal year 2006. Instead of insisting on 100 percent state flexibility in the use of federal funds, Boehner agreed that only 50 percent of federal funds would be without strings. He also dropped a provision that would have allowed federal funds to be used for after-school religious programs.[26]

Boehner included in the plan an option for parents of poor children to use federal money to pay for tuition at private schools. To Boehner's dismay, five committee Republicans joined with all committee Democrats in a vote that stripped the plan of the private school option.

Knowing that he could not insist on private school subsidies and expect to legislate, Bush encouraged Boehner to move the bill to the floor, where Bush would support, but not insist upon, an amendment to allow parents a private school option. The willingness of Bush to legislate on public education without any progress for private schools enraged many conservatives.[27]

Boehner and Miller moved the package through committee on a 41–7 vote. All but six Republicans voted for the bill, but some indicated that they did so only to provide a win for their new Republican president.[28] With such a decisive committee vote, favorable House floor action was preordained.

A House floor amendment to strip the mandatory annual testing was defeated 255 to 173. There were 52 Republicans who defied the White House and joined 119 Democrats and 2 independents against mandatory testing.[29]

Knowing that Bush would not insist on vouchers for private schools, the teachers' unions worked hard to defeat vouchers on the House floor. Dick Armey of Texas tried to reinstate some authorization of funding for parents interested in private schools. His amendment was defeated 273 to 155. Sixty-eight Republicans joined in the opposition; only two Democrats voted in favor of the Armey amendment. A more modest amendment to create five voucher demonstration projects was also defeated, 241 to 186. Even this amendment was opposed by thirty-seven House Republicans.[30]

The final vote on the House floor was 384 to 45 in favor of the bill. As Boehner predicted from the beginning, the opposition was concentrated among House conservatives. Of those who voted against the final bill, thirty-four were Republicans, ten were Democrats, and one was an independent.[31]

The Senate floor debate on NCLB consumed six weeks during May and June of 2001. With the Democrats controlling the floor (when James Jeffords switched from Republican to independent, the Democrats became the majority party), some expected progress on NCLB to stall. But Ted Kennedy of Massachusetts "took over as the bill's manager and remained on the floor throughout most of the proceedings."[32] When Democratic senator Paul Wellstone of Minnesota sought to weaken the bill's core testing provision, a bipartisan coalition led by Kennedy, Gregg, Bayh, and Lieberman blocked Wellstone's amendment.[33]

Some amendments were added that irked Senate conservatives. For example, Senators Tom Harkin of Iowa and Chuck Hagel of Nebraska required 40 percent of state and local costs for special education to be covered by the federal government. There was no similar provision in the House plan.[34] By the time the Senate completed floor debate, the number of categorical federal programs had increased to 89 compared to 55 under existing law and 47 in the House bill. The overall cost of the Senate plan was more than 50 percent larger than that of the House plan.[35]

The biggest disappointment for conservatives occurred when vouchers for private schools were debated. Senator Gregg proposed a demonstration project in three states and ten school districts where parents with children in failing schools could use federal assistance to enroll their children in another public school or help defray tuition costs at a private school. This amendment was defeated 58 to 41, despite support from the White House. Eleven Republicans defected; only three Democrats (Byrd of West Virginia, Carper of Delaware, and Lieberman of Connecticut) crossed over. The only consolation for parental-choice advocates was a voice-vote approval of a $125 million amendment by Senator Carper allowing children in underperforming public schools to attend other public schools.[36]

The huge bipartisan vote for NCLB in the Senate, 91 to 8, mirrored the lopsided House vote. But the legislators' task was far from over. The discrepancies between the House and Senate bills needed to be reconciled. Concerns from governors, teachers, and school officials were flooding into Washington. All this was occurring as the country experienced the shock of 9/11.

Reconciling Differences

During the summer of 2001, the thirty-nine House and Senate conferees on NCLB were facing 2,750 discrepancies between the two bills. Teachers' unions were appalled at the mandatory testing. Conservatives were upset about the large spending levels and the demise of the Bush voucher proposal. A bipartisan coalition of governors was concerned that the definition of "adequate yearly progress" was so stringent that too many schools would be dubbed "failing." The result could be costly corrective action plans and public embarrassment for schools, districts, and governors.[37] Despite the bipartisan spirit in Washington, many state and local officials of both parties were convinced that NCLB amounted to a big "unfunded mandate" for states and localities.[38]

House-Senate conferees did their best to hold the bipartisan coalition together. Conservatives were relieved when the mandatory special-education provision was dropped as well as much of the extra funding added by the Senate. The overall funding authorization for the poorest schools was set for 2006 at double the 2001 level. States were required to test all children within four years or lose small amounts of federal funds. States were required to design and administer the annual tests, but they also had to ensure that a sample of children from each state participated in a national test to check state results. States were required to set "proficiency" standards based on test scores and achieve 100 percent proficiency among children within twelve years, as Bush requested. Schools that consistently failed to meet proficiency goals faced restructuring and a loss of autonomy. More flexibility was provided to states in the use of federal funds as long as the poorest children were not shortchanged. A pilot program authorized seven states and up to 150 local districts to reallocate federal monies as long as test scores improved.[39]

The conference agreement was crafted primarily by Gregg, Kennedy, Boehner, and Miller. Because the bipartisan coalition held together, the favorable votes for the conference agreement in the House (381–41) and Senate (87–10) were never in doubt. When President Bush signed NCLB into law in January 2002, it was hard to believe that such a comprehensive reform of public education had occurred within twelve months, especially since Congress had been hopelessly polarized on these same issues in 1999–2000.[40]

The 1,100-page bill is summarized in table 4.1. Despite all the detailed legislative language, NCLB left many key issues unresolved. The Bush administration faced a huge implementation challenge. No one really knew whether it was feasible to achieve the idealistic goal of 100 percent proficiency in reading and math by the 2012–13 school year. The cost of achieving such a lofty goal was certainly a complete unknown. Skeptics noted that the terms of the bill left the states with enormous discretion in the implementation process. They were predicting that NCLB, though legislated like a lion, might be implemented like a lamb.[41]

Table 4.1. Highlights of the No Child Left Behind Act of 2002

Annual testing	Each state must design and administer annual statewide assessments in reading and mathematics for grades 3–8.
Performance standards	Each state must define minimum "proficiency" standards in each subject and ensure that all subgroups of students, including the disadvantaged, make "adequate yearly progress" until 100% proficiency is achieved by 2013–14.
Corrective action	Schools that fail to make adequate progress are subject to increasingly aggressive countermeasures: (1) two years of poor progress forces a school to offer parents the option of their child attending another public school; (2) three years of poor progress forces a school to offer supplemental services (e.g., tutoring) chosen by parents; (3) four consecutive years of poor progress triggers staff replacements and new curricula; and (4) five years of poor progress forces school restructuring.
Report cards	Each state and district must publish key data such as student achievement scores broken down by subgroups and grade.
Teacher quality	Each state must certify that all teachers in federally subsidized schools are "highly qualified."
Transferability	School districts may transfer up to 50% of selected fund monies from one use to another.
Flexibility Demonstration Projects	Up to 150 districts may consolidate several federal programs as long as student test scores continue to improve.
Graduation Rates	Requires states and schools to report high-school graduation rates, to the federal government, and plans to improve those rates.

Source: Adapted from Patrick J. McGuinn, *No Child Left Behind and the Transformation of Federal Education Policy* (Lawrence: University Press of Kansas, 2006), pp. 180–181 (Table 10.2).

Mandatory Testing: The Heart of NCLB

The mandatory annual testing of children by the states is the heart of NCLB because the performance of children on these tests is the critical measurement that identifies struggling schools and triggers remedial actions. When NCLB was signed into law, most states already were doing some testing but the quality and frequency of testing was uneven. Fewer than half the states were administering tests that were related to explicit academic standards. Many off-the-shelf tests in widespread use were not related to the curricula being taught to students in the classroom.[42]

The Bush administration was unequivocal that there would be no compromises on implementation of the core testing mandates. In March 2003, for
example, the Department of Education threatened to hold $783,000 in federal
funds from Georgia for the state's failure to meet testing requirements—requirements that had been in federal law since 1994.[43] Using executive powers, the Bush
administration also cracked down on states that were administering inadequate
tests of math and reading skills.[44] One of the early successes of NCLB is that all
fifty states ultimately came into compliance with the testing requirements.[45]

Under NCLB, all children in a state must take the same test, but each state
is permitted to design its own tests and define what constitutes "proficiency"
on those tests. Although some legislators had advocated for uniform national
tests, granting the states discretion to test children was seen as a necessary nod
to the principle of federalism. The authors of NCLB recognized that this would
create incentives for states with poor schools to "game" the system, either by
manipulating the difficulty of tests over time or by adjusting the definition of
"proficiency" so that marginal schools would pass. In order to ensure an independent check on state testing, NCLB required all fifty states, every two years,
to participate in the National Assessment of Educational Progress (NAEP).
Results from this national testing program were intended to serve as an independent measure of what was really happening in each state.

NAEP was not new. It was first administered in 1969 and had been conducted regularly in most states for twenty-five years. NAEP did not cover all
students. It was administered to a stratified random sample of 2,500 students
per grade (fourth and eighth grade) and per subject (reading and math). The
NAEP testing provided statistically representative results for each state, but
the NAEP subsamples were not large enough to be representative of individual
schools or school districts within a state.

The NAEP testing played exactly the role that was envisioned. For example,
in 2005 the State of Tennessee reported, based on state testing, that 87 percent of
eighth-graders were "proficient" in math while the NAEP results for Tennessee
found only 21 percent of eighth-graders "proficient" in math.[46] Tennessee was
not alone. Many states have found that their results on the national tests are
lower than their results on state exams.[47] For example, a 2006 study of twelve
states from 1992 to 2005 found that state testing was finding about twice as
many "proficient" children as the NAEP results, a gap that appeared to be widening in the early years after enactment of NCLB.[48]

Explanations for the discrepancies vary. One possibility is that scores on the national tests are lower than the scores on the state tests because students and teachers care more about the state tests because they matter. Another possibility is that state definitions of proficiency vary, even when state and national tests are of equal difficulty. One study found that on the 500-point NAEP scale, state standards of proficiency range from an NAEP-equivalent score of 242 in North Carolina to 314 in Missouri, a 72-point difference.[49] Some professionals believe that a "basic" level of performance on the NAEP test—a level of achievement below "proficient"—is actually equivalent to the "proficient" level on Tennessee's statewide test. Under this interpretation of what the two tests measure, Tennessee was performing 26 percentage points lower on the national test than on the statewide test.

The disparities between the state and NAEP testing results are a source of persistent controversy that damages public confidence in NCLB.[50] A growing number of experts are suggesting that, as NCLB is refined, uniform national tests, coupled with uniform definitions of proficiency on those tests, replace the current state-by-state approach to testing.[51]

A common complaint about NCLB is that teachers "teach to the test," since the scores from those tests are used to judge schools and school districts. In fact, some teachers and principals do become preoccupied with preparing children for specific kinds of questions or question formats at the expense of a quest for learning.[52] Substantial evidence from the field suggests that schools and districts are reallocating resources and revising curricula in ways that are designed to improve student performance on tests. In the process, teachers may neglect problem-solving skills that are not included on tests, and they may shortchange subjects other than reading and math, which are not tested.[53] Many schools are implementing interim tests or quarterly tests as a diagnostic tool rather than wait for the results of end-of-the-year testing. Thus, concerns are being raised that too much emphasis in schools is placed on testing.[54]

Paradoxically, some of these concerns are best addressed with improved and expanded testing programs. Multiple-choice questions may need to be supplemented with questions that ascertain proficiency at problem solving.[55] Coverage is being broadened to include more science and social studies as well as math and reading. The concerns of those who oppose greater emphasis on test scores are difficult to address unless other measures of student learning are developed and validated.

Designating Schools in Need of Improvement

When states set goals for adequate yearly progress under NCLB, it is not adequate if a state proves that the goals are met for the average child. They must also be met for each of four subgroups of children: students with disabilities, students with limited English proficiency (LEP), students from racial minorities, and students from low-income families. If a school fails to meet its goals in either subject (reading or math) in any of the four subgroups, the school is designated as "in need of improvement" for the next year. Such a designation, if it persists for two consecutive years, begins to trigger adverse publicity and mandatory remedial measures aimed at schools and school districts. The remedies are sequenced: school choice (year 2), tutoring services (year 3), staffing changes (year 4), and restructuring (year 5 and beyond).

Many state and local officials complained to President Bush that the insistence on 100 percent proficiency by 2013–14, in all of the four subgroups, will ultimately cause many good schools to be labeled as "in need of improvement." One survey in Michigan found that "many of the educators we interviewed continue to regard NCLB as a guarantee of failure for virtually all of the state's schools . . . there are nearly 50 ways to fail under NCLB, and only one way to succeed."[56]

Using executive powers, the Bush administration responded to these complaints by introducing some statistical flexibility in how the data on subgroups are collected, analyzed, and interpreted. Yet, Bush's commitment to seeing proficiency in each of the subgroups seemed unalterable. Later, as test scores from the subgroups produced disquieting results, states urged the Bush administration to permit a small percentage of students (such as those with cognitive disabilities) to take an alternative achievement test or be subjected to a modified achievement standard. Using executive powers, the Bush administration granted this permission. All states are now using alternative assessments and modified standards to some degree, though the Department of Education and the states continue to work on these special procedures.[57]

In the 2004–2005 school year, the share of high-poverty schools that failed to meet annual progress requirements increased from 6,000 to 9,000 out of 50,000 such schools nationwide.[58] Many schools without many impoverished students (2,370 in 2004–2005) were also found to be in need of improvement. In Florida, where the state gives each school a grade from A through F, 1,200 of the state's 3,050 schools earned an A in 2003. Yet 950 of those top-rated schools failed to meet the yearly progress goals approved by the state under NCLB. Often a school will miss only one or two of the progress targets for a few sub-groups of students. Perplexing contradictions in Florida's school performance data were evident in 2004, 2005, and 2006.[59] Florida governor Jeb Bush tried to persuade his brother, President Bush, that the problem was with NCLB, not the state of Florida.

As the accountability provisions of NCLB began to bite, resistance from states mushroomed. Some states passed resolutions or legislation objecting to the various provisions of NCLB. Other states passed laws prohibiting state funds to be expended on implementation of NCLB requirements.[60] The response of the Bush administration was firm: If states did not comply with NCLB, they might forfeit their access to federal financial assistance. Although the federal government provides less than 10 percent of the $500 billion expended annually on K–12 public education, the federal dollars are often the most flexible dollars for school districts and administrators. Many recalcitrant states folded. The Utah legislature was one that considered, but decided against, turning down federal funds in order to bypass the mandates of NCLB.[61]

A sustained pushback from governors—many of them Republican—cul-minated in a two-hour meeting with President Bush in the White House in 2005. The Department of Education pledged to take a new approach to imple-mentation of NCLB that was sensitive to the concerns of states and localities.[62]

Educational experts believe that a key design flaw in NCLB is how the "ad-equate yearly progress" (AYP) goal is defined. AYP is to be based on a student's or school's test performance relative to an absolute standard of proficiency, not on the change in performance over time. Experts generally prefer "growth-based" measurements of student achievement because they reflect the impact of teachers and curricula better than the absolute score, which may be as much affected by nonschool factors (for instance,, family support) as by the quality of the educational product.

Growth measurements have another big advantage: They allow consider-ation of progress by all students, whereas absolute proficiency standards en-courage teachers and schools to focus only on the "bubble kids"—those children who are scoring near the proficiency line.[63] Students who are scoring far below or far above the proficiency line may not seem worth the educational effort. Under growth-based models of achievement, each child's progress during a year (and over multiple years) is measured using a unique identification number for that child. Accountability schemes can be devised to reward progress (and penalize lack of progress) by all children covered by a growth model.

As the perversities of the absolute proficiency scheme were disclosed, the Bush administration was urged to permit states to implement growth-based learning models. The Department of Education responded cautiously by approving pilot projects with growth-based learning, even though some critics feared that growth-based thinking would turn NCLB into a search for "improvement" rather than "proficiency."[64] The pilot projects began in five states—Arkansas, Delaware, Florida, North Carolina, and Tennessee—and an additional eight states were considering pilot projects in 2008. Even as growth-based models were used to set AYP goals, President Bush never backed off the stipulation that 100 percent of children must be proficient, in absolute terms, by 2014.

An alternative approach that has been suggested is an integrated score for each school, where numeric weight is given to both the absolute level of proficiency and the improvement that has been accomplished over the last year.[65] If a school has made substantial progress from a poor base, they may be treated differently in designations from a school that has the same absolute score but has demonstrated no progress.[66] A related innovation might be to give substantial weight to subgroup scores but to allow outstanding performance in one subgroup to compensate for less-than-adequate performance in another subgroup. Bush consistently resisted these proposals on the grounds that they would divert schools and teachers from some students who need attention.

One of the beneficial by-products of NCLB is more capability to compare student performance over time using unique student identification numbers. Prior to NCLB, there was substantial resistance to such widespread use of such identification, even with assurances that privacy would be protected. Rich longitudinal databases are now being established around the country that will facilitate measuring how much "value added" to academic achievement is being provided by schools and individual teachers. It is "highly doubtful" that this trend would have occurred "without NCLB."[67]

Despite the complaints from the states, the truth is that states possess enormous discretion in the AYP determinations—discretion that is used to determine how many schools will be designated as "in need of improvement" in a given year. The AYP "design decisions" include the planned pace of student learning, the confidence intervals around testing results, and the percentage of children subjected to alternative tests or modified achievement standards. In 2004, for example, the State of Kentucky determined that 6 percent of Kentucky schools had failed to achieve their AYP target. But the school failure rate would have been 56 percent if the state had employed a different—yet plausible—set of design decisions. To a significant extent, states decide which schools will fail based on how they define the parameters of AYP.

As states get closer to the goal of 100 percent proficiency by 2014, it may become very difficult for many schools to meet plausible AYP requirements. Not even creative use of state discretion will be able to shield numerous fairly good schools from a designation of "in need of improvement." One scholar painted a stark future for AYP targets under NCLB: "If the AYP targets become completely unreasonable, they will become irrelevant."[68]

As the number of schools designated as in need of improvement grew, the Bush administration was faced with the reality of enforcing the accountability provisions and remedies under NCLB. As we shall see, the planned remedies did not always work as anticipated. In some cases, they did not work at all. Bush was again forced to use executive powers to bring some reality to accountability under NCLB. I consider the track record with three remedies: school choice, tutoring, and restructuring.

School Choice

Children are eligible for "school choice" when the federally funded school they attend has not met its performance (AYP) goals for two or more consecutive years. The child must be offered the option of transferring to another public school in the district that does not have a designation problem (based on state testing and yearly progress reports).

Schools are required to notify parents that their child is eligible to choose another school no later than the first day of the school year following the year when the school was identified as "in need of improvement." In addition to considering other public schools in a child's district, parents may have the option of placing their child in a public school outside of their district, especially if none of the schools in their district are performing adequately.

Unless a funding cap is exceeded, states must provide free transportation for all students who exercise the school choice option. The law requires that priority in school choice be given to the lowest-achieving children from low-income families. Federal funds under the "Voluntary Public School Choice" program are awarded to organizations that can establish or expand a public school choice program (for instance, by conducting public information campaigns to inform parents of their choices). But NCLB does not require that any local, state, or federal funds "follow the child" to his or her new school. Decisions about whether funds should be transferred are handled at the state and local level.

Many conservatives, already disappointed that private school choices were not included in NCLB, were further disappointed about how the school choice plan was implemented. Nationwide, the school choice option was used sparingly. In 2003–2004, for example, only about 31,500 eligible students—or about 1 percent of the 3.3 million students eligible for school choice under NCLB—were transferred to a different school.[69] In 2004–2005, 39 percent of the school districts required to offer choice did not do so at all.[70] In some entire states school choice was virtually nonexistent, despite the language in NCLB. Regrettably, school choice participation by African-American children was lower than the national average.[71]

It is extremely unlikely that school choice plans will have their intended competitive impact on public schools if they are rarely used. Some experts are already suggesting that school choice might need to be scaled back.[72] But the multiple reasons for the failure of school choice under NCLB need to be considered, since some of the reasons suggest that the choice option needs to be strengthened rather than weakened.

A fundamental problem has been the lack of timely parental notification, or any notification at all. One study found that sixteen states failed to identify their "need-improvement" schools from 2005–2006 prior to the September start of the 2006–2007 academic year.[73] Parents are unlikely to choose a different school after the school year has already started. Even when parents receive a notification, it may not be clear or encouraging.[74] Few efforts were made to expand capacity in better-performing schools while bureaucratic resistance to the choice option was evident in some parts of the country.[75] Even when parents were notified and placements in good schools were available, many parents were reluctant to exercise the choice option.[76]

The Bush administration took limited steps to enforce the choice option. One of the large fines issued under NCLB ($450,000) was levied against Texas for failing to inform parents quickly enough that their children were eligible under NCLB to transfer out of "needs improvement" schools.[77] In California, the Alliance for School Choice filed a complaint against the Los Angeles Unified School District. In 2005–2006, only 500 of the 250,000 students eligible for transfer in Los Angeles enrolled in a different public school. The complaint alleged that officials evaded deadlines for notifying parents, causing many parents to be unaware that their child was enrolled in a "needs improvement" school. Of those parents who were notified, many did exercise the choice option. Although the U.S. Department of Education threatened to take action against Los Angeles, little was done. In some cases, the department granted waivers to states and school districts that were obviously out of compliance with the school choice requirements.[78]

Supplemental Tutoring

Schools that do not meet their progress goals for three consecutive years are required to fund "supplemental services" (such as free tutoring) for children who need them. The authors of NCLB envisioned a novel experiment in educational entrepreneurship since tutoring was to be offered by private individuals and companies, who would be paid for their services with public funds.

Implementation of supplemental services did not occur quickly. In 2004, about two million children were eligible for supplemental services under NCLB but only 226,000 (about 12 percent) actually received them.[79] Participation among blacks was higher than among whites.[80] Many rural areas had access to only online services because the market was insufficient to attract local providers.[81] In addition, only a fraction of children who began private tutoring programs actually completed the programs as planned.

The offering of supplemental services started slowly, but participation grew steadily. The preliminary educational evaluations of supplemental tutoring are quite encouraging. In most districts, students served by supplemental tutoring increase their math and reading scores, especially if they remain in the tutoring program for at least two years.[82] Substantial gains have been demonstrated among African Americans, Latinos, students with disabilities, and other subgroups who tended to be among the lower achievers among the eligible students. The performance evaluations of students who use tutoring services are much more encouraging than the evaluations of students who transfer to a different school.[83]

The seemingly different results for school choice and tutoring led to a dilemma for the Bush administration. Should school districts be permitted to offer tutoring as well as school choice, even though NCLB requires choice to be offered one year before tutoring? School transfers may be less likely if parents believe their child will be tutored. Should schools in need of improvement be permitted to pay their own teachers to offer tutoring, rather than rely exclusively on private providers, as envisioned under NCLB? If teachers are not getting the job done in the regular school day, one can question whether they should receive federal funding to offer tutoring during after-school hours.[84]

Using executive-branch waiver authority, the Bush administration decided to permit pilot projects with supplemental tutoring that appeared to skirt the plain language of the law.[85] Five states were permitted to allow districts to offer supplemental tutoring a year earlier than specified by NCLB. Four large urban school districts identified as in need of improvement (including New York and Chicago) were permitted to allow schools in need of improvement to serve as providers of supplemental tutoring. Critics argued that, once again, the letter and intent of NCLB was watered down by the Bush administration during the implementation process.[86]

Teacher Qualifications and Merit Pay

Under NCLB any new or existing teacher working in a federally funded school must be "highly qualified," effective the 2005–2006 school year. As interpreted by the Department of Education, that means the teacher must hold at least a bachelor's degree, be fully licensed and certified by the state in the subject(s) they teach, and have passed a state test of subject knowledge. As an alternative to passing a state test, the qualifications of current teachers may be accessed through use of the "high, objective, uniform state standard of evaluation" (HOUSE). Components of HOUSE may include college coursework, advanced credentials, professional development, involvement in curriculum-related matters, student achievement, and years of experience.

Elementary school teachers must demonstrate knowledge of both reading and mathematics. New paraprofessionals must have two years of college or pass a test assessing their ability to assist teachers in reading, writing, and math instruction.

NCLB requires states to inform parents each year that they are entitled to know the qualifications of the teachers assigned to their children. Parents must be notified if their child is taught for more than four consecutive weeks by a teacher who is not "highly qualified." States must provide annual report cards about teacher qualifications, including the percentage of classrooms in the state not taught by highly qualified teachers.

Critics of the teacher quality standards argue that the criteria are unrelated to the quality of teaching in the classroom.[87] Some teachers who are not rated "highly qualified" may excel in the classroom while those who are "highly qualified" may perform poorly in the classroom.

The states also vary enormously in the content knowledge expected of teachers. About two-thirds of the states use the Educational Testing Service's Praxis II tests, but each state sets its own minimum standards for what test score a teacher must earn to be "highly qualified." On the math test for secondary school teachers the median score nationwide in one year was 143, but the "cut scores" varied from a low of 116 in Arkansas to a high of 156 in Colorado. At the middle school level, the median national score and the highest state cut score (Virginia) were equal: 163. The lowest cut score (in Nevada and South Dakota) was 139.[88] For existing teachers, states also vary considerably in how much weight is given to experience in the classroom versus direct indicators of subject knowledge.[89]

Even with the state discretion to set cut scores for new teachers, many states have experienced difficulty in hiring teachers who meet the federal requirements, especially in rural areas and in certain subjects (such as science). A July 2004 report by the Education Commission of the States found that none of the fifty states was on track to meet the law's requirement of a highly qualified teacher in every classroom or for providing professional development for teachers.[90] In response to complaints from states, the Department of Education adjusted the federal rule modestly to provide additional flexibility, but many teachers do not meet their state's qualification requirements.[91]

On the other hand, there is considerable criticism of how science teaching is being handled under NCLB. In addition to math and reading tests, states must ultimately test students in science at least once during grades 3–5, grades 6–9, and grades 10–12. The first science assessment was scheduled at the end of the 2006–2007 school year. A 2006 report from the National Academy of Sciences recommended urgent reform of the K–12 science curriculum in the United States, arguing that under NCLB the "bar is set too low."[92] Through executive order, President Bush in April 2006 created the National Math Panel to provide recommendations on how to improve math achievement in the United States. But recruiting enough qualified teachers in science subjects remains a large challenge in many regions of the country.

The Bush administration may have struggled on teacher qualifications, but President Bush set in motion some important policies aimed at rewarding teachers for superior performance. He persuaded the Congress to establish a Teacher Incentive Fund that provides financial incentives for teachers and principals in high-need schools who succeed at raising student achievement levels. Over $40 million was awarded to sixteen grantees in 2006. Another $43 million was awarded in 2007. Given the data on individual students and teachers that are now available under NCLB, it should be feasible to make more rigorous assessments as to whether performance pay for teachers leads to improved student achievement.

Restructuring Schools

If a school fails to meet its AYP goals for several years, despite the availability of school choice and supplemental tutoring, NCLB calls for the school or school district to be subjected to corrective action or be "restructured." What exactly this means is not entirely clear. In New Jersey, for example, restructuring may amount to modest curricular changes or perhaps the replacement of a principal.[93] One critic has commented that there is no evidence that NCLB "has cost a single educator a job or pay raise."[94] The preference appears to have been for the mildest forms of restructuring, though there is some evidence that the mere threat of restructuring brought a "sense of urgency" to troubled schools in Michigan and Kentucky.[95]

As more and more schools became eligible for restructuring, the Bush administration took some steps to avoid penalizing many schools that were designated as in need of improvement. For example, rather than crack down on all poorly performing schools, the Bush administration in 2008 gave permission to ten states to focus reform efforts on schools that are drastically underperforming and intervene less in schools that are raising the test scores of most students but struggling with only one subgroup of students. This program, which was applauded by the National Education Association, may have the effect of letting many suburban and rural schools off the hook for serious remedial action under NCLB.[96] Critics argued that the new policy is unfair to central city schools that serve many subgroups of students with learning problems.

If restructuring and other forms of accountability under NCLB are to be meaningful, it may be necessary for the state and federal governments to get serious. School superintendents and principals may need to be held personally responsible for the performance of schools under their supervision. This might be a form of merit pay (rewards and penalties) for managers, a practice that is quite common in the private sector of the economy. It may also be necessary to close some schools, launch some new charter schools, and reward good schools that are willing to enroll students from failing schools. Neither the Bush administration nor members of Congress from either party have demonstrated an appetite to get this serious about failing schools.

One of the more innovative suggestions has been to add some accountability at the level of the student as well as the school. For example, a high school student's score on state tests could be reported on the student's high school transcript or could count in some way toward the student's grades.[97] Such information might be quite useful to college admissions officials and employers, but President Bush and the Congress did not get that serious about accountability for performance.

Graduation Rates

NCLB required states and localities to report high school graduation rates to the federal government but allowed states to do so using their own formulas. In 2005 the National Governors Association (NGA) acknowledged inconsistencies in the state formulas and urged all states to consider use of a uniform, rigorous formula.

In 2008 the Bush administration used executive powers to require that all fifty states and 14,000 public schools use the more accurate formula recommended by NGA. Under that formula, the high school graduation rates in North Carolina and New York State are projected to drop from 95 percent and 77 percent to 68 percent and 65 percent, respectively.[98] It is expected that these sobering statistics will catalyze more improvement programs in public schools, beyond those already stimulated by the NCLB testing and accountability standards. Yet some experts question whether graduation in four years should be a uniform national goal.[99]

Federal Funding: How Much Is Enough?

Of the roughly $500 billion spent annually on public education in the United States, less than 10 percent is supplied by the federal government under the Elementary and Secondary Education Act.[100] Critics of NCLB argue that the new law has been chronically underfunded, which transforms the new federal requirements into a burdensome "unfunded mandate" on states, school districts, and schools.[101]

As evidence of underfunding, critics point to the fact that Congress has not appropriated, and Bush never requested, the amount of money that is authorized to be spent under NCLB. For example, in fiscal year 2006 the "authorization level" for NCLB's Title I programs was $22.75 billion, but Bush requested an appropriation from Congress of $13.3 billion. Each year since 2001, the amount actually appropriated for NCLB has been far less than what Congress authorized in 2001.

In assessing this concern, it is important to recognize that the authorization level is simply the maximum permissible amount that can be spent under NCLB. When Congress set the authorization levels in 2001, they were not based on any detailed cost analysis of how much it would cost to reach the goal of 100 percent student proficiency in the United States. The authorized amounts are politically negotiated figures set by members of Congress who know that the real budgetary decisions are made on an annual basis in the appropriations process. Under federal budgetary procedures, it is the norm that discretionary federal programs receive annual appropriations that are far smaller than the maximum permitted by authorization language.

From 2001 through 2009, NCLB has been one of the few sustained growth areas in discretionary federal spending at home. President Bush's fiscal year 2009 budget request called for an increase in total funding of NCLB programs to $24.5 billion, an increase of 41 percent over the fiscal year 2001 appropriation. Title I of NCLB, the program aimed at low-income students, was to receive a proposed $14.3 billion, a 63 percent increase over the 2001 appropriation.[102]

The city of Pontiac, Michigan, and the National Education Association sued the Department of Education about the large cost of NCLB. They argued that the federal government did not provide sufficient funds to cover the costs of compliance, which they interpreted as a violation of the Unfunded Mandates Act of 1995.

A federal judge dismissed the suit in late 2005 on the simple grounds that the federal government is permitted to set educational standards for states that choose to accept federal funds.[103] States always remain free to reject both federal funds and NCLB requirements and instead finance and operate their own public school systems. But this judge's decision was appealed to the Sixth Circuit Court of Appeals.

In early 2008, a divided three-judge panel reversed the lower court's opinion and upheld the challenges to NCLB. In an unexpected line of reasoning, the appeals court concluded that Congress, when it passed NCLB, violated the spending clause of the U.S. Constitution by failing to give states clear notice of their liabilities should they choose to accept federal funding under NCLB.[104] The precise impact of the appeals court decision is unclear because the court's opinion did not include a remedy and the opinion may be modified or overturned by the U.S. Supreme Court.

The big unanswered question about NCLB is how much it will cost—regardless of who pays—to achieve the idealistic goal of 100 percent proficiency by 2013–14. Some scholars view this as a largely symbolic goal, not as a true mandate, while the Bush administration treats the goal as a legal or civil right.[105] No one has even attempted to compute a cost estimate for 100 percent proficiency for a simple reason: Without improving the conditions for students in their homes and communities, it is not clear that even perfect public schools could achieve 100 percent proficiency among students in each subgroup specified in NCLB.[106]

Fixing Problems with NCLB

As the scheduled reauthorization of NCLB approached in 2007, the Bush administration and congressional leaders began to consider whether NCLB should be retained, modified, or repealed. To its credit, the Bush administration announced in 2007 that while progress was being made, unexpected problems with NCLB needed to be fixed.

Several of Bush's reform proposals flowed directly from the evaluations of data from state-by-state experiences with NCLB. They include the following:

- NAEP Test Results to Parents. States would be required to make NAEP results transparent and readily available to parents along with state testing results.

- Science Assessments. States would be required to include performance on science tests, as well as math and reading scores, in state accountability standards by the 2019–20 school year.
- Modified Testing. States would be permitted to test students with learning disabilities using an alternative test and/or modified achievement standards. More federal funding would be made available to help develop the tests and standards.
- Growth Measures of Learning. Qualified states would be permitted to meet the AYP requirements using a growth measure of learning rather than the absolute proficiency measure specified in the 2001 law. In order to be qualified, a state must have well-established testing systems, robust data systems, and goals for student progress that are based on proficiency rather than background characteristics of the students.
- School Choice Reforms. Schools would be required to notify parents of their right to transfer their children to better schools at least two weeks before the start of the new school year. More federal scholarships would be provided to facilitate parental choice, including more support for charter schools and flexibility for parents to consider private school options and public schools located outside the student's home district. When a child moved from one school to the next, federal dollars would move from the old school to the new school.
- Tutoring Reforms. When a school is in its first year of "need for improvement" status, the school would be permitted to use federal funds to offer tutoring services as well as school choice options. Under current law, federal funding of tutoring is not authorized until after a school's second year with "need for improvement" status. Larger tutoring subsidies per child would also be authorized for rural students due to the shortage of rural providers, and more tutoring services would be authorized for children with disabilities and limited English skills.
- Serious Restructuring. If schools do not meet their AYP requirements for five or more years, they must institute large staffing changes or a new governance structure. Exemptions are provided only for those schools that are in "need of improvement" status because of poor performance by one subgroup of students.

- High School Requirements. A uniform formula would be used by each state when computing the school's official dropout rate. New "college-ready" standards and assessments would begin in 2011–12 coupled with more federal funding for high schools with a large number of low-income students.[107]

But there was one crucial aspect of the 2001 NCLB law that Bush did not propose to modify: He reaffirmed the importance of measuring the achievement of all students, including the four student subgroups, and the goal of having every child performing at grade level or above by 2014.[108]

Congress was unable to reauthorize NCLB on schedule. The widespread dissatisfaction with NCLB at the state and local government level led to numerous proposals ranging from mild reform to outright repeal of the law. The National Education Association sought substantial changes to NCLB, many of which were opposed by the Bush administration.[109] In 2007 Representative George Miller of California did make a proposal to give states more discretion to measure progress, but his proposal was seen by civil rights groups as a step away from the ambitious goals established by Bush.[110]

The efforts to repeal or weaken NCLB faced an obvious difficulty: a formidable veto threat from President Bush through January 20, 2009.[111] More importantly, the bipartisan congressional coalition that established the core requirements of NCLB may be difficult to unravel. For example, immediately before the midterm elections in 2006, Senator Ted Kennedy of Massachusetts and Representative Miller signaled that they would seek to retain the core accountability provisions of NCLB as well as the annual testing requirements. More federal funding for NCLB was their highest priority.[112]

In 2008, recognizing that NCLB would not be reauthorized during his tenure, Bush instructed the Department of Education to make creative use of executive powers, thereby accomplishing some key refinements of NCLB without any congressional action. For example, states were required to notify parents earlier about school choice opportunities, more flexibility was provided in state use of federal money for tutoring, states were permitted to override some collective bargaining agreements when moving better teachers to needy schools, and authorization of merit pay for teachers was expanded.[113] Although some members of Congress expressed opposition to these policies, the Congress was too polarized to block Bush's executive actions.

The history of NCLB provides a revealing case study of how a president can overcome partisan polarization in Congress and institute a major reform of domestic policy. But presidents must choose their priorities wisely. For Bush, NCLB had both benefits and risks.

The upsides for President Bush in choosing public education as his top domestic priority were numerous. He "had a natural constituency among congressional Democrats" for a stronger federal role in education policy.[114] He and the first lady also had valuable experience working this issue in Texas, and the Bush campaign used the issue against Vice President Gore. Moreover, Bush's "standards and testing" approach to education policy reaffirmed his commitment to be a "compassionate conservative" and therefore set the stage for capturing key subgroups of voters (such as "soccer moms") in 2004.[115]

The downsides of education policy were that Congress was already polarized on this issue, making it uncertain whether Bush could deliver on his campaign commitment. Moreover, Bush's conservative base was destined to be offended by NCLB because Bush's views on this issue were far left of most conservatives.[116] The one idea conservatives cherished, federal vouchers for parents to enroll their children in private schools, was given away early in the deliberations because of the intense opposition from both moderate Republicans and Democrats, especially Jeffords and Lieberman.[117]

Conservatives argue that Bush compromised enormously, far too fast and too much, in order to sign a bill into law.[118] He lost his initiative on private school choice. He failed to achieve large-scale consolidation of federal education programs (for instance, the block grant idea). Only modest increases in state flexibility in the use of federal funds were accomplished. In fact, more categorical grant programs were added in the Senate to secure passage. While some accountability checks were included in NCLB (such as the ill-defined threat of "restructuring" for failing schools), Bush did not win any automatic loss of federal assistance to schools whose test scores showed consistently bad performance. Progress toward merit pay for teachers was at best modest.

What will matter in the long-term assessment of NCLB is whether it succeeds in improving the rate at which children learn in schools. The preliminary results from NAEP in the post-NCLB period are somewhat encouraging. Math scores are on the rise nationally, but less progress is apparent in reading scores.[119] In America's center-city school systems, the achievement gaps in both math and reading appear to be narrowing, including some encouraging progress among African-American children.[120]

Even if the lofty goal of NCLB (such as 100 percent proficiency in each subgroup by 2014) proves to be unattainable, NCLB has already made significant contributions. As one scholar put it, NCLB has "helped urban schools direct attention to students who, for far too long, were out of sight and out of mind."[121] The law has "brought attention to the inequality in achievement faced by students from racial, ethnic, and linguistic minorities."[122] From a scientific perspective, NCLB has also stimulated an explosion in the availability of useful data on children, teachers, and schools. From these data parents can make more informed choices about what makes sense for their children, and science-based evaluations may provide a better picture of what the next generation of NCLB should look like.

Could President Bush have achieved more of his education agenda with a truly cross-partisan strategy instead of allowing Senator Kennedy and Congressman Miller to play such strong roles? Bush paid a stiff price in cumbersome, equity-oriented provisions in order to achieve a bipartisan consensus in favor of NCLB. Following the model of his successes on tax cuts, Bush might have taken a more risky route to passage. He could have requested that House Republicans pass his version of NCLB (a partisan vote) and then the White House could have negotiated with a limited number of moderate crossover Democrats such as Senators Bayh of Indiana and Lieberman of Connecticut.

With tax policy, however, Bush knew that his Republican base in Congress, virtually all of the Republican members, would be with him. On education policy, there were anywhere from thirty to sixty conservative House Republicans who, unless a provision was made for school vouchers, were likely to vote against a big new role for the federal government in public education. Yet, the White House knew from the votes taken in 1997–99 that a significant number of Republicans—as well as virtually all Democrats—would vote to strip federal vouchers for private schools from Bush's package, both in a House committee vote and on the Senate or House floor. Thus, the only way to ensure passage of a voucher-less NCLB in the House was to negotiate with Miller and the House Democrats.[123]

Bush did not insist that vouchers for private schools be included in NCLB, but he continued to advocate them. For example, his fiscal year 2006 budget request to Congress included a $100 million voucher-demonstration program that was modeled after a small pilot program undertaken in the District of Columbia.[124] The $100 million would have financed vouchers for 28,000 children in poorly performing schools, providing $4,000 per child to help offset tuition expenses at private schools and $3,000 per child for tutoring services. In January 2007 Bush again advocated federal scholarships for private schools as part of the NCLB reauthorization debate. It was the Congress—both Democrats and a significant number of Republicans—who refused to enact federal vouchers for private schools.

Given the tenacious opposition to federal vouchers by NEA, the scientific case for vouchers needs to be more definitive. The data are not yet definitive. For example, the most recent statistics from the Department of Education indicate that, controlling for family characteristics, children in private schools do not perform much better than children in public schools.[125] This comparison might have been different if a more limited set of private schools had been used as the comparator. The political climate for vouchers are likely to remain unfavorable until the scientific case improves and until African-American and Hispanic parents become more determined to create a viable private school option for their children.[126]

President Bush overcame his low political standing and a polarized Congress to win his number one social policy priority: comprehensive reform of public K–12 education. In securing passage of NCLB, Bush allowed a cross-partisan strategy to evolve into a classic bipartisan effort, which irked his conservative base. On the other hand, the prompt, bipartisan success in Congress helped jump-start his presidency by enhancing his credibility as a political force in Washington, D.C.

The process of implementation, while difficult and controversial, further showcased President Bush's use of executive powers to advance his agenda and correct some of the unanticipated problems with the legislation. Although NCLB has plenty of warts and will surely be modified in the years ahead, it is now broadly accepted that Bush did more to reform public education in America than any president since Lyndon Baines Johnson.[127]

5

Drug Coverage for Seniors

Like education, health care is an issue that historically has been dominated by the Democratic Party. President Bush was not deterred by this history. He established principles for comprehensive Medicare reform but carved out a more targeted objective that was a direct outgrowth of a 2000 campaign pledge: a new prescription drug benefit under Medicare for expenses incurred outside of the hospital.

In selecting this issue as an administration priority, Bush took a significant political risk. He was bound to offend his conservative base by proposing expansion of an already large and rapidly growing federal entitlement program. Yet success in Congress was bound to be difficult given the obstacles faced by any major piece of health care legislation. As Hillary Clinton discovered in 1993, any major health care proposal triggers complex negotiations among powerful commercial interests such as insurers, physicians, managed-care organizations, employers, labor unions, patient advocacy groups, and pharmaceutical manufacturers. And one of the most powerful groups on this issue, the American

Association of Retired Persons (AARP), had built a long and trusting relationship with the Democratic Party.

In a fascinating series of legislative developments, Bush worked the polarized Congress to accomplish the first major reform of Medicare since the program was created more than a generation ago. The legislation did not pass quickly. It was not until three years into Bush's first term that Congress sent a bill to the Oval Office for the president's signature.

Once passed, the complex new law confronted major roadblocks during the implementation process. Early stumbles by the Department of Health and Human Services provided plenty of stories for reporters eager to identify flaws in the new program. Some conservatives called for suspension or repeal while some liberals called for a major overhaul of the new program just as it was beginning to take effect.

Using a wide range of executive powers, from rule making to public communications, the White House and the Department of Health and Human Services overcame the immediate obstacles, increased public satisfaction with the program, and demonstrated that a market-oriented approach to drug coverage can work effectively.

Why a New Drug Benefit Was Inevitable

When the Medicare program was created in 1965, the pharmaceutical revolution was only beginning. The public had already experienced the benefits of powerful new antibiotics and antidepressants, but the role of drugs in medicine was perceived to be quite limited. In 1965 Americans spent about $3.7 billion on pharmaceuticals, less than 5 percent of health care spending.[1] There was little impetus to extend Medicare coverage to drugs.

Over the last forty years, there has been dramatic progress in the development of new therapies: vaccines to protect against childhood diseases, immunosuppressant drugs for organ transplant recipients, drugs to manage asthma, clot-busting and blood-thinning drugs, antidepressants with less severe side effects, and remarkable treatments that combat HIV/AIDS and other infectious diseases. Surgical advances and lifestyle changes have also been valuable, but progress against America's largest killer, heart disease, has been aided by new drugs that control cholesterol levels, lower blood pressure, and combat irregular heartbeats.

By the year 2000 drug expenditures in the USA had soared to over $100 billion. Policy makers in 2000 were told that these expenditures were expected to grow to over $240 billion by 2008.[2] With more new drug breakthroughs based on gene therapy and biotechnology on the horizon, the only debate was about how fast drug expenditures would grow.

If the pharmaceutical marketplace was growing so handsomely, why was legislation inevitable? The answer lies in the fragmented nature of the health insurance industry and the challenges that American businesses face remaining competitive in a global economy.

In the fall of 1999, 38 percent of seniors and younger Medicare beneficiaries with disabilities had no insurance for drug coverage. A significant proportion of those uninsured were in rural areas (50%), near the poverty level (44%), and over the age of eighty-five (45%). The very poor, or at least those enrolled in the federal Medicaid program, had excellent drug coverage and few out-of-pocket expenses for drugs.[3]

The medication needs of the Medicare population are substantial. The average Medicare recipient had over twenty prescriptions in 1999. Those without insurance coverage had an average of eighteen prescriptions; those with coverage had an average of twenty-five.[4] From a medical perspective, there is a real concern that some patients do not take their drugs because they are so expensive. Among those without coverage, one-fifth of people with either congestive heart failure or diabetes report skipping doses to make prescriptions last longer.[5]

Not all seniors faced large drug-related costs. The majority of them reported average out-of-pocket drug costs of less than $100 per month. Yet 17 percent of those with coverage and 43 percent of those without coverage were paying more than $100 per month.[6]

As Congress deliberated on reform options, from 2000 to 2003 average spending on pharmaceuticals grew rapidly. Expenses rose 12 percent per year in a politically active population many of whose members were living on a relatively fixed income.[7] And the incidence of these costs was quite skewed, since 16 percent of Medicare eligibles were experiencing drug costs greater than $4,000 per year.

Those poor enough to be eligible for Medicaid were well covered. But they made up only about 12 percent of the Medicare-eligible population. Another 3 percent were covered generously by the Department of Defense, the Department of Veterans Affairs, or by selected states with special programs for the low-income elderly or the disabled.[8]

About 60–70 percent of the Medicare-eligible population did have some insurance for drug expenses, but the coverage was fragmented and beginning to erode.[9] Those who were covered depended primarily on employer-based coverage or private health insurance. About 95 percent of employer-sponsored plans provided some drug coverage, but many companies were beginning to reconsider, reduce, or eliminate such coverage.

The pressure on companies to cut health care costs was building. Starting in 1992 Financial Accounting Standards Board Statement No. 106 required that the unfunded liability of retiree health plans be reported on corporate balance sheets. And the increasingly global nature of the economy was causing U.S. firms to slash labor and benefit costs whenever possible. In the mid-1990s alone, the percentage of employers offering health benefits to their Medicare-eligible retirees dropped by 25 percent.

Many private health insurance plans added coverage for prescription drugs in the 1990s, but these plans often imposed caps on drug coverage and/or premiums that rose faster than the incomes of the retired population.[10] In 1999, 79 percent of Medicare+Choice plans offered at least $750 of prescription drug coverage; in 2003 only 39 percent of plans did so.[11]

Uncovered seniors could not go into the private market and purchase a drug-only policy to supplement their Medicare coverage. No such coverage was offered by the insurance industry because of concerns that it could not be offered profitably.

The sensitivity of elected officials to this growing concern of senior citizens should not be surprising. Seniors are prolific voters in the United States. In 2002, 70 percent of those age sixty-five and over voted; less than 52 percent of those under the age of sixty-five did so.[12] Prescription drug coverage was the top priority for the AARP, one of the most effective lobbies in Washington.

Political Stalemate

In 1999 President Clinton proposed that Medicare be expanded to cover prescription drugs used outside of the hospital.[13] The full details of the Clinton plan were never disclosed, perhaps because Senate Republican leaders insisted that the issue should be addressed as part of comprehensive Medicare reform.[14]

House Republicans were more nervous, and unlike their Senate colleagues, all of them were up for reelection in November 2000. One GOP pollster advised House Republicans that they had to have a plan passed prior to the November election.[15]

Under the leadership of Bill Thomas of California, chairman of the House Ways and Means Committee, the House passed in June 2000 a drug-benefits package based on federal subsidies to private insurers. In the face of criticism from many of the key interest groups, including insurers, AARP, and patient advocates, the Thomas plan passed the House on a shaky vote of 217 to 214. Ten House Republicans voted against the plan; only five Democrats voted in favor of it. The House leadership used procedural powers to prevent a vote on a government-run plan favored by the Democrats.[16] President Clinton was prepared to veto the Thomas plan and the Senate was not ready to pass any bill, so the issue died in Congress.

As the fall 2000 election campaign began, the partisan policy differences were large. There was no agreement about how many of the 33 million Medicare eligibles should be covered, how generous the coverage should be, whether the coverage should be provided through Medicare or through private insurers, and whether cost-containment measures aimed at the pharmaceutical industry should be imposed. There also remained the issue of whether to pass a stand-alone drug plan or a comprehensive overhaul of Medicare.

Gore Pressures Bush

Vice President Al Gore made prescription drug coverage for the elderly the centerpiece of his health policy in the 2000 campaign. Under Gore's plan, all seniors with incomes less than 135 percent of the federal poverty level would receive free coverage. Those above this threshold would pay premiums based on income. All drug costs over $4,000 per year would be covered by Medicare. The Gore campaign estimated that the plan would cost about $250 billion over ten years.[17]

In the summer of 2000, the position of the Bush campaign was less specific, but it became more specific in early fall, as Gore went on the offensive through television advertisements in the battleground states. Governor Bush started by saying that he favored a plan that would offer seniors a choice of different private insurance policies, including a scheme of competition between public and private plans. He also favored granting low-income seniors a subsidy that they could use to buy prescription drug insurance.[18]

At a campaign stop in Cranston, Pennsylvania, in September 2000, Governor Bush became more specific. He described a plan that was less costly than Gore's ($198 billion over ten years), but would guarantee full coverage for the poorest seniors (those with incomes below $11,300 per year) and subsidized premiums for the others. Bush proposed to implement the plan by building on the efforts of twenty-three states to subsidize prescription drug coverage for the low-income elderly and disabled. Bush's revised position was similar to a plan co-authored by Democratic senator John Breaux of Louisiana and Republican senator Bill Frist of Tennessee.[19]

Bush's pledge was not just another election year ploy. Soon after taking office, on January 29, 2001, Bush announced "Immediate Helping Hand," a prescription drug initiative mirroring his campaign position in some respects but also going further. Bush signaled his determination to provide prescription drug coverage for seniors as a stand-alone package, but he also left open the door to a broader Medicare overhaul as long as it included a prescription drug benefit.[20]

The details of the Bush plan included full drug coverage with zero monthly premiums for seniors with incomes up to $11,600 per individual and $15,700 per couple. A premium subsidy of at least 50 percent was provided for seniors with incomes up to $15,000 per individual and $20,300 per couple. The plan provided for full coverage of all costs above $6,000 per year.[21]

At this early stage, the White House envisioned that the plan would cost the federal government an additional $153 billion over ten years.[22] Looking for another legislative victory, Bush's health policy advisers engaged in extensive outreach to key interest groups such as insurers, drug makers, and AARP, as well as members of Congress.

Legislative Strategy

The White House decided against the classic bipartisan effort that evolved in support of No Child Left Behind. What unfolded was a risky cross-partisan strategy. It was risky because it was not clear that there would be enough Republican votes in the House to pass a drug bill, given the close House vote on the Thomas plan in 2000 and the loss of Republican seats in the 2000 election. Meanwhile, some conservative think tanks were questioning why the Republicans were in this game in the first place, blasting Bush's willingness to secure the new drug benefit without comprehensive Medicare reform.[23]

The Bush White House was wary of the politics of comprehensive reform since Republicans might push for benefit reductions and more private competition in Medicare while Democrats wanted price controls. Bush never presented the details of a comprehensive plan to reform Medicare.

Another Stalemate

Progress was slowed for a variety of reasons. In March 2001 the director of the Congressional Budget Office (CBO) testified that a comprehensive prescription drug benefit under Medicare could cost as much as $1 trillion over the next ten years. CBO estimated that a Democratic bill authored by Senator Bob Graham of Florida would cost $318 billion over ten years. A version of the Frist-Breaux plan was estimated at $176 billion, somewhat larger than the projection for the Thomas plan passed by the House in 2000.[24] Guided by the CBO numbers, the House and Senate passed a fiscal year 2002 budget resolution that included $300 billion for prescription drugs as part of a possible Medicare overhaul.

Majority Leader Tom Daschle indicated that prescription drug coverage was a priority for Senate Democrats. Although differences remained about whether the Senate should do a stand-alone drug benefit or a comprehensive Medicare overhaul, no practical path to comprehensive reform was charted by either party.

Recognizing the slow pace of progress and the difficulty of the issues, President Bush announced on July 12, 2001, some principles for any Medicare overhaul as well as an administrative plan to provide drug discount cards to seniors that would cut their drug bills by at least 20 percent. The administration plan died quickly when a federal district court judge ruled on September 6 that the card plan was illegal: It had not been authorized by Congress and proper regulatory procedures had not been followed.[25]

Quite understandably, 9/11 also slowed progress on Medicare and other domestic issues.[26] The weakening economy and the large size of the tax cuts raised concerns in Congress about the future of the federal budget. Yet House

Republicans were determined to deliver a prescription drug plan before the 2002 midterm elections. In contrast, the Democrats in Congress decided that an inadequate plan was worse than no plan.[27]

In the summer of 2002, the House Ways and Means Committee, led by chairman Bill Thomas of California, authorized a drug plan on a 22–16 vote. Billy Tauzin of Louisiana got a similar plan through the House Energy and Commerce Committee on a 30–23 vote. Both votes largely followed party lines. The House then passed a merged bill 221–208, with only eight Republicans and eight Democrats bucking their respective party positions.

This time the insurance industry became an enthusiastic advocate of the House plan, which included a more generous package of subsidies for insurers.[28] Drug makers also saw the House plan as the best defense against the possible price controls that could emerge from a Democratic plan in the Senate. AARP continued to criticize the bill on the grounds that the benefit structure and premiums were not adequate. In addition to passing a bill estimated to cost $350 billion over ten years, the House Republicans defeated on the floor a more generous Democratic plan estimated to cost $800 billion over ten years.[29]

Daschle did not want the Senate Democrats to enter the midterm elections without passing a prescription drug plan. He urged his chairman of the Senate Finance Committee, Max Baucus of Montana, to present a drug plan for Senate floor consideration.[30] Yet Baucus was struggling with a difficult dilemma.

Baucus knew that a majority of the Democrats in the Senate favored a government-run drug plan operated through the familiar fee-for-service Medicare program. He could not get such a plan through the committee because veteran Democrat John Breaux of Louisiana and James Jeffords of Vermont were inclined to join with committee Republicans on a private-sector approach.[31] Republican senators Don Nickles of Oklahoma and Olympia Snowe of Maine were criticizing Baucus for refusing to allow such a bill to move out of the committee for floor consideration.[32] Meanwhile, the American Medical Association, AARP, and other health groups were urging Daschle and Baucus to do something on prescription drugs. AARP was disappointed in the slow progress in the Senate.

Late in the session, Daschle tried to move a prescription drug bill directly to the Senate floor, without action by the Senate Finance Committee. For this maneuver to bypass a budgetary point of order, sixty votes were required.

A government-run plan sponsored by Democrats Bob Graham of Florida, Zell Miller of Georgia, and Ted Kennedy of Massachusetts lost on a 52–47 vote. A private-sector plan offered by Charles Grassley of Iowa, John Breaux of Louisiana, and James Jeffords of Vermont fell short, 51 to 48, as did a more limited Republican bill sponsored by Chuck Hagel of Nebraska and John Ensign of Nevada, also 51 votes to 48. A last-ditch effort co-sponsored by Democrat Bob Graham of Florida and Republican Gordon Smith of Oregon fell short, 50–49, despite an endorsement by the AARP.[33]

The failure of any bill to pass the 60-vote threshold was a setback not only for the White House but also for Daschle. The Senate Democrats with terms expiring were forced to enter the 2002 midterm elections with no prescription drug bill for seniors.

The Grassley-Baucus Alliance

When the Republicans regained control of the Senate in 2003, the prognosis for passing a health care bill was better.[34] Yet, the threat of a filibuster on the Senate floor was now facing the Republicans. The Senate was split 51–49 in 2003, meaning that the Republicans fell far short of the sixty votes needed to stop a filibuster.

In February 2003, the White House proposed a revised framework to modernize Medicare at a cost of $400 billion. The plan provided low-income Medicare beneficiaries a $600 annual subsidy for drug coverage. The White House urged Congress to provide drug discount cards immediately to all Medicare beneficiaries, estimating that a 10 to 25 percent saving could be realized. Medicare beneficiaries were given the option to voluntarily enroll in traditional Medicare plans or private health care plans that provide coverage for prescription drugs, preventive care, and high out-of pocket costs.[35]

President Bush had the good fortune to find a pair of Senate Finance Committee leaders, Republican Charles Grassley of Iowa and Democrat Max Baucus of Montana, who were moderate, practical, and without presidential ambitions or party-leading obligations. On June 12, 2003, Grassley and Baucus secured a bipartisan committee vote of 16 to 5 in favor of a bill that Bush considered promising.[36] Somewhat ominously, the five nay votes belonged to powerful senators: conservative Republicans Don Nickles of Oklahoma and Trent Lott of Mississippi and Democrats John Rockefeller of West Virginia, Bob Graham of Florida, and John Kerry of Massachusetts. But encouraging signals came from two unexpected sources: Ted Kennedy of Massachusetts and Tom Daschle of South Dakota.[37] Kennedy stated that the Grassley-Baucus bill was a "major step forward" and was worthy of further consideration and improvement.[38] Some liberal Democrats were furious at Kennedy for agreeing to work with the Republicans.[39] Two weeks later, a bill passed the Senate floor on a decisive 76–21 vote. The twenty-one opponents were an odd combination of senators from both ends of the ideological spectrum.[40]

One week after the Senate committee action, Bill Thomas of California, chairman of the House Ways and Means Committee, and Billy Tauzin of Louisiana, chairman of the House Energy and Commerce Committee, moved bills through their panels on largely partisan votes of 25–15 and 29–20, respectively.[41] Once again, Thomas did not negotiate with House Democratic leaders. But when Thomas and Tauzin sought to bring a unified bill to the House floor, they ran into a roadblock: substantial opposition from both conservative Republicans and a large majority of Democrats.

In the search for votes, more spending was offered. Critical support from Collin Peterson of Minnesota and other conservative Democrats was enlisted by adding $28 billion for rural health care delivery.[42] The House leaders also reassured conservatives by agreeing to spend $174 billion to expand tax-exempt health savings accounts for uninsured or self-insured individuals and their families.[43] But these add-ons increased the risk that the overall cost of the bill might exceed $400 billion.[44]

When the votes were counted on the House floor, it appeared that the bill might go down to defeat. A determined House Republican leadership, working on behalf of President Bush, was able to secure a 216–215 vote for passage.[45]

Reconciling Differences

The House and Senate versions of Medicare modernization were quite different, and merging the two bills was a complex task. Conference chairman Bill Thomas of California proceeded to develop the final bill with key House and Senate Republicans. Only two Democrats, both from the Senate, played a significant role: moderates Max Baucus of Montana and John Breaux of Louisiana.[46] Their colleagues, Tom Daschle and Jay Rockefeller, were excluded.[47] Not surprisingly, this conference strategy triggered complaints from the House and Senate Democratic leadership, including Ted Kennedy.

AARP, which had been courted persistently by the White House, indicated that they would support the product of the House-Senate conference (including a $7 million dollar advertising campaign), thereby enhancing enormously the compromise bill's prospects in the Senate.[48] The Senate Democratic leadership expressed outrage when an organization traditionally loyal to the Democratic Party backed the Thomas plan.[49]

But it would be erroneous to suggest that Democrats had no influence on the plan. In fact, Chairman Thomas and the White House were so intent on securing Senate passage that their concessions to Baucus, Breaux, and other moderates triggered a revolt among rank-and-file conservative Republicans.[50]

Once the House vote on the final conference report was under way on November 22, 2003, it appeared to be reaching the wrong answer for the White House. While searching for votes, the House leadership left the vote "open" for an unprecedented two hours and fifty-three minutes. What transpired during this period—and historians may never know the full story—resulted in the reversal of several votes. (It also triggered a House Ethics Committee inquiry in the months that followed.) When the roll-call vote was "closed," the conference report had passed the House 220 to 215, with exactly twenty-five Democrats and twenty-five Republicans defecting from their party's position.[51]

On the Senate floor, Ted Kennedy threatened a filibuster, but seventy out of the one hundred senators voted to limit debate. Tom Daschle raised budgetary issues, arguing that the plan violated the fiscal year 2004 budget resolution,[52] but the Senate waived budgetary concerns on a crucial 61-39 vote. Two Republicans defected (Hagel of Nebraska and McCain of Arizona) but twelve Democrats crossed over (Baucus of Montana, Breaux and Landrieu of Louisiana, Carper of Delaware, Conrad and Dorgan of North Dakota, Feinstein of California, Jeffords of Vermont, Lincoln of Arkansas, Miller of Georgia, Nelson of Nebraska, and Wyden of Oregon). Former Senate majority leader Trent Lott opposed the bill but supplied a crucial procedural vote to waive budgetary concerns.[53] The final vote for passage in the Senate was 54-44, with forty-two of fifty-one Republicans voting yes. On the substantive vote, the same twelve Democrats crossed over, but the number of defecting Republicans increased to nine: Chafee of Rhode Island, Ensign of Nevada, Gregg of New Hampshire, Graham of South Carolina, Hagel of Nebraska, Lott of Mississippi, McCain of Arizona, Nickles of Oklahoma, and Sununu of New Hampshire. Notably missing from the supporters was the Senate Democratic leadership, a reflection of the cross-partisan strategy employed by the White House.

The Design of the New Drug Benefit

The Medicare Prescription Drug, Improvement and Modernization Act of 2003 (called MMA for short) makes outpatient drug insurance available to all 43 million elderly and disabled Medicare beneficiaries. The voluntary drug benefit is offered through two types of private plans: a stand-alone insurance policy for drugs or a managed care plan that covers both drugs and other health care services. Those choosing a stand-alone plan typically combine it with the traditional fee-for-service Medicare coverage for other health care services.

Federal subsidies were provided to insurers to encourage participation.[54] In order to participate in the program, private plans had to offer the standard benefit or a benefit that is considered "actuarially equivalent."[55] For the standard benefit, the national average annual premium was $386 in 2006. The precise premiums are updated annually.[56] When the law took effect in January 2006, beneficiaries in most states had a choice of at least forty stand-alone drug plans and one or more managed care plans.[57]

As the program was implemented, plans began to compete on the offered benefit, and thus most did not offer the standard package. For example, a majority of plans had no deductible. The co-payments also varied substantially. Most plans did have a substantial coverage gap, and the plans varied considerably in the precise benefit design, the drugs that were covered, and the management tools applied to utilization (such as prior authorization policies, quantity limits, and step therapy).[58]

Low-income beneficiaries were provided substantial benefit subsidies. For those with incomes less than 135 percent of the poverty level ($13,230 per individual or $17,820 per couple) and limited assets (less than $7,500 per individual or $12,000 per couple), there were no deductibles, no monthly premiums, and only modest co-payments. A sliding scale of subsidized monthly premiums and larger co-payments was offered to those with incomes up to 150 percent of the poverty level and assets up to $11,500 per individual or $23,000 per couple. Medicare replaced Medicaid as the primary source of drug coverage for people who were previously eligible for both Medicaid and Medicare (the so-called "dual eligibles").[59]

If a beneficiary already had coverage from an employer or another source that is "creditable" (that is, at least as good as the standard Medicare drug benefit), that coverage suffices. Those who did not have such coverage faced a premium increase equal to 1 percent of the national average monthly premium for each month they delayed enrolling in one of the new drug plans. To encourage employers to offer such coverage to their retirees, employers were provided tax-free subsidies equal to 28 percent of costs between $250 and $5,000 in drug expenses per year per retiree.[60]

The law and implementing regulations imposed some stipulations as to which drugs must be covered. Plans had to cover all or most drugs in the following therapeutic classes: HIV/AIDs, antidepressants, antipsychotics, immunosuppressants, and anti-cancer agents. Congress later passed a specific prohibition on plans covering drugs approved for the treatment of erectile dysfunction. Aside from these stipulations, decisions about coverage of specific drugs were left for competition among plans.

The plans may use a formulary, which must include some, though not necessarily all, drugs within each therapeutic category and class. If a plan uses a formulary, it must be developed by a pharmacy and therapeutics committee. This committee is required to base coverage decisions on the strength of the scientific evidence and standards of medical practice, including findings in the peer-reviewed medical literature. The law authorizes consideration of data from randomized clinical trials, pharmacoeconomic studies, outcomes research data, and other appropriate information. U.S. Pharmacopoeia created a model formulary. If plans follow that model, then the plan is deemed to meet federal requirements. Plans are allowed to negotiate price with drug manufacturers independently.

The new law is financed by a combination of premiums paid by beneficiaries, state contributions (to at least maintain the state contributions previously made under Medicaid), and general federal revenue.[61] There is no dedicated financing mechanism, which means that expenditures under this program will exacerbate the long-term fiscal challenges caused by the projected growth of Medicare spending.

Federal Budgetary Impact

The projected cost of the new drug benefit to the federal government was a source of heated controversy. When the benefit was debated in Congress, the Congressional Budget Office initially reported a cost estimate of $395 billion over the initial ten years.[62] The chief actuary of the Medicare program has said that administration officials threatened to fire him if he disclosed his belief in 2003 that the new drug benefit would cost $534 billion over ten years.[63] (This estimate included full implementation for two years, 2004 and 2005, when the benefit was not expected to be fully implemented.) After the law was passed, CBO did raise its cost estimate from $395 billion to $436 billion in March 2005.[64] It is no exaggeration to say that the proposal might have been defeated in the House or Senate if a larger official cost estimate had been publicly available prior to the final votes.[65]

There is genuine uncertainty about how much this program will cost. The changing demographics of the population, which determine the number of eligible beneficiaries, can be projected reliably. But as patients experience a decline in out-of-pocket costs under the new law, utilization of drugs should increase. Analysts must project how many medications will be used by different beneficiaries and the prices of those medications. That calculation needs to consider the medications already approved by the Food and Drug Administration as well as to project new ones that may be approved for use over the next ten years.

There are some factors that work to keep costs lower than expected. Plans are likely to implement cost-management techniques to hold costs down (for instance, use of prior-authorization policies and cost-effectiveness analysis in deciding which drugs to cover). Competition between health plans and the resulting price pressure on pharmaceutical manufacturers appear to be exerting a downward influence on the pricing of new and existing products. On the other hand, some factors work to escalate costs. More mergers in the pharmaceutical industry could reduce competition in some markets and cause higher pricing of products. If some employers drop coverage (despite the availability of subsidies), more beneficiaries will need to be shifted from corporate plans to Medicare. If many Fortune 500 companies shed retiree health obligations to avoid financial distress, more retirees may turn to the new Medicare benefit for their coverage. But the increased use of union-supervised plans instead of employer plans for retirees may shield Medicare from additional costs. Thus, the actual costs of the new benefit will be continually revised and updated as experience with the program materializes.

Implementation Snafus

Whenever a complex new program is delivered to a politically active and vulnerable population, there is a significant risk that snafus will provoke a public backlash and lead to repeal of the law. For example, a 1988 catastrophic health insurance law was repealed by Congress soon after it was adopted due to public furor over the costs of the law.[66] The dangers are especially great in a polarized political environment where reporters are hungry to expose unanticipated flaws in a program and partisan critics are looking to stigmatize the new law.

The MMA itself was complicated, but many of the key issues were left unresolved by Congress and were not clarified until the Department of Health and Human Services (HHS) issued implementing regulations and guidance. In January 2005, just nine months before the enrollment period began and less than one year prior to the kickoff date (January 1, 2006) for the new benefit, HHS issued 1,162 single-spaced pages of rules and guidance.[67] The fine print affected virtually everyone involved: insurers, employers, states, pharmacies, doctors, drug manufacturers, and the 43 million Medicare beneficiaries.

Not surprisingly, implementation of the law was accompanied by substantial confusion. The good-faith efforts to implement the new program led to unanticipated mistakes and unnecessary hardships.

Hard Choices for Seniors

For starters, many seniors had difficulty understanding the new benefit and deciding whether to participate or retain their existing coverage. Those who were inclined to participate had difficulty choosing among the dozens of alternative plans, each with its own benefit structure and payment obligations.

A national survey in May 2006 found that 75 percent of people over age sixty-five found the new program difficult to understand.[68] HHS officials explained that the many individual drug plans were intended to provide coverage options and drive down costs through competition.[69] New online tools were made available to help seniors make choices among plans, but journalists wrote gripping stories of the very sick and mentally disabled who could not possibly make such a choice on their own.[70]

Recognizing an opportunity for profit, insurers engaged in aggressive marketing tactics to persuade seniors and the disabled to sign up with their plans. The customer service agents for insurers were accused of providing inaccurate and misleading information, making it difficult for people to make informed decisions.[71] HHS officials insisted that the rate of complaints from beneficiaries was relatively low (2.2 per 1,000) and inaccurate information from insurers was not a major reason for complaints.[72] Ultimately, HHS responded to complaints. Using executive powers, the Bush administration barred marketing agents from cold-calling, door-to-door marketing, cross-selling of non-health-related products, and unsolicited marketing in waiting rooms and senior centers.[73]

Overburdened Pharmacies

Once the plan took effect in early January 2006, some patients had difficulty getting the drugs they needed. Pharmacists were reportedly swamped with questions and complaints from beneficiaries. It was difficult to obtain the information needed to submit claims, verify eligibility, or calculate payments. Doctors prescribed drugs without knowing which plan a patient was on or which drugs were covered by the patient's plan. When doctors tried to call insurers for critical information as to which drugs were covered, delays could be as long as several hours.[74]

HHS responded. Hundreds of call operators were enlisted to help pharmacies respond to problems. HHS instructed insurers to cover thirty days' worth of any drug that a patient had been using just prior to January 1, 2006, even if the drug was not listed on the plan's formulary.[75]

Mix-ups

Insurers took on a large record-keeping function. Under the supervision of HHS, they were responsible for tracking each patient's out-of-pocket spending on drugs. They needed to account for the deductible, co-payments, spending in excess of the coverage limit, and any cost-sharing assistance provided to low-income beneficiaries. They also needed to exclude those out-of-pocket costs incurred for drugs not listed on the plan's formulary. Beneficiaries were then sent monthly statements listing prescriptions and amounts spent.

Early in the process, there were cases where insurers got mixed up and applied a series of medications to a beneficiary's spouse. That type of error could cause the spouse's drug spending to exceed the coverage limit (the "doughnut hole") too rapidly.[76]

Some beneficiaries told the federal government to withhold premiums under the new benefit from their monthly Social Security checks. This reasonable request required coordination between two federal agencies. The Social Security Administration did not always respond promptly to such requests, and would belatedly deduct multiple months' worth of premiums from a single month's Social Security check.[77]

Low-income seniors who were not already on Medicaid needed to apply for special low-income assistance at either a federal Social Security office or a state Medicaid office, demonstrating that they satisfied both the income and asset tests. When counting income against the thresholds ($14,700 for singles, $19,800 for couples in 2006), the income of a spouse was to be included but not the income of dependents or other co-occupants. Welfare payments, food stamps, and other forms of assistance were also excluded. The asset threshold was $10,000 for single persons and $20,000 for couples, excluding a senior's house, car, furniture, or any rental property that a senior would rely on for financial support. Included were stocks, bonds, mutual funds, IRAs, or any cash deposited at home or deposited elsewhere.[78]

About half of the applications submitted for low-income assistance were rejected due to excess assets. Some seniors apparently took the rejection letter to mean that they were not eligible to participate in the program at all, even though all Medicare beneficiaries are eligible.[79] Concerned that many eligible low-income seniors had failed to enroll in the program, SSA and HHS made special efforts to find and enroll an estimated 4 million low-income seniors and disabled persons.[80]

When the new drug benefit went into effect, it was estimated that 10,000 to 20,000 persons were receiving free cancer medications from the charity programs of drug manufacturers.[81] Some seniors apparently did not enroll because they feared they might lose their free access to anti-cancer drugs. Fortunately, studies undertaken after the law took effect found that some of the worst forecasts (for instance, less access to anti-cancer drugs) did not materialize.[82]

A much larger number of seniors were concerned that they would lose their employer-based drug coverage. Employers had three options: retain their coverage for retirees and obtain a subsidy from HHS, scale back the coverage to the minimum level prescribed by HHS rules and obtain a subsidy from HHS, or drop coverage altogether.[83] The second option (more money for companies, less coverage for retirees) attracted massive adverse media coverage.[84] Some employers considered dropping coverage but decided instead to pay part or all of their retirees' premiums in the new plan or provide other compensation.

Shifting Patients from Medicaid to Medicare

Medicare beneficiaries who were also on Medicaid ("dual eligibles"), an estimated 6.4 million Americans who are often among the country's oldest and sickest, ran into unexpected problems. When their drug coverage was automatically shifted from Medicaid to the new Medicare program, they were randomly assigned to one of the drug-only private plans.[85] Many dual eligibles experienced denials of coverage, inability to get the drugs they had been taking, and unexpected co-payments.[86]

In California it was estimated that of the one million dual eligibles, about 20 percent did not initially get all of their medications due to the limited coverage of drugs.[87] In Texas, patients had been accustomed to zero co-payments under Medicaid. When switched to Medicare, they faced co-payments of $1 to $5 for each prescription. For patients with ten or more prescriptions, the cost was substantial, unbudgeted, and sometimes unaffordable.[88]

Many states responded to the concerns raised by dual eligibles by providing additional coverage, at least on an emergency basis.[89] Over time, some patients switched to plans that better satisfied their needs. The Bush administration also agreed, in a 2008 class-action settlement, to provide extra help to low-income people who face large co-payments for their prescriptions.[90]

The authors of MMA foresaw some of these potential problems. For example, dual eligibles in nursing homes were exempted from co-payments. But mentally disabled persons living in residential care facilities were not exempt. The families of some patients wondered whether transfer to a nursing home would be more affordable than paying co-payments for numerous drugs. Some patients went to emergency rooms or hospitals to obtain free drugs.[91]

Press reports also highlighted the fact that the transfer of dual eligibles from Medicaid to Medicare allowed drug companies to charge higher prices for the same prescription. Under Medicaid, the states are the purchasers of drugs, and by law they must receive the lowest available prices. Yet MMA allows the price of drugs to be negotiated between manufacturers and health plans. The precise prices that are charged are reported to Medicare but remain confidential. HHS officials strived to reassure reporters and the public that the best plans were negotiating lower prices than those made available to commercial insurers and Medicaid.[92]

Prior Authorization

To keep costs down, many insurers implemented various "prior authorization" procedures.[93] Doctors and pharmacists were required to obtain prior approval from the insurer before specific drugs would be covered. For years commercial insurers and pharmacy benefit managers had used similar techniques. The rationale is that each drug has unique clinical criteria that must be met to justify its use. Insurers might have as many as thirty forms for prior authorization of different drugs. The forms serve as a checklist of necessary information needed for claims review by the insurer. On some forms, doctors are required to submit details of lab test results, office notes, or other data showing why the drug is needed.[94]

The process of prior authorization created delays, paperwork burdens, rejections of prescriptions not authorized by a plan, and frustration among doctors, pharmacists, and patients. Yet such procedures were clearly intended by Congress. The U.S. Congressional Budget Office reports that they play a role in keeping down the overall costs of the new drug benefit.[95]

The Furor Rises and Subsides

Soon after the new drug benefit began, the program became so controversial that its future was in question. Conservatives were arguing that the program should be suspended, repealed, or replaced with a smaller program aimed specifically at low-income seniors.[96] Liberals argued that the program must be simplified and made more generous. Conservatives feared that price controls on drugs would inevitably result; liberals argued that such controls were urgently needed to contain the costs of the new benefit.

Rather than reopen the entire law, Congress responded to the initial complaints by extending the signup period and giving the Department of Health and Human Services time to tackle unexpected problems.[97] As the implementation snafus were worked out, the controversy died down and it became apparent that the law was doing what it was intended to do: reduce the cost to seniors of taking prescription drugs outside the hospital setting. Even the more skeptical reporters began to write stories touting some of the law's successes.[98]

A June 2006 survey of Medicare eligibles by the Kaiser Foundation found that over 90 percent were covered and understood the program. More than 80 percent of those in drug plans were satisfied; 58 percent thought the new law was a major benefit. Only 20 percent of respondents had encountered a problem.[99] Even some skeptical conservatives began to acknowledge the plan was working better than expected.[100]

Each year, though, seniors are urged to redo their choice of plan. Premiums at some plans have reportedly risen between 30 percent and 60 percent in a single year. Some plans that covered the "doughnut hole," at least partially, have scaled back such voluntary coverage.[101] Critics argue that seniors may be victimized because they lack the ability to make the best choice each year.[102]

The history of Medicare from its inception in 1965 through the 2002 election "is littered with missed opportunities to add prescription drug coverage for beneficiaries."[103] In 2003 President Bush and Congress "seized a historic opportunity."[104]

From the standpoint of presidential leadership, the new Medicare drug benefit was a substantial accomplishment. Reasonable people can disagree about the merits of specific features of the benefit, but it is instructive to consider how Bush secured from a polarized Congress the most important piece of entitlement legislation since the Great Society programs of the 1960s.[105]

In making the drug benefit issue a legislative priority, Bush followed through on his campaign commitment from 2000. He also picked an issue with significant Democratic interest in the Congress. Thus, the idea of a new drug benefit for seniors had the potential to attract Democratic collaborators in a polarized Congress, even if comprehensive Medicare reform would prove to be too difficult to accomplish. And for those who regret that comprehensive reform was not accomplished, the responsibility for that failure rests at least as much with the Congress as with Bush.

By choosing a cross-partisan strategy instead of a bipartisan one, Bush took a substantial political risk. When he made the compromises in the Senate that were necessary to avoid a filibuster, he almost lost the entire initiative to opposition from rank-and-file Republicans on the House floor. If House and Senate conservatives had known that the full cost of the benefit was expected to be greater than $400 billion, who knows whether it would have passed.[106] Nonetheless, the cross-partisan strategy was effective in protecting Bush's private-sector approach to coverage, as a bipartisan approach would likely have resulted in a program with much more government control. And a decision to negotiate with Democratic Senate and House leaders would probably have led to a far more generous and expensive program.

The drug-benefit success is a powerful illustration of why it was crucial for the White House to reach out to key interest groups, especially those with strong ties to the opposite party. In this case, the interests of the AARP and the Democratic Party were not perfectly aligned, and the White House was able to exploit that wedge effectively in advancing a policy priority that Bush and AARP shared.

It was especially significant that the White House and congressional Republicans enlisted the support of all of the powerful interests: insurers, drug manufacturers, and physicians, as well as the AARP. Once it was clear that the coalition of powerful interests would hold, it became easier for the White House to attract the critical number of Democrats in the Senate while holding on to skittish Republicans. In this case, a broad coalition of interest groups became an ally of the White House, not the enemy.

Small-government conservatives argue that this entire reform package was a disaster and will be a huge negative on Bush's record.[107] They are certainly correct that the legislation illustrates why Bush was different in his domestic policy instincts from small-government conservatives such as Ronald Reagan and Newt Gingrich. At the same time, Bush can argue that the question was not whether a drug benefit would be added to Medicare but when the political inevitability would occur. By seizing the leadership role, Bush won a private-sector, choice-oriented plan that advances his vision of an ownership society where people take more responsibility for their own lives. Moreover, if the plan works, it will lay the groundwork for more privatization and competition in Medicare policy in the decades ahead.

The early actuarial experience with the new drug benefit suggests that the overall costs of the program to the federal government are less than were projected.[108] The rate of growth of prescription drug spending began to decelerate in 2005, and spending on drugs actually declined by 12 percent in fiscal year 2008 compared to 2007.[109] For the top twenty-five drugs used by seniors, the Medicare drug plans have negotiated prices that are, on average, 35 percent lower than the average cash price at retail pharmacies.

Projections of the cost of the Medicare prescription drug benefit for the fiscal year 2008 budget cycle are 30 percent below what was projected when Congress passed the benefit in 2003.[110] The explanations for the lower cost estimates are lower-than-projected enrollment in Part D and the low-income subsidy program, competitive bidding between plans, increased use of generics, and slower growth in prescription drug costs since the new benefit began.[111] Thus, the early budgetary impacts of the new drug benefit have not been as bad as originally projected.

6

Producing More Energy

President Bush's policies on tax cuts, public education, and prescription drugs emerged directly from his campaign positions against Vice President Al Gore. In some ways, the same can be said of energy policy. Bush campaigned on the need for more U.S. oil and gas production and "clean coal" technology while Gore favored renewable sources of energy. After the election, the Bush administration used both legislation and executive powers to improve the investment climate for production of fossil fuels. But there were also two big surprises in the energy industry in the Bush era: the rapid growth of renewables (especially ethanol) and a resurgence of interest in nuclear power as a source of electricity.

Ironically, it was Al Gore who pioneered ethanol advocacy in his unsuccessful bid for president in 1992, a bid that began with a strong showing in the Iowa caucuses. While Bush shared some of Gore's pro-ethanol rhetoric in the 2000 campaign, the Bush administration's pro-ethanol policies were far more aggressive than anyone expected. The shift in U.S. policy to favor nuclear energy was an even bigger surprise because neither Bush nor Gore spoke much about nuclear energy in the 2000 campaign. The third-party candidate, Ralph Nader, campaigned on a platform to ban nuclear power.

Early efforts to pass energy legislation failed due to determined Democratic opposition and defections among moderate Republicans in the Senate and House. The threat of a filibuster in the Senate was formidable. Bush's legislative success on energy came slowly, but it was ultimately accomplished through a crafty cross-partisan strategy. A dozen Democratic senators, most from the farm states of the Midwest, supplied Bush the crucial crossover votes he needed to overcome the loss of support from moderate Republicans, especially those from the Northeast. Organized farm interests with strong ties to the Democratic Party played a crucial role in delivering Senate votes for Bush's 2005 energy legislation.

As important as the 2005 energy bill was, it is only one facet of Bush's national energy policy. A full appreciation of this policy requires consideration of executive as well as legislative successes. As we shall see, rule making and other executive actions proved to be at least as important as the 2005 legislation.

Energy was also a key to the connection between policy making and re-election politics. Bush's energy policies helped buttress support for his re-election in such states as West Virginia and Ohio and the corn-producing regions of the Midwest. With the exception of Illinois, Bush either carried or was competitive in the significant midwestern corn-producing states.

In this chapter, I examine the fate of the Bush's agenda on energy production, covering fossil fuels, nuclear power, and renewables. Chapter 7 considers Bush's surprising record on energy conservation.

Bush vs. Gore on Energy

After almost two decades of low energy prices, the presidential election year of 2000 coincided with an unexpected surge in the world price of oil. From January 1999 to September 2000 the world oil price tripled due to strong world oil demand, cutbacks in oil production by OPEC, and poor weather in several regions of the world.[1] American motorists incurred a fifty-cent-per-gallon spike in the retail price of gasoline that persisted through the 2000 election. Since rising energy prices create risks and opportunities for politicians, energy policy became a major presidential election issue for the first time since 1980.

Governor Bush alleged that the Clinton-Gore administration had ignored the need for an energy policy for eight years. He outlined a ten-year plan to expand oil and coal production in the United States, build stronger relations with other energy-producing nations, implement conservation measures at home, and develop alternative sources of energy such as biofuels.[2] Gore countered with a campaign position that emphasized conservation and renewable sources of energy such as solar, wind, and biofuels.[3]

In the fall before the 2000 election, Vice President Gore advocated that oil from the Strategic Petroleum Reserve be made available to bring down oil prices before winter arrived. Bush countered that the reserve should be used as an "insurance policy" in the event of "a sudden disruption of our energy supply," not as a pre-election ploy.[4] What is really needed, Bush argued, is increased domestic oil exploration, referring to the Bush-Cheney position that permission is needed to drill for oil in the Arctic National Wildlife Refuge (ANWR) in Alaska and other forbidden locations. The Gore-Lieberman campaign countered that drilling in ANWR would lead to irreversible environmental damage.[5]

The mountains of West Virginia are home to coal and its miners. Although West Virginia is traditionally a Democratic state in presidential elections,[6] in 2000 Republican radio advertisements began two months before the Democratic ads. Governor Bush made two visits to the state before Vice President Gore arrived. Bush pledged a $2 billion federal "clean coal" program while criticizing the Clinton-Gore administration for "choking" coal with excessive regulation.[7] Gore did make two visits to the state in the week before the election, citing his support for "clean coal" and the endorsement of the United Mine Workers of America. But Gore's efforts were not enough to prevent Bush's upset victory in West Virginia. Bush's final margin of victory over Gore proved to be less than the state's five electoral votes.

The 2001 National Energy Policy

During his second week in office, Bush directed his policy advisers to develop a national energy policy. The policy document was prepared by a team of agency specialists and White House staff under the leadership of Vice President Cheney. Cheney chose to organize a process that relied on closely held dialogues with a selected number of stakeholders, especially leaders in the business community. Objecting to this process, organized environmentalists stimulated several years of controversy, congressional hearings, and litigation about Cheney's energy-policy process.[8]

Published in May 2001, the *National Energy Policy* report included 103 specific recommendations.[9]

Using this report as a blueprint, Bush directed his administration to

- expand domestic production of oil and natural gas while diversifying foreign sources of oil and gas;
- reduce dependence on natural gas in the electricity sector by expanding the use of coal, nuclear power, and renewables; and
- reduce demand for oil in the transport sector through conservation and alternative motor fuels (e.g., ethanol and hydrogen).

Since some of these policies could not be pursued under existing statutes, the White House urged Congress to pass the necessary energy legislation. Rather than submit detailed legislative language, Bush encouraged Congress to develop a comprehensive bill that met his expectations.

Legislative Strategy

Recognizing Bush's limited political standing and the divided Congress in 2001, the White House knew that any energy legislation would be vulnerable to Democratic opposition in the Senate. A comprehensive bill seemed more promising than a series of bills on different fuels because a broad and powerful coalition of supportive interest groups might be easier to enlist on a comprehensive bill. Such support might compensate for Bush's limited political standing.

In order to generate Democratic interest, the bill needed to contain either (1) provisions that would attract support from southern and/or farm-state Democrats, or (2) provisions that would attract support of greener Democrats from the East and West Coasts. The first strategy was more promising because organized environmental groups generally opposed Bush's interest in expanding the use of fossil fuels and nuclear power. For the same reason, a cross-partisan strategy aimed at a limited number of Democratic senators seemed more likely to succeed than a classic bipartisan strategy entailing concessions to Democratic leaders in both the House and the Senate.

An impressive business coalition was formed to support the White House initiative: agriculture, oil and gas, coal, nuclear, autos, ethanol, and manufacturing. The White House worked to rally all of these groups in support of energy legislation, thereby overcoming the historical disagreements between autos and oil, coal and nuclear, ethanol and oil, and agriculture and manufacturing. Although the cross-partisan strategy was buttressed by this coalition, it was complicated by Senator Tom Daschle's dual roles in the Senate. Daschle was both the elected leader of the Senate Democrats and the de facto leader of the chamber's farm-state Democrats. The pro-ethanol provisions in the energy bill advanced the interests of Daschle's home state of South Dakota, but the entire bill was likely to be opposed by a majority of Senate Democrats, most of whom were largely from the East and West Coasts. If Bush's cross-partisan strategy was to work, Daschle's home-state interest would have to outweigh Daschle's loyalty to the policy preferences of the Democratic Party in the Senate.[10]

First Try

In 2001 Billy Tauzin of Louisiana, chairman of the House Energy and Commerce Committee, maneuvered a comprehensive energy bill through his committee and on to the House floor. Knowing they could not defeat the bill, the House Democratic leadership proposed two amendments. One sought to block oil exploration in the Arctic National Wildlife Refuge; the other tightened mileage requirements for new cars and SUVs. Both amendments were opposed by the White House, in part because they were contrary to the 2001 National Energy Policy but also because they were creating tensions within the coalition of business and labor interests supporting energy legislation.

In order to defeat the ANWR amendment, business groups and the White House reached out to some industrial labor unions for help. These unions saw exploration in ANWR as a source of jobs as well as a contribution to energy security. The U.S. Department of Energy estimated that peak oil production from ANWR could reach 1.3 million barrels per day, or more than 20 percent of current U.S. production.[11]

Environmentalists, led by the Sierra Club, tenaciously.opposed drilling in ANWR. Even though only a small fraction of the acreage of ANWR would be impacted by drilling, the Sierra Club was successful in raising concerns about damage to wildlife and ecosystems. The amendment to strip the ANWR provision lost on the House floor by a surprisingly close vote: 223 to 206.[12] With such a small margin in the House, trouble was likely in the Senate, where environmental sensitivities were even stronger than in the House.

The other Democratic amendment would have raised the Corporate Average Fuel Economy (CAFE) standards for light trucks and SUVs from 20.7 miles per gallon (MPG) in model year 2004 to 27.5 MPG in model year 2007. Some moderate House Republicans supported it, but the auto companies, their dealers, and the United Auto Workers of America helped the White House enlist dozens of Democratic members in opposition. The margin of defeat was decisive: 269 to 160.[13] Meanwhile, as we shall see in chapter 7, the White House was working with the Department of Transportation on its own plan for tightening mileage rules for vehicles.

With its emphasis on more fossil fuel production, the bill passed the House by a solid margin: 240 to 189. The vast majority of House Republicans as well as several dozen moderate Democrats voted for it.[14] The bill's prompt passage of the House energy bill exerted pressure on the Democratic-controlled Senate, where progress was slow. Months of bickering occurred in the Senate Energy Committee. At the end of 2001, Majority Leader Daschle decided to take the leadership role on energy policy from the Senate Energy Committee. This maneuver sidestepped a committee vote on the ANWR issue, which the White House might have won, and allowed Daschle, who wanted an energy bill, to accelerate the pace of progress.

Daschle proceeded to floor-manage a bill in April 2002 that emphasized renewable sources of energy as well as fossil fuels. An effort by Republican senator Frank Murkowski of Alaska to permit drilling in ANWR was defeated 54 to 46, despite White House support.[15] The number of defecting Republicans (eight) exceeded the number of crossover Democrats (five).

On vehicle fuel economy, Senators John Kerry and John McCain considered offering an ambitious amendment to increase mileage standards for cars and light trucks by 50 percent, to 36 MPG by 2015. They decided not to proceed when a moderate provision on gas mileage offered by senior Democratic senator Carl Levin of Michigan passed 62 to 38. On this vote, nineteen crossover Democrats—many concerned that UAW might be harmed by CAFE—overwhelmed the six crossover Republicans who preferred Kerry-McCain or another plan. The Levin amendment gave the Bush administration the power to set mileage standards for cars and light trucks based on practical criteria. Since the White House was working on such a plan (see chapter 7), the White House helped marshal Republican votes for the Levin amendment.

The Senate bill passed on a bipartisan vote of 88 to 11.[16] The House bill emphasized fossil fuels while the Senate bill emphasized renewable sources of energy. But the energy issue lost its urgency later in 2002 as world oil prices and fuel prices declined steadily. Efforts to resolve the differences between the two bills were also poisoned by pre-election partisan bickering, coupled with regional conflicts pitting the Northeast and the West Coast against the rest of the country. Much to Bush's frustration, energy legislation was not passed prior to the November 2002 midterm election.

Second Try

The prospects of passing energy legislation improved in 2003 when the Republicans regained control of the Senate and enlarged their majority in the House. Yet the Republican margin in the Senate remained slight (51 to 49). Determined opposition in the Senate was expected from a coalition of liberal Democrats and New England Republicans. Would there be enough votes to block a filibuster on the Senate floor?

In April 2003 the House again passed, 247 to 175, an energy bill aimed primarily at spurring fossil fuel production. The big pro-energy vote in the House turned the spotlight on the Senate. Under the leadership of veteran Pete Domenici of New Mexico, the Senate Energy Committee worked for months on a bill with limited progress. At the suggestion of Minority Leader Daschle, who again wanted a bill, the Senate Republican leadership decided to pass the same bill that the Senate passed in 2002, when the Democrats led the Senate. This maneuver saved precious time, as both parties knew that House and Senate conferees would have to write a largely new bill anyway.

The lead Republican conferees were Domenici of New Mexico and Tauzin of Louisiana. On tax-related issues, the key Republicans were Senator Charles Grassley of Iowa and Congressman Bill Thomas of California. The Republican conferees decided to rewrite the bill themselves, without input from the Democrats, but consumed ten weeks without reaching agreement. Grassley and Thomas were divided over how ethanol should be treated with respect to federal taxation. Vice President Cheney stimulated a resolution that maintained a preference for ethanol over gasoline. But the toughest issue to resolve was an obscure one: how to address the use of methyl tertiary butyl ether (MTBE) as an additive to gasoline.

Made from petroleum products, MTBE is a competitor to corn-based ethanol. MTBE and ethanol were used in the 1990s to reduce urban air pollution, following a mandate in the Clean Air Act Amendments of 1990. MTBE was widely used on the Atlantic and Pacific coasts while ethanol captured the oxygenate market in the Midwest.

MTBE is a highly persistent substance that leaked from old underground storage tanks at fueling stations. When MTBE was detected as a contaminant of groundwater and surface water in 1995, questions were raised about odor, health risks, and environmental liability. The policy debate gradually shifted to whether MTBE use should be continued and who should pay for any liability resulting from contamination of water bodies.

Tauzin, backed by Majority Whip Tom DeLay of Texas, wanted to allow states to decide whether to ban MTBE and, more importantly, sought broad liability relief for producers of MTBE, since use of the additive had been spurred by a federal regulation. Senator Grassley, with backing from Daschle, sought a federal prohibition of MTBE use in gasoline and no liability waiver for MTBE producers. On October 6, 2003, as the energy conference was nearing conclusion, several New England states filed suit against twenty-two oil companies seeking compensation for MTBE contamination of water supplies.[17]

Frustrated with the slow pace of progress, Vice President Cheney and the Republican congressional leadership intervened to encourage resolution. To grease the wheels in the Senate, the conference report was revised. By dropping the House-passed ANWR provision (which proponents believed could be addressed through a different vehicle anyway), the Republican leadership hoped to soften Democratic opposition on the Senate floor. Conferees also tripled the mandatory use of renewable fuels, expecting that this would persuade Daschle and other farm-state Democrats to fight hard for passage of the conference report.[18] Conferees also repealed the "oxygenate" mandate in the Clean Air Act and added a phase-out of MTBE use in gasoline. A liability waiver for MTBE producers was included with a provocative wrinkle: A retroactivity provision for liability relief covered all MTBE lawsuits filed after September 5, 2003, which would effectively block the lawsuit against oil companies filed by several New England states on October 6. This provision irked a key Democratic constituency, the plaintiff's bar.

As expected, the House passed the energy conference report, 246 to 180. But Democratic senator Charles Schumer of New York expressed the sentiment of many Senate Democrats and New England Republicans when he threatened a filibuster. Meanwhile, Daschle indicated he would only "reluctantly" support the conference report, effectively releasing his Democratic colleagues to vote as they saw fit.[19]

When the revised conference report went to the Senate floor, a key vote to limit debate received twelve Democratic votes, predominately farm-state and southern Democrats. If the White House and Senate majority leader Bill Frist had delivered all fifty-one Republican Senators, then a filibuster would have been easily avoided. But Frist could not find enough Republican votes. When six Republican senators voted against cloture, the White House fell two votes short of the sixty needed to move the energy bill through the Senate. The final vote to limit debate was 57 to 40, as Frist cast his vote with the 40 in order to allow the issue to be reconsidered later if votes shifted.

Frist and Daschle did agree to one last-ditch effort in April 2004, when the energy bill was offered as an amendment to legislation on an internet tax moratorium. Daschle offered a version that consisted of only the ethanol mandate in the energy bill, trying to make clear to farm interests that he supported ethanol. His amendment was defeated, 59 to 40. Domenici again offered the comprehensive energy bill but with one deletion: the provision providing liability relief for MTBE production and use. Surprisingly, removing the MTBE liability relief actually cost more votes than it attracted because some oil-state senators defected, so that the bill ended up five votes short of the sixty required: 55 to 43.

The only consolation for the Bush administration was that some of the energy tax incentives in the failed energy bill were transferred to a corporate tax reform bill that passed the Congress just before the 2004 election. As described later in this chapter, those provisions were aimed at stimulating the supply of domestic energy, from both fossil fuels and renewable sources.

Third Try

In 2004 Bush won re-election by only a narrow margin, but the partisan picture in the Senate improved for the White House. Daschle was defeated in his re-election bid. His failure to deliver an ethanol mandate for farmers surely did not help his case. The Republicans enjoyed a net gain of four seats in the Senate and thus the new 55–45 Republican majority enhanced prospects for passing an energy bill.

Unfortunately for the White House, three of the new Republican senators replaced Democratic senators who had voted in favor of cloture in the previous Congress. Thus, it was not obvious that sixty votes were feasible.[20] Fortunately, another increase in fuel prices added a renewed sense of urgency in the Congress.

In the House, the new Energy and Commerce Committee chairman, Joe Barton of Texas, worked cooperatively with John Dingell of Michigan while Senate committee chairman Pete Domenici of New Mexico worked closely with Democratic senator Jeff Bingaman of New Mexico. This time the Senate acted promptly.

The Senate energy bill passed 85 to 12 but only after heated floor debates on a range of amendments. Despite White House opposition, Bingaman won, on a 52–48 vote, an amendment that required 10 percent of electricity to be derived from renewable sources (for instance, wind and solar power) by the year 2020. The other amendments, which were defeated, reflected a range of concerns about vehicle fuel economy, offshore siting of liquefied natural gas terminals, climate change, and offshore oil and gas drilling.[21]

The House made matters easier by passing an energy bill without any ANWR provision, hoping to address ANWR in a separate budget resolution. Thus, the House-Senate conferees faced four big issues: liability relief for MTBE producers (which was not addressed in the Senate bill), the size of the ethanol mandate, the renewable electricity mandate, and the size of the overall tax package.

Barton made the key compromise: He accepted removal of the MTBE liability waiver in exchange for permission to have some MTBE lawsuits heard in federal courts. Since the House had not passed a renewable electricity mandate and Bush opposed it, the Bingaman provision was dropped by conferees. The numeric differences on ethanol and taxes were resolved with compromise figures between the House and Senate positions.

When the conference report went back to the two chambers, it was passed 74 to 26 in the Senate and 275 to 156 in the House.[22] Thus, the Congress delivered Bush an energy bill for signature just prior to the August recess of 2005, more than four years after the group led by Vice President Cheney published its report, *National Energy Policy*.

ANWR Defeat

The Senate's supermajority (sixty-vote) requirement for major legislation was a formidable obstacle to passing ANWR legislation. Yet Senate Republicans did not give up. They included the permission to drill for oil in ANWR as part of the annual budget resolution. The rationale for this inclusion was that energy leases for ANWR drilling could raise $2.5 billion in federal revenue over five years. This clever procedural maneuver was attractive because the budget resolution was not subject to the filibuster threat. By Senate rules, the budget resolution requires only a majority vote to pass.

Senate Democrats did not capitulate. Led by Senator Maria Cantwell of Washington, the Democratic leadership sought to strip the ANWR provision from the budget bill. Cantwell's amendment was rejected 51 to 48, with forty-eight of the Senate's fifty-five Republicans joining three Democrats (Landrieu of Louisiana and Akaka and Inouye of Hawaii) to defeat it.[23] The defection of Republican moderates in the Senate foreshadowed a bigger surprise in the House, which had previously voted to support the White House on ANWR.

When the House leadership looked for votes to pass the budget resolution, the vote count was inadequate. Many moderate House Republicans, responding to complaints by national environmental groups, objected to the ANWR provision. The only way to pass the budget resolution in the House was to drop the ANWR provision.

There was no more determined advocate of drilling in ANWR than veteran Republican senator Ted Stevens of Alaska. He bounced back from the budget-resolution defeat with a new plan: Attach permission for ANWR drilling to a must-pass defense appropriations bill. With White House support, this plan worked in the House, but Stevens again faced the sixty-vote hurdle in the Senate. Stevens assumed that Senate Democrats would be reluctant to filibuster a defense appropriations bill that included both funds for the Iraq war and post-Katrina assistance for the Gulf Coast.

The Senate Democratic leadership delivered Senator Stevens what Stevens described as "the worst day of my life." He fell a few votes short of the necessary sixty. Although four Democratic senators (Akaka and Inouye of Hawaii, Landrieu of Louisiana, and Nelson of Nebraska) were persuaded to side with Stevens, two Republican senators defected (Mike DeWine of Ohio and Lincoln Chafee of Rhode Island). The loss for Stevens was also a big setback for Bush.[24]

In 2007–2008, as oil prices soared above $150 per barrel, Bush's allies in Congress made a last-ditch effort to secure permission to drill for oil and gas in ANWR. Since the Democrats were controlling the Senate floor, Republicans offered their ANWR amendment to a flood-insurance bill desired by the Democratic leadership. The Senate was evenly divided between the parties at the time but the amendment was defeated, 56 to 42. Only one Democrat (Landrieu) voted for the amendment while six Republicans (Coleman, Collins, Dole, Martinez, Smith, and Snowe) voted against it.

The ANWR issue was certainly a loser for Bush, but much progress was made on the president's larger energy agenda. I now turn to assessment of what was accomplished with the 2005 energy legislation as well as a variety of energy-related executive actions. I consider oil and gas, coal, nuclear energy, and then renewables.

Oil and Gas

Despite the legislative setback on ANWR, the White House and Congress took a variety of steps to encourage more production of oil and gas in the United States. Bush also used the persuasive powers of the presidency in foreign affairs to encourage more production of oil and gas in other countries.

The rationale for producing more oil and gas is that it will add to worldwide supplies and thus exert downward pressure on world prices. One estimate prepared by the RAND Corporation is that each 6 million barrels per day of additional oil supply (or reduced demand) is associated with a 6 to 10 percent drop in the world oil price.[25] (World oil demand in 2030 is projected to be about 118 million barrels per day.) The price response could be somewhat larger or smaller than RAND estimates, depending upon how the OPEC cartel reacts to the additional supplies. Although OPEC is sometimes portrayed as invincible, the cartel has difficulty controlling prices when demand falls or when production rises from non-OPEC sources.[26]

When fuel prices at the pump are over $3 per gallon, even a 10 percent change in price is equivalent to 30 cents per gallon at each fill-up, a significant amount of money for working-class and low-income families. Fuel expenses consume 9 percent of after-tax income for low-income households compared to 3 percent of after-tax income for the average U.S. household.[27] Thus, more oil supplies create tangible benefits for consumers.

TAX INCENTIVES

In the 2004 corporate tax reform bill, drilling for oil and gas became eligible for a "manufacturing" provision that cut the top corporate income tax rate from 35 to 32 per cent. The same bill authorized accelerated depreciation for the new Alaska natural gas pipeline,[28] which helped spur the project's commercial progress.[29] The 2005 energy bill also contained generous tax relief for oil and gas exploration in the deep waters off the Gulf of Mexico and for 50 percent of refinery investments that increase plant capacity by at least 5 percent or boost production of gasoline by at least 25 percent.

Encouraged by such incentives, Motiva Corporation undertook a $3.8 billion refinery expansion in Port Arthur, Texas,[30] while a consortium led by Chevron found between 3 billion and 15 billion barrels of oil in several fields 175 miles off-shore, 30,000 feet below the Gulf's surface.[31] In 2007–2008 the Democratic Congress sought to repeal or scale back these tax incentives but they were blocked by both a filibuster threat in the Senate and a Bush veto threat. In 2008 Bush and the Democratic Congress extended the refinery tax break until 2013.[32]

REGULATORY REFORMS

On the regulatory front, federal agencies took a variety of actions to encourage oil and gas exploration, production, and refining.[33] The procedures at the Department of Interior for the leasing of lands for exploration and development were streamlined. Drilling permits approved on federal lands in the West jumped from 3,540 in fiscal year 2002 to 7,018 in fiscal year 2005. About 2.6 million acres of the National Petroleum Reserve in Alaska were leased to energy companies for oil and gas exploration, although the Department of the Interior took regulatory steps to limit ecological impacts in sensitive areas (for instance, the land north of Teshekpuk Lake that supports migrating caribou and waterfowl).[34] In late 2008, another 350,000 acres near Arches National Park in Utah was released for leasing.[35] Using new authority in the 2005 energy law, the Department of the Interior also developed a leasing plan for oil shale development in the West, where an estimated 800 billion barrels of recoverable fossil fuels are located. Chevron and Royal Dutch Shell began to spend capital on pilot projects. In 2008, however, the Democratic Congress began to use appropriations riders to delay oil-shale development until environmental concerns are fully resolved.[36]

Clean-air rules and enforcement practices at the Environmental Protection Agency (EPA) were streamlined in 2002 to provide refineries with flexibility to make modernization investments as long as plant-wide emissions caps were respected. The corporate obligation to pay federal royalties was removed to spur natural gas production in deep-well facilities in the Gulf of Mexico. Proposals were made to lease oil-rich and gas-rich areas off the Gulf of Mexico and Virginia, especially "sale area 181," a chunk of 2 million acres about 100 miles off Pensacola, Florida. In order to bypass obstructionism from elected officials in Florida, an executive adjustment gave the pro-oil states of Mississippi, Alabama, and Louisiana more power in the leasing process.[37]

Executive refinements to rules under the Coastal Zone Management Act facilitated the siting of new LNG terminals. The 2005 energy bill went further, giving the federal government more authority to overcome local opposition to the siting of LNG terminals. The U.S. had only five LNG import facilities in 2001 (Everett, Massachusetts; Cove Point, Maryland; Elba Island, Georgia; Lake Charles, Louisiana; and the Gulf of Mexico) but all but one of them were expanded during Bush's tenure. Four completely new terminals are projected to be operational by 2010, doubling U.S. LNG capacity.[38] By 2006, a total of thirteen more (onshore and offshore) were in various phases of the government approval process,[39] though litigation slowed progress at some liquefied natural gas (LNG) sites.[40]

In 2007–2008, as oil prices climbed to record levels (near $150/barrel), the Bush administration pressured the Democratic Congress to lift outstanding bans on drilling for oil and gas in U.S. territorial waters.[41] While drilling is already permitted in the deep waters off the Gulf, the entire east and west coasts are off limits.[42] In many of these areas federal agencies are precluded from doing even rudimentary geological surveys to determine the extent of resources and the areas of most promise. Bush received a boost when Florida governor Charlie Crist reversed his stance and decided to support more offshore drilling. Even presidential candidate Barack Obama expressed openness to a compromise energy bill that would permit some offshore drilling.

The leading Democrats in Congress countered that more offshore drilling rights are unnecessary because oil companies have not yet exhausted the oil-rich areas that have already been leased, such as those near the southwestern Alaska coast.[43] They also argued that speculation, not supply shortfalls, was causing the 2008 spike in fuel prices.[44]

House Speaker Nancy Pelosi was strongly influenced by the oil spill off Santa Barbara, California, in 1969 and, early in her career, was a leader in opposition to offshore drilling in marine sanctuaries near her San Francisco congressional district.[45] She called Bush's oil-drilling plan a "hoax" that would do nothing to address the short-term spike in energy prices.[46] The opposition to Bush's initiatives by California politicians, including Republican governor Arnold Schwarzenegger, was damaging, in part because more than half of the oil-rich areas under debate were off the coast of California and, even under Bush's plan, the state would have retained the power to continue the drilling ban.[47]

Seeing Bush's plan as an election-year ploy rather than a serious proposal, the congressional Democratic leadership used their agenda-control powers to prevent it from coming to a vote in either the House or the Senate. (They also allowed the federal moratorium on drilling to expire in the fall of 2008.) In the summer of 2008 the White House and Senate Republicans forced a vote on oil drilling. They insisted that no consideration would be given to renewable-energy tax credits or business research and development credits until a vote occurred. But the Democrats prevailed 55–45 with four Republicans defecting (Coleman of Minnesota, Collins of Maine, Smith of Oregon, and Snowe of Maine). The Democrats were unanimous.[48]

When oil prices collapsed in the second half of 2008, Bush did not stop pressing for more drilling. As one of his final acts as president, he formally opened public comment on a rule making to allow leasing of all or some portions of twelve areas of the outer continental shelf.[49]

Bush's tax and regulatory reforms, coupled with the rise in world oil and gas prices, improved the investment climate for oil and gas development in the United States from 2001 to 2007. But it is doubtful that this climate will reverse the long-term decline in U.S. oil and gas production. The accessible reserves in the United States are too limited and often too costly to exploit.[50] Recognizing this, Bush also worked to encourage more oil and gas development around the world.

DIPLOMATIC INITIATIVES

The most straightforward approach was Bush's effort to persuade Saudi Crown Prince Abdullah to increase Saudi oil production.[51] The Saudis delivered on a $90 billion plan to increase production from 9.5 million barrels per day in

2004 to 12.5 million barrels per day by 2010 and to 15 million barrels per day by 2015.[52] Bush appealed to Saudi Arabia again in 2008 as world oil prices soared to record highs, causing fuel prices in the United States to approach $4 per gallon.[53] The Saudis were initially unresponsive, but later pledged another 500,000 barrels per day. In 2008 they reversed course in response to a weakening world economy and a slowing in the rate of GDP growth in China and India.[54]

In his relationship with Russian president Vladimir Putin, Bush consistently emphasized the importance of more Russian oil and gas production.[55] The case was made in both their personal deliberations and through meetings of the leaders of the G8 (the United States, the United Kingdom, Germany, Japan, Canada, France, Italy, and Russia).[56] But Russia's rate of growth in oil and gas production was disappointing.[57]

Expansion of Iraqi oil production was also a Bush priority because Iraq ranks fourth in the world in oil reserves yet has underutilized capability. Progress was slow due to sabotage, smuggling, and maintenance woes, but Iraqi production expanded steadily in 2007 until it actually surpassed pre-invasion levels.[58] In 2008 ten major oil companies (including Exxon Mobil, Shell, and Chevron) signed contracts that suggest private investment in Iraqi oil production will rise.[59] But the gains in Iraq were offset temporarily in 2008 when Nigerian oil production plummeted during attacks against Royal Dutch Shell's pipelines in western Nigeria.[60] Mexico also failed to revive its struggling oil industry, despite encouragement from President Bush.[61]

America's most secure long-term foreign supplier of energy may be Canada, whose reserves are second in size only to Saudi Arabia's. With growing production in Newfoundland and Nova Scotia to offset some declines in western Canada, Bush touted Canada as a significant and potentially growing source of oil and gas for the United States.[62] Spurred by Bush's policies, U.S. investors readied refineries in Ohio and Indiana to accommodate oil from Alberta's massive oil sands deposits.[63]

Bush also supported new pipelines around the world. Building pipelines from remote areas of the world to countries where energy is needed requires international cooperation. Bush reaffirmed President Clinton's support for a $3.9 billion pipeline to bring oil from the Caspian Sea to Western Europe; its route bypasses Russia and goes through Azerbaijan, the mountains of Georgia, and northern Turkey before hitting the Mediterranean coast. Oil started flowing through this 1,100-mile pipeline in June 2006 at a rate of 430,000 barrels per day and the volume is projected to rise to 1 million barrels per day. The United States is also encouraging construction of more pipelines through Bulgaria and across Turkey.[64]

SUMMARY

Bush used tax incentives, regulatory reforms, and diplomatic powers to stimulate more oil and gas production, both offshore and onshore. Although these efforts may have significant long-term value, they did not prevent the world price of oil from climbing well above $100 per barrel (and fuel prices from remaining well above $3 per gallon) for most of his second term in office. Despite the collapse of oil prices in 2008, the long-term projections for world oil and gas prices remain high.[65] The case for Bush's oil and gas policies is a subtle one: They may work to slow somewhat the rate of growth in world oil and gas prices in the next two decades.

Coal

In contrast to America's oil dilemma, where U.S. oil reserves are limited, coal is by far the most abundant fuel source in the U.S. At current rates of consumption, we have enough coal to last 250 years. Over 1 billion tons are mined each year in twenty-five states, with over 80 percent of this coal burned to produce electricity.[66] Coal accounts for about half of U.S. electricity generation, but the policies of the Clinton administration, discussed below, were not designed to promote investments in coal. Building on his pro-coal record in Texas, Bush embarked on an ambitious and controversial pro-coal policy.

MOUNTAINTOP MINING

During the 2000 Bush vs. Gore contest, the future viability of coal mining became a major issue, especially in West Virginia. In October 1999 a federal judge ruled that the practice of mountaintop surface mining, which is more economical and safer than underground mining, violated federal environmental laws. The judge responded to concerns of environmentalists that mountaintop mining scars mountains, pollutes rivers, and kills fish.[67]

The congressional delegation from West Virginia was shocked by this unexpected decision. When the coal-state members of Congress tried to reverse the judge's decision through direct legislation, the Clinton administration favored stringent environmental rules, even though key Democratic officials from West Virginia argued that such rules would harm their state economically.[68]

The Bush campaign was already planning to campaign in a state that has historically voted for the Democratic Party in presidential elections. Bush pledged support for mountaintop mining and argued for a "clean coal" future for America, while Al Gore was emphasizing solar and wind power.[69]

Bush ultimately defeated Vice President Gore in West Virginia, taking 52 percent of the vote to Gore's 46 percent, a "stunning upset" in a heavily Democratic state that had not voted for a Republican in an open presidential race since 1928.[70] As mentioned earlier, the resulting five electoral votes were essential to Bush's victory in the Electoral College, just as essential as winning Florida and the post-election U.S. Supreme Court case.

PRO-COAL INVESTMENT CLIMATE

When Bush took office in 2001, environmental enforcement policies were stifling investment in repairs at aging power plants while no new coal-fired plants were under construction or in the planning stages.[71] Moreover, the Clinton administration had worked internationally to help design the Kyoto Protocol on global climate change. The protocol required nations to reduce greenhouse gas emissions below their 1990 levels on a permanent basis. Since coal is relatively high in carbon content, and carbon dioxide is a major greenhouse gas, the Kyoto requirements were expected to erect a formidable barrier to the expansion of coal use. As a result, the investment climate for coal during the Clinton administration was poor.

Beginning in 2001, Bush made a series of executive decisions and legislative proposals aimed at enhancing the future of coal. Most importantly, Bush announced in early 2001 that he would not seek ratification of the Kyoto Protocol on climate change. (Chapter 8 examines Bush's climate-control policy.) This single executive decision was seen as lifting a major barrier to the growth of the U.S. coal industry. As one executive from a coal company described it: "Putting in place a global warming program is about putting limits on the coal business and low-cost energy."[72]

The Bush administration also used executive powers to clarify the rules covering mountaintop mining,[73] streamline clean-air enforcement policies, and provide investment flexibility in a rule aimed at reducing mercury emissions. These actions, combined with new rules to reduce sulfur and nitrogen emissions (see chapter 8), were aimed at allowing owners of coal-fired plants to make coordinated investments in pollution-control equipment, thereby providing a

Table 6.1. Pro-Coal Provisions in the 2005 Energy Bill

- Cost sharing of $200 million per year was authorized from 2006 to 2014 for demonstrations of commercial-scale advanced "clean coal" technologies.

- $3 billion was authorized to encourage new sources of advanced coal-based power and upgrades of existing coal plants with pollution-control equipment to improve air quality.

- $1.1 billion was authorized over fiscal years 2007–2009 for clean coal research.

- $90 million was authorized over fiscal years 2007–2009 to develop carbon-capture technologies that could be applied to the existing fleet of coal plants.

- Investment tax credits were authorized for advanced clean-coal facilities, including industrial coal gasification, and integrated gasification combined cycle projects.

- The current 160-acre cap on coal leases was repealed, allowing the advance payment of royalties from coal mines.

- The Department of the Interior was required to prepare an assessment of coal reserves on federal lands that are not national parks, providing important information to investors interested in the mining of coal on federal lands.

better regulatory climate for coal investors. Although some of this regulatory relief was ultimately defeated in lawsuits waged by environmental groups, the regulatory climate for coal investments improved from 2001 through 2006.

CLEAN-COAL TECHNOLOGY

At the same time that the Bush administration halted overly aggressive enforcement of environmental rules against the coal industry, Bush insisted that that there was no long-term future for coal unless it was clean coal. He therefore advocated expanded investment of federal money in innovative clean-coal projects. As table 6.1 demonstrates, the 2005 energy bill contained numerous pro-coal provisions aimed at mitigating coal's impact on climate change.[74]

Carbon dioxide is one of the most important gases linked to global climate change. A critical step toward "clean-coal" is commercial-scale demonstration of technology to capture carbon dioxide at a coal plant's boiler or stack, ship it by pipeline to a storage facility, and store the carbon dioxide underground in a safe geological repository.[75] Although this "clean-coal" technology is promising, private investors were hesitant to move forward without a predictable regulatory climate and federal financial support.[76] Indeed, some environmentalists insisted that "clean-coal" technology is a false hope that should not be subsidized.[77]

In 2005, the Bush administration established a public-private partnership, FutureGen, to build a $950 million prototype coal-gasification plant that would generate electricity and produce hydrogen to power motor vehicles without causing air pollution. Most importantly, FutureGen was designed to demonstrate the technical and economic feasibility of capture and permanent storage of carbon dioxide.[78] The project was to be implemented by a consortium that included the federal government, selected states, several coal producers and electric utilities, and even some international collaborators, including China. After a competitive bidding process, a decision was made to site the innovative plant in southern Illinois. Under a cost-sharing agreement, the industry consortium was to pay 26 percent of costs while the U.S. Department of Energy (DOE) was to pay 74 percent.

FutureGen was not simply a technical project promoted by the DOE and private industry. It was a presidential priority announced in Bush's 2003 State of the Union address and reaffirmed in five consecutive Bush budgetary requests to Congress. The Bush administration and other countries perceived Future-Gen as one of America's major contributions to the future of global climate policy. If the United States could demonstrate how to capture and store carbon dioxide on a large scale, the knowledge could then be transferred to coal users from China to Poland to Australia.

Although FutureGen was an inspiring idea, history provided ample reason to be somewhat skeptical of the venture.[79] In the 1970s President Carter backed a billion-dollar coal gasification experiment in Beulah, North Dakota, seeking to make use of the region's cheap lignite coal. The experiment failed in the marketplace because virgin natural gas proved to be far less expensive.[80]

FutureGen likewise proved to be a flop, again for economic reasons.[81] The projected costs of the idealistic venture rose steadily from 2003 to 2008, until Bush was informed by the Department of Energy that the true cost would ultimately be at least $1.8 billion, with most of the cost to be paid by taxpayers. At such a high cost, the plant was projected to have little commercial viability.[82]

In 2008 Bush accepted the department's recommendation to scrap FutureGen and reallocate the funds to a more practical, multi-site program along the lines suggested by a group of MIT scientists.[83] Instead of funding one huge experiment, the modified plan is to fund several smaller demonstrations of capture-and-storage technology at plants where private investors are already prepared to incur all of the costs of the new coal plant except for capture and storage.[84] The modified plan also decoupled clean coal and hydrogen, thus allowing federal financial support for carbon capture and control at a new coal plant that is not designed to produce hydrogen for use in transportation.[85] DOE estimates that subsidizing several modest demonstrations instead of one big one will achieve twice as much control of carbon dioxide and will do so faster, starting with plants that come online in 2015–16. Whether these estimates prove accurate depends on resolution of an array of economic, geological, and regulatory issues about carbon capture and storage.[86]

Bush was also persuaded to promote another promising but expensive coal-related technology. Coal is typically considered a source of electricity, but clean-coal enthusiasts also see promise in "coal-to-liquid" (CTL) technologies that produce a transport fuel to replace petroleum.[87]

No commercial-size CTL plants were operating in the U.S. when Bush took office,[88] but a Chinese plant making diesel fuel from coal was operating in Inner Mongolia. In 2007 Bush advocated CTL as part of his "20-in-10" initiative, which aimed to slash U.S. gasoline consumption by 20 percent (compared to projected levels) over ten years (for more detail, see chapter 7). The U.S. Air Force also promoted an ambitious program to make jet fuel from coal.[89] From an energy-security perspective, CTL technology is promising since it can help reduce U.S. dependence on oil. The technology is supported by a potent coalition of coal miners, coal producers, rail and shipping companies, and military contractors.

But CTL technology has a potential flaw that has been pointed out by environmentalists: By itself CTL does nothing to reduce carbon dioxide emissions. In fact, an enormous amount of energy is consumed in making the liquid fuel from coal. CTL technology is likely to produce more greenhouse gases than would result from refining oil into gasoline.[90] Fortunately, there are creative ways to pursue CTL that would actually reduce life-cycle carbon emissions (relative to petroleum), but these innovations (for instance, mixing biomass and coal prior to liquid production and/or storing carbon dioxide underground) raise significant cost issues.[91]

Congress ultimately decided against mandating greater use of CTL technologies.[92] In fact, the 2007 energy bill permits the Air Force to pursue CTL technology only if it results in a net decrease in life-cycle greenhouse gas emissions.

Despite the setbacks with FutureGen and CTL technology, Bush's pro-coal ambitions began to make progress in the marketplace. A doubling of natural gas prices from 1995 to 2005, coupled with the new policies of the Bush administration, stimulated more investor enthusiasm in new coal-fired power plants. The newest coal plants have significant efficiency improvements that bring their carbon dioxide emissions closer to the levels of gas plants.[93] In 2004 the federal government projected that by 2012 the U.S. would bring online seventy-two new coal-fired power plants instead of none (as projected in 1999). Several utility companies in the West announced in 2004 that they intended to shift planned investments from natural gas to coal, thereby launching the first new western coal plants in more than a decade.[94] As one indicator of coal's revival, the U.S. Energy Information Administration enlarged coal's projected market share in the U.S. electricity sector through 2030.[95] As recently as 2006, another hundred new coal plants were under consideration in the United States.[96]

BACKLASH AGAINST COAL

During Bush's last two years in office, his plans to expand coal use in the United States suffered some major setbacks.[97] A rapid rise in global coal prices, spurred by the growth in demand for coal in China and India, reduced coal's cost advantage compared to natural gas, nuclear, and renewables.[98] Wall Street investors also began to doubt coal's future because the major presidential candidates of both parties were favoring a mandatory climate-control plan that would hurt coal.[99] Meanwhile, environmental activists launched a grassroots campaign to dissuade electric utilities from building new coal plants without carbon capture and storage.[100] One attorney from the Sierra Club boasted that their anti-coal campaign would leave no new coal plant unchallenged.[101]

The activist campaigns led to a high-profile decision by a large Texas utility, TXU, to cancel eight of eleven planned coal plants. TXU was criticized by Environmental Defense, a national environmental group, and by a former EPA administrator, William Reilly, who was involved in a corporate buyout decision involving TXU.[102] Public officials in Florida, Kansas, North Carolina, and Oregon also agreed with activists in high-profile decisions against permission to build new coal plants.[103]

By the end of 2007, twenty-nine new coal plants had been challenged in U.S. court or administrative proceedings and a total of fifty plants were canceled or delayed.[104] According to the U.S. Department of Energy, more than two dozen new coal plants were scrapped toward the end of the Bush administration, usually due to environmental opposition or rising construction costs. By early 2008 investors were becoming more skeptical about the future of coal in the United States, even though coal use was booming throughout much of the world.[105]

The political power in Washington, D.C., also began to shift against coal. When the Democratic Party captured a majority of the Congress in November 2006, new congressional committee chairs Barbara Boxer of California in the Senate and John Dingell of Michigan in the House pledged to pass economywide programs to cap carbon dioxide emissions. Henry Waxman of California, an ardent environmentist, later replaced Dingell as chair of the key House Energy and Commerce Committee. Thus new policies are expected to hurt the competitive position of coal relative to other sources of power generation.[106] The only saving grace for pro-coal forces is that President Barack Obama has a pro-coal record; he campaigned in 2008 in favor of coal and may be inclined to rejuvenate FutureGen.[107]

Despite the uncertain economics and regulatory environment, several utilities moved forward with plans to build new coal plants, in some cases with concrete plans to capture and store carbon dioxide.[108] For example, Duke Energy is planning an advanced coal plant in Indiana that will gasify coal, control conventional air pollution, and capture and store carbon dioxide.[109] A CTL plant in West Virginia is also planned. Peabody, the largest U.S. coal producer, and its partners are also planning a new $3 billion coal plant in Illinois.[110]

The long-term viability of Bush's clean-coal agenda may hinge on whether plans for carbon capture and storage can overcome an array of technical, cost, regulatory, and public-acceptance hurdles.[111] If Bush's policies ultimately contribute to the commercialization of viable clean-coal technology, it will be a significant accomplishment with long-term, global ramifications.

Nuclear Power

Over a hundred plants producing nuclear energy account for about 20 percent of U.S. electricity supply, but many existing nuclear plants are nearing the end of their useful life. When President Bush took office in 2001, no new nuclear plants were under construction or under serious consideration.[112] Yet demand for electricity in the United States was growing at twice the overall rate of new supplies.[113]

In 2000 Governor Bush did not campaign on an explicit pro-nuclear platform against Vice President Gore. It was not until release of the 2001 National Energy Plan, spearheaded by Vice President Cheney, that revival of the nuclear power industry in the United States emerged as a priority of the Bush administration.[114] Much to the surprise of both industry executives and environmentalists, Bush became an ardent advocate of nuclear power. In his re-election bid against John Kerry in 2004, Bush campaigned aggressively on a pro-nuclear platform.

Working with Republican leaders in Congress, the White House took virtually every step in its power to enhance the future of nuclear power,[115] seeking to add the United States to a growing list of countries (Finland, China, Taiwan, Russia, India, South Korea, Great Britain, Bulgaria, the Czech Republic, Switzerland, Hungary, and Slovakia) that are expanding nuclear-generation capacity.[116] Even some countries with anti-nuclear policies (Italy for example) began to reverse course in favor of nuclear power.[117] But Bush's pro-nuclear policies were opposed by organized environmentalists on the grounds that nuclear energy is too risky and expensive. The environmentalists favored instead more reliance on conservation and renewable sources of electricity, such as wind and solar.[118]

Bush relied more on legislation than executive powers to promote nuclear power because the key regulatory agency, the Nuclear Regulatory Commission (NRC), is an independent agency—like the Federal Reserve Board—that operates outside the purview of formal White House oversight. He also relied heavily on a pro-nuclear champion in the United States Congress, Republican senator Pete Domenici of New Mexico. The relevant cabinet agencies, DOE and EPA, were also harnessed by the White House to support the administration's pro-nuclear agenda. Bush advanced the pro-nuclear policy on multiple fronts: waste disposal, radiation protection, reprocessing spent fuel, insurance for accidents, and financing of new reactors. I consider briefly Bush's progress and setbacks on each of these challenges.

STORING NUCLEAR WASTES AT YUCCA MOUNTAIN

One of the impediments to nuclear power in the United States is uncertainty about nuclear wastes, which are currently stored temporarily at 121 locations in 39 states. Without any approved permanent storage facility, most owners of nuclear plants are accumulating wastes in aboveground facilities. Temporary storage facilities are safe and economical, but a permanent burial place for highly radioactive wastes might improve public acceptance of nuclear power.[119] Some states will not even permit construction of new nuclear power plants until a permanent waste site is operational.[120]

As early as 1982, the U.S. Department of Energy began to study whether nuclear wastes could be stored safely in an underground site near Yucca Mountain, about 100 miles northwest of Las Vegas, Nevada. A comparative study of several sites determined that burial of wastes near Yucca was the most promising and was safer than the temporary storage facilities currently in use at operating reactors.[121] The site is located on federally owned land on the western edge of the Nevada Test Site in the Mojave Desert.

In the current repository design for Yucca, the radioactive material will be stored about 1,000 feet beneath the land surface and about 1,000 feet above the closest groundwater. The repository is designed to hold 70,000 metric tons of waste, 90 percent from nuclear power plants and 10 percent from Department of Defense projects. Since existing plants will generate 60,000 tons of waste by 2010, either Yucca will need to be expanded or additional sites found as the industry grows.[122]

Through legislative action, Congress in 1987 designated Yucca as the lone permanent burial site. Years of delay in planning the Yucca facility ensued. A critical turning point occurred in 2000 when Congress passed a law calling for completion of the siting and licensing of the facility.[123]

In 2002 President Bush gave the necessary executive approval to the DOE's plan to make Yucca Mountain the site of our nation's first and only permanent repository for nuclear waste.[124] Under the terms of federal law, the governor of Nevada and the Nevada state legislature, acting in unison, may veto the president's decision. And they did so. Nevada's veto could only be overridden by a majority vote of both the House and Senate. If such a vote did not occur within ninety legislative days of Nevada's veto, a new site would have to be identified.

Recognizing the importance of the Yucca repository to the future of nuclear energy, the White House helped rally congressional Republicans to ensure that the Nevada's veto was overridden. In May 2002, the House passed an override resolution 306 to 117.[125] Only 13 out of 216 Republicans defied the White House. The Democrats in the House were about evenly divided.

The vote in the Senate was expected to be closer because Majority Leader Tom Daschle and his whip, Harry Reid of Nevada, were ardent opponents of the Yucca project. On the Republican side, John Ensign, the junior senator from Nevada, tried to persuade his GOP colleagues to sustain the state's veto.

The Nuclear Waste Policy Act (1982) provided that any senator could request that an override resolution be considered on the Senate floor, even if the Senate majority leader did not want to schedule floor time. As a result, Daschle could not block a vote. Moreover, the expedited procedures blocked any filibuster threat, which meant that a simple majority vote would be sufficient to override Nevada's decision.

When the roll-call vote on Yucca was taken in the Senate in July of 2002, Nevada's veto was overridden 60 to 39.[126] Only three out of forty-eight Republicans voted to sustain Nevada's veto (Campbell of Colorado, Chafee of Rhode Island, and Ensign of Nevada). Fifteen of fifty Democratic senators also supported the override.[127] As decisive as this vote seemed, it was followed by annual skirmishes over whether the Yucca project would be funded.

In 2004 the White House proposed to obtain some of the funding for Yucca by tapping an off-budget trust fund that had accumulated revenues from periodic assessments on nuclear utilities. Minority Whip Harry Reid blocked this proposal in the Senate, hoping to starve the project of funds. In response, the White House worked with House and Senate Republican leaders to reallocate appropriations from other agencies in order to obtain enough funding for Yucca as part of an omnibus budget bill.[128]

The Democratic takeover of Congress after the November 2006 elections placed a cloud of uncertainty over Yucca. Led by Harry Reid, the new Senate majority leader, Congress cut Bush's funding request for Yucca from $494 billion to $386.5 billion, causing a halt in construction and the layoff of 900 Yucca personnel.[129] Under the best of circumstances, Yucca will open no sooner than 2020. Construction costs may total $70 to $80 billion. Political conflict over the future of Yucca is expected to continue, even though in June 2008 the Bush administration filed with the U.S. Nuclear Regulatory Commission a formal application to license the facility.[130]

PUBLIC HEALTH STANDARDS FOR YUCCA

In order to ensure the safety of the Yucca repository, the Bush administration established formal standards to protect public health. The development of standards was complex because federal authority over the management of nuclear wastes is split among three federal agencies: the Department of Energy is responsible for siting, building, and operating an underground repository for nuclear wastes; the Environmental Protection Agency is responsible for setting radiation standards for Yucca that would protect the public; and the Nuclear Regulatory Commission is responsible for implementing EPA standards through its licensing requirements for repositories. The Bush administration worked diligently to coordinate these efforts, even though NRC is an independent agency.

The Energy Policy Act of 1992 directed EPA to set standards based on a technical study to be undertaken by the National Academy of Sciences (NAS). Although NAS completed its study in August 1995,[131] EPA took four years to issue a rule-making proposal. When the Bush administration assumed power in 2001, EPA's final rule was not completed. At Bush's direction, EPA issued a final rule in June 2001.[132]

Complex litigation ensued. The State of Nevada and several environmental groups challenged these standards in federal court on the grounds that they did not adequately protect the public. The Nuclear Energy Institute, representing producers of nuclear power, challenged the standards on the grounds that they were unrealistically stringent and would increase cost and slow construction of the repository. Although the lawsuits were filed in July 2001, the case was so technically and legally complex that a decision was not issued by the D.C. Circuit Court of Appeals until January 2004.[133] The court upheld the EPA standards in all respects except for the time period over which regulatory compliance was expected.

In the June 2001 rule, EPA applied the radiation protection standards for "only" a 10,000-year period after the wastes were disposed at Yucca. The court, based on the NAS study, concluded that compliance with EPA's radiation standard must extend until the peak radiation dose is expected to occur, even if that peak is projected to occur after 10,000 years. The NAS determined that there is no scientific basis for limiting the period of compliance assessment to 10,000 years. The NAS further opined that compliance assessment is feasible over a 1,000,000-year period, the time scale of the long-term stability of the fundamental geologic regime at Yucca Mountain. NAS and the court were concerned that some radiation releases from the Yucca site may not occur until several hundred thousand years after the wastes are buried in the Yucca repository.

In light of the court's opinion, EPA modified the 2001 rule to account for the possibility that peak doses of radiation from Yucca could occur after 10,000 years.[134] If EPA's rule-making position survives further judicial scrutiny, the public health framework for permanent disposal of nuclear wastes will be set.

Meanwhile, the estimated costs of the entire project have continued to grow. Due to inflation, stricter design requirements, and larger volumes of spent fuel, the projected costs of building and operating the facility through 2133 have risen from $57.5 billion in 2001 to $96.2 billion in 2008. Although only 20 percent of the projected cost will be incurred by taxpayers (the remaining 80 percent will be built into electricity rates), the rising cost estimates play into the hands of anti-Yucca advocates who seek to delay or kill the project.[135]

REPROCESSING NUCLEAR FUEL

Recognizing that the Yucca project may not prove to be a comprehensive or acceptable solution to the waste-disposal challenge, Bush also proposed to reverse a 1978 prohibition on the reprocessing of nuclear fuels. President Jimmy Carter and the U.S. Congress banned reprocessing on the grounds that it might enhance the prospects for making nuclear weapons.

Since 1978, it has become more apparent that unauthorized persons do not need access to materials from a nuclear power plant in order to acquire the materials required to make a nuclear bomb. The added risk of nuclear proliferation from reprocessing is perceived to be slight or nonexistent. As a result, most countries in the world with substantial nuclear power capacity are already moving toward reprocessing as the primary way to manage nuclear wastes. When nuclear fuels are reprocessed and reused in nuclear reactors, the quantity of nuclear waste that requires permanent disposal is dramatically reduced.

If Congress should remove the prohibition on reprocessing and provide adequate funding for recycling,[136] the long-term future of nuclear power generation in the United States might be enhanced. President Bush's 2009 budget request to Congress continued to give priority to reprocessing, but the response of the Democratic Congress is uncertain, especially since some scientists and environmentalists continue to oppose reprocessing of nuclear wastes.[137] For example, a 2007 report from the National Academy of Sciences urged the federal government to scale back funding for reprocessing in favor of a more concerted effort to support construction of conventional nuclear power plants in the United States.[138] If reprocessing is not authorized and the Yucca project is scaled back, nuclear wastes can continue to be stored safely on-site at temporary storage facilities (for instance, in dry storage casks), or centralized dry-cask repositories can be established at several locations to manage wastes for the next few decades.[139]

FEDERAL INSURANCE FOR REACTOR ACCIDENTS

The Price-Anderson Act provides insurance protection for private investors in the event of a nuclear accident. It expired in 2003, and its renewal was critical to allaying investors' concerns about the risks of operating a nuclear reactor. At the encouragement of the Bush administration, the 2005 energy bill extended Price-Anderson protection for twenty years, the longest renewal in the act's fifty-year history.

The 2005 energy bill requires nuclear plant operators to purchase all of the private insurance available to them, or about $300 million in 2005. This private insurance serves as primary coverage in the event of an accident. If not sufficient to cover claims from an accident, a secondary level of coverage is provided from company contributions. The maximum fee for secondary coverage was raised from $63 million to $95.8 million per reactor. The annual secondary payout was raised from $10 million to $15 million per reactor, with payouts adjusted regularly to account for inflation. The renewal of Price-Anderson protection did not receive much public attention, but it was a necessary step toward a favorable investment climate for nuclear power in the United States.

SUBSIDIZING NEW NUCLEAR REACTORS

Bush took a strong interest in overcoming the financial barriers to the construction of new nuclear power plants. The 2005 energy bill encouraged new nuclear plant construction by authorizing a series of generous government loans, tax provisions, subsidies, and research and development funds. Table 6.2 summarizes the key pro-nuclear aspects of the energy bill.

The cumulative impact of these provisions was a shift in the investment climate for new nuclear-plant construction in the United States. For example, the U.S. Energy Information Administration has revised its projections and now forecasts an expansion of nuclear generation capacity in the United States by 2030.[140]

Table 6.2. Pro-Nuclear Provisions of 2005 Energy Bill

- The Department of Energy was authorized to loan up to 80% of the cost of a new nuclear plant, with full payment required within 30 years or 90% of the project's life.
- A production tax credit was made available for the first eight years of a new nuclear plant's operation, which mirrors the credit that had been made available for wind and biomass since 1992.
- The tax treatment of funds used to decommission nuclear plants was rationalized in a way that helps merchant companies planning to build new nuclear plants.
- The federal government was authorized to provide "standby support" for the first six new nuclear plants if there are unexpected delays during the construction of a new plant or during the initial phases of start-up. Delays are considered unexpected if they are attributable to slowness by the Nuclear Regulatory Commission or litigation. Reimbursement is provided to investors for any additional principal or interest on debt attributable to plant delays, including any costs incurred due to the obligation to pay for replacement sources of electricity. The delay-induced costs are reimbursed 100% for the first two new reactors, up to a limit of $500 million each, and 50% for plants three through six, up to $250 million each.
- The Congress authorized $2.95 billion for federal research and development into nuclear power and hydrogen, including $1.25 billion for construction of an advanced nuclear cogeneration reactor to produce electricity and hydrogen at the Idaho National Laboratory.

PROSPECTS FOR NUCLEAR POWER

The United States has not built a new nuclear plant since 1978 and, when Bush took office in 2001, none were in the planning stages. In fact, the longevity of the 103 existing nuclear plants was in doubt.

Due to more promising economics, streamlined rules at the U.S. Nuclear Regulatory Commission, and the supportive policies of Bush and the Congress, some energy specialists are beginning to speculate about a possible "renaissance" of nuclear energy. Half of the existing plants have already sought and received a twenty-year extension to their original forty-year licenses. The remaining plants are also expected to be relicensed. More importantly, by the end of 2006, twelve utilities had notified NRC of their plans to seek construction and operating licenses for as many as twenty-three new reactors. The first new plants could come online as soon as 2015.[141]

The NRC has already issued its first license for a major new commercial nuclear facility in thirty years. It is the $1.5 billion National Enrichment Facility, located in Eunice, New Mexico, which is scheduled to start selling enriched uranium to reactors in early 2009. The nuclear power industry viewed the licensing of this facility as a bellwether for the licensing of new nuclear reactors in the years ahead.[142]

The improved public policy environment, combined with high natural gas prices and rising coal prices, has stimulated investors to reconsider future investment.[143] Yet utilities are sharply divided on the future of nuclear power. Some companies are planning to expand nuclear capacity while others see new coal or gas plants as the fiscally responsible choice.[144] A growing number are turning to wind or solar for added peak-load capacity.[145] If Congress does establish a carbon tax or an economy-wide cap-and-trade program for greenhouse gases, the commercial prospects of nuclear power (which does not emit carbon dioxide) will be further enhanced.[146]

Investment in nuclear power is nonetheless risky. From 2006 to 2008 the projected costs of building a new nuclear power plant grew sharply, more than doubling from an estimated $5 billion per plant to $12 billion per plant. Rising costs are attributed to the spiraling costs of uranium, steel, cement, and copper coupled with a shortage of skilled labor and qualified suppliers.[147] Even if utilities can find the financing for large up-front costs, state public utility commissions may not be willing to pass on the costs to consumers in the form of higher utility bills.[148] Some utilities have backed away from their pro-nuclear plants due to escalating costs.[149]

President Bush's goal of seeing new nuclear power plants built and operated in the United States may ultimately be achieved. Three applications to NRC for new plants were made in 2007 and perhaps fifteen more are expected by the end of 2009. Both major-party presidential candidates in 2008, Barack Obama and John McCain, appeared to be open to a future role for nuclear power.[150] But most experts do not foresee nuclear power accounting for a growing share of U.S. power production through 2030 unless the price of carbon dioxide emissions under new federal policies becomes much higher than is now anticipated.[151]

Renewable Energy Sources

As the term is used in policy debates, "renewable" sources of energy typically include solar, wind, biomass, ocean, geothermal, and hydroelectric. Bush's 2001 National Energy Policy emphasized the importance of renewable sources of energy in the overall energy mix and recommended that their small share be enlarged.[152]

Some of the policy's pro-renewables recommendations were quite specific. Tax credits for renewable electricity (for instance, that produced by wind or biomass) were to be extended and expanded. A new tax credit of 15 percent (up to a maximum of $2,000) to stimulate residential applications of solar energy was suggested. Assuming Congress passed legislation permitting oil and gas drilling in ANWR, about $1.2 billion of the resulting revenues were to be used to fund expanded federal research programs into renewable sources such as wind, solar, geothermal, and biomass. Future research programs were to be funded through public-private partnerships based on anticipated performance.[153]

Despite the policy's support for renewable energy, organized environmental groups and the Democratic leadership in Congress were at odds with the White House over the key policy issues. The root of the disagreement was over priorities: Bush emphasized clean coal and advanced nuclear while environmental groups and Democratic leaders emphasized conservation and renewable sources. The disagreement played out in several ways.

The Bush White House often combined support for "renewable energy" with support for "alternative energy" ideas that included innovative applications of coal (for example, co-firing an electricity boiler with a mix of biomass and coal, or making hydrogen from coal to power cars, or making liquid jet fuel from coal to propel airplanes). Many environmental groups feared that too much emphasis on such ideas would slow the development of truly renewable sources.

A showdown on the Senate floor occurred in June 2007. Democratic senator Jeff Bingaman of New Mexico proposed a requirement that 15 percent of electric power be produced by "renewable" sources (such as wind and solar) by 2020. The amendment appeared to have majority support in the Senate. Republican senator Pete Domenici of New Mexico countered with a substitute plan that required 20 percent of electric power to be produced by renewable sources OR nuclear energy OR clean coal. Domenici's plan was tabled on a vote of 56 to 39, with all Democrats and seven Republicans (Collins, Grassley, Gregg, Smith,

Snowe, Specter, and Sununu) joined in opposition. As a result of this vote, the Senate Republican leadership, backed by the White House, retaliated. They informed Bingaman that his original 15 percent requirement would not survive a filibuster threat on the Senate floor.[154] On several other occasions during the Bush presidency, Congress came close to passing a renewable electricity mandate, but White House opposition played a key role in defeating it.[155]

The Bush administration's requests for federal funding of energy research also exposed disputes over priorities. The Bush budget requests to Congress were typically more generous to advanced fossil fuel and nuclear technologies than to renewables. In fact, when the federal budget situation was very tight in fiscal year 2009, President Bush's request to Congress called for an expansion of research-and-development (R & D) support for advanced nuclear and clean coal but a decline in R & D support for energy efficiency and solar energy research.[156]

Despite the policy disagreements about renewables, the Bush years proved to be an enormously good period for renewable sources of energy. The key reasons were the rising prices of oil, natural gas, coal, and nuclear energy. The 2004 corporate tax reform bill and the 2005 energy bill also contained key provisions that promoted renewables:

- Two billion dollars in tax-exempt bonds were authorized to finance private-sector real estate projects involving renewable energy.
- Production tax credits for renewable energy were extended for two additional years, with eligibility expanded to include hydropower on Indian reservations.
- The Renewable Energy Production Incentive was extended, making nonprofit electric utilities eligible to receive the renewable energy production tax credit.
- An investment tax credit was created for purchases of solar photovoltaic technologies and solar water heating, with a $2,000 cap for residential applications and no cap for commercial applications.
- The Department of the Interior was instructed to survey the potential to develop wind, solar, and ocean energy resources on federal land.
- The Department of Energy was directed to annually review the potential of renewable energy resources in the United States, including solar, wind, biomass, ocean, geothermal, and hydroelectric.

The federal tax policies were buttressed by many state and local policies that used tax incentives and regulatory requirements to spur the use of renewable energy sources in the power sector. As a result, investments in wind turbines and solar applications increased rapidly from 2000 to 2008.[157]

In 2008 the Bush administration used executive powers to begin leasing large segments of the outer continental shelf to companies seeking to build massive wind turbines. Developers have given priority to wind projects off the New England coast because the region has high electricity prices, large coastal cities, and some of the strongest winds in U.S. territory. Two dozen offshore wind projects are already operating in Europe. The U.S. Department of the Interior is performing environmental analyses to support proper leasing of ten offshore parcels.[158]

The Democrats in Congress, with acquiescence by Bush, used the 2008 financial bailout legislation as a vehicle to extend even more generous tax credits to renewable energy through 2016. For example, the $2,000 cap on the solar tax credit was removed, which means that a typical $60,000 solar installation will be eligible for a $18,000 credit. Taxpayers who don't owe that much tax in one year are entitled to carry forward any unused credit and use it in later years. They can also apply the credit to their alternative minimum tax bill as well as to their regular tax. For wind, a new $4,000 credit was made available for up to 30 percent of the cost of installing a home windmill system to generate electricity. Geothermal systems are also available for generous credits.[159] The new tax policies will partly offset the adverse effect that the credit crunch and low oil and gas prices have inflicted on renewables.[160]

President Bush left office with renewables taking a small but rapidly growing share of the electricity market. In the late 1990s, the official U.S. government projection was that the share of the electricity market accounted for by renewables (primarily wind, solar, and hydroelectric) would decline from 11.3 percent in 1998 to 9.5 percent in 2020.[161] By the end of the Bush administration, the official projection was that renewables would grow at a faster annual rate than any other source of electricity, capturing 18 percent of the market by 2030.[162] In 2007, 35 percent of the new electricity-generating capacity in the U.S. was from wind, more than from coal and nuclear combined. Had it not been for local opposition by environmentalists to wind turbines and solar transmission lines, the market penetration of wind and solar would have been even greater.[163]

While the Bush administration opposed mandates for renewable sources of electricity, Bush did support mandates for renewable energy in the transport sector of the economy. Working with a diverse coalition of farm, automotive, and environmental interests, the Bush administration instituted a mix of incentives and mandates to spur rapid expansion of biofuels to power motor vehicles.

Biofuels: Savior or Curse?

Biomass is organic matter that can be used to make energy. Since biomass can be converted directly into liquid fuels, it has tremendous promise as a way to meet our energy needs for transportation while reducing dependence on petroleum. The most common forms of these "biofuels" are ethanol and biodiesel. While ethanol is typically made from corn or sugar cane, biodiesel is made using vegetable fats (such as palm oil or rapeseed oil), animal fats, algae, or even recycled cooking greases.

Both ethanol and biodiesel can be used as fuel additives or "blenders," or they can be used in their pure form to fuel a vehicle. In some U.S. cities, local buses are powered on pure ethanol. Brazil already makes widespread use of ethanol made from sugar cane to power vehicles and has recently mandated that every liter of diesel fuel contain 5 percent biodiesel by 2013.[164] Sweden has required all large refueling stations to have at least one pump that supplies ethanol, biodiesel, or other clean fuels by 2009.[165] The European Union has mandated a rapid increase in biodiesel use by cars and trucks, since diesel fuel is more common in the EU than gasoline. But the U.S. interest in biofuels began with efforts to enhance urban air quality.

Ethanol vs. MTBE

When ethanol is added to gasoline (10 percent ethanol is a common blend), sometimes called "gasohol," it raises the oxygen level of the fuel, helping the fuel to burn more completely and cleanly. It also reduces engine knocking by raising a fuel's octane rating.

The 1990 Clean Air Act Amendments required urban areas to add oxygen to motor fuels, expecting these "oxygenated" fuels to help clear the air of harmful doses of carbon monoxide and ozone. In 2006, gasohol accounted for 40 percent of gasoline produced in the United States.[166]

A petroleum-derived oxygenate, MTBE, was the primary competitor to ethanol, especially on the East and West Coasts of the United States. Ethanol cannot be shipped through oil pipelines without corrosion and was more expensive to produce than MTBE. Thus, ethanol—which is made from corn in the U.S.—was sold primarily in the Midwest.

Before Bush took office in 2001, Congress passed a tax-preference scheme to reduce the cost advantage of MTBE over ethanol, thereby ensuring a market for ethanol in the Midwest. The federal excise tax on gasoline was 18.4 cents per gallon in the early 1990s. In order to reduce the price disadvantage of ethanol, Congress set the gasohol tax at only 13.2 cents per gallon, 5.2 cents less than the rate assessed on pure gasoline, including gasoline blended with MTBE. Congress later replaced the 5.2-cent excise tax reduction with a tax credit for gasohol blenders based on the volume of ethanol they use. Congress also allowed small ethanol producers to qualify for a federal income tax credit equal to 10 cents per gallon of pure ethanol. At least twenty states, predominantly those in the Midwest, enacted additional tax breaks or subsidies to encourage ethanol production and use.

As a result of favorable tax and regulatory policies, ethanol production grew rapidly from 660 million gallons in 1996 to 1.1 billion gallons in 2002. But prior to enactment of the 2005 energy bill, ethanol's market penetration was small compared to the 150 billion gallons of gasoline consumed in the United States in 2006.

As Bush's energy plan was initially considered by Congress in 2001–2002, public opposition to MTBE was growing due to reports of groundwater and surface water contamination. There was a strong push to prevent further MTBE contamination by eliminating or paring back the oxygenates mandate in the Clean Air Act. Yet farm groups and ethanol producers saw deregulation as a threat to the continued growth of ethanol, which was serving well as an oxygenate in many midwestern towns and cities. More ambitiously, ethanol advocates envisioned taking MTBE's market in the U.S. fuels business.

Grand Compromise

The key to passage of the 2005 energy bill was the Bush administration's handling of the ethanol issue. Without the support of the ethanol coalition, Bush did not have the votes in Congress to pass his agenda for oil, gas, coal, and nuclear power. What emerged was a grand compromise on ethanol that facilitated a successful cross-partisan strategy on energy legislation. Although the oil industry opposed ethanol mandates, the ethanol coalition was more diverse and potent than one might think.[167] It included corn producers, landowners in the Midwest, ethanol producers, rail and shipping interests, coal interests (since coal is often used to power ethanol plants), and the National Wildlife Federation and other environmental groups who favor renewables.[168]

For the Bush administration, the easier part of the policy decision was to favor ethanol over MTBE, since some states were already considering a ban on MTBE and the EPA was considering a prohibition of MTBE under the Toxic Substances Control Act. But a key question remained: Should the oxygenates mandate just be rescinded, or should it be replaced with something?

Working with Republican senator Charles Grassley of Iowa, the White House decided to use the energy bill as a vehicle to replace the oxygenates requirement in the Clean Air Act with a new requirement that refiners blend "renewable" fuels with gasoline. It was expected that the blending would occur primarily with ethanol made from corn, since other U.S.-based feedstocks were more expensive than corn. (Imported ethanol was discouraged with a tariff of $0.54 per gallon.) Many economists objected to this de facto mandate of corn-based ethanol, but it was this grand compromise which attracted midwestern Democrats to vote for Bush's overall energy plan.

In 2005 Congress required refiners to increase the volume of ethanol and other renewable fuels to 4 billion gallons in 2006 and 7.5 billion gallons in 2012. In January 2007 Bush urged the Democratic Congress to expand the renewable fuels requirement to 35 billion gallons in 2017.[169] Within a year Congress responded with a similar mandate: a 36-billion-gallon requirement by 2022. As mentioned earlier, Congress rejected Bush's suggestion that alternative fuels (such as CTLs) as well as renewable fuels be permitted to contribute to this petroleum-reducing policy.[170]

Coupled with the favorable tax policies, new federal loan guarantees, and rising oil prices, the renewable fuels mandates of 2005 and 2007 stimulated a powerful rate of growth in the U.S. ethanol industry. As of April 2008 a total of 124 ethanol plants were operating in 24 states, with most located in corn-growing states. Another 62 plants were under construction. According to one estimate for 2007, this relatively new industry in the United States contributed $47.6 billion in gross output and 238,000 new jobs in various sectors of the U.S. economy.[171] If anything, the ethanol industry may have grown too fast, as there was a period of overcapacity in 2007–2008 that led to some consolidation and diminished profit margins in the industry.[172]

Proponents of ethanol argue that the growing use of this gasoline substitute helped restrain the growth of world oil prices and gasoline prices. A substantial amount of energy is necessary to produce ethanol from corn, but the life-cycle effect of replacing gasoline with ethanol is a substantial net reduction in oil consumption.[173] An analyst for Merrill Lynch estimated that U.S. gasoline prices in 2007–2008 would have been 15 percent (45 cents per gallon) higher if biofuels had not been capturing an increasing fraction of the U.S. gasoline market.[174]

Critics counter that ethanol is so expensive to produce that it would never be competitive in the market without the tax preferences and regulatory favoritism provided by politicians. For example, a study by the International Monetary Fund found that corn-based ethanol is 18 percent more costly to produce than gasoline (assuming that the long-term price of oil is $65 per barrel).[175]

Pumping E85

In order to meet the 36-billion-gallon requirement by 2022, it will not be sufficient to expand the market share of E10—10 percent ethanol, 90 percent gasoline—from 60 percent to 100 percent. A substantial number of motor vehicles in the transport sector will need to operate on either pure ethanol or a more substantial ethanol blend. The Bush administration recognized this reality and sought to expand use of E85 (a blend of 85 percent ethanol and 15 percent gasoline). The administration drew from the experience of Brazil, where various ethanol blends, ranging from E10 to E95, are widely available and most cars are designed to accommodate them.[176]

Even before passage of the 2005 Bush energy plan, several U.S. vehicle manufacturers were producing new "flex-fuel" vehicles that can run on gasoline, E10, or E85. A flex-fuel vehicle costs an additional $150 to produce because the tank must be made from stainless steel (to withstand erosion) and a special sensor is required to adjust the engine cycle for the different fuels. In theory, the consumer could decide at the refueling station which fuel to purchase on any given day, based on their current prices.

Using executive powers, the Bush administration encouraged automakers to produce more flex-fuel vehicles by extending compliance credits for them under the Corporate Average Fuel Economy program (CAFE; see chapter 7 for further discussion). The credits are generous: A "flex-fuel" version of a Chevy S-10 that normally achieves 25 miles per gallon is counted for compliance purposes as if it gets 40 miles per gallon. The U.S. Department of Transportation offered the CAFE credits from model years 2004 to 2007, and the 2005 energy bill extended authorization of the credits through 2014. In 2007 Bush and the Democratic Congress agreed to extend at least some flex-fuel credits until 2020, though increasingly stringent caps were added to the amount of credit any single manufacturer can claim between 2014 and 2021.[177]

From 2001 to 2006 over 5 million new cars and light trucks were produced with flex-fuel capability. In model year 2007 alone, about 4–5 percent of the 17 million new vehicles sold in the United States were capable of running on E85, including 500,000 GM and 250,000 Ford vehicles. Daimler-Chrysler committed to expand offerings from 25,000 in 2006 to 500,000 in 2008. Nissan and Toyota also decided to offer some flex-fuel vehicles, leaving Honda as the only large manufacturer without a commitment to E85.[178]

Critics of Bush's flex-fuel policy argued that the capability to run a car on E85 is not useful because of the lack of availability of E85 pumps at refueling stations. In 2005 only about 800 of the 170,000 fueling stations in the nation offered E85.[179] Minnesota alone accounted for more than 200 of the E85 pumps. Critics also argued that the credits actually weaken the energy-security and environmental benefits of CAFE by allowing manufacturers to count flex-fuel credits toward fuel economy compliance, even when the drivers do not purchase and use E85.

The White House, Congress, industry, and the states took some steps to address these concerns. GM and Ford joined with ethanol producers to help convert more independent fueling stations to E85, contributing to a doubling of the number of such stations in 2005 alone. To enhance the availability of E85 on the West Coast, General Motors certified E85 vehicles for sale in California beginning with the 2006 model year and collaborated with Chevron to explore ways to open more E85 stations in California. In order to further stimulate the availability of E85 to consumers, the 2005 energy bill made fueling stations eligible for a tax credit covering 30 percent of the cost of installing E85 refueling stations through 2010, up to a cap of $30,000 per year per station. Sympathetic states also chipped in. For example, Indiana put up about $500,000 to help install pumps for E85 fuel while GM backed giveaways and discounts to local Indiana residents who use E85.[180] The National Ethanol Vehicle Coalition projects that the federal tax credits, coupled with some state tax incentives, may stimulate the building of as many as 2,000 additional E85 fueling stations in the years ahead.[181]

Interstate 65, which runs from Gary, Indiana, to Mobile, Alabama, is now called the "Biofuels Corridor" because a motorist can purchase E85 ethanol and B20 biodiesel from one end to the other. The thirty-one refueling stations on this stretch were aided by $1.5 million in subsidies contained in the 2005 energy bill.[182]

The business policies of major oil companies, however, do not always encourage the offering of E85. Most of the 170,000 refueling stations are not owned by oil companies, but they are often franchised from them or have long-standing business contracts with them. These arrangements may require stations to purchase gasoline, may limit advertising of E85, and may restrict credit card use to pay for E85. Some contracts require that if E85 is offered, it must be provided on a separate island rather than under the main canopy. Given these contractual obstacles, the pro-ethanol forces targeted refueling stations owned by big retailers such as Kroger and Wal-Mart.

As consumer use of E85 increased, the reactions of motorists to vehicle performance were generally good—indeed, the driving experience with E85 is generally indistinguishable from pure gasoline or E10. According to one estimate, the tailpipe emissions of conventional air pollutants—those related to smog and soot in urban air—were about 50 percent less with E85 than with E10.[183]

The big downside of E85 is the diminished energy value of the fuel, which means that a vehicle gets 25 percent fewer miles per gallon on E85 than it gets on E10. As a result, most consumers are unlikely to purchase E85 unless the price at the pump is significantly lower than the price of E10 or pure gasoline.[184]

The Bush administration argued that it might be useful for the United States to establish the capability to fuel vehicles without consuming as much oil. If the United States experiences sustained shortages of gasoline in the years ahead, the millions of flex-fuel vehicles on the road may be able to convert to E85, thereby reducing the vulnerability of American consumers and our national economy.[185] But if Bush's policies result only in an occasional use of E85 during extreme shortages, the contribution to energy security will be limited.

A more promising option than E85 may be a gradual increase in the ethanol blend from E10 to E15 or even E20. In 2008 the Department of Energy reported that a small test fleet of vehicles ran adequately on blends with as much as 20 percent ethanol. But automakers warn that long term use of E20 can damage fuel systems and catalytic converters in vehicles that were not designed to burn E20.[186]

Backlash against Corn-Based Ethanol

During his last two years in office, Bush's pro-ethanol policies began to generate substantial opposition. The backlash became so intense that twenty-four Republican senators, including presidential candidate John McCain, urged the Bush administration to use executive authority to ease the ethanol mandates.[187] The backlash was caused by new economic and environmental developments that began to strain the pro-ethanol coalition.

The price of corn rose rapidly and unexpectedly. From 2003 to 2006 the percentage of the U.S. corn crop allocated to ethanol production rose from 12 percent to 16 percent. (If even half of the 2022 biofuels mandate is met with corn-based ethanol, it will require almost 40 percent of that year's projected corn harvest.) Wholesale corn prices were $1.90 per bushel in 2005, $2.41 per bushel in 2006, and spot prices in 2007 soared above $4.00 per bushel.[188] As farmers shifted land from other grains to corn, the price of those grains also shot up. Consequently, the agricultural economy began to experience unexpected food price inflation, with overall food prices up 4 percent in 2007, the largest increase since 1900.[189]

Experts disagreed about the key causes of the food price inflation. While the ethanol mandates certainly played a role, other factors were the growing demand for food from China and India, higher world oil prices (as oil is a key input to agriculture), and less-than-expected supplies from Australia due to droughts.[190] Bush made a public statement disputing the notion that ethanol is "the main cost driver" for the inflation in food prices around the world.[191]

Livestock, meat, and poultry interests were hurt by the rising corn prices. They began to coordinate their anti-ethanol lobbying with the oil industry. Packaged food companies, hurt by the higher prices of corn and other grains, also fought back against the biofuels mandates. That brought large companies such as Dean Foods, Heinz, Kellogg's, Kraft, PepsiCo, and Coca-Cola into the anti-ethanol coalition.[192] The U.S. ethanol mandates also became a source of international controversy as critics linked them to everything from riots in Mexico to hunger in the developing world.[193]

Environmental scientists began to question the wisdom of mandating ethanol use. Even ignoring the amount of water used to grow corn, a typical ethanol plant consumes as much as four gallons of water to produce each gallon of fuel. Concerns were raised about the pressure being put on aquifers in the relatively dry farm belt region of the United States.[194]

More importantly, new studies found that a large expansion of ethanol use would increase, not reduce, the greenhouse gases linked to global climate change. The perverse effect occurs as farmers convert forest and grassland to new cropland. The absorption of carbon dioxide by forests and grassland is thereby diminished. Instead of reducing greenhouse gases by 20 percent (as previously predicted), a new study estimated that expanded use of corn-based ethanol would double the emissions of greenhouse gases over the next thirty years.[195] Environmentalists began to consider that some renewable fuels might not be good for the environment, a finding that caused further tension in the ethanol coalition.[196]

In the summer of 2008 Governor Rick Perry of Texas petitioned EPA to waive the agency's ethanol fuel-blending requirements, in effect reducing the ethanol mandate by 50 percent (from 9.0 billion to 4.5 billion gallons).[197] Perry argued that the requirement was causing "severe harm" to the economy, since corn was better suited for use as livestock feed than as fuel. The Bush administration rejected Perry's request, citing "no compelling evidence" of "severe harm."

A Future for Cellulosic Ethanol?

Bush was a strong advocate of corn-based ethanol, but he was an even stronger advocate of cellulosic ethanol, ethanol made from crop residues, wood chips, switchgrass, or even municipal garbage. If these techniques become commercially viable, they may diminish food price inflation.[198] They also tend to consume less energy and cause fewer adverse environmental impacts than corn-based ethanol. Unfortunately, "a viable cellulosic technology may be a decade or more from providing fuel at scale."[199] In 2007 the International Monetary Fund estimated that making cellulosic ethanol was about twice as expensive as making ethanol from corn.[200]

In order to lower the cost of making cellulosic ethanol, Bush expanded federal R & D investments in cellulosic ethanol, provided federal loan guarantees for the initial plants, and supported legislation that provided a minimum mandated market. For example, in his 2006 State of the Union message, Bush pledged $150 million for R & D aimed at lowering the cost of cellulosic ethanol, double the previous year's level.[201] The 2005 energy bill authorized federal loan guarantees for new cellulosic biorefineries. By 2013, refineries are required to use at least 250 million gallons of cellulosic ethanol. Bush's policies had a powerful side effect in favor of cellulosic ethanol: They helped persuade venture capitalists to open their wallets for cellulosic biorefineries.[202]

At the start of the Bush administration, the largest cellulosic ethanol facility was a demonstration-scale plant in Ottawa, Canada, built by Iogen Corporation. It is designed to produce 1 million gallons of ethanol per year, less than a commercial-scale plant, which would be expected to produce 40 million gallons per year.

The Department of Energy made unsuccessful attempts to launch pilot plants in the 1990s but it helped persuade Bush that another concerted effort should be made.[203] In fiscal year 2007 DOE awarded $385 million in grants to six companies working on cellulosic ethanol technology. Another $375 million was allocated to support three new federal bioenergy research centers. The Department of Agriculture also provided $161 million in financing for bioenergy projects, including $21 million in loan guarantees for cellulosic plants. It is estimated that in 2007 alone an additional $200 million in private monies flowed from venture capitalists and Wall Street banks to cellulosic ethanol interests. Even major oil companies, such as BP, Chevron, and ConocoPhillips, began to support bioenergy research programs at major U.S. universities.[204]

Before the results of these efforts were known, Bush and the Congress went further and required a large-scale increase in use of cellulosic ethanol. The 2007 energy bill, which Bush negotiated with the Democratic leaders in Congress, does not permit a majority of the 36-billion-gallon mandate to be met with corn-based ethanol. In fact, corn-based ethanol is capped in the legislation at 14 billion gallons per year in 2022. The remaining 22 billion gallons are envisioned to be met largely with cellulosic ethanol, unless the administrator of EPA makes a determination that feedstocks are not plentiful enough or prices are expected to rise significantly.[205] Since the structure of the bill provides a virtually certain market for cellulosic ethanol, one should expect that even more private money will be attracted. Time will tell whether Bush's gamble on cellulosic ethanol proves to be worthwhile.

Import Brazilian Ethanol?

The International Monetary Fund estimates that making ethanol from sugar cane is significantly less expensive than making either corn-based ethanol or cellulosic ethanol.[206] In Brazil, where the methods of making ethanol from sugar cane have been optimized, the output-input ratio for energy is 10 to 1, far better than the 2.5 to 1 ratio for corn-based ethanol.[207] Thus, the basic economics suggested an obvious policy to the Bush administration: rescind the U.S. tariff on imported ethanol and encourage the global expansion of ethanol production from sugar cane.[208]

Bush tried both initiatives but learned a basic lesson in cross-partisan politics: Do not expect to enact legislation that offends some of your best Republican allies as well as some of your most valued crossover Democrats. Bush made a short-lived suggestion that the 54-cent-per-gallon tariff on imported ethanol be rescinded. The farm state Democrats in Congress, the key crossover votes for Bush on energy and many other issues, were not impressed with Bush's free-trade idea. Bush was politely informed by the Speaker of the House—Republican Denny Hastert of Illinois—and Republican senator Charles Grassley of Iowa that this proposal was not helpful to their regions economically and would do nothing but create divisions within the valued pro-ethanol coalition.[209] Congress ignored Bush's suggestion and ultimately extended the tariff to 2010.[210]

In 2007 Bush also negotiated a "memorandum of understanding" with Brazil aimed at reducing demand for oil in the Western Hemisphere by promoting production and use of ethanol throughout Latin America and the Caribbean. The agreement should help other small sugar-cane-producing countries in the Caribbean and Central America become ethanol producers. Eventually it might spur ethanol production from sugar cane in Africa and Thailand through technology-transfer activities and venture-capital investments.[211]

Curiously, the U.S. tariff on imported ethanol applies to Brazil but not to Caribbean nations in the Central American Free Trade Agreement. Some poor countries lack the technology and capacity to carry out the last processing steps in ethanol production. Under the Caribbean Basin Initiative, countries can take partially processed Brazilian ethanol, carry out the last processing steps, and ship the ethanol to the U.S. with no tariff. Under the agreement, this tariff-free importation is limited to 7 percent of U.S. ethanol consumption.

A growing ethanol industry was also attractive to Brazil and the U.S. for a political reason: it might reduce the political influence of Hugo Chávez, president of oil-rich Venezuela, a member of the OPEC cartel. For the United States and Brazil, which account for 70 percent of global ethanol production, the agreement might also lead to more downward pressure on the world oil price, with both economic benefits at home and foreign policy benefits around the globe.

Once again, however, a meaningful agreement between Brazil and the United States would require congressional action, for instance, for the appropriation of U.S. funds to facilitate technology transfer in the Western Hemisphere. Key interest groups registered concerns about what Bush was up to. Environmentalists warned members of Congress that a surge in ethanol production in Latin or South America could result in a destruction of rain forests, as more farmland is needed to grow sugar cane. Senator Grassley joined U.S. corn interests in questioning why making more ethanol from sugar cane in the Western Hemisphere would be good for the U.S.-based ethanol industry. Not surprisingly, the final memorandum of understanding between Brazil and the United States ultimately contained no specifics about commitments of government dollars, no joint biofuels plants, and no relief from trade barriers.[212] The Bush White House was stymied because it had no political strategy for persuading the Congress to expand the non-U.S. ethanol industry in the Western Hemisphere.

Prospects for Ethanol

Bush's policies have already led to a large expansion of ethanol in the transport sector of the U.S. economy. A shift to universal ethanol blending (at least to E10) seems likely and has already been required by three states. But the negative side effects of reliance on corn-based ethanol are causing some second thoughts.

The 2008 farm bill, which was enacted over Bush's objections (for reasons unrelated to ethanol), signaled congressional interest in a rapid transition from corn to advanced biofuels with different feedstocks.[213] The tax credit for corn-based ethanol was clipped from $0.51 per gallon to $0.45 per gallon in order to help finance a series of generous incentives and subsidies for advanced biofuels.[214] A new $1.01-per-gallon tax credit was added for cellulosic ethanol (on top of the existing credit). A subsidy of $45 per ton was added for farmers who agree to collect biomass (for instance, switchgrass and sorghum) for energy production.[215] Builders of commercial-scale biorefineries will be eligible for $320 million in federal loan guarantees. To top it off, an additional $118 million was authorized for R & D into advanced biofuels.

Despite the commitment of politicians to ethanol, future growth of the industry is not assured. The extent of the young industry's growth hinges on four factors: the long-term path of world oil prices, the pace of technical progress in reducing the cost of making cellulosic ethanol and transporting it around the country, finding solutions to the greenhouse gas ramifications of cellulosic ethanol, and the willingness of consumers to purchase E85 at the pump.

The last point is so fundamental that it is easy to forget. The cost of a single E85 pump and related equipment at a refueling station can exceed $200,000.[216] Refueling stations will not invest this money, even with a large tax credit, if motorists do not want to purchase E85. But a vehicle must use 1.4 times as much ethanol as gasoline to go the same distance.[217] As a result, most motorists will not use E85 unless it is priced significantly below E10. Corn-based ethanol is actually more expensive to produce than gasoline, especially when oil prices are low. Unless Bush's R & D gamble on cellulosic ethanol pays off or unless future politicians are willing to force refueling stations to offer E85 at a relatively low price (as they are now doing in Sweden), Bush's pro-ethanol agenda, though significant, will not threaten the viability of petroleum as a transport fuel.[218]

Despite his limited political standing and an evenly divided Congress, Bush made substantial progress on his energy policy agenda. The 2005 legislation was the first major energy bill passed by the Congress in decades, and Bush's numerous executive actions were of equal or greater significance.

Legislatively, Bush succeeded in 2005 through a creative cross-partisan strategy that entailed some hefty compromises. Although his pro-oil, pro-gas, pro-coal, and pro-nuclear positions generated widespread Republican support in the Congress, he could not find sixty votes in the Senate without making three compromises: dropping the permission to drill for oil and gas in ANWR (which relieved Republican moderates and many Democrats), dropping the liability relief for MTBE producers (which offended the New England states and the trial lawyers, a key Democratic constituency), and—most importantly—including a requirement that refiners blend biofuels (which attracted the farm state Democrats). The rise and fall of Tom Daschle in the Senate is a vivid illustration of how a Congress polarized on partisan lines can make it difficult for a party leader to pursue the interests of their state or region.

Using executive action, Bush took numerous steps that were controversial in the Congress, especially among environmentalist Democrats and Republicans on the East and West Coasts. But the same coalition that passed the 2005 energy bill was available to protect Bush's executive actions (such as the rule makings in favor of fossil fuels) from congressional reversal. Environmentalists, however, did have significant success delaying or reversing some of Bush's executive actions through lawsuits, as in the case of the nuclear-waste-disposal plan for Yucca Mountain.

In the electricity sector, Bush sought to diversify our new sources of electric power, which became heavily oriented to natural gas in the 1990s. A key test of the success of Bush's policies will be whether the share of new power plants fueled by coal, nuclear energy, and renewables rises over the next twenty years. The early indications are that this trend is occurring for renewables and coal, though the long-term prospects for coal hinge on the uncertain future of carbon capture and storage technology.

Bush made only modest progress toward a revival of the nuclear power industry, in part because (ironically) the investment climate he created for coal was even more favorable than the climate for nuclear power. In chapter 7 we examine why Bush did not follow through on his 2000 campaign pledge to cap carbon dioxide emissions from the power sector. Had he done so, his vision of a revival of nuclear power might have been actualized by his policies, though at a price of a diminished future for coal.

In the transportation sector, where the United States is heavily dependent on petroleum, Bush sought to reduce oil use by increasing the use of biofuels as a near-term bridge to a hydrogen-based economy. Experts disagree about the practicalities of hydrogen. The collapse of FutureGen delays further the commercial future of hydrogen. Bush had some success expanding the use of gasohol and equipping millions of new vehicles to run on E85. The unfinished business on ethanol is to raise the blending to E15 or E20, or to modify our nation's refueling infrastructure so that consumers have a realistic option to use E85 at an attractive price. Unfortunately, a large-scale transition to the use of ethanol may not be wise unless low-cost cellulosic ethanol becomes a commercial reality and the greenhouse gases from ethanol use are addressed effectively.

All of Bush's energy policies appear vulnerable because of the collapse of world oil prices that began in mid-2008. From a peak of $145 a barrel, the global recession rapidly brought the price below $50 a barrel as Barack Obama was preparing to take office.[219]

Energy forecasters still project rising oil prices until 2030 (when the price may surpass $200 a barrel),[220] but low energy prices over the 2009–2015 period could undercut many of the investments Bush's policies strived to encourage, and politicians may lose their interest in energy policy until energy prices rise again.

7

Consuming Less Energy

The 2001 National Energy Policy emphasized the urgent need to increase oil production in the United States. Less well known is the fact that the policy also stipulated that "conservation and energy efficiency are important elements of a sound energy policy."[1] Even less well known is the fact (which this chapter reveals) that George W. Bush accomplished more to improve the fuel efficiency of future cars and light trucks (SUVs, vans, and pickup trucks) than any previous president.

Oil use in the U.S. is projected to increase 50 percent by 2025 as income and population growth cause consumers to demand more oil-consuming goods and services. Unless the growth in oil demand is curbed (and/or oil production expanded) through public policy, nearly 70 percent of the oil consumed in the U.S. in 2025 will be imported.[2] Transportation alone accounts for two-thirds of U.S. oil use as well as the majority of the projected growth in U.S. oil consumption through 2025.[3] Within the transportation sector, cars and light trucks account for most of the fuel consumption.[4] Thus, it was fuel use by cars and light trucks that dominated Bush's deliberations about energy conservation.

Curbing America's appetite for oil was considered beneficial for several reasons.[5] The United States alone accounts for almost 25 percent of world oil consumption, more than twice as much as the second largest consumer, China. If the U.S. can reduce its demand for oil (or even slow its rate of growth in consumption), it can apply downward pressure on the world price of oil, with corresponding benefits to consumers in the United States and around the world. Some Bush administration officials also perceived that lower world oil prices would diminish the flow of oil money to terrorists, to insurgents in Iraq and Afghanistan, and to regimes hostile to U.S. national interests, such as Iran and Venezuela.[6] From an environmental perspective, reducing oil consumption also curtails emissions of the greenhouse gases that are implicated in global climate change. All of these rationales were not equally persuasive to the Bush administration and to the Congress, but at least one of these rationales was usually considered compelling to the powerful actors.

One reason that Bush's record on energy conservation is so little known is that his accomplishments were initiated through federal rule making, an executive power that receives far less journalistic and scholarly attention than legislation. To achieve his energy-conservation agenda, Bush pursued rule making because, at least initially, he could not persuade the Congress to enact his preferred policy. He also used rule making as a device to persuade the Congress and the stakeholders (auto companies, the UAW, and environmentalists) that his conservation reforms were constructive and cost-effective. By the end of Bush's second term, a majority of congressional Republicans and Democrats, spurred by years of rising fuel prices, voted to grant the Bush administration new authority to enact his energy-conservation agenda in the transport sector.

Policy Options

The Bush administration considered and rejected the favorite tools of economists: higher gasoline taxes and "feebates" for fuel-efficient cars. (Under a feebate, purchasers of high-efficiency cars receive rebates while purchasers of gas guzzlers pay fees.) Gasoline taxes were perceived as unfair to rural and low-income households. It was widely thought that supporting them was political suicide for elected officials. Feebates were seen as a low-probability proposal in the U.S. Congress because they would require consideration by multiple committees in the House and Senate and would likely draw opposition from the major automakers, car dealers, and the United Auto Workers.

Revitalization and reform of the federal program of mileage regulations for new cars and light trucks became the heart of Bush's energy conservation agenda. A 2001 report from the National Academy of Sciences played a pivotal role in persuading the administration that the mileage rules should be fixed rather than scrapped. This report is discussed below.

In addition to modernizing the mileage rules, Bush helped persuade the Congress to create financial incentives for consumers to purchase vehicles with innovative technologies that save fuel. The 2001 National Energy Policy emphasized the promise of hybrid engines, as Honda, Toyota, and Ford had each introduced hybrids for consumer purchase, but Bush's policies were broadened to spur consumer interest in clean diesel technology, fuel cells, plug-in hybrids, and electric cars.

Through new federal highway legislation, the Bush administration also adopted policies to improve traffic flows, reduce congestion, and save fuel. Bush even scaled back one of his tax cuts to avoid undercutting his energy conservation policy. I begin by considering reform of the federal mileage program.

The CAFE Program

In May 2001 the White House directed the U.S. Department of Transportation (DOT) to review the Corporate Average Fuel Economy (CAFE) program. CAFE is a federal regulatory scheme that sets average miles per gallon (MPG) requirements for the new products of vehicle manufacturers. Each manufacturer must achieve the same minimum level of corporate average fuel economy, one level for cars built in the U.S., one for cars imported into the U.S., and one for light trucks as a class (regardless of where they are built). The levels are set by DOT through rule making.

The CAFE program was established during the energy crisis of the mid-1970s. With the help of a temporary surge in fuel prices, the fuel economy of new cars more than doubled, from 12.9 to 27.5 MPG, in less than a decade.[7]

By the 1990s, however, the program was dysfunctional. The combined fuel economy of cars and light trucks in model year 2005 was about 25 MPG, the same as it had been ten years earlier.[8] The 2001 National Energy Policy directed DOT to determine whether the CAFE program should be revived, reformed, or scrapped altogether.

Science Recommendations

When Bush assumed office in January 2001, standards for new vehicles were frozen at 27.5 MPG for cars and 20.7 MPG for light trucks, a freeze that Congress imposed through "riders" to appropriations bills in each fiscal year starting in 1996.[9] The riders reflected the fears of the Big Three (General Motors, Ford, and Daimler-Chrysler) and the United Auto Workers (UAW) that the Clinton administration might tighten the standards so aggressively that more vehicle production and jobs in Detroit would be lost to Toyota, Honda, and other primarily non-UAW manufacturers.[10] Environmentalists objected to the freeze, but the best they could negotiate was an evaluation of the CAFE program by the National Academy of Sciences (NAS).

In August 2001, the anticipated NAS report raised another concern: safety. Tighter CAFE standards for cars from 1975 to 1985 caused 2,000 additional traffic fatalities per year because cars were downsized in order to meet the required 27.5 MPG standard. The NAS suggested a new system that ties MPG rules to individual vehicle attributes such as size or weight. This reform was aimed at enhancing safety because vehicle manufacturers are encouraged to comply with new fuel-saving technology, such as hybrids or modern diesel engines, instead of with downsized vehicles.[11]

NAS also recommended that vehicle manufacturers be permitted to "trade" CAFE credits. A manufacturer that does better than the minimum MPG requirements could earn CAFE credits and sell them to another vehicle manufacturer having difficulty meeting the minimum requirements. NAS argued that the permission to "trade" CAFE credits would reduce the overall cost of complying with the program while spurring innovation, even among manufacturers that could easily meet any plausible industry-wide MPG requirement. To maximize the impact of credit trading, NAS suggested consolidation of the separate programs for domestic cars, foreign cars, and light trucks.[12]

Legislative Flop

The NAS recommendations did not generate any consensus among the key stakeholders.[13] The Big Three were not necessarily opposed to size- or weight-based standards, but they feared the regulatory mischief that could result from giving regulators this large-scale discretion. They also saw no value in the permission to trade credits with other companies, which they felt could only create a public relations bonanza for the Japanese transplants. The UAW, while supportive of modestly tighter mileage requirements, opposed the NAS recommendations for size-based reform because they feared that GM and Ford would respond by curtailing production of small cars in the United States. Honda favored size-based reforms but saw weight-based reforms as an obstacle to use of promising lightweight materials. Environmentalists objected that reforms might encourage more production of large SUVs and thereby undermine the fuel-saving impact of tighter CAFE standards.

Without much outreach to interest groups, the White House directed the DOT to ask Congress for new legislative authority to reform CAFE along the lines suggested by the NAS.[14] The request was made by the secretary of transportation in February 2002.

The Congress did not act for a simple reason: All of the important stakeholders—vehicle makers, the UAW, and consumer and environmental groups—lobbied Congress to retain the existing structure of the program. In other words, the Bush proposal was a flop, even though it was based on an authoritative NAS report.

Fortunately for the White House, the industry and the UAW agreed reluctantly with environmentalists that Congress should lift the "freeze" on future CAFE rule makings. Congress did so in 2002. In Sacramento, California, far from Washington, D.C., and Detroit, Michigan, lawmakers were passing far-reaching legislation that had the practical effect of softening Detroit's longstanding opposition to federal fuel economy regulation.

Origins of the California Plan

In the 1992 presidential election contest, the Clinton-Gore campaign ran on a pledge to increase CAFE standards from 27.5 MPG in 1992 to 40 MPG by 2000 and 45 MPG by 2015. This stance was quite popular in California, where environmental concerns are salient and where very few UAW members reside. In Michigan, though, another large state that leans Democratic, the CAFE program was perceived as a threat to the economic viability of the Big Three and the UAW.

After Clinton assumed office in 1993, a preliminary proposal to raise CAFE standards was released by DOT. Both Clinton and Gore were promptly informed by the UAW and congressional Democrats from industrial states that the initiative was both unacceptable on its merits and a political risk to the future of the Democratic Party in several key industrial states.

The Clinton White House and DOT quietly dropped the proposal.[15] What replaced it was a federal research and development program championed by Vice President Gore. It was called the Partnership for a New Generation of Vehicles. The immodest goal was to design, pilot-test, and produce by 2004 a car that got 80 MPG. Useful research was conducted on cleaner diesel engines and on advanced batteries for electric vehicles, but it is difficult to argue that the Partnership had a large commercial impact on the automotive industry.

When the Republicans seized control of the Congress in 1995, they encountered little opposition from either industrial-state Democrats or the Clinton administration when they slapped an annual freeze on CAFE standards during the appropriations process. Ralph Nader was not the only environmentalist who rapidly became disenchanted with the Clinton administration's stance on CAFE regulation.

Californians interested in cleaner, more fuel-efficient cars were convinced that neither party in Washington, D.C., would get the job done.[16] The primary concern in California was global warming and the need to regulate greenhouse gas emissions from new vehicles. With urgings from state and national environmental groups, the California legislature in Sacramento decided to launch its own CAFE-type program. Despite industry objections, the legislature passed an ambitious bill (AB 1493) to achieve about 36 MPG by 2016. With support from Republican governor Arnold Schwarzenegger, the California Air Resources Board published rules in 2004 calling for a 30 percent reduction in greenhouse gases from all new vehicles sold in California by 2016.[17]

From California's perspective, AB 1493 is an extension of the state's regulation of tailpipe pollutants, which began in the 1960s. Under the national Clean Air Act, California is entitled to issue its own regulations for tailpipe pollutants if the U.S. Environmental Protection Agency concurs that the conditions in

California are "compelling and extraordinary." Other states may either adopt the California standards or follow national tailpipe standards enacted by EPA. Given how smog-ridden Los Angeles was during much of the twentieth century, it became well accepted that cars sold in California needed to meet more stringent tailpipe standards than did cars sold in other states.

Legally, the California plan is actually broader than—and somewhat different from—CAFE because it regulates the emissions of greenhouse gases, such as carbon dioxide, from a vehicle rather than MPG. From an engineering perspective, however, the compliance strategies for AB 1493 overlap greatly with the compliance strategies for a strict CAFE mandate.

The California plan on carbon dioxide was a bombshell in Detroit. Part of the problem was that Detroit perceived the California plan to be costly and onerous. To make matters worse, other states around the country began to consider opting in to the California plan, sometimes with different penalties for noncompliance. Building a fleet to comply with California's 2004 rules would not necessarily be sufficient in an "opt-in" state because manufacturers might sell more gas-guzzling vehicles in the opt-in state than in California. A scenario began to unfold where each vehicle manufacturer might have to track dealer sales, compliance statistics, and fines for noncompliance in each state.

But the auto industry discovered a potential weakness in California's rationale: Unlike greenhouse gases, which are pollutants that mix globally, the tailpipe pollutants previously regulated by California caused localized air quality problems. According to industry experts, neither global climate change nor dependence on foreign oil seemed like appropriate rationales for California to launch its own carbon or mileage regulations. On this critical issue, the Bush administration concurred with the industry, though it was a complex legal question that was destined to be the subject of litigation and possibly an eventual Supreme Court decision.

Reluctantly but opportunistically, the auto industry began to perceive national CAFE reform as preferable to a California-driven policy. Not only were the California carbon emissions standards stringent and costly but the auto industry—Toyota as well as the Big Three—did not want to face two competitive regulatory bodies (the California Air Resources Board and U.S. DOT) serving basically the same function.[18]

In response to the California plan, the auto industry developed an advocacy position that called for state greenhouse gas or mileage programs to be preempted by the federal government on the grounds that the CAFE program was adequate. The 1974 federal CAFE law expressly prohibits any state rules "related to fuel economy." In order for the industry's preemption strategy to be credible, a meaningful federal CAFE program was desirable.

Bush's Reforms

When Congress lifted the freeze on CAFE standards in 2002, the Bush administration proceeded in two phases. Phase one, aimed at achieving prompt progress on conservation, tightened MPG standards under the traditional CAFE system. Priority was given to light trucks over cars because light trucks are much less fuel efficient than cars and account for almost half of new vehicle sales. Phase two, implementing the reforms suggested by NAS, was aimed at securing a more promising long-term future for the CAFE program. Bush instructed DOT to accomplish as much reform as possible using current legal authority.[19] Legislative reform—covering cars as well as light trucks— would be requested again later, once stakeholders became more familiar with the specifics of the Bush reform plan.

In 2003 the Bush administration raised CAFE's light truck standards for three consecutive model years (2005–2007), the first tightening of the standards in nearly a decade. The industry-wide standard was raised gradually from 20.7 MPG in 2005 to 22.2 MPG in 2007.[20]

Although the 1.5 rise in miles per gallon appears to be small, DOT estimated that it will translate into a savings of 3.6 billion gallons of fuel over the life of the affected vehicles. The MPG increases were feasible for the industry to accomplish at modest cost, and thus the risk of adverse safety consequences from downsizing were slight. DOT projected that the costs of fuel-saving technology, about $1.6 billion per year, were more than offset by the projected fuel-saving benefits to consumers over the lifetimes of the affected vehicles.

When the final rules were issued, the Bush administration warned that further increases in CAFE standards were unlikely without reform of the program along the lines suggested by NAS. As soon as the 2005–2007 standards were released, DOT began work on a more ambitious plan to reform the CAFE system for light trucks of model years 2008 and beyond.

In 2005, DOT proposed to restructure the CAFE program by setting different MPG targets for light trucks of different sizes, using a measure of size called "footprint" (roughly, the area between the four wheels).[21] Due to an oddity in the way the 1974 CAFE law was drafted, DOT lawyers concluded that sufficient legal authority was available to adopt size-based standards for light trucks but not for cars.

The adjustment of mileage rules based on vehicle size was not a minor technical refinement in the CAFE program. It was a profound change in policy because it reduced the safety risks of the unreformed system, and it spread the costs of compliance more broadly among vehicle manufacturers. For example, under the traditional CAFE system, virtually all of the compliance costs of tighter standards were incurred by two companies, GM and Ford, companies whose product mixes were geared toward relatively large SUVs and vans. Under a size-adjusted system, each vehicle manufacturer is required to make MPG improvements, even if it chooses to sell only smaller trucks. DOT found that, under the size-based reform, the unequal concentration of compliance costs under tighter CAFE standards began to lessen, especially at the financially troubled companies, such as GM and Ford, that sold predominantly large vehicles.[22]

DOT engineers designed the size-based system on the premise that it is easier (and less costly) to achieve good fuel economy in small vehicles. Thus, the MPG targets for small light trucks were set at more stringent levels than the targets for large light trucks. To achieve fuel savings, the MPG targets for vehicles of all sizes were tightened gradually from model years 2008 through 2011. The coverage of four model years provided more regulatory certainty to the industry, a clear signal that MPG must improve steadily. The largest passenger SUVs (for instance the Hummer) were also included in the CAFE program for the first time.

By model year 2011, when the size-based reform will be fully phased in, light trucks were projected by DOT to achieve 24.0 miles per gallon, about 16 percent more fuel economy than was required when Bush took office (20.7 MPG in model year 2004).[23] More fuel savings were expected from these rule makings than from any previous actions in the twenty-year history of the light truck CAFE program.[24] Although the fuel-saving technologies compelled by the 2011 standards are projected to cost $6.7 billion, an additional 10.7 billion gallons of fuel are projected to be saved.[25]

Environmental and consumer activist groups complained that the reformed standards were not stringent enough. A complex litigation strategy was launched to compel DOT to make the mileage standards even more stringent. One of the key arguments against DOT's rules is that they did not give quantitative consideration to the climate-change benefits of tighter mileage requirements. If the benefits of fewer greenhouse gases had been counted by DOT, in addition to the consumer fuel savings, the MPG standards might have been more stringent. DOT countered that the science of global warming is not precise enough to quantify these benefits and express them in monetary units.

Another Legislative Flop

Soon after Bush's re-election in 2004, gasoline prices again rose above $3 per gallon. The White House determined that the time was ripe to renew the request for legal authority from Congress to revamp the CAFE program.[26] As the size-based CAFE rules for light trucks were proposed, Bush sought similar authority to enact size-based standards for cars.

The CAFE standards for cars had not been upgraded in more than a decade. Several vehicle manufacturers were already close to (or exceeding) the outmoded 27.5 MPG standard for cars; in model year 2005, for example, the car fleets of Ford, Daimler, Honda, and Toyota were at 26.9, 26.6, 33.1 and 33.1 MPG, respectively.[27] The Bush administration was prepared to make the car standards progressively tighter if the Congress provided DOT with the necessary reform authority.

The vehicle manufacturers did not oppose this plan, but the White House was not successful in securing the support of UAW. When the House Energy and Commerce Committee chairman, Joe Barton, tried to move Bush's plan through the House, he confronted some stiff opposition. According to the UAW, size-based CAFE standards discourage small-car production in the United States, since the only reason GM and Ford make unprofitable small cars is to average their higher MPG figures against the lower MPG figures of profitable sedans. GM in particular was able to approach compliance with the 27.5 MPG car standard only by counting its highly fuel efficient small cars. The environmentalists, on the other hand, argued that Bush's plan did not go far enough and were favoring a rival bill offered by Democrat Edward Markey of Massachusetts that compelled large increases in fuel efficiency.

Barton worked with the White House, industry, and the UAW to defeat a Markey amendment that would have forced cars and light trucks to achieve

33 MPG by 2015. The committee's vote was 36 to 17, with ten Democrats voting with the Republicans.[28] But the only way Barton could move Bush's plan through committee was on a straight party-line vote (28 to 26). Given such a polarized vote and the anticipated opposition from some moderate Republicans on the House floor, Bush's CAFE reform plan never made it to the floor.[29]

In the Senate, the situation was even more complicated. The Senate Democratic leadership, apparently sensitive to the UAW's concerns, did not even mention CAFE legislation in the party's 2006 campaign platform. This stance annoyed environmentalists, but there were plenty of Democratic and Republican senators eager to work with the environmentalists on stricter CAFE legislation.

Democrat Dianne Feinstein of California and Republican Olympia Snowe of Maine sponsored a bill to compel automakers to raise the weighted average of car and light truck MPG from 25.2 in 2005 to 35.0 in 2017.[30] A bipartisan coalition led by Democrat Joe Biden of Delaware proposed to raise car and light truck CAFE requirements by 1 MPG per year for a decade. Under Biden's plan, tax incentives were offered to automakers to upgrade plants to build hybrids and flex-fuel vehicles, and size-based reform of CAFE standards was permitted. The co-sponsors of this bill included Democrats Dick Durbin and Barack Obama of Illinois, Tom Harkin of Iowa and Jeff Bingaman of New Mexico, and Republicans Richard Lugar of Indiana, Norm Coleman of Minnesota, and Gordon Smith of Oregon.

The White House was initially encouraged because a bipartisan pair, Republican Trent Lott of Mississippi and Democrat Mark Pryor of Arkansas, agreed to co-sponsor Bush's CAFE reforms in committee. Yet they also added some unique provisions sought by Nissan for how imported and domestic vehicles are counted. Nissan had moved its headquarters from California to Mississippi, and tended to lobby independently of the rest of the auto industry on many issues.[31] Some aspects of the Lott-Pryor plan began to create divisions among the vehicle manufacturers.

Given this wide range of legislative approaches, it was anyone's guess as to what would emerge from a Senate floor debate on CAFE. When fuel prices fell temporarily after the summer driving season of 2006, political interest in fuel economy legislation dissipated. Nothing was even considered on the Senate floor, in part because the November 2006 elections were on the horizon.

Judicial Wars

A series of complex lawsuits about CAFE regulation and global warming consumed much of Bush's second term. Basically, everyone was suing somebody.

A coalition of states concerned about global warming sued the auto industry on the grounds that the industry's failure to produce greener cars was harming the future well-being of those states. Automakers countered that the industry was already offering several dozen models with mileage ratings in excess of 30 MPG. The real problem, industry argued, was that consumers were choosing to purchase the low-MPG vehicles in much higher volume. For example, the pickup truck is the largest selling vehicle in America in spite of relatively low MPG ratings, accounting for far more sales than any small car (including the hybrid-equipped Prius). Even after small car sales surged and pickup truck sales plummeted in 2005–2008, due to rising fuel prices and rising unemployment, the pickup truck remained one of the largest-selling vehicles in America.[32] Citing market realities, a federal court ultimately dismissed the complaint of the states.[33]

Consumer and environmental groups persuaded a federal appeals court to strike down DOT's reformed CAFE program. The appeals court ruled that the Bush administration had not given sufficient consideration to the benefits of reducing greenhouse gas emissions. But the three-judge panel also had some good news for the Bush administration: It saw no basis for overturning the size-based reforms that DOT had devised. In effect, the court ordered DOT to reconsider the stringency of the model year 2011 standards for light trucks based on a more in-depth environmental benefits analysis.

Led by Massachusetts, a coalition of states sued EPA on the grounds that carbon dioxide is an air pollutant that should be regulated. In addition to federal regulation of fuel economy under the 1974 CAFE law, these states sought EPA regulation of greenhouse gas emissions from motor vehicles under the Clean Air Act. (The Massachusetts petition was actually initiated during the Clinton administration, but no decision was made until the Bush administration assumed power in 2001 and declined the petition.) The Bush administration won a 2–1 appeals court decision but later lost a 5–4 U.S. Supreme Court decision. EPA was instructed by the Court that it does have legal authority to regulate greenhouse gas emissions under the Clean Air Act. The Court instructed the

Bush administration to consider whether new regulations of carbon dioxide emissions from motor vehicles are necessary to prevent the dangers of global warming.

The Supreme Court opinion was seen as both an opportunity and a setback by the Bush administration. The setback was the Court's rejection of EPA's claim that it had no authority to regulate greenhouse gas emissions under the Clean Air Act (see chapter 8). The opportunity was found in the Court's expansive view of the president's power under current law. An opportunistic Bush administration began to consider that the legal authority they thought was missing under the 1974 CAFE law, meaning authority to implement all of the reforms to CAFE suggested by the 2001 NAS report, may already exist at EPA under the Clean Air Act!

Finally, the auto industry sought judicial relief from California's plan (AB 1493) on the grounds that the 1974 federal CAFE law preempts any state regulation related to fuel economy. The Bush administration supported this interpretation of federal law. But California and allied states won two rulings in federal district court that recognized California's authority to set carbon standards for motor vehicles under the Clean Air Act. Both district courts also conceded a key point: California would need to obtain a waiver from the federal government to apply standards that are different from those that U.S. EPA applies to the entire nation. (As discussed below, EPA later denied California's request for a waiver under the Clean Air Act.) Some legal experts believe that the contest between the auto industry and California is headed again for the U.S. Supreme Court.[34]

Why Not 35 Miles per Gallon by 2017?

When the Democratic Party regained a majority of the Congress in November 2006, the White House saw only a few opportunities for collaboration with the new Congress. CAFE reform was one of them, along with biofuels, as discussed in chapter 6, and immigration reform, as examined in chapter 9. Many members of both parties were itching to do something in response to the growing public concern about global warming and the rising gasoline prices that were straining family budgets and hurting long-haul truckers.

In conjunction with his January 2007 State of the Union address, Bush announced a new "Twenty in Ten" plan.[35] The ten-year goal was to reduce by 20 percent the projected rate of U.S. gasoline consumption in 2017. Three-quarters of the goal was to be accomplished by a stricter renewable-fuels standard: the 35-billion-gallon mandate discussed in chapter 6. The other quarter was to be accomplished by increasing vehicle mileage requirements under CAFE by 4 percent per year until 2017. That is equivalent to a savings of 8.5 billion gallons of fuel in 2017, or an average of 35 MPG by 2017, 40 percent more than the 2005 MPG level.

Setting a long-term, energy-savings goal for the CAFE program represented a significant shift from Bush's previous position on CAFE reform. The ambitiousness of the 2017 goal was similar to the recommendations of the non-partisan National Commission on Energy Policy, an expert commission that had been formed to urge congressional action on a variety of energy and environmental issues.[36] Officials throughout the auto industry (vehicle manufacturers, suppliers, dealers and the UAW) were stunned. The Bush plan's goal of 35 MPG by 2017 was similar to numbers in previous CAFE bills that the White House had worked repeatedly and successfully to defeat in Congress from 2001 to 2005. However, those had been legally binding numeric standards while Bush was now proposing a legislative goal that the executive branch could modify based on the findings of benefit-cost analysis.

Bush demonstrated that he was prepared to risk straining (or even losing) his alliance with the automakers and the UAW. He gambled that the public concern about rising gas prices and global warming would make his ambitious CAFE plan irresistible to the Democratic majority in Congress as well as to many Republicans.

The 35 MPG goal was coupled with a request that Congress provide DOT the necessary authority to achieve the 2017 goal through a reformed CAFE system, as suggested in the 2001 NAS report. Although Bush's request for authority to implement the NAS reforms was hardly new, DOT's light truck rule making was serving its intended purpose of dampening anxiety among some stakeholders (such as the Big Three and the UAW) about what a size-based CAFE program might look like. Moreover, the industry, the UAW, and the Bush administration saw a strong federal CAFE program as helpful in persuading the federal courts and many undecided states to favor national CAFE reform over California's plan.

Working a Democratic Congress

From the White House's perspective, the initial legislative response from the House of Representatives was not encouraging. During the first 100 days of the new Congress, Speaker of the House Nancy Pelosi of California and her colleagues focused on a new energy bill that replaced many oil and gas tax incentives (including some passed at Bush's request in 2004–2005) with new tax incentives for renewable energy and fuel-saving technologies. This bill stalled in the Senate due to a filibuster and a veto threat by President Bush.

The new chairman of the House Energy and Commerce Committee, John Dingell of Michigan, informed Speaker Pelosi that he intended to address CAFE later in the year at the same time that the committee prepared legislation addressing climate change. (As will be seen in chapter 8, the White House was opposed to economy-wide climate legislation.) Dingell, a veteran ally of the domestic auto industry and the UAW, was prepared to let the Senate act first on CAFE reform.

Unlike the House, the Senate did respond promptly.[37] Democrat Dianne Feinstein of California and Republican Ted Stevens of Alaska moved a CAFE reform bill through the Senate. It mandated an average of 35 MPG by 2020, providing three more years of compliance time than Bush proposed plus an additional 4 percent per year in MPG gains from 2020 to 2030. It also authorized DOT to establish the first CAFE-like programs for some pickup trucks and large commercial trucks.

The White House was pleased that the Senate bill provided DOT what the White House wanted most: authority to implement the key reforms suggested in 2001 by NAS, including size-based standards, credit trading among vehicle manufacturers, and consolidation of the separate standards for cars and light trucks. But the Senate plan did not pass without a tussle, as it was part of a larger energy bill.

The White House pointed out some weaknesses in the Senate CAFE bill, but the dreaded veto threat was reserved for some non-CAFE provisions in the draft energy bill, especially a 15 percent renewables mandate in the electricity sector and a repeal of tax incentives for oil and gas production. The White House not only saw these provisions as bad policy but also feared that they would stimulate formidable opposition and potentially doom the entire bill.

In order to avoid a filibuster and presidential veto, the Senate Democratic leadership ultimately agreed to discard those provisions. The auto industry mounted an effort to strip the CAFE provisions as well, or to replace them with an alternative plan prepared by Senator Carl Levin of Michigan, but the industry lost a key cloture vote 62 to 32, which allowed the bill to progress further. It was ultimately passed by the Senate 65 to 27.[38] Almost half of the Senate Republicans joined most Senate Democrats in these two votes.

The House CAFE deliberations were slowed by disagreements between Chairman Dingell and Speaker Pelosi.[39] Dingell annoyed the Speaker with an early draft plan that called for federal legislation to preempt state authority to regulate greenhouse gas emissions from motor vehicles. Pelosi indicated that no such language would be acceptable since it would undermine the California plan to reduce greenhouse gas emissions. Pelosi annoyed Dingell by announcing that she supported the 35 MPG language in the Senate bill, even before Dingell's committee delivered a detailed CAFE plan. Yet Dingell knew that Pelosi might be able to block (or obtain modification of) Dingell's CAFE language in the House Rules Committee, before it reached the House floor for a vote. Frustrated with the slow pace of action in the House, the Bush administration urged Pelosi to move a bill on biofuels and CAFE reform promptly, rather than wait for Dingell to address climate change and CAFE reform together in the fall.[40]

As Congress dithered, the Bush administration received an unexpected boost from the U.S. Supreme Court. In April 2007 the Court ruled that EPA did possess the necessary authority to regulate carbon dioxide emissions from motor vehicles. The White House promptly regrouped and charted a plan to achieve the "Twenty in Ten" goal without congressional action. Daring the Congress to join him, Bush issued an executive order calling for four federal agencies (EPA, DOT, USDA, and DOE) to prepare regulatory options for meeting the energy-saving goal in his 2007 State of the Union address. Bush made clear that he preferred congressional action, but that if necessary he was prepared to act alone using his executive powers.[41]

After months of bickering (including efforts by some Republicans to block any legislation), Pelosi took control of the process by passing an energy bill through the House that contained no provisions on CAFE or biofuels. She concluded that these issues were best addressed by a House-Senate conference committee, knowing that a majority of House members (including at least fifty industrial-state Democrats) might prefer a less ambitious CAFE bill than she did. Much to the dismay of the White House, the bill the House passed included both a 15 percent renewables electricity mandate and a repeal of tax incentives for oil and gas production. It passed on a vote of 235 to 181, aided by 221 out of 228 House Democrats. Fourteen Republicans defied the White House's veto threat by supporting the measure.[42] Tellingly, Pelosi did not muster the two-thirds margin that would be necessary to override a likely Bush veto.

The House-Senate conference consumed several months but finally reached a conclusion in December 2007. The White House won a big victory: the conference bill *included* both a biofuels mandate and CAFE reform and *excluded* both the renewables electricity mandate and the tax provisions on oil, gas, and renewables. On CAFE reform, Dingell conceded to Pelosi a 35 MPG requirement by 2020 but won four technical refinements: an extension of CAFE compliance credits for flex-fuel vehicles (see chapter 6), a requirement that cars and light trucks be regulated separately, maintenance of DOT's current definition of "feasible" mileage standards (which includes consideration of cost-benefit analysis), and a requirement that mileage standards be adjusted for the size and/or weight of the vehicle, which went beyond just giving permission for DOT to do so. It was also agreed that DOT, not EPA, would remain the lead regulatory agency for CAFE.[43]

The most important Senate vote in this process proved to be not a vote on CAFE reform but a cloture vote on whether to proceed with a version of the energy bill that included the tax provisions on oil, gas, and renewables favored by Speaker Pelosi. If this version had passed both the House and Senate and then been vetoed by President Bush, it is possible that no bill would have passed the Congress. But the cloture motion failed (by a single vote), persuading the Senate and House Democratic leadership that the tax issues should be pursued at another time through a different legislative vehicle. Only one Democratic senator crossed over (Landrieu of Louisiana) but the White House suffered nine defections (Coleman of Minnesota, Collins and Snowe of Maine, Ensign of Nevada, Grassley of Iowa, Hatch of Utah, Lugar of Indiana, Murkowski of Alaska, and Smith of Oregon).

Rejecting the California Plan

The California plan, though it technically regulates greenhouse gases, is roughly equivalent to a 36 MPG fuel economy requirement by 2016. That requirement is slightly more stringent than the 2007 CAFE legislation. It also becomes binding three years earlier. On the other hand, the California plan lacks both the safety-motivated adjustments for vehicle size and the generous flex-fuel incentives contained in the 2007 CAFE reform legislation. The

California plan provides incentives for E85 but only if a vehicle is powered continuously by E85.

The California plan was scheduled to take effect beginning with model year 2009, but the Bush administration did not respond to California's request for a waiver under the Clean Air Act until late 2007, less than a year before the beginning of model year 2009. As the Bush administration deliberated, a battle ensued in state legislatures around the country. The State of California and environmental groups urged other states to pass legislation enforcing the California plan. A coalition of vehicle manufacturers, the UAW, car dealers, farmers, and ethanol producers worked to discourage states from adopting the California plan.[44]

As of early 2008, fourteen states had joined, or announced their intention to join, the California effort: Connecticut, Massachusetts, Maryland, Maine, New Jersey, New York, Pennsylvania, Oregon, Rhode Island, Vermont, Washington, New Mexico, Florida, and Arizona. In other words, states that accounted for more than one-half of new vehicle sales in the U.S. were prepared to compel vehicle manufacturers to comply with the California plan in their states. Automakers, facing different consumer preferences in each state, were aghast at the prospect of facing uncoordinated compliance penalties in multiple states. Opponents of California's effort were successful in discouraging or blocking the California plan in most midwestern and southern states. For example, significant campaigns to join the California plan were defeated in both Minnesota and Arizona.[45]

In yet another bold use of executive power, Bush concurred with the Environmental Protection Agency in late 2007 that California's waiver petition should be denied. This decision was allegedly made over the objections of EPA's career technical and legal staff.[46] The EPA administrator concluded that California had failed to demonstrate that the state faced "extraordinary and compelling" conditions, as required by the Clean Air Act.

Denial of the waiver triggered outrage among the congressional Democratic leadership and environmental advocates. (The three remaining presidential candidates—John McCain, Barack Obama, and Hillary Clinton—each publicly expressed sympathy for California's position.) But it is far easier for politicians to criticize a presidential decision than it is to overturn it through roll-call voting in the Congress.

Senator Barbara Boxer of California, chair of the Senate Committee on Environment and Public Works, sought to overturn the waiver denial through legislation. The United Auto Workers joined the industry and the White House in vigorous opposition to Boxer's effort.[47] Her effort barely survived a roll-call vote (9 to 8) in her own committee. She acknowledged to the press that her effort would have to await a new president because she was unlikely to find the votes on the Senate floor that would be necessary to override a presidential veto.[48] What was left unstated is that she might also have found insufficient votes to override a filibuster threat on the Senate floor.

The California Air Resources Board (CARB), even if it loses the EPA waiver litigation, will remain a potent regulator of the auto industry. Through established authority under the Clean Air Act, CARB has the power to spur new technology by compelling automakers who sell products in California to offer zero emission vehicles (ZEVs). CARB has already required the automakers to produce at least 58,000 plug-in hybrids or other ZEVs by 2014.[49] Bush was never inclined to negotiate a deal with California over the future of auto regulation.

Are the Mileage Numbers Accurate?

The increase in gasoline prices before Hurricane Katrina stimulated consumer interest in fuel economy. The interest exploded in the months after Katrina, when fuel prices remained above the $3 per gallon mark for several months. As sales of large SUVs declined, sales of vehicles with hybrid engines grew rapidly. Consumers wanting to purchase a Prius faced long delays. Some consumers relied naively upon the official fuel economy figures stating how much fuel could be saved by a Prius.

For years, consumer groups have questioned the validity of the federal government's official fuel economy ratings, the city and highway MPG figures posted on the window stickers of new vehicles. The official ratings were based on a series of test procedures developed by the U.S. Environmental Protection Agency in the 1970s, with only a modest adjustment in the 1980s. The test procedures did not mirror real-world driving conditions.[50] In 2002 an environmental group, Bluewater Network, petitioned the Bush administration to fix the MPG figures.

The White House encouraged a team of engineers and policy analysts in EPA's Ann Arbor, Michigan, laboratory to move forward on Bluewater Network's request. Congress ultimately compelled this rule making to occur in the 2005 highway bill, but the congressional action simply forced a rule making that Congress knew EPA was about to propose.[51]

The old EPA test procedures had a top speed of 60 miles per hour and were conducted in mild climate conditions (75 degrees Fahrenheit). They used vehicles without fuel-consuming accessories such as air conditioning.[52] As a result, many vehicle owners who tracked their mileage and fuel consumption found that their MPG figures deviated from the official fuel economy figures that had been posted on the window sticker when the vehicle was sold.

According to studies by Consumers Union (CU), the city fuel economy figures derived from real-world experience were consistently below the official EPA city ratings.[53] Yet the CU-derived highway ratings were generally above the official EPA highway ratings. A different study, by the Automobile Association of America (AAA), found that the combined city/highway values based on real-world experience ranged from 40 percent lower to 22 percent higher than EPA's combined city/highway value, depending upon the vehicle.[54]

Owners of new hybrid vehicles were particularly frustrated with their experiences. The nature of the hybrid technology (the addition of a battery as a second source of power in addition to the internal combustion engine) suggests that fuel economy will be more sensitive to certain conditions such as high acceleration rates and cold temperatures. The features of the hybrid engine that save fuel tend to be less beneficial while driving aggressively, during colder temperatures, and when the air conditioner is turned on.

In a rule finalized in late 2006, EPA established a new method, rooted in their state-of-the-art emissions testing, to determine the official fuel economy label values.[55] The new methods accounted for higher speeds, more aggressive driving (for instance, higher acceleration rates), use of air conditioning at higher outside temperatures, and operation at colder temperatures.[56]

Based on a database of 423 recent model year vehicles, EPA determined that their proposal would have the effect of reducing the average MPG figures. For conventional vehicles with a gasoline-powered engine, the city and highway MPG label values would be reduced by 13 percent and 9 percent, respectively. The impact on hybrid vehicles was greater, averaging 23 percent lower in the city and 9 percent lower on the highway.[57] The ratings for the Prius declined from 60/51 MPG to 48/45 MPG.[58]

The Bush administration applied the new EPA ratings to the consumer labels but did not make any progress in modernizing the MPG values used in DOT's CAFE program. By law, Congress compels DOT to use the outmoded MPG values, so that the older MPG values continue to be used to determine whether vehicle manufacturers are in compliance under the CAFE program. In the future, congressional action will be required to harmonize the MPG values used in EPA's consumer labels with the MPG values used in DOT's CAFE compliance program.

Bush's Mileage Plan

On Earth Day 2008, the Bush administration announced a regulatory proposal to raise average MPG levels of cars and light trucks 25 percent by model year 2015. Average mileage levels for cars would rise from 27.5 MPG in 2009 to 35.7 in 2015; the levels for light trucks would rise from 23.5 MPG in 2010 to 28.6 MPG in 2015. This proposal amounts to an annual mileage upgrade of 4.5 percent per year, far more than the 3.3 percent per year that Congress required in the 2007 CAFE reform legislation.[59] In order to achieve the fleet-wide goal of 35 MPG by 2020, only a 2.2 percent annual improvement would be necessary between 2015 and 2020. Bush's proposal appeared to be aimed at meeting his original 2007 State of the Union proposal of 35 MPG by 2017, even though Congress refused to go that far.

This rule-making proposal was another shock to the auto industry: It occurred just as national auto sales were slumping due to rising gas prices and growing rates of home foreclosure.[60] Nonetheless, some environmental groups insisted that the Bush administration should have set even higher MPG requirements, such as 40 MPG by 2020 and more than 50 MPG by 2030.[61]

The details of the rule-making proposal provided some assistance to the industry and the UAW. The precise legal language in the proposal took another shot at the legal foundation of California's plan. The language states explicitly that the national CAFE rules preempt the California rules aimed at curbing carbon-dioxide emissions from new vehicles.[62]

Bush's rule making was not finished when President Obama took office. In his quest for the Democratic presidential nomination, Barack Obama offered a deal for the domestic automakers: If they would achieve 40 MPG by 2022, the

Table 7.1. Comparison of Average New Vehicles Sold in USA, 1997 vs. 2006

Vehicle Attribute	Average Values: New Cars and Light Trucks	
	1997 Vehicle	2006 Vehicle
Fuel Economy (MPG)	22.1	21.0
Horsepower	169	219
Weight (lbs.)	3,727	4,142
Acceleration (0–60 MPH in seconds)	11.0	9.7

Source: Gina Chon, "High Fuel Prices Don't Dent Love of Gas Guzzlers," *Wall Street Journal,* July 18, 2006, p. D1 (reprinting EPA data).

federal government would relieve the Big Three of 10 percent of their health-care obligations to retirees. Obama also offered tax incentives for retooling auto assembly plants for fuel efficient vehicles and more consumer tax credits for hybrid vehicles.[63] Thus, it remains to be seen whether Bush's CAFE reform effort will be durable.

Incentives to Purchase Fuel-Efficient Vehicles

Before the CAFE rules were tightened, the industry was already offering for sale more than ninety new vehicle models that achieved over 30 miles per gallon.[64] The barrier to saving fuel through new vehicle purchases was not primarily on the supply side of the market. As table 7.1 indicates, U.S. consumers have been less interested in fuel economy than horsepower, size, and acceleration capability. Economists argue that tighter CAFE rules are destined to create market inefficiency unless consumers are motivated to purchase fuel-efficient vehicles.

The White House helped persuade the Congress to stimulate consumer interest in energy conservation through adoption of new tax credits for consumers. The credits were designed based on a recommendation from a rare coalition of industry and environmental groups that worked with the White House on the president's May 2001 National Energy Policy.[65]

Congress responded. Income tax credits were authorized for consumers who purchase new vehicles with innovative engines and fuels. The credits took effect on January 1, 2006. If consumers purchase a car or light truck with a hybrid engine, the size of the income tax credit is based on how much fuel economy is achieved relative to a comparable vehicle from model year 2002. The basic credit ranges from $400 (for achieving 125 percent of the 2002 fuel economy) to $2,400 (for achieving 250 percent of the 2002 fuel economy). An additional "conservation" credit was authorized depending on the amount of fuel saved over the vehicle's lifetime. This bonus credit ranges from $250 to $1,000, depending upon the projected fuel savings.[66]

In response to a specific White House request, a similar credit was authorized by Congress for consumers who purchased a car or light truck with a modern diesel engine that meets stringent tailpipe pollution limitations.[67] Authorization for the credit was extended through calendar year 2009 (for hybrids) and 2010 (for clean diesels).[68] Thus Bush helped ensure that both clean diesels and hybrids received a boost in the market from tax policy.

Under the tax policy, each vehicle manufacturer is allowed to sell 60,000 vehicles with a hybrid or clean diesel engine before the tax credit is gradually reduced and phased out. Thus, the buyers who make the first purchases from a manufacturer are assured of a credit. The credits for Toyota's hybrids began to decline after October 1, 2006, because the 60,000-unit cap was exceeded quickly due to the popularity of the Prius. The Toyota credit became zero in 2007; Honda's credit began to decline in 2008.

Congress provided even more generous tax treatment for promising technologies that may become competitors to hybrids and diesels in the long run. For new cars and light trucks that are designed to run on alternate fuels (for instance, compressed natural gas), the size of the credit equals the incremental cost of the vehicle compared to a conventional model of the same year, up to a maximum of $5,000. This credit was authorized through 2010. For vehicles powered with fuel cells, arguably the most promising alternative to gasoline-powered engines, the authorized tax credits can be as much as $12,000, with credits available through 2014.[69]

When the Internal Revenue Service issued new tax rules in early 2006, purchasing a hybrid engine became much more attractive (see table 7.2). The new credit directly reduced the consumer's income tax liability and was therefore more generous than the previous $2,000 tax deduction for hybrids, which simply reduced the consumer's taxable income. The credits for advanced diesels were somewhat smaller but still significant.

Later, in 2008, Congress and the Bush administration agreed to another tax credit aimed at spurring sales of plug-in hybrids and electric vehicles from 2010

Table 7.2. Consumer Tax Credits for Hybrids and Diesels

Hybrid Vehicle	Estimated Tax Credit
2006 Honda Civic	$2,100
2006 Toyota Prius	
— Before 10/1/06	$3,150
— After 10/1/06	$1,575
2007 Toyota Camry	
— After 10/1/06	$1,300
2006 Ford Escape SUV	
— Two-wheel drive models	$2,600
— Four-wheel drive models	$1,950
2009 Volkswagen Jetta (diesel)	$1,300

Sources: Mike Specter, "Toyota Won't Cover Lost Tax Credits," *Wall Street Journal,* Sept. 26, 2006, p. D2; Joseph B. White, "Cheaper Gas Threatens Hybrid Goal," *Wall Street Journal,* Oct. 17, 2006, p. D7; Chris Woodyard, "IRS Setting Tax Breaks for Hybrids," USA Today, Jan. 16, 2006, p. 6B; James R. Healey, "Volkswagen's '09 Jetta Brings Diesel Back to U.S. Mainstream," *USA Today,* Dec. 19, 2008 (online).

to 2015.[70] The extended-range system that GM plans for the Chevy Volt (2010) might qualify for a $7,500 tax credit. Cars with smaller batteries might qualify for a $2,500 credit. These credits would be phased out once 250,000 plug-ins were sold in a single calendar year. In addition to GM, Toyota, Chrysler, Nissan, and Ford are planning to offer plug-ins or electrics, but it is unclear whether the batteries will have sufficient range, durability, or affordability.[71]

Scale Back Tax Cuts to Save Fuel

In January 2003 Bush announced an economic stimulus plan that included a new tax incentive to encourage small businesses to invest in new equipment. A year after it was enacted by Congress, the White House learned that the incentive had inadvertently created a perverse stimulus for businesses to purchase large, gas-guzzling SUVs. This was a clear case where Bush was tested on a conflict between his tax-cutting and energy-conservation goals. The story of how energy conservation won is an interesting one.

When Bush took office in 2001, the tax code permitted a small business to deduct, during the year of purchase, up to $25,000 of the cost of general capital equipment (for example, a new industrial boiler or a large pickup truck for use on the farm). At the same time, the code imposed a $7,660 limit on deductions for the cost of new vehicles weighing less than 6,000 pounds, such as a new sedan or small van. The original rationale for this structure was to allow investment in large pickups and other large work vehicles, without encouraging the purchase of luxury cars by salesmen, real estate agents, and business owners. This differential tax treatment began in 1986, before large SUVs surged in popularity.[72]

Bush's 2003 tax plan increased the maximum deduction from $25,000 to $100,000. However, no adjustment was made to the $7,660 limit for smaller vehicles. As a result, the 2003 tax plan created a huge and unintended incentive for businesses to purchase large SUVs and pickups, loaded with options, instead of smaller SUVs and cars.[73]

A variety of news articles reported that tax advisers were encouraging clients to either make additional investments in large new vehicles or shift their planned purchases from cars and small vans to large SUVs and pickups.[74] Not surprisingly, the consequences for vehicle fuel economy were decidedly negative. Trucks weighing between 6,000 and 8,500 pounds have average fuel economy ratings that are 35 percent lower than the average car.[75] Trucks weighing over 8,500 pounds were not even regulated for fuel economy and thus had no official MPG ratings.

Upon learning of this perverse effect, Bush insisted upon a policy reversal. The White House worked with Senator Charles Grassley of Iowa, chairman of the Senate Finance Committee, to reinstate the $25,000 cap on business deductions for new large vehicles in the American Jobs Creation Act of 2004.[76]

Congestion Management

Energy conservation in the transportation sector cannot be fully effective if it addresses only the design of new vehicles. Motorists need to have incentives to use their vehicles responsibly. Bush worked with Congress on a new highway bill, which he signed in 2005, that contains promising new authority for states to manage highway congestion.[77] The administration strived to make it easier for states to reduce traffic congestion, improve air quality, reduce travel times, and save energy.

The highway bill authorized states to assess tolls on high-occupancy vehicle (HOV) lanes on the interstate highway system.[78] The idea is to allow drivers to pay a toll to use HOV lanes, even if their vehicle does not meet the occupancy or other requirements. States are required to use automatic toll collection and to enforce violations. Drivers pay variable fees for highway use depending on congestion levels. If there are excess toll revenues, states are required to expend these funds on projects involving alternatives to single-occupancy vehicles (such as public transit) or to improve highway safety.

New technologies, such as those implemented on Interstate 15 in Southern California and Interstate 394 in Minnesota, permit road providers to price roads dynamically (every few minutes), depending upon traffic conditions.[79] As a result, charging tolls on interstate highways is also permitted in fifteen new demonstration projects authorized by the highway bill over fiscal years 2005 to 2009.[80] The projects are limited to highways, bridges, or tunnels that already collect tolls or already serve HOVs or are new facilities that create additional toll-collection capacity. If a toll is charged to use an HOV lane, pricing is to vary by time of day or by amount of traffic, as needed to reduce congestion and improve air quality. Revenues from tolls may only be used for debt service on the toll-charging facility or for a reasonable rate of return on private financing and operational costs. If the toll-charging facility is being adequately maintained, revenue from tolls may also be applied to any other federal highway or transit projects. The federal share of project costs for authorized facilities may not exceed 80 percent.

The highway bill also continues a congestion-pricing pilot program, now called the Value Pricing Pilot Program, at fifteen sites around the country.[81] Each site is experimenting with area-wide highway pricing: pricing of multiple or single facilities or corridors, single-lane pricing, and other market-based approaches to traffic management. New funds are set aside for innovative congestion-pricing projects at those sites that do not collect tolls. One study estimates that innovative congestion-management schemes in just a quarter of the nation could save 65,000 to 260,000 barrels of oil per day.[82] To build on these efforts, Bush's 2008 and 2009 budget requests called for an additional $175 million of federal funding to be redirected to an expanded program of congestion pricing.[83]

Despite the encouragement from Bush and the Congress, congestion management has encountered some opposition at local levels of government. Privacy advocates fear that continuous camera monitoring of motorists can be used (and abused) by government to invade the privacy of citizens.[84] When

Mayor Bloomberg of New York proposed a congestion-pricing plan based on the London experience, he was blocked by state politicians in Albany.[85] Defending the pocketbooks of commuters, state officials argued that commuters should not have to pay $8 to drive below 60th Street from 6 AM to 6 PM. As a result, New York City lost the opportunity to win $354 million in federal highway assistance.[86]

The Market Responds

The gradual tightening of CAFE standards from model years 2005 through 2015, combined with the new consumer tax credits for fuel-efficient vehicles, were designed to stimulate penetration of new fuel-saving technologies in the U.S. marketplace. Several unexpected developments occurred at the same time that the Bush administration was adopting these new policies. Fuel prices rose much more rapidly than experts expected, the financial woes at General Motors, Ford, and Chrysler worsened, and diesel fuel prices rose more rapidly than gasoline prices.

In August 2004, average fuel prices in the U.S. were well below $2.00 per gallon, where they had been through much of the 1990s. Fuel prices rose substantially to a national average of $2.61 per gallon by August 2005 and to over $3.00 per gallon in the months following Hurricane Katrina. Prices fell again below $2.30 per gallon at the end of 2005 but climbed steadily again in 2006 and 2007. During the summer 2006 and 2007 driving seasons, national average prices climbed over $3.00 per gallon before they again declined rapidly.[87] In the summer of 2008 they surpassed $4.00 per gallon before they collapsed in the fall of 2008 to levels below $2.00 per gallon.

The Chinese and Indian economies were growing at a clip of 7–10% per year,[88] and consuming a larger share of limited world oil supplies. In late 2005, the U.S. Energy Information Administration (EIA) began to revise upward its long-term forecast for the price of gasoline in the United States. In an unusually large adjustment, they raised the price forecasts from around $1.50 per gallon to $2.10 per gallon for 2010 to 2025.[89] In May 2008 EIA upped the price forecast again, to $2.36 per gallon in 2020 and $2.51 per gallon in 2030.[90]

Rising gas prices tend to curtail new vehicle sales and change the type of vehicle that consumers purchase. For example, sales of the Ford (F-series) pickup truck, the most popular vehicle in America, declined from a peak of

Table 7.3. New Hybrid and Diesel Offerings Planned by Vehicle Manufacturers

BMW
- Offered diesel-powered sedans and sport wagons

Daimler
- Offered diesel option on E-class sedan (E320 CDI, 2007)
- Plans to offer optional diesel-powered Smart Car in U.S. market
- Plans to offer diesel options on crossover SUVs (2009)

Ford Motor Company
- Sold 25,000 units of Hybrid Escape SUV in 2005
- Backed off pledge to produce 250,000 hybrid vehicles by 2010
- Expanded offerings of advanced diesel technology on large pickup trucks
- Plans to offer diesel option on the Fiesta subcompact (2010)
- Plans pure electric sedan (2011)

General Motors Corporation
- Offered hybrid version of Saturn Vue (a small SUV) in model year 2007
- Offered optional "two-mode" hybrid on several large SUVs and pickups (2008)
- Announced that a "plug-in" hybrid for the Chevrolet Volt is under development (2010)
- Plans to offer hybrid technology on as many as twelve GM vehicles (2010)
- Expanded advanced diesel offerings on large pickups and SUVs (2009–2010)

Honda Motor Company
- Delayed plans to offer diesel option on Acura TSX sedan and SUVs and vans
- Plans to replace 2-seat hybrid Insight with another hybrid-equipped small car (2009)
- Offered hybrid version of popular Honda Civic, selling 25,000 in 2006
- Honda Accord hybrid launched in late 2004, but terminated in 2007 due to insufficient sales

Nissan Motor Company
- Plans to offer diesel-powered Maxima sedan (2010)
- Announced plans to offer hybrids, plug-ins, and electric vehicles (2012)

Toyota Motor Company
- Hybrid-equipped Prius sold to 235,000 buyers in 2005
- Hybrid offerings made available on seven models in 2006
- First manufacturer to exhaust authorization of consumer tax credits (due to 60,000-unit limit)
- Plans to offer plug-in hybrid technology in 2010
- May offer diesel option on the Tundra pickup

Volkswagen
- Offered new diesel-powered Jetta sedan and wagon (2008)
- Offered diesel-powered SUV (2009)

939,463 in 2004 to less than 500,000 in 2008.[91] Some consumers shift from large SUVs, vans, and pickups to carlike SUVs (so-called "crossovers") and large sedans.[92] Others shift from a large car to a small car, or some small-car owners decide to buy another small car rather than bump up to a midsize or large car.

The shifting product mix was another nail in the coffin of Detroit. In 2005, for example, General Motors lost a staggering $10.6 billion.[93] Ford eked out a $2 billion profit in 2005 but lost $1.6 billion in North America. Ford followed in the first quarter of 2006 with a multibillion-dollar loss company wide.[94] Even Toyota, Honda, and Nissan experienced profit declines in 2007–2008 due to the global credit crunch and sharp contraction in overall U.S. vehicle sales.[95] From a peak annual sales rate of 17 million units, industry-wide sales were projected to be as low as 11 million in 2009.

The steep losses at GM and Ford amplified a long-term decline in their market shares and serious cost problems due to health and pension commitments to retirees and current employees.[96] Wall Street analysts responded by downgrading the debt ratings of both companies deeper into junk bond status.[97] If it had not been for the huge amount of cash on hand at both companies, near-term predictions of Chapter 11 would have been widespread.[98] The Big Three won some concessions from the UAW in 2007, but the cost savings from the concessions were overwhelmed in the near term by the overall decline in industry sales and the shift in product mix away from pickup trucks and large SUVs.

Despite the fiscal troubles in Detroit, competitive and regulatory pressures forced innovation in the industry. Investments in hybrid and diesel technology increased rapidly. See table 7.3.

Cautious analysts predicted that it will be difficult for hybrid sales to extend much beyond the two initial groups of buyers: "early adopters" (people who like to purchase the latest auto technology) and "greens" (people who will buy to save the planet, despite the premium price). The cautious analysts predicted modest growth of hybrid sales from 220,000 (1.3 percent of the market) in 2005 to 756,000 (4.2 percent of the market) in 2012.[99] A more optimistic view, based on the assumption that the costs of producing hybrids can be cut by another 50 percent through innovation and improved production techniques, is that hybrid sales may capture 26 percent of the light-duty market by 2012, even without considering the effects of tax credits and tighter fuel economy rules. But the optimistic view was undermined by the collapse of fuel prices in 2008.

Overall, the pace of hybrid penetration has been rapid. In the U.S., two hybrid models were offered in 2000, five in 2004, twelve in 2006, and about twenty in 2008.[100]

Advanced diesels emerged as a serious competitor to hybrid technology. A diesel-powered vehicle's economy is 20–40 percent better than that of a gasoline-powered counterpart. Performance is generally equivalent or even better, especially the added torque. Reliability and long-term maintenance are not a concern, except for the new emissions-control systems. Depending on the vehicle, the extra cost is $1,000 to $5,000 compared to a gasoline engine, a smaller cost disadvantage than hybrids.[101]

Sales of diesel vehicles are projected to accelerate in the U.S. market. Conservative projections are that diesel's share of the light-duty market will grow from 3 percent in 2006 to 7.6 percent in 2012.[102] More optimistic analysts project diesel capturing 31 percent of the market by 2012.[103] Since these projections do not account for tighter CAFE standards or consumer tax credits, the future of diesel in the U.S. light-duty passenger market seemed bright. But a big setback occurred in 2007–2008 as diesel fuel prices diverged from gasoline prices. The unexpected growth of the European economy (which depends on diesel fuel), combined with a global shortage of refining capacity dedicated to diesel, caused diesel fuel in the U.S. to carry a 40–50 percent price premium. Honda announced in late 2008 that it was delaying its plans to offer diesel-powered cars in the U.S.[104]

Beyond hybrids and diesels, vehicle manufacturers announced a wide variety of measures to enhance new-vehicle mileage. They included turbochargers, cylinder deactivation systems, lightweight aluminum and lightweight steels, improved vehicle aerodynamics, and fuel-saving tires.[105] Combined with the shift toward smaller vehicle offerings, these engineering improvements caused new U.S. cars and light trucks in model year 2007 to be the most fuel-efficient on record.[106]

Bush's legislative record on energy conservation was a mixture of success and failure. When he recognized his limited power, considered the need to forge coalitions with key interest groups, and timed proposals to maximize public support, he was successful. That is what happened with consumer tax credits for diesels and hybrids and with the 2007 energy bill. When he worked to add promising reforms (such as congestion pricing) to larger bills that were irresistible to the Congress or when he timed legislative proposals to capture public support (such as CAFE reform during a bout of high fuel prices in 2007), he was effective. When he proposed ambitious legislation without marshalling the support of any key interest groups, he was unsuccessful. That is what happened with his failed 2002 and 2005 efforts to reform CAFE legislatively.

Although less publicized, Bush's executive policies on CAFE reform played a pivotal role in his energy-conservation accomplishments. The administrative reform of the light-truck CAFE program gave a second life to a well-intentioned program that was essentially dead when Bush took office. The UAW started out opposing Bush's reforms of the CAFE program but was ultimately persuaded to support them, especially the adjustments for vehicle size.[107] By securing UAW support, Bush enhanced the odds that his CAFE reforms will endure as the Democrats take power in Washington. If the CAFE reform successfully preempts the California plan, it may emerge as one of Bush's most important achievements in domestic policy. Even if the California plan survives, it may be amended to accommodate the size adjustments that NAS, the UAW, the Big Three, and Bush supported.

Bush's overall record on energy conservation is more accomplished than most people realize.[108] Unlike his tax, education, and health-care accomplishments, which were each packaged in a single, high-visibility bill, Bush's conservation policies arose from a series of seemingly unrelated actions involving different bills, multiple rule makings, and different federal agencies. Conservation groups can certainly argue that Bush should have been even more activist on energy conservation than he was, but Bush's accomplishments were much greater than any president since the CAFE law was enacted in 1974.

8

Cleaner Air, Warmer Climate

When Bush took office in 2001, he sought to accelerate the progress on clean air that his father had spurred with the Clean Air Act Amendments of 1990. In contrast to leading European politicians and Vice President Al Gore, who saw global warming as the top environmental priority, Bush's priority was to reduce the soot and smog in the air that impairs the public's health.

The Bush administration devised Clear Skies, a legislative initiative to reduce air pollution from electric utilities through a national cap-and-trade program. Instead of focusing on the carbon dioxide emissions linked to global warming, Clear Skies was aimed at reducing three pollutants: sulfur dioxide, nitrogen dioxide, and mercury. The primary public health beneficiaries would be children, the elderly, and asthmatics of all ages.[1] In addition to reducing these three pollutants by 70 percent over fifteen years, Clear Skies called for elimination of a variety of federal and state regulatory programs covering the same pollutants. Clear Skies also provided some regulatory flexibility for industry: Utilities were authorized to participate in a national emissions-trading program instead of EPA's cumbersome, plant-by-plant permit reviews.

Bush's attempts at a cross-partisan strategy on Clear Skies failed in a key Senate committee. Rather than fold, Bush launched a series of clean-air rule makings aimed at achieving similar objectives. By relying on executive authority to implement his clean-air agenda, Bush's policies became vulnerable to a complex series of lawsuits by national environmental groups, the regulated industries, and the states. The Bush administration lost some important cases but won others. Thus, Bush's track record on clean air reveals both the promise and perils of executive policy making.

Stumble on Global Warming

Early in 2001, before the Bush administration proposed Clear Skies, Bush's credibility on environmental issues was tarnished. Part of the problem was a clumsy decision by the Bush administration to reconsider a regulation of arsenic in drinking water that was adopted in the waning days of the Clinton administration. (The Clinton EPA tightened the arsenic rule to protect public health, but the Bush EPA considered relaxing it due to its higher cost to rural communities.) Environmentalists argued that Bush was putting money ahead of health. But the bigger setback was the global reaction to Bush's handling of climate change.

The Kyoto Protocol on global climate change, championed by Vice President Al Gore, called for each industrialized nation to cut its greenhouse gas emissions to 7 percent below 1990 levels by 2012 or face even tougher emission-reduction targets at a later date.[2] The Clinton administration and the leaders of 167 other countries endorsed the global climate treaty in December 1997 in Kyoto, Japan.

Before the Kyoto Protocol can take effect in the United States, it must be submitted by the president to the Senate for ratification. During the Clinton administration, the Senate voted 95 to 0 for a "sense of the Senate" resolution expressing the view that any binding protocol should include developing nations such as China and India.[3] Minority Leader Tom Daschle urged President Clinton not to submit the treaty to the Senate for ratification until developing countries agreed to participate in a meaningful way.[4] Although there was no vote against ratification in the 1990s, strong concerns were registered in the

Senate. Not surprisingly, President Clinton never submitted the protocol to the Senate for ratification.

During the 2000 campaign, Governor Bush criticized Gore's support for the Kyoto Protocol.[5] Bush argued that the protocol's numeric targets were unrealistic and a threat to the continued growth of the U.S. economy. He also argued that the protocol would do little to combat global warming because the two fastest-growing economies in the world, China and India, were excluded from its mandates, along with the rest of the developing world.[6] At the time it was projected that China would be the world's largest emitter of carbon dioxide by 2009, but China actually earned this dubious distinction earlier then expected.[7]

In March 2001 Bush informed the Senate that he would not seek Senate ratification of the Kyoto Protocol.[8] This announcement should not have been surprising, but it triggered loud protests from organized environmentalists, their allies in the mass media, and many foreign leaders throughout the world.[9] Bush's announcement was particularly vulnerable to criticism because he had not announced an affirmative position on climate policy, and did not do so until much later. Months of speculation ensued about whether Bush believed in the science of global warming and what the United States would do, if anything, to address global concerns. Suspicions were aggravated by news reports that Bush administration officials were editing governmental science documents to downplay the risks of global climate change induced by human activity.

Rare Reversal of a Campaign Pledge

As the Clear Skies plan was developed by Bush's advisers in 2001, a question arose as to whether carbon dioxide should be one of the pollutants covered by the legislation. During a fall 2000 campaign speech in Saginaw, Michigan, Governor Bush spoke directly to this issue: "We will require all power plants to meet clean-air standards in order to reduce emissions of sulfur dioxide, nitrogen dioxide, mercury and carbon dioxide within a reasonable period of time."[10]

Carbon dioxide is the major greenhouse gas implicated in global warming. On the basis of Bush's rather clear campaign statement, EPA moved aggressively in early 2001 to begin work on a version of Clear Skies that included carbon dioxide as well as sulfur dioxide, nitrogen dioxide, and mercury. Conservative members of Congress and key business leaders had a different idea. They urged Bush to reconsider his position. Bush agreed. In the same March 2001 letter to the Senate that reaffirmed his opposition to the Kyoto Protocol, Bush reversed his campaign pledge on a four-pollutant bill by saying: "I do not believe, however, that the government should impose on power plants mandatory emissions reductions for carbon dioxide, which is not a 'pollutant' under the Clean Air Act."[11] Not surprisingly, this reversal sparked angry protests from organized environmentalists as well as their allies in Congress.

A Stance on Climate Change: Too Little, Too Late?

Bush ultimately did announce a new U.S. policy on climate change in February 2002, at the same time that he announced Clear Skies.[12] It was a modest yet constructive effort to advance climate science, promote new technology, and reduce the "carbon intensity" of the U.S. economy by 18 percent by 2012 through a combination of existing programs. Instead of pledging to reduce overall carbon emissions, Bush chose to reduce carbon emissions per unit of gross domestic product, thereby protecting the anticipated growth in the U.S. economy.

Bush's climate proposal was arguably too little, too late. It was too little to generate any enthusiasm among environmental advocates or the growing number of scientists concerned about the threat of climate change. More importantly, it came almost a year after the controversies about the Kyoto Protocol and Bush's reversal on the four-pollutant pledge. During that year, Bush was ridiculed by environmentalists and their congressional allies as an ignorant politician who did not believe in science and who cared more about the near-term profitability of the coal and oil industries than the future of the planet.[13]

Critics of Bush's climate policy argued that more research on climate science will not stimulate progress on emissions control without a regulatory framework.[14] Key members of the Senate, including Democrat Joe Lieberman of Connecticut and Republican John McCain of Arizona, were not persuaded by the Bush administration and continued work toward an ambitious economy-wide regulatory system.

Bush's modest policy did not include a forward-looking strategy for persuading countries around the world to consider and support the U.S. position. The reputation of the United States in many other countries suffered because we appeared to be uninterested in a dialogue with our global colleagues about the best way to address climate change. A key opportunity was missed to reach out to Russia, China, and other countries who had strong reservations about the climate policies advocated by European politicians.[15]

Bush was criticized for being too timid about responding to the threat of global climate change, but he was certainly not the only elected official in Washington who was wary of a mandatory, economy-wide regulation of greenhouse gas emissions. The McCain-Lieberman plan was defeated twice: 55 to 43 in 2003 and again in 2005, this time by a wider margin, 60 to 38.[16] Six Republican senators (Chafee of Rhode Island, Collins and Snowe of Maine, Gregg of New Hampshire, Lugar of Indiana, and McCain of Arizona) deviated from the White House position in the 2005 climate vote. But businesses, farmers, and industrial labor unions helped the White House by motivating eleven Senate Democrats to vote against the 2005 climate plan: Baucus of Montana, Boxer of California, Byrd of West Virginia, Dayton of Minnesota, Feingold of Wisconsin, Harkin of Iowa, Landrieu of Louisiana, Lincoln and Pryor of Arkansas, and Nelson of Nebraska. (Boxer of California voted against McCain-Lieberman because she had a more ambitious bill.) Even a modest "sense of the Senate" resolution calling for the United States to reduce the risks of climate change and engage in international negotiations was defeated, 49 to 46, in 2005.[17] This more party-line vote may have been attributable to the identity of the resolution's sponsor: Democrat John Kerry of Massachusetts.

Some environmentalists took solace in a 2005 voice vote supporting a "sense of the Senate" resolution introduced by Jeff Bingaman of New Mexico. The resolution favored a mandatory cap-and-trade program for greenhouse gas emissions, coupled with encouragement for similar action elsewhere in the world. An effort by Republican senator James Inhofe of Oklahoma to kill the Bingaman resolution was defeated 53 to 44.[18] All Democrats except Max Baucus of Montana and Ben Nelson of Nebraska opposed Inhofe's effort. Eleven Senate Republicans joined in the opposition: John McCain of Arizona, Olympia Snowe and Susan Collins of Maine, Judd Gregg of New Hampshire, Pete Domenici of New Mexico, Mike DeWine of Ohio, Arlen Specter of Pennsylvania, Lincoln Chafee of Rhode Island, Lindsey Graham of South Carolina, Lamar Alexander of Tennessee, and John Warner of Virginia.

The lack of adequate national leadership on climate policy created a vacuum that spawned a proliferation of state and local regulations.[19] Many states and cities protested the policies of the Bush administration by enacting their own rules to curb greenhouse gases.[20] For example, a group of ten northeastern states began to participate in the Regional Greenhouse Gas Initiative, a step toward a regional cap-and-trade system similar to the McCain-Lieberman plan. In 2006 California expanded its carbon-control plan for motor vehicles to include most factories and power plants. Under this plan, California emissions in 2020 are compelled to be no greater than 1990 levels, or about 25 percent lower than what was projected in 2020 without regulation. Prime Minister Tony Blair of the United Kingdom actually signed a climate-change agreement with the Republican governor of California, Arnold Schwarzenegger, rather than with the president of the United States.[21]

Before long, Bush's position began to lose credibility with the business and labor interests that it was designed to protect. The proliferation of state and local regulations, some of which conflicted with each other, were a nightmare for businesses that sold product across state lines. By losing control of the climate issue, Bush became vulnerable to the charge that his policies were generating the worst of possible outcomes: economic costs were being incurred in many states without generating any meaningful environmental progress on the global challenge.

Clear Skies: Apathy and Opposition

In order for Clear Skies to be enacted by Congress, it needed to first pass through two congressional committees: the Committee on Environment and Public Works in the Senate and the Energy and Commerce Committee in the House. It didn't get through either one. After James Jeffords of Vermont switched his party affiliation from Republican to independent and the Democrats assumed control of the Senate in 2001, he was named chair of the Committee on Environment and Public Works in May 2001. Jeffords was quite interested in passing clean-air legislation. Instead of working with the White House, though, he worked with Senate Democrats and national environmental groups on a competing plan that he intended to pass through his committee.

The Jeffords plan differed from Clear Skies in four key ways: It covered four pollutants (including carbon dioxide) rather than three, it had earlier deadlines and larger emissions reductions, it required each plant to reduce mercury emissions (without any permission to trade mercury allowances with other plants), and it did not provide business any relief from the morass of existing federal and state regulatory programs. The Jeffords plan was supported enthusiastically by the environmental advocacy community but was strongly opposed by business groups.

The Bush administration was slow in releasing details about Clear Skies to the Senate. As months passed in 2002 without enough specific information from the Bush administration, Jeffords decided to move his plan through his committee. In June 2002 the Jeffords plan was approved 10 to 9, with all Democrats except Max Baucus of Montana supporting it and all Republicans except Lincoln Chafee of Rhode Island opposing it.[22] The committee was so polarized that the Jeffords plan never reached the Senate floor. If it had done so, Democratic senators from coal-producing states might have had little difficulty mustering the votes to filibuster, and possibly defeat it outright.

When Bush finally released the details of Clear Skies in July 2002, the House leadership informed the White House that they had no intention of acting until after the November midterm elections and only after there was some evidence that the Senate was serious about passing Clear Skies. But Jeffords was strongly opposed to Clear Skies, and as committee chair he possessed the power to prevent Clear Skies from moving through his committee to the Senate floor. At this stage, the president and his advisers became ambivalent about Clear Skies, in part because they were not convinced the legislation could be passed but also because they feared that compromises to Jeffords and the Senate Democratic leadership would be necessary to advance the plan.

Bush's limited leadership on global climate change exacerbated the obstacles to passing Clear Skies. Environmentalists and their allies in Congress took the position that no clean-air bill was acceptable unless it also included mandatory regulation of carbon dioxide, as Governor Bush had pledged in the 2000 presidential campaign. Some White House advisers suspected that the environmentalists in Congress would never collaborate with Bush on clean-air legislation because they wanted to use the environmental issue to further damage his fragile political standing and thereby help defeat him in his 2004 re-election bid. That perception, regardless of whether it was accurate, dampened enthusiasm for making Clear Skies a first-tier legislative priority in the White House. It also caused business leaders to develop even more doubts as to whether passage of Clear Skies was realistic.

When the Senate returned to Republican control in 2003, Clear Skies was promptly re-introduced in Congress. Jeffords lost his chairmanship to conservative Senator James Inhofe of Oklahoma. Joe Barton of Texas assumed the leadership of the House Energy and Commerce Committee. Yet the new Republican committee chairs were reluctant to give priority to Clear Skies. The run-up to the 2004 election was felt to be the wrong time to move a divisive clean-air bill. The preferences of the business community were a relevant consideration, but businesses were divided: Some saw promise in Clear Skies; others saw peril in an unpredictable legislative process. Momentum was building behind solutions to clean-air issues that could be enacted with executive powers instead of through legislation.

Streamlining Reviews of Clean-Air Permits

One of the key points in Bush's clean-air agenda was replacement of plant-by-plant emission limitations with a national cap on emissions coupled with a flexible emissions trading program to minimize compliance costs. Rather than await passage of Clear Skies, the Bush administration irked environmentalists by trying to curb plant-by-plant permit reviews and enforcement actions through executive action.

The Clean Air Act of 1970 established a pair of New Source Review (NSR) programs to accelerate industrial investments in clean air. One program for new plants stipulated that a permit for plant construction should not be provided unless the plant is designed with advanced pollution control equipment. A second program for existing plants also required advanced emissions controls but only if the plant was being changed, in structure or operation, in a way that increases emissions. NSR review at existing plants was designed to stimulate investments in modern clean-up technology when a plant was modified or upgraded.

Toward the end of the Clinton administration, EPA brought a series of lawsuits against the owners of power plants based on a new, more aggressive interpretation of the agency's NSR authority, including a narrow view of the exemptions that plants could claim from NSR enforcement actions. The agency's enforcement staff filed fifty-one lawsuits against (mostly coal-fired) power plants, alleging that the plants were disguising major renovations as "routine maintenance" in order to skirt scrutiny under the NSR review program.[23] If the lawsuits were successful, EPA could force owners of power plants to invest billions of dollars in aging plants or shut them down. Some owners settled these lawsuits by making significant clean-air investments, but other plants went to court to challenge EPA's new legal theory.

Early in 2001, the White House and EPA faced a critical decision about what to do about current and future NSR lawsuits against coal plants, refineries, and other sources. One option favored by some EPA staff was to continue the NSR litigation until Congress passed Clear Skies. Alternatively, EPA could issue NSR reform rules that reduced litigation pressure on industry by providing for operational flexibility at plants and by providing exemptions for routine maintenance and repairs. Under either option, EPA could exercise enforcement discretion to temporarily relieve some of the pressure on industry, until new legislation or new rules were established. A very different approach would be for EPA to exert maximum litigation pressure on industry, thereby creating a strong incentive for plant owners to lobby Capitol Hill for passage of Clear Skies. Thus, the politics of Clear Skies and NSR reform became intermingled.

The Justice Department weighed in with a legal opinion that EPA had a reasonable basis for its aggressive NSR legal interpretation. But the Department of Energy informed the White House that the NSR program was having a perverse effect: Fear of enforcement actions was causing some coal plants and refineries to reduce (or defer) investments in maintenance and repairs. The report from the Department of Energy was quite disturbing because the White House was scrambling to find ways to expand energy production in the U.S. (see chapter 6).

Given the uncertain prospects for Clear Skies legislation, Bush chose the rule-making route, coupled with careful use of enforcement discretion. In 2002 EPA issued an NSR reform rule aimed at providing operational flexibility for oil refineries and factories.[24] In 2003 EPA issued another NSR reform rule providing an exemption for power plants and other facilities to make routine repairs without facing NSR enforcement litigation.[25] In 2006 EPA proposed a third NSR reform aimed at providing owners of complex facilities some flexibility to undertake "debottlenecking" (plant-efficiency) projects that enhance productivity without triggering NSR lawsuits.[26]

National environmental groups, in collaboration with a variety of (largely northeastern) states, opposed the NSR reforms on the grounds that they would allow plants to make physical changes that increase emissions, thereby undercutting the goals of the Clean Air Act. They sought to overturn the rule makings in Congress or in federal court on the grounds that EPA lacked the authority to issue them and they would increase air pollution.

Backlash against NSR Reforms

It is not easy to muster a sufficient congressional coalition to overturn an executive action, but that is what some Democrats in Congress tried to do. In 2002 Democratic senators Joe Lieberman of Connecticut and John Edwards of North Carolina organized a coalition to block the proposed rule-making reforms of NSR. They recruited thirty-nine other senators (including three Republicans) to sign a letter to President Bush urging that the NSR reforms be withdrawn.[27]

The White House noticed that the number of signatories fell short of the sixty votes that would be required to advance corrective legislation in the Senate and far short of the two-thirds majority that would be required to overrule a Bush veto. (A resolution of disapproval under the Congressional Review Act can pass with a simple majority, but the likely Bush veto would be sustained in Congress unless the required two-thirds override vote could be mustered.) An appropriations rider blocking the NSR reforms was another possibility, but Democrat Robert Byrd of West Virginia, chairman of the Senate Appropriations Committee, was a key name absent from the list of signatories on the Lieberman-Edwards letter. An appropriations rider without the support of Senator Byrd did not seem likely.

On the Senate floor, Edwards sought to delay the NSR reforms until a study of NSR was completed by the National Academy of Sciences (NAS). The Edwards amendment was defeated, despite support from six Senate Republicans (Chafee of Rhode Island, Collins and Snowe of Maine, Gregg and Sununu of New Hampshire, and McCain of Arizona). Bush's stand on NSR was protected by five crossover votes from Senate Democrats (Breaux and Landrieu of Louisiana, Lincoln and Pryor of Arkansas, and Miller of Georgia). Ultimately, Edwards was forced to settle for an NAS study of the NSR program without any delay in the two rule makings.[28]

Environmentalists achieved more success in their litigation counterattack. The 2002 rule, aimed at providing operational flexibility to refineries and factories, was partially upheld and partially struck down in a complex federal appeals court opinion.[29] The 2003 rule was immediately vacated by a federal appeals court and ultimately overturned on the grounds that Congress had not provided EPA with legal authority to provide NSR exemptions.[30]

Meanwhile, industry and environmentalists waged a separate litigation battle over whether the Clinton-era legal theory of NSR was defensible. The federal appeals courts split on this question, but the Supreme Court ultimately sided with the environmentalists.

In summary, the Bush administration devoted significant political capital trying to reform the NSR program using executive authority. Perversely, this effort may have undercut the momentum to pass Clear Skies, since businesses perceived they might win relief from onerous permit reviews without any legislation from Congress. In the final analysis, much (but not all) of the NSR reform effort was lost in litigation.

Last-Ditch Effort on Clear Skies

After Bush's re-election in 2004, a last-ditch effort was made to pass Clear Skies. Senate optimists pointed to the fact that the Republican vote margin in the Senate had grown from 51 to 49 to 55 to 45. More subtly, they argued that moderate Democrats in Congress might begin to give Clear Skies a fair hearing, since a vote in favor of Clear Skies would no longer be perceived as bolstering Bush's environmental credentials prior to his 2004 re-election bid. In other words, the removal of presidential politics from the Clear Skies deliberations might open the door for more Democratic crossover votes. When the Republican leadership in Congress urged the White House to give legislation one last try, Bush agreed to delay any additional clean-air rule makings until the spring of 2005.

Chairman Inhofe tried to move Clear Skies through the Senate Committee on Environment and Public Works in early 2005, hoping to force a prompt roll-call vote on the Senate floor. Much to Inhofe's dismay, the bill never made it to the Senate floor. Despite a concerted push by business groups and the White House, the committee deadlocked 9 to 9 along party lines with one key exception: Republican senator Lincoln Chafee of Rhode Island voted against Clear Skies.[31] The White House won no Democratic crossover votes for Clear Skies.

There were some discussions of a compromise plan, possibly engineered by Democratic senator Tom Carper of Delaware and Republican senator George

Voinovich of Ohio. Looking for a constructive compromise, Carper suggested a bill with voluntary carbon dioxide controls that would become mandatory if the voluntary controls did not work. After numerous meetings without progress, Voinovich explained why it was the climate-change issue that killed Clear Skies: "Chafee thinks this is the biggest problem facing the world, and the chairman [Inhofe] has a sign in his office saying this is a hoax."[32] By losing control of the climate-change issue, the Bush administration made passage of Clear Skies more difficult than it needed to be.

Clean Diesel Engines

In theory, a president has the power to reverse the executive actions of his predecessor. Such reversals do occur on occasion, but a new president may prefer to pursue his own agenda, or build on the accomplishments of his predecessor. The Bush administration raised some eyebrows by forcing oil refineries and engine suppliers to slash the amount of exhaust from diesel engines. Instead of pursuing legislation, Bush authorized rule makings to accomplish the same purpose based on existing authority in the Clean Air Act.

In 2000 the Clinton EPA had issued a new rule compelling a 90 percent reduction in the exhaust from highway diesel engines, especially the exhaust from heavy trucks, which are the largest consumers of diesel fuel on U.S. highways.[33] This was a capital-intensive regulation because it forced refineries to remove large amounts of sulfur from crude oil before making gasoline. It also forced diesel engine suppliers to add modern emission-control equipment. The deadline for compliance was set at the beginning of model year 2007 for all new heavy-duty diesel engines sold for use on highways.

As soon as Bush took office in 2001, the White House decided to review a large number of new "midnight" regulations that had been adopted late in the Clinton administration.[34] Some conservatives and owners of refineries saw Bush's election as a window of opportunity to reopen Clinton's highway diesel rule.[35] Many refineries had deteriorating equipment and a shortage of capital to invest in desulfurization technology. Relief from the highway diesel rule (such as delayed deadlines for compliance or less stringent desulfurization requirements) was seen as attractive. On the other hand, excessive amounts of sulfur in diesel fuel cause damage to modern emission-control systems. Diesel engine suppliers did not want to make investments in new emissions-control technology until adequate supplies of low-sulfur fuel were available for their new engines. Meanwhile, environmentalists were nervous about what might happen if the highway diesel rule was reconsidered by the Bush administration.

When EPA and OMB analyzed the issue, they came to a surprising conclusion. Rather than delay or weaken the highway diesel rule, the two agencies joined together in persuading the administration to retain the rule. More importantly, they decided to pursue an expansion of the rule's requirements to cover the large numbers of off-road diesel engines used in construction, agriculture, and mining.

Ultimately, a plan was developed by EPA and the Office of Management and Budget (OMB) to cut exhaust from non-road engines by 90 percent as well. In order to keep the cost of the rule as low as possible, trading of emission credits was permitted between engines of different sizes. Finalized in 2004, the "off-road diesel rule" is one of the most beneficial rule makings in the history of the U.S. Environmental Protection Agency. The rule is projected to cost about $2 billion per year, but the annual public health benefits are projected by EPA to be about $80 billion per year by 2015, when the rule takes full effect.[36] The rule was later extended to include diesel locomotives and marine engines.[37]

In addition to enacting strict emission limits on diesel engines, the Bush administration resisted efforts by some companies to soften the penalties for noncompliance under the highway diesel rule. An intra-industry squabble emerged among a handful of diesel engine suppliers who had signed a settlement with EPA during the Clinton administration. The settlement called for compliance with the highway diesel rule earlier than was required by law. The suppliers agreed to a three-year "pull-up" of the deadline in order to avoid EPA enforcement actions against them for their alleged failure to sell engines in previous years that met applicable tailpipe standards.[38]

As the "pull-up" deadline approached (model year 2004), some suppliers were ready with promising technology to comply with the standards while others were not quite ready with their new engines. The latter informed EPA that they intended to pay noncompliance penalties for at least a year rather than comply with the "pull-up" standards. A controversy erupted about how large the penalties should be.

The complying suppliers argued that the fines should be large, since all the suppliers had signed a consent decree indicating they would meet the accelerated deadline. The noncomplying suppliers were seeking smaller noncompliance penalties or a delay in the applicable standards.[39] The issue became politicized when the competing companies engaged sympathetic congressmen to lobby the White House on their behalf.

The resolution of the Bush administration was firm: Noncomplying firms should be penalized to whatever extent was necessary to ensure that they gained no competitive advantage relative to suppliers who had complied with the accelerated schedule. EPA and OMB performed a comprehensive calculation of the cost advantages that the noncomplying suppliers would achieve through delayed compliance, including the savings in fuel consumption over the life of the engines due to the absence of emission-control equipment. The result of these calculations justified a new noncompliance rule that imposed substantial fines on suppliers who decided to pay the fines rather than innovate with clean technology.[40] This enforcement rule sent a clear signal to industry that the Bush administration was prepared to enforce the clean diesel rules with rigor.

The Bush administration's strong stance against diesel engine exhaust stands in notable contrast to the tentative stances taken by the European Commission and the European member states. European rules against diesel engine exhaust are gradually becoming more demanding, but the precise deadlines, numeric limits, and compliance test conditions are less stringent than required by U.S. and California regulators.

Reducing Air Pollution at Coal Plants

While Congress was bickering over NSR reform and Clear Skies, Bush instructed EPA, OMB, and the Department of Energy (DOE) to develop a rule-making strategy to reduce air pollution from coal-fired power plants. When coal is burned to generate electric power without modern pollution controls, two key gases, sulfur dioxide and nitrogen dioxide, are emitted into the air through tall stacks and contribute to the formation of soot and smog. The tall stacks dilute the concentrations of pollution near the plants, but the huge height of the stacks contributes to the long-range transport of pollution, including the atmospheric transformation of gases into small particles (soot) and ozone (smog). Public health scientists have demonstrated that particles and ozone are more harmful to human health than the gases emitted from the stacks.[41]

Although most clean-air programs are administered by the fifty states, federal rules are needed to ensure that plants do not degrade air quality in downwind states. Environmental models show that coal-fired power plants sited east of the Mississippi River contribute to violations of air-quality standards throughout much of New England and parts of the Midwest. EPA analysts projected that these problems would persist through at least 2015 unless strong regulatory action was taken.

When the effort to pass Clear Skies faltered, Bush instructed EPA to design a regional regulation using market-based mechanisms. The regional cap was designed to reduce by 70 percent the amount of pollution from coal-fired power plants. Using existing legal authority aimed at reducing interstate transport of pollution, EPA's program covered twenty-eight states and the District of Columbia, including all of the operating coal plants that were causing air-quality problems in downwind states. Bush preferred a national program covering coal plants in all fifty states, but EPA lacked authority to enact a national program without passage of Clear Skies. The regional program was dubbed the Clean Air Interstate Rule (CAIR).[42]

By 2015, permanent caps on sulfur and nitrogen would reduce emissions in the CAIR region by 70 percent and 65 percent, respectively, compared to 2003 emissions levels. An interim 2010 cap was also established to ensure gradual progress. In order to encourage controls prior to 2015, plants were offered special credits if they undertook early emissions reductions, including an opportunity to bank those credits for use when complying with the 2015 cap. Each plant was allocated a limited number of emissions credits each year, but plants were permitted to trade credits with each other, as long as the overall regional cap on emissions was achieved. This trading mechanism was designed to stimulate innovation in emissions control and help keep down the costs of this expensive program.

At the time it was adopted in 2005, the CAIR rule was the most costly regulation of business issued during the Bush presidency.[43] EPA estimated that the utility industry and consumers will pay $2.4 billion per year in compliance costs by 2010 and $3.6 billion per year by 2015. The costs were justified by large public health and environmental benefits. Of those benefits that could be quantified, the annual totals were $60.4 billion per year in 2010 and $83.2 billion in 2015. These impressive estimates assume that, by 2015, the rule will prevent, each year, 17,000 premature deaths, 8,700 cases of chronic bronchitis, 22,000 nonfatal heart attacks, 10,500 hospitalizations among people with respiratory and cardiovascular conditions, and 510,000 lost school days among children with respiratory problems. The science underpinning these figures is by no means certain. Yet, a more conservative estimate of benefits prepared by EPA and OMB analysts was also larger than the projected costs of the rule. Moreover, it was not feasible for EPA to fully quantify some of the important environmental benefits of the rule: reductions in the acidification of lakes, streams, and forests, and reduced eutrophication in water bodies.

The CAIR rule had substantial support among states, environmentalists, and businesses. But there also were enough CAIR critics to stimulate complex litigation. Some critics of EPA insist that the CAIR rule did not go far enough and should have ordered reductions larger than 65–70 percent by 2015. From a strictly benefit-cost perspective, more emission reductions could have been achieved at a reasonable cost. Unfortunately, a more stringent rule might have placed the entire rule making at even greater risk of judicial reversal, since industry could have argued in federal court that reductions beyond 70 percent were not necessary to prevent air-quality problems in downwind states, which is the relevant legal test under the Clean Air Act. Some businesses argued precisely the opposite, that the rule is too stringent because the 2015 requirements do not help communities comply with scheduled air-quality goals, which are binding in 2010.

In 2008 a panel of federal judges overturned CAIR on the grounds that key provisions of the rule are not consistent with EPA's statutory authority. Instead of striking down the unsupportable provisions and leaving the rest of the rule in place, the appeals court ordered EPA to redo the entire rule making. The court's opinion is so complex that some experts believe the rule can only be resurrected through legislation along the lines of Clear Skies.[44] After a rehearing, the same court decided to let CAIR remain in effect until the legal flaws are corrected.

As EPA tightens the health-based air-quality goals for particles, more stringent clean-coal rules to reduce particles should be permissible. In 2007–2008 the Bush administration used executive authority to further tighten the health-based air quality standards for soot and smog, though the clean-air goals were not tightened as much as some scientists and environmental advocates recommended.[45] A federal appeals court was asked to resolve whether the stringency of the EPA's new clean-air goals need to be reconsidered by the Obama administration.

The Clean Air Mercury Rule

When a president decides to use executive powers instead of pursuing a legislative solution, a determination must be made as to whether the legal risks of executive action are acceptable. Even when the legal risks of executive action are substantial, a president may prefer his or her policy agenda in the face of those risks, rather than await new legislative authority from the Congress. This is precisely what happened with mercury, another air pollutant emitted by coal-fired power plants. In fact, mercury pollution emerged as a political issue during the 2004 presidential election campaign.

The mercury controversy is rooted in how the Clean Air Act is written, how the environmental science about mercury is interpreted, and whether the costs of controlling mercury at coal plants are justified by the anticipated public health benefits.

In the Clean Air Act Amendments of 1990, Congress ordered major industrial plants to install technology to reduce "hazardous" air pollution to the maximum extent feasible. Additional controls were to be implemented if EPA determined that they were necessary to protect the health of nearby residents. A "hazardous" air pollutant was defined as any one of 189 specific pollutants named in the law (or a pollutant later identified by EPA as "hazardous" within the meaning of the Clean Air Act). The term "hazardous" referred to severe health effects (such as cancer or birth defects) that might occur among highly exposed residents living near the plants. Mercury was one of the 189 pollutants listed by Congress.

Electric utilities emitted some of the same hazardous pollutants (including mercury) as industrial facilities, but Congress did not require EPA to regulate utilities in the same way that industrial sources are regulated. Instead, Congress required EPA to first perform a public health study to determine what hazards were reasonably anticipated to occur as a result of utility emissions. EPA was then instructed to consider alternative control strategies and to make a finding as to whether federal regulation of toxic emissions from utilities was appropriate and necessary. Congress directed EPA to complete the required study by November 1993, but no specific deadline was set for any necessary rule makings.

President Clinton's leadership team at EPA was slow in addressing mercury emissions from electric utilities. The required public health study was not completed on schedule, and no regulatory determination was made as Clinton's second term came to a close. Consequently, a coalition of environmentalists sued EPA, resulting in a consent-decree deadline for a rule-making decision about mercury from power plants, a deadline that was scheduled a few weeks after the November 2000 election.

In late 2000, at about the same time the U.S. Supreme Court resolved the presidential election dispute (but before President Clinton left office), EPA announced its intent to regulate mercury emissions from power plants. The agency concluded that it was "necessary and appropriate" to use the same legal framework that had been used previously to regulate industrial plants.[46] This framework compelled each plant to reduce emissions, with no flexibility for plants to trade emissions allowances in order to reduce compliance costs.

For industry and environmental groups, the belated decision by the Clinton EPA raised more questions than it provided answers. EPA did not specify the amount of emissions reductions that would be required, the anticipated costs of the contemplated controls, or the public health benefits that were reasonably anticipated to occur. These difficult issues were simply deferred to the incoming Bush administration.[47] Industrial interests immediately sued EPA on the grounds that the decision was arbitrary, but a federal court ruled that the suit was premature because EPA had not yet proposed a plan to reduce mercury emissions.[48]

Bush's leadership team at EPA worked with specialists from several agencies to re-examine the public health science on mercury and the available control strategies under the authority of the Clean Air Act. Industry officials argued that scarce capital expended on mercury was capital better spent on more sulfur or nitrogen controls. Environmentalists sought a 90 percent reduction in mercury emissions at each plant within five years. Bush's policy preference was to address mercury emissions through new Clear Skies legislation that coordinated industry investments in mercury control with the industry's investments in sulfur and nitrogen controls. Despite the advantages of a new legislative framework, Bush requested that EPA develop a mercury rule with OMB in the event that Congress didn't pass Clear Skies.

After extensive scientific analysis and consideration of the policy alternatives, EPA decided to reverse the determination that mercury from coal plants needed to be regulated in the same way that industrial plants are regulated.[49] Instead, EPA moved to regulate mercury through a market-based, cap-and-trade program that would potentially cover facilities in all fifty states. The authority for the plan rested on an innovative legal analysis that had been prepared by lawyers at the Office of Management and Budget during the Clinton administration.

EPA's reassessment found that mercury was emitted from utility plants in two forms: oxidized mercury and elemental mercury. The two forms of mercury behave differently in the atmosphere after they are emitted from the stack, although both are ultimately deposited into water bodies and can be transformed into the more toxic methylmercury.

When emitted from coal plants, oxidized mercury can raise localized health concerns because during periods of rainfall the mercury is deposited in nearby lakes and streams, causing contamination of fish. EPA scientists were concerned that local Indian tribes and avid recreational fishermen consume fish that are contaminated with mercury. How much of this mercury contamination was the result of utility emissions was unclear.

In contrast to oxidized mercury, elemental mercury, the pure gas, tends to be transported long distances in the atmosphere after it is emitted from the coal plant. It becomes part of the global pool of mercury, thereby contributing to the general background levels of mercury found in marine and freshwater fish throughout the world. Utility emissions in the United States are responsible for a small percentage of the global pool of mercury (considerably less than 5 percent), but the White House insisted that these emissions be reduced substantially, in part so that the U.S. would be in a credible position to urge other countries to reduce their contributions to the global mercury pool.

The Clean Air Mercury Rule (CAMR) mandated a reduction in mercury emissions from utility plants from a baseline level of 48 tons per year in 1999.[50] Fortunately, the same technologies that control sulfur and nitrogen emissions also control oxidized mercury. As a result, the controls imposed by the CAIR are projected to reduce mercury emissions from 48 tons to 38.0 tons in 2010, 34.4 tons in 2015, and 34.0 tons in 2020. However, the nonelemental forms of mercury (oxidized mercury plus small amounts of particle-bound mercury) will be reduced by more than 50 percent (from 22 tons per year to 9 tons per year) by 2015 as a "co-benefit" of the reduction in sulfur and nitrogen emissions. (Elemental mercury is more technically challenging and costly to control, since it is not captured in the stack by conventional control devices.) EPA projects that any regional health hazards caused by nonelemental mercury emissions from coal plants will be prevented by 2015, without mandating any specific investments in mercury control.

In order to reduce the contribution of U.S. utilities to the global mercury pool, CAMR created a permanent national cap on mercury emissions that would decline from a baseline of 48 tons per year to 15 tons in 2018, with an interim cap set at 38 tons in 2010, approximating the level of national mercury "co-benefits" accomplished by CAIR. The 2018 cap was projected to further reduce oxidized mercury emissions to 9 tons per year, 25 percent below the 12 tons per year projected to remain after the sulfur and nitrogen controls are implemented.

CAMR had several advantages over an alternative rule-making plan advocated by national environmental groups, a plan that would have ordered a 90 percent reduction in mercury emissions at each coal-fired power plant by 2008. First, CAMR contained a permanent national cap that ensured that national mercury emissions would not increase, even if the number of new coal-fired power plants were to grow significantly in the next twenty years. Second, CAMR avoided the disruption in the coal industry that the alternative plan might have caused, since there were no known technologies that could reduce mercury emissions by 90 percent from plants by 2008, especially at plants that burned certain kinds of coal (for instance, the subbituminous and lignite coals with significant mercury content). Finally, CAMR contained more realistic deadlines—2010 and 2018—than the 2008 target advocated by environmentalists, leaving more time for invention of innovative control technologies that might be effective at reducing multiple air pollutants, not just mercury, and might be less costly to industry and consumers.

Backlash against Mercury Rule

Despite these advantages, many national and local environmental groups were disturbed about CAMR. They argued that the emission targets were not ambitious enough, the deadlines were too lenient, and the trading provisions might permit "hot spots" of contamination to occur near some plants. Even before the rule was finalized, advocacy groups took these arguments to the public in the form of mass media campaigns and attack advertisements before the November 2004 presidential election.[51] After the election, they took these same arguments both to Congress and the federal courts, seeking to overturn the rule and replace it with a more stringent one.

Led by Democrat Patrick Leahy of Vermont, a coalition of senators introduced a resolution of disapproval of the mercury rule under the authority of the Congressional Review Act. Leahy was joined by Republican Susan Collins of Maine and fellow Vermont senator James Jeffords. A Senate floor debate and roll-call vote on the disapproval resolution occurred in September 2005. The mercury vote in the Senate was considered largely symbolic because no such action in the House was likely, and the White House could sustain a veto of any disapproval legislation that Congress might pass. Even though senators had a "free" vote, knowing the mercury rule would not be overturned by Congress, the disapproval legislation was defeated on the Senate floor 51 to 47.[52] A close look at the Senate vote reveals that the mercury issue was not a purely partisan one. In fact, the vote reflected regional interests as well as party affiliations. Nine Republican senators voted to disapprove the rule, but six Democratic senators, primarily from coal states, voted against the disapproval resolution.[53]

National environmental groups also worked tenaciously—and effectively—to overturn the mercury rule through litigation in federal courts. A federal appeals court declined an early opportunity to stay the rule, but after a long delay overturned the entire rule based on a different legal interpretation of a provision in the Clean Air Act. The appeals court did not address EPA's reanalysis of the public health science or the merits of a cap-and-trade program for mercury. Given the narrow foundation of the court's opinion, further litigation on mercury seems likely in the years ahead.

Environmental groups have also persuaded some states to set stricter plant-by-plant mercury rules instead of participating in EPA's national cap-and-trade program.[54] By the end of 2007, at least twenty-one states had enacted mercury rules that are inconsistent with EPA's cap-and-trade program. For example, New Jersey required a 90 percent reduction in mercury emissions from its ten coal plants by 2012, six years ahead of EPA's schedule.[55] Yet the states with the lion's share of coal-fired power generation in the U.S. appear to be waiting for a new national policy resolution.

Late Shift on Climate-Change Policy

Despite the opposition of the United States, a sufficient number of countries eventually ratified the Kyoto Protocol, allowing the protocol to take effect. Industrialized countries are required to reduce their overall emissions by 5 percent from 1990 levels by 2012. Developing countries are encouraged but not required to reduce their emissions of greenhouse gases. Under the Clean

Development Mechanism (CDM), which is monitored by the United Nations, industrialized countries can obtain credit for greenhouse gas emissions that are accomplished in the developing world with financial support from parties in the developed world.

The 2012 caps in the Kyoto Protocol are unlikely to be accomplished. Although some countries (including the United Kingdom) have made progress reducing their emissions under the Kyoto Protocol, many participating countries—including Canada, Japan, and much of the European Union (EU)—have not made adequate progress.[56] The EU enacted an innovative cap-and-trade program to control greenhouse gas emissions from power plants and factories, but some of this program's features allowed overall emissions to increase rather than decrease.[57] In the transport sector, the European Commission acknowledged that the EU's progress toward meeting the Kyoto goals was inadequate and therefore belatedly proposed to replace a voluntary program with a new mandatory rule.[58] As the EU's economic performance improved from 2005 to 2008, emissions grew more rapidly than expected.[59] The growing economies in eastern Europe pose especially serious problems for greenhouse gas control in the EU.[60] Meanwhile, serious questions have been raised about whether the CDM is producing meaningful emission reductions in the developing world.[61]

Worldwide, including both developing and developed countries, experts are projecting that greenhouse gas emissions may actually climb 50 percent above 1990 levels by 2030 (assuming no effective international agreement). Even Kyoto advocates recognize that the protocol needs to be modified with a new set of targets to replace the unrealistic 2012 ones.[62]

Recognizing that the international policy debate was open for new proposals, President Bush in June 2007 called on the fifteen countries with the largest greenhouse gas emissions to come together and establish a global goal for control of such emissions.[63] Once the goal was set, Bush emphasized, each country should be free to decide for itself how to reach it. For the first time in his presidency, Bush reached out to China, India, and the major European countries in an effort to stimulate constructive dialogue on the climate-change issue.[64] Bush's proposal was warmly received by the European Commission and leaders of EU member states from the UK to Germany.[65] In early 2008 Bush also directed the U.S. government to join a UN-led process to negotiate a post-2012 global climate plan that will cover developing as well as developed countries.[66]

A variety of factors may have influenced the White House calculations. The large increase in climate science research that the Bush administration funded from 2001 to 2007 produced results. Scientific advances further strengthened support for the view that human activities are spurring climate change while the adverse economic, human health, and ecological consequences of climate change became somewhat better understood.[67] A growing number of businesses and their trade associations shifted positions by recognizing the need for the United States to enact either a tax on greenhouse gas emissions or an economy-wide cap on emissions.[68] Public opinion was also changing. An international public relations campaign, assisted by former Vice President Al Gore, foundations, and organized environmental groups, raised public awareness of climate change among opinion leaders, elected officials, and the public. When the Democratic Party assumed control of Congress in January 2007 and placed climate change on the agenda of priority issues, the Bush administration was effectively forced to take another look at the White House position.

Leaders of environmental groups questioned whether Bush's new stance was meaningful. They complained that at the G8 summit in June 2007 the Bush administration blocked a proposal to cut by 50 percent (compared to 1990 levels) the volume of greenhouse gas emissions by 2050. They also accused the United States of trying to use dialogue as a device to scuttle a binding international agreement.[69] Some experts argued that the new U.S. position on climate change would not be taken seriously unless the U.S. adopted a mandatory, economy-wide, cap-and-trade program for greenhouse gas emissions.[70]

The Bush administration countered that, without vigorous participation by China and India, an economy-wide regulation in the United States would simply harm the distressed U.S. economy without making a meaningful dent in the global emissions problem. The International Energy Agency projected in 2007 that, over the next twenty-five years, the growth of China's greenhouse gas emissions would double the emissions of all Organisation for Economic Co-operation and Development (OECD) countries combined, including Europe, the United States, Japan, and South Korea.[71]

Bush proposed both carrots and sticks to persuade China and India to get serious about controlling greenhouse gas emissions. In his 2008 State of the Union address, Bush called for a global "clean technology" fund to speed deployment of new technologies in countries such as China and India. This fund would supplement a similar fund proposed by Japan. On the trade front,

Bush appealed to the World Trade Organization to pressure China and India to accept more green technologies. The proposal was supported by multinational companies such as General Electric Co., which plans to sell innovative, climate-friendly technologies throughout the world. In fact, the United States and the EU joined hands in an effort to persuade developing countries to drop tariffs and other trade barriers that discourage the diffusion of clean-energy technologies.[72]

By the last year of his second term, Bush was claiming progress toward his first-term (2002) goal of reducing the greenhouse gas intensity of the U.S. economy by 18 percent by 2012. A key shift in Bush's position in 2008 was a new focus on total greenhouse gas emissions, not simply their intensity relative to gross domestic product (GDP). The call to stop the growth of greenhouse gas emissions by 2025 (regardless of the extent of economic growth) was carefully qualified by an insistence that developing countries (including China and India) join in a similar effort.[73]

The Veto Threat

The modified Bush administration position on climate change was well timed to influence an intense controversy unfolding in the Democratic-led Congress. The April 2008 call for zero growth in emissions by 2025 was coupled with a series of principles about the "right way" and "wrong way" to confront global climate change.[74] In addition to being constructive, Bush sought to discourage Congress from acting unilaterally by passing a mandatory program to control greenhouse gases.

The Democratic leadership in Congress had a different idea. With encouragement from Majority Leader Harry Reid of Nevada, Senator Barbara Boxer of California moved a cap-and-trade plan through her Committee on Environment and Public Works with the support of John Warner, the senior Republican senator from Virginia.

The Boxer plan called for a 66 percent reduction in greenhouse gas emissions in the United States by 2050. About 500 pages of draft legislative language covered a wide range of provisions concerning which industry sectors would be covered, how emission allowances would be allocated initially, how revenues raised from industry would be allocated, and the ground rules for emissions trading within the United States and globally. Unfortunately for Boxer, the beginning of the floor debate occurred at precisely the same time that fuel prices burst over $4 per gallon for the first time and the U.S. unemployment rate recorded its largest quarterly rise in decades, from 5.0 to 5.5 percent.[75]

A brief Senate floor debate occurred on the Boxer plan in June 2008, but the bill was never subjected to a vote because it confronted insurmountable obstacles. A majority of Senate Republicans, backed by a veto threat from President Bush, pledged to filibuster the bill unless Reid and Boxer agreed to permit a series of amendments to be considered on the Senate floor. A cloture motion to limit the number of amendments failed, 48 to 36 (60 votes were required to proceed). A proper count of missing senators (John McCain and Barack Obama among them) might have brought the vote as high as 54, still 6 short.[76] In addition, ten Democratic senators from industrial states wrote Reid and Boxer on June 6, 2008, indicating that they could not support the Boxer plan "in its current form," even though some had supported the procedural motion. The letter raised eight complex concerns about the Boxer plan such as cost, the impact on competitiveness of U.S. industry, and the need for harmonization of federal and state laws covering greenhouse gas emissions. Reid and Boxer reluctantly agreed to defer further consideration of climate-change legislation until the new administration and new Congress.[77]

Bush's stance against the Kyoto Protocol on global climate change tends to dominate his image as an environmental policy maker in both the United States and abroad. European authorities are beginning to acknowledge, perhaps grudgingly, that the Kyoto targets were implausible and are unlikely to be achieved in much of the world. While Europe has been a consistent leader in the international dialogue on climate change, Bush is justly criticized for not working aggressively enough with the international community, including Russia, China, and India, on a viable alternative to Kyoto. Only late in Bush's second term did he move in this direction.[78] By then, his diminished clout as a lame-duck president, combined with the constrained time frame, created clear incentives for Democrats and leaders of other countries to await a new president and Congress.[79]

The climate saga also illustrates how a president who neglects a festering issue can lose control of policy to other actors in the political process. While

Bush's veto threat was used effectively in 2008 to obstruct congressional action on climate change, Bush was ineffective at discouraging many governors, mayors, and state legislatures from enacting a plethora of climate-change regulations. By allowing state and local politicians to fill the policy vacuum he left on climate change, Bush made it more difficult for future presidents to regain U.S. leadership on this international challenge.

Bush's clean-air record also reveals how mishandling one issue, in this case global climate change, can have adverse ramifications for the White House's ability to succeed on related issues. From the very beginning of his administration, Bush struggled to find a defensible U.S. position on global climate change. His credibility on the issue was damaged when he reversed a campaign pledge to regulate carbon dioxide emissions from electric utilities. By losing credibility on the issue, Bush made it more difficult to move his Clear Skies initiative through Congress, even though the initiative contained some good policy that was unrelated to climate change.

If Bush had simply honored his original 2000 campaign pledge, which was to enact a cap-and-trade program for carbon emissions in the electricity sector, his credibility as an environmental policy maker would have been enhanced at home and abroad. Arguably, he could have persuaded Congress to enact a modest cap on carbon emissions in the electricity sector without causing economic turmoil in the coal and manufacturing sectors. Given how critical West Virginia and Ohio were to Bush's re-election in 2004, one can certainly appreciate why the White House was adamantly opposed to enacting a costly climate plan along the lines suggested by Senator Jeffords and national environmental groups.

In part due to his questionable handling of the climate issue, Bush was not able to move Clear Skies through the Congress using a cross-partisan strategy. In the crucial Senate committee vote that killed Clear Skies, Bush lost one Republican vote without winning any Democratic votes. Had Clear Skies included carbon dioxide as the fourth covered pollutant, Clear Skies might have passed the Congress with provisions for removal of cumbersome New Source Review (NSR) permit reviews and plant-by-plant mercury regulation.

Despite this setback, Bush did not let Congress have the last word on Clear Skies. The rule makings he authorized—the NSR reform rules, the Clean Air Interstate Rule, and the Clean Air Mercury Rule—were designed to achieve much of the policy reform he hoped to accomplish through legislation. Bush's rule making to curb diesel engine exhaust also helped curb emissions that were exacerbating soot and smog in many of America's metropolitan areas. Taken together, Bush's clean-air rule makings were predicted to produce the largest advances in air quality and public health since the Clean Air Act Amendments were passed by Congress in 1990.

Weaknesses in Bush's clean-air rule makings were exposed by the federal judiciary. Much of the NSR reform agenda, the Clean Air Mercury Rule, and parts of CAIR were delayed or lost to court challenges. While the litigation will continue for years, it appears likely that Bush's rules to reduce the soot and smog caused by diesel engines and coal plants will be durable accomplishments.

9

Illegal Immigration: Punishment or Amnesty?

One of George W. Bush's fascinating failures was his bold legislative proposal to reform federal immigration law. Instead of combining a unified Republican base with a limited number of crossover Democrats, the Bush White House sought to combine widespread Democratic support for his plan with support from a limited number of Republicans in Congress.

There was some creativity in Bush's losing strategy. The supporting interest groups ranged from civil rights and Hispanic groups to large segments of business and organized labor. The White House worked effectively with Democrat Ted Kennedy and Republican John McCain in the Senate.

President Bush's proposal failed in Congress for a simple reason: He could not persuade his conservative base, including the Republican leadership of the U.S. House of Representatives and a majority of Senate conservatives, to enact a guest worker program for foreign workers.

Bush certainly tried to enlist their support by authorizing a wide range of executive actions to enhance the security of the border. Those actions included more inspections at the borders, more deportations of apprehended migrants, and more enforcement actions against businesses that employ illegal immigrants. Bush even supported 770 miles of new fencing along the U.S.-Mexico border. Despite these security measures, Bush could not persuade a majority of Republicans in Congress to support (or even tolerate) his proposal for a guest worker program.

The lesson from this chapter is simple yet powerful: A Republican president should not expect to get a bill through a polarized Congress when the bill is opposed intensely by a majority of congressional Republicans, not to mention the radio talk-show hosts, commentators, and bloggers who are capable of energizing opposition from the grassroots activists in the Republican Party.

In order to appreciate why Bush failed on immigration reform, it is essential to recognize that the split on immigration within the Republican Party did not begin with George W. Bush. In this chapter I begin by tracing the modern history of the immigration issue through the Clinton administration. I argue that Bush's sympathetic views toward immigration were developed while he was governor of Texas, were made clear during his campaign against Vice President Gore, and were reflected in his early presidential decisions to uphold pro-immigrant policies crafted by the Clinton administration.

Those views and actions may have helped Bush defeat John Kerry in 2004. They may also be a harbinger of how national Republican leaders need to address immigration in the decades ahead. But I argue that Bush was not an effective policy maker on immigration because he did not fully appreciate the sensitivity of the issue to a majority of congressional Republicans. The chapter concludes on a speculative but optimistic note because the executive actions Bush took to help secure the border may lay the groundwork for comprehensive reform legislation in the decade ahead.

Reagan-Era Immigration Reforms

The last major overhaul of federal immigration law, which passed in 1986 after five years of congressional stalemate, occurred with the support of Republican president Ronald Reagan. It was spurred by growing political pressure from southern and western states where more foreign workers were needed to support the agricultural sector of the economy. Opponents of liberalized immigration policy feared that the 1986 legislation would simply entice millions of additional migrants to enter the country, illegally or legally.

Supporters of immigration won two reforms in 1986: temporary resident status for up to 350,000 foreigners who could show that they had worked in the U.S. at least ninety days between May 1985 and May 1986 and a pathway to permanent legal status for millions of migrants who had resided continuously in the United States from 1982 to 1986. Opponents of illegal immigration secured the first penalties (largely fines) against employers for knowingly hiring undocumented aliens.[1]

A close look at the roll-call voting reveals that opposition to the 1986 reforms was concentrated among Republicans, despite the support of the Reagan White House. The vote on final passage was 230 to 188, with 105 out of 167 Republicans voting against the bill. An even closer vote occurred just prior to passage on the House floor. Conservative Republicans championed an amendment that would have rescinded the pathway to permanent legal status for resident illegal migrants. The conservatives argued that offering amnesty is a "rolling enticement" for people to come into the country.[2] The amendment was barely defeated, 199 to 192, with 124 of 164 Republicans voting to strip the alleged "amnesty" from the bill.

One of the emerging leaders of the anti-immigration movement in Congress was Jim Sensenbrenner, from suburban Milwaukee, Wisconsin. Elected to Congress in 1978 after service in the Wisconsin legislature, Sensenbrenner representing a predominantly white district where a plurality of residents are of German ancestry.[3] Twenty years later, it was Sensenbrenner who led the effort to block Republican president George W. Bush's proposal to enact reforms similar to those passed in 1986.

California's Proposition 187

The early 1990s brought a wave of public concern about immigration. A grassroots movement that began in California eventually captured a substantial segment of the national Republican Party. As we shall see, this movement had roots in economic, racial, and cultural concerns.

The 1990–1993 recession was the deepest and longest in California since the Great Depression. Two-thirds of all U.S. job losses during this period occurred in California, as the state's unemployment rate hit a peak of 9.2 percent in 1993—the second highest jobless rate in the country.[4] Although much of the economic turmoil is attributable to a contraction in the aerospace and military sectors, many other businesses moved out of California in search of more favorable tax, regulatory, and investment climates.

The recession was preceded by a period of steady growth in the number of illegal immigrants settling in California. The immigrants were predominantly Mexican and thus the public schools, medical facilities, and criminal justice facilities handled a steady increase in the number of Spanish-speaking people. Concerns among California's white majority were stimulated, particularly a concern about the need to preserve American culture and identity as many Mexican immigrants did not become proficient in English and tended to socialize only with other Hispanics.

In the 1992 presidential primary season, populist conservative Patrick Buchanan challenged incumbent Republican president George Herbert Walker Bush. Buchanan highlighted illegal immigration as a major issue. He called for a trench to be dug along the U.S.-Mexico border and for military troops to be used to deter illegal migration from Mexico. He also called for a constitutional amendment to deny U.S. citizenship to children born in the U.S. to undocumented parents. Although Buchanan lost California by a wide margin to Bush, exit polls found that Buchanan actually won a majority of primary voters who saw immigration as the key issue in California.

From 1990 to 1995 the number of Californians expressing restrictionist views on immigration grew, including a large growth in the fraction of people who held these views with intensity.[5] Public officials in California expressed frustration about their inability to control the flow of immigrants into California, since border security and immigration control are responsibilities of the federal government. Yet the state of California, already in fiscal trouble because of the deep recession, was bearing some unexpected costs in public education, health care, and criminal justice.

In 1993 the Republican governor of California, Pete Wilson—a former mayor of San Diego—was plagued with the lowest approval ratings of any governor in the state's history.[6] With Wilson's first term expiring at the end of 1994, one survey found him down 22 points to Kathleen Brown, a possible Democratic challenger and sister of former governor and presidential candidate

Jerry Brown. One of Wilson's re-election strategies was to raise the saliency of illegal immigration.

Instead of an explicit focus on racial concerns, Governor Wilson attacked illegal immigration on economic grounds. He argued that "illegals" take more money for public services than they contribute in taxes. In an August 9, 1993, letter to President Clinton, Governor Wilson urged the federal government to (1) deny citizenship to children born into the United States to undocumented parents, (2) introduce a legal residency card to stop illegals from taking jobs and welfare payments, (3) deny public education and health care to illegals, and (4) use federal trade powers under NAFTA to discourage the flow of illegal immigration from Mexico to the United States.[7]

Since the federal government was not controlling the border, Wilson insisted that it should reimburse California for the costs of educating, caring for, and incarcerating illegal migrants. Wilson authorized a litigation strategy against the federal government seeking fiscal compensation as a remedy for the growing state expenditures on illegal migrants.

At about the same time that Wilson began to highlight the immigration issue, a group of grassroots, anti-immigrant activists came together behind Proposition 187, a ballot initiative aimed at denying public benefits to illegal immigrants and public school access to undocumented students. Although Wilson was not the author of Prop. 187, he championed it in the public debate and allowed his public persona to be linked closely with its fortunes.

President Clinton joined most Democrats, including the two Democratic senators from California, Dianne Feinstein and Barbara Boxer, and Democratic gubernatorial candidate Kathleen Brown, in opposition to Proposition 187. Even some national Republican leaders, such as conservatives William Bennett and Jack Kemp, argued that the initiative was inconsistent with basic American values. The Republican candidate for governor of Texas, George W. Bush, publicly opposed Proposition 187 as he reached out to Hispanic voters in a successful 1994 campaign against incumbent Democratic governor Ann Richards.

Both Proposition 187 and Governor Pete Wilson were successful at the polls in 1994. The ballot initiative passed by a large margin (59% to 41%) while Wilson won a surprisingly decisive victory against Kathleen Brown. Strictly speaking, both Proposition 187 and Wilson's lawsuits against the federal government were ultimately losers in federal court: they were never implemented.[8]

But these judicial setbacks only inflamed the sentiments of anti-immigrant activists, spurring a broader national movement for corrective legislation. After his re-election, Wilson went to Washington in November 1995 and advocated national legislation along the lines of Prop. 187 at a conference convened by the conservative Heritage Foundation.[9] Wilson also began a campaign to succeed Bill Clinton as president of the United States.

Clinton and Immigration

Newt Gingrich's "Contract with America" did not mention the word "immigration," but when the Republicans seized a majority in Congress in November 1994, Gingrich delegated power to members with strong anti-immigrant sentiments. They included Representative Lamar Smith of Texas and Representative Elton Gallegly of California. Their efforts were buttressed by two reports from the bipartisan U.S. Commission on Immigration Reform, which was chaired by a Democrat, former Texas representative Barbara Jordan. What became known as the Jordan Commission called for a wide range of anti-immigration measures, including some more radical than those provided by Proposition 187, such as a significant decline in legal as well as illegal immigration.[10]

While Clinton and his cabinet campaigned unsuccessfully against Proposition 187, the Clinton White House understood the power behind the movement that Pete Wilson was riding and leading. In order to be positioned properly for his 1996 re-election bid, including a contest in the key state of California, Clinton moved to the right on immigration. In his January 1995 State of the Union message, he acknowledged that Americans were "rightly disturbed by the large numbers of illegal aliens entering our country."[11]

In the 1996 Personal Responsibility and Work Opportunity Reconciliation Act—the Welfare Reform Act—President Clinton agreed with congressional Republicans that even legally resident permanent immigrants should be excluded from Medicaid, Supplemental Security Income (SSI), and food stamps. The Congressional Budget Office estimated that this provision would save taxpayers $23.7 billion over six years. Clinton also signed the Illegal Immigration Reform and Responsibility Act of 1996, which accelerated the expulsion process for illegal migrants and for unsuccessful asylum applicants residing in the country.[12] Thus, much of the national legislation that Clinton supported can be traced to Proposition 187.

1996 vs. 2000 Republican Presidential Politics

A comparison of presidential campaign positions in the Republican primaries in 1996 and 2000 reveals how unstable the party's stance was on immigration. In 1996 the emphasis was anti-immigration; in 2000 it was pro-immigration.

Pete Wilson's 1996 campaign for the Republican nomination died early, despite the fact that concerns about immigration and affirmative action were at the heart of his candidacy. Part of Wilson's troubles related to personal issues (among other things, it was disclosed that he had employed an illegal migrant as a housekeeper in the 1970s), but Wilson was also perceived as sympathetic to liberal views on taxes, homosexuality, and gun control. More important, his competitors made it difficult for him to own the immigration issue.

Patrick Buchanan ran to Wilson's right, calling for a five-year moratorium on legal immigration while reinforcing his previous calls for a trench at the U.S.-Mexico border. The Buchanan rhetoric was hardly nuanced: "What we have is a lawless situation on the southern border of the United States where this country is literally being overrun by people who are violating our immigration laws and defying the American Constitution. I will stop it cold." Another hopeful, Senator Phil Gramm of Texas, opposed the Wilson and Buchanan positions on citizenship but supported a reduction in legal immigration. Front-runner Bob Dole joined all the candidates in favoring stricter border control as well as measures to make it difficult to counterfeit citizenship documents. In the campaign in California, Dole went out of his way to claim that he had backed Proposition 187 before Buchanan did. He went on to defeat Buchanan, receiving 66 percent of the vote to Buchanan's 18 percent.[13]

In contrast to 1996, the leading Republican candidates in 2000—George W. Bush and John McCain—ran on largely pro-immigration platforms. Both emphasized the need for more visas for highly skilled workers. McCain sought to restore welfare benefits for legal immigrants while Bush advocated a new guest worker program for Mexicans. Bush went out of his way to tout his opposition to California's Proposition 187, both when visiting California and in other states.[14]

Those who have followed Bush's career on immigration issues see nothing but consistency. In 1994 Bush made national headlines by vocally opposing California's Proposition 187.[15] In fact, Bush annoyed California governor Pete Wilson by traveling from Texas to California to campaign against it. As governor of Texas, George W. Bush established a good relationship with leaders of the Hispanic community. He constantly strived to strengthen ties between Mexico and the United States, recognizing that many families have members on both sides of the Rio Grande.

In his 1999–2000 campaign for the presidency, Bush repeatedly appealed to Hispanic leaders and their communities for support. He was fond of making these appeals in Spanish as well as English. Bush emphasized the experience he had acquired as governor of a border state, especially his appreciation of the benefits legal immigrants bring to America. Although he opposed illegal immigration, Bush argued that more should be done to welcome legal immigrants, including removal of needless obstacles to legal migration and family reunification.[16]

This stance on immigration was portrayed by the Bush campaign as one of the several ways in which Bush was a different kind of Republican—a "compassionate conservative." Indeed, one is hard-pressed to discern a large difference between the campaign positions of Vice President Gore and Governor Bush on the subject of immigration.

The Demographics of Illegal Immigration

As of March 2000, about 10.4 percent of the U.S. population was foreign-born. The immigrant share is by no means the highest in American history (for example, the percentage of immigrants hovered around 15 percent from 1870 to 1920). Yet the number of immigrants residing in the U.S. has tripled since 1970, from 9.6 million to 28.4 million; the percentage of immigrants in the total population doubled from 4.7 in 1970 to 10.4 in 2000. Overall, immigrants and their children were responsible for 70 percent of U.S. population growth from 1990 to 2000.[17]

The precise number of illegal immigrants residing in the United States is not known. Arizona, a state with 6 million residents and a long, largely unfenced border with Mexico, is estimated to be home to 500,000 illegal immigrants. The most frequently cited estimate is that 12 million illegal immigrants reside in this country on a sustained basis.[18] The yearly flow of new illegal immigrants is believed to have increased from 280,000 in the early 1990s to 750,000 in 2005.[19] By way of comparison, the federal government grants only 5,000 permanent visas each year for low-skilled workers.[20]

About 80–85 percent of the new immigrants from Mexico lack legal documentation. Their primary motive for coming to the United States is clear: money. The median hourly wage of Mexican-born workers in the USA was $9 per hour in 2004; the corresponding wage in Mexico was 21 pesos (about $1.86 per hour in 2004). Overall, the combined annual gross income of all U.S. workers born in Latin America, both legal and illegal, is estimated at $450 billion, of which about 93 percent is spent in the United States.[21]

Most illegal immigrants are believed to enter the United States through Mexico, but they are not necessarily Mexicans. The U.S.-Mexican border has become a conduit for illegal immigrants from all over the world. Official lists of undocumented adults held in Mexico at migrant detention centers reveal people from more than sixty countries, with a disproportionate share from the "global south"—the nations of Central and South America, Africa, and parts of Asia. Tight visa restrictions prevent these people from traveling directly to the United States, but Mexico is widely perceived as a gateway to the United States.[22]

Illegal migrants may typically enter the USA via Mexico, but they are no longer settling primarily in Texas, Arizona, California, Florida, New Jersey, and New York. Since 2000, they have become more dispersed around the country, including areas that are not accustomed to dealing with foreign-born populations. For example, from 2000 to 2005 the foreign-born population grew by 48 percent in South Carolina and 34 percent in Nebraska. As a result, the share of the foreign-born population residing in Arizona, California, Texas, New York, New Jersey, and Florida declined from 80 percent in 1990 to 60 percent in 2005.[23]

Migrants have become increasingly sophisticated about entering the United States and manipulating the U.S. judicial system. They make widespread use of counterfeit documents. The courts are often overloaded with deportation cases. The House Judiciary Committee reported that the number of petitions for judicial review of deportation orders exploded from 1,654 in 2001 to 10,681 in 2004.[24] When illegal Mexican migrants are caught, they are deported, but many non-Mexican detainees are released after being given summonses, due to a severe shortage of detention spaces. Many non-Mexican detainees (often over 90 percent) ignore their summonses and never appear on their court date. Critics of U.S. immigration law call this a "catch and release" policy.

U.S. households and businesses need illegal immigrants: They account for one in four farmworkers, one in six cleaning workers, and one in seven construction workers. Until recently, employers faced a small and declining risk of punishment for hiring illegal immigrants. In 1999 the government issued 417 notices of intent to fine employers for hiring undocumented workers. By 2004 that number had dropped to three. The number of arrests of unauthorized workers at work sites declined from 2,849 in 1999 to 445 in 2003.[25] Even when employers were caught hiring illegal aliens, the resulting penalties were typically minor.[26]

As long as U.S. businesses need and welcome illegal immigrants, efforts to migrate will persist. And the success rate is large for those who are determined. Over 90 percent of those who try to enter the U.S. make it by the fourth try. A majority make it by the second. Less than 10 percent give up after one failed attempt.[27]

Meanwhile, many state and local authorities believe that illegal migrants are a drain on public treasuries because they use public services such as education and health care while paying little or no taxes (since their wages are often "under the table").[28] There is also concern that illegal workers are stimulating crime and depressing wages and employment opportunities for U.S. citizens. As a result, there is palpable anger in some regions of the United States about how the federal government is managing immigration policy. According to Republican congressman J. D. Hayworth of Arizona, "With all due respect, this is not a political problem to be managed. This is an invasion to be stopped."[29]

Some state and local politicians have responded to the anger. The city of Hazleton, Pennsylvania, enacted an ordinance imposing heavy fines on landlords caught renting to illegal immigrants or businesses caught hiring them.[30] Although this ordinance was overturned by a federal judge, over a hundred municipalities in the United States have enacted restrictionist ordinances. In 2007 alone, 1,169 bills and resolutions related to immigration were introduced in state legislatures. Most of these bills sought to punish or restrict immigration.[31]

Pro-immigration advocates counter that much of the opposition to immigration is a "mean-spirited" impulse that is inconsistent with America's historical record of "generosity in the admission of immigrants."[32] After all, they argue, virtually all Americans have immigrants in their family tree.[33]

Immigration Reform Caucus

In May 1999 the Immigration Reform Caucus of the U.S. House of Representatives was established under the leadership of Republican Tom Tancredo of Colorado. Tancredo represented a predominantly white district in the southern suburbs of Denver that is considered relatively safe for a Republican nominee. From 1999 to 2007, Tancredo was considered the leading voice in the House on tougher border security. He publicly criticized Bush's "open door" stance toward immigration. He went so far as to advocate imposing taxes on the checks that illegal immigrants send back to their families south of the U.S.-Mexico border. He was criticized by House majority leader Tom DeLay for setting up a political action committee to fund anti-immigration challengers to incumbent Republicans in the House.[34] In 2007–2008 Tancredo made an unsuccessful run for the Republican presidential nomination.

The caucus grew rapidly under Tancredo's tenure to include almost a hundred House members, about 90 percent of whom were Republicans. The caucus emphasized border security, work verification, and enforcement of immigration laws.[35] Much to Bush's dismay, the caucus became a significant barrier to enactment of the president's immigration-reform agenda.

Language Assistance for Migrants

Bush was not reluctant to reverse Clinton administration policies, even popular ones, when he objected to them. Thus, it is instructive that his administration chose not to reverse a Clinton-era policy that intersected with the immigration issue: subsidized foreign-language assistance for immigrants who do not have good English skills. The administration's support for this Clinton-era reform foreshadowed Bush's bitter conflicts with House conservatives.

In August 2000 President Clinton issued an executive order aimed at providing language-assistance services to people living in the United States who do not speak English proficiently because the United States is not their country of birth.[36] Persons with limited English proficiency (LEP) may have difficulty reading, writing, speaking, or understanding English. According to the Census Bureau, somewhere between 10 and 20 million persons living in the United States do not speak proficient English.[37]

The LEP executive order was applied to all organizations in the United States that provide services to persons with limited English proficiency and receive federal funds. Such organizations include food stamp offices, hospitals, health clinics, police stations, motor vehicle registries, immigration offices, and polling places. The executive order requires organizations to provide language-assistance services to these people in their native tongue, which is most commonly Spanish but could be any one of twenty other foreign languages spoken by persons living in the United States (French, German, Italian, Chinese, Tagalog, Polish, Korean, Vietnamese, Portuguese, Japanese, Greek, Arabic, Hindi, Russian, Yiddish, Thai, Persian, French Creole, and Armenian).[38]

Clinton's LEP order sparked controversy. Leaders of the "English-first" movement argued that it was inappropriate for U.S. taxpayers to support language assistance when English is clearly the dominant language of the United States. More practical concerns were raised by organizations covered by the order. For example, the American Medical Association and other health groups raised concerns about the significant costs the order would impose on the delivery of health care. As Bush took office in 2001, federal agencies were in the early stages of implementing of the executive order.

The White House soon heard from a member of Congress who was deeply disturbed about the order. Ernest Istook of Oklahoma, a devout conservative from a safe Republican district encompassing Oklahoma City, expressed the view that the Clinton LEP order was ill-advised and should be repealed. Istook's district was not devoid of persons who might have limited English proficiency: The racial/ethnic distribution of his Oklahoma City constituents was 67.7 percent white, 13.6 percent black, 8.3 percent Hispanic origin, 4.4 percent Native American, 2.5 percent Asian, and the remainder belonging to two or more races.[39] But Istook's position was partly philosophical and partly practical. He had sympathy with the English-first perspective, and he also heard from the medical community that the LEP order could prove to be a nightmare at physician's offices, health clinics, and hospitals.

There are 435 members of the House of Representatives, but Istook sat on a perch that made it easy for him to get the attention of the White House. Istook was chair of the House Subcommittee on Appropriations, which possessed jurisdiction over the Executive Office of the President, including the Office of Management and Budget (OMB).

Istook became frustrated that that he did not have an ally in the White House. As governor of Texas, George W. Bush had taken an "English-plus" stance on language issues, far different from the "English-first" perspective that Istook favored. Rather than rescind the LEP executive order, as Istook requested, the White House agreed to perform a benefit-cost analysis of the order, coupled with a revised plan aimed at reducing any unnecessary costs associated with implementation.

OMB's analysis concluded that the costs of implementing the order might indeed be quite significant, particularly in the health care sector. But the benefits of language-assistance services to migrants could also be significant.[40] For example, medical errors often result from miscommunication between patients and their physicians. Patients who do not speak English as their primary language are more likely to experience adverse drug reactions and other medical complications.[41] Moreover, language-assistance services for LEP persons may decrease the rate of noncompliance with medical instructions, resulting in better therapy and improved health. The availability of trained interpreters in the health care setting causes both an increase in the use of primary and preventive care and a reduction in emergency room visits.[42]

The findings of the OMB analysis reinforced the White House's determination to retain the LEP executive order. OMB did work with the Justice Department and other federal agencies to clarify, through formal guidance, what is expected of organizations under the order and what measures could be undertaken to ensure that language assistance was provided in the most cost-effective manner.[43]

Chairman Istook was not satisfied with OMB's handling of this matter. While he chaired OMB's appropriations subcommittee, his unhappiness contributed to OMB's flat level of appropriations from the Congress. (Istook later lost his chairmanship when the House committees were reorganized by the House Republican leadership in collaboration with the Bush White House.) Nonetheless, the Bush White House's support for the limited-English proficiency executive order was only the beginning of years of conflict between Bush and anti-immigrant conservatives in Congress.

Early Skirmish on Legislation

An obscure section of federal immigration law, Section 245(i) of the Nationality and Immigration Act, allows immigrants who are eligible for residency but who have overstayed their visas to pay a $1,000 fine and complete their residency application in the United States. They must also be sponsored by an employer or family member who is a legal resident or U.S. citizen. Without 245(i), immigrants would have to return to their home countries and apply from there. Due to their illegal status in the United States, they could be barred from returning to the U.S. for up to ten years.

The 245(i) program was revived by the Clinton administration in the 1990s, but it expired on April 30, 2001, before the Immigration and Naturalization Service was able to issue a regulation to extend the program. Thus, the Bush White House was drawn into a legislative squabble about the future of 245(i), well before the administration resolved its own legislative agenda on immigration reform.

The White House began by backing a Senate measure aimed at extending the program for a year. In the House, though, only a four-month extension was under consideration. The House was scheduled to have a floor vote on this issue on September 11, 2001. Instead, the Capitol was evacuated. The vote was never taken.[44]

Later in 2001, a criminal justice spending bill was passed by the Senate with a provision providing for an indefinite extension of 245(i). It was ultimately dropped from the bill, despite White House support, when objections were raised by conservative Republican Jim Sensenbrenner of Wisconsin, leader of the House Judiciary Committee.

Another effort was made in 2002, this time as part of a "border security" bill motivated by 9/11. Despite the support of Majority Leader Tom Daschle, the 245(i) extension provision was dropped when Democrat Robert Byrd of West Virginia, chair of the Senate Appropriations Committee, raised concerns that the 245(i) program was a form of "amnesty" for illegal immigrants.[45] Thus, it was apparent that some leading Democrats as well as Republicans did not share Bush's somewhat permissive views on immigration.

Bush's Guest Worker Plan

Bush did not dispute that border security measures were needed, but he believed security measures should be coupled with a bold plan to bring the 12 million illegal immigrants out of the shadows and into lawful society. Early in his first term, Bush met with President Vicente Fox of Mexico and pledged to work on liberalization of federal immigration law. But Bush's progress was slowed by 9/11 and the heightened concerns about border security, even though data suggest that few terrorists enter the U.S. via the Mexican border.[46]

In January 2004 Bush proposed legislative principles that might lead to the Fair and Secure Immigration Reform. A key feature of the plan, though it was sketchy, was a new temporary guest worker program. The idea was to match foreign workers with American employers for those jobs that American workers were unwilling to take. Temporary workers, defined as people who are currently illegal immigrants living in the United States, would be permitted to register for legal status for a fixed period of time and then would be required to return to their home country. Bush's proposal did not create an automatic path to citizenship and, from Bush's perspective, no amnesty was authorized. To permit efficient work-site enforcement of the guest worker program, tamper-proof identification cards were to be made available to each legal temporary worker. The plan also envisioned an increase in the number of "green cards" issued to legal immigrants.

The guest worker plan was intended to respond to the huge demand for unskilled workers in the growing U.S. economy. It would also allow honest workers to provide for their families without fear of violating the law while permitting workers to travel back and forth between the U.S. and their home country. Bush also argued that this program would assist in efforts to secure U.S. borders since the increased level of legal immigration, and the corresponding growth in the number of green cards, would reduce pressure on the border.

Bush's proposal was received warmly by immigrant communities. It also had the desired effect of stimulating congressional interest in comprehensive immigration reform. Senators John McCain of Arizona and Ted Kennedy of Massachusetts accelerated work on a bill that combined enhanced border security with a guest worker program.

Bush's more conservative allies in the Senate were frustrated that the White House would not provide more specifics. In fact, Republican senators Jon Kyl of Arizona and John Cornyn of Texas were rebuffed by the White House when they requested the opportunity to sponsor the "president's bill." Momentum was lost, in part because key House members were appalled.

The Immigration Reform Caucus was outraged that a U.S. president would make such a proposal. As one anti-immigrant activist put it: "It's an amnesty, no matter how much they dance around the fact. It's legalizing illegal immigrants."[47] Conservatives were aghast that Bush would make a proposal whose practical effect would be to encourage more illegal immigration in the future.

More generally, Bush's proposal was not well received among rank-and-file House Republicans because they sensed a rising anger toward immigrants among many Americans, especially among whites in the Republican base but also among some African Americans. Many House members feared that the economic security of Americans was threatened by "aliens," even though the evidence to support this fear was inconclusive.[48] Many states and localities, responding to grassroots fears, were moving in the opposite direction from Bush and cracking down on undocumented immigrants.[49]

Conservatives Ignore Bush

In 2004, House conservatives chose to ignore Bush's proposal. Instead they exploited lingering concerns about 9/11 to advance their own legislative agenda. House Judiciary Committee chair Jim Sensenbrenner of Wisconsin led the effort to draft an intelligence bill to strengthen the Patriot Act by cracking down on illegal immigration. The bill allowed deportation of undocumented aliens without judicial review; created new federal standards governing issuance of driver's licenses, ID cards, and birth certificates; and authorized more border security and immigration enforcement agents. On behalf of these provisions, Sensenbrenner reminded the House that "the nineteen 9/11 hijackers had 63 validly issued U.S. driver's licenses."[50]

The Senate version of the intelligence bill included no language similar to the Sensenbrenner provisions. In the House-Senate conference, the Sensenbrenner provisions were dropped almost completely. To justify this action, Senate leaders pointed to the fact that none of the controversial provisions were recommended by the National Commission on Terrorist Attacks upon the United States, an independent bipartisan body charged with making recommendations to policy makers after 9/11.

Needless to say, Sensenbrenner was outraged. To address Sensenbrenner's concerns about the conference, House Speaker Denny Hastert pledged that the new Congress in 2005 would begin with a legislative initiative along the lines favored by Sensenbrenner and the Immigration Reform Caucus. That is exactly what transpired.

Bush's Re-election

Immigration reform was not a key issue in the 2004 presidential election, in part because the differences between Bush and Kerry on immigration were slight. But there is no question that Bush's stance on immigration issues was appreciated by the Latino community. Exit polls indicate that the percentage of Latinos voting for Bush rose significantly from 2000 to 2004. By way of comparison, Bush made smaller gains among whites, Asians, and African Americans.

Soon after his re-election, Bush established immigration reform as one of his top second-term domestic priorities. House conservatives saw the election differently. They were also re-elected by large margins, which they interpreted as validation of their views on immigration.

The House Version of "Immigration Reform"

In his February 2, 2005, State of the Union message, Bush emphasized the need for a guest worker program as well as stronger border security measures. Ignoring this request, Sensenbrenner revived his provisions from the previous Congress. With aggressive support from the Immigration Reform Caucus, a border security bill passed the House 261 to 161 one week after the State of the Union address. The bill was supported by 219 out of 227 House Republicans as well as 42 House Democrats.

Senator Majority Leader Bill Frist tried to resist the Sensenbrenner provisions but was not successful, in part because the White House was reluctant to oppose the House leadership. Frist decided instead to insist upon a new provision allowing more temporary workers into the United States. Frist won a higher cap on the number of seasonal workers in the United States as well as an enlarged flow of skilled workers and foreign nurses. The entire package was incorporated into a fiscal year 2005 emergency supplemental appropriations bill for Iraq, which Bush signed into law in May 2005.

In the summer of 2005, illegal immigration received national attention due to the Minuteman Project, an effort by "hundreds of armed American citizens to patrol the U.S.-Mexico border in Arizona in an effort to repel what they perceived to be an alien invasion."[51] The Democratic governors of Arizona and New Mexico declared states of emergency along the border with Mexico. Claiming that the federal government had not done enough to curb illegal immigration, the governors sought emergency federal funding.[52] After a visit to the border, Bush responded with resource commitments for more border agents and detention beds.

Table 9.1. Key Provisions of House Immigration Bill

- Employers would be required to check the Social Security numbers of alien employees against Social Security Administration and Department of Homeland Security records in order to weed out fraudulent numbers and ensure that employees are not working in the United States illegally.
- Mandatory minimum sentences would be required for individuals convicted of alien smuggling and for individuals caught re-entering the United States after they have been removed.
- The Department of Justice would be authorized to designate alien street gangs based on specified criteria. Gang members would be inadmissible and deportable. Detention of gang members would be required and humanitarian benefits would be denied to gang members.
- Refugees and asylees with aggravated felony convictions would be barred from receiving green cards.
- Local sheriffs in the 29 counties along the southern border of the United States would be reimbursed by the federal government for the costs of detaining illegal aliens prior to transfer to federal custody.
- The Department of Homeland Security's authority to detain dangerous aliens indefinitely and to remove a previously deported alien would be clarified.
- Aliens who are security threats or terrorists would be barred from becoming U.S. citizens.
- Multiple DUI offenses would become a deportable offense for aliens.

Later in 2005 Sensenbrenner defied Bush again and passed an even more ambitious "enforcement only" approach to immigration reform. This bill is summarized in table 9.1. It included virtually the entire agenda of the Immigration Reform Caucus except for Tancredo's plan to end birthright citizenship.

The bill also authorized $2.2 billion in federal spending to build five double-layer border fences covering 698 miles in Arizona and California. Enforcement authorities were to be provided new high-tech tools to combat illegal immigration: sensors, radar, satellites, and unmanned drones to enhance the efforts of patrols along the border.

The House Judiciary Committee passed the bill on a party-line vote on December 8, 2005, while also rejecting, 22 votes to 13, a guest worker amendment proposed by Democrat Howard L. Berman of California. The entire bill passed, 239 to 182, on the House floor. The House Republican leadership used agenda-control powers to forbid consideration of any amendments to create a guest worker program, whether along the lines favored by President Bush or those favored by House Democrats.

The House vote was remarkable given the potent and diverse lineup of interest groups in opposition: ethnicity-based groups, such as the National Council of La Raza; business groups, who argued the verification provisions were impractical; labor unions, who said the measure was too harsh on illegal immigrants; and religious groups, who saw the measure as overly punitive.

The House leadership countered that the bill responded to a widespread fear in the United States about the growth of undocumented aliens. Republican congressman Tom Tancredo of Colorado was proud of the bill: "For the first time, I can go out on the stump and say our party has done right on the issue of immigration. And I feel good about it."[53]

The Sensenbrenner-Tancredo bill posed a difficult dilemma for the White House. Bush could have killed the bill with a veto threat (or even a statement of opposition). But the White House decided to support the House bill, hoping that the Senate would add Bush's guest worker plan. The theory was that the White House would help shape the final bill by mediating the anticipated disagreements in a complex House-Senate conference.

Immigrant Communities Respond

The House plan to criminalize undocumented migration and construct a border fence triggered a backlash of angry sentiments in Mexico and in Latin and Asian communities throughout the United States. About 300,000 people protested in Chicago on March 10, 2006. Two weeks later another 500,000 protested in Los Angeles and hundreds of thousands more in other cities across the United States. A National Day of Action for Immigrant Justice was called on April 10, 2006, as 500,000 people protested in Dallas, Texas.

Sensenbrenner made a clumsy yet conciliatory effort in response to the protests. He proposed that his bill be amended to make illegal residency a misdemeanor punishable by a six-month prison term, rather than a felony. The House rejected the amendment, with many Democrats eager to keep the bill as bad as possible to encourage further criticism prior to the November 2006 midterm elections. Several dozen Republicans voted against the bill because they opposed the milder penalty.

Despite the demonstrations, Bush followed through on the border fence to reassure conservatives. About 267 miles of the project in California, Arizona, New Mexico, and Texas was slowed by complicated environmental laws.[54] In 2008 the Department of Homeland Security used executive waiver authority to bypass thirty laws and regulations in an ambitious effort to finish the project by the end of 2008.

Another Bush-Kennedy Collaboration?

A bipartisan coalition led by Senators John McCain and Ted Kennedy had drafted a bill along the lines of Bush's 2004 proposal but with even more permissive legalization opportunities. A more conservative bill drafted by Jon Kyl of Arizona and John Cornyn of Texas included a guest worker program but no automatic pathway to citizenship (that is, no "amnesty"). But little progress was made in the Senate in 2005.

The Sensenbrenner bill was referred to the Senate in January 2006 and stalled. An enforcement-only approach seemed to have little traction in the Senate until Majority Leader (and presidential hopeful) Bill Frist introduced a limited bill criminalizing illegal residency. Frist accelerated deliberations by threatening to bring his bill to the Senate floor unless a bipartisan comprehensive bill could achieve widespread support in the Senate.

In April 2006 President Bush endorsed a comprehensive bill drafted by Senators Chuck Hagel of Nebraska and Mel Martinez of Florida that was somewhat similar to the McCain-Kennedy bill. In May 2006 Bush went on national television for the first time to make a case for a domestic legislative proposal.[55] He supported both a guest worker plan and a pathway to citizenship but sided with House conservatives on the need for stronger border security provisions. His speech came two weeks after a boycott in Los Angeles, called "Day Without Immigrants," that drew 650,000 people. Yet Bush's speech was immediately attacked both by conservative talk-show hosts (who used the word "amnesty") and by some liberals who felt that deploying the National Guard on the border amounted to another militaristic act by the Bush White House.

Bush followed up his speech with news conferences, meetings with lawmakers, and aggressive deployment of his close advisers and cabinet officers.[56] It is difficult to isolate the effectiveness of Bush's actions in themselves, but the circumstantial evidence suggests they had an impact. A motion to limit debate taken before his intense involvement failed 60 to 39 (with all 55 Republicans voting against the motion). Minority Leader Harry Reid complained at the time that Bush was failing to deliver the necessary Republican votes. After Bush's intense involvement, a motion to limit debate passed 73 to 25, with many Senate Republicans and most Democrats allowing the debate to proceed.

On the Senate floor, a series of amendments offered by Democrats and Republicans scaled the bill back modestly. One amendment limited the number of migrants who could obtain green cards to work in the U.S. Another amendment barred illegal migrants from collecting tax refunds or filing for other tax benefits for the pre-2006 period. But the amendment that most concerned the White House was offered by Democratic senator Byron Dorgan of North Dakota. It would have inserted a "sunset" of the guest worker program after five years. This amendment was defeated by a single vote (49 to 48). One of the most effective defenders of the guest worker plan on the Senate floor was Ted Kennedy.[57]

The amended bill passed the Senate 62 to 36. Analysis of the vote count reveals that it passed with more Democratic support (39 Democrats voted for it and only 4 against) than Republican support (23 Republicans supported the bill; 32 opposed it).[58] The complex bill included many border security measures that House conservatives could support, but it also liberalized immigration law in the following ways:

- A guest worker program for 200,000 workers interested in non-agricultural jobs, each eligible for a three-year visa that could be renewed once and could lead to an application for permanent residence after four years.
- Eligibility for 1.5 million agricultural workers to seek permanent legal residence if they had worked in the U.S. prior to enactment of the bill and pledged to work three to five more years in agriculture.
- A permanent residence option for all eligible illegals.[59]

After the Senate bill passed, the Congressional Budget Office (CBO) delivered some unwelcome news. It estimated that over the next ten years, the bill would cost the federal government $47.5 billion in tax credits (earned income and child credits), Medicaid, Social Security, Medicare, and food stamps. An additional $9.8 billion would be expended by 2011 on 870 miles of border fence, detention facilities for 20,000 inmates, a new employment eligibility verification system, 100 new helicopters and 250 new powerboats, and 1,000 additional Border Patrol agents. CBO projected that the bill would add 24.4 million persons to the U.S. population by 2026.[60] The large fiscal consequences of the Senate bill only emboldened conservative opposition while complicating the House-Senate conference for Bush and Kennedy.

The Conference That Never Happened

Despite the huge chasm between the comprehensive Senate bill and the "enforcement-only" House bill, Bush urged House and Senate leaders to meet promptly and resolve their differences. The House Republican leadership balked. In June 2006 House Speaker Denny Hastert announced that House Republicans would instead hold public hearings on immigration over the summer recess, just prior to the November 2006 elections. Tancredo made it clear that these hearings were a "nail in the coffin" to Bush's plan for "amnesty."[61]

Hastert's view was that the first legislative priority was tighter border security, coupled with a crackdown on employers who hire illegal migrants. He insisted that he wanted to see a measurable drop in illegal border crossings before the House would even consider Bush's guest worker idea. Sensenbrenner indicated a willingness to consider a guest worker program but was adamantly opposed to amnesty. The House position aroused both the Hispanic community and many Americans who harbored anti-immigration sentiments just prior to the 2006 elections.[62]

In a gesture of cooperation with the House leadership, Bush and the Senate Democratic leadership allowed a bill to pass that authorized construction of 700 miles of fencing along the Mexican border plus a "virtual fence" operated with cameras and sensors. This was the only significant immigration legislation to pass in 2006, despite an enormous investment of White House energy.[63] Conservatives could not understand why Bush was prepared to invest so much political capital in an issue that was so divisive in his own party.[64]

Administrative Crackdowns

Bush was not enthusiastic about cracking down on illegal immigrants, but he realized that tougher border security policies were needed. More importantly, he took House leaders at their word, perhaps naively, thinking that tougher border security policies would soften conservative opposition to his guest worker plan.

In 2005 Bush announced that the "catch and release" policy would be replaced by expanded use of "expedited removals," without an immigration hearing. Several airplane flights per week were filled with deportees bound for their home countries of Guatemala, Brazil, El Salvador, and Honduras.

The new policy was part of Bush's Secure Border Initiative, which was aimed at keeping both terrorists and illegal immigrants out of the country. Under this policy, anyone caught within 100 miles of the border and within 14 days of entering the U.S. illegally was subject to expedited removal. Illegal immigrants were entitled to a hearing before an immigration judge if they had a credible case of subjection to persecution or torture. Human Rights First and other refugee advocates complained that these safeguards were not always honored.[65]

Construction also began on new detention centers. In the interim, there was widespread leasing of private prisons to house illegal migrants who were awaiting their deportation hearings. By the fall of 2006, the number of immigrants in detention was expected to increase from 6,700 to 27,500.[66]

Investments in border security had begun to expand after 9/11. The number of agents along the northern and southern borders of the U.S. increased from 9,500 in 2001 to 11,000 in 2006.[67] What was missing was pressure on employers to stop recruiting and hiring illegal aliens.

In April 2006 the Department of Homeland Security announced a new campaign to crack down on employers. Those suspected of violations linked to felony charges faced large financial penalties and possible seizure of assets. Only 25 criminal charges were filed against employers in 2002, but that figure was upped to 716 in 2006. Most of the 2,700 illegal immigrant workers caught during these employer actions were promptly deported.[68] In fiscal year 2007, the number of arrests at U.S. plants and factories climbed to more than 4,000, a tenfold increase over 1999.[69] The crackdown on employers continued in 2007 and 2008.[70]

By late summer 2006, preliminary signs indicated that the number of border crossings was declining. Apprehensions of illegal migrants caught crossing the border were down 25 percent in the summer of 2006 compared to the summer of 2005. Border crossing fell again in 2007 and 2008.[71] As the U.S. economy weakened in 2008, the growth of America's foreign-born population slowed to 500,000, about half the annual average from 2000 to 2007.[72]

On the Mexican side of the border, the number of immigrants in staging areas fell from 1,000 to 200 persons per day.[73] The number of released detainees plummeted from 1,055 per week in the summer of 2005 to seven in a week in early August 2006. The decline may have been partly due to the demise of the "catch and release" policy. Some specialists suggested that the stronger Mexican economy, coupled with some slowing in the U.S. economy, also played a role.[74]

Despite Bush's administrative crackdowns, the House Republican leadership refused in 2006 to join with Senate conferees in a discussion of a comprehensive immigration reform bill. Last-ditch efforts at a compromise led by Republican senator Kay Bailey Hutchison of Texas and Republican representative Mike Pence of Indiana could not find a unified position.[75]

Collaboration with Democrats?

When the Democrats captured control of the Congress in November 2006, Bush saw opportunity on immigration reform. He responded by highlighting immigration in his 2007 State of the Union address and reaching out to the congressional Democratic leadership. Bush and Kennedy had already met on January 7, 2007, to reaffirm their alliance. Both sought a bipartisan agreement on immigration reform, knowing that Hispanic groups and businesses were eager for a deal. It appeared that immigration might be one of the few issues where the Democrats in Congress and Bush could find some common ground.[76] Since some anti-immigrant conservatives were defeated in the 2006 elections, among them J. D. Hayworth of Arizona, the theory was that the dwindling number of Republicans in Congress might be more cooperative.[77]

For congressional Democrats, feelings about cooperating with the White House were quite mixed. Some Democrats were not eager to cooperate with Bush on any of his key second-term priorities, especially since they had already worked successfully to kill his Social Security initiative. An immigration victory would only revive Bush's credibility, which was declining steadily. An ineffective, weakened Bush was seen as a plus entering into the 2008 presidential election season.

Resisting the temptation to obstruct, Democratic leaders agreed with Bush on a Senate-first strategy to deliver a bill that combined more border security with a pathway to citizenship for illegal immigrants.[78] The bipartisan team crafting the bill was led by Ted Kennedy and two Senate conservatives: Jon Kyl of Arizona and Lindsey Graham of South Carolina. The addition of Kyl was notable because he had voted against the 2006 bill that passed the Senate.[79]

Kyl won some important concessions: heightened border security, stronger requirements for employers to verify the status of workers, and a shift from family connections to skills in evaluating visa applications. Kyl also won several "triggers"—conditions that would have to be met before any guest worker program could begin, such as the hiring of more border agents and implementation of an employer-verification system. Majority Leader Reid, however, was quite skeptical of the triggers.

Pro-immigrant advocates also gained some ground. Fines on illegal immigrants seeking to legalize their status were reduced to $5,000, provisions for temporary workers were liberalized (the cap was raised from 400,000 to 600,000 per year), and workers were allowed to have more than one tour of work in the United States.

When the new reform plan was released, virtually every interest group found something to complain about. The AFL-CIO objected that the guest worker program would create a permanent underclass of workers that would depress wages for all Americans. Businesses raised questions about how the verification system would work. Yet the most damaging objections came from the ideological right, which again charged that the plan provided de facto "amnesty" for millions of illegal immigrants.

Proponents of the reform plan, including Senator Dianne Feinstein of California, sought to explain that there was no amnesty because payment of a fine was a precondition to receiving legal status. Moreover, the plan required each applicant to demonstrate proficiency with the English language, regardless of how many years he or she had lived and worked in the United States.

Bush exacerbated tensions in his own party on May 29, 2007, when he attacked the "empty political rhetoric" of opponents of comprehensive reform. His speech at the Federal Law Enforcement Training Center in Georgia accused opponents of trying to scare people through use of the word "amnesty." In Bush's view, the bill did not contain amnesty for illegal aliens.[80]

Some opinion polls found that the plan engineered by Kyl and Kennedy had a majority of supporters among both Democrats and Republicans in the United States. A guest worker program was also favored in polls. Yet results from polls on immigration are highly sensitive to how questions are worded. Thus, a majority of Americans also agreed that illegal immigrants should be considered for citizenship only after consideration of legal immigrants who have played by the rules. And the American people seemed divided about whether the rapid rise in immigration is good for the country.[81]

Senator Kyl became a target for criticism and ridicule in his home state. Protesters outside his Phoenix office waved signs reading "Recall Kyl," according to the local radio station KTAR. Republican state representative Russell Pearce charged that Kyl is "at the table with La Raza and other far left groups crafting this legislation with the Ted Kennedys of the world. That's absolutely not acceptable."[82] Kyl received warm support from the Arizona business community for his efforts, but the tenaciousness of his critics was more evident than the enthusiasm of his allies.

When the Kyl-Kennedy plan was considered on the Senate floor, it was subjected to a slew of amendments.[83] A proposal to eliminate the guest worker program failed 64–31. A proposal to sunset the program again failed, 49–48, but critics ultimately won a 50 percent reduction in the number of guest workers permitted under the plan.[84]

As the number of amendments offered by conservatives proliferated, Majority Leader Harry Reid tried three times to limit debate. On the third vote (the best for the White House), the cloture motion was defeated 45 to 50—a full fifteen votes short of the sixty required.

Reid faulted Bush for failing to deliver Republican support for the bill, since thirty-eight of the fifty no votes were cast by Senate Republicans. Even Jon Kyl of Arizona voted against the cloture motion: He asked why Reid was refusing to permit votes on more amendments sought by conservatives. Reid countered that he had allowed debate on twenty-one amendments, ten of which were adopted.[85]

The White House responded to the impasse by delivering President Bush to a meeting of congressional Republican leaders.[86] Bush urged another attempt at compromise. He sought to reassure social conservatives by offering $4.4 billion in new border security initiatives and more active enforcement of immigration laws against businesses that hire undocumented workers.[87] A White House–engineered public relations campaign was also launched to promote the plan.[88]

On June 26, 2007, the Senate voted 64–35 to reconsider the immigration package. This impressive vote found 39 Democrats, 24 Republicans, and one independent voting "yes." The encouraging mood did not last long. An organized rebellion of grassroots conservatives was stepped up to counter Bush's efforts.

In 2007 the grassroots opponents of a liberalized immigration policy were far more dedicated and passionate than its proponents. In the seven weeks prior to the Senate floor debate, immigration was the second most popular topic on talk radio, trailing only the 2008 presidential campaign.[89] Organizations such as Numbers USA, Grassfire.org and Federation for American Immigration Reform were rallied by conservative bloggers and radio talk-show hosts. Grassfire.org alone gathered more than 700,000 signatures on petitions opposing the Senate bill; the signatures were delivered to the home-state senators of the signatories. Conservative Republican and Democratic senators were also bombarded by phone calls and e-mail messages protesting amnesty, the result of a coordinated, internet-based campaign.[90]

In a New Hampshire primary debate on June 5, 2007, the bill was mentioned. Former New York City mayor Rudy Giuliani described it as "a typical Washington mess" while Representative Duncan Hunter of Colorado called it a "disaster." Earlier, former Massachusetts governor Mitt Romney had attacked McCain for collaborating with Ted Kennedy on an "amnesty" bill.[91] Of the ten Republican presidential candidates, only McCain endorsed the Senate reform bill.

Recognizing the tension in the Republican Party, Majority Leader Reid worked to ensure that the Democratic Party would gain politically (or at least not be harmed). Reid went out of his way to portray the Senate bill as "Bush's plan" rather than a Democratic initiative. If it passed the Senate, Reid and the Democrats would be credited for an act of bipartisanship. If it failed, Reid was preparing to blast Bush for failing to deliver enough Republican votes and thereby to persuade more Hispanics to support the Democratic Party.

In the House, Speaker Pelosi was already setting expectations that Bush would need to deliver at least seventy Republican votes in the House to overcome conservative Democratic opposition.[92] Given the strength of the Immigration Reform Caucus in the House, Pelosi's requirement would not be easy for Bush to meet.

When Majority Leader Reid called for a vote on the final cloture motion on June 28, 2007, the motion failed 53 to 46 (33 Democrats, 12 Republicans, and 1 independent voted yes). This count was only one vote closer to the sixty required than it had been prior to Bush's personal efforts. The additional Republican vote was provided by Jon Kyl, the architect of the compromise. Eighteen of the twenty-one Republican senators seeking re-election in 2008 voted against cloture. In effect, the vast majority of Senate Republicans voted against Bush's hope for a second-term domestic policy accomplishment.[93]

Indirectly, House Republicans contributed to Bush's defeat in the Senate. Over the objections of the White House, House Republicans voted a party resolution criticizing the Senate immigration plan. The party caucus vote leaked out just prior to Reid's call for a vote to end debate in the Senate. House Republican leaders argued that they faced strong pressure from rank-and-file members who demanded a vote that would dissociate them from the Senate bill prior to the July 4 recess.[94] Some senators cited the hostile House vote to support the view that a yes vote for the Kyl-Kennedy plan was futile, since it would die in the House anyway.[95]

As soon as it was clear that the Senate bill was dead, Majority Leader Reid moved to the blame game. He suggested to reporters that the headline should be "The President Fails Again."[96] Grassroots conservatives offered a different spin. In the final week of Senate deliberations, 75 percent of all talk-show time devoted to immigration was controlled by Lou Dobbs, Rush Limbaugh, and Sean Hannity. Rush Limbaugh's website proclaimed: "We did it. Amnesty bill goes down."[97]

Will the Crackdowns Continue?

In late 2008 the Department of Homeland Security (DHS) completed 500 miles of fencing along the southwest border, 170 miles short of its legislated goal. Congress set aside $2.7 billion for the fence in 2006, but an additional $400 million was needed in 2008 due to higher costs for fuel, steel and labor.[98] An additional 100 miles of fence was scheduled to be completed by January 20, 2009.[99] Fence advocates cite data from the San Diego border suggesting that a double-layer fence cut crossings by 80 percent.[100]

Toward the end of 2008, DHS shifted priorities away from a "smart" (high-tech) fence to completion of the physical barrier, even though the Democrats in Congress favored electronic surveillance.[101] DHS also reached an agreement with the Interior Department on funding to protect public lands near the fence.[102] As the Bush administration drew to a close, completion of the fence was not a certainty as local opposition was growing in El Paso.[103]

In June 2008 President Bush issued an executive order requiring companies that deal with the federal government to use an electronic system to verify that their workers are in the country legally. Known as E-Verify, the system has already been used by some states seeking to deter illegal immigration. Using a worker's name and Social Security number, the system searches for a "nonconformation." When one is detected, the individual is barred from working until he or she can submit documents to facilitate manual verification.[104]

It is not clear that the new Congress will continue these policies. In the 2008 elections, ten of the House Republicans who lost their seats were members of the Immigration Reform Caucus. The founder of the caucus, Tom Tancredo of Colorado, retired, as did his California ally, Duncan Hunter. One study of twenty 2008 races where the candidates drew sharp distinctions on immigration found punishment-oriented candidates losing in eighteen of them.[105]

Bush's plan to modernize immigration law set in motion a fascinating battle that was quite different from any other battle Bush faced during his eight years in office. It became apparent that his views on immigration were starkly different from the views of mainstream conservatives in the South and West, where the Republican Party is strong. Bush was accused of being pro-amnesty, but he denies it. He argues it is not amnesty because he stipulated fines and English proficiency as conditions of citizenship. In any event, Bush found himself working a polarized Congress from a different direction: The political muscle behind his proposal was a coalition of liberal Democrats in the Senate such as Ted Kennedy and moderate Republicans such as John McCain of Arizona.

It is certainly true that the unexpected events of 9/11 delayed and complicated Bush's effort to enact immigration reform. Grassroots conservatives were able to use the threat of terrorism as yet another reason to oppose liberalization of federal immigration law. But the modern history of the immigration issue in the Republican Party, including the Reagan years and California's Proposition 187, suggests that Bush's stance would have been highly divisive in his party, even if the 9/11 attacks had not happened.

In a creative use of executive powers aimed at advancing his legislative initiative, Bush instructed the Department of Homeland Security to accomplish enhanced border security through expedited removals of illegal immigrants caught at the border and crackdowns on employers who hired illegal immigrants. Despite some progress at the border, and a record number of criminal prosecutions of immigrants,[106] Bush could not overcome the tenacious opposition of grassroots conservatives. He tried to launch some guest worker programs administratively but his authority was constrained.

A strong case can be made for the merits of Bush's guest worker proposal, but it is questionable whether a president should invest so much political capital in a controversial plan that is opposed—sometimes strenuously—by the majority of the members in his own party. In a polarized environment, a president who relies on the opposing party to enact a significant proposal is not likely to succeed. Even if the effort meets with some success, it will annoy the natural allies that the president needs when the going gets tough on many key votes.

A better strategy for Bush might have been to offer a more detailed, thirty-page blueprint after the 2002 midterm elections, coupled with a strong push for quick passage by early 2004. Bush knew he could mobilize business, Hispanic and religious groups, and sympathetic unions. By stretching the period of deliberation over almost three years, Bush gave opponents too much time to raise money and organize. Bush could have insisted to Hastert and Sensenbrenner that he needed the bill—and the support of the Hispanic community—to support his 2004 re-election effort.

In short, Bush's personal effort to pass immigration legislation during his second term did more to further alienate his base and undermine his credibility as a policy maker than it accomplished in liberalization. The short-term impact of Bush's executive policies was to actually increase punishment of illegal immigrants. It is possible, however, that Bush's border security policies will pave the way for modernization of federal immigration law over the next decade.

10

Tort and Regulatory Reform

In 2000 and again in 2004 Bush campaigned on the need to curb the unnecessary burdens caused by America's complex tort liability system. Bush also criticized the excessive regulatory and paperwork burdens imposed on businesses and state and local governments, and called for special consideration of the need to nurture and support small businesses.

In 2001, the best estimate was that federal regulations imposed several hundred billion dollars per year in compliance and paperwork burdens on the private sector of the U.S. economy.[1] No such estimates exist for the cumulative burden of tort suits in America, but there was a concern that the amount of innovation in the American economy was suppressed due to the financial burdens (and fear) of lawsuits.[2]

Some sectors of the economy are disproportionately impacted by regulation and lawsuits. Medical providers argue that malpractice litigation contributes to defensive medicine, unproductive paperwork, and higher costs for the delivery of health care.[3] In the manufacturing sector, both small and large businesses argue that reform of our regulatory and tort systems is necessary to enhance the ability of U.S. firms to compete in an increasingly global economy.[4]

The White House strategies for making policy in these two areas were strikingly different. Bush made many speeches about tort reform and collaborated with Republican leaders in Congress on a variety of legislative proposals. But he decided against any generic legislative proposals on regulatory reform and instead authorized executive actions by the Office of Management and Budget. It is instructive to compare the degree of success of the two approaches.

Tort Reform

To pass tort reform legislation, the White House and congressional Republicans attempted the same cross-partisan strategy that had succeeded on tax cuts, energy, and health care. But the search for cooperative Senate Democrats proved frustrating. Even some Republicans saw national tort reform as an intrusion on states' rights.

One certainly cannot blame the House of Representatives for failing to act. The House passed several tort reform bills. One restrained class-action lawsuits by moving large cases from the plaintiff-friendly state court systems to federal courts. Another capped damage awards in medical malpractice cases. And yet another increased sanctions on lawyers who file meritless lawsuits and curtailed the discretion of judges to refrain from punishing lawyers who engage in such behavior. In order for any of these bills to get to the Oval Office for signature, they needed to move through what proved to be a plaintiff-friendly forum: the United States Senate.

With heart surgeon Bill Frist as Senate majority leader in 2004, one might have thought that medical liability reform would be a promising priority. That is certainly what Frist hoped as he decided to focus Senate floor consideration on what some considered a modest proposal: caps on damage awards in medical malpractice lawsuits against obstetricians and gynecologists. In several states where litigation was particularly onerous, such as Pennsylvania, there were widely publicized reports of physicians leaving their practices due to litigation concerns, making it more difficult for women to obtain quality care.[5]

When this modest bill reached the Senate floor on February 24, 2004, opponents of tort reform flexed their muscles. The vote was 48 to 45, far short of the 60 votes required to block a filibuster. A close look at the roll-call vote reveals the sobering reality: There were more Republicans voting to support a filibuster (Senators Richard Shelby of Alabama, Mike Crapo of Idaho, and Lindsey Graham of South Carolina) than there were Democrats voting to stop a filibuster (Robert Byrd of West Virginia).[6]

Frist tried again to bypass the filibuster threat on April 7, 2004. This time the scope of the reform bill was expanded to include protection of emergency room medical personnel and trauma center staff as well as obstetricians and gynecologists. The margin in favor of limiting debate was again meager (49 to 48), with the same three Republicans voting to support a filibuster. Again, only one Democrat, this time Zell Miller of Georgia, voted for cloture.[7]

A more concerted effort at tort reform was launched by a coalition of businesses and insurance companies who faced substantial liability for asbestos-related diseases among workers. This effort was not launched by the Bush administration, but it was encouraged by the Senate Republican leadership and tolerated by the White House. The basic idea was to create a no-fault federal fund to compensate victims of asbestos exposure in exchange for relief from business and insurer liability.[8]

After several years of tough slogging in the Senate Judiciary Committee, committee chairman Orrin Hatch cleared a bipartisan bill out of the committee in 2004 with an estimated $158 billion price tag. Yet even this bill continued to spark disputes among businesses, insurers, and labor unions about such basic issues as the size of the fund and the criteria for designating beneficiaries. Meanwhile, business groups, Senate conservatives, and the White House were concerned about the overall cost of the bill. The White House frustrated proponents of the bill by failing to take a strong position until after positions on the Hill had hardened.

Frist and Hatch trimmed the bill to $118 billion before bringing it to the Senate floor. In the face of a filibuster threat from the Democratic leadership, Frist called for a vote to limit debate on April 22, 2004. A bare majority, 50–47, supported limiting debate, far short of the required 60 votes.[9] Although Republican senators were unanimous on this vote, only one Democratic Senator (Zell Miller of Georgia) defected. Given the difficulties in the Senate, the House never expended effort on the issue.

In 2006 another asbestos compensation bill was considered on the Senate floor. Republican Senator Arlen Specter of Pennsylvania, with encouragement from the White House, sought to create a $140 billion fund to compensate victims of asbestos-related diseases. The plan triggered opposition from conservatives, who feared long-term budgetary consequences, and from liberals, who thought the plan was not generous enough. The floor vote (58 to 41) was really only one short of the 60 necessary to waive a budgetary point of order since Majority Leader Frist voted against the measure only to reserve his procedural right to reconsider the matter at a later time.[10] But the 60th vote was never found. The bill died. Even if a budgetary objection had been waived, the bill remained even more vulnerable to a filibuster threat, which some conservative Republicans were prepared to support.

Bush's only legislative success on tort reform came in early 2005, after the president's re-election, Daschle's defeat, and the significant Republican gains in the Senate. The seeds of this success were planted in 2003–2004, when the House passed a bill authorizing more cases to be heard in federal courts and a similar bill had majority support in the Senate.

The rationale for reform was that trial lawyers engage in "venue shopping," filing cases in those state courts with a reputation for delivering big-dollar judgments against defendants.[11] Existing law allowed such cases to be heard in federal courts only in exceptional circumstances. On June 12, 2003, the House passed, 253 to 170, a bill authorizing more liability cases to be heard in federal courts.[12]

In the Senate, Judiciary Committee chairman Orrin Hatch collaborated with Democratic senator Herbert Kohl of Wisconsin on a bill to allow large class-action lawsuits to be handled in federal court. The covered cases needed to involve at least 100 plaintiffs and $5 million of alleged damages, and have fewer than two-thirds of the plaintiffs living in the same state as the defendant. Democratic senator Dianne Feinstein of California agreed to support the bill when two restrictive amendments she offered were accepted. The bill cleared the committee on a bipartisan vote of 12 to 7.[13]

Majority Leader Frist brought this bill to the Senate floor on October 22, 2003. When the votes were counted, Frist was one vote short of the required sixty. All Senate Republicans except Richard Shelby of Alabama and nine Democrats voted to limit debate.[14]

Frist brought the bill to the floor again later in the session, believing that there were sixty-two senators, including eleven Democrats, prepared to invoke cloture and pass the bill. But the Democratic leadership devised a new way to stop the bill. Frist reluctantly pulled the bill from floor consideration when it became apparent that the Democratic leadership was prepared to offer unrelated amendments aimed at extending unemployment insurance and raising the federal minimum wage.[15] The Senate Republicans did not want to take recorded votes on these issues.

After the November 2004 election, Senate Democrats were more cooperative on this issue. One of the first bills Bush signed into law in early 2005 was a bill allowing large class-action suits to be heard in the federal courts. The bill again passed the House and sailed through the Senate 72 to 26. All Republican senators present and nineteen Democratic senators (including Jim Jeffords) voted in favor of passage.[16]

The new cooperative attitude toward tort reform did not extend to other reforms. In August 2005 the House again passed, on a 230–194 vote, a bill limiting economic and punitive damages to $250,000 in medical malpractice cases. This vote closely followed party lines: Nine Republicans voted against it while fourteen Democrats voted in favor of it.[17] Predictably, the measure ran into partisan gridlock on the Senate floor, as there was unanimous Democratic opposition to time limits on floor debate.[18]

Recognizing the obstacles to passing tort reform legislation, the White House began to look for administrative strategies. Bush authorized his agency heads to search for more creative approaches to tort reform that did not require congressional action.

Using the executive's authority to interpret statutes, federal agencies began to assert legal authority to preempt lawsuits that were proceeding under state law.[19] In carefully worded regulatory language, federal agencies such as the National Highway Traffic Safety Administration and the Food and Drug Administration began to signal that compliance with federal regulatory requirements would be considered a viable defense against some tort suits launched under the common laws of the fifty states.[20] By the end of 2008, it was estimated that the Bush administration had written "preemption" language into fifty rules.[21] The new regulatory language was significant because judges are generally expected to defer to the president's legal interpretation of statutes passed by Congress.

It is too early to say how important these acts of administrative tort reform will be. Even careful legal interpretations are far less potent than new tort reform legislation, but the new interpretations may tip some future liability cases in the favor of defendants.[22] When all is said and done, Bush may have accomplished as much tort reform through executive action as he accomplished through legislation. But Obama and the new Congress may seek to reverse some of Bush's pro-business actions on tort reform through legislation.[23]

Regulatory Reform

In 1995, after the Republicans took control of the Congress for the first time in decades, there was a major push, led by House Speaker Newt Gingrich and Majority Leader Bob Dole, to pass comprehensive regulatory reform legislation. The basic idea was to require rigorous cost-benefit analysis in support of expensive new regulations while creating new ways for businesses and states to petition federal regulators to reconsider outmoded rules. If regulators did not take these new responsibilities seriously, the reform bills authorized affected parties to seek relief in federal court.[24]

A comprehensive regulatory reform bill, based on language in Newt Gingrich's Contract with America, passed the House in March 1995.[25] The leader of the Senate effort, Robert Dole of Kansas, found himself several votes short of the margin necessary to block a filibuster on the Senate floor, even though Republicans possessed a 54–46 majority in the Senate.[26] As a result, in July 1995 regulatory reform legislation died on the Senate floor.

Pro-regulation advocates—environmentalists, consumer advocates, and public health groups—had opposed the Dole bill tenaciously. They argued that it would tie the hands of regulators, preventing issuance of valuable lifesaving rules. They raised both ethical and practical objections to using benefit-cost analysis for food safety, health, and environmental rules.

The George W. Bush administration reconsidered the prospects of passing regulatory reform legislation in both 2001 and 2005. The business community was disorganized on this issue, still smarting from the 1995 defeat and lacking confidence that such legislation could avoid partisan gridlock. Moreover, at the start of both his first and second terms, President Bush had other legislative interests that were higher priority than regulatory reform legislation. A strategic decision was made to focus regulatory reform efforts on executive actions, placing the Office of Management and Budget (OMB) in the lead.

Anticipating Bush's strategy, pro-regulation groups worked to kill my nomination to the post of administrator, Office of Information and Regulatory Affairs (OIRA) in OMB.[27] They attacked my academic writings, my speeches, my corporate funding sources, and my support of benefit-cost analysis in regulatory policy. As my academic colleagues defended my personal integrity, the White House launched a cross-partisan strategy to secure the nomination. After several months of delay, I was confirmed in July 2001 on a 61–37 vote. No Republicans defected (though two were absent from the vote for unrelated reasons) while fourteen Democrats (including Jeffords) crossed party lines to support Bush's OIRA nominee.

My challenge was to bring discipline to the review of new regulations while stimulating federal agencies to modernize or streamline the sea of existing rules. Reform in this area had to be executed with care because some federal regulations were necessary to accomplish well-accepted public objectives such as health, safety, environmental protection, and homeland security.

Slowing the Growth of the Regulatory State

Using a "smart regulation" approach, OMB took steps to restrain the flow of expensive new regulations.[28] OMB's actions were based on President Clinton's 1993 executive order on regulatory planning coupled with creative use of OMB's existing statutory authority. No moratorium on new regulations was imposed, since OMB approved new rules, even expensive ones, if the agency's benefit-cost analysis was compelling.

First, regulators were informed by OMB that valid benefit-cost analyses would be required in support of any expensive new rule. Even if the agency's underlying statute prohibited cost-benefit considerations, OMB compelled agencies to publish a benefit-cost analysis, thus providing the public and Congress access to data about the projected economic impact of the rule.[29] During the first year of Bush's presidency, OMB demonstrated that it was prepared to use its executive-order authority to "return" rules to agencies when OMB judged the analyses to be of inadequate quality: It publicly returned about two dozen rules to agencies for reconsideration, more than the total number of rules returned in the eight years of the Clinton administration.[30] As a result of this early demonstration of clout, OMB rarely needed to exercise its return authority in subsequent years. The regulators were instead willing to fix the rules based on suggestions from OMB, or persuade OMB that the problems were not significant enough to justify return of the rule for reconsideration.

The criteria for sound benefit-cost analysis were defined by OMB in the obscure but important Circular A-4, a new formal guidance document that was developed through an open process, including comments from stakeholders, academic experts, and analysts within the regulatory agencies. For rules with large economic impacts, the circular imposed increasingly stringent analytic requirements on regulators.[31]

Pro-regulation groups opposed the issuance of A-4 because they feared it was too burdensome on the agencies. They also raised ethical objections to cost-benefit analysis.

Second, in order to combat the "garbage in, garbage out" syndrome in regulatory analysis, OMB developed new government-wide standards for information quality.[32] These standards were designed to enhance the technical quality of the data and models used in benefit-cost analysis. Before regulatory agencies were permitted to disseminate key data and models, they were required to have such information peer-reviewed by specialists outside the federal government.[33] Once scientific information was disseminated, agencies were also required to provide the public an opportunity to seek prompt correction of misleading or erroneous technical information.[34]

The revitalized OMB review process was not the only factor suppressing the proliferation of expensive new regulations. In making appointments to regulatory agencies, President Bush looked for candidates who understood the need to approach federal regulation from a benefit-cost perspective. Moreover, the Republican leaders of the House and Senate were generally disinclined to pass expensive new regulatory legislation without compelling justification.

As a result of these new restraints on the regulatory state, the growth rate of costly new rules declined rapidly under the Bush administration, especially rules that imposed costs on the private sector or state and local governments (so-called "unfunded mandates"). Between 1981 (when OMB's regulatory review office was created) and 2005, federal regulators imposed an additional $140 billion in costly "major" rules (that is, unfunded mandates). The growth rate of new regulatory costs was not uniform throughout this twenty-five-year period. In fact, the annual rate of growth in regulatory costs was reduced 70 percent in 2001–2006 compared to previous Democratic and Republican administrations.[35]

Costly new rules were not always avoided. The Bush administration continued to permit, and indeed encourage, development of new rules with strong benefit-cost rationales. This was sometimes accomplished in the form of a "prompt letter" from the White House budget office to the appropriate federal regulatory agency. For example, the Food and Drug Administration was encouraged to require that foods be labeled for their "trans fat" content in order to promote "heart-healthy" diets. The Environmental Protection Agency (EPA) required that the amount of diesel exhaust from off-road engines be cut by 90 percent through use of low-sulfur diesel fuel and cleaner engine technology (see chapter 7). And when the Congress failed to pass Bush's Clear Skies initiative, Bush authorized EPA to issue the Clean Air Interstate Rule, which contained cuts in air pollution from coal plants by 70 percent through a new "cap-and-trade" program. Although these rules were expensive for businesses, OMB shared the view of regulators that the public health benefits of the rules would be greater than the costs to industry and consumers. As a result of a handful of highly beneficial new rules, the overall net benefits from major rules were projected to be greater during 2001–2006 than during the 1990s.[36]

Modernizing the Sea of Existing Regulations

Since OMB began to keep records in 1981, federal regulatory agencies have adopted 114,000 new regulations. About 20,000 of them were significant enough to require OMB review. About 1,100 of these were estimated, when they were adopted, to have at least a $100 million impact on the American economy. For the vast majority of these rules, no effort was ever made to determine whether the rules accomplished their objectives or what the actual benefits and costs of the rules were.

An immediate effort to review the vast number of existing rules would require far more analytic resources than regulators and OMB possessed. Consequently, OMB launched an annual, open process whereby the public could nominate specific rules and paperwork requirements that needed to be reconsidered or reformed. In 2001, 2002, and again in 2004, OMB solicited nominations of such rules and requirements. OMB then worked with regulators to ensure that these reform nominations were evaluated on the basis of benefit-cost criteria, with public decisions made as to which of the reform ideas would be pursued.

Pro-regulation advocates objected to this initiative because they perceived it to be biased in favor of business. They also argued that regulators should be free to set their own priorities.

In 2001, 23 of 71 nominated rules and requirements were targeted for agency action. In 2002, over 100 of 316 nominations were targeted for agency action. In 2004, when OMB focused on reform of the manufacturing sector of the U.S. economy, 76 of 189 nominations were targeted for agency action. Agency progress on these regulatory reforms was reported annually in OMB's *Report to Congress on the Costs and Benefits of Federal Regulation.*[37] Although the number of existing rules subject to reconsideration was limited, this was the first serious effort at regulatory modernization since the early days of President Reagan's first term.

Agencies and their pro-regulation advocates resisted modifications to many of these rules, and dragged OMB out through extensive and repeated meetings. Some rules were modernized, but nothing happened on the majority of public nominations.

U.S.-EU Regulatory Cooperation

In addition to overseeing U.S. regulators, OMB launched a multi-year dialogue with regulatory officials from the European Commission in Brussels. The aim was to rationalize regulatory procedures and policies on both sides of the Atlantic. The OMB initiative began informally in 2002 and was accelerated and formalized when European Commission president Jose Barrosso took office in 2004.

Part of the motivation was to prevent another mess similar to the regulatory dispute over genetically modified seeds. The United States, Canada, and Australia persuaded most of the world that the seeds were safe for widespread use. The European Union (EU) blocked their registrations in member countries on various grounds ranging from assertions of danger to concerns about how the quality of farm life might be hurt. The U.S. ultimately won a multi-year case against the EU in the World Trade Organization (WTO), but the remedy was ineffective. OMB sought to prevent future WTO cases.

The annual United States–European Union summit began to set milestones on regulatory cooperation. Although it is too early to assess the long-term impact of this effort, U.S. and EU officials found some common ground: Prosperity and jobs could be enhanced if firms doing business on both sides of the Atlantic could expect harmonized regulatory systems and procedures for assuring regulators that firms were in compliance.

Specific Achievements and Setbacks

In the effort to curb the increase in costly rules and to streamline existing ones, the Bush administration can point to achievements as well as setbacks. I begin by considering Bush's supportive role in a congressional action to reverse a controversial ergonomics rule. I then consider how the Bush administration revised rules governing overtime pay and the finances of labor unions. I conclude with two setbacks, cases where the Bush administration ultimately worked with Congress to create vast new regulatory programs.

Reversal of the Ergonomics Rule

Toward the end of the Clinton administration, the Occupational Safety and Health Administration (OSHA) completed a large rule making about ergonomics. The rule imposed three major new requirements on employers: to educate workers about how to prevent repetitive motion injuries; to reconfigure the workplace if a worker reports an ergonomic injury; and to provide compensation for injured workers, at a level up to 90 percent of the worker's salary, if such injuries last longer than seven days and up to ninety days. The rule was estimated to cost businesses $8 billion per year, but OSHA, over OMB objections, insisted that the benefits of the rule might be larger. With encouragement from organized labor, the Clinton White House chose to issue the rule.

When Bush took office in 2001, the new OSHA rule was scheduled to take effect January 16, with enforcement scheduled to begin on October 14. Republican leaders in the House and Senate, with encouragement from the White House, decided to seek reversal of the ergonomics rule under a little-used law called the Congressional Review Act (CRA).

The CRA allows lawmakers to overturn a newly adopted regulation through a simple majority vote of both houses of Congress. It was passed by Congress in 1996 as part of the Gingrich-era reforms but had never been used by the Congress. Since the president retains the power to veto a CRA disapproval resolution, a two-thirds majority in both the House and Senate is necessary to overturn a veto by a determined president. Thus, the CRA was not of much use to congressional Republicans while Clinton was president.

Spearheaded by Senator Don Nickles of Oklahoma, Republicans in the Senate worked with the business community and the White House to win a critical floor vote, 56 to 44, at the start of Bush's first term in office. In a rare display of unity, all fifty Republican senators voted to overturn the ergonomics resolution. They were joined by six moderate Democrats: Baucus of Montana, Breaux and Landrieu of Louisiana, Hollings of South Carolina, Lincoln of Arkansas, and Miller of Georgia.[38] Even if none of the Democrats had voted to disapprove the rule, Vice President Cheney could have cast the tie-breaking vote in favor of disapproval. In the House, the resolution of disapproval passed 223 to 206. Only 13 of 219 Republicans and 16 of 208 Democrats defied their party leadership on this vote.[39]

These floor votes effectively terminated federal ergonomics regulation for the foreseeable future because the Congressional Review Act prohibits the executive branch from reissuing the rejected rule "in substantially the same form." Consequently, OSHA decided to address ergonomic injuries through a series of voluntary guidelines that were tailored to the conditions in specific occupations and industry sectors. The demise of OSHA's ergonomics rule was arguably more a win for the Republican Congress than it was for the Bush White House. It is certainly a rare case where congressional Republicans and the Bush White House won a legislative issue through a purely partisan strategy.

Modernization of Overtime Rules

In 2001 Bush also authorized the Department of Labor to undertake a rule making to modernize our nation's overtime regulations.[40] This is a case where Bush used his executive powers to achieve an important policy reform, despite tenacious labor opposition that generated opposition from both parties in both houses of Congress.

The Fair Labor Standards Act generally requires that covered employers pay employees at least the federal minimum wage for all hours worked, and overtime premium pay of "time-and-a-half" (1.5 times the rate of regular pay) for all hours worked over 40 in a single workweek. Exemptions are provided for executive, administrative, professional, and certain sales and computer employees. The "white collar" exemptions had not been updated in decades.

Under the Fair Labor Standards Act, employees cannot be classified as exempt from the minimum wage and overtime requirements unless they are guaranteed a minimum weekly salary and perform certain job duties. The minimum salary level, only $155 per week ($8,060 per year), had not been updated since 1975.

The new rule guaranteed overtime protection for all workers earning less than $455 per week ($23,660 per year). For comparison, a minimum-wage employee currently earns about $10,700 per year. Due to the increased salary level, overtime protection was upgraded for more than 6.7 million salaried workers who earn between $155 and $455 per week. There were also adjustments made to the rules to clarify who is an "executive" and which jobs are "administrative" or "professional." These clarifications were aimed at reducing confusion among employers and employees and curbing litigation costs for employers due to the ambiguity about the terms.

Some employees who currently qualified for overtime were expected to lose overtime pay. For example, under the "highly compensated" test, about 107,000 employees who earn over $100,000 per year would lose overtime protection. Labor union leaders feared that a much larger number of workers, running into the millions, would lose overtime eligibility if their jobs were reclassified as professional or leadership positions.

In response to the concerns of organized labor, the scope of modernization was limited to ensure that existing overtime pay was protected. The new exemptions did not apply to manual laborers or other "blue collar" workers who perform work involving repetitive operations with their hands. Moreover, the modernized exemptions did not apply to police officers, firefighters, paramedics, and emergency medical technicians.

Overall, the final rule was estimated to cost employers up to $375 million in yearly payroll costs and $739 million in one-time implementation costs. Clarifications and diminished litigation were projected to save employers about $252 million per year. The modernization was supported by the business community because it offered a more predictable system that could lead to unambiguous resolution of disputes.[41]

Organized labor worked tenaciously against the modernization of overtime rules. Rather than use a disapproval resolution under the Congressional Review Act, which could be vetoed by President Bush, the unions sought riders on bills that would prevent the Department of Labor from implementing the rule. If a rider could be attached to a bill that Bush wanted, the theory was that Bush would be reluctant to veto the entire bill.

The opposition mobilized in 2003 as the new overtime rules were scheduled to take effect in August 2003. An omnibus budget bill moving through the Congress was an inviting target. Democratic senator Tom Harkin won a 54–44 vote on the Senate floor for a rider that blocked the new overtime rules.[42] In October 2003 the House adopted a nonbinding resolution supporting Harkin's amendment by a vote of 221 to 203.[43] When Republican senators Arlen Specter and Ted Stevens sought to include the Harkin rider in the omnibus budget bill crafted by House and Senate conferees, the White House responded with a veto threat. At Bush's insistence, the rider was dropped.

The story in 2004 was similar. In the Senate, Harkin targeted a corporate tax reform bill with a rider that would have prevented any worker from losing overtime eligibility under the modernized rules. The Senate has few germaneness rules, and thus Harkin was entitled to offer his labor policy amendment to a bill dealing with corporate tax reform.

The Senate voted 52 to 47 in favor of Harkin's amendment. The 52 yes votes included all Democratic senators (except Miller of Georgia) plus five Republican senators (Campbell of Colorado, Chafee of Rhode Island, Murkowski of Alaska, Specter of Pennsylvania, and Snowe of Maine).[44]

In the House, the Democrats took a more straightforward strategy: A rider was added to the 2005 appropriations bill for the Department of Labor. Championed by David Obey of Wisconsin, it passed the House 223 to 193. In an impressive show of unity, all 200 Democratic members voted in favor of the rider, joined by 22 Republicans and an independent.[45]

Since both the House and Senate voted for a similar rider, the conventional wisdom was that organized labor would prevail. But Bush responded with a threat to veto the entire bill if the Harkin rider was not stricken. The House-Senate conferees, recognizing that the votes did not exist to override a veto, struck the Harkin rider, and the modernized overtime rules went into effect.

The saga of the overtime regulation reveals how difficult it is for a polarized Congress to block an executive action by a determined president. As long as the president is prepared to veto contrary legislation, it will be extremely difficult for Congress to overturn his executive action. With some confidence that its regulatory reforms would not be overturned by Congress, the Bush administration also began to modernize financial-reporting rules for labor unions.

Financial Disclosures by Labor Unions

Like corporations, labor unions are regulated to deter fraud and abuse by their leaders. Detecting improprieties requires that the public, including rank-and-file union members, have access to information about a union's finances. Democratic presidents may be reluctant to regulate in this arena because labor unions are a powerful constituency of the Democratic Party. If stronger laws aimed at disclosing union finances are to be adopted, they may need to be engineered by a Republican president.

Early in his first term, Bush authorized the Department of Labor to undertake a rule making to expand the annual financial reports that labor unions make available to the government and the public. The more detailed, electronic disclosures were designed to be more useful to union members and to more effectively deter fraud while making it easier to discover fraud when it occurs.

Each labor organization with annual receipts above $250,000 was already required to file an LM-2, a standardized financial disclosure form. All receipts and disbursements of $5,000 or more were to be itemized on the form in specified categories. Investments with a book value above $5,000 and beyond 5 percent of the union's total investments were to be reported on the LM-2. Information on large trusts were also required on a separate form.

The new rule modernized the requirements established by the Labor-Management and Disclosure Reporting Act of 1959.[46] The rule implemented the law's purpose of requiring unions to inform their members on a yearly basis about the financial condition and operations of the union.

The revised reporting regime had the effect of bringing financial reporting by labor unions closer to the reporting already required of publicly owned companies. Financial transparency encourages union leaders and corporate directors, who are elected by union members and corporate shareholders, to conduct the business of their organizations in the best interests of the people who provide the operating funds. The rule tightens financial reporting requirements on labor unions, but it does not provide the same depth or breadth in financial reporting that is required of large and small public companies. In fact, corporate disclosure requirements are becoming even more detailed as a result of the recent legislation and related rules issued by the Securities Exchange Commission (SEC) in the wake of the Enron scandal (see chapter 11).

What was required of labor unions in financial accounting does not even approach what is now required of publicly owned companies. Labor unions must file only once a year while public companies file both annual and quarterly reports. Unions need not disclose any qualitative information while the corporate law compels companies to disclose any "material" qualitative data (such as detailed explanations of internal controls and procedures as well as information on material legal proceedings and property holdings that may affect the company's future well-being). Unions are not required to conduct certified audits of their financial statements, but public companies must certify audits of the accuracy of the information in their annual and quarterly reports. The enforcement environments are also quite different. The SEC performs reviews on public companies not less than once every three years, whereas labor unions can expect to be audited by the Department of Labor approximately once every 150 years.

Organized labor nevertheless went to Congress and the courts, seeking to make the case that the Bush administration behaved in a punitive manner toward labor unions, presumably for political reasons. In response, the Department of Labor limited LM-2 reporting requirements to information related to the financial integrity of union behavior. Several of the paperwork and record-keeping requirements in the proposed rule were lightened to reduce the burden of compliance on unions. Ultimately, it is instructive that no vote was taken in the House or Senate to block implementation of the rule. When organized labor sued the Department of Labor in federal court, seeking reconsideration of the rule, the court upheld the key provisions of the rule except for an overly ambitious effective date.[47]

Homeland Security

Bush campaigned in 2000 on a platform aimed at relieving states and businesses of unnecessary regulatory burdens. By the end of 2001, however, Bush was issuing far-reaching new regulations spawned by the unexpected events of September 11, 2001.

In the first year after 9/11, federal agencies issued fifty-eight significant new regulations aimed at preventing future attacks or providing relief to those harmed directly or indirectly by the events of 9/11.[48] The counterterrorism rules were often costly and intrusive. They entailed monitoring of communications between inmates and their attorneys, tighter security at America's borders, new airline security policies, meticulous monitoring of suspicious transactions in the banking sector, and closer scrutiny of foreigners seeking to enroll at U.S. educational institutions. The compensation rules provided money to any individual killed or physically injured as a result of terrorist-related airplane crashes on 9/11, financial assistance to airlines and travel agents who experienced abrupt declines in business, and assistance to New York City and the surrounding communities.

Although these rules were typically reviewed through OMB's process, the political demand for the rules was so great that they were often promulgated with less scrutiny than is typical of new federal regulations. By 2004, roughly half of the cost of new federal regulations in the United States was attributable to new homeland security rules. The benefits of these rules cannot be fully quantified because it is difficult to assess the probability of future terrorist attacks, the likely damage from such attacks, and the effectiveness of new rules in reducing either the probability or the severity of future attacks.[49] OMB did work with the new Department of Homeland Security to establish more systematic procedures for developing and analyzing new regulations.

Corporate Fraud Regulations

Another wave of new federal regulations during the Bush administration was aimed at restoring public confidence in corporate accounting and the stock market. They were an outgrowth of the accounting scandals at Enron, World-Com, and Xerox. Bush began by arguing that new legislation might not be necessary but he ultimately supported the Sarbanes-Oxley Act.

The year 2001 was not just about 9/11. It also brought into public view the Enron fiasco. Just months before Enron declared bankruptcy, it was widely regarded as one of the most innovative and successful companies in the world. The leader of the company, Kenneth Lay, had roots in Texas and had developed associations with numerous politicians in Washington, D.C., including President Bush and former president George H. W. Bush.[50] But Enron's apparent financial success was shown to be largely the result of questionable accounting schemes that moved massive amounts of debt off Enron's books into a series of obscure special partnerships. The shady bookkeeping was sanctioned by one of the country's most respected accounting firms, Arthur Andersen LLP, which was performing millions of dollars' worth of consulting work for Enron each year. The Enron fiasco created widespread fears on Wall Street and launched a potent public demand for punishment of fraud and new steps to prevent future Enrons.[51]

The Securities and Exchange Commission (SEC), an independent regulatory agency outside the purview of presidential oversight and OMB review, called for creation of a new private-sector body to bring more discipline to the auditing profession. SEC also issued new rules to increase corporate disclosures about the financial health of companies. But SEC's actions were not sufficient to address public and congressional concerns.

In March 2002 President Bush sought to shape an emerging debate in Congress by releasing ten recommendations.[52] Bush's plan relied substantially on stronger SEC enforcement of existing law, but it also contained two points that would soon find their way into legislation: CEOs should personally vouch for the accuracy of their financial statements, and an independent regulatory body should be created to ensure that accounting practices satisfy basic ethical standards.

In the Congress, key Democrats were advocating a much stronger federal regulatory response while many Republicans were arguing that better enforcement of existing laws would address most of the problem. Federal Reserve Board chairman Alan Greenspan entered the debate with the argument that market mechanisms were already responding to the Enron fiasco and addressing many of the problems that had been uncovered. But the Congress was convinced that new regulatory legislation was urgently needed.

Bush initially backed a legislative proposal engineered by Republican Michael Oxley of Ohio and passed by the Republican-controlled House.[53] But the Senate, led by Democrat Paul Sarbanes of Maryland, began to move a more aggressive bill, despite vigorous opposition from the accounting industry. With the 2002 midterm elections fast approaching and Republicans unlikely to benefit from controversy about corporate fraud, Senate Republicans worked out a compromise with Sarbanes that brought an aggressive regulatory bill out of the Senate on a unanimous bipartisan vote.

In July 2002 Bush went to Wall Street and called for a doubling of prison sentences for mail and wire fraud and a tightening of existing law on the shredding of documents. Bush also used his executive powers to accelerate investigation and punishment of perpetrators of corporate fraud.[54]

The House responded quickly by passing another bill with the authority that Bush requested. The House-Senate conference produced a bill tilted toward the Sarbanes approach, because time was on the side of the Democrats and new revelations about fraud at WorldCom and Xerox were motivating Republicans to find a deal. Bush signed the landmark Sarbanes-Oxley legislation in late July of 2002.[55]

The Sarbanes-Oxley law is one of the most complex pieces of regulatory legislation passed by the Congress in the last generation.[56] It creates a new independent board to police the accounting industry, the Public Company Accounting Oversight Board, under the purview of the SEC. It has highly prescriptive provisions designed to ensure auditor independence and objectivity. CEOs and CFOs are required to certify the accuracy of corporate financial statements, and publicly owned companies are required to institute a variety of internal controls designed to ensure the company's financial integrity. Stronger penalties against corporate fraud are authorized as well as additional funding for SEC implementation and enforcement of the law.

If the success of Sarbanes-Oxley is measured by the impressive performance of the stock market in the several years after July 2002, one is tempted to conclude that Sarbanes-Oxley did buttress investor confidence in our economy.[57] But many questions remain about whether the specific provisions of the law, and the SEC implementing regulations, are overly prescriptive, costly, and potentially damaging to foreign investment in the U.S. economy.

"Midnight" Regulations

In the last few months of a presidential administration, it is typical for regulators to issue a flood of new rules that have been under development for years. Not all of these rules are well analyzed or properly vetted with stakeholders. To discourage hasty rules, OMB issued on May 9, 2008, a memorandum setting November 1, 2008, as a deadline for the federal government to take final action on new regulations (barring "extraordinary circumstances").

Despite OMB's effort, media reports indicated that a variety of final rules were issued after the November 1 deadline. Those rules generally advanced long-standing Bush administration priorities such as opening some federal lands for oil shale development, allowing truckers to drive for longer periods, and streamlining family and medical leave rules covering businesses.[58] Whether the Obama administration will invest political capital in reversing these actions is unclear.

The contrast between Bush's track records on tort reform and regulatory reform illustrates the potential effectiveness of executive powers when the president faces a polarized Congress. Bush's rhetoric on tort reform was lofty but the amount of legislative accomplishment was minimal. In contrast, Bush made no formal legislative proposal on regulatory reform and instead worked within the existing authority provided by Congress and an executive order penned by President Clinton.

Bush's progress in reducing the growth in regulatory costs was substantial (a 70 percent decline relative to the administrations of the first President Bush and President Clinton). During the same period, the total benefits of regulation to consumers and the public were increased. Overall, Bush issued fewer costly rules than President Clinton or the first President Bush, but those rules that were issued had more impressive benefits than those issued by his two predecessors.

Reform of regulatory policies was a priority for George W. Bush even though he confronted the classic tension between the interests of organized labor and those of business, and the alignment of these two powerful interests with the two political parties. In the reversal of President Clinton's ergonomics regulation, the Republicans bypassed the Senate filibuster threat by using majority-vote authority in the 1996 Congressional Review Act. Republicans in the Senate and House demonstrated remarkable unity in this vote. With the benefit of hindsight, it appears that they might have won this reversal without any Democratic crossovers.

The modernization of overtime pay was an administrative initiative that encountered determined opposition from organized labor. Since the Bush administration possessed the power to initiate rule making, labor was forced into a reactive strategy. The White House lost significant majority votes in both the House and Senate, as the Democrats in Congress proved to be more unified on this issue than the Republicans. Organized labor, though ultimately unsuccessful in blocking the rule making, did win some compromises in how the final rule was crafted. The final rule was ultimately protected against opposition in Congress by Bush's threat to veto legislation that would override it. Since organized labor had no hope of winning a two-thirds override vote in an evenly divided, polarized Congress, the overtime reform survived substantial bipartisan opposition.

The revised financial disclosure rules again saw a Bush initiative supported by business groups but attacked by organized labor. Rather than pursue congressional reversal, labor chose a litigation strategy that might delay, reverse, or lead to modification of the rule. When the issues were thoroughly vetted in court, the federal judiciary found no substantive problems with the rule except for the ambitiousness of the effective date.

The major setbacks in Bush's regulatory reform record arose from the public emotions surrounding 9/11, the Enron fiasco, and the 2008 financial meltdown. The Bush White House was partly responsible for a vast increase in federal regulatory activity concerning homeland security, corporate fraud, and financial deals. While the goals of the rules are laudable, it will take many years to determine whether these rules have sufficient benefits to justify their rather significant costs.

11

Meltdown and Bailouts

The last year of a president's second term is supposed to be a dud because Congress has no incentive to negotiate or cooperate with a lame duck. Bush's persistently low public approval ratings in his second term (they sagged below 30 percent in many polls) certainly removed any fear of him among Democrats. Indeed, Bush became so unpopular that neither Democrats nor moderate Republicans—at least those up for re-election in 2008—were eager to publicly collaborate with him.

Interestingly, the disturbing economic developments of 2008 forced a degree of bipartisan collaboration in Washington that was unprecedented during Bush's eight years in office. As a result, the housing and financial legislation of 2008 may have more long-term impact on the United States than even the flurry of bipartisan legislation that was passed in the months after 9/11, including the Patriot Act and the creation of the Department of Homeland Security. As we shall see, Bush's final year was one of activist legislation that underscores the perception that he was a "big government" conservative, even though he may have been a reluctant collaborator in some of the 2008 "bailouts."

Housing Bust

The United States experienced a housing boom from the late 1990s until 2006. Real home prices in the USA climbed an average of 85 percent.[1] They more than doubled in cities as diverse as Providence, Naples, Minneapolis, Tucson, Salt Lake City, and Sacramento.[2] During the same period, U.S. homeownership rates rose in all regions of the country, all age groups, all racial groups, and all income groups. The overall 11 percent rise in U.S. homeownership, from 65.7 percent to 68.9 percent, conceals even larger gains in the West, among people under the age of thirty-five, among Hispanics and blacks, and among those with below-median incomes.[3] National records were shattered for housing construction, remodeling jobs, housing-related employment, and housing prices.[4] In what should have been a warning sign, housing prices shot up far faster than household incomes or rents. The price boom was certainly not explainable by a rapid rise in the cost of building homes.[5]

The first signs of a "correction" appeared in the spring of 2005 in Boston and San Diego.[6] After several years of rising home prices and rising interest rates, even outsized mortgages were not large enough to make homes affordable. Bidding wars among home buyers vanished, many sellers could not get their listing prices, and the number of unsold properties on the market mounted.[7]

Lenders countered by pushing more adjustable-rate mortgages with interest rates that started near zero ("teasers") but quickly grew thereafter.[8] This practice grew nationally and stimulated a large number of refinancings. Refinancings jumped from $14 billion in 1995 to nearly $250 billion in 2005.[9] Borrowers were able to shift their cash into new car purchases and other forms of spending.[10]

The early signs of a bust were dismissed because localized or regional housing busts are not uncommon in the history of the U.S. housing market. What never happens is a decline in the national average value of homes. As of 2006 the consensus among housing forecasters was that average housing prices in the USA could not possibly decline because that never happens. In fact, since the Great Depression, average house prices nationwide had not declined in any single year.[11]

By mid-2006 it was apparent that a national housing slump was under way, though there were different forecasts about how long and severe it would be.[12] From mid-2006 to early 2008, Standard and Poor's U.S. National Home Price Index declined 16 percent. In some cities, prices had already fallen nearly halfway down to their "pre-bubble" levels by mid-2007, and the rate of fall appeared to be accelerating.[13]

Roughly speaking, the rate of decline was inversely proportional to the speed of the increase.[14] For example, the tier of houses with the lowest prices experienced the largest percentage rise before the bubble burst; they also experienced the largest percentage decline during the bust. Cities with more stable pre-bubble pricing trends, such as Chicago and New York, experienced smaller declines but the cities with large pre-bubble price booms, among them Las Vegas, Miami, and San Francisco, saw housing prices decline rapidly and steeply.[15]

Since many people were using loans against their home equity to support their consumption, the rapid decline of housing prices forced millions of families into financial problems. For example, the number of properties in foreclosure rose from 71,507 in January 2005 to 261,255 in May 2008.[16] The rate of foreclosure was particularly high among Hispanic households that had been targeted by an organized campaign to increase their rates of home ownership.[17]

The troubles spread to financial markets. Many home builders had established their own mortgage-lending affiliates, and they were hard-hit. As losses mounted, mortgage lenders did their best to sell out to investment banks or anyone (usually Wall Street firms) with confidence and liquidity. Mortgage lenders who did not find buyers faced bankruptcy and, ultimately, liquidation. Financial markets began to experience stress in August 2007, and the stress deepened in the second half of 2008.[18]

Wall Street's exposure to the risk of subprime mortgages was so widespread and substantial that a range of financial institutions began hemorrhaging cash. Some of the large hedge funds were facing failure. As fear spread through Wall Street, some banks stopped issuing mortgage-backed securities, particularly those backed by subprime loans. Money-market funds and other investors began to lose faith in banks. The credit default swap market was hit because it was full of insurance contracts on mortgage-backed bonds. And the impacts rippled around the globe, as financial institutions from Europe to Asia were invested in the U.S. housing market or were otherwise dependent on Wall Street. The U.S. recession deepened in 2008 to the point that it is expected to be the worst since 1945.[19]

While it is fashionable to blame bad economic news on the current president, especially an outgoing and unpopular one, the prevailing theories of what caused the housing crisis and the global financial meltdown have little to do with any specific policy of the George W. Bush administration. Indeed, an event as calamitous as the 2008 meltdown could not have happened unless a variety of factors, some long-term and some short-term, had not interacted in unanticipated ways.

Prevailing Causation Theories

A new book a week is being written on what caused the 2008 housing bubble and the global financial meltdown. It may take a generation or more for scholars to sort it all out. (New views of what caused or exacerbated the Great Depression continue to be published.) Thus, what I highlight below should be understood only as the preliminary conjectures at this time.

LOW INTEREST RATES AFTER 9/11

In the early 1980s, interest rates on a thirty-year fixed mortgage exceeded 18 percent, but that rate declined steadily to 10 percent in the early 1990s and to 8 percent by 2000.[20] A key decision for the Federal Reserve Board (FRB) was how to manage the nation's money supply after the stock market bubble of 2000 and the economic uncertainties following 9/11.

Alan Greenspan, chairman of the Federal Reserve Board, was most worried about a syndrome of deflation and deeper recession. He responded with an unprecedented series of reductions in interest rates. Between New Year's Day 2001 and Memorial Day 2003, the Fed orchestrated a dramatic decline in the benchmark lending rate for banks from 6.5 percent to 1 percent, the lowest rate since the early 1960s.[21]

The actions by the Fed helped drive the thirty-year fixed mortgage rate to as low as 5.25 percent during the invasion of Iraq, but a rate around 6 percent persisted through much of the 2003–2006 period.[22] Using the bully pulpit, Greenspan also urged lenders to fashion more creative alternatives to the thirty-year fixed mortgage, and Greenspan—backed by the research of FRB economists—promoted the promise of adjustable-rate mortgages. Historically, an adjustable-rate mortgage starts a full two percentage points lower than the thirty-year fixed rate, though it was once offered only to low-risk borrowers. Very low initial interest rates grew in popularity as lenders sought to attract borrowers to the adjustable-rate format.[23]

As important as the cuts in interest rates were, they are not the entire explanation. Skeptics argue that the boom period for housing prices was three times as long as the period of low interest rates, and housing prices were accelerating when the Federal Reserve Board was increasing interest rates briefly in 1999.[24] Even proponents of the Austrian business cycle theory, who give primary emphasis to interest rates, are not convinced that they have the entire explanation. There appears to be more to the story than low interest rates.

SUBPRIME BORROWING PRACTICES

A subprime mortgage is simply a loan made to someone with a weak or troubled credit history. Subprime lending jumped from an annual volume of $145 billion in 2001 to $650 billion in 2005. The rate of growth was particularly large in California, Florida, Detroit, and the border areas of Texas.[25]

The FICO score (named after the Fair Isaac Corporation) is the most common system used to evaluate the credit risk of borrowers, and the scores range from a low of 350 to a high of 850. The average national credit score across all borrowers is about 700. Lenders and their regulators consider someone with a score less than 620 to be subprime.

The market-wide risk from the growth in subprime lending was partially concealed by the fact that the average FICO score among subprime borrowers was rising (to 650 in 2006). It turns out that lenders were also pushing subprime loans to people who were eligible for less expensive, conventional mortgages because the subprime loans carried higher rates and fees.[26] Thus, the aggregate data on FICO scores did not disclose to the market some of the risk that was occurring.

Lenders peddled adjustable-rate mortgages to higher-risk borrowers. This practice should have raised a red flag because, even in periods of prosperity, the delinquency rate on adjustable-rate mortgages is 50 percent greater than on fixed loans. But everyone was expecting housing prices to continue their inexorable rise. If the adjustable rate rose after its two-year "reset," borrowers could refinance using the equity they had acquired. In 2006 about 90 percent of subprime loans carried adjustable rates.[27] Creative features were added to many of these loans to keep down the initial monthly payments. For example, "interest-only" formats allowed borrowers to forgo principal payments. But these formats caused larger increases in monthly payments in later years. Surveys have found that many adjustable-rate borrowers misunderstood the key features of these loans.[28]

SMALL DOWN PAYMENTS

It used to be that the down payment was the principal barrier to purchasing a home; lenders might require a 20 percent down payment. However, this requirement has gradually eroded since the 1980s, first to 10 percent, then 5 percent, and ultimately—during the most recent housing boom—to virtually zero. Nor were those who put nothing down always required to purchase mortgage insurance. Instead, lenders might devise a two-loan package, with the second "piggyback" loan covering the fraction of the price that the first loan did not cover. Under this arrangement, essentially all of the money paid to the seller of the house was borrowed.

Prior to the recent housing bubble, the average U.S. mortgage equaled about 65 percent of a home's market price (excluding homes whose mortgages were already paid off entirely). By 2006, the average subprime borrower had incurred mortgage debt equal to 95 percent of the home's value. More than one-third of the subprime loans were for 100 percent of the home's value—more than 100 percent when fees were added. Red flags should have been waving. If home prices fell, these owners would owe more on their loans than their homes were worth.[29]

WEAK INCOME VERIFICATION

It was once typical for lenders to ask for a W-2 form or tax return to verify a borrower's income. During the recent housing boom, some lenders stopped asking for income verification. In 2006 over half of the subprime loans were based on "stated income," which means that the lender simply accepted the number stated by the borrower.[30] For sure, some of the borrowers were people buying second homes or seeking to "flip" a house for investment purposes. The recent housing boom witnessed a large growth in buyers approaching a home purchase entirely or primarily from an investment perspective.[31] But these borrowers are perfectly capable of fibbing or exaggerating their income, and some did. During the recent housing boom, the transition was from mortgages with "light documentation" to "ninja" loans—no income, no job, no assets.[32]

BUNDLING MORTGAGES AND SELLING THEM LIKE STOCKS

Residential mortgage bankers developed creative schemes to package loans and "securitize" them (that is, sell them off to pension funds and other investors), building on a concept that originated in the 1970s. The vast majority of subprime loans are now securitized. In other words, mortgage bankers shift much or all of the risk of lending to other investors while making their real money on fees charged when a mortgage agreement is signed.[33] With little skin in the game, mortgage bankers are motivated to sign as many new mortgage agreements as possible, since they can typically sell them off and avoid risk.[34] It is instructive that housing bubbles also occurred in the United Kingdom, Australia, Spain, and other countries where residential lending became highly permissive.[35]

But securitization was commonly viewed as a good thing among economists and financial analysts. For those who originated loans, securitization reduced their risk and freed up cash for additional lending. Borrowers found it easier to get the money they needed. And for investors around the world, it provided an opportunity to purchase from a much richer variety of assets. In theory, these investors could tailor the amount of risk in their portfolios to their risk preferences.

RELAXED REGULATORY POSTURE TOWARD FINANCIAL INSTITUTIONS

With the possible exceptions of health care and education, banking is arguably the most regulated sector of the U.S. economy. But during the 1980s and 1990s, Congress wrote a series of new laws with a largely deregulatory impact on the financial sector.[36] The distinctions between commercial banks, investment banks, and insurance companies were gradually eroded, but the regulatory regimes covering these institutions were not rationalized accordingly.

For example, in 1999 Congress relaxed the law by allowing banks to enter the securities business. Historically, commercial banks were regulated strictly by the Federal Reserve Board and the Federal Deposit Insurance Corporation. Bank deposits were insured by the federal government in exchange for adherence to strict capital requirements and public access to the books of these institutions. Investment banks, which underwrote only corporate and government securities, were regulated more loosely by the Securities Exchange Commission (SEC). They were not insured but also did not face compulsory capital requirements or stringent public disclosure obligations.[37] In 1999, Congress basically allowed investment banks and commercial banks to play in the same sandbox without equivalent regulatory regimes.[38]

Insofar as regulatory oversight existed, it was a mishmash of state and federal agencies that operated largely outside the purview of the White House. New Century Financial, for example, made some of the most questionable subprime loans before it went bankrupt. It fell under the jurisdiction of California's state regulators and the SEC, yet neither group has much expertise or political accountability for the mortgage lending practices of an individual company.[39]

Meanwhile, the real estate investment trust became a largely unregulated vehicle to reap profits from the mortgage-lending business. Some of the most aggressive—and arguably egregious—participants in the recent housing boom were trusts: American Home Mortgage, New Century Financial, and NovaStar.[40]

To make a long story short, when the housing bust occurred in 2006, the most exposed institutions were weakly regulated private mortgage lenders, real estate investment trusts, hedge funds, money-market funds, and investment banks. Prime examples were New Century Financial and Bear Stearns.

The structure of the U.S. regulatory system cannot possibly be the sole explanation. The European financial sector is regulated quite differently but experienced similar problems.

WEAK OVERSIGHT OF FANNIE MAE AND FREDDIE MAC

As government-sponsored entities (GSEs), Fannie Mae (the Federal National Mortgage Association) and Freddie Mac (the Federal Home Loan Mortgage Corporation) as of 2008 owned or guaranteed half of the $12 trillion mortgage market in the United States.[41] Although they deal only in "conforming loans" (not jumbo loans), Fannie Mae and Freddie Mac were considered a source of systemic risk in financial markets because they buy mortgages from lenders, package them, and sell them to investors as mortgage-backed securities with guaranteed yield payments.[42] Fannie Mae and Freddie Mac have special privileges that other financial institutions don't. They are exempt from typical capital-reserve requirements that provide cushions against unforeseen financial blows, and they have lines of credit with the U.S. Treasury Department. It was widely perceived that their debt was backed by the federal government even though no formal guarantee was established when they were launched.[43] The

Bush administration floated a proposal in 2003 to tighten oversight of Fannie Mae and Freddie Mac through new regulatory powers at Treasury but this proposal was "dead on arrival" in Congress due to opposition from home builders, supporters of low-income housing, and leading Democrats in Congress.[44] Many of the politicians in Washington, from President Bush to the liberal Democrats, pressured the GSEs to help expand rates of home ownership in low-income and minority communities. In this respect, Bush and the Congress exacerbated the foreclosure crisis.

DUBIOUS RATING-AGENCY BEHAVIOR

In the absence of federal regulation, market participants tended to rely on the rating agencies, which are sometimes perceived as objective arbiters, like a "financial Supreme Court."[45] But rating agencies are also businesses, and their biggest clients were the big banks and investment houses. Between 2002 and 2006, for example, Moody's doubled its revenue and tripled its stock price.

Experts allege that the rating agencies slanted their ratings of companies with large stakes in bundles in order to please their clients. What we know for sure is that agencies persisted in giving AAA ratings to mortgage securities that were ultimately shown to be vulnerable.[46]

HUGE FOREIGN INVESTMENTS IN THE U.S. ECONOMY

The rapid growth of the Chinese economy from 2000 to 2008, combined with the large flow of oil revenues to the Middle East, contributed to large foreign investments in the U.S. economy. In effect, investors worldwide were drawn into the U.S. financial meltdown because they—knowingly or not—purchased a stake in the future of U.S. housing prices and the ability of U.S. home buyers to make their mortgage payments. When U.S. housing prices fell, the ripple effects in financial markets were felt worldwide.

HERD PSYCHOLOGY AND DIFFUSION OF ACCOUNTABILITY

Hard-nosed economists resist allowing a role for psychology, but an irrational enthusiasm for housing investments among all market participants may have been a core of the problem.[47] Lenders and borrowers alike assumed that housing prices could only go up and up, causing them to minimize the risks of large, poorly backed loans. Indeed, the perception was not entirely unreasonable, since by the end of 2005 there had been a fourteen-year run of mostly accelerating increases in home prices.[48]

The transfer of risk from initial lenders and borrowers to global investors diffused accountability for bad loans. No person had enough financial stake in any single loan to make sure that it had plausible backing. The complex process of securitization and diversification of risk among global investors caused everyone to count on everyone else, arguably with no one really regulating risk. Indeed, some investors may have perceived that it was "rational" to overinvest in U.S. housing, since they may have been confident that they would pull out before other investors realized it was necessary.

Bipartisan Response

When bad events occur, the initial response in a polarized environment is for each political party to point the finger at the other party, and that goes on for a while. But when it becomes clear that bad events are building into a global financial crisis, possibly along the lines of another Great Depression, even polarized parties find a way to work together on public policy reforms.

For Bush and the Democratic leaders of Congress, bipartisanship was the only hope in 2008 because the Republican Party did not control the floor of the House or the Senate and the Democratic Party did not control the White House. And the collaboration on this issue was even more complex because the Federal Reserve Board, acting as an independent agency, was effectively a third player in the collaboration.

The Housing Sector Bailout

To assist troubled homeowners, the initial response from the Bush administration was modest, much more modest than what many Democrats in Congress thought was necessary.[49] First, Bush proposed a legislative amendment to federal tax law making it easier for financially strapped homeowners to sell out before they faced foreclosure. (The tax system had discouraged sellouts by treating any mortgage debt forgiven by a lender as taxable income.) Second, Bush unveiled FHA Secure, a new program designed to help homeowners who were delinquent on their loans due to a reset of the mortgage interest rate. This plan had limited impact because many distressed homeowners could not meet the program's down payment and income requirements. Finally, Bush subsequently proposed Hope Now, a consortium of market participants who would work to find a way to modify mortgage loans. But the negotiated repayments did not help very much, and in some cases the required payments were larger because missed payments and penalties were wrapped into repayment plans. Moreover, Hope Now did not address what was emerging as a bigger problem than the interest-rate resets: negative mortgage equity, meaning a home market value that is less than the size of the loan(s). What was needed was a way to prevent foreclosures and keep people in their homes.

The 2008 stimulus package (see chapter 2) provided a modest boost to the housing and lending sectors. In addition to a $168 billion package of individual and business tax cuts, the bill authorized higher caps (around $729,000) on loans by the Federal Housing Administration (FHA), Fannie Mae, and Freddie Mac. This action was helpful because it replaced some of the private lending that was disappearing as the credit crunch unfolded, especially in regions of the country where high housing prices required large home loans, such as California, Washington, D.C., New York City, and southern Florida. The agreement to this provision was a stark reversal by the Bush administration, which had been seeking reforms of these institutions before supporting larger lending authority.[50]

As the crisis worsened in 2008, the Bush administration made a dramatic shift in position: Bush asked for unlimited authority from Congress to lend money to Fannie Mae and Freddie Mac, including the option to buy their stock. The two organizations owned $5 trillion out of the $12 trillion in residential mortgages nationwide but were saddled with $1.5 trillion in outstanding debt. Each company lost 80 percent of its stock market value from July 2007 to July 2008.[51] Given the practical realities, letting Fannie Mae and Freddie Mac fold was not an option. As a consolation prize, Bush won a long-standing administration request: a revitalized regulatory authority within the Treasury.

Bush also dropped his threat to veto a plan aimed at rejuvenating FHA. FHA mortgages were restructured to make them more competitive in the real estate market. FHA was also authorized to insure up to $300 billion in new, refinanced loans to borrowers who were struggling to make their current payments.[52] In an effort to boost the depressed housing sector, Bush and the Congress also agreed on a $15.1 billion one-time tax break for first-time home buyers: an interest-free loan of up to $7,500 through July 1, 2009.

This huge legislative package is the largest legislative reform of the housing sector in a generation. Yet it passed with remarkable speed and bipartisan support (272–152 in the House and 72–13 in the Senate). The opposition was concentrated among House Republicans, who voted against the package 149 to 45.[53] The only opposing votes in the Senate were Republicans.[54] Bush emerged again as the "big government" conservative.

Wall Street Bailout

In March 2008 the Federal Reserve Board stepped in to engineer the sale of Bear Stearns to J. P. Morgan Chase. On September 15, 2008, Lehman Brothers, the fourth-largest Wall Street investment house, declared bankruptcy. The nation's largest insurance company, AIG, was kept afloat on September 16 only by an $85 billion loan from the Federal Reserve Board.

In the midst of the fall 2008 presidential campaign, the financial meltdown forced another round of comprehensive legislation. It was again acts of bipartisanship by Bush and the Democratic leadership in Congress that spurred passage. The White House was concerned that the leading financial institutions on Wall Street, as well as others around the globe, were reeling from bad mortgage debt and a crisis in confidence on the part of investors. Fear had shut off ordinary loans to businesses, creating an economy-wide liquidity crisis.

Bush's initial legislative proposal to Congress, the Troubled Asset Relief Program (TARP), with a $700 billion authorization, was criticized by leaders of both parties. It gave enormous power to the Department of the Treasury with few checks and accountability provisions. But the Bush proposal served as the foundation for refinements. Congress added limits on executive pay at recipient companies, and an ownership stake for the federal government in return for the investments. Periodic reports from the U.S. General Accountability Office were required to keep Congress informed of Treasury's implementation of the package. Nor did Congress authorize the entire $700 billion without a check. Treasury was required to ask Congress for the second $350 billion, which Treasury would receive automatically (upon request) if both houses of Congress did not pass disapproval resolutions within fifteen days.

The White House successfully resisted efforts by congressional Democrats to enact much more sweeping provisions (such as providing to all first-time home buyers an entirely new mortgage). Democrats pledged that more legislation would be passed when Bush left office.[55]

But Bush and congressional leaders found that passing a Wall Street rescue package was not easy. Members were well aware of polls showing that substantial segments of the public were intensely opposed to a Wall Street bailout. Despite the bipartisan leadership agreement, the House actually voted the rescue package down, 228 to 205. Democratic leaders witnessed 95 defections (including all African-American members) while Republicans rejected the package 133 to 65.[56]

Needless to say, investors were not reassured by the House's action. On the day of the House vote, the Dow plummeted a record 778 points or 7 percent.[57] The stock market losses spread worldwide, especially in the emerging economies (Brazil's stock market, for example, fell 9 percent). Soon after the vote, some members were already reconsidering their position.

Despite the setback, Bush redoubled efforts to find more Republican votes while House Speaker Nancy Pelosi (and even presidential candidate Barack Obama) did the same among House Democrats. Using an old-fashioned yet effective tactic, the Senate added a sweetener: $150 billion in popular tax breaks and spending earmarks for various sectors of the economy, including temporary relief from the alternative minimum tax (see chapter 2).

When the House voted again four days later, the measure passed 263 to 171. During this eventful week, 33 Democrats and 24 Republicans reversed their positions.[58] Bush and the Congress launched the largest relief package for the financial sector in American history.

Under the terms of the legislation, the Department of the Treasury was granted broad authority to respond to the financial crisis, including an authorization of $700 billion in potential relief for financial institutions. The expectation in Congress was that Treasury would use the funds to take troubled assets off the balance sheets of banks.

Soon after the plan was enacted, Treasury changed direction.[59] It instead used the broad grant of authority to purchase $125 billion in shares of the nine largest banks in the United States. Treasury also used the funds to encourage stronger banks to acquire weaker ones; for instance, PNC Financial of Pittsburgh purchased National City, a troubled Ohio bank.

Interestingly, the outline of Treasury's actual relief efforts tracked closely the thinking of Democratic senator Charles E. Schumer of New York and the policy directions of several European countries. The Bush administration shifted course to ensure that U.S. banks were able to compete internationally on a level playing field.[60]

Implementation of the Wall Street rescue package quickly became a source of controversy. The Government Accountability Office (GAO) reported in December 2008 that Treasury did not have the tools in place to determine whether banks were using the funds to support lending to consumers and small businesses. Recipient firms would state only that they used the funds to support their "balance sheets."[61]

Congressional frustration with Treasury became so widespread that it was uncertain whether Bush would even ask for the second installment of $350 billion to support TARP. But Bush received encouragement from a potent source: President-elect Barack Obama. When Obama made it clear to Congress that he needed the $350 billion, and he pledged to expend it with more transparency, neither chamber of Congress voted to deny him the funds.[62] Legislators in both parties began to introduce legislation that would force public disclosure of how the rescue funds were being spent. Some legislators sought to require that funds be used for more lending.[63] Meanwhile, conservatives began to search for an "exit strategy," a way for the federal government to terminate some of the bailout programs before they were institutionalized as a large new feature of the federal government.[64]

Bush and Congress did not act alone to bolster Wall Street and the entire financial sector of the economy. The Federal Reserve, which operates outside the purview of the White House, took aggressive steps to re-establish the flow of funds in the economy.

Beginning in early August 2007, the Fed loaned $185 billion in Treasury securities to Wall Street firms in exchange for riskier securities. By the end of 2008 the Fed had committed $1.9 trillion to support financial markets. How much of this money will be recovered (with or without interest) is unknown.

The Fed raised bank reserves from $13 billion at the end of 2007 to $848 billion by the end of 2008 while increasing the Fed's balance sheet from $892 billion to $2.247 trillion. Short-term interest rates were cut by the Fed to near zero while its loan facilities were extended to accept as collateral a variety of assets that had been shunned by private investors.

Despite the Fed's actions, surveys in late 2008 revealed that many senior loan officers at financial institutions were not yet ready to resume lending to consumers. Some Wall Street firms that had received TARP funds indicated that they planned to hold the funds or pay off debts rather than expand lending to businesses.[65] As the Obama administration took office in early 2009, the Fed and Congress were still looking at new strategies to boost financial markets. Similar efforts were under way in governments around the world.[66]

Bailing Out Detroit

The Big Three automakers were steadily burning cash in 2007–2008 but had product plans ready for an economic recovery. Unexpectedly, the count of new vehicle sales fell off a cliff in the fall of 2008 during the credit crunch. The number of consumers looking to buy a new car plummeted. Among those looking, many could not obtain financing. From a peak of 17 million new vehicle sales in 2006, the U.S. annualized sales rate was down to almost 11 million by the end of 2008. In late 2008 profit margins at Toyota and Honda disappeared while the steady cash burn at the Big Three turned quickly into a liquidity crisis.[67]

Ford Motor Company, with substantial cash on hand ($18.9 billion) and a $10.7 billion line of credit with private lenders, felt it could keep running through 2009 without government assistance.[68] But Ford had already incurred $24 billion in losses since 2006—$8.7 billion in the second quarter of 2008 alone—and was not sure how bad 2009 might be. GM had less cash on hand than Ford and had reported a stunning loss of $15.5 billion in the second quarter of 2008 ($4.4 billion from operating losses and the remainder from write-offs related to buyouts of hourly workers and problems at its supplier Delphi).[69] Chrysler did not disclose financials but was well known to be more dependent on light truck sales than Ford and GM, and Chrysler had far fewer sales than Ford and GM outside North America, where markets were growing. If conditions did not change quickly, Chapter 11 bankruptcy was in Detroit's future.

The Big Three perceived their individual fates to be intertwined. If any one of the three collapsed, the failure of shared suppliers might push all three into bankruptcy. They were also concerned about what the stigma of bankruptcy might do to their future vehicle sales. Would consumers be willing to buy a new car from a bankrupt company that was rapidly closing dealerships?

The imminent failure of the Big Three also threatened to exacerbate difficulty in the already stressed financial markets. At the end of 2008, the Big Three owed more than $100 billion to bankers and bondholders. Bankers feared they might never see repayment. For example, in 2005 Bank of America bought $55 billion in loans from GMAC (GM's financing arm) and sold most of them to investors. In June 2008 Bank of America helped GMAC finance $60 billion of debt.[70] Likewise, Goldman Sachs and Morgan Stanley were among the banks that arranged $11.5 billion in financing for the takeover of Chrysler by the financial firm Cerberus. The auto debts were then spread among a wide range of insurance companies, pension funds, and hedge funds.[71]

More important from a political perspective, the United Auto Workers (UAW), which represented workers at the Big Three but not at Toyota, Honda, Nissan, and the European manufacturers, feared what might happen in Chapter 11 proceedings. In its 2007 contract negotiations with the Big Three, the UAW made major concessions on legacy costs, wage rates for new hires, and some work rules.[72] The Big Three had already shed 100,000 high-paying hourly jobs since 2006, and the UAW was determined to minimize future layoffs.

In the fall of 2008, the Big Three and the UAW requested that the Bush administration and Congress provide temporary loans to enable the companies to weather the deep recession.[73] An initial industry request for loans of $25 billion was later enlarged to $34 billion. And this request was on top of $25 billion in low-interest loans that Congress had already authorized in 2007, though that pot of money was restricted to retooling expenses for "green" vehicles and was made available to a wide range of manufacturers and suppliers, not just the Big Three. In fact, only firms that were financially sustainable were eligible, and Detroit was not looking sustainable!

Conservatives in the Congress, particularly those from the South where non-union auto plants operate profitably for Honda, Toyota, Nissan, and others, opposed federal financial assistance for the Big Three. They argued that Detroit cannot be saved. GM's market share, for example, had already declined from a peak of 53 percent to 20 percent over a forty-year period. Yet GM continued to offer eight brands (Cadillac, Saab, Buick, Pontiac, GMC, Saturn, Chevy, and Hummer) while Toyota (with 19 percent market share) offered three and Honda (with 11 percent market share) offered two.[74] GM had 7,000 dealers. Toyota had fewer than 1,500 and Honda about 1,000. And the work rules at southern, non-union auto plants are more flexible about layoffs during adverse market conditions than the work rules at UAW-organized plants.[75]

GM's basic wage under its UAW contract was $28.69 per hour, or $59,675 per year. In a new non-union Honda plant in Greensburg, Indiana, 2009 hires will earn $18.55 per hour, or about $38,500 per year.[76] Considering cash and non-cash benefits, a study by the Economic Policy Institute found that a typical UAW member costs $71 per hour in total compensation compared to $49 per hour for a typical worker at a Japanese plant in the U.S.[77]

Given these circumstances, conservatives argued that federal assistance for the Big Three would simply delay the hard decisions that needed to be made. Reorganization under bankruptcy, they argued, was the best way to force the hard decisions.

Senators from the South were aware that a more rapid shift of market share from the Big Three to non-union automakers would boost their states. Volkswagen, Toyota, and Kia Motors are planning new plants in Chattanooga, Tennessee; Blue Springs, Mississippi; and West Point, Georgia, respectively.[78] Toyota already operated production facilities in seven states and R & D facilities in three others. Honda was already operating facilities in five states. These "foreign" auto companies (and their suppliers) were employing 402,800 workers in the United States, at an average annual compensation of $63,538.[79] Interestingly, no large non-union automakers were seeking federal assistance.

The Big Three and the UAW countered that many hard decisions had already been made. The 2007 UAW contracts with the Big Three permitted new hires to start at an hourly wage as low as $14 per hour, at least on subassembly lines where new work is brought to the plant.[80] Since 2006, Ford had sold off three of its brands, shed 40,000 workers, and shifted its mix to include fewer light trucks and more small cars.[81] Ford's new "EcoBoost" systems—modifications to the gasoline engine—will improve mileage by 20 percent at less cost than a new hybrid or diesel engine. From 2000 to 2008, GM reduced its hourly workforce by 52 percent and its salaried workforce by 45 percent.[82] GM also rolled out award-winning new vehicles such as the Saturn Aura, the Cadillac CTS, and the Buick Enclave. The new Chevy Malibu led the midsize segment in fuel economy at 33 miles per gallon. GM was planning to offer by 2010 the first plug-in hybrid vehicle with advanced innovative lithium-ion batteries (the Volt) and a new small car for the global market (the Chevy Cruze).

Fiscal conservatives were worried. If the Big Three were rescued, other companies would request assistance. For example, many auto suppliers were also bleeding. The Motor and Equipment Manufacturers Association informed Congress and the Bush administration that auto parts suppliers employ 600,000 workers in the U.S., triple the number employed by the Big Three.[83] And if the auto sector were to be fully rescued, one could expect numerous failing companies in many sectors of the economy to request aid as well as state and local governments.[84]

Bush originally expressed skepticism about assistance for the Big Three. Yet he reluctantly agreed, with the strong encouragement of Vice President Cheney, to a legislative proposal that would allow the $25 billion authorized in 2007 to be reallocated to the near-term liquidity needs of the industry. House Speaker Pelosi, with support from environmentalists, quickly objected to this plan on the grounds that the $25 billion had been intended only for retooling expenses for "green" vehicles.[85] She argued that the Bush administration and Congress could instead reallocate some of the $700 billion already made available for the financial sector to assist Detroit. The Bush administration countered that those funds needed to be reserved for the uncertain future of financial institutions.[86]

When Senate Majority Leader Harry Reid announced that the Pelosi plan could not pass the Senate, Pelosi relented and it appeared that Bush's preferred solution would prevail.[87] Yet the Bush White House soon learned that they did not have adequate support from Senate Republicans, who refused to cooperate with any bailout plan for Detroit. They threatened to filibuster to ensure that no plan would pass the Senate.[88] In a crucial Senate vote in December 2008, only ten Republican senators were willing to support Bush on his Detroit rescue plan.[89] Republican senator Bob Corker of Tennessee did offer a rescue plan that included steep cuts in wages, but the UAW objected to it.[90] GM began to consult Chapter 11 attorneys.[91]

In his final weeks in office, Bush was faced with the choice of letting the Big Three enter bankruptcy at a time when confidence in the economy was already low, or using executive authority and some of the $700 billion to assist the Big Three until the Obama administration took office. In his first visit with Bush in the White House, Obama had already urged Bush to assist the Big Three.[92]

Soon after the Senate blocked his legislative relief plan, Bush announced that the Treasury would lend $17.4 billion to General Motors and Chrysler in exchange for financial concessions from workers, suppliers, dealers, and other stakeholders. GM would receive $13.4 billion and Chrysler $4 billion. The stipulations in the loans were generally nonbinding, and considerably more permissive than the plan that the Senate had blocked days earlier.[93] In effect, the auto loan package drained what was left in the first $350 billion already provided to the

Treasury for the financial sector, and the remainder would be provided to GM when Congress provided the Treasury the second installment of $350 billion.

The Bush plan was described as a short-term loan that would take GM and Chrysler through the end of March. The Obama administration would then be expected to decide whether the assistance would continue. Obama publicly supported Bush's action.

Later in December, the Treasury allocated another $6 billion to GMAC, GM's financing arm—$5 billion directly to GMAC and another $1 billion to GM, which, in turn, would be invested in GMAC. As a result, GMAC resumed offering loans to borrowers with credit scores of 621 or higher, an easier threshold than the 700 they had required two months earlier as they strived to stay afloat. (About 60–75 percent of GM buyers tend to have credit scores below 700, with about 40 percent between 621 and 700.) Critics questioned the Treasury decision since GMAC had lost nearly $8 billion in the previous fifteen months, and was vulnerable because it had expanded into home as well as car loans during the recent economic boom.[94]

The Federal Reserve ruled separately that GMAC could become a bank holding company.[95] In order to qualify, GMAC persuaded 75 percent of its bondholders to restructure outstanding debt. As a result, GMAC gained access to $30 billion in additional low-interest capital from the Fed.[96] This was a critical step because GMAC faced $1.8 billion of unsecured debt that matured at the end of 2008, $12.8 billion in 2009, and another $8.8 billion in 2010.[97]

In early January 2009, the Treasury Department issued auto sector guidelines that allowed even more companies and industries to apply for TARP money. In effect, any company that the Treasury deems important to the making or financing of cars is potentially eligible.[98] Critics argued that the Bush administration was falling down a slippery slope, but Treasury officials responded that an orderly restructuring of the industry may require temporary assistance of suppliers and financing arms as well as vehicle manufacturers.

The Treasury followed in January 2009 with $1.5 billion in emergency loans to Chrysler Financial LLC, Chrysler's lending arm. The move was in response to concerns from Chrysler that the Treasury's loans to GMAC were placing Chrysler products at a competitive disadvantage vis-à-vis GM products.[99]

It is hard to be confident that Bush's auto bailout will work. Despite recent plant closures, it is estimated that vehicle production capacity in North America in 2009 will be 16.9 million units. Consumer demand is projected to justify output of only 9.5 million units, for a capacity utilization rate of 56 percent. A return to a profitable utilization rate of 85 percent is not expected until 2012 at the earliest.[100] Overcapacity is also a serious problem on a worldwide basis.[101] Thus, unless Obama is prepared to keep numerous non-operating plants afloat, large-scale layoffs of auto workers in North America appear to be inevitable.

President Bush certainly was dealt his share of crises: 9/11, Katrina, and then a recession as deep as any experienced since World War II. The housing bust, financial meltdown, and auto depression occurred with such speed and severity that Bush and the Congress were forced into a series of bipartisan responses.

While Bush was as lame as a lame duck can be, and his popularity was at rock bottom, he continued to be influential in shaping—however hastily—a series of rescue packages. From the perspective of Bush's own agenda, the housing relief package is the most promising because it contains the new regulatory system for Fannie Mae and Freddie Mac that Bush first proposed in 2003. On the other hand, the financial and auto relief packages were completely reactive and accomplished none of Bush's planned domestic agenda.

It is hard to argue that some form of housing and financial relief was not absolutely necessary. Whether the details of what Bush did was exactly right, who knows? The bailout of the Big Three automakers, though, is far more questionable. It is nonetheless a fascinating extension of a series of Bush administration policies that have protected or aided one of the most loyal and resourceful forces in the Democratic coalition: the United Auto Workers.

Not surprisingly, the projected federal deficit in fiscal year 2009 will be over $1 trillion. But maybe the deficit matters less than the stimulus. If Obama and the Democratic Congress are able to build on Bush's rescue efforts and bring the economy back to prosperity, history may look kindly on Bush's last-minute behavior as a "big government" conservative. It is no overstatement to suggest that another Great Depression may have been prevented by Bush, the Fed, Obama, and the Democratic Congress.

12

Taking Stock, with Lessons for Future Presidents

George W. Bush's domestic policies receive far less attention than his foreign policies, especially the military operations in Afghanistan and Iraq.[1] Any president's foreign policies certainly deserve sustained scrutiny, but this book has supplied a wealth of evidence that Bush was also a bold and activist president on traditional domestic issues. In light of the partisan divide in the Congress and Bush's limited political standing throughout most of his presidency, it is remarkable how ambitious he was and how much of his domestic agenda was enacted and implemented, whether by legislative or executive actions, and yet these accomplishments, by and large, have not been recognized.

In this final chapter, I offer my own evaluation of Bush's domestic record. What were his most important achievements? Which of his enacted reforms are likely to prove problematic? Did he propose any policies that, though blocked by effective opposition, are promising enough that they should be reconsidered in the future? What were some key opportunities that Bush missed, opportunities that future presidents may wish to consider? And which of Bush's policies are likely to be reversed by the Obama administration and the Democratic-controlled Congress? In answering these questions, I draw on the case studies of specific Bush initiatives described in chapters 2 through 11.

More important, this chapter offers some lessons for future presidents. It is never easy to serve as president, and the challenge is exacerbated when the Congress often seems to be dysfunctional because of a decline in bipartisanship and the constant threats of filibuster in the Senate. How should a president, Democrat or Republican, go about making domestic policy in this polarized era of American politics? If American politics remains polarized, as seems likely, future presidents will face similar dilemmas unless their parties acquire such large majorities in the Congress that one-party lawmaking is feasible. I offer eight constructive lessons from Bush's experience that may be helpful in the future.

Taking Stock

In chapters 2 through 11, I traced the origins and content of Bush's agenda, including both the successful initiatives and those that were not enacted or were overturned. Now I turn to an evaluation of this record.

Significant Achievements

I employ three criteria in the evaluation: whether the reform is promising, whether it is primarily attributable to the efforts of the Bush administration, and whether the reform is likely to reshape public debate on the issue for many years in the future. The last criterion is the most exacting because policy making in the United States is typically incremental, with each policy reform making only modest adjustments to previous policies.[2] If a president's reform causes a fundamental change in how an issue is perceived and debated, as was the case with LBJ's Great Society, it is especially noteworthy.

Pathbreaking achievements are defined as those that may ultimately satisfy all three of the evaluative criteria. My tentative evaluations are summarized in table 12.1. They are tentative because few of the Bush reforms have been subjected to careful policy evaluation based on real-world experience. Many of Bush's reforms may meet at least two of the three criteria, but only a handful have a

Table 12.1. Evaluation of the Domestic Policies of George W. Bush

Policy Reform	Promising?	Evaluative Criteria Attributable to Bush?	Reframe Future Policy Debates?
2001 Tax Cut	Yes	Partly[a]	No
2003 Tax Cut	Yes	Yes	Yes
No Child Left Behind	Yes	Yes	Yes
Drug Coverage-Medicare	Yes	Yes	Yes
Oil and Gas Promotion	Yes	Yes	No
Pro-Coal Policies	Uncertain	Yes	No
Pro-Nuclear Policies	Yes	Yes	Maybe
Pro-Ethanol Policies	Uncertain	Yes	Maybe
Renewable Electric Power	Yes	Partly[b]	No
Reform of Automobile Mileage Rules	Yes	Yes	Maybe
Clean Air Rules	Yes	Yes	No
Immigration Crackdowns	Uncertain	Partly[c]	Maybe
Overtime Reforms	Yes	Yes	No
Union Disclosures	Yes	Yes	No
Regulatory Reforms	Yes	Yes	No
Sarbanes-Oxley Law	Uncertain	Partly[d]	Maybe
Reform of Housing Sector	Uncertain	Yes	Maybe
Reform of Financial Sector	Uncertain	Yes	Maybe
Big Three Bailout	Uncertain	Yes	No
Wall Street Bailout	Uncertain	Yes	No

a. The GOP Congress did heavy lifting for the 2001 tax cut in earlier battles against Clinton.
b. The Congress was a stronger pro-renewables force than Bush.
c. The House GOP was a stronger force than Bush behind immigration crackdowns.
d. Congress was a more significant force for the Sarbanes-Oxley law than Bush.

chance of satisfying all three. And unpredictable actions by future presidents, Congresses, and judges may affect—negatively or positively—how Bush's reforms play out in the long run.

For example, the Bush administration's clean-air rule makings (especially the new emission controls on diesel engines and coal plants) are projected to have impressive public health and environmental benefits that justify their expense. Yet these rules were implemented using existing legal authority and are incremental extensions of previous policies. Thus, since the clean-air rule makings are unlikely to reframe future public policy debates about environmental policy, they are not, according to application of the criteria, "pathbreaking achievements."

Likewise, the Bush administration's reform of federal overtime law meets the first two of the three criteria for a pathbreaking achievement. Yet it is difficult to argue that such an incremental reform has fundamentally changed public debate about labor policy.

Some conservatives hold the view that Bush's multiple rounds of tax cuts stand out as his pathbreaking achievement. Even those who oppose the size or distribution of the tax cuts grant that they were major political victories for Bush.

The reality is that the 2001 tax cuts were not entirely a Bush administration achievement. Much of the substance of the agenda was defined in the 1990s. The groundwork for Bush's 2001 tax cut was established by congressional Republicans in the 1999–2000 battle with Clinton. Yet Bush certainly played a critical role. If McCain or Gore had been elected president in 2000, the 2001 tax-cut package would have been much smaller (assuming any tax cut was enacted). One also can argue that Bush intimidated Gore and congressional Democrats into advocating much larger tax cuts than Clinton supported in the late 1990s. But there is nothing groundbreaking about a newly elected Republican president pursuing tax cuts.

Where Bush changed the future of political debate on tax policy was with his second round of tax cuts: the 2003 reduction in taxes on stock dividends and capital gains. Although Bush did not win the elimination of these taxes that he proposed, they were reduced to their lowest levels since the 1920s. Prior to Bush's bold proposal, the conventional wisdom was that elimination of the "double taxation" of corporate profits—while certainly based on good economics—is too difficult to explain to the public and too politically sensitive for a party worried about being tagged as pro-business and biased in favor of the wealthy, investor class. Bush rejected this skepticism and successfully launched pro-growth arguments in favor of cutting taxes on capital gains and stock dividends. Our nation's solid economic performance from 2003 to 2007 provides circumstantial evidence that the policies were an economic success. Obama may seek to raise these taxes back to their earlier levels, but he will not succeed without a political bloodbath.

A second candidate for pathbreaking achievement is the federal government's new role in K–12 public education that Bush engineered with the Congress in 2001 and implemented from 2002 to 2008. Prior to Bush, most Republicans did not advocate a significant role for the national government in public education. At Bush's insistence, the No Child Left Behind (NCLB) legislation brought standards, testing, and accountability in public education under the purview of the federal government.

For the first time, the federal government compelled states and localities to set explicit standards for math and English knowledge, test students regularly for performance, and implement systems of accountability for schools and districts. As federal spending on public education expands, and I expect it will grow significantly in the years ahead, the federal government's role in public education also will grow.

NCLB is certainly far from perfect. Reforms of NCLB are likely as grassroots opposition to some aspects of NCLB is burgeoning in both parties. The school-choice provisions did little to create new opportunities for parents. The lack of uniform national tests caused inconsistency and mischief at the state level. The primary focus on math and reading may be shortchanging science, history, physical education, and the arts. And the exclusive focus on children at the border of proficiency may be diverting resources from other children at the top and bottom of the achievement ladder. But none of these objections is an argument against federal responsibility or accountability. Indeed, the objections suggest a need for more comprehensive federal responsibilities.

NCLB is a fundamental change because it shifts the public debate from *whether* the federal government should be involved in public education to *how* the federal government should hold states and localities accountable for the scope and extent of learning in their schools. Some Republicans may envision a return to the day when public education is addressed entirely by local communities, but it seems highly unlikely that the federal responsibilities under NCLB will be eliminated or pared back. Since Senator Ted Kennedy of Massachusetts is no longer in the Senate to defend NCLB, I do expect significant modifications and refinements, as should be expected after any policy reform of this magnitude.

My third candidate for significant achievement is the private-sector model for health care reform that Bush and the Congress adopted with the new prescription drug benefit under Medicare. The fact that Medicare was expanded to include outpatient drug coverage was not so significant because I believe it would have happened sooner or later, regardless of who became president in 2001. The House Republicans were already scrambling to enact such a benefit before Bush was elected. The potent political power of seniors, combined with rapidly rising pharmaceutical expenditures, ensured that Medicare would be expanded to cover outpatient drugs.

What Bush did was demonstrate the viability of a competitive, private-insurance model of health care reform. As citizens and politicians become more comfortable with the new prescription drug benefit, it may become feasible to further privatize Medicare and extend the competitive, consumer-oriented model of health care. If the implementation of this reform continues to improve and if senior citizens become satisfied with it, the single-payer model of health care that has dominated progressive thinking for decades will have no future in the United States.

Bush's policies to revive nuclear energy as a source of electricity in the United States are potentially a fourth significant pathbreaking achievement. Through new policies on insurance for large-scale accidents, loan guarantees and subsidies for construction costs, and new waste-management strategies, the Bush administration helped foster an improved investment climate for nuclear power. Preliminary evidence indicates that utilities are already acting to lengthen the lives of existing reactors while considering expansion of nuclear capacity at existing and new sites. These policies are promising because nuclear energy has few of the environmental problems associated with fossil-fuel combustion, including none of the carbon dioxide emissions linked to global climate change.

Bush's pro-nuclear policies are classified as a pathbreaking achievement with two qualifications. First, Bush's pro-coal policies were at least as influential as his pro-nuclear policies. Nuclear power may therefore make only marginal gains over time. Second, the durability of Bush's pro-nuclear policies is questionable given the Democratic takeover of the Congress and the opposition of many Democrats to nuclear power and to Yucca Mountain as a permanent burial site for nuclear wastes. Without a permanent solution to the waste problem, the future of nuclear power in the U.S. will remain in doubt. But Bush has certainly persuaded the Republican Party that it is not suicidal to be pro-nuclear in an era of growing concern about global climate change. John McCain aggressively advocated nuclear power during the 2008 presidential campaign. And even President Obama appears to be somewhat open-minded about a nuclear future.

Finally, Bush's energy conservation policies in the transport sector, both the modernization of federal mileage standards and the demonstrations of congestion pricing, have the potential to be pathbreaking achievements. The only question on auto mileage is whether the California rules on carbon dioxide emissions will overshadow or undermine the federal auto mileage reforms. A key question for Obama is whether he is prepared to let California, rather than Washington, chart regulation of the automotive industry. The future of congestion pricing is also somewhat uncertain. It hinges on whether local politicians and their constituencies will support such worthy measures, even though they are unpopular among some motorists.

Enacted Yet Dubious Policies

It is unfortunate that the Bush administration initiated or aligned itself with some domestic policy initiatives that are of dubious value. The two that are most striking are the mandate of ethanol as a petroleum substitute and the Sarbanes-Oxley legislation aimed at deterring corporate fraud. Neither policy arose from a careful campaign position. Both evolved from complex political considerations.

Bush's most important objectives on the supply side of energy policy were to expand production of oil, gas, coal, and nuclear power. Such legislation was vulnerable to widespread Democratic opposition on the Senate floor. The opposition was overcome when Bush agreed to mandate a large increase in the use of ethanol as a substitute for petroleum, recognizing that corn-based ethanol (not cellulosic ethanol) would dominate the ethanol industry for the next decade. Indeed, it was ethanol's economic boost to the corn-growing states that helped deliver the votes of farm-state Democrats for Bush's energy bill.

The case for Bush's ethanol program was that it reduced the rate of growth of U.S. oil consumption and therefore exerted downward pressure on the world price of oil, with potential benefits for consumers throughout the developing and developed world. If Bush's ethanol plan is replicated in other parts of the world, building on the pro-ethanol policies of Brazil and Sweden, the energy security benefits for the world may be substantial.

Unfortunately, the Bush ethanol program has some serious flaws. The cost of making ethanol from corn has declined somewhat in recent years due to productivity improvements, but higher corn prices nullified those efficiency gains.

On an energy-equivalent basis, it still costs at least $1 per gallon more to use ethanol then gasoline. Furthermore, the rapid growth of the ethanol industry is causing environmental damage that is not yet fully understood or appreciated, such as water shortages and carbon emissions due to land-use changes. And higher food prices are an adverse side effect of the ethanol mandate that is only beginning to be considered by policy makers. In short, the de facto mandate of corn-based ethanol, without removal of tariffs on ethanol imports, appears to be causing a range of unintended adverse consequences. One can only hope that Bush's faith in the future of cellulosic ethanol—a faith that is shared by a surprising number of venture capitalists—proves to be warranted.

The Sarbanes-Oxley legislation, like the ethanol mandate, did not result from a campaign commitment by Governor George W. Bush. Nor was it part of Bush's planned domestic agenda. It arose instead from the public outrage caused by the unexpected Enron scandal and other highly publicized incidents of corporate fraud. The Bush administration could have stopped or scaled back such legislation with a veto threat but chose not to do so, possibly to avoid controversy for congressional Republicans prior to the 2002 midterm elections, and to protect Bush himself from public criticism.

The benefits and costs of the Sarbanes-Oxley law were never estimated before it was adopted and are still largely unknown. The law may have had its intended short-term effect (2002–2004) of restoring investor confidence in securities markets. But the long-term consequences of such a massive and complex regulatory program are only beginning to be understood. Concerns have been raised that the law has discouraged private companies from going public, redirected foreign investment away from the United States, and imposed needless costs and rigidities on the operation of publicly owned companies in the United States.

Promising Failures

When a White House proposal is blocked in Congress or in the courts, it may be worthwhile to reconsider the proposal in the future. Some of Bush's failed policy initiatives were promising. Indeed, table 12.2 summarizes the failed Bush initiatives that were examined in chapters 2 through 11. A plausible case can be made for a number of these policies: federal vouchers for low-income parents who seek to enroll their children in private schools, flexibility for young workers to invest some of their Social Security taxes in private investment accounts, more per-

Table 12.2. The Fate of the Failed Domestic Policies of George W. Bush

Policy	Attempted Method of Enactment (L=Legislative: A=Administrative)	Comment
Social Security Reform	L	Never reached House or Senate floor
Subsidized Vouchers for Private Schools	L	Defeated in House and Senate floor votes
Permission to Drill for Oil in Alaska (ANWR)	L	Defeated by Senate filibuster
Removal of Tariffs on Imported Ethanol	L	Never reached House or Senate floor
Mercury "Cap-and-Trade" Rule	A	Struck down by federal judiciary
Clear Skies	L	Never reached House or Senate floor
New Source Review Reforms	A	Struck down by federal judiciary
Guest Worker Program for Illegal Immigrants	L	Blocked by House Republicans
Medical-Malpractice Reform	L	Defeated by Senate filibuster
Caps on Damage Awards	L	Defeated by Senate filibuster
Asbestos Compensation Plan	L	Defeated by Senate filibuster

mission for companies to drill for oil and gas in an environmentally responsible manner (onshore and offshore), and removal of tariffs on Brazilian ethanol.

Of the promising proposals that failed to pass Congress, the one that is the most significant and commendable in my opinion is the guest worker program for foreign nationals. This legislation could have included both a program for the 12 million illegal immigrants currently living in the United States and a program for unskilled and skilled workers who are seeking to enter the United States to work for several years before returning home.

I recognize that the guest worker idea is controversial. Opponents of this plan may be correct that we need more secure borders before we can start issuing millions of work permits for guest workers. Illegal immigrants and the businesses who hire them do need to pay a price for violating immigration laws! But our economy urgently needs this additional supply of labor. Much more of it will be needed in the years and decades to come.

What Bush proposed may prove to be several years or, more likely, a decade ahead of his time. Ironically, in an interview given during the last week of his presidency, Bush expressed regret that he had not begun his second term with immigration reform instead of Social Security reform. My own hunch is that Bush's political party—exemplified by the House Republican leadership—was not ready for, and would not have permitted, reform of federal immigration law.

Missed Opportunities

No president can possibly advance a policy agenda on every legitimate concern of the public. Where we should fault an administration is when the scientific community and our closest allies around the world are begging for leadership from the United States but the administration does not respond adequately.

Bush was on solid ground in rejecting ratification of the Kyoto Protocol on global climate change because it was unrealistic, economically dangerous, and ineffective (due to the exclusion of the rapidly growing developing world from mandatory programs). Bush should be faulted for failing to seek a viable alternative to the Kyoto Protocol, a more practical international regime for addressing global climate change. In particular, the United States should have reached out to China, Russia, and other countries with reservations about the Kyoto Protocol and then led a process to develop a more realistic yet promising international strategy. Fortunately, the international dialogue was re-energized by Bush in 2007–2008—a dialogue that he could have fostered six years earlier.[3]

Bush's mismanagement of the global climate issue was not simply bad for the global environment and bad for the reputation of the United States around the world. It inadvertently placed American businesses, workers, and consumers at risk of economic harm because of the proliferation of ill-considered state and local regulatory policies that were advocated by frustrated environmentalists. A more proactive national policy on climate change by the Bush administration would have been more cost-effective than the policies that California and other states are now forcing on the rest of the country. Bush would also have preserved presidential leadership on an international issue that President Obama will now have to wrest away from the governors of several states. In short, Bush could have preempted the overly aggressive, wasteful climate policies that are now looming on the horizon while moving the planet gradually toward a less carbon-intensive future.

Another opportunity that was missed was a reduction in the tax rate applied to corporate income. Among countries in the Organisation for Economic Co-operation and Development (OECD), U.S. corporate income taxes are among the most punitive. The loss of revenue from lower rates could have been offset by a broadening of the base (as President Reagan and the Congress accomplished in 1986 and as Democratic senator John Breaux proposed to the George W. Bush administration). Corporate tax cuts might also have been combined with a small but gradually rising tax on carbon dioxide emissions in the U.S. economy. By linking a new carbon fee to corporate tax reform, the president could have simultaneously advanced both economic and environmental policy objectives.[4]

In summary, a careful evaluation of Bush's domestic record reveals that, despite his limited political standing and a polarized Congress, he instituted numerous promising reforms and several potentially pathbreaking achievements. Some of his improvised policies—among them the ethanol mandate, the Sarbanes-Oxley law, and the GM-Chrysler bailout—are objectionable, but he also proposed a variety of promising policies that were blocked in Congress or the courts, such as the guest worker program for immigrants and Social Security reform. His most important missed opportunities were his belated leadership on global climate change and his decision not to pursue corporate tax reform.

First Term vs. Second Term

Bush's first-term record in domestic policy had numerous successes because he recognized his limited political standing and the polarized Congress, and devised his agenda accordingly. His early successes on tax cuts and education enhanced his credibility as a leader and established that he knew how to make things happen in Washington. Bush entered the 2004 re-election cycle as a serious, accomplished politician who had proven he could overcome the polarization in Washington, D.C., at least on several key domestic issues.

Bush's second term was less successful because his agenda was "more assertive than conditions appeared to warrant."[5] The choice of legislative priorities in the second term failed to account for the president's limited political standing and the ability of the (diminished) Democratic minority in the Senate to unite and block his lawmaking ambitions. And Bush appeared to take the Republicans in Congress for granted rather than deliberate about whether Social Security and immigration should be the top second-term priorities. But Bush did win an energy bill in his second term as well as some tort reform, a comprehensive reform of auto mileage standards, and some reform of the housing and financial sectors.

The fact that Bush experienced a case of "second-term blues" is well recognized, but many of the explanations for his problems are off the mark. The alleged mismanagement of Hurricane Katrina, the prolongation of the Iraq war, and the corruption in Congress certainly complicated Bush's second term. They surely reduced his popularity and the credibility of the Republicans in Congress. But these serious difficulties were not the principal causes of Bush's second-term failures in domestic policy. The failure of Bush's agenda was apparent before these complications unfolded.

Bush's second-term domestic agenda failed because he did not select issues that were likely to stimulate Republican support while appealing to some Democrats. Without any initiatives similar to the first-term reforms of taxes, education, and health care, Bush's second-term agenda was counterproductive, especially Social Security reform. What Bush proposed actually made it easy for Democratic congressional leaders to unify their members against his priorities and weaken his presidency.[6]

Immigration reform was a second term priority that did appeal to many Democrats, but it suffered the opposite problem: tenacious opposition inside the president's Republican base, including the Republican leadership in the House. In fact, immigration reform was so offensive to conservative Republicans that Bush created a dynamic where his base attacked one of his major second-term priorities, and Bush responded by attacking the motives of his base. By exposing such salient divisions in the Republican Party, Bush inadvertently played into the hands of the Democratic leadership in Congress.

A strength of Bush's second term is poorly appreciated: a renewed emphasis on fiscal responsibility. In 2001 Bush inherited from President Clinton a weakening economy that caused the federal budget to shift rapidly from surplus to deficit. The revenue shortfalls from a slumping economy and the Bush tax cuts were exacerbated by weak spending restraint during Bush's first term. For example, the wars in Afghanistan and Iraq cost an average of $93 billion from fiscal years 2003 to 2005. The first deficit since 1997 occurred in 2002, and the red ink grew from −$158 billion in 2002 to −$413 billion in 2004.

Recognizing that the deficits were not sustainable, Bush pledged to cut them in half by the end of his second term. As the economy recovered, perhaps in part due to the tax cuts, federal tax revenues grew rapidly. Meanwhile, Bush held the rate of growth of (non-security) discretionary spending below the rate of inflation for three consecutive years. The net effect of the slower rate of spending growth and the surge in tax revenues was a plummeting deficit. It fell to $318 billion in 2005, $248 billion in 2006, and $163 billion in 2007.[7] Prior to the 2008 recession, the Congressional Budget Office (CBO) projected that Bush would leave his successor with a budget deficit equal to less than 1.5 percent of GDP, which is lower than the forty-year historical average. Although the deficits in 2008 and 2009 ballooned to huge levels, they resulted not from poor fiscal planning but from the unexpected housing bust, the financial meltdown, the severe recession, consequent bursts in entitlement spending, and the necessity to nurse the economy with additional tax cuts and bailouts.

The Bush deficit would have been eliminated by 2007 if two unexpected events had not occurred: Hurricane Katrina and the prolonged military activities in Afghanistan and Iraq. Katrina was the smaller of the two adverse factors, causing an estimated $128 billion in unanticipated expenditures (and tax relief) over the 2005–2007 period.[8] Much larger expenditures were made in Afghanistan and Iraq, ballooning to $120 billion in 2006 and an estimated $170 billion in 2007.[9] The 2008 request rose again to $195 billion, and experts say the 2009 costs may exceed $200 billion.[10]

Many conservatives criticize Bush for his failure to restrain discretionary domestic spending. But Bush's second term is not very vulnerable to that criticism. The real issue in the second term is whether the priorities were right. In effect, new corporate tax cuts and a normal growth rate in discretionary domestic programs were sacrificed to pay for the unexpected growth in military expenses in Iraq and Afghanistan and the Katrina relief. The annual deficit declined rapidly, both in absolute terms and as a share of GDP, until the Democrats took control of the Congress and the economy cratered due to the housing bust and the financial meltdown.

One can certainly argue that Bush should have opposed the bailouts of the housing sector, Wall Street, and the Big Three. (He probably should have held his ground against the bailouts of GM and Chrysler.) He reluctantly agreed to them for a defensible reason: Our economy appeared to be facing a possible repeat of the Great Depression.

Obama and Polarization

The sharp partisan polarization in American politics during the presidency of George W. Bush has two primary explanations. One view is that Bush caused or fueled polarization.[11] An alternative view is that Bush, like his predecessor, governed in one of the most polarized periods in American history.[12] Just as Clinton was despised by many Republicans, Bush was despised by many Democrats. And these two explanations are not mutually exclusive, as Bush's style, policy agenda, and political strategies may have exacerbated a growing division in American political culture that has been building for at least a generation.[13]

If one subscribes to the first view, it is tempting to believe that polarization in Congress can be overcome in the near future by a different form of presidential leadership. For example, there may be another Teddy Roosevelt–like figure who builds a "centrist coalition" from parts of the Republican Party and the independent sector.[14] Alternatively, a future Democratic president may offer a more inclusive, less confrontational leadership style that stimulates more genuine deliberation and consensus building. This unifying theme was part of the campaign strategy of Barack Obama.[15]

Obama's clear victory at the polls in 2008 has been attributed to many factors: His success at tapping anti-war sentiment; the grassroots proficiency of his campaign organization; his remarkable rhetorical skills and apparent confidence and ease with himself; the huge fundraising advantage he built over McCain; Biden's fewer negatives compared to Palin; Obama's able performance in the presidential debates; Obama's success at reaching out to the supporters of Hillary Clinton; and the simple fact that Obama was not affiliated with George W. Bush or the Republican Party. Under the circumstances, it is hard to imagine that the 2008 presidential election was ever in doubt.

But there was doubt. As of mid-September 2008, after the glow of the two conventions faded, McCain and Obama were in a dead-even race. Serious questions were raised about Obama's experience while Palin was stimulating enthusiasm where McCain was weak: the conservative base. Indeed, some experts were predicting another razor-close finish similar to 2000 and 2004. On the day in September that Lehman Brothers collapsed, one national poll showed McCain with a slight lead over Obama.

Just as Senator McCain was driving home his message that the fundamentals of the U.S. economy were sound, the financial meltdown occurred. In the last eight weeks of the campaign, Obama pulled away from McCain and went on to a clear victory.

According to the exit polls, Republicans voted overwhelmingly for Mc-Cain, Democrats for Obama. The independent voters, whom Bush lost to Kerry in 2004, went for Obama by an even larger margin. Obama's advantage among Hispanics and African Americans was also larger than Kerry's.[16] Overall turn-out was slightly higher in 2008 than 2004, but in several key upset states (such as Indiana and North Carolina) Obama's organization appeared to turn out large numbers of young people and African Americans. McCain was less successful turning out his Republican base than Bush was in 2004.

Unlike Bush's slim victories in 2000 and 2004, Obama's margin of victory in the Electoral College was significant, 365 to 173. But Obama's margin was smaller than that of both Clinton victories (1992, 1996), George Herbert Walker Bush's victory over Michael Dukakis (1988), and both Reagan victories (1980, 1984).

The electoral map in 2008 had strong resemblances to the 2000 and 2004 maps. The West Coast and Northeast are solid blue while much of the South and the Rocky Mountain West is red. How was the 2008 result different? McCain lost nine states that Bush won at least once, and McCain won no state that Bush lost.

Colorado, Florida, Nevada, and Ohio were close in 2000 and 2004. It is not surprising that Obama won them in a strong Democratic (anti-Republican) year. The big upsets for Obama occurred in five states that typically vote Republican in presidential races: Indiana, Iowa, New Hampshire, North Carolina, and Virginia.

In the House of Representatives, the Democrats solidified their majority by picking up 21 seats. They began 2009 with a large partisan advantage: 257 to 178. The bigger story occurred in the Senate, where the Democratic margin mushroomed from 51–49 to 59–41 (counting the two independents with the Democrats). With Republicans facing another difficult election in 2010 (when more Republican than Democratic Senate seats will be up for competition), the Democratic Party has a realistic chance of acquiring 60 or more seats in the Senate for the last two years of Obama's four-year term.

Obama's clear 2008 victory and the Democratic gains in Congress certainly put many Bush policies at significant risk. In table 12.3 I offer my own predictions of specific Bush policies that seem to be prime candidates for reversal by the Obama administration or the Democratic Congress.

Table 12.3. Bush Domestic Policies Most Vulnerable to Reversal

Policy	Predicted Change
2001 Tax Cut	Larger marginal tax rates in the two higher-income brackets
Estate tax repeal (2010)	Likely to be reinstituted
Shift in federal spending mix from non-defense to defense	Less emphasis on defense and homeland security spending
NCLB	More federal funding, broader focus than math and reading, more weight to uniform national tests, and more use of "growth-based" measures of learning.
Drug coverage	Controls on drug pricing, more regulation of insurers, elimination of the "doughnut hole."
Oil and gas drilling	More environmental restrictions, fewer tax incentives
Coal	More environmental regulation
Nuclear power	Delay or termination of the Yucca Mountain project; less emphasis on reprocessing of wastes
Renewables	R & D shift from advanced nuclear and fossil fuels to renewables; federal mandate of renewables in the electric power sector; more tax incentives for renewables.
Climate policy	Shift from voluntary measures to mandatory cap-and-trade program. New international strategy. Approve California plans.
Mercury pollution	Shift from cap-and-trade program to plant-by-plant technology standards.
Immigration	Halt completion of fencing on Mexican border and diminish the crackdowns in factories.
Tort reforms	Less assertion of federal preemption of state laws
Regulatory reform	New executive order on regulatory analysis; less emphasis on monetary aspects of benefit-cost analysis; less review of existing rules.
Wall Street bailout	Shift of funding emphasis from banks to homeowners with financial problems; new financial regulatory system.

Will Obama de-polarize American politics and facilitate more bipartisan lawmaking in the Congress? Like Bush in 2000, Obama campaigned in 2008 as a uniter. However, the polarizing forces described in chapter 1 remain a fundamental feature of American politics, and they may be larger than any presidential personality can overcome. Moreover, the 2006 and 2008 elections should not necessarily be interpreted as a public call for bipartisanship. The 2006 results reflected voter weariness with the Iraq war, Bush's unpopularity, and the corruption in Congress.[17] The 2008 election results were driven primarily by the uncertainty created by the financial meltdown and Bush's personal unpopularity.

President Obama will confront resistance from both the left and right if he seeks bipartisan consensus before making new laws. The Republican leadership in Congress will be under pressure from party activists to block a liberal policy agenda through filibuster threats in the Senate while Democratic Party activists will become angry if Obama compromises with Republican leaders in Congress. While Obama may find a few bipartisan wins early in his tenure, we should expect widespread GOP opposition if he pursues a legislative agenda aimed at pleasing Democratic Party activists.

A more likely scenario is that Obama and the Democratic leaders in Congress will seek to overwhelm the GOP with Democratic votes in the House and Senate, while reaching out to a small number of Senate Republicans. All Obama will need, if the Democrats are fairly disciplined, is a handful of GOP votes in the Senate (to provide an insurance policy against several defections among Democratic senators). Much will depend on the precise content of Obama's lawmaking agenda and how well it is communicated and worked out with powerful interest groups.

Competitive Party Politics

A close election is not necessarily polarized, and a polarized election is not necessarily close.[18] Our two parties are competitive both in their ability to win presidential elections and in their capacity to seize a majority in one or both houses of the Congress. The Republicans captured the Congress in 1994 and enlarged their margins in 2002 and 2004. The Democrats acquired the upper hand in 2006 and 2008, and they may make further gains in 2010. But those gains may be difficult to sustain thereafter. Anyone who thinks it is impossible for a Republican candidate to win the White House in 2012 does not appreciate the competitiveness of American politics.

Table 12.4. Electoral College: States with Partisan Leanings, 1992–2004

Leans Democratic (Votes)	Leans Republican (Votes)	Battleground States (Votes)
California (55)	Alaska (3)	Colorado (9)
Connecticut (7)	Alabama (9)	Florida (27)
D.C. (3)	Arkansas (6)	Iowa (7)
Delaware (3)	Arizona (10)	Missouri (11)
Hawaii (4)	Georgia (15)	Montana (3)
Illinois (21)	Idaho (4)	New Hampshire (4)
Massachusetts (12)	Indiana (11)	New Mexico (5)
Maryland (10)	Kansas (6)	Nevada (5)
Maine (4)	Kentucky (8)	Ohio (20)
Michigan (17)	Louisiana (9)	West Virginia (5)
Minnesota (10)	Mississippi (6)	
New Jersey (15)	North Carolina (15)	
New York (31)	North Dakota (3)	
Oregon (7)	Nebraska (5)	
Pennsylvania (21)	Oklahoma (7)	
Rhode Island (4)	South Carolina (8)	
Vermont (3)	South Dakota (3)	
Washington (11)	Tennessee (11)	
Wisconsin (10)	Texas (34)	
	Utah (5)	
	Virginia (13)	
	Wyoming (3)	
TOTAL: 248	TOTAL: 194	TOTAL: 96

Notes: Assignments of states were based on presidential election results in 1992, 1996, 2000, and 2004. With a few exceptions, all states listed as leaning Democratic (Republican) voted for the Democratic (Republican) candidate in all four elections. Four states are listed as leaning Republican even though they voted for Clinton in 1992 and/or 1996: Arkansas, Kentucky, Louisiana, and Tennessee. All four were won by George W. Bush in 2000 and 2004.

No presidential candidate since 1988 has won more than 53 percent of the popular vote.[19] With viable general-election candidates, both parties appear to have a strong chance of winning 175–200 votes in the Electoral College (see table 12.4). In fact, it is difficult to envision how a viable presidential candidate from either party could be trounced, given that New York and California will likely vote Democratic and much of the South and Rocky Mountain West will likely vote

Republican. Roughly ten states become "the battleground," especially Florida and the Midwest from Ohio to Iowa.

House races tell the story of competitiveness more clearly. In 1994 Newt Gingrich and the Republicans seized control of the House, receiving 52 percent of the popular vote to the Democrats' 45 percent. Since 1994, the popular vote was evenly split in 1996, with 49 percent for each major party; the Republicans won 49 percent to the Democrats' 48 percent in 1998 and 2000; and the Republicans edged out the Democrats 51 percent to 46 percent in 2002 and 50 percent to 48 percent in 2004. Even with the huge Democratic congressional sweep in 2006, the popular vote margin in House races was a modest eight percentage points: 53 percent to 45 in the Democrats's favor. The 2008 congressional margin was similar. Control of the White House and the Congress are being determined by relatively small margins, which itself helps explain why the partisan dimension of American politics has become so tenacious.[20]

Given this political history, it is likely that future presidents will face a divided electorate and a Congress where the opposing political party has substantial power, even if it is in the minority in both chambers. Balanced polarization causes virtually all policy issues to be examined by party leaders through the lens of potential partisan gain or loss. Consequently, politicians are under increasing pressure to make decisions according to partisan criteria rather than from an assessment of their constituents' interests or an analysis of the virtues of a particular policy.

Guidance for Future Presidents

If polarization is unavoidable in modern American politics, how should activist presidents go about their business of making public policy? In chapters 2 through 11, I explored how George W. Bush fared on a wide range of domestic policy issues. Here I argue that much can be learned from Bush's experience, both his successes and his failures.

LESSON #1: A WHITE HOUSE EFFORT TO PASS LEGISLATION THROUGH
THE CONGRESS ON A PARTY-LINE VOTE IS UNLIKELY TO SUCCEED.

Legislative proposals by the president that please the party faithful are destined to die in a polarized Congress unless they attract some support from the opposing party. Even if the president's party has a clear majority in both the House and Senate, a party-line vote will typically not be sufficient to invoke cloture and prevent a filibuster in the Senate by members of the opposing party.

When Bush made legislative proposals that did not attract any Democratic support, those proposals failed to pass the Congress. That is why Bush failed to make progress on Social Security reform and tort reform (with the exception of the transfer of some class-action suits from state to federal courts).

There are some exceptions to this lesson. In 2001, for example, congressional Republicans repealed the Clinton-era ergonomics regulation through a largely partisan strategy (see chapter 10). The legislative vehicle for repeal was the 1996 Congressional Review Act (CRA), which dispensed with the sixty-vote requirement to end debate in the Senate and provides that a simple majority vote in the House and Senate, coupled with the president's signature, is sufficient to overturn a recently enacted regulation.

The CRA is unlikely to have widespread use in the future because presidents have little reason to seek legislative reversal of rules that they have engineered and supported. The repeal of the ergonomics rule was an aberration because the rule was issued at the end of one president's term and was opposed by the incoming president, and the new president's party also happened to possess a majority in both the House and Senate. A similar pattern could occur early in the Obama administration against some high-profile rules issued in the waning months of the Bush administration (for instance, Bush's last-minute effort to ease rules under the Endangered Species Act could be reversed under the CRA), but most likely the CRA will be useful only in a handful of cases.

Similarly, the budget reconciliation procedures in the Congress permit some fiscal policies to be adopted on majority votes. Even when Bush used this procedure aggressively on tax cuts, he typically needed some Democratic votes to offset defecting Republicans.

Bush's early legislative successes with Congress may have reflected some learning from Clinton's difficulties, as Clinton was arguably the first president to serve in the modern era of polarization.[21] In 1993, the congressional Republicans sought to deny Clinton his first major legislative package: a stimulus plan for the economy. The stimulus passed the House 218–215, without a single Republican vote. (At the time, the Democrats had 258 seats.) It then passed the Senate on a 51–50 vote, with Vice President Gore casting the tie-breaking vote. Although Clinton won the stimulus package, he later lost his top domestic policy initiative, health care reform, to unified Republican opposition.[22]

The Democratic Party may deliver Obama at least sixty Senate seats in 2010 and tempt Obama and the Democrats to practice partisan lawmaking like LBJ did in the 1960s. Even with sixty to sixty-five Democratic members of the Senate, Obama (or any future president) will find significant insurance value in at least a handful of votes in the Senate from the opposing party (since some defections by members of the majority party should be expected).

In a balanced polarized setting, the opposing party has a strong strategic incentive to block any legislative proposal from the White House aimed primarily at pleasing the president's base.[23] A realistic White House should expect unified and effective opposition to such proposals.

LESSON #2: THE START OF A PRESIDENT'S FOUR-YEAR TERM—FIRST OR SECOND TERM—SHOULD BEGIN WITH A DOMESTIC LEGISLATIVE SUCCESS, EVEN IF SUCCESS ENTAILS A HIGH DEGREE OF COMPROMISE WITH SELECTED MEMBERS OF THE OPPOSING PARTY AND A RISK OF OFFENDING SEGMENTS OF THE PRESIDENT'S BASE.

All presidents, but especially those who enter the Oval Office with thin margins of victory in the popular vote and the Electoral College, need to demonstrate early in their term that they can move legislation through Congress. Since presidents possess limited constitutional powers in domestic policy, their real power is rooted in their ability to set the agenda, persuade, cajole, and bargain.[24]

A president's reserve of political capital is almost never greater than soon after his or her election or re-election.[25] Yet, honeymoon periods for presidents have become shorter, especially in America's polarized politics. An early legislative win establishes the president's credibility and creates political momentum for the administration's entire domestic agenda.[26] Thus, one of the key considerations at the start of a four-year term is the practicality of the president's top legislative priorities.

Tax cuts are certainly a base-pleasing proposal for any Republican president, and Bush quickly proposed a large tax cut in 2001. If tax cuts had required sixty votes in the Senate, the Democrats might have succeeded in blocking Bush's agenda. Using the reconciliation procedure, only a majority vote was required. With the Democratic threat of filibuster removed, Bush got four rounds of tax cuts from 2001 to 2006, each time with the same cross-partisan strategy. The number of supportive Democrats declined with each successive tax cut, but Bush was always able to attract at least one Democratic vote to compensate for each defecting Republican. Thus, the tax cuts were a successful strategy for Bush because they both pleased his base and attracted the necessary Democratic support.

The education issue also proved to be a sound choice for Bush but for a very different reason. The national Democratic Party was already sympathetic to the need for a stronger federal role in public education. It was certainly not a surprise priority, since Governor Bush had highlighted his commitment to public education repeatedly during the 2000 campaign. The number of powerful interest groups with a stake in the issue (i.e., just the teachers' unions) was limited, and the president and the first lady had acquired significant knowledge of the issue from their experiences in Texas.[27]

Nonetheless, choosing education as a top legislative priority created political risks for Bush. His conservative base was offended because there was little conservative interest in either a stronger federal regulatory role in public education or an expansion of federal funding for public schools. Even worse, the one idea that could have enlisted an enthusiastic response among conservatives—a government-supported voucher that parents could use to send their children to private schools—was not a Bush priority. The voucher concept was so controversial (especially with teachers' unions) that it was perceived to be a show-stopper among House and Senate Democrats and many Republicans. When Bush signaled early in 2001 that he was willing to sign an education bill that did not include vouchers for private schools, he bargained away the favorite policy innovation of conservatives.

Passage of the No Child Left Behind Act did irk Bush's conservative base, but it boosted Bush's credibility in Washington, D.C. A major legislative success in early 2002, coupled with Bush's 2001 victory on tax cuts, created valuable momentum going into the rest of the first term. This momentum was established largely in the pre-9/11 period and, in any event, Bush's temporary boost in popularity after 9/11 did little to assist him on policies not related to national security.

At the start of the second term, Bush's top domestic priority was a reform of Social Security that would permit workers to place part of their Social Security taxes in private investment accounts. Although this proposal was grounded in sound economics, it was politically dubious. The razor-close 2004 election result did not suggest that Bush had acquired a mandate from the public to begin a process of privatizing Social Security.[28] Perversely, the proposal helped unify the Democrats in opposition (rather than divide them) and was quite frightening to nervous congressional Republicans. Bush's proposal never made it to a committee vote in either the House or the Senate, despite the fact that Bush devoted much of the first year of his second term to speaking on this topic throughout the country.[29]

Sometimes it is a good idea for the president to advocate a promising proposal that cannot be passed in Congress. For example, a president may seek to stimulate public debate, showcase an idea for the future, or verify to a segment of the public that he is on their side. In this case, however, Bush's failure on Social Security reform did nothing positive for his political standing or for the idea of investment accounts in an ownership society.[30] Based on Bush's track record, few Republicans will be inclined to promote the idea in the future, and we can be sure that the national Democratic Party will not advance the idea.

Losing opportunity in the first year of a second term is especially harmful because second-term presidents are plagued by the "lame duck" perception.[31] Unlike the first term, when Bush's momentum was palpable,[32] Bush's second term got off to a poor start. Given the continued fragility in Bush's political standing and the very real filibuster threat in the Senate, Bush's top legislative priority in the second term should have been an initiative with obvious attraction to at least a handful of Senate Democrats.

A number of possibilities might have worked better. For example, a revenue-neutral proposal to reform the corporate income tax by combining lower rates with a broader tax base (such as closing of loopholes) might have attracted substantial Democratic support while maintaining enthusiasm among the Republican voter base. Similarly, an energy plan aimed at reducing oil use in the transport sector of the economy, perhaps along the lines that Bush proposed in January 2007, would have sparked some bipartisan interest in 2005. A more ambitious policy to slow global climate change, accompanied by a new international climate strategy, would have been more risky with the president's base, but by 2005 thoughtful business leaders knew that states and localities were forcing the issue. By including federal preemption of state and local policies in a new national climate plan, Bush might have attracted some critical business allies and the support of the United Auto Workers and United Mine Workers. Business and industrial labor unions might then have helped deliver crossover Democrats for the White House effort.

Once Bush's top second-term priority was well on its way to success in Congress, Bush could then have introduced his more risky Social Security initiative from a posture of reinforced credibility and momentum. Admittedly, it is possible that the Democrats would have unified to oppose whatever Bush proposed at the start of his second term. In order to discourage unified Democratic opposition, Bush needed to make a proposal that contained an olive branch to at least a significant segment of Senate Democrats. It is rarely wise for a re-elected president to announce a top second-term priority that is promptly rejected by the Congress.

LESSON #3: BARRING UNUSUAL CIRCUMSTANCES, THE CLASSIC BIPARTISAN APPROACH TO PASSING LEGISLATION IS AN UNATTRACTIVE CHOICE FOR A PRESIDENT FACING A POLARIZED CONGRESS.

The classic bipartisan approach is an effort by the president to engage the leadership of the two parties, in both the House and the Senate, in a cooperative effort to pass legislation. It is distinguished from a purely partisan approach, where the president seeks to legislate based solely on votes from his party, or a "cross-partisan" approach, where the president recruits a limited number of supporters from the opposing party without engaging their leadership.[33]

In a polarized setting, a request by the president for bipartisan cooperation in the Congress is likely to require large compromises with leaders of the opposing party in order to succeed. The opposing leaders will be under pressure from their strong partisans to resist cooperation and refuse compromises with "the enemy."[34] The only real way for cooperation to be a "win" for the leaders of the opposing party is if they can persuade their activists that the president capitulated to their legislative demands. Otherwise, their cooperation may be seen as helping the president establish (or re-establish) himself as an effective leader.[35]

If the president makes the request for bipartisan legislation and the opposing leaders decline to cooperate (explicitly or implicitly), then the president's legislative initiative has failed. A blame game will ensue. The president can make an effort to blame the lack of progress on the Congress, but it is possible that the public will conclude instead that the president was not effective in working with the Congress.

There are unusual circumstances that may justify use of a bipartisan strategy. A tragic incident may occur that induces leaders of both parties to believe that it is essential that they work together cooperatively. Bush's homeland security legislation was passed in this fashion after 9/11, as was the Sarbanes-Oxley law after the Enron fiasco and the 2008 housing and finance laws after the financial meltdown.

Another infrequent justification for the bipartisan strategy may emerge when a president is seeking to pass domestic legislation that is more popular among the opposing party than among his own party. Bush almost lost his prescription drug benefit on the House floor because he did not pursue a bipartisan strategy. The drug benefit barely survived defections among rank-and-file House Republicans. Had Bush used a bipartisan approach to pass the prescription drug benefit, he might have better ensured legislative success, but the resulting bill might have been much more expensive, including fewer private-sector options and mandatory price controls on the pharmaceutical industry. Bush was fortunate that his cross-partisan strategy captured just enough votes to win in both chambers.

Some (including Bush himself) have speculated publicly that Bush's second term should have begun with making the immigration reform proposal the president's top legislative priority and coupling it with a bipartisan strategy. A case can be made for this view, following the successful experience with NCLB in Bush's first term. In my view, however, immigration reform was not a promising candidate for bipartisanship because it was opposed so strenuously by many party activists and opinion leaders in the Republican base—much more so than NCLB.

LESSON #4: ALTHOUGH IT DOES NOT ALWAYS WORK, A CROSS-PARTISAN STRATEGY BY THE WHITE HOUSE CAN OFTEN BYPASS THE POLARIZATION IN CONGRESS.

The cross-partisan strategy makes three critical assumptions: (1) The president can pass his favored plan in the House, (2) a limited number of Senators from the opposing party can be persuaded to support the initiative or bargain for a tolerable refinement, and (3) the number of defections in the Senate from the president's party can be kept to a tolerable level, given the number of crossovers from the opposing party. When the differences between the House and Senate versions of a bill are reconciled, the conference agreement must be able to attract a majority of House members as well as sixty or more senators (absent special procedures). If the leadership of the opposing party in Congress can enlist perfect discipline from its members, cross-partisanship can never work for the president.

In this book, we have reviewed Senate voting on forty-two measures where a White House initiative or position was at stake, and where crossover behavior can be examined. Table 12.5 summarizes these forty-two measures, including the overall Senate result as well as the number of Republican and Democratic crossovers. Votes where a three-fifths majority was required (explicitly or implicitly) are designated as "F" (filibuster). The other votes, designated "P," required a simple plurality, a majority of those voting. Votes that represent a win for the Bush White House are coded "W." In votes that were 51–50, Vice President Cheney cast the deciding vote, per Senate voting rules.

The number of crossover votes on each issue varies enormously, though most counts range from zero to fifteen per party. In a clear majority of cases (about five out of eight), the crossover count for a party is five votes or less, which is a clear indication of partisan unity in the Senate.

When there are more than fifteen crossover votes from a party, there are clear explanations. For example, it may be that the Democratic leadership in the Senate removed any pressure for party unity (as, for instance, in the final passage votes on energy and class-action reform in 2005). In the case of immigration, Bush's initiative had stronger support among Senate Democrats than Senate Republicans.

Some of the vote counts in table 12.5 refer to procedural matters (such as budgetary waivers and cloture motions) while others concern substantive issues. Sometimes party discipline is greater on procedural motions than on matters of policy, which is why I have included some critical procedural motions. Party leaders may expect more discipline on procedural votes since constituents and reporters may not fully understand their ramifications. Of course, insiders know that procedural votes often determine policy outcomes.

The forty-two measures in table 12.5 are not all of the legislative proposals during the Bush administration. Some are bills or amendments that would weaken, block, or rescind a Bush administration policy. In several cases, more than one vote addressed the same issue (for instance, permission for companies to drill for oil and gas in the Arctic National Wildlife Refuge [ANWR]). But most of the votes relate to Bush's legislative initiatives that provoked significant opposition. Overall, the position of the Bush administration prevailed on half of the issues.

We observed that Bush used the cross-partisan strategy on numerous occasions, and with notable success on tax cuts, prescription drug coverage, and

Table 12.5. Crossover (CO) Senate Vote Counts on 42 Key GWB Issues[a]

Vote	Issue	Rep CO	Dem CO	Overall Vote[b]	Required Majority[c]	Outcome for GWB[d]
1	Reduce 2001 Tax Cut	4	1	53–47	P	L
2	Shift Some 2001 Tax-Cut Dollars to Education	5	1	54–46	P	L
3	Final 2001 Tax Cut	0	12	62–38	P	W
4	2002 Budget Resolution	2	5	53–47	P	W
5	2004 Budget Resolution	2	1	51–50	P	W
6	2005 Budget Resolution	3	0	52–47	P	W
7	2007 Budget Resolution	5	1	51–49	P	W
8	Repeal Estate Tax	2	9	54–44	F	L
9	Reduce 2003 Tax Cut	3	0	51–48	P	L
10	Final 2003 Tax Cut (Passage)	3	2	51–50	P	W
11	Final 2005 Tax Cut (Passage)	3	3	54–44	P	W
12	Repeal Estate Tax	2	4	57–41	F	L
13	Social Security Petition[e]	NA	3	NA	NA	L
14	Vouchers: Private Schools	11	3	58–41	P	L
15	Prescription Drugs (Budget Waiver)	2	11	61–39	F	W
16	Final Drug Bill (Passage)	9	12	54–44	P	W
17	ANWR (Cloture)	8	5	54–46	F	L
18	CAFE—Pres. Discretion	6	19	62–38	P	W
19	Energy Bill (Cloture)	7	12	57–40	F	L
20	Energy Bill (Passage)	6	25	74–26	F	W
21	ANWR (Passage)	7	3	51–48	P	L
22	ANWR (Cloture)	3	4	56–44	F	L
23	Expand Oil & Gas Leases	4	0	55–45	P	L
24	Approve Yucca Project	3	15	60–39	P	W
25	Add Nuclear & Clean Coal to Renewables Mandate	7	0	56–39	P	L
26	Immigration (Cloture)	32	38	62–36	F	W
27	Immigration Bill (Passage)	37	34	53–46	F	L
28	Remove Energy Tax Reforms	9	1	59–40	F	W
29	Climate "Cap & Trade" Bill	6	11	60–38	F	W
30	Kill Climate Resolution	11	2	53–44	P	L
31	Delay NSR Reform	6	5	50–46	P	W
32	Reverse Mercury Rule	9	6	51–47	P	W
33	Climate Bill (Cloture)	7	4	48–36	F	W

Table 12.5. Crossover (CO) Senate Vote Counts on 42 Key GWB Issues[a] (cont.)

Vote	Issue	Rep CO	Dem CO	Overall Vote[b]	Required Majority[c]	Outcome for GWB[d]
34	Tort Reform, Gynecologists	3	1	48–45	F	L
35	Tort Reform, ER	3	1	49–48	F	L
36	Asbestos Bill (Cloture)	0	1	50–47	F	L
37	Asbestos Bill (Passage)	11	14	58–41	F	L
38	Tort Reform, Class Action	1	9	59–39	F	L
39	Tort Reform Class Action (Passage)	0	18	72–26	F	W
40	Disapproval of Ergonomics Rule	0	6	56–44	P	W
41	Block Overtime Reforms	5	1	52–47	P	L
42	Confirm OIRA Administrator	0	14	61–37	F	W

a. All of these issues and votes are covered in chapters 2 through 11. The order tracks their sequence in the book.

b. Some vote counts do not add up to 100 because some members did not vote.

c. "P" means only a plurality (usually a simple majority vote) was required; "F" means that a "filibuster-proof" 60-vote majority may have been required.

d. "W" is a win for GWB position; "L" is a loss for GWB position.

e. Issue no. 13 is a petition from Democratic senators to Bush, not a roll-call vote.

energy.[36] To execute cross-partisanship, the White House typically began with the outline of a legislative proposal (or some broad principles), but not necessarily with detailed, draft legislation. A White House–favored bill was passed in the House, and then a limited number of compromises were made with Senate Democrats in order to garner enough votes to reach a simple majority or the sixty-vote majority necessary to prevent a filibuster.[37]

The Bush White House typically assumed that a vague proposal was preferable to a more specific one because it left room for bargaining in Congress and afforded the White House more room to claim a legislative victory. Vagueness proved to be a liability in several cases. For example, the vagueness in Bush's initiatives on Social Security, immigration, and clean air may have hurt Bush's chance of success by slowing the deliberative process and providing time for the president's opponents to raise money, mobilize, and defeat his initiatives. The Bush White House needed a more informed basis for deciding when to focus on the general themes of legislative proposals and when to be highly specific with legislative language.

The cross-partisan strategy is promising, but it does not always work. In the case of immigration reform, the White House could not persuade House Republicans to pass Bush's key proposal: a guest worker program for the millions of illegal immigrants already residing in this country. Bush's failed efforts to reform medical malpractice law, embodied in multiple bills passed by the House, could not attract even a handful of Democratic senators in roll-call votes on the Senate floor. And the key votes on ANWR fell short for Bush due to defections by several Republican senators as well as virtually unanimous Democratic opposition.

Party discipline is easier to accomplish if the members of Congress are ideologically similar. As the number of Senate Democrats dwindled from 2001 to 2005, the surviving Democratic senators were more homogeneous, liberal, and unified. When the White House was effective, it was usually through attracting support from farm-state and southern Democrats. That was the key to Bush's success on energy. Bush's regional strategy on energy did trigger some losses among New England and northwestern Republicans (recall the environmental votes on ANWR, New Source Review, and mercury), but the gains among Democrats were sometimes more than adequate to compensate for the losses among Republicans.

If the president's party controls the Senate but not the House, a cross-partisan strategy is not likely to work because, under House rules, the House leadership can block the president's plan from reaching the House floor. Bush never faced this precise situation. If the president's party controls neither chamber, the cross-partisan strategy is usually infeasible because the leaders of the opposing party can use their agenda-control powers to block consideration of the president's plan. This is the conundrum that President Clinton faced from 1995 to 2000 and Bush faced from 2007 to 2008. Thus, the cross-partisan strategy has limited applicability.

LESSON #5: INSTEAD OF SEEING CROSSOVER VOTING IN THE SENATE AS RANDOM, THE WHITE HOUSE SHOULD SEE IT AS SOMEWHAT PREDICTABLE AND MANIPULABLE.

There were a handful of Republican and Democratic senators who frequently made crossover votes on Bush's domestic-policy agenda. Table 12.6 identifies those two groups of senators in both parties: those most likely and least likely to support the White House position on the forty-two measures covered in this book.

The Bush White House believed that one of the factors that predicted crossover potential was Bush's popular vote in a senator's home state. And there is some circumstantial evidence that validates this belief. For example, Republican senator Lincoln Chafee of Rhode Island repeatedly voted against the position of the Bush White House. Democrats Zell Miller of Georgia and Ben Nelson of Nebraska often voted in favor of the White House position. Notice in Table 12.6 that Bush ran poorly in Rhode Island in both 2000 and 2004 whereas he won Georgia and Nebraska comfortably in both elections.

A major exception to this pattern was the voting behavior of Republican senator John McCain, Bush's principal adversary for the Republican nomination in 2000. McCain frequently voted against Bush's domestic agenda, even though Bush carried Arizona easily in both elections. Given these data, it is surprising how often McCain was accused in 2008 of being another version of Bush! These data also help explain why some activist Republicans who were sympathetic to Bush's agenda harbored fears of McCain as president.

What can a president do to reduce defections by senators of his own party while increasing the number of crossover votes from the opposing party? On this critical question, the Bush experience offers several insights.

First, the president can make a direct appeal to the public or party activists in a senator's home state. Bush frequently traveled to the home state of a Democratic or Republican senator and made a public appeal on an issue to the local media, party activists, and voters.[38] Bush sometimes bypassed the national media entirely and gave privileged access to local media elites in a key state. Bush was not popular among Democrats, but his high favorability rating among Republicans helped him unify Senate Republicans and attract crossover Democrats representing GOP-leaning states.

Senators do take some political risk when they defy a request from a president who is popular in their state, or when they defy a president on an issue that is important to party activists in the senator's own party. Insofar as presidential popularity matters to crossover voting, what matters is the president's popularity in the home state of the senator who is considering a crossover vote. It is no accident that Republican senator Rick Santorum of Pennsylvania was defeated in his 2006 re-election bid. His voting record certainly left him vulnerable, since

Table 12.6. U.S. Senators with Highest Crossover Voting Rates on Bush's Democratic Priorities

Republicans	Crossover Rate (%)	GWB Vote in 2000/2004 (%)	Democrats	Crossover Rate (%)	GWB Vote in 2000/2004 (%)
1. Lincoln Chafee, RI	74	39, 32	1. Zell Miller, GA	85	58, 55
2. Olympia Snowe, ME	45	45, 44	2. Mary Landrieu, LA	45	57, 53
3. John McCain, AZ	43	55, 51	3. Blanche Lincoln, AR	45	54, 51
4. Susan Collins, ME	38	45, 44	4. Ben Nelson, NE	45	66, 62
5. John Sununu, NH	28	49, 48	5. John Breaux, LA	38	57, 53
6. Judd Gregg, NH	26	49, 48	6. Max Baucus, MT	38	59, 58
7. Gordon Smith, OR	26	47, 47	7. Mark Pryor, AR	21	54, 51
8. Norm Coleman, MN	18	48, 46	8. Tim Johnson, SD	20	60, 60
9. Lindsey Graham, SC	17	58, 57	9. Herbert Kohl, WI	20	49, 48
10. Mike DeWine, OH	17	51, 50	10. Evan Bayh, IN	18	60, 57
			11. Tom Carper, DE	18	46, 42

U.S. Senators with Lowest Crossover Voting Rates on Bush's Democratic Priorities

Republicans	Crossover Rate (%)	GWB Vote in 2000/2004 (%)	Democrats	Crossover Rate (%)	GWB Vote in 2000/2004 (%)
1. Sam Brownback, KS	0	62, 58	1. Harry Reid, NY	0	50, 50
2. Pat Roberts, KS	0	62, 58	2. Hillary Clinton, NY	0	40, 35
3. Mitch McConnell, KY	0	60, 57	3. John Kerry, MA	0	37, 33
4. Kay Bailey Hutchison, TX	0	61, 59	4. Frank Lautenberg, NJ	0	46, 40
5. Ted Stevens, AK	0	61, 59	5. Jon Corzine, NJ	0	46, 40
6. Wayne Allard, CO	0	52, 51	6. Charles Schumer, NY	2.56	40, 35
7. Larry Craig, ID	0	68, 67	7. Barbara Boxer, CA	2.56	44, 42
8. Robert Bennett, UT	0	72, 67	8. John Reed, RI	2.70	39, 32
9. George Allen, VA	0	54, 52	9. Patty Murray, WA	2.78	46, 45
10. Rick Santorum, PA	0	48, 46	10. Paul Sarbanes, MD	2.94	43, 40

Note: 1. Others with a crossover rate of zero: Saxy Chambliss, GA; James Talent, MO; Richard Burr, NC; Thomas Coburn, OK; John Cornyn, TX.

he rarely defected from Bush's agenda even though Bush's performance at the polls in Pennsylvania was weak in both 2000 and 2004 (see table 12.6).

Making numerous crossover votes creates a different kind of political problem: Party loyalists seek to dislodge the disloyal member. Republican senator Lincoln Chafee of Rhode Island was targeted by Club for Growth (a well-financed conservative group), was damaged by this primary opposition, and then lost his 2006 general election bid.

When a president's popularity is low (especially among voters aligned with the opposing party), the leader of the opposing party may find it easy to enlist or impose discipline. Bush experienced this conundrum as his popularity declined steadily during his second term. Finding crossover Democrats became more difficult, in part because Senate Democrats realized that the White House sought to exploit crossover Democrats to boost Bush's credibility and compensate for his limited political standing.

Second, a president can optimize crossover voting by mobilizing interest groups on his behalf. Thus, the Bush White House collaborated with key interest groups with ties to wavering Democrats, such as the auto workers and coal miners on environmental votes and the AARP on the prescription drug votes.

When executing a cross-partisan strategy, the positions of key interest groups with ties to the opposing party are especially critical. A White House of one party may discover that a particular group's interest in legislation conflicts with the opposing party's strategic interest in blocking the president's agenda. Even if personal appeals by a Republican president cannot win the vote of a Democratic senator, interest groups with ties to that senator may be able to deliver his or her vote. Since interest groups typically care more about the welfare of their members than they do about partisan politics, they play a key role in cross-partisan strategies. If a senator does not respond to interest-group pressure, he creates re-election risk for himself. One of the reasons that Democrat Tom Daschle of South Dakota lost his re-election bid in 2004 is that farm interests perceived that he had failed to work effectively with Bush on pro-ethanol policies.

A White House held by one party should not be timid about opening dialogue with interest groups that typically support politicians of the other party. For it is those dialogues that lead to some of the most creative cross partisan strategies.

Finally, classic logrolling—offering members support on unrelated issues—can be exploited to encourage loyalty by members of one's own party or support by members of the opposing party. We saw various forms of logrolling in chapters 2 through 11. By adding subsidies for rural health care to the prescription drug bill, additional votes were garnered in the House. By adding more money for the states to a budget resolution, the White House recruited badly needed Senate votes for Bush's second round of tax cuts. The terms of logrolling tend to be kept secret, and thus the pervasiveness of this age-old legislative tactic is not known with certainty. If one thinks of the inducement as a "side payment," then larger side payments may be required in polarized settings. Now that party leaders have more powers and resources to induce loyalty from their members, the side payments necessary to induce crossover behavior can be quite large.

LESSON #6: THE CROSS-PARTISAN LEGISLATIVE STRATEGY IS ATTRACTIVE TO THE WHITE HOUSE BECAUSE IT MINIMIZES THE NUMBER OF COMPROMISES THAT MUST BE MADE TO MEMBERS OF THE OPPOSING PARTY, AND MINIMIZES INTRAPARTY CRITICISM OF THE PRESIDENT.

Compared to classic bipartisanship, the cross-partisan strategy was attractive to the Bush White House for a variety of reasons. Most important, it protected Bush's policy agenda from excessive modification because the number of compromises necessary to pass the bill in Congress was minimized. A more subtle attraction is that the strategy reaped political intelligence about when members are "cross-pressured." For example, it exposed vulnerable members of the opposing party who were under pressure to shortchange the interests of their constituents in favor of national party preferences. Democratic senator Tom Daschle of South Dakota was exposed in this way on the energy bill, and he was ultimately defeated in his 2004 re-election bid. Cross-partisanship also exposes members of the president's party who are inclined to be disloyal to the president (such as Lincoln Chafee of Rhode Island), thereby directing intraparty criticism at the disloyal members rather than at the president.

When the president seeks a bipartisan rather than a cross-partisan solution, he may subject himself to severe criticism from within his own party, as numerous compromises are made to meet the demands of the leadership of the opposing party. When Bush allowed the NCLB deliberations to become virtually bipartisan, the resulting compromises annoyed conservatives. Since fragile presidents are in a poor position to withstand intraparty criticism, they should prefer cross-partisan to bipartisan strategies. That is why some scholars refer to the cross-partisan strategy as "cheap bipartisanship."[39]

The cross-partisan strategy is a creative and powerful tool for the White House, but it is not a panacea for a president dealing with a polarized Congress. It is not easy for the White House to execute this kind of strategy because many factors influence the voting behaviors of individual members of Congress. Moreover, the margins of victory and defeat may be small, which means that the White House will face considerable uncertainty as to whether a desired initiative will be enacted. Nonetheless, compared to a partisan or bipartisan strategy, the cross-partisan strategy will usually be the most promising for a president who is governing in a competitive, polarized setting.

LESSON #7: THE EXECUTIVE TOOLS OF POLICY MAKING CAN BE QUITE EFFECTIVE IN A POLARIZED ENVIRONMENT, EVEN THOUGH THEY ARE LESS VISIBLE THAN PASSING LEGISLATION.

In virtually all areas of domestic policy, presidents can use executive powers, limited as they are, to reform public policy. Those powers include executive orders, rule making, information campaigns, and enforcement activities. Executive action can be an alternative to the controversy and time associated with legislation, a fallback in the event that a proposal fails to move in the Congress, a way to complement or implement legislative action, or a tool to enhance the prospects for future legislative action.

There are two key assumptions behind the executive strategy: The president's appointees have sufficient control of the bureaucracy to undertake desired executive action, and the lawyers in the agencies or the White House can craft a legal case that gives the executive action a decent chance to survive litigation in the courts by opponents of the president's action. Although these conditions may seem obvious, they are not always satisfied. For instance, agencies with recalcitrant civil servants may not work productively for the president's policy priorities.

Executive actions can certainly be overturned by a determined Congress. But when the Congress is polarized, it may be quite difficult for opponents of an executive action to accomplish a reversal in both the House and Senate, especially if opponents face a presidential veto. We saw this scenario unfold when Bush modernized overtime pay, despite substantial opposition in both the House and the Senate.

A future president can also reverse or modify a predecessor's executive action, but new presidents are often more interested in expending political capital on their own agenda. Of the numerous "midnight regulations" passed by the Clinton administration in 2000, only a handful were overturned by the Bush administration. Even when a new president reverses a predecessor's rule making, the courts may review the action with special scrutiny, because hasty actions attract the attention of careful judges.[40]

Holding back executive initiatives to wait for a doomed legislative proposal is rarely advisable. For example, as early as 2003 the Bush administration was prepared to make several administrative reforms to the Endangered Species Act (ESA), such as clarifying the processes for listing or delisting a species and designating critical habitat that requires protection. These administrative reforms were continually delayed on the dubious theory that Congress might address the problems through an ambitious legislative reform of the Endangered Species Act. Although legislative action in the House was plausible (and in fact a limited bill passed the House in 2005), there was never a realistic possibility that legislation would pass the Senate. That is largely because Lincoln Chafee of Rhode Island had a pivotal role in the Senate Committee on Environment and Public Works and was not enthusiastic about ESA reform.[41] Late in 2008, the Bush administration made a hasty effort to reform some aspects of the ESA through rule making, but this belated effort is vulnerable to reversal.[42]

In the case of Clear Skies, Bush started with a legislative proposal but was aware that the Congress might not be receptive. He instructed his advisers to prepare a series of rule makings aimed at accomplishing much of what Clear Skies would do. Some of these rule makings (for example, reform of industrial permits under New Source Review) began before the fate of Clear Skies was apparent, while others were held back until Bush's allies in the Senate agreed that there was no remaining hope for Clear Skies. Some of the clean-air reforms, among them NSR reform and the mercury trading rule, were unpopular among many Democrats and New England Republicans, but Bush had sufficient support in the polarized Congress to protect them from legislative reversal.

Even in situations where a legislative proposal is the centerpiece of the president's initiative, passage of the legislation does not necessarily implement the president's policy. The fine print of legislation does not resolve all the issues, leaving key matters to be resolved through executive action. Each of Bush's successful legislative proposals was accompanied by a less visible yet important implementation process that was accomplished through public information, rule makings, and enforcement actions.

In the cases of education reform and the new prescription drug benefit, there were key executive actions following passage of the legislation that facilitated implementation of these complex programs. For example, the executive actions under NCLB established the ground rules for what school districts must do to comply with the new law. On prescription drugs, the executive actions played an important role in making sure that the marketplace responded with an adequate diversity of insurance plans. Information campaigns also helped many senior citizens understand their options and become more familiar with the new plan. Without these executive actions, Bush's education and health reforms may have encountered insurmountable opposition in the implementation phase.

Executive actions can also be used by the president to move modestly on an issue, thereby helping the White House block (or delay) overly ambitious legislative proposals in the Congress or in the states. Bush's auto mileage rules, which steadily improved the fuel economy of SUVs and pickup trucks through model year 2011, accomplished several purposes. They advanced the president's energy-conservation agenda, they strengthened the case against unrealistic legislative proposals in the Congress, and they helped provide a rationale for preemption of the proliferation of conflicting programs at the state level, such as California's program to regulate greenhouse gas emissions from new vehicles.[43]

By using executive power to build trust among key interest groups, the president can pave the way for landmark legislation. The auto mileage rule makings were an interesting case where the Bush White House was able to use a limited rule making on light trucks as a forum to familiarize the United Auto Workers, the Big Three and some moderate environmental groups with his reform plan. Several years later, when fuel prices were high and Congress was attentive, Bush won a major legislative victory on the reform of auto mileage standards.

Executive powers also need to be used to restrain inappropriate or hostile actions by state and local policy makers. In areas of federal responsibility, it is crucial for the president to consider when strong federal actions should be used to preempt a plethora of costly and contradictory state and local programs.[44] Bush used rule-making power to preempt state and local action in policy areas ranging from auto mileage requirements and food safety to the warning labels (package inserts) on prescription drugs.

In unusual circumstances, executive actions can also be used by the president as a tool to enhance the prospects of the president's legislative agenda. In immigration policy, for example, House Republicans argued that the border should be secured before Congress passed Bush's guest worker program. Sensing the key role of border security in the debate, Bush in 2005 authorized the Department of Homeland Security to expedite removals of illegal immigrants at the border and to punish employers who are hiring illegal immigrants. By taking executive actions that addressed some of the concerns of the House conservatives, Bush enhanced the chances that the House and Senate could find a compromise on immigration. Although the House did not budge, the executive actions may help pave the way for comprehensive immigration legislation in the future.

Thus, although executive action is less publicized than legislation and of less interest to scholars, it is one of the president's most powerful and versatile tools. It is especially important in a polarized setting when legislative reform is unrealistic but Congress is too divided to block the president's executive action.

LESSON #8: WHEN CREATIVE RULE-MAKING STRATEGIES ARE CONSIDERED TO ACHIEVE POLICY GOALS, THE PRESIDENT SHOULD REALIZE THAT THERE ARE SIGNIFICANT RISKS OF JUDICIAL REVERSAL BUT BE PREPARED TO TAKE THOSE RISKS WHEN THE POLICY PAYOFFS ARE HIGH AND THE COSTS OF AN UNFAVORABLE JUDICIAL OUTCOME ARE LOW.

The president will frequently face circumstances where the Congress is too polarized to pass desired legislation. At the same time, the Congress may be too polarized to block an assertive president from achieving the same policy goals through rule-making action. Precisely this scenario unfolded for Bush on several occasions: reform of overtime law, control of mercury pollution from coal plants, reform of clean-air permitting at power plants and oil refineries, and modernization of mileage standards for motor vehicles.

When it is not clear whether the president possesses the legal authority to undertake rule-making action, and where opposing interests are likely to challenge a new rule in federal court, the White House faces significant risk from judicial review. It is inexpensive for opposing interests to litigate the president's decision, and such litigation is common.

In theory, the federal judiciary is supposed to afford some degree of deference to presidential discretion, especially when the relevant statutes are silent, confusing, or conflicting. In reality, the federal judiciary—like the Congress—has also become somewhat polarized on partisan and ideological grounds.[45] As a result, the White House may not know the degree of legal risk they are facing until a final rule is issued and a specific judge or three-judge panel has been assigned to their case. Bush lost some important cases on clean-air and auto mileage standards where the panels were not favorable to the president from a partisan or ideological perspective.

Even when a court does not have a partisan orientation, the reasoning of judges can be speculative and unpredictable. For example, on Bush's decision not to regulate carbon dioxide as an air pollutant under the Clean Air Act, Bush won a 2–1 decision in a federal appeals court but then lost a 5–4 decision in the U.S. Supreme Court. Neither court was stacked against the White House on partisan or ideological grounds, but the opinions of both courts were unpredictable. Surprisingly, the Supreme Court's decision ultimately provided an avenue for Bush to accomplish at the Environmental Protection Agency the same policy outcome he was trying to accomplish at the Department of Transportation! Thus, in the course of blocking a rule making, a court may allow the president power that he did not realize was available—in effect, the president wins by losing.

Many government lawyers will urge caution in the face of legal risks, but it is often wise for an assertive president to move forward despite the legal risks. Since rule making and judicial review often take multiple rounds to reach resolution, a persistent president can win a substantial percentage of the time.

If the president loses the first round of litigation but a court's reasoning is questionable, the president may do better after a rehearing or after an appeal to a higher court. Bush's Clean Air Interstate Rule was found to be legally deficient by a federal appeals court. After a rehearing, the same court decided to allow the rule to remain in place until the specific flaws were corrected by the agency. Even if a rule is overturned on legal grounds, the typical remedy ordered by a court is reconsideration of the issue. A court will rarely decide whether a rule must be issued and will almost never order exactly how a rule must be written.

If the president gambles for 100 percent of his policy in an initial rule making and loses in court, the president can come back with a revised rule that accomplishes, say, 70 percent or 80 percent of the president's policy. In the case of mercury pollution, the Bush administration tried to establish a pollution trading regime under a little-used section of the Clean Air Act. The court overturned the rule on narrow legal grounds. If time had permitted, Bush could have crafted a similar policy with a different legal rationale. Unfortunately, by delaying the mercury rule making until it was clear that Clear Skies would not move in the Congress (2005), Bush lost precious time to work the federal judiciary in his favor. Now it appears the issue will be resolved by the Obama administration.

Interest groups opposed to the president's policy will frequently threaten litigation against a rule making. The White House should not be intimidated by such threats since the White House may win the litigation, as it won against labor's lawsuit contesting the rule to disclose more financial information about the operation of labor unions. Even if a court blocks a rule, it may not offer a rationale that threatens the core of the president's policy; this was the case with the judicial reversal of Bush's mileage standards for light trucks, which did not upset Bush's safety-oriented, size-based reforms. If a court issues a bad opinion, it may change the dynamics in Congress and allow a congressional resolution to occur. Some specialists predict that Congress will ultimately pass Bush's Clean Air Interstate Rule, even though the court found legal flaws in the rule under existing statutory authority.

The key lesson from the George W. Bush years is one familiar to presidential scholars: Presidents are "well advised to be stubbornly realistic in understanding who they are, how they came to be in the Oval Office and what their own strengths and weaknesses are . . ."[46] Bush was most effective as a policy maker when he recognized his limited political standing, analyzed the polarization in Congress, and devised an agenda that Republicans could support and Democrats found difficult to oppose in a united way. Bush also used executive powers to institute policies that a polarized Congress could not block.

When Bush was least effective, it was because he either offended large segments of his base, as on immigration reform; made proposals that pleased his base without attracting even limited Democratic support, such as Social Security reform; or pursued dubious legislation when rule making was a more promising strategy, as with reform of endangered species rules. When Bush lost control of key issues to Congress, the states, or the courts, as happened with climate policy, bad results often resulted for his base as well as the nation.

Bush's bold foreign policies will continue to attract most of the ink, but his domestic policies on taxes, education, health care, energy, clean air, labor, and regulatory reform are likely to change this country for many years.[47] Unlike the case of Iraq and Afghanistan, where the merits of U.S. policy remain in doubt (especially considering the large cost of the prolonged occupation of Iraq), what Bush accomplished in domestic policy is often quite promising. Where his domestic policies prove to be insufficient or imperfect, it should be feasible for those policies to be refined or fixed without changing Bush's fundamental policy direction. Obama and the Democratic Congress will certainly reverse some of Bush's policies, but refinements may be more common than reversals. Thus, Bush's activism in domestic policy may outperform his activism abroad.

Notes

1. Ambiguous Mandate, Polarized Congress

1. Susan Page, "Bush's Disapproval Rating Worst of Any President in 70 Years," *USA Today,* April 22, 2008, p. 7A.

2. "The Bush Legacy: War Horse," *Economist,* March 1, 2008, pp. 90–91; John D. McKinnon, Alex Frangos, and Elizabeth Holmes, "Can Bush Transcend His Own Record?" *Wall Street Journal,* Jan. 28, 2008, p. A6.

3. The typically light treatment of Bush's domestic policies is evident in Jonathan Rauch, "Small Ball After All?" *National Journal,* Sept. 20, 2008, pp. 22–28.

4. Jacob Weisberg, "The Bush Who Got Away," *New York Times,* Jan. 28, 2008 (online) (Bush was "too distracted by war and foreign policy"); Peter Wallsten and James Gerstenzang, "Bush's Agenda Loses Focus," *Los Angeles Times,* March 19, 2006, p. 1; Jim Vandetti and Mike Allen, "A Domestic Policy in Sharp Focus," *Washington Post,* Dec. 10, 2004, p. A01; Susan Page, "Conflict Will Define Bush's Role in History," *USA Today,* March 14, 2006, p. A1.

5. Dana Milbank, "Bush's Domestic Policy Gap," *Washington Post,* Oct. 12, 2004, p. A21.

6. Dana Milbank and Jonathan Weisman, "Conservatives Restive about Bush Policies: Fresh Initiatives Sought on Iraq, Domestic Issues," *Washington Post,* May 10, 2004, p. A01; Gary Mucciaroni and Paul J. Quirk, "Deliberations of a 'Compassionate Conservative,'" in *The Bush Presidency: Appraisals and Prospects,* ed. Colin Campbell and Bert A. Rockman (Washington, D.C.: CQ Press, 2004), 182–83.

7. Karen M. Hult, "The Bush White House in Comparative Perspective," in *The George W. Bush Presidency,* ed. Fred I. Greenstein (Baltimore: Johns Hopkins University Press, 2003), 65–66 (discussing turnover in Bush's domestic policy and economic advisers).

8. Wallsten and Gerstenzang, "Bush's Agenda," p. 1 (quoting a quip from Michael Tanner, director of health and welfare studies at the libertarian Cato Institute: "You mean they have a domestic policy?").

9. Dan Balz, "Bush's Ambitious Second-Term Agenda Hits Realities," in *Second-Term Blues: How George W. Bush Has Governed,* ed. John C. Fortier and Norman J. Ornstein (Washington, D.C.: American Enterprise Institute and Brookings Institution Press, 2007), pp. 17–18; Sean Wilentz, "The Worst President in History," *Rolling Stone,* May 2, 2006, p. 34 (Bush's weakness was an "unswerving adherence to a simplistic ideology"; he chose "rigid ideology" over leadership that might have built a national consensus).

10. Mucciaroni and Quirk, "Deliberations," pp. 162, 182.

11. Ronald Brownstein, "A Possible Fatal Flaw in GOP Formula for Success," *Los Angeles Times,* Oct. 22, 2006, p. A18; "Job Performance Evaluations: The President," Editorial, *Los Angeles Times,* Dec. 31, 2006, p. M5. Joshua Green, "The Rove Presidency," *Atlantic,* September 2007, pp. 53–72.

12. One writer makes a similar point: "Paradoxically, this chief executive who prided himself on assertive, even aggressive leadership proved to be not a weak strong president but a surprisingly strong weak president." Jonathan Rauch, "Small Ball After All?" *National Journal,* Sept. 20, 2008, p. 25

13. For an edited volume on many aspects of the Bush presidency, see Gary L. Gregg II and Mark J. Rozell, eds., *Considering the Bush Presidency* (New York: Oxford University Press, 2004); for a more journalistic account of deliberations inside the Bush White House, see Robert Draper, *Dead Certain: The Presidency of George W. Bush* (New York: Free Press, 2007).

14. John P. Burke, *Becoming President: The Bush Transition, 2000–2003* (Boulder, Colo.: Lynne Rienner, 2004).

15. Fred I. Greenstein, ed., *The George W. Bush Presidency: An Early Assessment* (Baltimore: Johns Hopkins University Press, 2003).

16. John C. Fortier and Norman J. Ornstein, eds., *Second-Term Blues: How George W. Bush Has Governed* (Washington, D.C.: American Enterprise Institute and Brookings Institution Press, 2007).

17. Fred Barnes, *Rebel-in-Chief: Inside the Bold and Controversial Presidency of George W. Bush* (New York: Crown Forum, 2006).

18. Fred I. Greenstein, *The Presidential Difference: Leadership Style from FDR to George W. Bush* (Princeton, N.J.: Princeton University Press, 2004); Donald F. Kettle, *Team Bush: Leadership Lessons from the Bush White House* (New York: McGraw-Hill, 2003).

19. Lou Cannon and Carl M. Cannon, *Reagan's Disciple: George W. Bush's Troubled Quest for a Presidential Legacy* (New York: Public Affairs, 2008).

20. Gary Jacobson, *A Divider, Not a Uniter: George W. Bush and the American People* (New York: Pearson Education, 2007).

21. George C. Edwards III, *Governing by Campaigning: The Politics of the Bush Presidency* (New York: Pearson-Longman, 2007).

22. George C. Edwards III and Desmond S. King, eds., *The Polarized Presidency of George W. Bush* (New York: Oxford Press, 2007).

23. As background in preparing this book, I found the following scholarship on presidential power to be particularly helpful: Richard E. Neustadt, *Presidential*

Power: The Politics of Leadership (New York: Wiley, 1960); Stephen Hess, *Organizing the Presidency,* 3rd ed. (Washington, D.C.: Brookings Institution Press, 2002); James P. Pfiffner, *The Strategic Presidency,* 2nd ed. (Lawrence: University Press of Kansas, 1996); and especially Charles O. Jones, *The Presidency in a Separated System,* 2nd ed. (Washington, D.C.: Brookings Institution Press, 2005). On congressional power, I gained insight from Keith Krehbiel, *Pivotal Politics: A Theory of Lawmaking* (Chicago: University of Chicago Press, 1998), and David Mayhew, *Congress: The Electoral Connection,* 2nd ed. (New Haven, Conn.: Yale University Press, 2004).

24. Jones, *The Presidency in a Separated System,* pp. 243, 319; Charles O. Jones, *Separate but Equal Branches: Congress and the Presidency* (Chatham, N.J.: Chatham House Press, 1995), p. 28 (since World War II, the most lawmaking occurred in the Nixon-Ford years, a period of split-party control, even more than occurred during the Kennedy–LBJ era of single-party control); also see David R. Mayhew, *Divided We Govern: Party Control, Lawmaking, and Investigations, 1946–1990* (New Haven, Conn.: Yale University Press, 1991), esp. pp. 52–73.

25. Other writers attribute Bush's first-term success to his ability to energize the Republican Party and keep it unified. William A. Galston and Pietro S. Nivola, "Delineating the Problem," in *Red and Blue Nation? Characteristics and Causes of America's Polarized Politics,* ed. Pietro S. Nivola and David W. Brady (Washington, D.C.: Brookings Institution Press, 2006), p. 3.

26. Jones, *The Presidency in a Separated System,* pp. 131–32; also see George C. Edwards III, "Riding High in the Polls: George W. Bush and Public Opinion," in *The George W. Bush Presidency: Appraisals and Prospects,* ed. Colin Campbell and Bert A. Rockman (Washington, D.C.: CQ Press, 2004), pp. 40–41 (the politics of the war on terror did not fundamentally alter the politics of traditional domestic issues).

27. "The Constitution remains largely silent on the nature and extent of presidential authority, especially in domestic affairs." Terry M. Moe and Scott A. Wilson, "Presidents and the Politics of Structure," *Law and Contemporary Problems* 57 (2) (Spring 1994): 23; Mark A. Peterson, "The President and Congress," in *The Presidency and the Political System,* 5th ed., ed. Michael Nelson (Washington, D.C.: CQ Press, 1998), pp. 472–73; Jones, *The Presidency in a Separated System,* p. 24.

28. The only president in the post–World War II period who had the luxury of pursuing "noncompetitive partisanship" in lawmaking was Lyndon Baines Johnson. The bargaining over legislation occurred primarily in the dominant Democratic Party. Jones, *The Presidency in a Separated System,* pp. 26–30; also see Jones, *Separate but Equal Branches,* p. 42.

29. Bush received broad bipartisan support after 9/11 for the authorization of force in Afghanistan, airline security legislation, and the Patriot Act. Thomas E. Mann and Norman J. Ornstein, *The Broken Branch: How Congress Is Failing and How to Get It Back on Track* (New York: Oxford University Press, 2006), p. 129.

30. A key feature of "cross-partisanship" is that collaboration with members of the other party may not occur until late in the process, and may occur in only one of the two chambers (where votes are short). See Jones, *Presidency in a Separated System,* pp. 26–30.

31. Mann and Ornstein, *Broken Branch,* p. 128.

32. Cindy Skrzycki, *The Regulators: The Anonymous Power Brokers Who Shape Your Life* (New York: Rowman and Littlefield, 2003).

33. On Reagan's new assertion of presidential authority over federal regulators, see Moe and Wilson, "Presidents and the Politics of Structure," pp. 1–44. On Clinton's assertion of such authority, see Elena Kagan, "Presidential Administration," *Harvard Law Review* 114 (8) (June 2001): 2245–2385.

34. Toward the end of 2000, the Clinton administration issued numerous new regulations. Most were not changed by the incoming Bush administration. See "Delay of Effective Dates of Final Rules Subject to the Administration's Jan. 20, 2001 Memorandum," U.S. General Accounting Office, Washington, D.C., January 2002 (GAO-02-370R).

35. See "Faith-Based Charities Bill Idles," *Congressional Quarterly Almanac,* 2001, vol. 57 (Washington, D.C.: CQ Press, 2002), pp. 17-3 to 17-5; Anne Farris, Richard P. Nathan, and David J. Wright, "The Expanding Administrative Presidency: George W. Bush and the Faith-Based Initiative," Roundtable on Religion and Social Welfare Policy, Rockefeller Institute of Government, August 2004 (available online at http://www.religionandsocialpolicy.org/docs/policy/FB_Administrative_Presidency_Report_10_08_04.pdf).

36. For a proponent of this view, see Fred Barnes, *Rebel-in-Chief,* p. 202 ("On domestic policy, Bush is more important for what he proposed and fought for than for what he achieved.").

37. The American people differ from political elites in that their policy views are not constrained or ordered by coherent ideology. Morris P. Fiorina, Paul E. Peterson, D. Stephen Voss, and Bertram Johnson, *America's New Democracy,* 3rd ed. (New York: Penguin Academics, Pearson-Longman, 2006), p. 107.

38. Exit polls in 2004 found a breakdown of 45% moderates, 34% conservatives, and 21% liberals, a breakdown "practically indistinguishable from thirty years ago." Galston and Nivola, "Delineating the Problem," p. 5.

39. James E. Campbell, "Polarization Runs Deep, Even by Yesterday's Standards," in *Red and Blue Nation? Characteristics and Causes of America's Polarized Politics,* ed. Pietro S. Nivola and David W. Brady (Washington, D.C.: Brookings Institution Press, 2006), p. 158.

40. Public views on abortion were stable from 1972 to 2002: Morris P. Fiorina et al., *America's New Democracy,* p. 102. More generally, see David C. King, "The Polarization of American Political Parties and Mistrust in Government," Working Paper, Politics Research Group, Kennedy School of Government, Harvard University, Cambridge, Mass., 2006.

41. Fiorina et al., *America's New Democracy,* p. 167. If we look to exit polls instead of party registration, it appears that in 2004 the number of self-described Republicans was about equal to the number of self-described Democrats. Michael Barone, *The Almanac of American Politics, 2004* (Washington, D.C.: National Journal Group, 2005), p. 25; also see Donald Green, Bradley Palmquist, and Eric Schickler, *Partisan*

Hearts and Minds: Political Parties and the Social Identities of Voters (New Haven, Conn.: Yale University Press, 2002), pp. 13, 15, 144–45.

42. In 2006 self-described independents made up 25% of the electorate, according to exit polls conducted by the Associated Press and the major television networks. See Susan Page, "Election '06: Lessons Learned by Dissecting Votes," *USA Today*, Nov. 27, 2006, p. 6A.

43. Galston and Nivola, "Delineating the Problem," p. 10; William G. Mayer, "What Exactly Is a Swing Voter? Definition and Measurement," in *The Swing Voter in American Politics*, ed. W. G. Mayer (Washington, D.C.: Brookings, 2008), pp. 9–10.

44. Anthony Downs, *An Economic Theory of Democracy* (New York: Harper and Row, 1957); for a modern view, see Morris Fiorina and Paul Peterson, *The New American Democracy* (Needham Heights, Mass.: Allyn and Bacon, 2006).

45. Gary C. Jacobson, "Party Polarization in National Politics: The Electoral Connection," in *Polarized Politics: Congress and the President in a Partisan Era*, ed. Jon R. Bond and Richard Fleisher (Washington, D.C.: CQ Press, 2000), p. 19; Sean M. Theriault, *Party Polarization in Congress* (New York: Cambridge University Press, 2008), p. 95.

46. Gary C. Jacobson, "The Bush Presidency and the American Electorate," in *The George W. Bush Presidency: An Early Assessment*, ed. Fred I. Greenstein (Baltimore: Johns Hopkins University Press, 2003), pp. 197–227; also in *Presidential Studies Quarterly* 32 (December 2003): 701–729.

47. Turnout rates in U.S. elections declined steadily from 1960 to 1990, and then stabilized. The turnout rate then rose markedly to 50% in 2000 and to 59% in 2004. It topped 60% in 2008. Associated Press, "Voter Turnout Reached 40-Year High," *Indianapolis Star*, Dec. 15, 2008, A3. Morris P. Fiorina et al., *America's New Democracy*, p. 135.

48. Gary C. Jacobson, "The Bush Presidency and the American Electorate," pp. 197–227; Morris P. Fiorina and Matthew S. Levendusky, "Disconnected: The Political Class versus the People," in *Red and Blue Nation? Characteristics and Causes of America's Polarized Politics*, ed. Pietro S. Nivola and David W. Brady (Washington, D.C.: Brookings Institution Press, 2006), p. 108.

49. Jones, *Presidency in a Separated System*, p. 2.

50. Fiorina and Levendusky, "Disconnected," p. 49.

51. Jones, *Presidency in a Separated System*, p. 53.

52. Ibid.

53. For an excellent survey of research on partisan polarization in Congress, see Theriault, *Party Polarization in Congress*.

54. Geoffrey C. Layman, Thomas C. Carsey, and Juliana Menasce Horowitz, "Party Polarization in American Politics: Characteristics, Causes and Consequences," *Annual Review of Political Science* 9 (2006): 83–100.

55. James Q. Wilson, "How Divided Are We?" *Commentary* 121(2) (February 2006): 15–21; Sunil Ahuja, *Congress Behaving Badly: The Rise of Partisanship and Incivility and the Death of Public Trust* (Westport, Conn.: Praeger, 2008).

56. Shanto Lynegar and Richard Morin, "Polarization across Party Lines, or Politics as Contact Sport," *Washington Post,* March 29, 2006.

57. Gerald F. Seib, "Hopes Quickly Fade for a Postpartisan Era," *Wall Street Journal,* Oct. 14, 2008 (online).

58. Theriault, *Party Polarization in Congress,* pp. 3, 113.

59. Fiorina et al., *America's New Democracy,* p. 1887 (especially table 8.3); also see Green et al., *Partisan Hearts and Minds,* p. 218.

60. King, "Polarization of American Political Parties."

61. Alan I. Abramowitz, "Disconnected, or Joined at the Hip?," comments on Fiorina and Levendusky's "Disconnected: The Political Class versus the People," in *Red and Blue Nation? Characteristics and Causes of America's Polarized Politics,* ed. Pietro S. Nivola and David W. Brady (Washington, D.C.: Brookings Institution Press, 2006), p. 73; Theriault, *Party Polarization in Congress,* pp. 3–4.

62. Abramowitz, "Disconnected, or Joined at the Hip?," p. 85; but there is dispute about whether the definitions of "strong partisans" and "campaign activists" are too inclusive. See Fiorina and Levendusky, "Disconnected," pp. 99–107.

63. Ronald Brownstein, *The Second Civil War: How Extreme Partisanship Has Paralyzed Washington and Polarized America* (New York: Penguin Press, 2007).

64. The influence of party activists drives primary candidates to the extremes. Fiorina et al., *America's New Democracy,* 2006, pp. 182–87. Also see Barry C. Burden, "The Polarizing Effects of Congressional Primaries," in *Congressional Primaries and the Politics of Representation,* ed. Peter F. Galderisi, Marni Ezra, and Michael Lyons (New York: Rowman and Littlefield, 2001), 95–115.

65. Bill Bishop, *The Big Sort: Why the Clustering of Like-Minded America is Tearing Us Apart* (Boston: Houghton Mifflin, 2008); Galston and Nivola, "Delineating the Problem," p. 5; Fiorina and Levendusky, "Disconnected," p. 69.

66. Theriault, *Party Polarization in Congress,* p. 89.

67. Fiorina and Levendusky, "Disconnected," p. 108.

68. Alan I. Abramowitz, "Disconnected, or Joined at the Hip?," p. 75; Fiorina and Levendusky, "Disconnected," p. 55.

69. Party unity refers to whether members of Congress vote as preferred by their party's leadership. Abramowitz, "Disconnected, or Joined at the Hip?," p. 75; Fiorina and Levendusky, "Disconnected," p. 55. Also see Steven S. Smith, "Parties and Leadership in the Senate," in *The Legislative Branch,* ed. Paul J. Quirk and Sarah A. Binder (New York: Oxford University Press, 2005), p. 261; Theriault, *Party Polarization in Congress,* pp. 35, 102.

70. Fiorina et al., *America's New Democracy,* p. 244 (especially figure 9.2).

71. Sarah Binder, "The Disappearing Political Center: Congress and the Incredible Shrinking Middle," *Brookings Review* 14(4) (Fall 1996): 36–39; Sarah Binder, "Going Nowhere: A Gridlocked Congress," *Brookings Review* 18(1) (Winter 2000): 16–19; Sarah A. Binder, "Elections, Parties and Governance," in *The Legislative Branch,* ed. Paul J. Quirk and Sarah Binder (New York: Oxford University Press, 2005), pp. 148–70, esp. pp. 153–54; Theriault, *Party Polarization in Congress,* p. 226.

72. Thomas E. Mann, "Polarizing the House of Representatives: How Much Does Gerrymandering Matter?," in *Red and Blue Nation? Characteristics and Causes of America's Polarized Politics,* ed. Pietro S. Nivola and David W. Brady (Washington, D.C.: Brookings Institution Press, 2006), p. 263.

73. Page, "Election '06," p. 6A; Pam Belluck, "A GOP Breed Loses Its Place in New England," *New York Times,* Nov. 27, 2006, pp. A1, A19.

74. King, "Polarization of American Political Parties"; Mann and Ornstein, *Broken Branch,* pp. 80–81.

75. Byron E. Shafer and Richard Johnston, *The End of Southern Exceptionalism: Class, Race and Partisan Change in the Post-War South* (Cambridge, Mass.: Harvard University Press, 2006), p. 178.

76. Donald Green, Bradley Palmquist, and Eric Schickler, *Partisan Hearts and Minds: Political Parties and the Social Identities of Voters* (New Haven, Conn.: Yale University Press, 2002), p. 13; Nicole Mellow, *The State of Disunion: Regional Sources of Modern American Partisanship* (Baltimore: Johns Hopkins University Press, 2008).

77. E. J. Dionne Jr., "Polarized by God? American Politics and the Religious Divide," in *Red and Blue Nation? Characteristics and Causes of America's Polarized Politics,* ed. Pietro S. Nivola and David W. Brady (Washington, D.C.: Brookings Institution Press, 2006), pp. 175–205.

78. Ibid., p. 183.

79. Ibid.; also see Laurie Goodstein, "In Poll, Republican Party Slips as a Friend of Religion," *New York Times,* Aug. 25, 2006, p. A12; Peter Wallsten, "Conservatives Put Faith in Church Voter Drives," *Los Angeles Times,* Aug. 15, 2006, p. 1.

80. Goodstein, "In Poll, Republican Party Slips," p. A12.

81. Nolan McCarthy, Keith T. Poole, and Howard Rosenthal, *Polarized America: The Dance of Ideology and Unequal Riches* (Cambridge, Mass.: MIT Press, 2006).

82. Rich states (e.g., Connecticut) tend to be more liberal and Democratic then poor states but, within a state, voters with more income are likely to be pro-Republican in their voting behavior. Andrew Gelman, *Red State, Blue State, Rich State, Poor State: Why Americans Vote the Way They Do* (Princeton, N.J.: Princeton University Press, 2008).

83. Nick Timirosa, "Hispanic Voters Flex Political Muscle," *Wall Street Journal* Sept. 15, 2007, p. A7 (Hispanics account for 14% of the U.S. population but only about 9% of the electorate).

84. Diana C. Murtz, "How the Mass Media Divide Us," in *Red and Blue Nation? Characteristics and Causes of America's Polarized Politics,* ed. Pietro S. Nivola and David W. Brady (Washington, D.C.: Brookings Institution Press, 2006), pp. 223–48.

85. Barone, *Almanac of American Politics, 2004,* pp. 34–35; also see Fiorina et al., *America's New Democracy,* p. 130.

86. Robert D. Putnam, *Bowling Alone: The Collapse and Revival of American Community* (New York: Simon and Shuster, 2002); also see Fiorina et al., *America's New Democracy,* pp. 146–48.

87. Pietro S. Nivola, "Thinking about Polarization," Policy Brief no. 139, January 2005, Brookings Institution, Washington, D.C.; for a skeptical view, see Mann, "Polarizing the House of Representatives," pp. 263–83.

88. Steven Hill, "Divided We Stand: The Polarizing of American Politics," *National Civic Review* 94(4) (Winter 2005): 3–14; Theriault, *Party Polarization in Congress,* pp. 3, 83, 221.

89. Mann and Ornstein, *Broken Branch,* pp. 12, 212; Mann, "Polarizing the House of Representatives," pp. 279–80; Fiorina and Levendusky, "Disconnected," pp. 70–71.

90. See preceding note.

91. Associated Press, "Voter Turnout Reached 40-Year High," *Indianapolis Star,* Dec. 15, 2008, p. A3.

92. Bipartisanship is rare in polarized, narrow-margin politics. Jones, *Presidency in a Separated System,* p. 336.

93. King, "Polarization of American Political Parties"; also see Binder, "Elections, Parties and Governance," pp. 163–65.

94. David W. Brady and Hahrie C. Han, "Polarization Then and Now: A Historical Perspective," in *Red and Blue Nation? Characteristics and Causes of America's Polarized Politics,* ed. Pietro S. Nivola and David W. Brady (Washington, D.C.: Brookings Institution Press, 2006), pp. 119–51.

95. Page, "Election '06," p. 6A (citing exit polls by Associated Press and major television networks); Gary C. Jacobson, "Referendum: The 2006 Midterm Congressional Elections," *Political Science Quarterly* 122(1) (2007): 1–24.

96. Thomas B. Edsall, "Why Other Sources of Polarization Matter More," in *Red and Blue Nation? Characteristics and Causes of America's Polarized Politics,* ed. Pietro S. Nivola and David W. Brady (Washington, D.C.: Brookings Institution Press, 2006), p. 294.

97. Galston and Nivola, "Delineating the Problem," p. 10, n. 25.

98. James E. Campbell, "Polarization Runs Deep, Even by Yesterday's Standards: Comment," in *Red and Blue Nation? Characteristics and Causes of America's Polarized Politics,* ed. Pietro S. Nivola and David W. Brady (Washington, D.C.: Brookings Institution Press, 2006), p. 158.

99. Party unity scores in Congress are rising both among members from competitive districts and among members from safe districts. One possible explanation is that more members play "base politics." Theriault, *Party Polarization in Congress,* p. 102.

100. Mann, "Polarizing the House of Representatives," pp. 279–80.

101. Galston and Nivola, "Delineating the Problem," p. 26.

102. Kathryn Pearson, "Party Loyalty and Discipline in the Individualistic Senate," in *Why Not Parties? Party Effects in the United States Senate,* ed. Nathan W. Monroe, Jason M. Roberts, and David W. Rohde (Chicago: University of Chicago Press, 2008), pp. 100–20.

103. Amanda Cox, Matthew Ericson, and Archie Tse, "Voters Shift the House to Democrats," *New York Times,* Nov. 9, 2006, p. 2.

104. The empirical research is mixed, but it does show adverse electoral effects of party-line voting when the incumbent senator represents a mixed-ideology, competitive state. Jamie L. Carson, "Electoral Accountability, Party Loyalty, and Roll-Call Voting in the U.S. Senate," in *Why Not Parties? Party Effects in the United States Senate,* ed. Nathan W. Monroe, Jason M. Roberts, and David W. Rohde (Chicago: University of Chicago Press, 2008), pp. 36–37.

105. Carl Hulse, "Moderate Republicans Feeling Like Endangered Species," *New York Times,* Oct. 28, 2006, p. A11; Jacobson, "Referendum," pp. 1–24.

106. Michael Tomasky, "How the Dems Did It," *Los Angeles Times,* Nov. 12, 2006, p. M1.

107. Peter Wallston and Janet Hook, "Liberal Groups Insist on Results," *Los Angeles Times,* Nov. 12, 2006, p. 1.

108. The loss of five Senate seats by a winning president was the largest "negative coattail" in modern U.S. history. Mann and Ornstein, *Broken Branch,* p. 123.

109. Jacobson, "Bush Presidency and the American Electorate."

110. In fact, in early 2001 Speaker Hastert "proudly announced that his primary responsibility was to pass the President's legislative program." Mann and Ornstein, *Broken Branch,* p. 213.

111. Nothing in the U.S. Constitution guarantees that a minority of senators may block action. The custom only exists in Senate rules. Fiorina et al., *America's New Democracy,* p. 231.

112. Michael Barone, *The Almanac of American Politics, 2003* (Washington, D.C.: National Journal Group, 2004), p. 43.

113. Mann and Ornstein, *Broken Branch,* p. 10; more generally, see Sarah A. Binder and Steven S. Smith, *Politics or Principle: Filibustering in the U.S. Senate* (Washington, D.C.: Brookings Institution Press, 1992).

114. Michael Barone, *The Almanac of American Politics, 2002* (Washington, D.C.: National Journal Group, 2003), p. 45; also see Trent Lott, *Herding Cats: A Life in Politics* (New York: HarperCollins, 2005), p. 212.

115. Fiorina et al., *America's New Democracy,* p. 171.

116. Since the 1980s the parties in Congress have given their respective leaders greater power to determine and enforce party positions: Paul J. Quirk, "Deliberation and Decision Making," in *The Legislative Branch,* ed. Paul J. Quirk and Sarah A. Binder (New York: Oxford University Press, 2005), p. 323. Also see Gary C. Jacobson, "Modern Campaigns and Misrepresentation," in *The Legislative Branch,* ed. Paul J. Quirk and Sarah A. Binder (New York: Oxford University Press, 2005), pp. 109–47, esp. pp. 123–30.

117. Smith, "Parties and Leadership in the Senate," pp. 255–78; Frances E. Lee, "Agreeing to Disagree: Agenda Content and Senate Partisanship, 1981–2004," *Legislative Studies Quarterly* 33 (2008): 199–222; Kathryn Pearson, "Party Loyalty and Discipline in the Individualistic Senate," in *Why Not Parties? Party Effects in the United States Senate,* ed. Nathan W. Monroe, Jason M. Roberts, and David W. Rohde (Chicago: University of Chicago Press, 2008), pp. 100–120; Theriault, *Party Polarization in Congress,* pp. 138, 143, 154.

118. Jason M. Roberts and Lauren Cohen Bell, "Scoring the Senate: Scorecards, Parties, and Roll-call Votes," in *Why Not Parties? Party Effects in the United States Senate*, ed. Nathan W. Monroe, Jason M. Roberts, and David W. Rohde (Chicago: University of Chicago Press, 2008), pp. 52–70.

119. Bruce I. Oppenheimer, Marc J. Hetherington, "Catch-22: Cloture, Energy Policy, and the Limits of Conditional Party Government," in *Why Not Parties? Party Effects in the United States Senate*, ed. Nathan W. Monroe, Jason M. Roberts, and David W. Rohde (Chicago: University of Chicago Press, 2008), p. 222.

120. Charles O. Jones, "The U.S. Congress and Chief Executive George W. Bush," paper presented at the Conference on Politics and Polarization: The George W. Bush Presidency, May 26–27, 2007, pp. 393, 404. Burke, *Becoming President*, p. 54.

121. Theriault, *Party Polarization in Congress*, pp. 155, 180, 223.

2. Lower Taxes, More Spending

1. N. Gregory Mankiw, *Macroeconomics*, 6th ed. (New York: Worth, 2007), pp. 406–54.

2. Michael J. Boskin, "How Not to Fix the Economy," *Wall Street Journal*, Dec. 13, 2007, p. A23; Keith Hennessey, "Keep Taxes Low," *USA Today*, June 30, 2008 (online).

3. Larry M. Bartels, *Unequal Democracy: The Political Economy of the New Gilded Age* (Princeton, N.J.: Princeton University Press, 2008).

4. Robert H. Frank, "Why Wait to Repeal Tax Cuts for the Rich?" *New York Times*, Dec. 7, 2008 (online); Linda J. Bilmes and Joseph E. Stiglitz, "The $10 Trillion Hangover: Paying the Price for Eight Years of Bush," *Harper's Magazine*, January 2009, pp. 31–35.

5. James Q. Wilson, *American Government*, 10th ed. (Boston: Houghton Mifflin, 2006), 255–59.

6. Ibid., pp. 500–501.

7. Keith Marsden, "Bush Has a Good Economic Record," *Wall Street Journal*, Sept. 3, 2008, p. A23.

8. It is plausible to argue that Bush's pressure on Fannie Mae and Freddie Mac for more minority home ownership, coupled with congressional pressure in the same direction, may have contributed to the housing crisis. See chapter 11.

9. Boskin, "How Not to Fix the Economy," p. A23.

10. Edmund L. Andrews, "Greenspan Concedes Error on Regulation," *New York Times*, Oct. 24, 2008 (online); Kara Scannell and Sudeep Reddy, "Greenspan Admits Errors to Hostile House Panel," *Wall Street Journal*, Oct. 24, 2008 (online); Greg Ip, "His Legacy Tarnished, Greenspan Goes on the Defensive, *Wall Street Journal*, April 4, 2008, p. A1.

11. Julie Hirschfield, "Former SEC Chief Says Agency Dropped Ball," *USA Today*, Oct. 21, 2008 (referring to congressional testimony by former SEC chairman Arthur Levitt).

12. Even scholars who prefer a bipartisan approach to legislation acknowledge that Bush's cross-partisan strategy on tax cuts was as successful as it was bold. For a critical view of the legislative tactics used by the Bush White House and the congressional Republicans to enact tax cuts, see Thomas E. Mann and Norman J. Ornstein, *The Broken Branch: How Congress Is Failing America and How to Get It Back on Track* (New York: Oxford University Press, 2006), pp. 124–28, 218–20.

13. Clea Benson, "For Deficit Hawks, Better Dead than Red," *Congressional Quarterly Weekly Report,* July 28, 2008, pp. 2035–36.

14. Russ Sobel, "Can Public Choice Theory Explain the U.S. Budget Surpluses of the 1990's?" *Journal of Public Finance and Public Choice* 23(3) (2004): 169–182.

15. Gary L. Gregg II and Mark J. Rozell, *Considering the Bush Presidency* (New York: Oxford University Press, 2004), p. 147 (describing the role of the CBO forecasts in the tax-policy debate, including an updated forecast issued ten days after Bush took office). Also see "The Budget and Economic Outlook: An Update," Congressional Budget Office, Washington, D.C., July 2000.

16. Beth Fouhy, "Tax Cuts Likely to Be an Issue in 2000 Elections," *CNN.com,* July 28, 1999, http://www.cnn.com/ALLPOLITICS/stories/1999/07/28/president.2000/tax .candidates/ (accessed Jan. 17, 2008).

17. "Bush-Gore Debate: Money; Part 1: Taxes and the Surplus," *About.com,* Oct. 4, 2000, http://usgovinfo.about.com/library/weekly/aa100600a.htm (accessed Jan. 17, 2008).

18. Jacob S. Hacker and Paul Pierson, *Off Center: The Republican Revolution and the Erosion of American Democracy* (New Haven, Conn.: Yale University Press, 2005), pp. 50–51.

19. For a vivid portrayal of how Senate and House Republicans sought to block Clinton's initial 1993 budget plan, see Mann and Ornstein, *Broken Branch,* pp. 91–93 (describing a new Republican leadership strategy of "trying to deny any [Republican] votes for crucial presidential priorities" during President Clinton's first two years in office). Also see Gary C. Jacobson, *A Divider, Not a Uniter: George W. Bush and the American People* (New York: Pearson Education, 2007), p. 208 (n. 11: not a single Republican in either chamber voted for Clinton's 1993 budget, which accomplished deficit reduction through tax hikes and spending cuts).

20. John P. Burke, *Becoming President: The Bush Transition, 2000–2003* (Boulder, Colo.: Lynne Rienner, 2004), 136 (discussing Jeffords's and Chafee's complaints about the size of Bush's tax-cut plan).

21. For a lucid description of how tax cuts became a central element of the budget process, including reconciliation legislation, see Allen Schick, "Bush's Budget Problem," in *The George W. Bush Presidency: An Early Assessment,* ed. Fred I. Greenstein (Baltimore: Johns Hopkins University Press, 2003), p. 99.

22. Mann and Ornstein, *Broken Branch,* p. 128 (contrasting the speed of the 2001 tax cuts with Reagan's 1981 tax cut, which occurred after a landslide election victory).

23. Burke, *Becoming President,* p. 136 (discussing Bush's resistance to inclusion of business tax cuts in the 2001 package).

24. For an account that roots Greenspan's reversal in private discussions between Greenspan and Treasury Secretary Paul O'Neill, see Ron Suskind, *The Price of Loyalty: George W. Bush, the White House, and the Education of Paul O'Neill* (New York: Simon and Schuster, 2004), pp. 40–42, 45–46, 48–49, 60–64. On how Greenspan's testimony undermined Democratic opposition, see Gary Mucciaroni and Paul J. Quirk, "Deliberations of a 'Compassionate Conservative,'" in *The George W. Bush Presidency: Appraisals and Prospects,* ed. Colin Campbell and Bert A. Rockman (Washington, D.C.: CQ Press, 2004), p. 166. For Greenspan's account, see Alan Greenspan, *The Age of Turbulence: Adventures in a New World* (New York: Penguin Press, 2007), pp. 206–25.

25. It appears that Baucus's decision to work promptly with Grassley was made over the objections of the Senate Democratic leadership. Mann and Ornstein, *Broken Branch,* p. 127.

26. Although George W. Bush is often described as inflexible, his behavior on the 2001 tax cuts clearly demonstrated an ability to compromise when he felt it was advisable. Fred I. Greenstein, "The Leadership Style of George W. Bush," in *The George W. Bush Presidency: An Early Assessment,* ed. Fred I. Greenstein (Baltimore: Johns Hopkins University Press, 2003), p. 9 (noting how Bush compromised on the size of the 2001 tax-cut package, accepting reductions from $1.6 trillion to $1.35 trillion).

27. On the Democratic leadership's opposition to the size, breadth, and duration of the Bush's 2001 tax-cut proposal, see John C. Fortier and Norman J. Ornstein, eds., *Second-Term Blues: How George W. Bush Has Governed* (Washington, D.C.: American Enterprise Institute and Brookings Institution Press, 2007), pp. 148–49 (describing how Tom Daschle in the Senate and Charles Rangel in the House developed smaller tax-cut plans aimed more at lower-income Americans).

28. For a scholarly account of liberal opposition to the Bush tax-cut agenda, see William Gale and Peter Orszag, "An Economic Assessment of Tax Policy in the Bush Administration, 2000–2004," *Boston College Law Review* 45(5) (September 2004): 1157–1232.

29. Hacker and Pierson, *Off Center,* pp. 65–66.

30. Some scholars have characterized the extent of Bush's 2002 campaigning as "unprecedented" for a midterm election. There were 90 campaign appearances, including 23 for House candidates and 16 for Senate candidates. Bush attended nearly 75 fund raisers and helped raise $144 million. Mann and Ornstein, *Broken Branch,* pp. 133–34.

31. One view is that the Democrats fielded weak candidates in 2002 because Bush's post-9/11 popularity was so high in the time period when Democratic challengers made their decisions about running. Jacobson, *A Divider, Not a Uniter,* pp. 88–89.

32. On the key role of CEA in advocating repeal of taxes on capital gains and dividends, see Suskind, *Price of Loyalty,* p. 306.

33. U.S. Council of Economic Advisers, *Annual Report of the Council of Economic Advisers* (Washington, D.C.: Government Printing Office, 2003), pp. 22, 37–38, 202–204.

34. U.S. Council of Economic Advisers, *Economic Report to the President,* 2003, Washington, D.C., p. 22.

35. U.S. Council of Economic Advisers, *Economic Report to the President,* 2008, Washington, D.C., pp. 115–36.

36. Joel Friedman, "Dividend and Capital Gains Tax Cuts Unlikely to Yield Touted Economic Gains," rev. Oct. 7, 2005, Center for Budget and Policy Priorities, http://www.cbpp.org/3-10-05tax.htm (accessed Jan. 17, 2008).

37. Fairness objections to both the 2001 and 2003 tax cuts are summarized in Schick, "Bush's Budget Problem," p. 92.

38. Burke, *Becoming President,* p. 190 (discussing Thomas's concern about the size of Bush's tax-cut plan).

39. Gary L. Gregg II and Mark J. Rozell, *Considering the Bush Presidency* (New York: Oxford University Press, 2004), p. 147 (Bush campaigned for his tax-cut plans in states that he carried but were also represented by Democratic senators); Burke, *Becoming President,* p. 191 (Bush pressed his case publicly in Ohio and Nebraska).

40. Floyd Norris, "Investment Tax Cuts Help Mostly the Rich," *New York Times,* Jan. 10, 2009, p. B3.

41. Joseph J. Schatz, "The Power of the Status Quo," *Congressional Quarterly Weekly Report,* Feb. 6, 2006, p. 322.

42. Michael T. Darda, "The Inflation Threat to Capital Formation," *Wall Street Journal,* April 10, 2008, p. A15 (Darda is chief economist, MKM Partners); Stephen J. Entin, "The Folly of 'Family Friendly' Tax Policy," *Wall Street Journal,* April 9, 2008, p. A15. (The pro-growth elements of the Bush tax cuts, the reductions in the top income tax rates, the lower taxes on capital gains and dividends, and the additional expensing of equipment "are what turned the economy around." Entin is president of the Institute for Research on the Economics of Taxation.)

43. These types of tax cuts, though popular, may have little long-run economic benefit. Entin, "Folly of 'Family Friendly' Tax Policy," p. A15.

44. Jacobson, *A Divider, Not a Uniter,* 2007, p. 205. (Referring to the 2004 Bush-Kerry race, there is not much evidence of a "mandate for a domestic agenda" . . . "Had terrorism not been in the picture and the election hinged on domestic issues, Kerry would almost certainly have won.")

45. Kevin Hassett, "Tax Policy Taking the U.S. Down the Road to France," Bloomberg.com, July 2, 2007 (noting that politics of tax policy are changing quickly as Democrats, now in control of the Congress, are considering letting many of the Bush tax cuts expire in 2010). Robert H. Frank, "Why Wait to Repeal Tax Cuts for the Rich?" *New York Times* Feb. 7, 2008 (online).

46. Bill Archer and James Carter, "Tax Challenges for the New President," *Wall Street Journal,* Jan. 8, 2008, p. A21; John F. Cogan and R. Glenn Hubbard, "The Coming Tax Bomb," *Wall Street Journal,* April 8, 2008, p. A21.

47. Douglas Holtz-Eakin, "Security Is Job One," *Wall Street Journal,* Feb. 1, 2008, p. A15.

48. Arthur B. Laffer, "The Tax Threat to Prosperity," *Wall Street Journal,* Jan. 25, 2008, p. A15.

49. Len Berman, "Make the Tax Cuts Work," *New York Times,* Jan. 23, 2008 (online).

50. Gerald F. Seib, "Tax Cuts Gain Relevance as Outlook Dims," *Wall Street Journal*, Nov. 27, 2007, p. A2; Joseph E. Stiglitz, "How to Stop the Downturn," *New York Times*, Jan. 23, 2008 (online).

51. Jennifer Waters, "Tax Rebates May Be Used to Cut Debt this Time," *Wall Street Journal*, Jan. 22, 2008, p. D5.

52. John Sullivan, "Tax Rebates in $168 Billion Stimulus Plan Begin Arriving in Bank Accounts," *New York Times*, April 29, 2008 (online); Sarah Lueck, John D. McKinnon, and Michael M. Phillips, "Bush, Democrats Rush to Roll Out Stimulus Plan," *Wall Street Journal*, Jan. 18, 2008, p. A1 (Bernanke favored a package that would target those who "live paycheck to paycheck").

53. Sarah Lueck, Timothy Aeppel, and Michael M. Phillips, "Washington Sets $150 Billion Plan to Jolt Economy," *Wall Street Journal*, Jan. 25, 2008, p. A1.

54. Kelly Evans, "Stimulus Checks Bolster Retail Sales, *Wall Street Journal*, June 13, 2008, p. A3.

55. U.S. Council of Economic Advisers, *Economic Report of the President*, 2008, Washington, D.C., pp. 115–17.

56. Schick, "Bush's Budget Problem," pp. 92–93 (the Bush tax policy "impedes efforts to restore budgetary balance"), p. 99 (expecting Bush tax cuts to create federal budgetary deficits for as long as the eye can see, just as happened after the Reagan tax cuts); Robert E. Rubin, Peter R. Orszag, and Allen Sinai, "Sustained Budget Deficits: Longer-Run U.S. Economic Performance and the Risk of Financial and Fiscal Disarray," paper presented at the AEA-NAEFA Joint Session, Allied Social Science Associations Annual Meetings, Andrew Brimmer Policy Forum on National Economic and Financial Policies for Growth and Stability, San Diego, Calif., Jan. 4, 2004.

57. Mucciaroni and Quirk, "Deliberations of a 'Compassionate Conservative,'" p. 168; Bilmes and Stiglitz, "$10 Trillion Hangover," pp. 31–35.

58. John D. McKinnon and Deborah Solomon, "As Deficit Shrinks, Battle Looms," *Wall Street Journal*, July 12, 2007, p. A4; online at http://online.wsj.com/article/SB118415891916263140.html?mod=home_whats_news_us (accessed Oct. 18, 2007).

59. John D. McKinnon, "Federal Deficit Soars to Nearly $455 Billion," *Wall Street Journal*, Oct. 15, 2008 (online); Louis Uchitelle and Robert Pear, "Deficit Rises, and Consensus Is to Let It Grow," *New York Times*, Oct. 20, 2008 (online).

60. Clea Benson, "For Deficit Hawks, Better Dead than Red," *Congressional Quarterly Weekly Report*, July 28, 2004, p. 2035–36.

61. Michael M. Phillips, "Budget Gap Sets Record as Corporate Profits Fall," *Wall Street Journal*, April 11, 2008, p. A12.

62. David Clarke, "Patient Opposition Greets Bush Budget," *Congressional Quarterly Weekly Report*, Feb. 11, 2008, pp. 366–73.

63. David M. Herszenhorn, "Estimates of Iraq War Cost Were Not Close to the Ballpark," *New York Times*, March 19, 2008 (online).

64. Steven Lee Myers, "Bush's Request for Wars Increases to $196 Billion," *New York Times*, Oct. 23, 2007 (online).

65. Janet Hook, "Bush Boxed in His Congressional Foes," *Los Angeles Times*, Dec. 21, 2007 (online).

66. David Baumann, "Purse Strings: A Tangled Mess," *Congressional Quarterly Weekly Report,* May 19, 2008, pp. 1336–42.

67. In the discretionary outlays, the ratio of non-defense to defense outlays shifted from 343/306 = 1.12 in 2001 to 520/553 = 0.96 in 2008. U.S. Congressional Budget Office, Letter from Peter R. Orzag to the Honorable Robert C. Byrd, March 3, 2008 (attached table).

68. Michael M. Phillips and John D. McKinnon, "Legacy of Deficits Will Constrain Bush's Successor," *Wall Street Journal,* Feb. 1, 2008, p. A3.

69. William Ahern, "Comparing the Kennedy, Reagan and Bush Tax Cuts," Fiscal Fact No. 15, Aug. 24, 2004, http://taxfoundation.org/news/show/323.html (accessed July 13, 2007).

70. For a conceptual case for the 2003 package, and an early analysis suggesting some positive effects, see Alan Auerbach and Kevin Hassett, "The 2003 Dividend Tax Cuts and the Value of a Firm: An Event Study," OTPR/Burch Center Conference, May 2005; also see Edward P. Lazear, "Conference on Corporate Income Taxation and the U.S. Economy," American Enterprise Institute, Washington, D.C., June 2, 2006 (explaining how the 2003 tax cuts have spurred growth, productivity, and wages).

71. Kevin A. Hassett, "The Audacity to Succeed: Bush's Tax Cuts Have Worked, and This Has Stirred the Pot," *National Review* (online), Dec. 8, 2003. (The Bush tax cuts were well-timed medicine for an ailing economy. The first tax cut stimulated consumption at just the right time. The second tax cut helped boost the stock market and spur business investment.) Also see Kevin Hassett, "Let's Give John Snow the Praise He Has Earned," *Bloomberg.com,* July 2, 2007.

72. Chris Edwards, "Corporate Tax Reform: Kerry, Bush, Congress Fall Short," Cato Institute Tax and Budget Bulletin, No. 21, September 2004. Also see "We're Number One, Alas," Review and Outlook, *Wall Street Journal,* July 13, 2007, p. A12 (citing studies from OECD and AEI suggesting that the corporate income tax rate in the United States is larger than in any other OECD country).

73. Deborah Solomon and Sarah Lueck, "Democrats Outline Tax Approach," *Wall Street Journal,* Sept. 19, 2007, p. A6; Sarah Lueck, "Rangel Expresses Openness to Corporate-Tax Rate Cut," *Wall Street Journal,* Sept. 20, 2007, p. A7.

3. The Social Security Debacle

1. Board of Trustees, "2004 Annual Report of the Board of Trustees of the Federal Old-Age and Survivors' Insurance and Disability Insurance Trust Funds" (Washington, D.C.: Government Printing Office, 2004).

2. For an insightful case study of the history of the Social Security program, including Bush's inability to reform it, see Fiona Ross, "Policy Histories and Partisan Leadership in Presidential Studies: The Case of Social Security," in *The Polarized Presidency of George W. Bush,* ed. George C. Edwards III and Desmond S. King (New York: Oxford University Press, 2007), pp. 419–46.

3. Ibid., p. 421.

4. Ibid., pp. 422–23.

5. Some scholars speculate that President Bush intended to pursue Social Security reform during his first term but was derailed in that effort by the 2001–2002 recession, 9/11, the cost of the war on terror, and the growing budget deficits. According to this theory, when the projected budget surpluses vanished (the surpluses that might otherwise have been used to finance private accounts for young workers), the plans for Social Security were shelved indefinitely. See Allen Schick, "Bush's Budget Problem," in *The George W. Bush Presidency: An Early Assessment,* ed. Fred I. Greenstein (Baltimore: Johns Hopkins University Press, 2003), pp. 89–90. But if this theory is correct, it is hard to explain why Bush launched Social Security reform under similar conditions at the start of his second term. A more parsimonious explanation is that Bush cared more about other domestic priorities (tax cuts, education, and prescription drugs) and knew he could not do everything in his first term. Moreover, there would be no presidential re-election ramifications at the start of his second term.

6. "Report of the President's Commission on Strengthening Social Security and Creating Personal Wealth for All Americans," President's Commission on Strengthening Social Security, Washington, D.C., Dec. 21, 2001.

7. Ross, "Policy Histories and Partisan Leadership," p. 423.

8. Joshua Green, "The Rove Presidency," *Atlantic,* September 2007, p. 62.

9. Cynthia Bowers, "The Issues: Social Security," *CBS Evening News,* Sept. 23, 2004; online at www.cbsnews.com/stories/2004/09/23/eveningnews/main645305 .shtml (accessed July 16, 2007).

10. David M. Halbfinger, "Campaigning Furiously, with Social Security in Tow," *New York Times Online,* Oct. 18, 2004, http://www.nytimes.com/2004/10/18/politics/ campaign/18trail.html?fta=y (accessed July 16, 2007); Matt Moore, "The Scare-Seniors Card," *National Review,* Sept. 24, 2004; online at www.nationalreview.com/nrof_ comment/moore200409240818.asp (accessed July 16, 2007).

11. Lawrence R. Jacobs, "The Promotional Presidency and the New Institutional Toryism: Public Mobilization, Legislative Dominance, and Squandered Opportunities," in *The Polarized Presidency of George W. Bush,* ed. George C. Edwards III and Desmond S. King (New York: Oxford University Press, 2007), pp. 313–14 (prior to the 2002 midterms, some congressional Republicans pleaded with Bush to "stop talking about Social Security reform"; quoting one Republican leader in 2005 as saying that Bush's Social Security proposal in 2005 "pushed the GOP way out there beyond our defenses").

12. "Lieberman's 'Enron-Inspired' Turn against Social Security Reform Unfounded, Cato Experts Say," Press Release, Cato Institute, Feb. 13, 2002 (tracing Lieberman's support of private accounts under Social Security to an interview Lieberman gave to Cox News Service on May 4, 1998).

13. See, for example, Tim Penny, "Social Security Reform Can Be Bipartisan," *Christian Science Monitor* (online), Aug. 3, 2005.

14. Jacobs, "Promotional Presidency," p. 314.

15. Bush traveled to dozens of cities but apparently never made it to sixty of them. Jacobson, *A Divider, Not a Uniter,* pp. 207–208.

16. Jacobs, "Promotional Presidency," p. 314.

17. Ross, "Policy Histories and Partisan Leadership," p. 425.

18. Jacobs, "Promotional Presidency," p. 316.

19. Ross, "Policy Histories and Partisan Leadership," p. 434.

20. Jacobson, *A Divider, Not a Uniter,* pp. 210–17 (presenting data suggesting that public support for private accounts and Bush's position on Social Security actually declined from January to May of 2005).

21. Ross, "Policy Histories and Partisan Leadership," p. 434.

22. Nick Fram, "Dems Win on Social Security? Democrats Bet the Farm on Keeping the Status Quo," *Stanford Daily,* Feb. 16, 2005, online at http://www.stanforddaily .com/cgi-bin/?p=1016839 (accessed July 16, 2007) ("I would prefer that history not tell the story that Bush was the one who saved Social Security. Yes, that is partisan . . . That's the nature of the political game . . . Hopefully, Democrats realize that by sticking to their guns now and taking this issue away from the GOP, they have a good shot at long-term party revitalization"); Ross, "Policy Histories and Partisan Leadership," p. 438 (describing "strongest" opponents of Social Security reform: Democratic lawmakers and their interest-group network, possessing "clear strategic and ideological incentives to block path-breaking reform by a Republican president"); Dan Balz, "Bush's Ambitious Second-Term Agenda Hits Realities," in *Second-Term Blues: How George W. Bush Has Governed,* ed. John C. Fortier and Norman J. Ornstein (Washington, D.C.: American Enterprise Institute and Brookings Institution Press, 2007), p. 28 ("By early 2005 Democrats were ready for a fight . . . If there was any political risk, Democratic leaders concluded, it was with cooperating with Bush.")

23. Dan Balz, "Social Security Stance Risky, Democrats Told," *Washington Post,* March 8, 2005, p. A3 (noting that Lieberman was once attracted to private accounts and is actively working with Republicans on Social Security reform plans).

24. David D. Kirkpatrick and Carl Hulse, "On Social Security, Lieberman the Centrist Ruffles Democratic Feathers," *New York Times,* March 7, 2005, online at http://www.nytimes.com/2005/03/07/politics/ 071lieberman.html (accessed Jan. 17, 2007).

25. Paul Krugman attacked Lieberman continuously on Social Security. See, for example, Paul Krugman, "Talk-Show Joe," May 22, 2006; online at http://select.nytimes .com/2006/05/22/opinion/22krugman.html?_r=1 (accessed June 23, 2009).

26. "Lieberman Joins Senate Democrats in Opposing Bush Social Security Privatization Plan," Press Release, Office of Joe Lieberman, March 4, 2005, online at http:// lieberman.senate.gov./newsroom/release.cfm?id=232853 (accessed July 16, 2007.

27. Richard W. Stevenson, "Despite Problems, Bush Continues to Make Advances on His Agenda," *New York Times,* July 29, 2005, online at http://www.nytimes .com/2005/07/29/politics/29assess.html (accessed Jan. 17, 2007) (Republicans as well as Democrats in Congress were reluctant to consider Bush's Social Security reform proposal); Jacobs, "Promotional Presidency," p. 316 (Republican legislators were convinced that there would be clear costs to the president's reform proposal, costs that would be traced back to them, to their electoral detriment); Ross, "Policy Histories and Partisan Leadership," p. 426 (describing view of key Republican senator, Charles

Grassley of Iowa, that there was widespread disinterest in Congress about addressing Social Security reform).

28. Dan Balz, "Bush's Ambitious Second-Term Agenda," p. 33 ("Republicans [in the House] were loath to vote on a plan that could subject them to negative ads in 2006 when there was no prospect it would ever pass the Senate"); Jacobs, "Promotional Presidency," p. 314 (asserting that Republican leaders actually refused to bring Bush's plan to a vote on the floor of either the House or Senate).

29. Ross, "Policy Histories and Partisan Leadership," p. 425 (discussing Bush's willingness to consider "progressive indexing," which would adjust Social Security payments for wealthier citizens by the rate of inflation, not the larger rate of wage growth applicable to other beneficiaries); Jacobs, "Promotional Presidency," pp. 315–16 (discussing Bush's willingness to work with Republican senator Lindsey Graham of South Carolina on a plan to help pay for the costs of private accounts by raising the income ceiling for payroll taxes applied to higher-income workers).

30. Jacobson, *A Divider, Not a Uniter,* p. 208 (the Democrats were determined to force Bush and the Republicans to initiate the unpopular steps necessary to reform Social Security).

31. Ross, "Policy Histories and Partisan Leadership," p. 425 (describing Tom De-Lay's hostile reaction to Bush's willingness to consider raising the $90,000 cap on payroll taxes).

4. Making Sure Kids Learn

1. Andrew Rudalevige, "The Politics of No Child Left Behind," *Education Next* 3(4) (Fall 2003): 62–69; online at http://www.hoover.org/publications/ednext/3346601 .html (accessed October 19, 2006).

2. Patrick J. McGuinn, *No Child Left Behind and the Transformation of Federal Education Policy, 1965–2005* (Lawrence: University Press of Kansas, 2006), pp. 153–54.

3. J. R. Campbell, C. M. Hombo, and J. Mazzeo, *NAEP 1999 Trends in Academic Progress: Three Decades of Student Performance,* U.S. Department of Education, National Center for Education Statistics, NCES 2000-469, Washington, D.C., 2000; Krista Kafer, "No Child Left Behind: Where Do We Go from Here?," Backgrounder No. 1775, The Heritage Foundation, July 6, 2004, online at http://www.heritage.org/ Research/Education/bg1775.cfm (accessed Jan. 17, 2008).

4. Margaret Spellings, "Building on Results: A Blueprint for Strengthening the No Child Left Behind Act," U.S. Department of Education, Washington, D.C., January 2007, p. 1.

5. Andrew C. Porter, "NCLB Lessons Learned: Implications for Reauthorization," in *Standards-Based Reform and the Poverty Gap: Lessons for No Child Left Behind,* ed. Adam Gamoran (Washington, D.C.: Brookings Institution Press, 2007), pp. 300–302.

6. For example, a July 1999 national survey by the Pew Research Center found that more respondents, by a 52–29% margin, trusted Democrats (52%) than Repub-

licans (29%) to do a good job on education. Rudalevige, "Politics of No Child Left Behind," p. 65; also see McGuinn, *No Child Left Behind*, p. 152 (table 9.2)

7. The National Commission on Excellence in Education spotlighted high rates of illiteracy, falling test scores, and poor training of teachers. See "A Nation at Risk: The Imperative for Education Reform," National Commission on Higher Education, April 1983; also see McGuinn, *No Child Left Behind*, pp. 39–47.

8. Maris A. Virioyskis, *The Road to Charlottesville: The 1989 Education Summit,* paper prepared for National Educational Goals Panel, September 1999; online at http://govinfo.library.unt.edu/negp/reports/negp30.pdf (accessed Jan. 17, 2008).

9. On April 18, 1991, President George H. W. Bush unveiled his "America 2000" proposal calling for standards in five core subjects (English, math, science, history, and geography), voluntary national testing of fourth-, eighth-, and twelfth-graders, and permission for parents to use federal assistance to enroll disadvantaged students into other public or private schools. Congressional Democrats countered with a plan that excluded national testing and withheld permission for parents to use federal dollars at private schools. Bush threatened to veto the Democratic plan, which fell one vote short of overcoming a filibuster threat in the Senate. "Hill Counters President's Education Plan," *CQ Almanac* (Washington, D.C.: CQ Press, 1991), pp. 377–81; "Scorned School Bill Dies in the Senate," *CQ Almanac* (Washington, D.C.: CQ Press, 1992), pp. 455–60.

10. Rudalevige, "Politics of No Child Left Behind"; Kafer, "No Child Left Behind."

11. Rudalevige, "Politics of No Child Left Behind," p. 64.

12. Andrew Rotherham, "Toward Performance-Based Federal Education Funding," Policy Report, Progressive Policy Institute, April 1, 1999, online at http://www .ppionline.org/ndol/print.cfm?contentid=1249 (accessed Jan. 17, 2008); also see McGuinn, *No Child Left Behind*, p. 140.

13. "House Passes Bills to Reauthorize Elementary and Secondary Education Act," *CQ Almanac* 1999 (Washington, D.C.: CQ Press, 1999), pp. 10-3 to 10-21.

14. "Lawmakers Extend Some ESEA Programs as Part of Omnibus Spending Package," *CQ Almanac* (Washington, D.C.: CQ Press, 2000), pp. 9-3 to 9-13.

15. Ibid., p. 9-4.

16. Ibid, pp. 9-4 to 9-5.

17. "The President's Big Test," interview by Wen Stephenson with *New Yorker* correspondent Nicholas Lemann, *Frontline,* March 28, 2002; online at http://www .pbs.org/wgbh/pages/frontline/shows/schools/nochild/lemann.html (accessed Nov. 14, 2005).

18. McGuinn, *No Child Left Behind*, pp. 146–64

19. David S. Broder, "Long Road to Reform: Negotiators Forge Education Legislation," *Washington Post,* Dec. 9, 2001; Rudalevige, "Politics of No Child Left Behind," p. 66.

20. Broder, "Long Road to Reform," p. A01; also see Charles O. Jones, *The Presidency in a Separated System* (Washington, D.C.: Brookings Institution Press, 2005), p. 205.

21. Broder, "Long Road to Reform"; Rudalevige, "Politics of No Child Left Behind"; on Miller's background, see Michael Barone, *The Almanac of American Politics, 2005* (Washington, D.C.: National Journal Group, 2006), pp. 183–84.

22. Rudalevige, "Politics of No Child Left Behind," p. 64; on the similarity of Bush's proposal to the ide(accessed the Progressive Policy Institute, see McGuinn, *No Child Left Behind*, p. 155.

23. John P. Burke, *Becoming President: The Bush Transition, 2000–2003* (Boulder, Colo.: Lynne Rienner, 2004), p. 138 (Bush signaled early and often that he would not insist on vouchers: Andy Card's remarks on inauguration day, the confirmation hearings of Roderick Paige, and the president's own words on Jan. 24, 2001).

24. Rudalevige, "Politics of No Child Left Behind," p. 66; Broder, "Long Road to Reform"; McGuinn, *No Child Left Behind*, p. 167.

25. "Landmark Education Bill Signed," *CQ Almanac* (Washington, D.C.: CQ Press, 2001), pp. 8-6 to 8-10.

26. Ibid.

27. Ibid.

28. Ibid.

29. Ibid.

30. Ibid.

31. Ibid.

32. Ibid., p. 8-7

33. Rudalevige, "Politics of No Child Left Behind," p. 67.

34. "Landmark Education Bill Signed," p. 8-7.

35. Rudalevige, "Politics of No Child Left Behind," p. 67.

36. "Landmark Education Bill Signed," p. 8-7.

37. Rudalevige, "Politics of No Child Left Behind," p. 68.

38. Ibid., p. 69.

39. "Landmark Education Bill Signed," pp. 8-8 to 8-9.

40. Ibid., p. 8-7

41. Paul E. Peterson and Martin R. West, "No Child Left Behind: The Politics and Practice of Accountability," Transcript of Briefing, Brookings Institution, Dec. 11, 2003; online at www.brookings.edu/events/2003/1211education.aspx (accessed Oct. 19, 2006).

42. Kafer, "No Child Left Behind."

43. McGuinn, *No Child Left Behind*, p. 183, esp. n. 41.

44. Sam Dillon, "Most States Fail Demands Set Out in Education Law," *New York Times*, July 25, 2005, p. A14 (Education Department flatly rejected testing systems in Maine and Nebraska).

45. Laura S. Hamilton, Brian M. Stecher, Georges Vernez, and Ron Zimmer, "Passing or Failing? A Midterm Report Card for 'No Child Left Behind,'" *RAND Review,* (Fall 2007): 17–25.

46. Sam Dillon, "Students Ace State Tests, but Earn D's from U.S.," *New York Times*, Nov. 26, 2005, p. A1.

47. Ibid.

48. Paul Basken, "'No Child' Leads States to Weaken Student Tests, Study Finds," *Bloomberg.com,* July 5, 2006 (referring to 12-state study by Professor Bruce Fuller of the University of California–Berkeley); online at http://www.bloomberg.com/apps/news?pid=20601087&sid=aUT15ttmRntY&refer=home (accessed May 20, 2009).

49. Hamilton et al., "Passing or Failing?," p. 19.

50. On the need for standardization of state tests, see Brian Stecher, "Revamp NCLB to Fulfill Its Promise," *Baltimore Sun,* Sept. 16, 2007, p. 17A. Also see Chester E. Finn Jr., "Dumbing Education Down," *Wall Street Journal,* Oct. 5, 2007, p. A16.

51. Frederick M. Hess and Chester E. Finn Jr., "Conclusion: Can This Law Be Fixed? A Hard Look at the NCLB Remedies," in *No Remedy Left Behind: Lessons from a Half-Decade of NCLB,* ed. Frederick M. Hess and Chester E. Finn Jr. (Washington, D.C.: AEI Press, 2007), p. 320.

52. Hamilton et al., "Passing or Failing?," pp. 17–25.

53. "Choices, Changes and Challenges: Curriculum and Instruction in the NCLB Era," *From the Capital to the Classroom: Year 5 of the No Child Left Behind Act,* Center for Education Policy, Washington, D.C., July 2007 (62% of districts report more class time spent on reading and math; 44% report cutting time elsewhere).

54. Porter, "NCLB Lessons Learned," p. 296.

55. Ibid.

56. David N. Plank and Christopher Dunbar Jr., "Michigan: Over the First Hurdle," in *No Remedy Left Behind: Lessons from a Half-Decade of NCLB,* ed. Frederick M. Hess and Chester E. Finn Jr. (Washington, D.C.: AEI Press, 2007), p. 222.

57. Porter, "NCLB Lessons Learned," p. 297; Spellings, "Building on Results" (many states still working on technical aspects of state assessments and standards as they are applied to students with disabilities and students with limited English proficiency).

58. Susan Saulny, "Tutor Program Offered by Law Is Going Unused," *New York Times,* Feb. 12, 2006, p. 1.

59. Sam Dillon, "As 2 Bushes Try to Fix Schools, the Tools Differ," *New York Times,* Sept. 28, 2006, p. A1.

60. McGuinn, *No Child Left Behind,* pp. 184–85.

61. The Utah House of Representatives amended its strongly worded resolution against NCLB to allow the state to continue to receive federal funds. Kafer, "No Child Left Behind."

62. McGuinn, *No Child Left Behind,* p. 186. For example, the Department of Education allowed two states, North Carolina and Tennessee, to track how individual students advance year by year in reading and math rather than track whether a growing fraction of children pass exams each year. Diana Jean Schemo, "Flexibility Granted 2 States in No Child Left Behind," *New York Times,* May 18, 2006, p. A19.

63. Porter, 2007, p. 319; Hamilton et al., and others, RAND Review, 2007, pp. 17–25.

64. Porter, "NCLB Lessons Learned," p. 298.

65. Hamilton et al., "Passing or Failing?," pp. 23, 24–25.

66. Porter, "NCLB Lessons Learned," p. 298.

67. Ibid., p. 298.

68. Ibid., p. 319.

69. Ibid.; Dillon, "As 2 Bushes Try to Fix Schools," p. A1.

70. Porter, "NCLB Lessons Learned," p. 312.

71. Patrick McGuinn, "New Jersey: Equity Meets Accountability," in *No Remedy Left Behind: Lessons from a Half-Decade of NCLB,* ed. Frederick M. Hess and Chester E. Finn Jr. (Washington, D.C.: AEI Press, 2007), pp. 172–73; Alex Medler, "Colorado: The Misapplication of Federal Power," in *No Remedy Left Behind: Lessons from a Half-Decade of NCLB,* ed. Frederick M. Hess and Chester E. Finn Jr. (Washington, D.C.: AEI Press, 2007), p. 199; Hamilton et al., "Passing or Failing?," p. 19.

72. For a view that school-choice provision in NCLB is ineffectual, see Brian Stecher, "Revamp NCLB to Fulfill Its Promise," *Baltimore Sun,* Sept. 16, 2007, p. 17A.

73. Frederick M. Hess and Chester E. Finn, eds., *No Remedy Left Behind: Lessons from a Half-Decade of NCLB* (Washington, D.C.: AEI Press, 2007, p. 323.

74. Hamilton et al., "Passing or Failing?," p. 20 (20% of districts did not notify parents about the transfer option in a clear, timely manner).

75. For examples of how some schools subtly discourage parents from seeking transfers, see Kafer, "No Child Left Behind."

76. Hamilton et al., "Passing or Failing?," p.20; Julian Betts, "California: Does the Golden State Deserve a Gold Star?" in *No Remedy Left Behind: Lessons from a Half-Decade of NCLB,* ed. Frederick M. Hess and Chester E. Finn Jr. (Washington, D.C.: AEI Press, 2007), p. 150.

77. McGuinn, *No Child Left Behind,* p. 187.

78. Clint Bolick, "Four Million Children Left Behind," *Wall Street Journal,* Sept. 7, 2006, p. A21.

79. Susan Saulney, "Tutor Program Offered by Law Is Going Unused," *New York Times,* Feb. 12, 2006, pp. 1, 27.

80. Hamilton et al., "Passing or Failing?," p. 19.

81. Stephen Clements, "Rural Kentucky Districts: 'Do-It-Yourself' School Improvement," in *No Remedy Left Behind: Lessons from a Half-Decade of NCLB,* ed. Frederick M. Hess and Chester E. Finn Jr. (Washington, D.C.: AEI Press, 2007), p. 243.

82. Hamilton et al., "Passing or Failing?," p. 19.

83. Ibid., pp. 17–25; Debra Viadero, "NCLB Tutoring, but Not Transfers, Found to Help Student Scores," *Education Week,* June 28, 2007.

84. Hess and Finn, *No Remedy Left Behind,* p. 310 (expressing concern that most federal monies for supplemental tutoring flow back to local teachers).

85. Bolick, "Four Million Children Left Behind," p. A21.

86. "Spellings Exemptions," Editorial, *Wall Street Journal,* Oct. 31, 2006, p. A18; Jason L. Riley, "A Law Best Left Behind," *Wall Street Journal,* Sept. 28, 2007, p. A14.

87. Kafer, "No Child Left Behind."

88. Porter, "NCLB Lessons Learned," p. 294.

89. Hamilton et al., "Passing or Failing?," p. 20.

90. *ECS Report to the Nation: State Implementation of the No Child Left Behind Act,* Education Commission of the States, Denver, Colo., 2004.

91. Dillon, "As 2 Bushes Try to Fix Schools"; Kafer, "No Child Left Behind"; Hamilton et al., "Passing or Failing?," pp. 17–25. But see Gregg Toppo, "Report, Suit Question Teacher Qualifications," *USA Today,* Aug. 22, 2007; online at http://www.usatoday.com/news/education/2007-08-21-teachers-lawsuit_n.htm (accessed Jan. 18, 2008).

92. Valerie Strauss, "Report Calls for Improvement in K–8 Science Education," *Washington Post,* Sept. 22, 2006, p. A9.

93. McGuinn, "New Jersey: Equity Meets Accountability," p. 177.

94. Hess and Finn, *No Remedy Left Behind,* p. 310.

95. Ibid., p. 313.

96. Sam Dillon, "U.S. Eases 'No Child' Law as Applied to Some States," *New York Times,* March 19, 2008 (online).

97. Porter, "NCLB Lessons Learned," p. 317.

98. Sam Dillon, "U.S. to Require States to Use a Single School Dropout Formula," *New York Times,* April 1, 2008 (online); Associated Press, "New Rule: States, High Schools Must Improve Dropout Rates, *Herald Times* (Bloomington, Ind.), Oct. 29, 2008 (online).

99. Ashley Johnson, "Next Frontier: High Schools," *National Journal,* Jan. 10, 2009, pp. 48–49.

100. Rudalevige, "Politics of No Child Left Behind."

101. William J. Mathis, "No Child Left Behind: Costs and Benefits," *Kappan Professional Journal* 84(9) (2003): 679–86; online at http://www.pdkintl.org/kappan/k0305mat.htm (accessed Jan. 18, 2008).

102. Budget of the U.S. Government, Fiscal Year 2009, U.S. Office of Management and Budget, Washington, D.C., Jan. 31, 2008 (see summary of Discretionary Funds for the U.S. Department of Education).

103. *School District of the City of Pontiac v. Spellings,* U.S. Dist. LEXIS 29253 (D. Mich. 2005).

104. *School District of the City of Pontiac, et al. v. Secretary of the U.S. Department of Education,* 512 F.3d 252 (6th Cir. 2008), Jan. 7, 2008.

105. Hess and Finn, "Conclusion: Can this Law be Fixed?," p. 309.

106. The 2005 national tests showed persistent gaps between racial groups, but some progress in math scores. Sam Dillon, "Schools Slow in Closing Gaps between Races," *New York Times,* Nov. 23, 2006, p. A1.

107. Ashley Johnson, "Next Frontier: High Schools," *National Journal,* Jan. 10, 2009, pp. 48–49.

108. Margaret Spellings, "Building on Results: A Blueprint for Strengthening the No Child Left Behind Act," U.S. Department of Education, Washington, D.C., January 2007.

109. Phil Davis, "NEA to Challenge NCLB," *Boston Globe,* July 3, 2006; online at http://www.boston.com/news/nation/articles/2006/07/03/nea_to_challenge_no_child_left_behind/ (accessed Jan. 18, 2008).

110. Diana Jean Schemo, "Teachers and Rights Groups Oppose Education Measure," *New York Times,* Sept. 11, 2007; online at http://www.nytimes.com/2007/09/11/education/11child.html?_r=1&ref=education&oref=slogin (accessed June 23, 2009).

111. On the cloudy prospects for reauthorization of NCLB, see Diana Jean Schemo, "Crucial Lawmaker Outlines Changes to Education Law," *New York Times,* July 31, 2007; online at www.nytimes.com/2007/07/31/washington/31child.html?scp=1&sq=Crucial+Lawmaker+Outlines+Changes+to+Education+Law (accessed Jan. 18, 2008).

112. Alyson Klein, "Political Shift Could Temper NCLB Resolve," *Education Week* 26(5), Sept. 27, 2006, pp. 1, 24.

113. Libby George, "His Permanent Record: Bush Mints a Legacy," *Congressional Quarterly Weekly Report,* Feb. 18, 2008, p. 427; Sam Dillon, "Education Secretary Offers Changes to 'No Child' Law," *New York Times,* April 23, 2008 (online).

114. Thomas E. Mann and Norman J. Ornstein, *The Broken Branch: How Congress Is Failing and How to Get It Back on Track* (New York: Oxford University Press, 2006), p. 128.

115. McGuinn, *No Child Left Behind,* p. 158 (especially table 9.3).

116. Animosity toward NCLB among some conservatives did not dissipate with time. See Charles Murray, "Acid Tests," *Wall Street Journal,* July 25, 2006, p. A12.

117. Burke, *Becoming President,* p. 138 (discussing how Bush signaled early in 2001 that he would not insist on vouchers).

118. Kafer, "No Child Left Behind."

119. Porter, "NCLB Lessons Learned," p. 290.

120. Michael Casserly, "America's Great City Schools: Moving in the Right Direction," in *No Remedy Left Behind: Lessons from a Half-Decade of NCLB,* ed. Frederick M. Hess and Chester E. Finn Jr. (Washington, D.C.: AEI Press, 2007), p. 43.

121. Ibid., p. 65.

122. Adam Gamoran, "Introduction: Can Standards-Based Reform Help Reduce the Poverty Gap in Education?" in *Standards-Based Reform and the Poverty Gap: Lessons for No Child Left Behind,* ed. Adam Gamoran (Washington, D.C.: Brookings Institution Press, 2007), p. 15.

123. Jones, *Presidency in a Separated System,* pp. 205, 326.

124. Bush's $100 million voucher proposal in 2006 was modeled on a pilot project that congressional Republicans launched in 2004. Diana Jean Schemo, "Republicans Propose National School Voucher Program," *New York Times,* July 19, 2006, p. A17; Greg Toppo, "Spellings Promotes Voucher Program," *USA Today,* July 19, 2006, p. 6D.

125. Schemo, "Republicans Propose National School Voucher Program" (summarizes findings of Department of Education study of 700,000 fourth- and eighth-graders in public schools and 25,000 in private schools).

126. On the growing interest in vouchers among African Americans and Latinos, see McGuinn, *No Child Left Behind,* p. 159.

127. Broder, "Long Road to Reform," p. A01.

5. Drug Coverage for Seniors

1. Robert D. Reischauer, "Prescription Drugs: What We Know and Don't Know about Seniors' Access to Coverage," Hearings before the Subcommittee on Health

and Environment of the Committee on Commerce, House of Representatives, 106th Congress, First Session, Sept. 28 and Oct. 4, 1999 (Washington D.C.: U.S. Government Printing Office, 1999), p.60.

2. Ibid.

3. "Medicare: The Prescription Drug Benefit" Fact Sheet, Henry J. Kaiser Family Foundation, Menlo Park, California, April 2003. Available online at http://www.kff .org/medicare/upload/Medicare-and-Prescription-Drugs-Fact-Sheet-Fact-Sheet.pdf (accessed Aug. 27, 2006).

4. Ibid.

5. D. G. Safran, P. Neuman, C. Schoen, et al. "Prescription Drug Coverage and Seniors: Findings from a 2003 National Survey," *Health Affairs,* April 19, 2005; available online at http://content.healthaffairs.org/cgi/content/full/hlthaff.w5.152/DC1 (accessed Jan. 18, 2008): even with a drug benefit, some seniors quit taking their drugs when they exceed their plan's annual spending limit. "Prescription Spending Caps Cause Some Seniors to Quit Taking Medicines for Chronic Illnesses," RAND News Release, Sept. 11, 2007, online at http://www.rand.org/news/press/2007/09/11/ index.html (accessed Sept. 12, 2007).

6. "Medicare: The Prescription Drug Benefit."

7. Ibid.

8. Ibid.

9. M. A. Laschober, M. Kitchman, P. Neuman, and A. Strabic, "Trends in Medicare Supplemental Insurance and Prescription Drug Coverage, 1996–1999," *Health Affairs,* Suppl Web Exclusive: pp. W127–38, Online at http://content.healthaffairs.org/ cgi/content/full/hlthaff.w2.127v1/DC1 (accessed Jan. 18, 2008); T. R. Oliver, P. R. Lee, and H. L. Lipton, "A Political History of Medicare and Prescription Drug Coverage," *Milbank Quarterly* 82(2) (2004): 340.

10. Reischauer, "Prescription Drugs," p. 62.

11. L. Achman and M. Gold, "Medicare+ Choice Plans Continue to Shift More Costs to Enrollees," report prepared by Mathematica Policy Research, for the Commonwealth Fund. New York, April 2003.

12. Drew E. Altman, "The New Medicare Prescription-Drug Legislation," *New England Journal of Medicine,* January 2004, 305(1): 9–10.

13. National Economic Council, Domestic Policy Council, "The President's Plan to Modernize and Strengthen Medicare for the 21st Century: A Detailed Description" (Washington, D.C.: White House, July 2, 1999).

14. "House-Passed Bill Looks Good to Insurers for Drug Plans; No Parallel Bill in the Senate," *CQ Almanac Plus,* 2000 (Washington, D.C.: CQ Press, 2001), p. 12-16.

15. Ibid., pp. 12-16 to 12-19.

16. Ibid., pp. 12-16 to 12-19.

17. Kevin Sack, "The 2000 Campaign: The Vice President; Gore, in Attack on Drug Industry, Focuses on Two Medicines," *New York Times,* Aug. 29, 2000, p. A19.

18. Ibid.; Oliver, Lee, and Lipton, "Political History of Medicare," p. 307.

19. Anne E. Kornblut, "Campaign 2000: Bush Airs $198B Plan for Drug Coverage," *Boston Globe,* Sept. 6, 2000, p. A1.

20. John P. Burke, *Becoming President: The Bush Transition, 2000–2003* (Boulder, Colo.: Lynne Rienner, 2004), pp. 146–47 (discussing how Grassley in the Senate and Thomas in the House believed comprehensive Medicare reform should be pursued).

21. "Medicare Drug Coverage Stalls," *CQ Almanac Plus,* 2001 (Washington, D.C.: CQ Press, 2002), p. 12-7.

22. President G. W. Bush, "A Blueprint for New Beginnings: A Responsible Budget for America's Priorities," The President's FY02 Budget Submission to Congress (Washington, D.C.: U.S. Government Printing Office, 2001), p. 8.

23. For example, see news release, "Cato Expert: Medicare Drug Benefit 'A Terrible Mistake,'" Cato Institute, Washington, D.C., Nov. 18, 2003.

24. "Medicare Drug Coverage Stalls," p. 12-8.

25. *National Association of Chain Drug Stores v. The Honorable Tommy G. Thompson, et al.,* No. 01-1554 (D.D.C. 2001); *National Association of Chain Drug Stores v. The Honorable Tommy G. Thompson, et al.,* No. 01-1554 (D.D.C. 2003).

26. Charles O. Jones, *The Presidency in a Separated System* (Washington, D.C.: Brookings Institution Press, 2005), p. 173.

27. Oliver, Lee, and Lipton, "Political History of Medicare," p. 308.

28. "No Deal on Prescription Benefit," *CQ Almanac Plus,* 2002 (Washington, D.C.: CQ Press, 2003), p. 10-4.

29. Ibid., p. 10-3.

30. M. A. Carey, "Medicare Deal Is Possible, as Senate Studies Bipartisan Plan," *Congressional Quarterly Weekly Report,* July 27, 2002, pp. 2042–43.

31. "Medicare Overhaul," *Congressional Quarterly Weekly Report,* Nov. 30, 2002, p. 3135.

32. "Medicare Overhaul," *Congressional Quarterly Weekly Report,* Oct. 19, 2002, p. 2749.

33. "Medicare Overhaul," *Congressional Quarterly Weekly Report,* Nov. 30, 2002, pp. 2135–36.

34. Oliver, Lee, and Lipton, "Political History of Medicare," p. 328.

35. The White House, "Fact Sheet: Framework to Modernize and Improve Medicare," Washington, D.C., March 4, 2003, online at http://georgewbush-whitehouse.archives.gov/news/releases/2003/03/20030304-1.html (accessed May 25, 2009); G. W. Bush, "President Announces Framework to Modernize and Improve Medicare," March 4, 2003, online at http://georgewbush-whitehouse.archives.gov/news/releases/2003/03/20030304-5.html (accessed May 25, 2009).

36. "Medicare Revamp Cuts It Close," *CQ Almanac Plus,* 2003 (Washington, D.C.: CQ Press, 2004), pp. 11-4 to 11-5; Oliver, Lee, and Lipton, "Political History of Medicare," p. 310.

37. Oliver, Lee, and Lipton, "Political History of Medicare," p. 311.

38. "Medicare Revamp Cuts It Close," p. 11-5.

39. Mann and Ornstein, *Broken Branch,* p. 137

40. "Medicare Revamp Cuts It Close," p. 11-5.

41. Ibid., p. 11-6.

42. Republican Joanne Emerson of Mississippi was reportedly persuaded to change her vote from nay to yea: Mann and Ornstein, *Broken Branch*, p. 137; "Medicare Revamp Cuts It Close," p. 11-7.

43. Congressional Budget Office (CBO), "Cost Estimate for H.R.1, Medicare Prescription Drug and Modernization Act of 2003, as passed by the House of Representatives on June 27, 2003, and S.1, Prescription Drug and Medicare Improvement Act of 2003, as passed by the Senate on June 27, 2003, with a modification requested by Senate conferees," Washington, D.C., July 22, 2003.

44. Oliver, Lee, and Lipton, "Political History of Medicare," p. 315.

45. "Medicare Revamp Cuts It Close," p. 11-7; A. Goldstein, "For GOP Leaders, Battles and Bruises Produce Medicare Bill," *Washington Post*, Nov. 30, 2003, p. A8; K. Schuler and M. A. Carey, "Estimates, Ethics, and Ads Tarnish Medicare Overhaul," *Congressional Quarterly Weekly Report*, March 20, 2004, p. 699.

46. M. A. Carey, "Medicare Deal Goes to Wire in Late-Night House Vote," *Congressional Quarterly Weekly Report*, Nov. 22, 2003, p. 2879.

47. Mann and Ornstein, *Broken Branch*, p. 137.

48. "Medicare Revamp Cuts It Close," p. 11-7; Oliver, Lee, and Lipton, "Political History of Medicare," p. 334; D. S. Broder, "AARP's Tough Selling Job," *Washington Post*, March 18, 2004, p. A31; R. Pear and R. Toner, "Medicare Plan Covering Drugs Backed by AARP," *New York Times*, Nov 18, 2003, p. A1.

49. D. S. Broder, and A. Goldstein, "AARP Decision Followed a Long Courtship," *Washington Post*, Nov. 20, 2003, p. A1; B. C. Vladeck, "Plenty of Nothing: A Report from the Medicare Commission," *New England Journal of Medicine* 340(9) (May 13, 1999): 1503–1506.

50. Oliver, Lee, and Lipton, "Political History of Medicare," p. 320.

51. "Medicare Revamp Cuts It Close," p. 11-8; D. S. Broder, "Time Was GOP's Ally on the Vote," *Washington Post*, Nov. 23, 2003, p. A1; Carey, "Medicare Deal Goes to Wire," p. 2879.

52. "Medicare Revamp Cuts It Close," p. 11-8.

53. M. A. Carey, "GOP Wins Battle, Not War," *Congressional Quarterly Weekly Report*, Nov. 29, 2003, p. 2956.

54. Oliver, Lee, and Lipton, "Political History of Medicare," p. 318.

55. The key features of the standard drug benefit (2006) were as follows: (a) $250 deductible and co-insurance of 25% after the deductible, up to an initial coverage limit of $2,250 in total drug expenses per year; (b) coverage gap (the "doughnut hole") between $2,250 and $3,600 (i.e., enrollees pay 100% of drug expenses); and (c) plan pays 95% of drug expenses above $3,600 per year.

56. "Medicare: The Prescription Drug Benefit."

57. Ibid.

58. Ibid.

59. Ibid.

60. Ibid.; Oliver, Lee, and Lipton, "Political History of Medicare," p. 318.

61. Oliver, Lee, and Lipton, "Political History of Medicare," p. 317.

62. Congressional Budget Office (CBO), "Cost Estimate for H.R. 1, Medicare Prescription Drug and Modernization Act of 2003, as passed by the House of Representatives on June 27, 2003, and S. 1, Prescription Drug and Medicare Improvement Act of 2003, as passed by the Senate on June 27, 2003, with a modification requested by Senate conferees," Washington, D.C., July 22, 2003.

63. Cici Connolly and Mike Allen, "Medicare Drug Benefit May Cost $1.2 Trillion," *Washington Post,* Feb. 9, 2005, p. A01; A. Goldstein, "Foster: White House Had Role in Withholding Medicare Data," *Washington Post,* March 19, 2004, p. A2; S. G. Stolberg, "Senate Democrats Claim Medicare Chief Broke Law," *New York Times,* March 19, 2004, p. A14.

64. Douglas Holtz-Eakin, Director, Congressional Budget Office, Letter to Honorable Joe Barton, Chairman, House Energy and Commerce Committee, March 4, 2005, Available at http://www.cbo.gov/ftpdocs/61xx/doc6139/03-04-BartonMedicare.pdf (accessed Sept. 4, 2006).

65. S. G. Stolberg and R. Pear, "Mysterious Fax Adds to Intrigue over the Medicare Bill's Cost," *New York Times,* March 18, 2004, p. A1; Schuler and Carey, "Estimates, Ethics, and Ads," p. 699.

66. Oliver, Lee, and Lipton, "Political History of Medicare," pp. 299–301.

67. "42 CFR Parts 400, 403, 411, 417, and 423 Medicare Program; Medicare Prescription Drug Benefit; Final Rule," Centers for Medicare and Medicaid Services, Department of Health and Human Services, *Federal Register,* Jan. 28, 2005, 70(18): 4193–4742.

68. Robert Pear, "In Texas Town, Patients and Providers Find New Prescription Drug Plan Baffling," *New York Times,* June 11, 2006, pp. 1, 32.

69. Richard Wolf, "Government Trying to Simplify Drug Plan, Medicare Official Says," *USA Today,* Feb. 9, 2006, p. 10A.

70. Robert Pear, "States Protest Contributions to Drug Plan," *New York Times,* Oct. 18, 2005, p. A24.

71. Robert Pear, "States Look to Rein In Private Medicare Plans," *New York Times,* May 5, 2008 (online).

72. "Medicare Details Steps Taken to Improve Customer Service by Drug Plans: Data Shows Improvements in Plan Call Center Wait Times," Centers for Medicare and Medicaid Services, *Medicare Daily News,* June 29, 2006, Available at http://www.cms.hhs.gov/apps/media/press/release.asp?Counter=1890 (accessed Sept. 3, 2006).

73. Jane Zhang and Vanessa Fuhrmans, "Proposal Would Limit Medicare-Plan Marketing," *Wall Street Journal,* May 9, 2008, p. B81.

74. Robert Pear, "Medicare Woes Take High Toll on Mentally Ill," *New York Times,* Jan. 21, 2006, p. A1.

75. "Medicare: Federal Officials Acknowledge Problems with Medicare Prescription Drug Benefit, Propose Fixes," Kaiser Daily Health Policy Report, Henry J. Kaiser Family Foundation, Menlo Park, Calif., Jan. 18, 2006; online at http://www.kaisernetwork.org/Daily_reports/rep_index.cfm?DR_ID=34849 (accessed Sept. 3, 2006).

76. Robert E. Moffit, "High Anxiety: Implementing the Medicare Prescription Drug Program," Heritage Foundation, Backgrounder #1860, Washington, D.C., June

14, 2005; online at http://www.heritage.org/Research/HealthCare/bg1860.cfm (accessed Aug. 28, 2006).

77. Pear, "In Texas Town," pp. 1, 32.

78. "Getting Help with Medicare Prescription Drug Plan Costs Income and Resource Limits 2006," Social Security Administration, Washington, D.C., Publication No. 05-10115, March 2006.

79. Pear, "In Texas Town," pp. 1, 32.

80. "Final Medicare Enrollment Effort Begins Monday across the U.S.," *Senior Journal,* April 12, 2006, online at http://www.seniorjournal.com/NEWS/MedicareDrugCards/6-04-12-FinalMedicare.htm (accessed Aug. 27, 2006); Richard Wolf, "Feds Push to Enroll More in Prescription-Drug Plans," *USA Today,* June 12, 2006, p. 4A.

81. Alex Berenson, "Co-Pay Means Many Don't Get Cancer Pills," *New York Times,* April 8, 2006, p. C1.

82. Steven Reinberg, "Medicare Drug Plan Helps Patients Fight Cancer," HealthDay.com, Sept. 12, 2006 (online).

83. Pear, "In Texas Town," pp. 1, 32.

84. Robert Pear, "Employers Can Get Medicare Subsidies for Lower Benefits," *New York Times,* Jan. 31, 2005, p. A1; Theo Francis and Ellen E. Schultz, "Rules Let Firms Get Subsidy For Retirees' Drug Costs," *Wall Street Journal,* Jan. 28, 2005, p. A4; Robert Pear, "Medicare Law Is Seen as Leading to Cuts in Drug Benefits for Retirees," *New York Times,* July 14, 2005, p. A1.

85. Moffit, "High Anxiety."

86. "The New Medicare Prescription Law: Issues for Enrolling Dual Eligibles into Drug Plans," Henry J. Kaiser Foundation, January 2006; online at http://www.kff.org/medicare/upload/The-New-Medicare-Prescription-Drug-Law-Issue-for-Enrolling-Dual-Eligibles-into-Drug-Plans-Issue-Paper.pdf (accessed Sept. 3, 2006).

87. Barbara F. Ostrov, "Emergency Drug Aid for Seniors: California Orders Prescription Payments amid Medicare Glitches," *San Jose Mercury News,* Jan. 13, 2006, p. 1A.

88. Pear, "In Texas Town," pp. 1, 32.

89. "New Medicare Prescription Law."

90. Robert Pear, "Settlement to Ease Drug Costs for Some on Medicare," *New York Times,* June 20, 2008 (online).

91. Pear, "Medicare Woes Take High Toll," p. A1.

92. Mirt Freundheim, "A Windfall from Shifts to Medicare," *New York Times,* July 18, 2006, p. C1.

93. Pear, "In Texas Town," pp. 1, 32.

94. Robert Pear, "Rules of Medicare Plans Slow Access to Benefits," *New York Times,* Feb. 14, 2006, p. A17.

95. "A Detailed Description of CBO's Cost Estimate," p. ix.

96. Moffit, "High Anxiety"; George Reisman, "Kill the Prescription Drug Benefit," Ludwig von Mises Institute, March 1, 2005, online at http://mises.org/story/1752 (accessed Sept. 3, 2006); Oliver, Lee, and Lipton, "Political History of Medicare," p. 320.

97. Peter Wallsten and James Gerstenzang, "Critics Say U.S. Domestic Focus Getting Blurred," *Los Angeles Times,* March 19, 2006, p. A24.

98. As a result of competition, plans are adding more drugs, removing unpopular options, and providing more options with advanced coverage. In 2007, more plans began to close the "doughnut hole." Robert Pear, "Medical Insurers to Offer More Drugs and Options in 2007," *New York Times,* Oct. 1, 2006, p. A14. Richard Wolf, "Medicare Drug Premiums Steady," *USA Today,* Sept. 29–Oct. 1, 2006, p. A1. However, the largest plan dropped coverage of brand drugs in the doughnut hole: Ricardo Alonzo-Zaldiver, "Insurer Scales Back Widening Medicare Prescription Gap," *Los Angeles Times,* Nov. 29, 2006, p. A31.

99. Christopher Lee, "Surveys Show Satisfaction with Medicare Drug Plan," *Washington Post,* Aug. 1, 2006, p. A5.

100. "Markets and Medicare," Editorial, *Wall Street Journal,* Oct. 4, 2006, p. A14; David Wessel, "Once Unloved, Medicare's Prescription Drug Program Defies Critics, but Issues Remain," *Wall Street Journal,* Dec. 7, 2006, p. A2.

101. Jane Zhang, "Expect Changes in Drug Co-Pays for Medicare," *Wall Street Journal,* Nov. 4, 2008 (online).

102. Ibid.

103. Oliver, Lee, Lipton, "Political History of Medicare," p. 341.

104. Ibid.

105. The new drug benefit is the biggest expansion of Medicare since the creation of the federal health program for the elderly and disabled in 1965. Lee, "Surveys Show Satisfaction," p. A5.

106. Oliver, Lee, and Lipton, "Political History of Medicare," p. 323.

107. Reisman, "Kill the Prescription Drug Benefit."

108. Mike Leavitt, "Medicare and the Market," *Washington Post,* Jan. 11, 2007, p. A25. Also see "Fact Sheet: Setting the Record Straight—Medicare Drug Benefit Estimates Unchanged," The White House, Feb. 9, 2005, online at http://georgewbush-whitehouse .archives.gov/infocus/bushrecord/factsheets/medicare.html (accessed May 25, 2009).

109. Dennis Cauchon, "Medicare Drug Program Snips $6B from Year's Tab," *USA Today,* Oct. 31, 2008, p. 1.

110. Lynne Taylor, "U.S. Prescription Drug Spending Growth Continues to Fall," www .pharmatimes.com, Oct. 1, 2007; online at http://www.natap.org/2007/newsUpdates/ 011207_04.htm (accessed Oct. 16, 2007).

111. "Fact Sheet: Medicare Spending and Financing," Henry J. Kaiser Family Foundation, Menlo Park, Calif., June 2007.

6. Producing More Energy

1. U.S. Energy Information Administration, Annual Oil Market Chronology, Overview: World Nominal Oil Price Chronology, 1970–2006, Washington, D.C., July 2007 (online).

2. Frank Bruni, "Bush, in Energy Plan, Endorses New U.S. Drilling to Curb Prices," *New York Times,* Sept. 30, 2000 (online).

3. "Excerpts from the Vice President's Speech on Energy Policy," *New York Times,* June 28, 2000 (online).

4. Alison Mitchell, "Bush Criticizes Gore for Wanting to Use Petroleum Supply," *New York Times,* Sept. 22, 2000 (online).

5. Bruni, "Bush, in Energy Plan."

6. Janet Battaile, "Gore Is Trying to Catch Up in Democrat-Dominated State," *New York Times,* Nov. 5, 2000 (online).

7. Frank Bruni with Katharine Q. Seelye, "Pump Propels Bush toward Contest of Words," *New York Times,* Oct. 3, 2000 (online).

8. Vice President Cheney's energy policy group denied the public access to a variety of deliberative documents associated with the group's work. Separately, both the U.S. Government Accountability Office and a coalition of advocacy groups initiated litigation to obtain deliberative materials. The administration won the lion's share of the resulting litigation, which took years to resolve and generated considerable negative press for the Bush administration. See *Cheney, Vice President of the United States v. U.S. District Court for the District of Columbia,* U.S. Court of Appeals for the District of Columbia, Number 03-475, June 24, 2004. For a critical view of Cheney's handling of the energy policy group, see Mark A. Peterson, "Bush and Interest Groups: A Government of Chums," in *The George W. Bush Presidency: Appraisals and Prospects,* ed. Colin Campbell and Bert A. Rockman (Washington, D.C.: CQ Press, 2004), pp. 245–46.

9. *National Energy Policy,* Report of the National Energy Policy Development Group (Washington, D.C.: U.S. Government Printing Office, May 2001).

10. In the terminology of political science, Daschle was "cross-pressured." Jamie L. Carson, "Electoral Accountability, Party Loyalty, and Roll-Call Voting in the U.S. Senate," in *Why Not Parties? Party Effects in the United States Senate,* ed. Nathan W. Monroe, Jason M. Roberts, and David W. Rohde (Chicago: University of Chicago Press, 2008), p. 29.

11. *National Energy Policy,* p. 5-9.

12. *CQ Almanac,* 2001, pp. 9-3 to 9-9.

13. Ibid.

14. Ibid.

15. *Congressional Quarterly Weekly Report* (Washington, D.C.: CQ Press, April 27, 2002), pp. 1118–20.

16. Ibid.

17. Ibid.

18. Bruce I. Oppenheimer and Marc J. Hetherington, "Catch-22: Cloture, Energy Policy and the Limits of Conditional Party Government," in *Why Not Parties? Party Effects in the United States Senate,* ed. Nathan W. Monroe, Jason M. Roberts, and David W. Rohde (Chicago: University of Chicago Press, 2008), pp. 214–15.

19. Ibid.

20. Oppenheimer and Hetherington, "Catch-22," p. 217.

21. *Congressional Quarterly Weekly Report,* July 4, 2005, p. 1827.

22. *Congressional Quarterly Weekly Report,* Aug. 1, 2005, p. 2108.

23. The defecting Republicans were Burns of Montana, Chafee of Rhode Island, Coleman of Minnesota, Collins and Snowe of Maine, DeWine of Ohio, and McCain of Arizona.

24. *CQ Almanac,* 2005, p. 8-18.

25. James T. Bartis, "Policy Issues for Coal-to-Liquid Development," Testimony Presented before the Senate Energy and Natural Resources Committee, U.S. Congress, Washington, D.C., May 2007, CT-281, RAND, p.4.

26. Jad Mouawad, "OPEC, Struggling to Move in Concert, Considers Cutting Output," *New York Times,* Nov. 30, 2008, p. 11; Spencer Swartz and Neil King Jr., "OPEC Faces Tough Call on Depth, Timing, of Export Cut," *Wall Street Journal,* Oct. 14, 2008 (online); Neil King, Jr. and Spencer Swartz, "OPEC Expects to Cut Output in Bid to Prop Up Oil Prices," *Wall Street Journal,* Oct. 21, 2008 (online); Spencer Swartz and Neil King Jr., "OPEC Ministers Weigh Another Oil-Production Cut," *Wall Street Journal,* Dec. 1, 2008 (online).

27. The poorest 25% of U.S. wage earners devote the largest percentage of their income to energy. See David B. Cashin and Leslie McGlanahan, "Household Energy Expenditures," *Chicago Fed Letter,* June 2006, No. 227, pp. 3–4; also see Gary Stoller, "Gasoline Prices Can Have a Punishing Impact," *USA Today,* June 4, 2007, pp. B1, B2 (citing data from the Bureau of Labor Statistics and the Energy Information Administration).

28. *CQ Almanac,* 2004, p. 9-5.

29. Russell Gold, "Conoco Phillips, BP Plan Pipeline for Alaska Gas," *Wall Street Journal,* April 9, 2008, B1.

30. John M. Biers and Jessica Resnick-Ault, "Energy Firms Keep Taxes at Bay," *Wall Street Journal,* July 18, 2006, p. A5.

31. Clifford Krauss, "Big Oil Find Is Reported in Gulf of Mexico Waters," *New York Times,* Sept. 6, 2006, p. C7.

32. Richard Rubin, "The Pre-Election Tax Package," *Congressional Quarterly Weekly Report,* Oct. 20, 2008, pp. 2832–33.

33. *National Energy Policy Status Report on Implementation of NEP Recommendations,* U.S. Department of Energy, Washington, D.C., January 2005; Tom Kenworthy, "Some in GOP Fighting Western Energy Drilling," *USA Today,* July 21, 2006, p. 3A.

34. The National Petroleum Reserve is located near the Arctic National Wildlife Refuge in northwest Alaska. See Paul Leavitt, "Area Near Refuge to Be Opened For Drilling," *USA Today,* Aug. 24, 2006, p. 6A; Felicity Barringer, "Interior Department Opens 2.6 Million Acres for Oil Exploration," *New York Times,* July 17, 2008 (online).

35. Ben Casselman, "New Administration Would Risk Backlash with Gas-Drilling Reversal," *Wall Street Journal,* Nov. 11, 2008 (online).

36. Avery Palmer, "The Shale of Things to Come," *Congressional Quarterly Weekly Report,* April 28, 2008, pp. 1075–76; Ben Casselman, "Squeezing Oil from Stone," *Wall Street Journal,* July 18, 2008, p. A9.

37. John J. Fialka, "Interior Department Seeks New Offshore Leasing," *Wall Street Journal,* Feb. 9, 2006, p. A4.

38. U.S. Energy Information Administration, "What Is LNG?," Fact Sheet, July 10, 2008. Available online at http://tonto.eia.doe.gov/energy_in_brief/liquefied_natural _gas_lng.cfm (accessed June 13, 2009).

39. Spencer Jakob, "Energy Firms Have Big Bets on LNG Imports," *Wall Street Journal,* March 14, 2006, p. A13.

40. Jan Talley, "Federal Court Rejects Dominion's LNG Expansion," *Wall Street Journal,* July 21, 2008, p. B2.

41. Henri J. Pulizzi and Siobhan Hughes, "Bush, in New Tactic, Lifts Ban on Offshore Drilling," *Wall Street Journal,* July 15, 2008, p. A3.

42. Ben Casselman, "Lifting Ban Wouldn't Be Immediate Fix for Oil," *Wall Street Journal,* June 19, 2006, p. A6.

43. Siobhan Hughes and Ian Talley, "Democrats and GOP Battle over Oil Exploration," *Wall Street Journal,* July 18, 2008, A3.

44. Jad Mouawad and Diana B. Henriques, "Speculators Aren't Driving Up Oil Prices, Report Says," *New York Times,* July 23, 2008 (online).

45. Carl Hulse, "For Pelosi, a Fight Against Offshore Drilling, "*New York Times,* July 17, 2008 (online).

46. Steven Lee Myers and Carl Hulse, "Bush Acts on Drilling, Challenging Democrats," *New York Times,* July 15, 2008 (online).

47. Richard Simon and James Gerstenzang, "Bush Lifts Ban on Offshore Drilling," *Los Angeles Times,* July 15, 2008 (online).

48. Richard Rubin and David Clarke, "Extenders Measures Get Caught Up in Senate's Partisan Showdown," *National Journal,* Aug. 4, 2008, p. 2133.

49. Stephen Power, "Bush Seeks Offshore Drilling in Former Off-Limits Areas," *Wall Street Journal,* Jan. 17, 2009 (online).

50. Edmund L. Andrews, "Study Suggests Incentives on Oil Barely Help U.S.," *New York Times,* Dec. 22, 2006, pp. A1, C4; Guy Chazan, "IEA Says Fading Oil Production Threatens Supply, *Wall Street Journal,* Nov. 13, 2008 (online).

51. "Bush Urges Saudis to Increase Oil Production," *CNN.com,* April 25, 2005; online at http://www.cnn.com/2005/US/04/25/bush.saudi/index.html (accessed Jan. 20, 2008).

52. John D. McKinnon, "In Mideast, Cheney Backs Saudis over Oil Production," *Wall Street Journal,* March 25, 2008, p. A12.

53. James R. Healey, "Gas Sets Another Economic-Battering-Ram of a Record," *USA Today,* May 13, 2008, p. B1.

54. John D. McKinnon, Stephen Power, and Neil King Jr., "Saudis Rebuff Bush on Oil," *Wall Street Journal,* May 17–18, 2008, pp. A1, A7; Spencer Swartz, "IEA Slashes Forecast of Oil-Demand Growth," *Wall Street Journal,* April 12, 2008, p. A4; Jad Mouawad, "Plan Would Lift Saudi Oil Output," *New York Times,* July 14, 2008 (online); Spencer Swartz, "OPEC to Meet in Attempt to Halt Oil-Price Decline," *Wall Street Journal,* Nov. 13, 2008 (online).

55. Associated Press "Putin Assures Bush on Oil Production," *Forbes,* Aug. 22, 2004.

56. Andrew E. Kramer, "From Group of Eight, Energy Focus Is On," *New York Times,* July 17, 2006, p. A11.

57. Neil King Jr. and Spencer Swartz, "Some See $150 a Barrel This Year," *Wall Street Journal,* May 7, 2008, p. A3 (Goldman Sachs report indicates that Russian oil production has been less than projected).

58. Chip Cummins and Hassan Hafidh, "Iraqi Lifts Oil Output in South," *Wall Street Journal,* July 19, 2006, p. A4; Walter Pincus, "Corruption Cited in Iraq's Oil Industry," *Washington Post,* July 17, 2006, p. A12; Hassan Hafidh, "Iraqi Oil Is Easing Supply Strain," *Wall Street Journal,* Dec. 13, 2007, p. A4.

59. Charles Levinson, "Hope Arises for Iraqi Oil Production," *USA Today,* June 30, 2008 (online).

60. Guy Chazan and Neil King, "Oil Nears $120 on Nigerian Unrest," *Wall Street Journal,* April 29, 2008, p. C12.

61. David Luhnow and Peter Millard, "Mexico Is Near Easing Oil Laws in Bid to Attract Foreign Firms," *Wall Street Journal,* Oct. 22, 2008 (online).

62. Ibid.

63. Russell Gold, "Oil Companies Stake Future on Canada," *Wall Street Journal,* July 11, 2007, p. A8.

64. Louis Meixler, "Oil Pipeline Opens at Opportune Time," *Buffalo News,* July 16, 2006.

65. Neil King Jr. and Spencer Swartz, "Some See $150 Barrel This Year," *Wall Street Journal,* May 7, 2008, p. A3 (Goldman Sachs report predicts possible "super spikes" of $150–$200 per barrel as China and India continue to grow rapidly and OPEC holds with its decision not to add much production capacity beyond 2009).

66. National Research Council, *Coal: Energy for the Future,* (Washington, D.C.: National Academy Press, 1995), pp. 38–53; U.S. Department of Energy, *Annual Energy Outlook 2006* (Washington, D.C.: GPO, 2006) (Table 15: "Coal Supply, Disposition, and Prices").

67. "Battle of the Mountain Tops," *Economist,* May 26, 2007, p. 32.

68. Michael Barone, *The Almanac of American Politics, 2004* (Washington, D.C.: National Journal Group, 2003), p. 1709.

69. Christopher Cooper, "Coal Country Lacks Consensus on a Nominee," *Wall Street Journal,* May 19, 2008, p. A5.

70. Barone, *Almanac of American Politics, 2004,* p. 1709.

71. U.S. Energy Information Administration, *Annual Energy Outlook, with Projections to 2020,* December 1999, DOE/EIA-0383, pp. 65–72.

72. Kimberley Strassel, "Coal Man," *Wall Street Journal,* May 19, 2007, p. A9.

73. Juliet Eilperin, "Rule Would Ease Mining Debris Disposal," *Washington Post,* Dec. 3, 2008, p. A6.

74. Remarks by Energy Secretary Samuel Bodman to the National Coal Council, U.S. Department of Energy, June 9, 2005 (online).

75. "The Future of Coal," An Interdisciplinary MIT Study, Massachusetts Institute of Technology, 2007, pp. 43–62. Available online at http://web.mit.edu/coal/ (accessed June 13, 2009).

76. Leila Abboud, "Why Burying CO2 Gets Wide Interest," *Wall Street Journal,* April 26, 2007, p. B3; Hiranya Fernando, John Venezia, Clay Rigdon, and Preeti Ver-

ma, *Capturing King Coal: Deploying Carbon Capture and Storage Systems in the U.S. at Scale* (Washington, D.C.: World Resources Institute, 2008).

77. Emily Rochon, "False Hope: Why Carbon Capture and Storage Won't Save the Climate," Greenpeace International, May 2, 2008. Available online at http://www.greenpeace.org/usa/press-center/reports4/false-hope-why-carbon-capture (accessed June 13, 2009).

78. U.S. Department of Energy, *FutureGen—A Sequestration and Hydrogen Research Initiative,* Project Update, December 2006 (touting a 275-megawatt prototype plant that produces both electricity and hydrogen with zero emissions).

79. John J. Fialka, "Kyoto Questioned as U.S. Moves on Coal," *Wall Street Journal,* Dec. 6, 2005, p. A2.

80. Ibid.

81. H. Josef Hebert, "U.S. Scraps Futuristic Coal Plant," *USA Today,* Jan. 30, 2008 (online).

82. Rebecca Smith and Stephen Power, "After Washington Pulls Plug on Future-Gen, Clean Coal Hopes Flicker," *Wall Street Journal,* Feb. 2, 2008, p. A7.

83. John Deutsch and Ernest Moniz, "A Future for Fossil Fuel," *Wall Street Journal,* March 15, 2007, p. A17.

84. U.S. Department of Energy, Fossil Energy Techline, "DOE Announces Restructured FutureGen Approach," Jan. 30, 2008. Available online at http://www.energy.gov/news/5912.htm (accessed June 13, 2009).

85. Steven Mufson, "Plan for Carbon Storage Dropped," *Washington Post,* Jan. 31, 2008, p. A7.

86. International Risk and Governance Council, *Regulation of Carbon Capture and Storage,* Policy Brief, Geneva, Switzerland, 2007 (www.irgc.org).

87. Frank Camm, James T. Bartis, and Charles J. Bushman, "Federal Incentives to Induce Early Experience Producing Unconventional Liquid Fuel," RAND Corporation, DRR-4328-AF/NETL, October 2007.

88. John J. Fialka, "Energy Mandates Fuel a Rift," *Wall Street Journal,* Jan. 26, 2007, p. A4.

89. Yochi J. Dreazen, "U.S. Military Launches Alternative-Fuel Push," *Wall Street Journal,* May 21, 2008, p. A1.

90. Jeff Logan and John Venezia, "Coal-to-Liquids, Climate Change, and Energy Security," World Resources Institute, May 13, 2007 (online).

91. James T. Bartis, "Policy Issues for Coal-to-Liquid Development," Testimony before the Senate Energy and Natural Resources Committee, U.S. Congress, May 24, 2007, RAND Corporation, CT-281, pp. 6–8.

92. CTL advocates in the Senate tried to mandate that at least 6 billion gallons of fuel per year from CTL be blended with gasoline by 2022. Successful opposition was engineered by Friends of the Earth, the Sierra Club, Greenpeace, and US PIRG. The proposal was defeated 55 to 39 on the Senate floor, with only Republicans voting for the proposal. A federal subsidy plan for CTL that generated significant Democratic support was defeated 61 to 33 on the Senate floor. Jeff Tollefson, "Senate Passes Compromise Bill," *Congressional Quarterly Weekly Report,* June 25, 2007, pp. 1920–24.

93. Ed Crooks and Rebecca Bream, "Best Alternatives," *Financial Times,* Dec. 2, 2008, pp. 32–33.

94. Associated Press, "Natural Gas Prices Rise, Utilities Plan New Coal-Fired Plants," March 20, 2004 (online); Rebecca Smith, "As Emission Restrictions Loom, Texas Utility Bets Big on Coal," *Wall Street Journal,* July 21, 2006, p. 1.

95. U.S. Energy Information Administration, *Annual Energy Outlook, 2007* (electricity sector projections). Available online at http://tonto.eia.doe.gov/ftproot/forecasting/0383(2007).pdf (accessed June 13, 2009).

96. Mark Clayton, "New Coal Plants Bury Kyoto," *Christian Science Monitor,* Dec. 23, 2004, p. 1.

97. Matthew L. Wald, "Mounting Costs Slow the Push for Clean Coal," *New York Times,* May 30, 2008 (online).

98. David Strahan, "Coal Prices May Triple as Supply Crisis Deepens," *Energy Bulletin,* Feb. 4, 2008, online at http://www.energybulletin.net/node/39870 (accessed June 13, 2009); Clifford Krauss, "An Export in Solid Supply," *New York Times,* March 19, 2008 (online).

99. Jeffrey Ball, "Wall Street Shows Skepticism over Coal," *Wall Street Journal,* Feb. 4, 2008, p. A6.

100. Judy Pasternak, "Global Warming Has a New Battleground: Coal Plants," *Los Angeles Times,* April 14, 2008 (online); Edmund L. Andrews, "Senate Democrats Propose Loans for Coal-Based Fuel Plants," *New York Times,* June 13, 2007, p. A16.

101. Bobby Carmichael, "Opposition Takes On Coal Plants," *USA Today,* Nov. 1, 2007 (online).

102. Andrew Ross Sorkin, "A Buyout Deal That Has Many Shades of Green," *New York Times,* Feb. 26, 2007, pp. A1, A19.

103. "North Carolina Coal Project Hits Resistance," *Wall Street Journal,* March 1, 2007 (online); Rebecca Smith, "Coal's Doubters Block New Wave of Power Plants," *Wall Street Journal,* July 25, 2007, p. A1; Stephen Power, "Kansan Stokes Energy Squabble with Coal Ruling," *Wall Street Journal,* March 19, 2008, p. A6.

104. Rebecca Smith and Stephen Power, "After Washington Pulls Plug on Future-Gen, Clean Coal Hopes Flicker," *Wall Street Journal,* Feb. 2, 2008, p. A7; "Coal Power: Still Going Strong," *Economist,* Nov. 17, 2007, pp. 71–72.

105. Jeffrey Ball, "Wall Street Shows Skepticism over Coal," *Wall Street Journal,* Feb. 4, 2008, p. A6; Elisabeth Rosenthal, "Europe Turns Back to Coal, Raising Climate Fears," *New York Times,* April 23, 2008 (online). Matthew L. Wald, "Mounting Costs Slow the Push for Clean Coal," *New York Times,* May 30, 2008 (online).

106. *The Future of Coal,* an Interdisciplinary MIT Study, Massachusetts Institute of Technology, 2007, p. 11 (figure 2.5), available online at http://web.mit.edu/coal/The_Future_of_Coal.pdf; U.S. Congressional Budget Office, *Nuclear Power's Role in Generating Electricity,* Washington, D.C., May 2008, pp. 27–30, available online at http://www.cbo.gov/ftpdocs/91xx/doc9133/05-02-Nuclear.pdf.

107. Stephen Power, "Big Coal Campaigning to Keep Its Industry on Candidates' Minds," *Wall Street Journal,* Oct. 20, 2008 (online); Siobhan Hughes, "'Clean Coal' Backers Pitch Project for Stimulus Plan," *Wall Street Journal,* Dec. 18, 2008 (online).

108. Clifford Kraus and Matthew L. Wald, "TXU Announces Plans for 2 Coal Plants Designed to Be Cleaner-Burning," New York Times, March 10, 2007, p. B3; "AEP to Install Carbon Capture on Two Existing Power Plants; Company Will Be First to Move Technology to Commercial Scale," AEP Press Release, Columbus, Ohio, March 15, 2007 (online); David Biello, "'Clean Coal' Power Plant Canceled—Hydrogen Economy, Too," Scientific American, Feb. 6, 2008 (online) (noting that the Southern Company is proceeding with a carbon capture and storage demonstration project).

109. Duke Energy, "Indiana Utility Regulators Approve Duke Energy Clean Coal Power Plant," Duke Energy press release, Plainfield, Ind., Nov. 20, 2007; WebWire, "Duke Energy Files Progress Report, Cost Update for Clean Coal Gasification Plant," May 3, 2008 (online).

110. Paul Davidson, "Coal King Peabody Cleans Up," USA Today, Aug. 19, 2008, p. 1B.

111. Intergovernmental Panel on Climate Change, Carbon Dioxide Capture and Storage, Summary for Policymakers and Technical Summary, UNEP, IPCC Special Report, 2006. Available online at http://www.ipcc.ch/pdf/special-reports/srccs /srccs_summaryforpolicymakers.pdf (accessed June 13, 2009).

112. National Energy Policy, 2001, p. 5-15; U.S. Energy Information Administration, Annual Energy Outlook 2000, With Projections to 2020, December 1999, DOE/ EIA-0383, pp. 65–72.

113. Rebecca Smith, "Electricity Demand Is Far Outpacing New-Supply Sources," Wall Street Journal, Oct. 17, 2007, p. A17.

114. National Energy Policy, p. 5-17.

115. "Energy Security for the 21st Century: Nuclear Power," The White House, 2006, online at http://georgewbush-whitehouse.archives.gov/infocus/energy/.

116. Alan Cowell, "British Review of Energy to Include Atomic Power," New York Times, Nov. 30, 2005, p. A12; Lizette Alvarez, "Finland Rekindles Interest in Nuclear Power," New York Times, Dec. 12, 2005, p. A10.

117. Elisabeth Rosenthal, "Italy Plans to Resume Building Atomic Plants," New York Times, May 23, 2008 (online).

118. See, for example, "Clean Energy; Nuclear Plant Risk Studies: Failing the Grade," Union of Concerned Scientists, Washington, D.C., Aug. 10, 2005, Jan. 20, 2008, online at http://www.ucsusa.org/assets/documents/nuclear_power/nuc_risk.pdf (accessed May 25, 2009).

119. Ed Crooks and Rebecca Bream, "Best Alternatives," Financial Times, Dec. 1, 2008, pp. 32–33.

120. Mark Stencil, "Waste Not, Want Not," Congressional Quarterly Weekly Report, April 28, 2008, p. 1084.

121. Fact Sheet #1: Background on Proposed Facility at Yucca Mountain, U.S. Environmental Protection Agency, EPA 402-F-05-025, Washington, D.C., October 2005, www.epa.gov/radiation/yucca (accessed Jan. 20, 2008).

122. Stencil, "Waste Not, Want Not," p. 1084.

123. Congressional Quarterly Weekly Report, April 13, 2002, pp. 984–85; CQ Almanac, 2000, p. 10-3

124. *Congressional Quarterly Weekly Report,* March 9, 2002, p. 654.

125. *Congressional Quarterly Weekly Report,* May 11, 2002, p. 1234.

126. *Congressional Quarterly Weekly Report,* July 13, 2002, p. 1880.

127. The crossover Democrats were Bingaman of New Mexico, Cleland of Georgia, Durbin of Illinois, Edwards of North Carolina, Graham and Nelson of Florida, Hollings of South Carolina, Kohl of Wisconsin, Landrieu of Louisiana, Leahy of Vermont, Levin of Michigan, Lincoln of Arkansas, Miller of Georgia, Murray of Washington, and Nelson of Nebraska.

128. *CQ Almanac,* 2004, p. 2-19.

129. Katie Mulik, "Six Years On, Yucca Mountain Nuclear Repository Slowly Moves Forward," NewsHour with Jim Lehrer, May 16, 2008; available online at http://www.yuccamountain.org/docs/doe_051908.pdf.

130. Siobhan Hughes, "Yucca Move Is Part of Nuclear Agenda," *Wall Street Journal,* June 4, 2008 p. A18.

131. *Technical Bases for Yucca Mountain Standards,* National Academy of Sciences (Washington, D.C.: National Academy Press, 1995).

132. *Federal Register,* vol. 66 (Washington, D.C.: U.S. Government Printing Office, June 13, 2001), pp. 32073–32074.

133. *Nuclear Energy Institute v. EPA,* 373 F.3d 1 (D.C. Circuit, 2004).

134. "Public Health and Environmental Protection Standards for Yucca Mountain Nuclear Proposed Rule," U.S. EPA, *Federal Register,* vol. 70 (Washington, D.C.: U.S. Government Printing Office, Aug. 22, 2005), p. 49014.

135. Siobhan Hughes and Stephen Power, "White House Increases Cost Estimate for Nuclear Storage," *Wall Street Journal,* Aug. 6, 2008, p. A12.

136. Jeff Tollefson, "Nuclear Waste Key in Energy-Water Bill," *Congressional Quarterly Weekly Report,* May 29, 2006, p. 1477.

137. Steve Fetter and Frank von Hippel, "Is U.S. Reprocessing Worth the Risk?" Arms Control Association, September 2005 (online).

138. National Research Council, *Review of DOE's Nuclear Energy Research and Development Program* (Washington, D.C.: National Academies Press, 2007).

139. Mark Stencil, "Waste Not, Want Not," *Congressional Quarterly Weekly Report,* April 28, 2008, p. 1084.

140. U.S. Energy Information Administration, *Annual Energy Outlook 2008,* March 2008, DOE/EIA-0383(2008).

141. James A. Lake, "The Renaissance of Nuclear Energy," *Clean Energy Solutions: Economic Perspectives,* State Department, July 2006, p. 14, http://www.america.gov/publications/ejournalusa/0706.html (accessed May 25, 2009); Rick Lyman, "Town Sees Nuclear Plant as a Boon, Not a Threat," *New York Times,* April 10, 2006, p. A20; David R. Francis, "America Warms Up to Nuclear Power," *Christian Science Monitor,* Feb. 6, 2006, p. 15; Richard W. Cortright Jr., "Nuclear Power Is Heating Up Again," *Business Week Online,* June 27, 2006, online at http://www.businessweek.com/investor/content/jun2006/pi20060627_680870.htm (accessed May 25, 2009); Matthew L. Wald, "Nuclear Power Venture Orders Crucial Parts for Reactor," *New York Times,* Aug. 4, 2006, p. C2.

142. Associated Press, "U.S. Grants First License for Major Nuclear Plant in 30 Years," *Washington Post*, June 25, 2006, p. A10.

143. Rebecca Smith, "Nuclear Energy's Second Act?" *Wall Street Journal*, Sept. 25, 2007, p. B1.

144. Rebecca Smith, "TXU Sheds Coal Plan, Charts Nuclear Path," *Wall Street Journal*, April 10, 2007, p. A2. Rebecca Smith, "New Hurdle for Nuclear Plants," *Wall Street Journal*, Oct. 15, 2007, p. A8.

145. Rebecca Smith, "Electricity Demand Is Far Outpacing New-Supply Sources," *Wall Street Journal*, Oct. 17, 2007, p. A17.

146. Rebecca Smith, "Carbon Caps May Give Nuclear Power a Lift," *Wall Street Journal*, May 19, 2008, p. A4; U.S. Congressional Budget Office, *Nuclear Power's Role in Generating Electricity*.

147. Rebecca Smith, "Costs to Build Power Plants Pressure Rates," *Wall Street Journal*, May 27, 2008, p. B3.

148. Rebecca Smith, "New Wave of Nuclear Plants Faces High Costs," *Wall Street Journal*, May 12, 2008 (online).

149. Rebecca Smith and Stephen Power, "After Washington Pulls Plug on Future-Gen, Clean Coal Hopes Flicker," *Wall Street Journal*, Feb. 2, 2008, p. A7 (mentioning that two companies have "pulled back" from new nuclear plants due to cost concerns).

150. Judy Pasternak, "Nuclear Power Gets Boost from Candidates," *Los Angeles Times*, Dec. 30, 2007 (online).

151. Matthew L. Wald, "Nuclear Power Venture Orders Crucial Parts for Reactor," *New York Times*, Aug. 4, 2006, p. C2; Matthew L. Wald, "Even the Utilities Differ over Whether Nuclear Is the Answer: Slow Start for Revival of Reactors," *New York Times*, Aug. 22, 2006, p. C1; Matthew L. Wald, "Reactors Prone to Long Closings, Study Finds," *New York Times*, Sept. 18, 2006, p. A19; U.S. Energy Information Administration, *Annual Energy Outlook 2008* (Early Release), March 2008, DOE/EIA-0383(2008) (projecting by 2030 that 2005 energy bill will help stimulate 8 gigawatts of new nuclear capacity plus another 9 gigawatts of new capacity that will not be eligible for tax credits but even with these expansions the nuclear share of the 2030 electricity market will be only 18%).

152. *National Energy Policy*, pp. 6-1 to 6-18.

153. Ibid., pp. 6-17 to 6-18.

154. Jeff Tollefson, "Renewable-Power Dispute Stalls Senate," *Congressional Quarterly Weekly Report*, June 18, 2007, pp. 1852–53.

155. For example, in 2007 a renewable electricity requirement and some generous tax incentives for renewables were stripped in a House-Senate conference bill at the insistence of the White House and many Republicans. Diana Cappiello, "Slimmer Energy Bill Nears Finish Line," *Congressional Quarterly Weekly Report*, Dec. 17, 2007, pp. 3722–23.

156. Lois R. Ember, David J. Hanson, Glenn Hess, Cheryl Hogue, Jeff Johnson, and Susan P. Morrissey, "2009 R+D Budget a Tough Sell," *Chemical and Engineering News*, Feb. 18, 2008, pp. 27–34.

157. Mark Landler, "Sweden Turns to a Promising Power Source, with Flaws," *New York Times*, Nov. 23, 2007 (online) (in 2006 the U.S. added more wind-generating capacity than any year on record); Clifford Kraus, "Where Now, for the Wind?" *New York Times*, June 1, 2007, pp.C1, C8; Leila Abboud, "Solar Companies of All Sizes Race to Develop Cheap, Efficient Panels," *Wall Street Journal*, June 14, 2007, p. B1.

158. Jeffrey Ball, "Wind Power May Gain Footing Off Coast of U.S., *Wall Street Journal*, Sept. 3, 2008, p. A4.

159. Ashlea Ebeling, "The Green Tax Gusher," *Forbes*, Nov. 24, 2008, pp. 150–52.

160. Tom Wright, "Winds Shift for Renewable Energy as Oil Price Sinks, Money Gets Tight," *Wall Street Journal*, Oct. 20, 2008 (online).

161. U.S. Energy Information Administration, *Annual Energy Outlook 2000*, with Projections to 2020, December 1999.

162. U.S. Energy Information Administration, *Annual Energy Outlook 2008*, With Projections to 2030, December 2007.

163. Gregg Hitt, "Green Activists Generate Splits in Activist Groups," *Wall Street Journal*, Dec. 13, 2007, p. A1; Peter Applebome, "Town Divided over Wind Farm Project Finds Pitfalls Getting to Green Future," *New York Times*, Oct. 28, 2007, p. 25; Stephen Power, "First Offshore Wind Farm Is Meeting Stiff Resistance," *Wall Street Journal*, Jan. 13, 2009 (online).

164. Monte Reel, "Brazil's Road to Energy Independence," *Washington Post*, Aug. 20, 2006, p. A14; Marla Dickerson, "Farmers Hopes Sprout as Brazil Bets on Biodiesel," *Los Angeles Times*, Sept. 19, 2006, pp. C1, C9.

165. Jenny Clevstrom, "Sweden Grabs 'Clean Car' Steering Wheel," *Wall Street Journal*, Oct. 3, 2006, p. A6.

166. Robert Tomsho, "Some Boat Owners with Gunky Motors Sing Ethanol Blues," *Wall Street Journal*, Sept. 2–3, 2006, pp. A1, A6.

167. John J. Fialka, "Coalition Pushes Wider Ethanol Use," *Wall Street Journal*, Feb. 28, 2007, p. A6.

168. John Cochran, "Fuel from the Farm," *Congressional Quarterly Weekly Report*, Aug. 7, 2006, pp. 2167–74; Ilan Brat and Thaddeas Herrick, "Ethanol Boom Fuels Brisk Sales of Midwest Farmland," *Wall Street Journal*, March 7, 2007, p. B6.

169. Edmund L. Andrews, "Bush Makes a Pitch for Amber Waves of Homegrown Fuel," *New York Times*, Feb. 23, 2007 (online).

170. "Twenty in Ten: Strengthening America's Energy Security," *State of the Union 2007 Policy Initiatives*, WhiteHouse.gov, Jan. 23, 2007, online at http://georgewbush-whitehouse.archives.gov/stateoftheunion/2007/initiatives/energy.html.

171. Bob Dinneen, "Today's U.S. Ethanol Industry," Renewable Fuels Association, Washington, D.C., April 8, 2008 (online).

172. Douglas Belkin and Joe Barrett, "An Ethanol Glut Hits Home in Bio Town," *Wall Street Journal*, Nov. 1, 2007, p. B1; Lauren Etter, "Ethanol Craze Cools as Doubts Multiply," *Wall Street Journal*, Nov. 28, 2007, p. 1.

173. Alexander E. Farrell, Richard J. Plevin, Brian T. Turner, Andrew D. Jones, Michael O'Hare, and Daniel M. Kammen, "Ethanol Can Contribute to Energy and Environmental Goals," *Science* 311 (5760) (Jan. 27, 2006): 506–508.

174. Patrick Barta, "As Biofuels Catch On, Next Task Is to Deal with Environmental, Economic Impact," *Wall Street Journal,* March 24, 2008 (online).

175. Bob Davis and Lauren Etter, "Brazil's Sugar-Cane Ethanol Gets a Boost from IMF Report," *Wall Street Journal,* Oct. 18, 2007, p. A4.

176. José Goldemberg, "The Ethanol Program in Brazil," *Environmental Research Letters* 1(2006): 1–5.

177. Dina Cappiello, "Details of the Energy Overhaul," *Congressional Quarterly Weekly Report,* March 31, 2008, pp. 830–33.

178. James B. Treece, "Nissan Plans Hybrid, Clean Diesels in 2010," *Automotive News,* Dec. 18, 2006, p. 31.

179. John D. McKinnon and Laura Meckler, "Bush Eschews Harsh Medicine in Treating U.S. Oil Addiction," *Wall Street Journal,* Aug. 9, 2006, p. 1.

180. Associated Press, "Rush to Ethanol Could Produce Glut," *Los Angeles Times,* June 14, 2007, p. C2; Douglas Belkin and Joe Barrett, "An Ethanol Glut Hits Home in Bio Town," *Wall Street Journal,* Nov. 1, 2007, p. B1.

181. Joe Poncer, "Ethanol Boom Fuels Agribusiness Gains," *Wall Street Journal,* Dec. 7, 2005, p. B3A; Sharon Silke Carty, "Automakers Fast-Track Ethanol Use," *USA Today,* Feb. 9, 2006, p. A1; Karen Lundegaard, "Ford, GM Make Big Push to Promote 'Flex-Fuel' Vehicles," *Wall Street Journal,* Jan. 10, 2006, p. B1; Alex Barrionvevo, "Fill Up on Corn If You Can," *New York Times,* Aug. 31, 2006, pp. C1, C4.

182. "I-65's Ramps to the Future: E85, B20," *Automotive News,* Oct. 13, 2008, p. 62.

183. Matt Vella, "Biofuel or Bust: On the Road with E85," *Wall Street Journal,* June 19, 2007, p. D2.

184. Ryan Keefe, Jay Griffin, and John D. Graham, "The Benefits and Costs of New Fuels and Engines for Cars and Light Trucks," Working Paper WR-537-PRGS, RAND Corporation, Santa Monica, Calif., November 2007.

185. U.S. Department of Transportation, "Effects of the Alternative Motor Fuels Act: CAFE Incentives Policy," Report to Congress, Washington, D.C., March 2002. Available online at http://www.nhtsa.dot.gov/cars/rules/rulings/CAFE/alternativefuels/index.htm (accessed June 13, 2009).

186. Harry Stoffer, "Bush Team Tests Higher Ethanol Blends," *Automotive News,* Oct. 13, 2008, 6.

187. Siobhan Hughes, Ian Talley, and Anjali Cordeiro, "Corn Ethanol Loses More Support," *Wall Street Journal,* May 3, 2008, p. A4.

188. William K. Caesar, Jens Riese, and Thomas Seitz, "Betting on Biofuels," *McKinsley Quarterly,* June 4, 2007 (online); Lauren Etter, "Ethanol Craze Cools as Doubts Multiply," *Wall Street Journal,* Nov. 28, 2007, p. 1.

189. Hughes, Talley, and Cordeiro, "Corn Ethanol Loses," p. A4.

190. Robert McFarlane, "Don't Give Up on Energy Independence," *Wall Street Journal,* May 7, 2008, p. A17.

191. Hughes, Talley, and Cordeiro, "Corn Ethanol Loses," p. A4.

192. Etter, "Ethanol Craze Cools," p.1.

193. Matthew L. Wald and Alexei Barrionuevo, "Chasing a Dream Made of Waste," *New York Times,* April 17, 2007, pp. C1, C5.

194. Review and Outlook, "Ethanol's Water Shortage," *Wall Street Journal,* Oct. 17, 2007, p. A18.

195. Timothy Searchinger, Ralph Heimlich, R. A. Houghton, Fengxia Dong, Amani Elobeid, Jacinto Fabiosa, Simla Tokgoz, Dermot Hayes, and Tun-Hsiang Yu, "Use of U.S. Croplands for Biofuels Increases Greenhouse Gases through Emissions from Land Use Changes," *Science Express* 319(5867) (Feb. 7, 2008): 1238–40; online at http://www.sciencemag.org/cgi/content/abstract/1151861.

196. Patrick Barta and Jane Spencer, "As Alternative Energy Heats Up, Environmental Concerns Grow," *Wall Street Journal,* Dec. 5, 2006, pp. A1, A13.

197. David Streitfeld, "Uprising against the Ethanol Mandate," *New York Times,* July 23, 2008 (online).

198. Life-cycle emissions of greenhouse gases may still be higher for cellulosic ethanol made from switchgrass but should be lower if made from wastes. Searchinger et al., "Use of U.S. Croplands."

199. Matthew A. Kromer and John B. Heywood, *Electric Powertrains: Opportunities and Challenges in the U.S. Light-Duty Fleet,* Sloan Automotive Laboratory, MIT, Cambridge, Mass., LFEE 2007-03 RP, May 2007, p. 20.

200. Bob Davis and Lauren Etter, "Brazil's Sugar-Cane Ethanol Gets Boost from IMF Report," *Wall Street Journal,* Oct. 18, 2007, p. A4.

201. John J. Fialka and Scott Kilman, "Big Players Join Race to Put Farm Waste into Your Gas Tank," *Wall Street Journal,* June 29, 2006, pp. A1, A12.

202. Elizabeth Douglass, "Private Funds Fuel Clean Energy," *Los Angeles Times,* Aug. 1, 2006, p. C1; Rebecca Adams, "Gas Prices Rise Along with Ethanol Use," *Congressional Quarterly Weekly Report,* April 24, 2006, pp. 1070–71.

203. Matthew L. Wald and Alexei Barrionuevo, "Chasing a Dream Made of Waste," *New York Times,* April 17, 2007, pp. C1, C5.

204. Malia Wollan, "Alternate-Fuel Hunt Gives Plant Biologist a Lift," *Wall Street Journal,* July 10, 2007, p. B1.

205. Associated Press, "U.S. Energy Bill Mandate for Corn-Free Ethanol Presents Huge Opportunity, Challenge for Industry," *International Herald Tribune,* Dec. 18, 2007 (online).

206. Davis and Etter, "Brazil's Sugar-Cane Ethanol," p. A4.

207. Goldemberg, "Ethanol Program in Brazil," pp. 1–5.

208. David Jackson, "U.S., Brazil Plan Ethanol Partnership," *USA Today,* March 2, 2007, p. 6A.

209. Laura Meckler and John J. Fialka, "Energy May Still Stall Refreshed Congress," *Wall Street Journal,* June 24, 2006, p. A4; Jackson, "U.S., Brazil Plan Ethanol Partnership," p. 6A.

210. Philip Brasher, "Farm Bill Emphasizes New Types of Ethanol," *Des Moines Register,* May 21, 2008 (online).

211. Antonio Regalado, "U.S., Brazil Weigh Ethanol Pact," *Wall Street Journal,* March 7, 2007, p. A2.

212. John D. McKinnon, "Biofuels Pact Likely to Hit Hurdles," *Wall Street Journal,* March 10, 2007, p. A2.

213. Marjorie Korn, "Cellulosic Ethanol Gets Big Push in Farm Bill," *Medill Reports,* Chicago, Ill., May 20, 2008 (online).

214. Catharine Richert, "Farm Bill Conferees in the Home Stretch," *Congressional Quarterly Weekly Report,* May 5, 2008, p. 1182.

215. Brasher, "Farm Bill Emphasizes."

216. Jeffrey Ball, "How California Failed in Efforts to Curb Its Addiction to Oil," *Wall Street Journal,* Aug. 2, 2006, pp. A1, A6.

217. James R. Healey, "Cost of E85 Fuel Is Higher than Gasoline," *USA Today,* Feb. 15, 2006, http://www.usatoday.com/money/industries/energy/2006-02-14-e85-usat_x.htm accessed(accessed Jan. 20, 2008); Sharon Silke Garty, "Automakers Fast-Track Ethanol Use," *USA Today,* Feb. 9, 2006, p. A1.

218. Even Republican senators such as Richard Lugar are suggesting that refueling stations be required to add E85 pumps. Gitte Laasby, "Biofuels Get Political Boost," *Indianapolis Star,* Oct. 8, 2008 (online).

219. Brian Baskin and Carolyn Cui, "Oil Drops under $40 on Demand Fears," *Wall Street Journal.* Dec. 19, 2008 (online).

220. Guy Chazan, "IEA Says Fading Oil Production Threatens Supply," *Wall Street Journal,* Nov. 13, 2008 (online).

7. Consuming Less Energy

1. "Using Energy Wisely," *National Energy Policy,* Report of the National Energy Policy Development Group (Washington, D.C.: U.S. Government Printing Office, May 2001), pp. 4.1–4.12.

2. U.S. Energy Information Administration, *Annual Energy Outlook 2004,* Washington, D.C.

3. Ibid.

4. Ibid.

5. National Commission on Energy Policy, *Oil, Consumer and Other Benefits from the Energy Independence and Security Act of 2007,* Washington, D.C., Dec. 13, 2007 (online).

6. Robert McFarlane, "The Right Is Wrong on McCain," *Wall Street Journal,* Feb. 11, 2008 (online) (the $300 billion per year the U.S. spends on foreign oil helps fund Al Qaeda and other terrorist groups and funds "both sides" of the war in Iraq).

7. National Research Council, *Effectiveness and Impact of Corporate Average Fuel Economy (CAFE) Standards* (Washington D.C.: National Academy Press, 2002); Robert Bamberger, *Automobile and Light Truck Fuel Economy: The CAFE Standards* (Washington, D.C.: Congressional Research Service, Sept. 25, 2002).

8. "'06 Fuel Economy Unchanged from Decade Ago, EPA Says," *Los Angeles Times,* July 18, 2006, p. C3; *Light-Duty Automotive Technology and Fuel Economy Trends: 1975 through 2006,* U.S. Environmental Protection Agency, EPA420-R-011, July 2006.

9. National Highway Traffic Safety Administration, "CAFE Overview: Frequently Asked Questions," online at http://www.nhtsa.dot.gov/cars/rules/cafe/overview.htm (accessed Jan. 20, 2008).

10. Harry Stoffer, "Auto Industry Hopes Next President Will Replay Clinton's CAFE Flexibility," *Automotive News*, Feb. 11, 2008 (online).

11. National Research Council, *Effectiveness and Impact.*

12. Ibid., p. 87.

13. U.S. Department of Transportation, "Request for Comments; National Academy of Sciences Study and Future Fuel Economy Improvements, Model Years 2005–2010," *Federal Register* 67(26) (Feb. 7, 2002): 5767.

14. U.S. Department of Transportation, *Study of Feasibility and Effects of Reducing Use of Fuel for Automobiles,* Report to Congress, August 2006, p. 8 (referring to DOT's February 2002 letter to Congress).

15. Stan Luger, *Corporate Power, American Democracy, and the Automobile Industry* (New York: Cambridge University Press, 2000), pp. 175–77.

16. Union of Concerned Scientists, "California Regulates Global Warming Emissions: California's Vehicle Global Warming Law," Oct. 28, 2005; online at http://www.ucsusa.wsm.ga3.org/clean-vehicles/vehicles-health/californias-global-warming-vehicle-law.html.

17. California Environmental Protection Agency, *ARB Approves Greenhouse Gas Rule,* news release, Sept. 24, 2004; online at http://www.arb.ca.gov/newsrel/nr092404.htm (accessed Jan. 20, 2008).

18. Harry Stoffer, "Toyota Joins Big Three in CAFE Fight," *Automotive News,* July 30, 2007 (online).

19. Advance Notice of Proposed Rulemaking on CAFE Reform, U.S. Department of Transportation, *Federal Register* 68 (Dec. 29, 2003): 74908.

20. U.S. Department of Transportation, "Light Truck CAFE Standards for Model Years 2005–2007," *Federal Register* 68 (2003): 16868.

21. U.S. Department of Transportation, "Proposed Light Truck CAFE Standards for Model Years 2008–2011," *Federal Register* 70 (Aug. 30, 2005): 51414; Karen Lundegaard, "Crash Course: How U.S. Shifted Gears to Find Small Cars Can Be Safe, Too," *Wall Street Journal,* Sept. 26, 2005, pp. A1, A14, online at http://www.wsjclassroomedition.com/archive/05nov/auto_related_crashcourse.htm (accessed Jan. 20, 2008).

22. Lundegaard, "Crash Course."

23. U.S. Department of Transportation, "Average Fuel Economy Standards for Light Trucks, Model Years 2008–2011," Final Rule, *Federal Registry* 71 (April 6, 2006): 17566.

24. Laura Meckler, "Fuel Standards Set for Auto Makers," *Wall Street Journal,* March 30, 2006, p. A2.

25. U.S. Department of Transportation, *Study of Feasibility and Effects of Reducing Use of Fuel for Automobiles,* Report to Congress, Washington, D.C., August 2006, p. 13.

26. "Fact Sheet: CAFE Reform for Passenger Cars," press release, the White House, April 28, 2006; online at http://georgewbush-whitehouse.archives.gov/news/releases/2006/04/20060428-9.html.

27. Matthew L. Wald, "Plan to Reshape Mileage Standards Could Buoy Detroit," *New York Times,* May 7, 2006, p. 27.

28. Kathleen Hunter, "New CAFE Standards for Automobiles Allowed under House Measure," *Congressional Quarterly Weekly Report,* May 15, 2006, p. 1332.

29. Ibid.

30. Ken Thomas, "Senators Push for Higher Fuel Economy Standards," *Boston Globe,* June 20, 2006; online at http://www.boston.com/news/local/maine/articles/2006/06/20/senators_push_for_higher_fuel_economy_standards/ (accessed Jan. 20, 2008).

31. Amanda Griscomb Little, "Gauge Match: Push to Raise Fuel-Economy Standards Gaining New Support," *Grist,* May 11, 2006, online at http://www.grist.org/news/muck/2006/05/11/cafe/ (accessed Jan. 20, 2008); Harry Stoffer, "Lobby Group: Senate Bill Gives Nissan a Freebie," *Automotive News,* July 2, 2007 (online).

32. Ford Motor Company's F-150 pickup truck was the number one monthly seller for three decades, until May 2008, when it was finally overtaken by a Toyota sedan. Josee Valcourt and Matthew Dolan, "Truck Sales Sink, Shaking Up Auto Market," *Wall Street Journal,* June 4, 2008, p. B5. Also see Neal E. Boudette, "GM Market Share May Fall below Milepost," *Wall Street Journal,* June 2, 2008, p. B3.

33. Adam Liptak, "Suit Blaming Automakers over Gases Is Dismissed," *New York Times,* Sept. 18, 2007 (online).

34. Mike Spector and Jeffrey Ball, "Court Roils Auto-Rules Debate," *Wall Street Journal,* Sept. 13, 2007, p. A9.

35. White House, "Twenty in Ten: Strengthening America's Energy Security," Washington, D.C., January 2007 (online).

36. National Commission on Energy Policy, *Energy Policy Recommendations to the President and the 100th Congress,* Washington, D.C., April 2007 (online).

37. Rebecca Adams, "Big Three on the Defensive," *Congressional Quarterly Weekly Report,* June 18, 2007, pp. 1825–31.

38. Jeff Tollefson, "Senate Passes Compromise Bill," *Congressional Quarterly Weekly Report,* June 25, 2007, pp. 1920–22.

39. Coral Davenport, "A Battle of House Titans," *Congressional Quarterly Weekly Report,* June 18, 2007, p. 1829.

40. Rebecca Kimitch and Jeff Tollefson, "Wrangling over Energy Package Continues at House Markup," *Congressional Quarterly Weekly Report,* July 9, 2007, p. 2043.

41. White House, "Twenty in Ten"; John D. McKinnon, John J. Fialka, and Mike Spector, "Bush Orders Stricter Rules on Auto Mileage," *Wall Street Journal,* May 15, 2007, p. A1; Jim Rutenberg and Edmund L. Andrews, "Bush Calls for Work for Higher Efficiency," *New York Times,* May 15, 2007 (online).

42. Richard Rubin and Jeff Tollefson, "Energy Package Generates Conflict," *Congressional Quarterly Weekly Report,* Aug. 13, 2007, pp. 2466–67.

43. Dina Cappiello, "Slimmer Energy Bill Nears Finish Line," *Congressional Quarterly Weekly Report,* Dec. 17, 2007, pp. 3722–23.

44. Stephen Power, "Auto Industry Focuses on States," *Wall Street Journal,* May 5, 2008, p. A4.

45. Bobby Carmichael, "California Gears Up for Car Emissions Fight," *USA Today,* Oct. 29, 2007 (online).

46. Janet Wilson, "EPA Chief Is Said to Have Ignored Staff," *Los Angeles Times,* Dec. 21, 2007 (online).

47. Stephen Power and Siobhan Hughes, "Emissions Bill Divides UAW, Democrats," *Wall Street Journal,* May 20, 2008, p. A4.

48. Frank Davies, "Senate Panel Approves California Waiver on Emissions," *San Jose Mercury News,* May 21, 2008 (online).

49. Lisa Margonelli. "The Plug-In Paradox," *Forbes,* Nov. 24, 2008, p. 78.

50. Mark Cooper, "Time to Change the Record on Oil Policy," Consumers Union.org, August 2006, p. 8; online at http://www.consumersunion.org/pub/time tochangetherecordonoilpolicy.pdf (accessed Jan. 20, 2008) ("Congress has not allowed EPA to update its fuel economy data on window stickers since the 1980s. Even more faulty numbers, which date back to 1970s, are used by the National Highway Traffic Safety Administration to enforce compliance with the federal miles per gallon standards.")

51. Harry Stoffer, "Would You Buy a Prius That Gets Only 45 MPG in Town," *Automotive News,* Dec. 18, 2006, p. 4.

52. "Regulatory Announcement: EPA Proposes New Test Method for Fuel Economy Window Stickers," Environmental Protection Agency, January 2006; online at http://www.epa.gov/fueleconomy/420f06009.htm (accessed Jan. 20, 2008).

53. Consumers Union, "How We Test: Fuel Economy," *Consumer Reports,* July 24, 2006. Available online at http://blogs.consumerreports.org/cars/2006/07/how_we_test_fue.html (accessed June 13, 2009).

54. James R. Healey, "AAA Calls for EPA to Do 'Real-World' Mileage Tests," *USA Today,* March 2, 2005 (updated March 4, 2005); online at http://www.usatoday.com/money/autos/2005-03-02-aaa-usat_x.htm (accessed Jan. 20, 2008).

55. James R. Healey, "Fuel Economy Calculations to Be Altered," *USA Today,* Jan. 10, 2006 (updated Jan. 13, 2006); online at http://www.usatoday.com/money/autos/2006-01-10-epa-fuel-economy-ratings_x.htm (accessed Jan. 20, 2008).

56. Matthew L. Wald, "EPA Revises Its Formula to Calculate Auto Mileage," *New York Times,* Dec. 12, 2006, p. C4.

57. Ibid.

58. Harry Stoffer, "Lower Fuel Ratings Take Effect," *Automotive News,* Oct. 15, 2007 (online).

59. Jayne O'Donnell, "Higher Fuel Standards Proposed by Feds," *USA Today,* April 23, 2008, p. B1.

60. Eric Dash, "Auto Industry Feels the Pain of Tight Credit," *New York Times,* May 27, 2008 (online).

61. Adriel Bettelheim, "Regulations Provide Fuel for Federalism," *Congressional Quarterly Weekly Report,* May 5, 2008, pp. 1154–5.

62. Christopher Conkey and Stephen Power, "Auto Fuel Efficiency Goals Revised," *Wall Street Journal,* April 23, 2008, p. A2.

63. Steven Mufson, "Obama Makes Push for Fuel Efficiency," *Washington Post,* May 8, 2007, p. A03.

64. Harry Stoffer, "Lower Fuel Ratings Take Effect," *Automotive News*, Oct. 15, 2007 (online) (the number of new vehicles rated over 30 MPG declined from 200 to about 90 when EPA's rating system was modernized).

65. *National Energy Policy*.

66. U.S. Department of the Treasury, "Credit for New Qualified Alternative Motor Vehicles," September 2006; Online at http://www.treas.gov/press/releases/reports/alt%20ener%20veh%20guidance.pdf (accessed Jan. 20, 2008).

67. Paul Courson, "'Clean Diesel Technology' Showcased," CNN.com, April 28, 2005; online at http://www.cnn.com/2005/POLITICS/04/28/diesel/ (Bush called for his original tax-credit proposal to be expanded to include new clean diesel technology).

68. U.S. Department of Energy, "The Energy Policy Act of 2005: What the Energy Bill Means to You," no date; online at http://www.energy.gov/taxbreaks.htm (accessed Jan. 20, 2008).

69. Chris Woodyard, "IRS Setting Tax Breaks for Hybrids," *USA Today*, Jan. 16, 2006, p. 6B.

70. Ken Thomas, "Tax Credits Offer Incentives for Plug-In Hybrids," MLive.com, Oct. 27, 2008; online at http://mlive.com/business/index.ssf/2008/10/tax_credits_offer_incentives_f.html.

71. Chris Woodyard and James R. Healy, "Local Authorities Get In On Push for Electric Cars," *USA Today*, Nov. 28, 2008, p. 4B (noting that 14 major companies and some smaller ones have announced plans to offer electric cars by 2012).

72. Danny Hakim, "Bush Proposal May Cut Tax on S.U.V.'s for Business," *New York Times*, Jan. 21, 2003; online at http://www.nytimes.com/2003/01/21/business/bush-proposal-may-cut-tax-on-suv-s-for-business.html (accessed Jan. 20, 2008).

73. Ibid.

74. Ibid.

75. Ibid.

76. National Business Association, "Recent Changes May Affect Your 2004 Taxes," online at http://www.nationalbusiness.org/nbaweb/newsletter/1081.htm (accessed June 13, 2009).

77. The White House, "President Signs Transportation Act," press release, Aug. 10, 2005; online at http://georgewbush-whitehouse.archives.gov/news/releases/2005/08/20050810-1.html (accessed Jan. 20, 2008).

78. Federal Highway Administration, "A Summary of Highway Provisions in Safetea-LU," Aug. 25, 2005; online at http://www.fhwa.dot.gov/safetealu/summary.htm (accessed Jan. 20, 2008) (The new Express Lanes Demonstration Program will allow a total of 15 demonstration projects through 2009 to permit tolling to manage high levels of congestion, reduce emissions in a nonattainment or maintenance area, or finance added interstate lanes for the purpose of reducing congestion. A state, public authority, or public or private entity designated by a state may apply. Eligible toll facilities include existing toll facilities.)

79. U.S. Department of Transportation, *Study of Feasibility and Effects of Reducing Use of Fuel for Automobiles*, Report to Congress, Washington, D.C., August 2006, p. 22.

80. Ibid.

81. Ibid.

82. Charles Komanoff, *Costs and Benefits of Congestion Pricing Policies in Selected U.S. Cities,* Report to the National Commission on Energy Policy, June 2, 2004; online at http://www.energycommission.org/files/finalReport/III.5.b%20-%20 Congestion%20Pricing%20Policies%20.pdf (accessed Jan. 20, 2008).

83. White House, "Twenty in Ten."

84. Holman W. Jenkins Jr., "Bloomberg vs. The Car," *Wall Street Journal,* July 11, 2007, p. A14.

85. Ray Rivera, "Transit Deficit Yields New Focus on Congestion Pricing," *New York Times,* Aug. 3, 2008, p. 21.

86. U.S. Watch, "Lawmakers Reject Traffic Fee Proposal," *Wall Street Journal,* April 8, 2008, p. A2.

87. Steve LeVine and Christopher Conkey, "Gasoline Prices Could Fall More," *Wall Street Journal,* Oct. 5, 2006, p. C1; Ronald D. White, "Enjoy Cheaper Gasoline for Now," *Los Angeles Times,* Sept. 19, 2006 p. C4.

88. David Barboza, "China's Surge Raises Fears of Runaway Economy." *New York Times,* July 19, 2006, p. C3.

89. Energy Information Administration, "Annual Energy Outlook," online at http://www.eia.doe.gov/ (accessed Jan. 20, 2008); Adriel Bettleheim, "Going for the Guzzler," *Congressional Quarterly Weekly Report,* May 15, 2006, pp. 1298–1305 (EIA oil forecast for 2025 upped to $54/barrel from $33/barrel in 2005).

90. Adriel Bettelheim, "Regulations Provide Fuel for Federalism," *Congressional Quarterly Weekly Report,* May 5, 2008, pp. 1154–55.

91. Jamie LaReau, "F-Series Sales: Steep Descent to Below 500,000?" *Automotive News,* Oct. 13, 2008, p. 6.

92. Sholnn Freeman, "Truck and SUV Sales Plunge as Gas Prices Rise; GM, Ford Hit Hardest," *Washington Post,* Oct. 4, 2005, p. D01; Neal E. Boudette and Jeffrey C. McCracken, "Detroit's Cash Cow Stumbles," *Wall Street Journal,* Aug. 1, 2006, p. B1.

93. Christine Tierney, "GM Loss Up $2B," *Detroit News,* March 17, 2006 (GM revised its loss for 2005 upward from $8.6 billion to $10.6 billion).

94. Chris Woodyard, "Ford Will Cut 25,000 to 30,000 Jobs, Close 14 Plants," *USA Today,* Jan. 23, 2006; online at http://www.usatoday.com/money/companies/ earnings/2006-01-23-ford-q4_x.htm (accessed Jan. 20, 2008).

95. Neal E. Boudette and Norihiko Shirouzu, "Car Makers' Boom Years Now Look like a Bubble," *Wall Street Journal,* May 20, 2008, p. A1.

96. Associated Press, "GM Chief to Address Senate on Health Care," Global Action on Aging, July 13, 2006; online at http://www.globalaging.org/health/us/2006/ addresshealth.htm (accessed Jan. 20, 2008).

97. Greg Schneider, "GM, Ford Bond Ratings Cut to Junk Status," *Washington Post,* May 6, 2005, p. E1.

98. Sharon Silke Carty, "GM CEO Rebuffs Chapter 11 Theory," *USA Today,* Nov. 17, 2005.

99. Sholnn Freeman, "Ford Abandons Pledge on Hybrid Production," *Washington Post,* June 30, 2006, p. D1 (cautious view by J. D. Power Automotive Forecasting); J. D. Power and Associates, "Global Markets for Diesel-Powered Light Vehicles to 2017," December 2007, online at http://www.jdpowerforecasting.com/services/syndicated12.htm (accessed June 13, 2009).

100. Jonathan Walsh, "For GM's First Hybrid SUV, a Promising Half Step," *Wall Street Journal,* Sept. 1, 2006, p. W4; Dan Leinert, "Diesel Power," Forbes.com, Jan. 9, 2006, online at http://www.forbes.com/vehicles/2006/01/06/diesels-cars-hybrids-cx_dl_0109feat_ls.html (accessed Jan. 20, 2008); Jack Peckham, "Ricardo Sees Diesel Surge Accelerating In Europe," *Diesel Fuel News,* online at http://find articles.com/p/articles/mi_m0CYH/is_8_6/ai_85046035 (accessed Jan. 20, 2008); Peter Ford, "Gas Prices Too High: Try Europe," *Christian Science Monitor,* Aug. 26, 2005, online at http://www.csmonitor.com/2005/0826/p01s03-woeu.html (accessed Jan. 20, 2008).

101. J. D. Power and Associates Automotive Forecasting Services, March 2006. http://www.findarticles.com/p/articles/mi_m3102/is_3_125/ai_n16348026.

102. Ibid.

103. Miguel Llanos, "Carmakers Eye Green Pastures," *MSNBC,* May 4, 2006; online at http://www.msnbc.msn.com/id/9762170/page/2/ (accessed Jan. 20, 2008).

104. James R. Healey, "Honda Rethinking Diesel Cars," *USA Today,* Dec. 9, 2008 (online).

105. Jonathan Welsh, "Putting a Muzzle on Guzzlers," *Wall Street Journal,* Aug. 1, 2007, p. D1; Mike Spector and Terry Kosdrosky, "A Green Ride for Investors?" *Wall Street Journal,* Sept. 25, 2007, p. C1; Harry Stoffer, "New CAFE Law Opens the Door to Industry Surprises," *Automotive News,* Feb. 11, 2008 (online).

106. Joseph B. White, "The Good News and Bad News on U.S. Fuel Economy Trends," *Wall Street Journal,* Oct. 1, 2007 (online).

107. Nick Bunkley, "Detroit Finds Agreement on the Need to Be Green," *New York Times,* June 1, 2007, p. 13.

108. For example, political scientists at Brookings write that the Bush administration's energy proposals "reflected . . . no meaningful pressure to conserve [oil]" William A. Galston and Pietro S. Nivola, "Delineating the Problem," in *Red and Blue Nation? Characteristics and Causes of America's Polarized Politics,* ed. Pietro S. Nivola and David W. Brady (Washington, D.C.: Brookings Institution Press, 2006), p. 28.

8. Cleaner Air, Warmer Climate

1. National Research Council, *Estimating the Benefits of Proposed Air Pollution Regulations* (Washington, D.C.: National Academies Press, 2002).

2. Michael Grubb, Christiaan Vrolijk, and Duncan Brack, *The Kyoto Protocol: A Guide and Assessment* (London: Royal Institute of International Affairs and Earthscan Publications, 1999).

3. S. Res. 89, introduced by Senators Robert Byrd (D-W. Va.) and Chuck Hagel (R-Neb.) was passed by a vote of 95–0 on July 25, 1997. *Congressional Quarterly Almanac,* 1997, pp. 4-13 to 4-15 and p. S-36.

4. Ibid., p. 4-14.

5. Kevin Finneran, "The Hidden Presidential Campaign Issues," *Issues in Science and Technology,* National Academy of Sciences, Fall 2000.

6. Charli E. Coon, "Why President Bush Is Right to Abandon the Kyoto Protocol," Heritage Foundation, May 11, 2001; online at http://www.heritage.org/Research/EnergyandEnvironment/BG1437.cfm (accessed Jan. 20, 2008).

7. Keith Bradsher, "China to Pass U.S. in 2009 in Emissions," *New York Times,* Nov. 7, 2006, pp. C1, C4; Elisabeth Rosenthal, "China Increases Lead as Biggest Carbon Dioxide Emitter," *New York Times,* June 14, 2008 (online).

8. Letter from the president to Senators Hagel, Helms, Craig and Roberts, the White House, March 13, 2001.

9. "Dismay as US Drops Climate Pact," CNN.com, March 29, 2001; online at http://archives.cnn.com/2001/WORLD/europe/italy/03/29/environment.kyoto/index.html (accessed Jan. 20, 2008).

10. Seth Borenstein, "Bush Changes Pledge on Emissions," *Philadelphia Inquirer,* March 14, 2001.

11. Letter from the President, March 13, 2001.

12. "President Announces Clear Skies and Global Climate Change Initiatives," news release, Feb. 14, 2002; online at http://georgewbush-whitehouse.archives.gov/news/releases/2002/02/20020214-5.html (accessed May 25, 2009).

13. Margaret Kriz, "Heating Up," *National Journal,* Aug. 5, 2005; online at http://www.nationaljournal.com/members/news/2005/08/0805nj1.htm (accessed June 13, 2009).

14. Sebastian Mallaby, "It's Not California Dreaming: Carbon-Policy Fixes and Biofuel: The Right Engine Mix," *Washington Post,* July 24, 2006, p. A19.

15. Richard B. Stewart and Jonathan B. Wiener, *Reconstructing Climate Policy: Beyond Kyoto* (Washington D.C.: American Enterprise Institute, 2003).

16. *Congressional Quarterly Weekly Report,* June 27, 2005, p. 1773.

17. Ibid.

18. Ibid.

19. Deborah Schoch and Janet Wilson, "Governor, Blair Reach Environmental Accord," *Los Angeles Times,* Aug. 1, 2006, p. B3; Jeffrey Ball and Jim Carlton, "California Pact Would Place Cap on Emissions," *Wall Street Journal,* Aug. 31, 2006, pp. A1, A7; Felicity Barringer, "Officials Reach California Deal to Cut Emissions," *New York Times,* Aug. 31, 2006, p. A1; Felicity Barringer, "States' Battles over Energy Grow Fiercer with U.S. in a Policy Gridlock," *New York Times,* March 20, 2008 (online).

20. Juliet Eilperin, "Cities, States Aren't Waiting for U.S. Action on Climate," *Washington Post,* Aug. 11, 2006, p. 1; Jeffrey Ball, "California Emission Plan Needs Allies," *Wall Street Journal,* Sept. 1, 2006, p. A6.

21. Eric Herrero-Martinez, "States Study Carbon Trading," *Wall Street Journal,* Aug. 1, 2007, p. B5A.

22. *Congressional Quarterly Weekly Report,* June 29, 2002, pp. 1742–43; Cat Lazaroff, "Senate Committee Backs Power Plant Emissions Bill," *Environment News Service,* June 28, 2002, online at http://www.ens-newswire.com/ens/jun2002/2002-06-28-06.asp (accessed Jan. 20, 2008).

23. *CQ Almanac,* 2002, p. 2119; Rebecca Adams, "Democrats Decry Bush's Clean Air Plan as Favoring Industry over Environment," *Congressional Quarterly Weekly Report,* Aug. 3, 2002, pp. 2119–2120.

24. U.S. Environmental Protection Agency, *Federal Register* 67 (Dec. 31, 2002): 80186.

25. U.S. Environmental Protection Agency, *Federal Register* 68 (Oct. 27, 2003): 61248.

26. U.S. Environmental Protection Agency, "EPA Proposes Steps to Improve New Source Review," Press Release, Sept. 8, 2006; online at http://yosemite.epa.gov/opa/admpress.nsf/ 8822edaadaba0243852572a000656841/674450d6221951d1852571e3005 22424!OpenDocument (accessed Jan. 20, 2008).

27. Adams, "Democrats Decry Bush's Clean Air Plan," p. 2120.

28. National Research Council, *New Source Review for Stationary Sources of Air Pollution* (Washington D.C.: National Academies Press, 2006).

29. *New York v. EPA,* 413 F.3d. 3 (D.C. Cir. 2005).

30. *New York v. EPA,* 443 F.3d. 880 (D.C. Cir. 2006).

31. Shankar Vedantan, "Senate Impasse Stops 'Clear Skies' Measure," *Washington Post,* March 10, 2005, p. A04.

32. Ibid.; *Congressional Weekly Report,* Sept. 5, 2005, p. 2314; *Congressional Weekly Report,* Sept. 19, 2005, p. 2507.

33. "Highway Diesel Rule," U.S. Environmental Protection Agency, *Federal Register* 65 (October 2000): 59896.

34. On the Jan. 20, 2001, memo from White House chief of staff Andrew H. Card to federal agencies, see *Making Sense of Regulation,* Report to Congress, U.S. Office of Management and Budget, Washington D.C., 2001, p. 34.

35. See, for example, U. S. Office of Management and Budget, *Making Sense of Regulation,* Report to Congress, Washington D.C., 2001, p. 105; "Diesel Blues," Editorial, *Wall Street Journal,* Aug. 25, 2006, p. A14.

36. U.S. Environmental Protection Agency, "Control of Emissions of Air Pollution from Nonroad Diesel Engines and Fuels; Final Rule," *Federal Register,* June 29, 2004, p. 38958. In 2007 EPA extended similar requirements to diesel locomotives and marine vessels. Felicity Barringer, "Environmental Agency Proposes Strict Standard for Some Diesel Engines," *New York Times,* March 3, 2007, p. A12.

37. Barringer, "Environmental Agency Proposes," p. A12.

38. U.S. Environmental Protection Agency, "Regulatory Announcement: Non-Conformance Penalties for Heavy-Duty Diesel Engines," Washington, D.C., August 2002 (EPA 420-F-02-025).

39. Cat Lazaroff, "EPA Refuses to Delay Diesel Rule," *Environmental News Service,* Aug. 2, 2002, online at http://www.ens-newswire.com/ens/aug2002/2002-08-02-06.asp (accessed Jan. 20, 2008).

40. U.S. Environmental Protection Agency, *Final Technical Support Document: Nonconformance Penalties for 2004 Highway Heavy Duty Diesel Engines,* Washington, D.C., August 2002 (EPA 420-R-02-021).

41. National Research Council, *Research Priorities for Airborne Particulate Matter,* Washington D.C.: National Academies Press, 2004.

42. U.S. Environmental Protection Agency, "Rule to Reduce Interstate Transport of Fine Particulate Matter and Ozone (Clean Air Interstate Rule); Final Rule," *Federal Register* 70 (May 12, 2005): 25162.

43. U.S. Office of Management and Budget, *Validating Regulatory Analysis,* Report to Congress, Washington D.C., 2005.

44. Rebecca Adams, "Clean Air Policy Gets a Little Murky," *Congressional Quarterly Weekly Report,* Aug. 4, 2008, pp. 2102–2104.

45. Juliet Eilperin, "EPA Cuts Soot Level Allowable Daily in Air," *Washington Post,* Sept. 22, 2006, p. A3.

46. U.S. Environmental Protection Agency, "Regulatory Finding on the Emissions of Hazardous Air Pollutants from Electric Utility Steam Generating Units," *Federal Register* 65 (Dec. 20, 2000): 79825.

47. Ted Gayer and Robert Hahn, "The Political Economy of Mercury Regulation," *Regulation,* Summer 2005, pp. 26–33.

48. *UARG v. EPA,* 291 F.3d 1 (D.C. Cir. 2005).

49. U.S. Environmental Protection Agency, "Revision of December 2000 Regulatory Finding on the Emissions of Hazardous Air Pollutants from Electric Utility Steam Generating Units," *Federal Register* 70 (March 29, 2005): 15994.

50. Ibid., p. 28621.

51. "The Bush Record: Mercury Pollution," Natural Resources Defense Council (no date); online at www.nrdc.org/bushrecord/health_mercury.asp (accessed Jan. 20, 2008).

52. *Congressional Quarterly Weekly Report,* Sept. 19, 2005, p. 2507.

53. The defecting Republicans were Alexander of Tennessee, Chafee of Rhode Island, Coleman of Minnesota, Collins and Snowe of Maine, Gregg and Sununu of New Hampshire, McCain of Arizona, and Smith of Oregon. The crossover Democrats were Baucus of Montana, Byrd of West Virginia, Conrad and Dorgan of North Dakota, Nelson of Nebraska, and Pryor of Arkansas.

54. Rebecca Adams, "State Dropout Rate High for Bush Mercury Plan," *Congressional Quarterly Weekly Report,* May 29, 2006, pp. 1456–57.

55. Larry Wheeler, "Power Plants Are Focus of Drive to Cut Mercury," *USA Today,* Nov. 1, 2007 (online).

56. John J. Fialka, "Emissions of CO2 Continue to Rise Despite Pledges," *Wall Street Journal,* Oct. 31, 2006, p. A6; Jeffrey Ball and Leila Abboud, "EU Aims to Toughen Approach on Emissions," *Wall Street Journal,* Nov. 30, 2006, p. A6.

57. Jeffrey Ball, "Kyoto's Caps on Emissions Hit Snag in Marketplace," *Wall Street Journal,* Dec. 3, 2007, p. A1; William Echikson and Adam Cohen, "EU Leaders Agree on Climate Plan," *Wall Street Journal,* March 10, 2007, p. A5; James Kanter, "The Trouble with Markets for Carbon," *New York Times,* June 20, 2008 (online).

58. William Echikson, "Many Auto Makers Miss Targets for Emissions Cuts in Europe," *Wall Street Journal,* Oct. 25, 2006, p. A8; "EU Warns Makers on Emissions," *Wall Street Journal,* Aug. 30, 2006, p. A6.

59. Leila Abboud, "EU Greenhouse-Gas Emissions Rose 1.1% Last Year," *Wall Street Journal,* April 3, 2008, p. A8; Leila Abboud and Stephen Power, "U.S. Aims to Skirt Flaws in Europe's Carbon Limits," *Wall Street Journal,* May 30, 2008, p. A4.

60. Charles Forelle and John W. Miller, "EU Backs Emissions Proposal After Concessions to Industry," *Wall Street Journal,* Dec. 12, 2008 (online).

61. Jeffrey Ball, "U.N. Effort to Curtail Emissions in Turmoil," *Wall Street Journal,* April 12, 2008, p. A1; Jeffrey Ball, "Two Carbon-Market Millionaires Take a Hit as U.N. Clamps Down," *Wall Street Journal,* April 14, 2008, p. A1.

62. Eileen Claussen, president, Pew Center on Global Climate Change, remarks to Global Climate Change and Coal's Future, Spring Coal Forum, American Coal Council, May 18, 2004.

63. John D. McKinnon, "Bush Alters Climate Dynamics," *Wall Street Journal,* June 1, 2007, p. A6.

64. Associated Press, "EU Welcomes U.S. Climate Proposal," *Wall Street Journal,* June 1, 2007 (online).

65. John D. McKinnon and Marcus Walker, "Market Supports Bush Plan for Climate Summit," *Wall Street Journal,* June 12, 2008, p. A6.

66. James L. Connaughton and Daniel M. Price, "The Bush Plan for Climate Change," *Wall Street Journal,* Jan. 26, 2008, p. A10.

67. *Understanding and Responding to Climate Change: Highlights of National Academies Reports* (Washington, D.C.: National Academies Press, March 2006); Intergovernmental Panel on Climate Change, *Climate Change 2007: The Physical Science Basis,* Summary for Policy Makers, Geneva, Switzerland, February 2007.

68. Nick Timirao, "Businesses Rethink Carbon Curbs," *Wall Street Journal,* March 3–4, 2007, p. A7.

69. Judy Pasternak, "It's Bush's Turn to Air Ideas for Dealing with Warming," *Los Angeles Times,* Sept. 26, 2007, p. A16.

70. John J. Fialka, "Leaders Weigh Emissions Fund," *Wall Street Journal,* Sept. 28, 2007, p. A3.

71. Shai Oster, "China Seems Poised to Pass U.S. as Top Greenhouse-Gas Emitter," *Wall Street Journal,* April 24, 2007, p. A6.

72. Jeffrey Ball, "Climate-Control Talks to Address Barriers to Green-Technology Profit," *Wall Street Journal,* Jan. 30, 2008, p. A15.

73. Sheryl Gay Stolberg, "Bush Sets Greenhouse Gas Emissions Goal," *New York Times,* April 17, 2008 (online).

74. White House, "Fact Sheet: Taking Additional Action to Confront Climate Change," Washington, D.C., April 16, 2008.

75. Siobhan Hughes, "Gas Prices Help Defeat Senate's Climate Bill," *Wall Street Journal,* June 7, 2008, p. A3.

76. Avery Palmer, "Climate Change Bill Stalls at Start," *Congressional Quarterly Weekly Report,* June 9, 2008, pp. 1544–45.

77. Siobhan Hughes and Stephen Power, "Climate Bill Appears Headed for Defeat," *Wall Street Journal,* June 6, 2008, p. A4; David M. Herszenhorn, "After Verbal Fire, Senate Effectively Kills Climate Change Bill," *New York Times,* June 7, 2008 (online).

78. John J. Fialka, "U.S. Plans on CO2 Percolate," *Wall Street Journal,* Sept. 25, 2007, p. A6.

79. Elisabeth Rosenthal, "Amid a Hopeful Mood, U.N. Talks Set Countries on Path Toward a Global Climate Treaty," *New York Times,* Dec. 13, 2008 (online).

9. Illegal Immigration

1. "Congress Clears Overhaul of Immigration Law," *Congressional Quarterly Almanac,* 1986, pp. 61–67.

2. Ibid., p. 63.

3. Michael Barone, *The Almanac of American Politics, 2005* (Washington, D.C., National Journal Group, 2006), pp. 1823–25.

4. Andrew Wroe, *The Republican Party and Immigration Politics: From Proposition 187 to George W. Bush* (New York: Palgrave Macmillan, 2008), pp. 29–30.

5. Ibid., pp. 2, 32, 36–37.

6. Ibid., pp. 42–43.

7. Ibid., pp. 42–43.

8. *League of United Latin American Citizens v. Wilson,* 908 F. Supp 755 (C.D. Cal 1995); *Wilson v. U.S.* 104 F.3d 1086 (9th Circuit 1997).

9. Wroe, *Republican Party and Immigration Politics,* pp. 117–18.

10. U.S. Commission on Immigration Reform, *U.S. Immigration Policy: Restoring Credibility,* September 1994; U.S. Commission on Immigration Reform, *Legal Immigration: Setting Priorities,* June 1995.

11. President Clinton's State of the Union Address, Jan. 24, 1995.

12. Wroe, *Republican Party and Immigration Politics,* pp. 133–46.

13. Ibid., p. 157.

14. Ibid., p. 179.

15. Fred Barnes, *Rebel-in-Chief: Inside the Bold and Controversial Presidency of George W. Bush* (New York: Crown Forum, 2006), p. 174.

16. "George W. Bush 2000 On the Issues: Immigration," 4President.org, no date; online at http://www.4president.org/issues/bush2000/bush2000immigration.htm (accessed Jan. 20, 2008).

17. U.S. Census Bureau, *The Foreign-Born Population of the U.S.* (Washington D.C.: GPO, March 2003), p. 20.

18. Lauren Etter, "After Port Fracas, Congress Tackles Immigration," *Wall Street Journal,* March 11–12, 2006, p. A7; June Krunholz and David Rogers, "Immigration Splits Republican Lawmakers," *Wall Street Journal,* March 29, 2006, p. A4.

19. Etter, "After Port Fracas," p. A7; Krunholz and Rogers, "Immigration Splits Republican Lawmakers," p. A4; Haya El Nasser, "Census: Newest Arrivals Fan Out," *USA Today,* Aug. 15, 2006, p. 1.

20. Michael A. Fletcher and Darryl Fears, "Analysts: Crackdown Won't Halt Immigration," *Washington Post,* Dec. 18, 2005, p. A11.

21. Nathan Thornburgh, "Inside the Life of the Migrants Next Door," *Time,* Feb. 6, 2006, pp. 38–30; Joel Millman, "As U.S. Debates Guest Workers, They Are Here Now," *Wall Street Journal,* Sept. 18, 2006, pp. A1, A16.

22. Michael Flynn, "Who's Trying to Cross Our Southern Border," *Washington Post,* Dec. 11, 2005, p. B1.

23. Haya El Nasser, "Census: Newest Arrivals Fan Out," *USA Today,* Aug. 15, 2006, p. 1.

24. Jonathan Weisman, "House to Take Up Stricter Immigration Measure," *Washington Post,* Dec. 11, 2005, p. A8.

25. Etter, "After Port Fracas," p. A7.

26. Fletcher and Fears, "Analysts: Crackdown Won't Halt Immigration," p. A11; Lauren Etter, "After Port Fracas," p. A7.

27. Miriam Jordan, "New Rules at the Border," *Wall Street Journal,* Feb. 21, 2006, p. B12.

28. Weisman, "House to Take Up," p. A8

29. Ibid.

30. Michael Sandler, "An Immigration Court Sequel," *Congressional Quarterly Weekly Report,* Aug. 6, 2007, p. 2343.

31. Damien Cave, "States Take New Tack on Illegal Immigration," *New York Times,* June 9, 2008 (online).

32. Kevin R. Johnson, *Opening the Floodgates: Why America Needs to Rethink Its Borders and Immigration Laws* (New York: New York University Press, 2007), p. 2.

33. Ibid.

34. Barone, *Almanac of American Politics, 2005,* p. 337.

35. The Immigration Reform Caucus maintains a website at http://www.house .gov/bilbray/irc/.

36. "Improving Access to Services for Persons with Limited English Proficiency," Presidential Executive Order No. 13166, August 2000.

37. One question on the decennial Census asks for the respondent's ability to speak English. It allows four responses: Very well, Well, Not well, and Not at all.

38. U.S. Office of Management and Budget (OMB), *Assessment of the Total Benefits and Costs of Implementing Executive Order No. 13166: Improving Access to Services for Persons with Limited English Proficiency,* Report to Congress, Washington D.C., March 14, 2002.

39. Michael Barone et al., *The Almanac of American Politics, 2005* (Washington, D.C.: National Journal Group, 2006), pp. 1379–82.

40. OMB, *Assessment of the Total Benefits and Costs.*

41. Ibid., p. 21.

42. Ibid., pp. 21–22.

43. U.S. Department of Justice, "Commonly Asked Questions and Answers Regarding Executive Order 13166," Oct. 26, 2001. Available online at http://englishfirst .org/13166/13266doj102601Q&A.htm (accessed June 13, 2009).

44. "245(i) Extension Left Unfinished," *Congressional Quarterly Almanac*, 2001, pp. 14-13 to 14-15.

45. "Cracking Down on Border Security," *Congressional Quarterly Almanac*, 2002, pp. 13-7 to 13-8.

46. Johnson, *Opening the Floodgates*, p. 33.

47. Wroe, *Republican Party and Immigration Politics*, p. 191.

48. Kim Hart, "Study Finds Immigrants Don't Hurt U.S. Jobs," *Washington Post*, Aug. 11, 2006, p. D1.

49. Miriam Jordan, "States and Towns Attempt to Draw the Line on Illegal Immigration," *Wall Street Journal*, July 12, 2006, pp. A1, A10.

50. "Intelligence Overhaul Enacted," *Congressional Quarterly Almanac*, 2004, pp. 11-3 to 11-13.

51. Wroe, *Republican Party and Immigration Politics*, p. 194.

52. Johnson, *Opening the Floodgates*, pp. 5, 153.

53. Jonathan Weisman, "House Votes to Toughen Laws on Immigration," *Washington Post*, Dec. 17, 2005, p. A1.

54. U.S. Watch, "Government to Use Waivers to Speed Border-Fence Work," *Wall Street Journal*, April 2, 2008, p. A2.

55. Wroe, *Republican Party and Immigration Politics*, p. 198.

56. "Guest Worker, Citizenship Issues Divide GOP and Stymie Overhaul," *Congressional Quarterly Almanac*, 2006, pp. 14-3 to 14-8.

57. Ibid., pp. 14-4 to 14-5.

58. Michael Sandler, "Tough Immigration Conference Looms," *Congressional Quarterly Weekly Report*, May 22–26, 2006, p. 1473.

59. "Guest Worker, Citizenship Issues Divide GOP and Stymie Overhaul," *Congressional Quarterly Almanac*, 2006, p. 14-3.

60. Jonathan Weisman, "Cost of Immigration Bill Put at $126 Billion," *Washington Post*, Aug. 22, 2006, pp. A1, A4.

61. Wroe, *Republican Party and Immigration Politics*, p. 199.

62. Kathy Kiely, "Border Security Should Be Priority, Hastert Says," *USA Today*, July 21, 2006, p. 4A; Darryl Fears, "Hispanics Cite Rise in Discrimination," *Washington Post*, July 14, 2006, p. A9; Emily Bazar, "Immigrant Activism Takes a Bold Turn," *USA Today*, Sept. 12, 2007.

63. "Congress Calls for Border Fence," *Congressional Quarterly Almanac*, 2006, pp. 14-7 to 14-8.

64. Wroe, *Republican Party and Immigration Politics*, p. 200.

65. Miriam Jordan, "New Rules at Border," *Wall Street Journal*, Feb. 21, 2006, p. B1; June Kronholz, "China Tests U.S. Immigration Plan," *Wall Street Journal*, July 31, 2006, p. A4.

66. Meredith Kolodner, "Private Prisons Expect a Boom," *New York Times*, July 19, 2006, p. C1.

67. Etter, "After Port Fracas," p. A7; David Rogers, "House, Senate Near Agreement on Homeland Security Budget," *Wall Street Journal*, Sept. 19, 2006, p. A8.

68. Julia Preston, "U.S. Puts Onus on Employers of Immigrants," *New York Times,* July 31, 2006, pp. A1, A15; Spencer S. Hsu, "Immigration Arrests Down 8% for Year," *Washington Post,* Oct. 31, 2006, p. A5.

69. Miriam Jordan, "Factories Turn to Refugee Workers," *Wall Street Journal,* June 6, 2008, A1; Julia Preston, "More Illegal Crossings Are Criminal Cases, Group Says," *New York Times,* June 18, 2008 (online).

70. Julia Preston, "Immigration Sweep Ends in 280 Arrests at Five Plants," *New York Times,* April 17, 2008, p. A19.

71. Miriam Jordan, "Crossings by Migrants Slow as Job Picture Dims," *Wall Street Journal,* April 9, 2008, p. A1.

72. Miriam Jordan and Conor Dougherty, "Immigration Slows in Face of Economic Downturn," *Wall Street Journal,* Sept. 23, 2008 (online).

73. Maura Reynolds and Richard Marosi, "Drop In Illegal Border Crossings a Sign of Success, Bush Aide Says," *Los Angeles Times,* Aug. 24, 2006, pp. A1, A16.

74. Ibid., p. A16.

75. Jonathan Weisman, "Immigration Plan Gets a Boost," *Washington Post,* Aug. 24, 2006, p. A4; Carl Huse and Rachel Swarns, "GOP Lawmakers Set Aside Work on Immigration," *New York Times,* Sept. 5, 2006, p. A18.

76. Wroe, *Republican Party and Immigration Politics,* pp. 200–206.

77. Ibid., p. 200.

78. David Rogers, "Progress Made on Immigration Bill," *Wall Street Journal,* May 15, 2007, p. A6.

79. Sarah Lueck, "Kyl Hits Immigration Head Wind," *Wall Street Journal,* May 23, 2007, p. A5.

80. Wroe, *Republican Party and Immigration Politics,* p. 209.

81. Julia Preston and Marjorie Connelly, "Immigration Bill Provisions Gain Wide Support in Poll," *New York Times,* May 25, 2007, p. A1.

82. Sarah Lueck, "Odd Bedfellows," *Wall Street Journal,* May 23, 2007, p. A5.

83. Robert Pear and Michael Luo, "Senate Votes 64–31 to Retain Temporary Worker Program in Immigration Measure," *New York Times,* May 23, 2007, p. A17; Sarah Lueck, "Immigration Measure Lives On," *Wall Street Journal,* May 25, 2007, p. A6.

84. "Immigration: Of Fences and Visas," *Economist,* May 26, 2007, pp. 27–28.

85. Michael Sandler, "Reid Pulls Immigration Overhaul," *Congressional Quarterly Weekly Report,* June 11, 2007, pp. 1746–47.

86. Carl Hulse and Jeff Zeleny, "Bush Lobbies GOP Senators for Stalled Immigration Bill," *New York Times,* June 13, 2007; Sarah Lueck, "Reviving the Immigration Bill," *Wall Street Journal,* June 13, 2007, p. A6.

87. Michael Sandler and Martin Kady II, "Immigration Bill Gets Second Chance," *Congressional Quarterly Weekly Report,* June 18, 2007, pp. 1850–51.

88. Michael Sandler, "Immigration Overhaul Stymied," *Congressional Quarterly Weekly Report,* July 9, 2007, pp. 2028–29.

89. Elizabeth Wasserman, "Pundit Power," *Congressional Quarterly Weekly Report,* July 9, 2007, p. 2006.

90. Julia Preston, "As Immigration Plan Folded, Grass Roots Roared," *New York Times,* June 10, 2007, pp. 1, 24; Wroe, *Republican Party and Immigration Politics,* p. 206.

91. Wroe, *Republican Party and Immigration Politics,* pp. 204, 208–209.

92. Michael Sandler, "For Reid, a Tricky Course to Democratic Victory," *Congressional Quarterly Weekly Report,* June 18, 2007, pp. 1819–20.

93. Michael Sandler, "Reid Pulls Immigration Overhaul," *Congressional Quarterly Weekly Report,* June 11, 2007, pp. 1746–47.

94. David Rogers, "Republicans Add Further Pressure on the White House," *Wall Street Journal,* June 26, 2007, p. A6.

95. David Rogers, "Beleaguered Immigration Bill Faces Do-or-Die Vote," *Wall Street Journal,* June 28, 2007, p. A2.

96. Michael Sandler, "For Reid, a Tricky Course to Democratic Victory," *Congressional Quarterly Weekly Report,* June 18, 2007, pp. 1819–20.

97. Elizabeth Wasserman, "Pundit Power," *Congressional Quarterly Weekly Report,* July 9, 2007, p. 2006.

98. Karoun Demirjian, "Balancing Border Security," *Congressional Quarterly Weekly Report,* Oct. 20, 2008, 2811–16; August Cole, "Virtual Fence for Mexico Border Is Put Off," *Wall Street Journal,* Sept. 10, 2008, p. A3.

99. Associated Press, "U.S. Fence at Border with Mexico Hits 500-Mile Mark," *Indianapolis Star,* Dec. 17, 2008, p. A4.

100. Demirjian, "Balancing Border Security," p. 2816.

101. Ibid., pp. 2811–16; August Cole, "Virtual Fence for Mexico Border Is Put Off," *Wall Street Journal,* Sept. 10, 2008, p. A3.

102. Randal C. Archibold, "Border Plan Will Address Harm Done at Fence Site," *New York Times,* Jan. 17, 2009 (online).

103. Thomas Frank, "Tensions Up with Border Fence," *USA Today,* Dec. 29, 2008, p. 3A.

104. Miriam Jordan, "Bush Orders Some Firms to Show Workers' Status," *Wall Street Journal,* June 10, 2008, p. A6.

105. Joel Millman and June Kronholz, "Economic Crisis Will Take Precedence over Near-Term Immigration Overhaul," *Wall Street Journal,* Nov. 12, 2008 (online).

106. Julia Preston, "More Illegal Crossings are Criminal Cases, Group Says," *New York Times,* June 18, 2008 (online).

10. Tort and Regulatory Reform

1. W. M. Crane and T. D. Hopkins, *The Impact of Regulatory Costs on Small Firms,* Report to the Office of Advocacy, U.S. Small Business Administration, Washington D.C., 2001.

2. Committee for Economic Development, *Breaking the Litigation Habit: Economic Incentives for Legal Reform,* New York, 2006; online at http://www.ced.org/images/library/reports/legal_reform/report_legalfull.pdf (accessed Jan. 20, 2008).

3. Jeffrey H. Birnbaum and John F. Harris, "President's Proposed Remedy to Curb Medical Malpractice Lawsuits Stalls," *Washington Post*, April 3, 2005, p. A5; Daniel P. Kessler and Mark McClellan, "Is Medical Malpractice Reform Good Medicine?" Stanford Graduate School of Business, Palo Alto, Calif., February 2005.

4. U.S. Manufacturing Council, "Focus: Tort Reform," Report of Subcommittee on U.S. Competitiveness, Washington D.C., Sept. 21, 2004; U.S. Council of Economic Advisers, "Who Pays for Tort Liability Claims," Executive Office of the President, Washington, D.C., April 2002; Towers Perrin, *U.S. Tort Costs and Cross-Border Perspectives: 2005 Update*, 2006, Online at http://www.towersperrin.com/tp/getwebcachedoc?webc=TILL/USA/2006/200603/2005_Tort.pdf (accessed Jan. 20, 2008).

5. "Fact Sheet: Pennsylvania Medical Liability Environment," Pennsylvania Hospitals and Health Systems, Dec. 31, 2005; online at http://www.pahospitalsadvocacy.org/hap/Medical_Liability.pdf (accessed Jan. 20, 2008).

6. *Congressional Quarterly Almanac*, 2004, p. 12-7.

7. Ibid.

8. *Congressional Quarterly Almanac*, 2004, pp. 12-6, 12-7.

9. *Congressional Quarterly Almanac*, 2004, p. 5-18.

10. Stephen Labaton, "Asbestos Bill Is Sidelined by the Senate," *New York Times*, Feb. 15, 2006, p. C1.

11. *Congressional Quarterly Almanac*, 2003, pp. 13-10, 13-11.

12. Ibid.

13. Ibid.

14. The crossover Democrats were Bayh of Indiana, Carper of Delaware, Feinstein of California, Jeffords of Vermont, Kohl of Wisconsin, Lieberman of Connecticut, Lincoln of Arkansas, Miller of Georgia, and Nelson of Nebraska.

15. *Congressional Quarterly Almanac*, 2004, p. 12-7.

16. *Congressional Quarterly Weekly Report*, Feb. 14, 2005, pp. 404–405.

17. *Congressional Quarterly Weekly Report*, Aug. 1, 2005, p. 2142.

18. Kate Schuler, "Health Care Agenda Falters in Senate," *Congressional Quarterly Weekly Report*, May 15, 2006, pp. 1334–35.

19. Scott Gottlieb, "Trial-Lawyer Kowtow," *Wall Street Journal*, Sept. 20, 2007, p. A12 (describing FDA's new preemption doctrine); Anna Wilde Mathews, Christopher Conkey, and Stephen Power, "State, Federal Power Collide," *Wall Street Journal*, Feb. 1, 2008, p. A8.

20. Rebecca Adams, "Washington's Rules Put the Squeeze on States," *Congressional Quarterly Weekly Report*, March 6, 2006, pp. 586–87.

21. Alicia Mundy, "Bush Rule Changes Could Block Product-Safety Suits," *Wall Street Journal*, Oct. 15, 2008 (online).

22. In 2007 the opponents of federal pre-emption sought to reverse some of the Bush legal interpretations in a new FDA reform bill. See Anna Wilde Matthews, Sarah Rubenstein, and Heather Won Tesoriero, "Bill Raising FDA's Powers Nears Passage," *Wall Street Journal*, Sept. 20, 2007, p. A6.

23. Nick Timiraos, "Lawyers Aim to Roll Back Curbs on Lawsuits," *Wall Street Journal,* Nov. 3, 2008 (online).

24. Rogelio Garcia, "Federal Regulatory Reform: An Overview," Issue Brief for Congress, U.S. Congressional Research Service, Library of Congress, Washington D.C., updated May 22, 2001.

25. Ibid.

26. Ibid.

27. "Nominations of Angela B. Styles, Stephen A. Perry, and John D. Graham," Hearing before the Senate Committee on Governmental Affairs, U.S. Congress, Washington, D.C., May 17, 2001.

28. U.S. Office of Management and Budget, *Stimulating Smarter Regulation,* 2001 Report to Congress, Washington D.C., 2000, pp. 39–51.

29. Ibid.

30. Stephen Power and Jacob M. Schlesinger, "Bush's Rules Czar Brings Long Knife to New Regulations," *Wall Street Journal,* June 12, 2002, pp. 1, A6.

31. U.S. Office of Management and Budget, "Regulatory Analysis," Circular A-4, Washington, D.C., 2003.

32. U.S. Office of Management and Budget, "Information Quality Guidelines," *Federal Register* 67 (Feb. 22, 2002): 84522.

33. U.S. Office of Management and Budget, "Final Information Quality Bulletin on Peer Review," Washington, D.C., Dec. 15, 2004; online at http://cio.energy.gov/documents/OMB_Final_Info_Quality_Bulletin_for_peer_bulletin(2).pdf (accessed Jan. 20, 2008).

34. U.S. Office of Management and Budget, "Implementation of the Information Quality Act," chapter 4 in *Validating Regulatory Analysis,* 2005; Report to Congress on the Costs and Benefits of Federal Regulations and Unfunded Mandates on State, Local, and Tribal Entities, Washington D.C., 2005, pp. 55–77.

35. U.S. Office of Management and Budget, "Trends in Federal Regulatory Activity," chapter 2 of *Validating Regulatory Analysis: Report to Congress,* Washington, D.C., 2005, pp. 35–39.

36. John D. Graham, Paul R. Noe, and Elizabeth L. Branch, "Managing the Regulatory State: The Experience of the Bush Administration," *Fordham Urban Law Journal* 32(4) (May 2006): 953–1002.

37. U.S. Office of Management and Budget, "Appendix D: Regulatory Reform in the Bush Administration," *Validating Regulatory Analysis: Report to Congress on the Costs and Benefits of Federal Regulations and Unfunded Mandates on State, Local, and Tribal Entities,* 2005, pp. 107–126; online at http://www.whitehouse.gov/omb/inforeg/2005_cb/final_2005_cb_report.pdf (accessed Jan. 20, 2008).

38. *Congressional Quarterly Almanac,* 2001, p. 13-3.

39. Ibid.

40. U.S. Department of Labor, "Defining and Delimiting the Exemptions for Executive, Administrative, Professional, Outside Sales and Computer Employees; Final Rule," *Federal Register* 69 (April 23, 2004): 22191.

41. Ibid.

42. *Congressional Quarterly Almanac,* 2004, p. 8-5.

43. Ibid.

44. Ibid.

45. Ibid.

46. U.S. Department of Labor, "Labor Organization Annual Financial Reports; Final Rule," *Federal Register* 68 (Oct. 9, 2003): 58374.

47. "Federal Appeals Court Upholds Authority of Secretary of Labor to Strengthen Union Financial Disclosure Laws," News Release, National Right to Work Legal Defense Foundation, Inc., June 1, 2005 (citing unanimous three-judge panel of the U.S. Court of Appeals for the District of Columbia).

48. U.S. Office of Management and Budget, *Stimulating Smarter Regulation,* 2002, pp. 7–11.

49. U.S. Office of Management and Budget, *Informing Regulatory Decisions: 2003 Report to Congress on the Costs and Benefits of Federal Regulations and Unfunded Mandates on State, Local, and Tribal Entities,* 2003, pp. 64–86; online at http://www .whitehouse.gov/omb/inforeg/2003_cost-ben_final_rpt.pdf (accessed Jan. 20, 2008).

50. Ibid., pp. 64–86.

51. "New Rules for Corporations," *Congressional Quarterly Almanac,* 2002, pp. 11-3 to 11-10.

52. The White House, "President's Ten-Point Plan," no date; online at http:// georgewbush-whitehouse.archives.gov/news/releases/2002/03/20020307-3.html (accessed May 25, 2009).

53. On Bush's initial stance against a strong corporate reform bill, see Gary Mucciaroni and Paul J. Quirk, "Deliberations of a 'Compassionate Conservative,'" in *The George W. Bush Presidency: Appraisals and Prospects,* ed. Colin Campbell and Bert A. Rockman (Washington, D.C.: CQ Press, 2004), p. 267.

54. Alex Berensen, "A U.S. Push on Accounting Fraud," *New York Times,* April 9, 2003, p. Cl; Stephen Labaton, "Bush Proposes Big Increase in SEC Budget," *New York Times,* Feb. 4, 2003, p. Cl.

55. Elizabeth Bumiller, "Corporate Conduct: The President; Bush Signs Bill Aimed at Fraud in Corporations," *New York Times,* July 31, 2002, p. Al.

56. For a review of the key provisions of Sarbanes-Oxley, see the testimony of SEC chairman William H. Donaldson before the House Committee on Financial Services, Washington, D.C., April 21, 2005; online at http://www.sec.gov/news/testimony/ ts042105whd.htm (accessed Jan. 20, 2008).

57. "Not Everyone Hates SarbOx: The Much Maligned New Rules Are a Big Hit with Investors," *Business Week Online,* Jan. 29, 2007; online at http://www.business week.com/magazine/content/07_05/b4019053.htm (accessed Jan. 20, 2008); Thomas J. Healey, "SarbOx Was the Right Medicine," *Wall Street Journal,* Aug. 9, 2007, p. A13.

58. Stephen Power, Elizabeth Williamson, and Christopher Conkey, "White House Pushes through a Flurry of Rule Changes Sought by Business," *Wall Street Journal,* Nov. 20, 2008 (online).

11. Meltdown and Bailouts

1. Robert J. Schiller, *The Subprime Solution* (Princeton, N.J.: Princeton University Press, 2008), p. 32.

2. Mark Zandi, *Financial Shock* (Upper Saddle River, N.J.: Pearson Education, 2009), p 15.

3. Schiller, *Subprime Solution,* p. 5.

4. Charles R. Morris, *The Trillion Dollar Meltdown* (New York: *Public Affairs,* 2008), p. 66.

5. Schiller, *Subprime Solution,* p. 33.

6. Zandi, *Financial Shock,* p. 16.

7. U.S. Congressional Budget Office, *The Budget and Economic Outlook: Fiscal Years 2009 to 2019,* Washington, D.C., January 2009, p. 5.

8. Zandi, *Financial Shock,* pp. 16–17.

9. Morris, *Trillion Dollar Meltdown,* p. 67.

10. Zandi, *Financial Shock,* p. 15.

11. Ibid., p. 13.

12. Schiller, *Subprime Solution,* p. 7.

13. Ibid., p. 29.

14. Jack Healy, "Home Prices Fell at Sharpest Pace in October," *Wall Street Journal,* Dec. 31, 2008 (online).

15. Ibid.

16. Adriel Bettelheim and Benton Ives, "The Crisis of Choice," *Congressional Quarterly Weekly Report,* July 7, 2008, pp. 1834–40.

17. Susan Schmidt and Maurice Tamman, "Housing Push for Hispanics Spawns Wave of Foreclosures," *Wall Street Journal,* Jan. 5, 2009 (online).

18. CBO, *Budget and Economic Outlook,* p. 6.

19. Ibid., p. 1.

20. These are nominal interest rates, with no adjustment for inflation.

21. Zandi, *Financial Shock,* p. 69.

22. Ibid., p. 65.

23. Peter S. Goodman and Gretchen Morgenson, "Saying Yes, WaMu Built Empire on Shaky Loans," *New York Times,* Dec. 28, 2008 (online).

24. Schiller, *Subprime Solution,* p. 39.

25. Zandi, *Financial Shock,* pp. 32–33.

26. Ibid., p. 33.

27. Ibid., p. 37.

28. Ibid., p. 54.

29. Ibid., p. 40.

30. Ibid., p. 39.

31. Ibid., p. 60.

32. Morris, *Trillion Dollar Meltdown,* p. 69.

33. Ibid., p. 71.

34. Goodman and Morgenson, "Saying Yes."

35. Morris, *Trillion Dollar Meltdown*, p. 67.

36. Benton Ives, "Mortgage Relief on the Horizon," *Congressional Quarterly Weekly Report*, July 28, 2008, pp. 2056–58.

37. Elizabeth Wasserman, "The Banking World Turns Upside Down," *Congressional Quarterly Weekly Report*, June 2, 2008, pp. 1482–91.

38. Ives, "Mortgage Relief on the Horizon," pp. 2056–58.

39. Zandi, *Financial Shock*, p. 147.

40. Ibid., p. 106.

41. CBO, *Budget and Economic Outlook*, p. 26.

42. Matt Andrejczak, "White House Warns of GSE Risks," *Marketwatch*, Nov. 6, 2003 (online) (CEA chairman Gregory Mankiw referred to Fannie Mae and Freddie Mac as a "source of systemic risk for our financial system").

43. U.S. Congressional Budget Office, *Assessing the Public Costs and Benefits of Fannie Mae and Freddie Mac*, Washington, D.C., May 1996; Congressional Budget Office, *Federal Subsidies and Housing GSEs*, Washington, D.C., May 2001.

44. Stephen Labaton, "New Agency Proposed to Oversee Freddie Mac and Fannie Mae," *New York Times*, Sept. 11, 2003 (online) (proposal drawn from previous bill by Congressman Richard H. Baker, R-La.; opposition led by Congressman Barney Frank, D-Mass.).

45. Morris, *Trillion Dollar Meltdown*, p. 77.

46. Schiller, *Subprime Solution*, pp. 50–51.

47. Ibid., pp. 41–43, 45.

48. Ibid., p. 65.

49. Zandi, *Financial Shock*, pp. 191–212.

50. Ibid., p. 206.

51. John Cranford, "Dimensions of a Crisis," *Congressional Quarterly Weekly Report*, July 21, 2008, pp. 1970–80.

52. Ives, "Mortgage Relief on the Horizon," p. 2056.

53. Ibid.

54. Ibid., pp. 2056–58.

55. Edmund L. Andrews, "Treasury Has Spent $350 Billion of Bailout Fund," *New York Times*, Dec. 20, 2008 (online); Deborah Solomon and Damian Palatta, "Paulson Wants Rest of TARP Funds from Congress," *Wall Street Journal*, Dec. 20, 2008 (online).

56. Jonathan Weisman, "House Rejects Financial Rescue, Sending Stocks Plummeting," *Washington Post*, Sept. 30, 2008, p. A01.

57. Ibid.

58. David M. Herszen-Horn, "Bailout Plan Wins Approval," *New York Times*, Oct. 3, 2008 (online).

59. Clea Benson, "Rescue Takes On a New Purpose," *Congressional Quarterly Weekly Report*, Oct. 20, 2008, pp. 2804–2805.

60. Ibid.

61. Diana B. Henriques, "Blunt Advice for Treasury on Progress of the Bailout," *New York Times*, Dec. 11, 2008 (online).

62. Deborah Solomon and Damien Paletta, "U.S. Seeks Rest of Bailout Cash," *Wall Street Journal,* Jan. 13, 2009 (online).

63. Associated Press, "Congress to Crack Down on Bailout Recipients," *MSNBC,* Dec. 23, 2008 (online).

64. Christopher Cox, "We Need a Bailout Exit Strategy," *Wall Street Journal,* Dec. 11, 2008 (online).

65. Mike McIntire, "Bailout Is a Windfall to Banks, if Not to Borrowers," *New York Times,* Jan. 18, 2009 (online).

66. Deborah Solomon, Jon Hilsenrath, and Damien Paletta, "U.S. Plots New Phase in Banking Bailout," *Wall Street Journal,* Jan. 17, 2009 (online).

67. Associated Press, "Toyota Projects Its First Loss," *Indianapolis Star,* Dec. 23, 2008 (online).

68. Bill Vlasic, "A Risk for Ford in Shunning Bailout, and Possibly a Reward," *New York Times,* Dec. 20, 2008 (online).

69. Bill Vlasic, "Automakers Race Time as Their Cash Runs Low," *New York Times,* Aug. 2, 2008 (online).

70. Zachary Kouwe and Louise Story, "Big Three's Troubles May Touch the Financial Sector," *New York Times,* Nov. 24, 2008.

71. Bill Vlasic, "A Ford Scion Looks Beyond Bailout to a Green Agenda," *New York Times,* Nov. 24, 2008, p. B1.

72. Matthew Dolan and John D. Stoll, "UAW Faces Prospect of More Concessions," *Wall Street Journal,* Nov. 18, 2008 (online).

73. Ken Bensinger, "Detroit Pushes for a $50-Billion Bailout," *Los Angeles Times,* Aug. 23, 2008, p. C4.

74. Michael E. Levine, "Why Bankruptcy Is the Best Option for GM," *Wall Street Journal,* Nov. 17, 2008 (online).

75. Paulo Prada and Dan Fitzpatrick, "South Could Gain as Detroit Struggles," *Wall Street Journal,* Nov. 20, 2008 (online).

76. Ted Evanoff, "Economy Nixes Talk of Honda Expansion," *Indianapolis Star,* Nov. 17, 2008 (online).

77. Ted Evanoff, "UAW Official: Big Three Pay Not Higher," *Indianapolis Star,* Dec. 23, 2008 (online).

78. Prada and Fitzpatrick, "South Could Gain as Detroit Struggles."

79. Matthew J. Slaughter, "An Auto Bailout Would Be Terrible for Free Trade," *Wall Street Journal,* Nov. 20, 2008 (online).

80. Evanoff, "Economy Nixes Talk of Honda Expansion."

81. Vlasic, "Ford Scion Looks Beyond," p. B1.

82. Rick Wagoner, "Why GM Deserves Support," *Wall Street Journal,* Nov. 19, 2008 (online).

83. Elizabeth Williamson and Greg Hitt, "Auto-Parts Suppliers Push for Aid," *Wall Street Journal,* Nov. 17, 2008 (online).

84. John D. McKinnon, Deborah Solomon, and Greg Hitt, "Detroit Gets Access to Bailout Funds," *Wall Street Journal,* Dec. 13, 2008 (online).

85. Sharon Silke Carty and Chris Woodyard, "Environmental Groups Irked," *USA Today*, Dec. 18, 2008 (online).

86. Greg Hitt, John D. McKinnon, and Matthew Donlan, "Bailout Turns on Auto Makers' Viability," *Wall Street Journal*, Nov. 13, 2008 (online).

87. Greg Hitt, "Negotiations on Auto Aid Show Bush's Influence in Final Days," *Wall Street Journal*, Dec. 8, 2008 (online).

88. Nafti Bendavid, "Shelby, South Lead Resistance to Rescue," *Wall Street Journal*, Dec. 12, 2008 (online).

89. The auto-rescue package passed the House first, 237–170, but only 32 Republicans supported it. The plan failed to achieve the required 60 votes in the Senate (52–35), as three out of four Senate Republicans (31 of 41) voted no. Associated Press, "Senate Roll Vote on $14B Auto Bailout," *San Francisco Chronicle*, Dec. 11, 2008 (online).

90. Evanoff, "UAW Official: Big Three Pay Not Higher."

91. Jeffrey McCracken, John D. Stoll, and Greg Hitt, "GM Retains Bankruptcy Counsel," *Wall Street Journal*, Dec. 12, 2008 (online).

92. Jonathan Weisman and John D. McKinnon, "Obama Prods Bush to Aid Detroit," *Wall Street Journal*, Nov. 11, 2008 (online).

93. John D. McKinnon and John D. Stoll, "U.S. Throws Lifeline to Detroit," *Wall Street Journal*, Dec. 20, 2008 (online).

94. Vikas Bajaj and Nick Bunkley, "GMAC Cuts a Barrier to Car Loan," *New York Times*, Dec. 31, 2008 (online).

95. Ted Evanoff, "Bailout Boom?" *Indianapolis Star*, Jan. 4, 2009 (online).

96. Sharon Silke Carty, "GMAC, Key to GM's Survival, Gets $5 Billion in Federal Aid," *USA Today*, Dec. 30, 2008, p. 3B.

97. Bradford Wernie and Jamie LaRue, "Rescue Raises Thorny Issues," *Automotive News*, Dec. 22, 2008 (online).

98. Rebecca Christie, "More Businesses Deemed Eligible for Bailout Aid," *USA Today*, Jan. 5, 2009 (online).

99. Josh Mitchell and Jeff Bennett, "Chrysler Financial Gets Loan," *Wall Street Journal*, Jan. 17, 2009; Bill Vlasic, "$1.5 Billion U.S. Loan to Chrysler Financial," *New York Times*, Jan. 17, 2009 (online).

100. Liam Denning, "Detroit Is Facing a Scary New Normality," *Wall Street Journal*, Jan. 12, 2009 (online).

101. Kate Linebaugh and Norihiko Shirouzu, "Global Auto Contraction Ahead," *Wall Street Journal*, Dec. 13, 2008 (online).

12. Taking Stock, with Lessons for Future Presidents

1. Gary Mucciaroni and Paul J. Quirk, "Deliberations of a 'Compassionate Conservative,'" in *The George W. Bush Presidency: Appraisals and Prospects,* ed. Colin Campbell and Bert A. Rockman (Washington, D.C.: CQ Press, 2004), p. 181 ("many citizens will probably continue to judge Bush's performance primarily on his response to terrorism, including his handling of the Iraq crisis . . .").

2. Charles Lindblom, "The Science of Muddling Through," *Public Administration Review* 19 (Spring 1959): 74–88.

3. Judy Pasternak, "It's Bush's Turn to Air Ideas for Dealing with Warming," *Los Angeles Times,* Sept. 26, 2007, p. A16.

4. On the case for a carbon tax, see David Frum, *Comeback: Conservatism That Can Win Again* (Garden City, N.Y.: Doubleday, 2008).

5. Charles O. Jones, *The Presidency in a Separated System* (Washington, D.C.: Brookings Institution Press, 2005), p. 64.

6. As the pool of Senate Democrats dwindled, they recognized that it would be easier to stick together and block Bush's policy ambitions. Jacob S. Hacker and Paul Pierson, *Off Center: The Republican Revolution and the Erosion of American Democracy* (New Haven, Conn.: Yale University Press, 2005), p. 173.

7. OMB's official tally put the fiscal year 2007 budget deficit at $162.8 billion, the lowest level in five years. John O. Buckley, "Budget Deficit Lowest in Five Years," *USA Today,* Oct. 12, 2007, p. 4A.

8. CBO estimates $94.8 billion in expenditures, $17 billion in extra borrowing, and $16 billion in tax relief were attributable to Hurricanes Katrina, Rita, and Wilma. U.S. Congressional Budget Office, Letter to Hon. John M. Spratt Jr. from Peter R. Orszag re: response to questions about federal relief funds for hurricane relief, Washington, D.C., Aug. 1, 2007; online at http://www.cbo.gov/ftpdocs/85xx/doc8514/08-07-Hurricanes_Letter.pdf (accessed Jan. 20, 2008).

9. U.S. Congressional Budget Office, *The Budget and Economic Outlook: An Update,* Washington, D.C., August 2007.

10. Julian E. Barnes, "Budget for War Jumps in 2008," *Los Angeles Times,* Sept. 22, 2007, pp. A1, A9.

11. Bush was referred to as a president "whose style and substance of governing is extremely polarizing." Thomas E. Mann, "Polarizing the House of Representatives: How Much Does Gerrymandering Matter?" in *Red and Blue Nation?,* ed. Pietro S. Nivola and David W. Brady (Washington, D.C.: Brookings Institution Press, 2006), pp. 278–79; also see Thomas E. Mann and Norman J. Ornstein, *The Broken Branch: How Congress Is Failing and How to Get It Back on Track* (New York: Oxford University Press, 2006), p. 124.

12. Both Clinton and Bush are often referred to as polarizing presidents. "An alternative explanation suggests itself: that the last two presidents inhabited a polarized political environment—and that instead of being its architects, they were its victims." Carl M. Cannon, "Polarization Runs Deep, Even by Yesterday's Standards; Comment," in *Red and Blue Nation? Characteristics and Causes of America's Polarized Politics,* ed. Pietro S. Nivola and David W. Brady (Washington, D.C.: Brookings Institution Press, 2006), p. 166. For a view that Republican leaders in Congress, more than Bush, fueled polarization, see Hacker and Pierson, *Off Center,* pp. 18–20.

13. ". . . and explanation of polarization should not focus solely on Bush, but on patterns of elite politics more generally." Morris P. Fiorina and Matthew S. Levendusky, "Disconnected," in *Red and Blue Nation: Characteristics and Causes of Amer-*

ica's Polarized Politics, ed. Pietro S. Nivola and David W. Brady (Washington, D.C.: Brookings Institution Press, 2006), p. 110.

14. This is a scenario suggested by Thomas E. Mann, "Polarizing the House of Representatives," in *Red and Blue Nation? Characteristics and Causes of America's Polarized Politics*, ed. Pietro S. Nivola and David W. Brady (Washington, D.C.: Brookings Institution Press, 2006), pp. 281–82.

15. David Brooks, "The Politics of Cohesion," *New York Times*, Jan. 20, 2009 (online).

16. Ronald Brownstein, "Demography and Destiny," *National Journal*, Jan. 10, 2009, p. 60.

17. Jonathan Chait, "That Grinding Sound Is the GOP Shifting Gears," *Los Angeles Times*, Nov. 4, 2006, p. M4 (nonideologic reasons for Democratic victory in 2006 include voter frustration with Iraq, the mishandling of Katrina, and corruption in Congress); Gary C. Jacobson, "The War, the President, and the 2006 Midterm Congressional Elections," speech delivered at the Annual Meeting of the Midwest Political Science Association, Palmer House Hilton, Chicago, Ill., April 12–15, 2007.

18. William A. Galston and Pietro S. Nivola, "Delineating the Problem," *Red and Blue Nation? Characteristics and Causes of America's Polarized Politics*, ed. Pietro S. Nivola and David W. Brady (Washington, D.C.: Brookings Institution Press, 2006), p. 3 (referring to the 1960 presidential election as close without being polarized and the 1964 election as deeply polarized without being close).

19. Susan Page, "Election '06: Lessons Learned by Dissecting Votes," *USA Today*, Nov. 27, 2006, p. 6A.

20. Galston and Nivola, "Delineating the Problem," p. 21.

21. Hacker and Pierson, *Off Center*, pp. 169–70.

22. Mann and Ornstein, *Broken Branch*, pp. 92–93.

23. Barbara Sinclair, "Context, Strategy and Chance: George W. Bush and the 107th Congress," *The George W. Bush Presidency: Appraisals and Prospects*, ed. Colin Campbell and Bert A. Rockman (Washington, D.C.: CQ Press, 2004), pp. 106–107.

24. Richard Neustadt, *Presidential Power: The Politics of Leadership* (New York: Wiley, 1960).

25. Paul C. Light, *The President's Agenda: From Kennedy to Carter* (Baltimore: Johns Hopkins University Press, 1982).

26. James P. Pfiffner, *The Strategic Presidency: Hitting the Ground Running* (Lawrence: University Press of Kansas, 1996), p. 112.

27. On Bush's ease with the education issue, see Robert Draper, *Dead Certain: The Presidency of George W. Bush* (New York: Free Press, 2007), pp. 113–20.

28. Jones, *Presidency in a Separated System*, p. 195 (arguing there was no real domestic policy mandate in Bush's reelection victory).

29. It is hard to take seriously the assertion that Social Security reform did not pass because Bush did not give it sufficient priority, a view expressed by Fred Barnes, "It Didn't Have to Be Sufficient That Way," *Wall Street Journal*, Nov. 6, 2004, p. A14.

30. It is notable that none of the Republican presidential candidates in the 2008 race gave much emphasis to private investment accounts under Social Security. Gerald F. Seib and John Harwood, "Bush's Taxing Legacy," *Wall Street Journal,* Oct. 9, 2007, p. A4.

31. "Because presidents are term limited, it is highly probable that their status in Washington will erode during their second terms." Jones, *Presidency in a Separated System,* p. 44.

32. "The idea of momentum connotes a sense of power of the new president and of the inevitability of his successes." Pfiffner, *Strategic Presidency,* p. 113.

33. Mann and Ornstein, *Broken Branch,* p. 124 (the Bush White House was seen "circumventing Senate Democratic leaders by seeking a handful of Democratic defectives on an issue-by-issue basis"); more generally, see Jones, *Presidency in a Separated System,* pp. 26–30.

34. A characteristic feature of polarization is that leaders of one party view leaders of the other party as enemies, often with a sense of moral right and wrong. James Q. Wilson, "How Divided Are We?" *Commentary,* February 2006, p. 16.

35. Sinclair, "Context, Strategy and Chance," pp. 106–107, 111.

36. One of the myths about the Bush presidency is that Bush was not inclined to reach out to Democratic members of Congress who were sympathetic on policy. See, for example, Ronald Brownstein, "A Possible Fatal Flaw in G.O.P. Formula for Success," *Los Angeles Times,* Oct. 22, 2006, p. A18; "Job Performance Evaluations: The President," Editorial, *Los Angeles Times,* Dec. 31, 2006, p. M5.

37. Jones, *Presidency in a Separated System,* p. 337.

38. Mann and Ornstein, *Broken Branch,* pp. 124–28 (describing how, on tax cuts, Bush went directly to voters in states that he had won where there were also wavering Democratic senators); George C. Edwards III, "Riding High in the Polls: George W. Bush and Public Opinion," in *The George W. Bush Presidency: Appraisals and Prospects* (Washington, D.C.: CQ Press, 2004), pp. 32–34 (documenting how Bush's travel schedule and speeches were aimed at states where moderate Republican or Democratic senators were important to Bush's agenda).

39. Hacker and Pierson, *Off Center,* p. 171.

40. The U.S. Supreme Court blocked the Reagan administration's hasty decision in 1981 to rescind the automobile airbag regulation. *Motor Vehicle Manufacturers Association v. State Farm Mutual Automobile Insurance Company,* 103 S. Ct. 2856 (1983).

41. Jeff Tollefson, "House Passes Species Act Rewrite," *Congressional Quarterly Weekly Report,* Oct. 3, 2005, p. 2663.

42. Dina Cappiello, "Bush to Relax Rules Protecting Species," *Indianapolis Star,* Aug. 12, 2008, p. A3.

43. The initial judicial decision on CAFE did not favor the Bush administration's preemption stance, but appeals are likely. Mike Spector and Jeffrey Ball, "Court Roils Auto-Rules Debate," *Wall Street Journal,* Sept. 13, 2007, p. A9.

44. Juliet Eilperin, "Cities, States Aren't Waiting for U.S. Action on Climate," *Washington Post,* Aug. 11, 2006, p. 1.

45. Cass R. Sunstein, David Schkade, Lisa M. Ellman, and Andres Sawicki, *Are Judges Political? An Empirical Analysis of the Federal Judiciary* (Washington, D.C.: Brookings Institution Press, 2006).

46. Jones, *Presidency in a Separated System,* p. 355.

47. Even liberal scholars who oppose much of Bush's domestic agenda acknowledge that the major changes have occurred largely "beneath the radar screen." Hacker and Pierson, *Off Center,* p. 228.

Index

Page numbers in italics refer to tables.

Abdullah of Saudi Arabia, 129
accountability, 77–78, 280–81. *See also* standards and testing movement
accounting standards, 268
achievement gaps, 63–64, 91. *See also* education reform
activism: and base politics, 18; and bipartisanship, 315; and consumer activists, 171–72; and crossover voting, 321; and party activists, 18–19; and political polarization, 13. *See also* environmental issues and activism
"adequate yearly progress" (AYP) standard, 77–79, *79–81*, 88
adjustable-rate mortgages, 273, 276–77
affirmative action, 9
Afghanistan: and budget deficits, 50; and the Bush legacy, 292, 331; and evaluation of Bush policies, 303–304; and military spending, 303; and oil prices, 164; and tax policy, 44
AFL-CIO, 245
Africa, 158, 229
African Americans, 67–68, 80–81, 91–92, 306
age issues, 95
agenda-control powers, 239, 320–24

agricultural interests, 116, 151, 155, 241, 323. *See also* ethanol
AIG, 283
air quality issues, 207–209, 210–13, 214–17. *See also* environmental issues and activism
Akaka, Daniel, 125
Alabama, 128
Alaska, 117, 120, 127, 128
Alexander, Lamar, 198
Allard, Wayne, *322*
Allen, George, *322*
Alliance for School Choice, 81
alternative minimum tax (AMT), *38*, 44, 45, 148, 284
American Association of Retired Persons (AARP), 59, 93–94, 97, 100, 103, 113
American Home Mortgage, 279
American Jobs Creation Act, 187
American Medical Association (AMA), 100, 232
anti-immigration sentiment, 223, 225–26, 234, 242
antiwar sentiment, 305
appointment powers, 325
appropriations bills, 166, 203, 237
Archer, Bill, 55

Arches National Park, 127
Arctic National Wildlife Refuge
(ANWR): and crossover voting, *318,*
320; and cross-partisanship, 317; and
energy policy, 119, 120, 122, 124, 125–
26; and failed Bush initiatives, *300;*
negotiations on, 160; and renewable
energy, 146; and the 2000 election,
117
Arizona, 180, 228, 229, 240
Arkansas, 83
Armey, Dick, 66, 70
arsenic, 195
Arthur Andersen LLP, 267
asbestos lawsuits, 253–54, *300, 319*
Asia, 229, 239
Australia, 155, 278
Automobile Association of America
(AAA), 182
automobile industry: and the California
Plan, 167–70, 175; and energy conservation, 166; and evaluation of Bush
policies, *294;* and executive powers,
327; and the federal bailout, 286–89,
291; and mileage requirements, 119;
and Twenty-in-Ten initiative, 176. *See
also* Big Three automakers
Azerbaijan, 130

Bank of America, 286–87
Barone, Michael, 22
Barrosso, Jose, 260
Barton, Joe, 124, 172–73, 201
base politics, 17–21. *See also* partisanship; polarization
battleground states, *309*
Baucus, Max: and Clear Skies initiative,
200; and crossover voting, *322;* and
ergonomics rules, 262; and global
climate change, 198; and prescription
drug benefits, 100–103; and tax cuts,
36, 37, 39, 45
Bayh, Evan, 39, 68, 69, 71, 91, *322*
Bear Stearns, 279, 283

benefit-cost analyses, 257–58, 258–59,
299
Bennett, Robert, *322*
Bennett, William, 225
Berman, Howard, 238
Bernanke, Ben, 46–47
Biden, Joe, 173, 305
Big Three automakers, 169, 291, *294;* and
CAFE standards, 167, 168; and executive powers, 327; profits and losses,
191; and Twenty-in-Ten initiative, 176.
See also specific companies
Bingaman, Jeff, 124, 146–47, 173, 198
biofuels: backlash against, 155–56; and
Brazilian ethanol, 157–58; and cellulosic ethanol, 156–57; compromise
on, 150–52; and E85, 152–55; and
environmental legislation, 178; ethanol vs. MTBE, 149–50; and mileage
standards, 175; prospects for ethanol,
158–59
Biofuels Corridor, 154
biomass power, 147, 159
bipartisanship: and base politics, 18–19;
and crossover voting, 314; and cross-
partisan strategy, 324; declines in,
293; and education reform, 68, 92;
and energy policy, 119; and financial
crises, 281; and good governance, 5;
and immigration policy, 247; and lessons for the future, 293; and regulatory reform, 272; and reversal of Bush
policies, 308; shortcomings of, 315–16;
and the subprime lending crisis, 282;
and the Wall Street bailout, 283–84
Blair, Tony, 199
Bloomberg, Michael, 189
Bluewater Network, 181–83
BMW, *190*
Boehner, John, 68, 69–70, 72
Border Patrol, 242
border security: and administrative
crackdowns, 242–44, 248; and executive powers, 328; and guest worker

programs, 246; and homeland security, 250; and House proposals, 237; and immigrant communities, 239, 240; and immigration policy, 240–42, 244–45; negotiations on, 242; and terrorism, 234
Boston, Mass., 273
Boxer, Barbara: and CAFE standards, 181; and climate-change initiatives, 217, 218; and crossover voting, *322;* and energy policy, 137; and global climate change, 198; and immigration policy, 225
Brazil, 149, 152, 158, 298, 300
Breaux, John: and clean-air permits, 203; and crossover voting, *322;* and ergonomics rules, 262; and filibuster threats, 23; and prescription drug benefits, 98–103; and tax policy, 37, 42, 302
Brown, Jerry, 225
Brown, Kathleen, 224–25
Brownback, Sam, *322*
Buchanan, Patrick, *19,* 224, 227
budget, federal: and budget bills, 263; and deficits, 27, 47–51, *48,* 303–304; discretionary spending, *49;* and energy policy, 140; and federal tax burden, 47–51; and legislative reconciliation, 311; mandatory spending, *49;* and national debt, 32; outlays, *48, 48, 49;* and prescription drug benefits, 99–100, 106–107, 113–14; procedures for, 86; resolutions on, 125, *318;* revenues, *48;* and spending politics, 51–52; and surpluses, 32
Bulgaria, 131
bundling of mortgages, 278
Burr, Richard, *322*
Bush, George H. W., *12,* 65, 224, 267, 306
Bush, George W.: and base politics, 18; and fiscal policy, 52–53; and party loyalty, *19;* and political polarization, 16–17; and "political standing," *12;* and prescription drug benefits, 97–98; and tax policy, 32–33. *See also specific policy areas*
Bush, Jeb, 77
business interests: and Clear Skies initiative, 200; and energy policy, 119; and immigration policy, 239, 250; and prescription drug benefits, 93; and regulatory reform, 256. *See also specific industries*
Byrd, Robert, 71, 198, 203, 234, 253

California: and climate change issues, 199, 301; and education reform, 80; and energy conservation, 327; and ethanol fuels, 153; and evaluation of Bush policies, 298; and the housing crisis, 282; and immigration policy, 223–26, 229, 240, 249; and mileage standards, 167–70, 175, 176, 179–81, 298; and political polarization, *309;* and prescription drug benefits, 110; and subprime lending crisis, 276; and traffic management, 188
California Air Resources Board (CARB), 181
California Plan, 167–70, 175, 176, 179–81, 298
California Resources Board, 168
Campbell, Ben Nighthorse, 140, 264
Campbell, Larry, 42
Canada, 130, 215
Cantwell, Maria, 125
cap-and-trade program: and Bush's legacy, 219, *300;* and Bush's proposals, 198–99; and Clear Skies initiative, 194; and greenhouse gas emissions, 216; and the Kyoto Protocol, 215; and mercury emissions, 211–12; and regulatory reform, 259
capital gains taxes, 43–44, 44–45
carbon dioxide emissions: and Bush campaign pledges, 219; and CAFE

standards, 174–75, 178; and Clear
Skies initiative, 199, 200, 205; and
coal, 133; and ethanol, 156; and global
warming, 196–97; and mileage standards, 298; and nuclear energy, 145,
297; and tax policy, 302

Caribbean Basin Initiative, 158

Carnahan, Jean, 37

Carper, Tom, 24, 71, 103, 204–205, *322*

Carter, Jimmy, *12*, 35, 134, 142–43

case-study approach, 24–26

Cato Institute, 55

cellulosic ethanol, 156–57, 161

Census Bureau, 231

Central America, 229

Central American Free Trade Agreement (CAFTA), 158

centrism, 15, 20. *See also* bipartisanship

Cerberus, 287

Chafee, Lincoln: and clean-air permits,
203; and Clear Skies initiative, 200,
204; and crossover voting, 321, *322,*
323; and cross-partisan strategy, 324;
and energy policy, 125, 140; and executive powers, 326; and the federal
budget, 51; and filibuster threats,
34; and global climate change, 198;
and overtime rules, 264; and party
loyalty, *19,* 20; and prescription drug
benefits, 104; and tax cuts, 37, 38, 39,
42, 43, 45

Chambliss, Saxy, *322*

charter schools, 85. *See also* voucher
programs

Chávez, Hugo, 158–59

Cheney, Dick: and the auto industry
bailout, 289; and cross-partisanship,
317; and energy policy, 117–18, 121–22,
124; and filibuster threats, 22, 34; and
tax cuts, 41–42, 43

Chevrolet, 186

Chevron, 127, 130, 153

Chicago, Ill., 274

Children's Defense Fund, 64

China: and Bush's fiscal policies, 31;
and climate change, 218; and coal,
134, 136; and energy policy, 134, 136;
and food price inflation, 155; and fuel
prices, 189; and greenhouse gas emissions, 215, 216, 217; and the Kyoto
Protocol, 195, 196, 301; and the mortgage crises, 280; and oil consumption, 30, 164

Christians, 16

Chrysler, 189, 286, 289, 302

Chrysler Financial LLC, 290

Circular A-4, 257–58

citizenship issues, 224, 225, 234. *See
also* immigration policy

civil rights, 221

civil servants, 325

class-action lawsuits, 252, 254–55. *See
also* tort reform

Clean Air Act: Bush's emphasis on,
194; and CAFE standards, 174–75,
180; and the California Plan, 168–69,
180; and campaign pledges, 197;
and clean-air permits, 203; and coal
plants, 209; and diesel engine regulations, 205, 220; and energy policy
reform, 122; and evaluation of Bush
policies, *294;* and executive rule-
making power, 329–30; and mercury
emissions, 210, 211, 214; and MTBE,
149–50; and "renewable" fuels, 151

Clean Air Interstate Rule (CAIR), 208–
209, 212, 219–20, 259, 329–30

Clean Air Mercury Rule (CAMR),
212–13, 213–14, 219–20

clean air permits, 201–203

clean air rules, 8, 128, 208, 294–95, 319.
See also global climate change

clean coal, 117, 133–36, *318*

Clean Development Mechanism, 214–15

Clear Skies initiative: attempt to save,
204–205; and Bush's legacy, 219; and
campaign pledges, 196–97; and clean-
air permits, 201–203, 204; described,

194–95; and executive powers, 259, 326; and failed Bush initiatives, *300;* and mercury emissions, 211; opposition to, 199–201

Cleland, Max, 37, 39

climate change. *See* global climate change

Clinton, Bill: and air quality issues, 201–202, 204, 210–11; and the California Plan, 167–68; and diesel engine regulations, 205–206; and economic performance, 31, 32, 47, 303; and education reform, 64, 66, 67; and election results, 10; and energy policy, 130, 131, 132; and ergonomics rules, 261; and the federal budget, 51; and fiscal policy, 34; and immigration policy, 222, 225, 226, 231, 234; and the Kyoto Protocol, 195; and midnight regulations, 326; and political polarization, 305, 306, 311; and political standing, *12;* and prescription drug benefits, 96–97; and regulatory reform, 257, 270; and Social Security reform, 54, 58; and tax cuts, 39, 295; and veto power, 32

Clinton, Hillary, 46, 93, 180, 305, *322*

cloture votes: and CAFE standards, 177–78, 179; and climate-change initiatives, 218; and energy policy reform, 124; and immigration policy, 247–48; and partisanship, 311; rules for, 23; and tort reform, 253

Club for Growth, *19,* 323

coal: and air quality, 207–209; backlash against, 136–37; and Bush priorities, *307;* and clean coal technology, 133–36; and crossover voting, *318;* and energy policy, 131–37, *133;* and evaluation of Bush policies, 161, *294;* and investment climate, 132–33; and presidential elections, 117; and the 2000 election, 118

coal-to-liquid (CTL) technology, 135–36

Coastal Zone Management Act, 128

Coburn, Thomas, *322*

cognitive disabilities, 76

Coleman, Norm, 126, 129, 173, 179, *322*

Collins, Susan M.: and CAFE standards, 179; and clean-air permits, 203; and the Congressional Review Act, 214; and crossover voting, *322;* and energy policy, 126, 129; and filibuster threats, 35; and global climate change, 198; and renewable energy, 146; and tax cuts, 43

Colorado, 83, 306

commercial banking, 279

Committee on Environment and Public Works, 199, 204, 217

Committee on Health, Education, Labor and Pensions, 67

"compassionate conservatism," 67, 228

compromise, 312–15

conference committees. *See* legislative reconciliation

confirmation votes, *319*

conflict extension, 13–14

Congressional Budget Office (CBO): and budget deficits, 49–50; and immigration policy, 226, 241–42; and prescription drug benefits, 99, 106, 111; and Social Security, 32; and tax revenues, 304

Congressional Review Act (CRA), 214, 261, 263, 270, 311

Connecticut, 180

Conrad, Kent, 60, 103

conservation efforts, 118

conservatives: and the auto industry bailout, 287, 288; and border security, 250; and cross-partisan strategy, 8; and domestic spending, 304; and education reform, 63, 66, 67, 69, 71, 90; and immigration policy, 223, 235, 246–47, 248; and political partisanship, 14–15; and prescription drug benefits, 99, 103, 111–12, 113; and school choice program, 80; and the subprime lending crisis, 283; and the Wall Street bailout, 285

consumer advocacy, 171–72, 256

Consumers Union (CU), 182

Contract with America, 226, 256

Corker, Bob, 289

corn-based ethanol, 298–99

Cornyn, John, 234, 240, *322*

corporate accountability, 268

Corporate Average Fuel Economy (CAFE): and Bush's reforms, 170–72, 183–84; and the California Plan, 167–70, 175, 179–81; and crossover voting, *318*; and energy policy reform, 120–21; establishment of, 165–66; and ethanol, 152–53; future standards, 175–76; and judicial conflicts, 174–75; and legislative failures, 167, 172–73; and legislative negotiation, 176–79; and science recommendations, 166; and special interests, 193

corporate fraud, 267–69, 268

corporate profits, 295

corporate tax reform, 264, 302

Corzine, John, *322*

Council of Economic Advisors (CEA), 40

counterfeiting, 229

counterterrorism, 266

Craig, Larry, *322*

Crapo, Mike, 253

credit default swaps, 274

Crist, Charlie, 128

crossover voting, 21, 23, 25–26, *318,* 320–24, *322. See also* cross-partisan strategy

cross-partisan strategy: advantages of, 324–25; and case-study approach, 24–25; and clean-air initiatives, 195; and climate-change initiatives, 219; conditions for, 316–20; described, 5–7; and education reform, 68, 91, 92; and energy policy, 116, 118–19, 160;

and ethanol compromise, 151; and the federal budget, 51; and filibuster threats, 34–35; and fiscal policy, 27; and prescription drug benefits, 98–99, 104, 112–13; and regulatory reform, 257; and Social Security reform, 59–61, 61–62; and tax policy, 312–13; and tort reform, 252

curriculum standards, 83–84. *See also* education reform

Daimler-Chrysler, 153, 172, 186, 189, *190*

Daschle, Tom: and crossover voting, 323; and cross-partisan strategy, 324; and energy policy, 119–21, 123–24, 139–40; and filibuster threats, 23; and immigration policy, 234; and the Kyoto Protocol, 195; and political polarization, 160; and prescription drug benefits, 99–100, 102–103; and tax cuts, 36, 37, 39; and tort reform, 254

"Day Without Immigrants," 240

Dayton, Mark, 198

Dean, Howard, 60

defense policy, *49,* 50, 125, 291. *See also* homeland security

deficits, 27, 47–51, *48,* 303–304

DeLay, Tom, 21, 122, 231

Democratic Leadership Council, 65–66, 69

Democratic Party: and AARP, 94; and cross-partisanship, 313, 314; and education, 64, 90; and the Electoral College, *309;* and energy policy, 116, 137; and governing strategies, 6–7; and interest groups, 4, 59; and labor unions, 265; and midterm elections, 1–2; and partisanship, 14; and party loyalty, 20; and political polarization, 15, 16; and prescription drug benefits, 93, 112–13; and Social Security reform, 59–61, 62. *See also specific individuals*

demographics, 106, 228–30

deregulation, 278–79

desulfurization technology, 205
detention centers, 243
Detroit, Mich., 169, 276
developing countries, 155, 195, 214–15, 215–16
DeWine, Mike, 20, 51, 125, 198, *322*
diesel fuel and vehicles, 185, *186,* 189, *190,* 192, 205–207, 220
Dingell, John, 124, 137, 177–79
diplomacy, 129–31
direct appeals, 321
disabled students, 76, 81–82
discretionary spending, *49*
District of Columbia, 92
Dobbs, Lou, 248
Dole, Bob, 126, 227, 256
Domenici, Pete, 121, 124, 138, 146, 198
Dorgan, Byron, 103, 241
dot-com bubble, 29
double-tracking, 22
Dukakis, Michael, 306
Duke Energy, 137
Durbin, Dick, 173

economic performance: and immigration policy, 223–24, 229–30; and presidential power, 28–31; recent indicators, 30; and supply-side economics, 39–44; and tax policy, 47
Economic Policy Institute, 288
economic stimulus: and assessment of Bush presidency, 4; and Clinton, 32, 311; and supply-side economics, 39–40; and tax credits, 186–87; and tax cuts, 28, 36, 46–47
Education Commission of the States, 83
education reform: and achievement gaps, 63–64; "adequate yearly progress" (AYP) standard, 77–79; and bipartisanship, 316; and Bush's terms compared, 302; and crossover voting, *318;* and cross-partisan strategy, 324; and educational gaps, 74; and evaluation of Bush policies, *294,* 296; and

failed Bush initiatives, 299–300, *300;* and failing schools, 76–79; and federal funding, 86–87; and graduation rates, 85; and immigration policy, 230; and Kennedy-Miller alliance, 69–71; and mandatory testing, 73–75; and partisanship, 66–67; problems with, 87–89; and school choice, 79–81, 88, 296; and school restructuring, 84–85, 88; and standards and testing, 65–66, 67, 71–72, *73,* 73–75, 76–79, 87–88, 90, 296; and supplemental tutoring, 81–82; and teacher qualifications, 82–84
education savings accounts (ESAs), *38*
Educational Testing Service, 83
Edwards, John, 203
E85 fuel, 152–55, 160, 180
Eisenhower, Dwight, *12*
El Paso, Tex., 249
elections: and base politics, 17–21; battle ground states, *309;* Bush reelection, 123; and Democratic gains, 1–2; and legislative agenda, 312–15; and political polarization, 9–10, 16–17; and prescription drug benefits, 97–98
Electoral College, 5, 10, 11, 39, 132, 306, *309*
electric power, *294,* 297. *See also* energy production policy
electric vehicles, 168, 185–86
elemental mercury, 212
Elementary and Secondary Education Act (ESEA), 64, 66, 86
emissions, 205–207, 220, 259. *See also* air quality issues; environmental issues and activism
employer-based drug coverage, 109–10
Endangered Species Act, 311, 326
Energy and Commerce Committee, 124, 199
energy conservation policy: Bush's emphasis on, 163–64; and CAFE standards, 165–66, 170–72, 183–84,

184–86, 193; and the California Plan,
167–70, 179–81; and future standards,
175–76; and judicial conflicts, 174–75;
and legislative failures, 166, 172–73;
and mileage calculation, 181–83; and
policy options, 164–65. *See also* energy production policy
Energy Policy Act, 141
energy production policy: and the
Arctic National Wildlife Refuge
(ANWR), 125–26; and assessment
of Bush presidency, 4, *294,* 303; and
Bush's proposal, 117–18; and coal,
131–37, *133;* and crossover voting, *318,*
318–19; and cross-partisanship, 317;
and diplomatic initiatives, 129–31;
and executive powers, 327; and legislative strategy, 118–24; and presidential elections, 116–17; and regulatory
reforms, 127–29; and security, 154;
and tax incentives, 127. *See also* energy conservation policy
Enron scandal, 266, 267, 271, 299, 316
Ensign, John, 101, 104, 140, 179
entitlements, 28, 304
Environmental Defense, 136
environmental issues and activism:
and air quality issues, 207–209,
211–13; and ANWR, 119–20; and
the auto industry bailout, 287, 289;
and the Bush energy policy, 118; and
CAFE standards, 172–73, 174–75,
193; and carbon dioxide, 196–97;
and clean diesel engines, 205–207,
220; and clean-air permits, 201–204;
and Clear Skies initiative, 199–201,
203–205; and climate change,
197–99, 214–17, 217–18, 219; and coal
energy, 133–34, 207–209; and energy
conservation, 166; and energy production policy, 136, 161; and ethanol
fuels, 156, 159, 160; and evaluation of
Bush policies, *294,* 297; and global
climate change, 195–96, 197–98;

and the Kyoto Protocol, 214–17; and
mercury emissions, 210–13, 213–14;
and mileage standards, 171–72; and
mountaintop mining, 131–32; and oil
exploration, 127–28; and regulatory
reform, 256
Environmental Protection Agency
(EPA): and clean-air permits, 201–
202, 204; and coal plant regulations,
207–209; and diesel engine regulations, 205–207; and executive rule-
making power, 329; and mercury
emissions, 210–11, 214; and mileage
standards, 182–83; and regulatory
reform, 259
ergonomics rules, 261–62, 270, 311, *319*
estate taxes, 36–39, *38,* 45, *307, 318*
ethanol: backlash against, 155–56; Brazilian sources, 158; E85 blends, 152–
55; and energy policy, 119, 121, 123–24,
149; and evaluation of Bush policies,
161, *294,* 298–99, 302; and failed Bush
initiatives, *300;* and Gore, 115–16; and
MTBE, 149–50; political compromise
on, 150–52; and presidential election,
118; prospects for, 159–60
Europe: and diesel engine regulations,
207; and ethanol use, 149; and fuel
prices, 192; and greenhouse gas emissions, 215, 216; and regulatory reform,
260
European Commission, 207, 215, 260
European Union, 149, 215
evangelical Christians, 16
E-Verify, 249
Executive Office of the President, 232
executive powers: and air quality, 210;
and the Bush legacy, 330–31; and
Bush's reliance on, 8; and CAFE
standards, 178, 180; and change in
presidency, 294–95; and clean-air
initiatives, 195, 201–203, 204; and the
Congressional Review Act, 214; and
diesel engine regulations, 205–207;

and education reform, 64–65, 74, 76, 82, 85, 89; and energy policy, 132, 161, 209; and ethanol, 152, 155; and governing strategies, 7; and immigration policy, 222, 231–32, 233, 249–50; and overtime rules, 264; and political polarization, 325–28; and prescription drug benefits, 108; and regulatory reforms, 256, 257, 269–70; and reversal of Bush actions, 306–308; and tort reform, 252, 255–56

Exxon, 130

Fair and Secure Immigration Reform, 234

Fair Labor Standards Act, 262

faith-based initiatives, 7–8

Fannie Mae, 279–80, 282, 291

farm interests, 116

Federal Deposit Insurance Corporation (FDIC), 278

Federal Home Loan Mortgage Corporation, 279

Federal Housing Administration (FHA), 282

Federal Law Enforcement Training Center, 245

Federal Mortgage Association, 279

Federal Reserve System: and the auto industry bailout, 290; independence of, 138; and presidential power, 28–29; and regulatory reform, 268, 275–76, 278, 281; and the Wall Street bailout, 283, 285–86

Federation for American Immigration Reform, 247

Feingold, Russ, 198

Feinstein, Diane: and CAFE standards, 177; and immigration policy, 225, 245; and mileage standards, 173; and prescription drug benefits, 103; and tax cuts, 37; and tort reform, 254

FHA Secure, 281

FICO scores, 276

filibusters: and the auto industry bailout, 289; and CAFE standards, 177, 181; and Clear Skies initiative, 200; and climate-change initiatives, 218; and cross-partisan strategy, 317, 319; and education reform, 67; and energy policy, 116, 121, 123–25; and good governance, 6; and governing strategies, 5; and nuclear energy, 140; overcoming filibuster threats, 22–24; and party voting, 311; and prescription drug benefits, 101, 103, 113; and presidential agendas, 22; and regulatory reforms, 270; and reversal of Bush policies, 308; and tax cuts, 33–35, 41; and tort reform, 253

Financial Accounting Standards Board, 95–96

financial crisis and bailout: and bipartisanship, 281; and the Bush agenda, 291; and Bush's terms compared, 303; and evaluation of Bush policies, 294, 304; and housing sector bailout, 281–83; and regulatory reforms, 271; and reversal of Bush policies, 307

financial disclosures, 264–66, 270

flex-fuel vehicles, 152

Florida: and CAFE standards, 180; and education reform, 76–77; and energy policy, 136; and immigration policy, 229; and presidential elections, 10–11, 306; and the subprime lending crisis, 276, 282

food prices, 155, 156, 299

food stamps, 226, 241

Ford Motor Company: and auto industry bailout, 286, 288; and CAFE standards, 167, 172; and diesel vehicles, 190; and ethanol vehicles, 153; and fuel prices, 189; and hybrid vehicles, 186, 190; and mileage standards, 171; profits and losses, 191

foreign investments, 280

Fox, Vicente, 234

France, 29
Freddie Mac, 279–80, 282, 291
Frist, Bill: and energy policy, 123; and
    immigration policy, 237; and pre-
    scription drug benefits, 98, 99; and
    tax cuts, 45; and tort reform, 252–54
fuel cell technology, 185
fuel economy ratings, 186–87. *See also*
    Corporate Average Fuel Economy
    (CAFE)
fuel prices: and CAFE standards, 173;
    and climate-change initiatives,
    218; collapse of, 191–92; and market
    forces, 189; and presidential election,
    116–17; and speculation, 128
fuel-saving technologies, 177
FutureGen, 134, 136, 137, 161

Gallegly, Elton, 226
gangs, *238*
gas exploration, *307, 318. See also* natu-
    ral gas
"gasohol," 150. *See also* ethanol
gasoline consumption, 175–76
gasoline prices, 152, 154, 172, 181–83
G8, 130, 216
General Accountability Office, 283, 285
General Electric (GE), 217
General Motors (GM): and the auto
    industry bailout, 286–87, 289–90,
    302; and CAFE standards, 167; and
    diesel vehicles, *190;* and ethanol
    vehicles, 153; and fuel prices, 189;
    and hybrid vehicles, 186, *190;* and
    mileage standards, 171; profits and
    losses, 191
General Motors Acceptance Corpora-
    tion (GMAC), 287, 290
geography, 15
Georgia (country), 130
Georgia (state), 321
geothermal power, 146, 147, 148
Germany, 29
gerrymandering, 16–17

gift taxes, *38*
Gingrich, Newt, 113, 226, 256, 310
Giuliani, Rudy, 247
global climate change, 194, 195–96, 214–
    17, 297; and Bush's legacy, 218–20; and
    clean coal technology, 133; and Clear
    Skies initiative, 205; and crossover
    voting, *318;* and ethanol fuels, 156;
    and the Kyoto Protocol, 218, 301; and
    reversal of Bush policies, *307;* and
    veto threats, 217–18
globalization, 29
Goldman Sachs, 287
Gore, Al: and base politics, 18; and the
    California Plan, 167–68; and educa-
    tion reform, 90; and energy policy,
    115, 116–17, 132, 138; and global warm-
    ing, 194; and immigration policy,
    222, 228; and the Kyoto Protocol, 195,
    196, 216; and party loyalty, *19;* and
    prescription drug benefits, 97–98;
    and presidential election, 10; and So-
    cial Security reform, 58; and stimulus
    package, 311; and tax policy, 32–33,
    295
governing strategies, 5–7
government-sponsored entities (GSEs),
    279–80
governors, 77
Graham, Bob, 99, 101–102
Graham, Lindsey: and crossover voting,
    322; and global climate change, 198;
    and immigration policy, 245; and
    prescription drug benefits, 104; and
    Social Security reform, 60; and tort
    reform, 253
Gramm, Phil, 227
Grassfire.org, 247
Grassley, Charles: and CAFE standards,
    179; and energy policy, 121, 122; and
    ethanol, 151, 158, 159; and fuel econ-
    omy, 187; and prescription drug ben-
    efits, 101–102; and renewable energy,
    146; and tax cuts, 36, 37, 42–43

Great Depression, 291
Great Society, 293
green cards, 234, 241
green vehicles, 287, 289
greenhouse gas emissions, 156, 160, 169, 196–97, 214–17, 327. *See also* carbon dioxide emissions; global climate change
Greenspan, Alan, 31, 36, 268, 275
Gregg, Judd: and clean-air permits, 203; and crossover voting, *322;* and education reform, 67–69, 71–72; and global climate change, 198; and prescription drug benefits, 104; and renewable energy, 146
gross domestic product (GDP), 47
growth-based models of achievement, 77–78
guest worker programs: and border security, 250; and Bush's proposal, 234–36; and crossover voting, 320; and Democratic support, 245–46; and executive powers, 328; and failed Bush initiatives, 221, 300, *300;* and House proposals, 237–39; and immigration policy, 240; and missed opportunities, 302
Gulf of Mexico, 127, 128

Hagel, Chuck, 71, 101, 103, 104, 240
Hall, Ralph M., 42
Hannity, Sean, 248
Harkin, Tom, 71, 173, 198, 263–64
Hartford Courant, 60
Hastert, Dennis, 21–22, 56, 158, 235, 242, 250
Hatch, Orrin, 179, 253, 254
Hayworth, J. D., 230, 244
health care reform, 230, 232–33, 311–12
health insurance industry, 95
hedge funds, 279
Heritage Foundation, 226
high occupancy vehicle (HOV) lanes, 187–88

Hispanic populations, 92, 221, 228, 250, 306
Hollings, Ernest, 262
home equity loans, 274
homeland security, 266–67, 315–16. *See also* U.S. Department of Homeland Security
Honda Motor Company: and the auto industry bailout, 286, 287; and CAFE standards, 167, 172; and diesel vehicles, *190;* and ethanol vehicles, 153; and hybrid technology, 185, *190;* profits and losses, 191
Hope Now, 281–82
House Energy and Commerce Committee, 102, 119, 172, 201
House Judiciary Committee, 229, 238
House Rules Committee, 6, 178
House Subcommittee on Appropriations, 232
House Ways and Means Committee, 97, 100, 102
housing crisis and bailout, 30–31, 273–81, *294, 303, 304*
Human Rights First, 243
Hunter, Duncan, 247, 249
Hurricane Katrina: and Bush's terms compared, 303; and evaluation of Bush policies, 25–26, 304; and fuel prices, 181, 189; and tax policy, 44–45
Hutchinson, Kay Bailey, 244, *322*
hybrid technology, 182, 184–86, *186, 190,* 288
hydroelectric power, 146, 147, 161
hydrogen, 118, 135

Idaho National Laboratory, *144*
ideology: and assessment of Bush presidency, 2–3; and base politics, 18; and crossover voting, 320; and political partisanship, 14–15; and the U.S. population, 9. *See also* conservatives; liberals

Illegal Immigration Reform and Responsibility Act of 1996, 226
Immediate Helping Hand initiative, 98
Immigration and Naturalization Service (INS), 234
immigration policy: and administrative crackdowns, 242–44; backlash against, 239–40; and bipartisanship, 244–48, 316; and Bush-Kennedy collaboration, 240–42; and Bush's reelection, 235–37; and Bush's terms compared, 303; and California, 223–26; and crossover voting, *318, 320*; and cross-partisanship, 317; and evaluation of Bush policies, *294;* and executive powers, 328; and guest worker programs, 234–36; and House reforms, 237–39, *238;* and language assistance, 231–33; and legislative reconciliation, 242; and missed opportunities, 302; prospects for, 248–49; and Reagan, 222–23; and reversal of Bush policies, *307*
Immigration Reform Caucus, 231, 234–35, 237–38, 247, 249
income inequality, 16, 28, 79–80
income tax, *38,* 61, 184–86. *See also* tax policy and reform
independents, 17, 18
India: and Bush's fiscal policies, 31; and climate change, 218; and energy policy, 136; and food price inflation, 155; and fuel prices, 30, 189; and greenhouse gas emissions, 215, 216, 217; and the Kyoto Protocol, 195, 196
Indiana, 130, 153–54, 306
industrial interests, 211
industrialized countries, 214–15
inflation: and assessment of Bush presidency, 53; and Bush's fiscal policies, 29, 31–32, 49; and discretionary spending, 304; and food prices, 155, 156; and Yucca Mountain, 142, 143
inheritance tax, 35

Inhofe, James, 198, 201, 204
Inouye, Daniel, 125
insurance industry, 95, 100, 104, 113, 143
interest groups: and base politics, 18; and CAFE standards, 193; and crossover voting, 323; and cross-partisanship, 313; and the Democratic Party, 4; and energy policy, 116; and executive powers, 327, 330; and governing strategies, 6; and immigration policy, 221, 239; and party loyalty, 21; and prescription drug benefits, 113. *See also specific groups*
interest rates, 275–76
International Energy Agency, 216
International Monetary Fund (IMF), 152, 156, 158
International Revenue Service (IRS), 185
interstate highway system, 187–88
investment banking, 279. *See also* financial crisis and bailout
Iogen Corporation, 157
Iowa, 306
Iraq: and budget deficits, 50; and energy policy, 130; and evaluation of Bush policies, 1, 292, 303–304, 331; and immigration reform, 237; and military spending, 303; and oil prices, 164; and policy reversals, 308; and tax policy, 44
Istook, Ernest, 232
Italy, 29

J. P. Morgan Chase, 283
Japan, 29, 215, 216
Jeffords, James: and Clear Skies initiative, 199, 201; and climate-change initiatives, 219; and the Congressional Review Act, 214; and education reform, 67, 68, 69, 70–71, 90; and filibuster threats, 22–23, 24, 34; and prescription drug benefits, 100, 101, 103; and tax cuts, 37; and tort reform, 255

Johnson, Lyndon, *12,* 64, 293, 312
Johnson, Nancy, 20
Johnson, Tim, 37, *322*
Jordan, Barbara, 226
Jordan Commission, 226
judiciary, federal, 7, 328–30. *See also*
    U.S. Supreme Court

Kaiser Foundation, 112
Kansas, 136
Kemp, Jack, 225
Kennedy, John F., *12,* 52, 102, 103
Kennedy, Ted: and education reform,
    68–69, 72, 89, 91; and immigration
    policy, 221, 234, 240–42, 244–45,
    247–49; and prescription drug ben-
    efits, 101
Kentucky, 79, 84
Kerrey, Bob, 34
Kerry, John: and crossover voting,
    322; and energy policy, 120, 138;
    and global climate change, 198; and
    immigration policy, 222, 235–36;
    and political polarization, 16; and
    prescription drug benefits, 102; and
    presidential elections, 11; and Social
    Security reform, 57, 58, 62
Kia Motors, 288
Kohl, Herbert, 24, 37, 254, *322*
Kolbe, Jim, 55
Korean War, 1
Krugman, Paul, 60
KTAR, 246
Kyl, Jon: and immigration policy, 234,
    240, 245–46, 248; and tax cuts, 45
Kyoto Protocol, 132, 195–97, 214–18, 301

labor unions, 239, 250, 264–66, *294,* 314
Labor-Management Disclosure Report-
    ing Act, 265
Laffey, Stephen, *19*
lame duck presidency, 272, 314
Landrieu, Mary: and CAFE standards,
    179; and clean-air permits, 203; and

crossover voting, *322;* and energy
    policy, 125, 126; and ergonomics
    rules, 262; and global climate change,
    198; and prescription drug benefits,
    103; and tax cuts, 39
Las Vegas, Nev., 274
Latin America, 229, 239
Latinos, 67–68, 81
Lautenberg, Frank, *322*
Lay, Kenneth, 267
Leach, Jim, 20
Leahy, Patrick, 213–14
legislative reconciliation: and cross-
    partisan strategy, 316; described,
    21–22; and education reform, 71–73;
    and energy policy, 122, 124; and im-
    migration policy, 242; and prescrip-
    tion drug benefits, 102–104; and tax
    cuts, 41, 46
Lehman Brothers, 283, 305
lending practices, 277, 278. *See also* fi-
    nancial crisis and bailout
Levin, Carl, 120–21, 177–78
liberals, 14–15, 21
Lieberman, Joe: and clean-air per-
    mits, 203; and education reform,
    65–66, 68–69, 71, 90–91; and filibus-
    ter threats, 24; and global climate
    change, 197–98; and party loyalty, *19;*
    and Social Security reform, 58, 60
lignite coal, 134, 212
Limbaugh, Rush, 248
limited-English proficiency, 76, 231–33
Lincoln, Blanche: and crossover vot-
    ing, *322;* and ergonomics rules, 262;
    and global climate change, 198; and
    prescription drug benefits, 103; and
    Social Security reform, 60; and tax
    cuts, 37, 45
liquefied natural gas (LNG), 128
LM-2 disclosure forms, 265
loan guarantees, 159
local actions, 327–28
logrolling, 324

Los Angeles, Calif., 81, 169
Los Angeles Unified School District, 81
Lott, Trent: and CAFE standards, 173; and education reform, 67; and filibuster threats, 23; and prescription drug benefits, 101, 103, 104; and Social Security reform, 56; and tax cuts, 37, 45
Louisiana, 128
Lugar, Richard, 173, 179, 198

Maine, 180
Majority Report, 60
mandatory spending, *49*
marginal income tax rates, 27
Markey, Edward, 172
marriage penalty, *38*
Martinez, Mel, 126, 240
Maryland, 180
mass media, 13
Massachusetts, 174, 180
McCain, John: and CAFE standards, 180; and clean-air permits, 203; and climate-change initiatives, 218; and crossover voting, 321, *322*; and energy policy, 120; and evaluation of Bush policies, 297–98; and global climate change, 197–98; and immigration policy, 221, 227, 234, 240, 247, 249; and nuclear energy, 145; and political polarization, 306; and prescription drug benefits, 103, 104; and presidential campaign, 13, 305; and tax cuts, 38–39, 42–43, 46, 295
McConnell, Mitch, *322*
media, 13, 16, 213–14
Medicaid, 28, 105, 109–11, 226, 241
medical malpractice reform, 251–52, *300*
Medicare: background of, 94–96, 112; and Clinton, 96–97; and conservatives, 99; and evaluation of Bush policies, 28, 296–97; and the federal budget, 106, 114; and immigration policy,

241; and Medicaid patients, 110–11; and poverty, 105; and presidential elections, 93
Medicare Prescription Drug, Improvement and Modernization Act of 2003 (MMA), 104–105. *See also* prescription drug benefits
Medicare reform, *294*
Medicare+Choice plans, 96
mercury emissions, 194, 199–200, 219, *300, 307,* 330
mergers, 106
merit pay for teachers, 82–84, 85
meritless lawsuits, 252
methyl tertiary butyl ether (MTBE), 122–24, 149–50, 160
methylmercury, 212
Mexico, 155, 224, 228–29, 239, 244
Miami, Fla., 274
Michigan, 84, 168
Middle East, 280
midnight regulations, 205, 326
midterm elections, 299
Midwest, 208
mileage standards: and the CAFE program, 165–66; and the California Plan, 167–70; and energy policy reform, 119; and estimation methods, 181–83; and evaluation of Bush policies, 170–72, 183–84, *294,* 303; and executive powers, 327; and future standards, 175–76; and legislative failures, 172–73; and Twenty-in-Ten initiative, 176. *See also* Corporate Average Fuel Economy (CAFE)
military spending, 50, 135
Miller, George, 68, 69–71, 72, 89, 91, 101
Miller, Zell: and crossover voting, 321, *322*; and education reform, 68; and ergonomics rules, 262; and filibuster threats, 23; and overtime rules, 264; and prescription drug benefits, 103; and tax cuts, 36–37, 39, 42–43; and tort reform, 253

minimum wage, 262–63
Minnesota, 153, 180, 188
minority populations, 63–64, 67–68, 81, 91, 92. *See also* immigration policy
Minuteman Project, 237
Mississippi, 128
Mobil, 130
moderates, 18, 20–21. *See also* bipartisanship
monetary policy, 28–29, 53
money-market funds, 279
Moody's, 280
Morgan Stanley, 287
mortgage insurance, 277
mortgage-backed securities, 279–80
Motiva Corporation, 127
Motor and Equipment Manufacturers Association, 288
mountaintop mining, 131–32
Moynihan, Daniel Patrick, 56–57, 58
Murkowski, Frank, 120, 179, 264
Murray, Patty, *322*

Nader, Ralph, *19,* 116, 168
A Nation at Risk, 65
National Academy of Sciences (NAS): and CAFE standards, 177; and clean-air permits, 203; and education reform, 83–84; and mileage standards, 165, 166, 170; and nuclear waste, 141, 142
National Assessment of Educational Progress (NAEP), 74–75, 87, 90–91
National Commission on Energy Policy, 176
National Commission on Excellence in Education, 65
National Commission on Terrorist Attacks upon the United States, 235
National Council of La Raza, 239, 246
National Day of Action for Immigrant Justice, 239
national debt, 32

National Education Association (NEA), 66, 84–85, 86, 89, 92
National Energy Plan, 138
National Energy Policy (report), 118, 124, 163, 165–66, 184
National Enrichment Facility, 145
National Ethanol Vehicle Coalition, 153–54
National Governors Association (NGA), 85
National Highway Traffic Safety Administration, 255
National Math Council, 84
National Petroleum Reserve, 127
national security, 51–52. *See also* defense policy; homeland security
National Wildlife Federation, 151
natural gas, 118, 128, 134, 147, 161, *307, 318*
Nebraska, 229, 321
Nelson, Ben: and crossover voting, 321, *322;* and energy policy, 125; and global climate change, 198; and prescription drug benefits, 103; and Social Security reform, 60; and tax cuts, 37, 39, 43, 45
Nelson, Bill, 39, 45
Nevada, 83, 138–40, 141, 306
New Century Alliance for Social Security, 59
New Century Financial, 279
New Deal, 15
New England, 148, 208
New Hampshire, 247, 306
New Jersey, 84, 180, 214, 229
New Mexico, 180, 240
New Source Review (NSR) programs, 201–203, 203–204, 219, *300,* 326
New York City, 274, 282
New York State, 180, 229, *309*
New York Times, 60
Newfoundland, 130
Nickles, Don, 42, 100–101, 104, 261–62
Nigeria, 29, 130

Nissan Motor Company: and the auto industry bailout, 287; and CAFE standards, 173; and diesel vehicles, *190;* and ethanol vehicles, 153; and hybrid vehicles, 186, *190;* profits and losses, 191

nitrogen dioxide, 194, 207

Nixon, Richard, *12,* 13

No Child Left Behind (NCLB) legislation: and bipartisanship, 316; and the Bush electoral campaign, 67–69; and cross-partisan strategy, 324; and cross-partisanship, 313; and enforcement mechanisms, 80–81; and evaluation of Bush policies, *294,* 296; and executive powers, 327; and failing schools, 76–79; and federal funding, 86–87; and graduation rates, 85; and Kennedy-Miller alliance, 69–71; key features, *73;* and legislative reconciliation, 71–73; mandates of, 64; and mandatory testing, 73–75; problems with, 87–89; and reversal of Bush policies, *307;* and school choice, 79–81; and school restructuring, 84–85, 88; and standards and testing, 65–66; and supplemental tutoring, 81–82; and teacher qualifications, 82–84

North American Free Trade Agreement (NAFTA), 225

North Carolina, 136, 306

Nova Scotia, 130

NovaStar, 279

nuclear energy: and crossover voting, *318;* and energy policy reforms, 137–45; and evaluation of Bush policies, *294,* 297; and fuel reprocessing, 142–43; and the Price-Anderson Act, 143; prospects for, 144–45; and renewable energy, 147; and reversal of Bush policies, *307;* subsidies for new reactors, 143–44; and the 2000 election, 115–16, 118; and waste disposal, 138–40, 140–42, 161, 297

Nuclear Energy Institute, 141

nuclear proliferation, 142

Nuclear Regulatory Commission (NRC), 138

Nuclear Waste Policy Act, 140

Numbers USA, 247

Nussle, Jim, 41–42

Obama, Barack: and air quality issues, 209; and the auto industry bailout, 289, 290–91; and Bush policies, 293, 331; and CAFE standards, 173, 180, 183; and climate-change initiatives, 218, 301–302; and energy policy, 128, 137, 162; and environmental issues, 298; and fiscal policy, 52; and midnight regulations, 269; and nuclear energy, 145; and political polarization, 4, 15, 305–308; and "political standing," *12;* and presidential election, 2, 13; and tax cuts, 46, 295; and tort reform, 256; and the Wall Street bailout, 284, 285–86

Obey, David, 264

Occupational Safety and Health Administration (OSHA), 261, 262

ocean power, 146, 147

Office of Information and Regulatory Affairs (OIRA), 256

Office of Management and Budget (OMB): and air quality issues, 212; and coal plant regulations, 207; and counterterrorism, 267; and diesel engine regulations, 206–207; and ergonomics rules, 261; and immigration reform, 232–33; and midnight regulations, 269; and regulatory reform, 256–57, 259–60; and "smart regulation," 257–59; and tort reform, 252

offshore drilling, 128

Ohio, 11, 116, 130, 219, 306, 310

oil consumption: and assessment of Bush presidency, 53; and consumption levels, 164; and energy policy,

126, 129, 161–62; and ethanol, 152;
and the National Energy Policy, 163;
and presidential elections, 116–17;
and renewable energy, 147; and tax
policy, 314
oil exploration and production: and
crossover voting, *318;* and energy
policy reform, 126–31; and evaluation
of Bush policies, *294, 298;* and failed
Bush initiatives, *300;* and oil shale
development, 127; and political polarization, 160; and presidential election,
118; and production levels, 130–31;
and reversal of Bush policies, *307*
Oregon, 136, 180
Organisation for Economic Cooperation and Development (OECD), 216,
302
Organization of the Petroleum Export-
ing Countries (OPEC), 30, 116, 126,
159
organized labor, 59, 221, 263, 270
overtime pay, 270, *294,* 295, *319*
oxidized mercury, 212

Palin, Sarah, 305
Parsons, Richard, 56–57
partisanship: and activism, 18–19;
and education reform, 66–67; and
filibuster threats, 34; and Obama
presidency, 308–10, 312; and OSHA
rules, 262; and party affiliations,
9–10; and party discipline, 23; and
party loyalty, *19,* 20; and party-line
voting, 310–12; and prescription drug
benefits, 97; by state, *309. See also*
polarization
Partnership for a New Generation of
Vehicles, 168
Patriot Act, 235
Peabody, 137
Pelosi, Nancy, 129, 177–79, 284, 289
Pence, Mike, 244
Pennsylvania, 180, 252

Penny, Tim, 58
Perot, H. Ross, *19*
Perry, Rick, 156
Personal Responsibility and Work Opportunity Reconciliation Act, 226
Peterson, Collin, 102
Petri, Tom, 66
pharmaceutical industry, 94–95,
108, 113. *See also* prescription drug
benefits
physicians, 113
pipeline construction, 130
plug-in hybrids, 185–86
polarization: and assessment of Bush
presidency, 2–3; and bipartisanship,
315–16; and the Bush legacy, 330–31;
Bush terms compared, 302–304;
causes of, 15–17; and cross-partisan
strategy, 316–20; defining, 13–14; and
education reform, 89, 90; and executive powers, 325–28, 328–30; and immigration policy, 222, 249, 250; and
legislative agendas, 310–12; and lessons for the future, 293; and Obama,
4, 305–308; party-line voting, 310–12;
and political parties, 14–15; and prescription drug benefits, 107, 112; and
regulatory reform, 264
"political standing," 11–13, *12*
population growth, 228
Port Arthur, Tex., 127
poverty, 76–77, 95, 104, 109
Praxis II, 83
prescription drug benefits: and bipartisanship, 316; as Bush priority, 93–94;
and crossover voting, *318;* and cross-
partisanship, 317; design of program,
104–105; and evaluation of Bush
policies, *294,* 296–97; and the federal budget, 99–100, 106–107, 113–14;
and Gore, 97–98; and the Grassley-
Baucus alliance, 99–101, 101–102; and
implementation problems, 107–11;
inevitability of, 94–96; and legisla-

tive reconciliation, 102–104; legislative strategy for, 98–99; opposition, 111–12; political stalemate on, 96–97, 99–101; and reversal of Bush policies, *307;* support for, 94–96; and the 2000 election, 97–98
primary elections, 14, 19–20
prior authorization, 111
Prius hybrids (search), 181, 182, 185
privacy issues, 78, 188–89
private school vouchers, 66–67, 69–72, 79–81, 91–92
privatization, 58, 59–61, 113
procedural votes and motions, 8, 25, 103, 125, 218, 317
Progressive Policy Institute (PPI), 65–66
prompt letters, 258–59
Proposition 187, 223–26, 227, 249
Pryor, Mark, 45, 173, 198, *322*
Public Company Accounting Oversight Board, 268
public education. *See* education reform; No Child Left Behind (NCLB) legislation
public health, 140–42, 256. *See also* health care reform; prescription drug benefits
public opinion: and assessment of Bush presidency, 1, 9; and clean air initiatives, 213–14; and crossover voting, 321, 323; and education reform, 64; and ideological polarization, 3; and immigration policy, 245; and the Kyoto Protocol, 216; and Social Security reform, 56, 58
public services, 230
public transit, 188
Putin, Vladimir, 130

RAND Corporation, 126
rating agencies, 280
Reagan, Ronald: and assessment of Bush presidency, 2, 3; Bush con-
trasted with, 113; and immigration policy, 222–23, 249; "political standing," *12;* and presidential campaigns, 306; and regulatory reform, 260; and tax policy, 35, 39, 52, 302
real estate investment trusts, 279
recession, 30, 40, 223–24, 304
redistricting, 16–17, 21
Reed, John, *322*
Regional Greenhouse Gas Initiative, 199
regulatory reforms: achievements and setbacks, 261–69; and the Bush agenda, 269–70, 291; and climate change issues, 301; cooperation with Europe, 260; corporate fraud, 267–69; and energy policy, 131; and ergonomics rules, 261–62; and ethanol, 152; and evaluation of Bush policies, *294;* history of, 256–59; and homeland security, 266–67; and labor unions, 264–66; and midnight regulations, 269; and modernization of regulations, 259–60; and oil exploration, 127–29; and overtime rules, 262–66; and reversal of Bush policies, *307;* and subprime lending crisis, 278–79; and tort reform, 251–56. *See also specific policy arenas*
Reid, Harry: and the auto industry bailout, 289; and climate-change initiatives, 217, 218; and crossover voting, *322;* and energy policy, 139–40, 140; and immigration policy, 241, 245–48
Reilly, William, 136
religious groups, 239, 250
renewable energy: and CAFE standards, 177, 178; and energy policy reforms, 120, 146–49; and evaluation of Bush policies, *294;* and presidential elections, 115–16, 118; and reversal of Bush policies, *307;* and Twenty-in-Ten initiative, 176
Renewable Energy Production Incentive, 147

Report to Congress on the Costs and Benefits of Federal Regulation, 260

Republican Party: and Bush's terms compared, 303; control of Congress, 4; and education reform, 64; and the Electoral College, *309;* and ideological polarization, 3; and immigration policy, 222–24, 227, 234–35, 249, 301; and political polarization, 14, 16; and prescription drug benefits, 113. *See also specific individuals*

research and development, *144,* 147, 156–57, 159, 168

retirement, *38,* 55, 96, 106–107, 299–300

reversal of Bush policies, 306–308, *307*

Rhode Island, 180, 321

Ricardian equivalence, 47

Richards, Ann, 225

riders, legislative, 166, 264

Roberts, Pat, *322*

Rockefeller, Jay, 101, 102

Romney, Mitt, 247

Royal Dutch Shell, 127, 130

rule-making powers, 164, 202, 327–28, 328–30

rural areas, 95

Russia, 130, 197, 218, 301

San Diego, Calif., 248, 273

San Francisco, Calif., 274

Sanders, Bernie, 23

Santorum, Rick, 321–23, *322*

Sarbanes, Paul, 268, *322*

Sarbanes-Oxley Act, 267–68, *294,* 298–99, 302, 316

Saudi Arabia, 129–30

Schumer, Charles, 123, 284, *322*

Schwarzenegger, Arnold, 129, 168, 199

seasonal workers, 237

Secure Border Initiative, 243

Securities and Exchange Commission (SEC), 31, 265–66, 267–69, 278–79

securitization of loans, 281

Senate Appropriations Committee, 203

Senate Committee on Environment and Public Works, 22–23, 181, 326

Senate Energy Committee, 120

Senate Finance Committee, 43, 100

Senate Judiciary Committee, 253, 254

seniors, 95, 96, 107–108, 109

Sensenbrenner, Jim, 223, 234–35, 237, 239, 242, 250

sentencing standards, *238*

September 11 terrorist attacks: and assessment of Bush presidency, 1, 4, 25–26; and homeland security, 315–16; and regulatory reforms, 266, 271; and Social Security reform, 56

Shaw, E. Clay, Jr., 55

Shays, Christopher, 15

Shelby, Richard, 253, 254

Shell, 130

Sierra Club, 119–20, 136

Sixth Circuit Court of Appeals, 87

Smith, Gordon: and CAFE standards, 173, 179; and crossover voting, *322;* and energy policy, 126, 129; and prescription drug benefits, 101; and renewable energy, 146

Smith, Lamar, 226

smog, 207, 209, 220

Snowe, Olympia: and CAFE standards, 179; and clean-air permits, 203; and crossover voting, *322;* and energy policy, 126, 129; and filibuster threats, 35; and global climate change, 198; and mileage standards, 173; and overtime rules, 264; and prescription drug benefits, 100; and renewable energy, 147; and tax cuts, 42, 43, 45

social inequality, 16

Social Security reform: and assessment of Bush presidency, 7–8, 330–31; and Bush's fiscal policies, 28; and Bush's priorities, 56–57, 57–59, 315; and Bush's terms compared, 56–57, 57–59, 303; and Clinton, 55–56; and crossover voting, *318;* and cross-partisan strategy, 313–14, 319; and Democratic opposition, 59–61, 62; and failed Bush initiatives, 299, *300;* and immigration policy, *238,* 241, 244, 249; and missed opportunities, 302; and party voting, 311; and prescription drug benefits, 109; problems of, 54–55; and tax policy, 32–33, 36

Social Security Trustees Report, 54

solar power, 132, 145–48

soot, 207, 209, 220

South America, 229

South Carolina, 229

South Dakota, 83, 119

South Korea, 216

Spain, 278

Spanish-speaking populations, 224

special education, 22, 69, 71–72

Specter, Arlen: and filibuster threats, 34; and global climate change, 198; and overtime rules, 264; and party loyalty, *19,* 20; and renewable energy, 147; and tax cuts, 36–37; and tort reform, 253–54

spending, 304

sport utility vehicles, 171, 187

stabilization policies, 27

Standard and Poor's U.S. National Home Price Index, 274

standards and testing movement: conservative support for, 67; and election constituencies, 90; and evaluation of Bush policies, 296; and failing schools, 76–79; and legislative reconciliation, 71–72; and No Child Left Behind mandates, *73,* 73–75; support for, 65–66; and transparency, 87–88

state actions, 327–28

State of the Union addresses, 157, 183, 216, 226, 237, 244

states' rights, 252

Stenholm, Charles, 55

Stevens, Ted, 125–26, 177, 264, *322*

stimulus packages: and assessment of Bush presidency, 4; and Clinton, 32, 311; and supply-side economics, 39–40; and tax credits, 186–87; and tax cuts, 28, 36, 46–47

stock dividends, 43–45

stock market, 57, 267–69

Strategic Petroleum Reserve, 117

subbituminous coal, 213

subprime lending crisis, 30, 274, 276–77, 280–81

subsidies, 104, 111–12, 143–44, 150, 324

sulfur dioxide, 194, 207

sunset provisions, 34

Sununu, John, 104, 147, 203, *322*

Supplemental Security Income (SSI), 226

supply-side economics, 28, 39–44, 46–47, 298

Sweden, 149, 298

Talent, James, *322*

Tancredo, Tom, 231, 238, 239, 242, 249

tariffs, 158, *300*

Tauzin, Billy, 100, 121, 122

tax policy and reform: and assessment of Bush presidency, 27, 52–53; and budget deficits, 48, *48;* and Bush's fiscal policies, 31; and Bush's tax cuts, 35–38, 44–46; and CAFE standards, 173, 177, 178, 179; and crossover voting, *318;* and cross-partisan strategies, 6, 317; and economic performance, 47; and energy legislation, *144;* and energy policy, 123, 131, 147, 148, 164–65, 184–86; and ethanol, 150, 152, 154; and evaluation of Bush policies, *294,* 295, 302, 304, 312–13; and filibuster threat, 33 35; and fuel efficiency, 186–87; and fuel prices, 189; and greenhouse gas emissions,

216; and immigration policy, 231, 241; and missed opportunities, 302; and oil exploration, 127; and renewable energy, 146; and reversal of Bush policies, *307;* and Senate votes, 38–39; and stock dividends, 43–45; and supply-side economics, 39–44; and tax cuts, *38;* and the Wall Street bailout, 284

Teacher Incentive Fund, 84

technology transfer, 158

temporary workers, 237

Tennessee, 74

terrorism, 164, *238,* 315–16

Teshekpuk Lake, 127

testing. *See* standards and testing movement

Texas, 80, 90, 110, 229, 240, 276

Thailand, 158

therapeutic drugs, 105

Thomas, Bill, 37, 43, 97, 99–100, 102–103, 121

Toomey, Pat, *19*

Torricelli, Robert, 34, 37

tort reform: and Bush's terms compared, 303; and crossover voting, *319;* and cross-partisanship, 317; and failed Bush initiatives, *300;* and party voting, 311; and reversal of Bush policies, *307*

Toxic Substances Control Act, 151

Toyota Motor Company: and the auto industry bailout, 286, 287, 288; and CAFE standards, 172; and the California Plan, 169; and diesel vehicles, *190;* and ethanol vehicles, 153; and hybrid technology, 185, 186, *190;* profits and losses, 191

traffic congestion, 165, 187–89, 193

transportation sector, 149, 161, 163, 314. *See also* automobile industry

Troubled Asset Relief Program (TARP), 283, 285, 290, 291

Truman, Harry, 1

Turkey, 130–31

turnover in the White House, 2

tutoring, 81–82, 88

Twenty-in-Ten initiative, 135, 175–76

245i program, 233–34

TXU, 136

unemployment, 28, 47, 53

unfunded mandates, 86, 258

Unfunded Mandates Act, 86

unions, 239, 250, 264–66, *294,* 314

United Auto Workers of America (UAW): and the auto industry bailout, 287–88, 291; and concessions to automakers, 191; and crossover voting, 314; and energy policy reform, 120; and executive powers, 327; and mileage standards, 167, 168, 172–73, 176, 181, 183, 193

United Kingdom (UK), 29, 199, 215, 278

United Mine Workers, 117, 314

United Nations (UN), 215

unskilled workers, 234

U.S. Air Force, 135

U.S. Commission on Immigration Reform, 226

U.S. Congress, 2–3, 15, 90, 308, 330. *See also* U.S. House of Representatives; U.S. Senate

U.S. Constitution, 87

U.S. Department of Agriculture (USDA), 157, 178

U.S. Department of Defense, 95–96, 139, 153

U.S. Department of Education, 63, 68, 74, 76–78, 81–83, 86. *See also* education reform

U.S. Department of Energy, 141, 154–55; and ANWR, 119; and CAFE standards, 178; and clean-air permits, 202; and coal energy, 134, 137, 207; and ethanol fuels, 157; and nuclear power, 139, *144*; and renewable energy, 147

U.S. Department of Health and Human Services (HHS), 94, 107–108, 109, 111

U.S. Department of Homeland Security: and immigration reform, *238*, 240, 243, 248, 250, 328; and regulatory reform, 257, 266–67; and reversal of Bush policies, 307

U.S. Department of Justice (DOJ), 202, 233, *238*

U.S. Department of Labor, 262, 263, 264, 265, 266

U.S. Department of the Interior, 127, *133*, 147, 148, 248

U.S. Department of the Treasury, 279, 283, 284, 290

U.S. Department of Transportation (DOT): and CAFE standards, 165–66, 167, 170, 172, 174, 178; and energy policy reform, 120; and executive rule-making power, 329; and Twenty-in-Ten initiative, 176

U.S. Department of Veterans Affairs, 95–96

U.S. Energy Information Administration (EIA), 136, 143–44, 189–91

U.S. Environmental Protection Agency (EPA): and CAFE standards, 174, 178, 180; and the California Plan, 168–69; and clean-air rules, 128; and nuclear waste disposal, 141–42

U.S. Food and Drug Administration (FDA), 106, 255, 259

U.S. House of Representatives: and Bush's fiscal policies, 31–33; and crossover voting, 320; and governing strategies, 5; and immigration policy, 231–32, 237–39, *238*; and presidential agendas, 21–22; and tax cuts, 36, 39; and 2008 election, 306; voting rules, 33. *See also specific individuals and committees*

U.S. Nuclear Regulatory Commission (NRC), 140–41, *144*, 144–45

U.S. Pharmacopoeia, 105

U.S. Senate: and crossover voting, *318–19, 322*; and cross-partisanship, 317; and elections, 306; and energy policy reform, 120; and filibusters, 22–24, 33–35, 125; and governing strategies, 5; and presidential agendas, 21–22; and tax cuts, 36; and tort reform, 252. *See also specific individuals and committees*

U.S. Supreme Court: and air quality issues, 211; and Bush v. Gore, 11; and CAFE standards, 174–75, 178; and the California Plan, 169; and clean-air permits, 204; and education reform, 68; and executive rule-making power, 329

Utah, 77

utility companies, 136, 207–209, 219, 297. *See also* energy production policy

Value Pricing Pilot Program, 188

Venezuela, 159, 164

venture capital, 157

Vermont, 180

veto power: and CAFE standards, 177, 178–79, 181; and climate-change initiatives, 217–19; and the Congressional Review Act, 214; and education reform, 89; and tax cuts, 32

Virginia, 83, 128, 306

Voinovich, George, 34, 42–43, 45, 204–205

Volkswagen, *190*, 288

Voluntary Public School Choice program, 80

voter turnout, 10

voucher programs: conservative support for, 66–67; and crossover voting, *318*; and cross-partisanship, 313; and education reform, 69, 91–92; and failed Bush initiatives, 299, *300;* and legislative reconciliation, 71–72; negotiations on, 69–71

Wall Street bailout, 283, 285–86, *307.* *See also* financial crisis and bailout
Wallace, George, 15
Warner, John, 198, 217
Washington, D.C., 282
Washington (state), 180
water safety, 195
Waxman, Henry, 137
welfare, 109, 225–26
Welfare Reform Act, 226
Wellstone, Paul, 71

West Virginia, 116–17, 131–32, 137, 219
White House budget office, 258–59
Wilson, Pete, 224–28
wind power, 132, 145–48
World Trade Organization (WTO), 217, 260
WorldCom, 267, 268
Wyden, Ron, 39, 103

Xerox, 267, 268

Yucca Mountain, 138–40, 140–42, 161, 297, *318*

zero emission vehicles (ZEVs), 181

JOHN D. GRAHAM is Dean of the Indiana University

School of Public and Environmental Affairs (Bloomington and Indianapolis). He is the author of seven books and two hundred articles on health, safety, and environmental issues.

Graham founded and led the Harvard Center for Risk Analysis from 1990 to 2001. In 2005 he was elected president of the Society for Risk Analysis, an international membership organization of 2,400 scientists and engineers. Graham reached out to risk analysts in Europe, China, Japan, and Australia as he helped organize the first World Congress on Risk Analysis (Brussels, 2000). From 2001 to 2006, Graham served as the Senate-confirmed Administrator of the Office of Information and Regulatory Affairs, White House Office of Management and Budget. From March 2006 to July 2008 he was the dean of the Frederick Pardee RAND Graduate School at the RAND Corporation in Santa Monica, California.